KU-617-906

THE
ARCHITECTURE OF EUROPE

also by Doreen Yarwood

ENGLISH HOUSES
ENGLISH COSTUME
OUTLINE OF ENGLISH COSTUME
THE ENGLISH HOME
ARCHITECTURE OF ITALY
(Chatto and Windus)
ROBERT ADAM
(J. M. Dent)

THE
ARCHITECTURE OF EUROPE

Doreen Yarwood

SPRING
BOOKS

First published in Great Britain in 1974 by
B. T. Batsford Limited

This edition published in 1987 by Spring Books
An imprint of Octopus Publishing Group PLC
59 Grosvenor Street
London W1

Distributed by Hamlyn Publishing Group Ltd
Bridge House, London Road,
Twickenham, Middlesex, England

© Doreen Yarwood 1974

ISBN 0 600 55430 9

Printed in Great Britain

Contents

Preface

This book has been planned as a companion volume to my *Architecture of England*, first published in 1963. There are many books available on the architecture of Europe. Most of these cover a specific area or period and a number present the subject in a general way. None so far published in the English language deals with Europe as a whole; generally only western Europe is discussed and, within this context, a carefully chosen selection of western European countries. This is understandable, especially in the light of the older, academic approach to the subject, for it was long considered that only countries such as France, Italy and possibly Germany and the Low Countries had been instrumental in influencing and forming British architectural history.

Since 1945, with increasing leisure time, the expansion of higher education and, above all, a greater facility of travel, the whole of Europe has become opened up to tourists and students. There are still difficulties and frustrations in visiting eastern Europe, but this is possible and more people each year go to the Soviet Union and the satellite countries. In the light of these factors, it was decided by the publishers and I that I should write a book which would narrate simply and chronologically the history of European architecture within the geographical boundaries of modern Europe and showing the architectural development and interdependence of the 23 countries concerned from the time of Ancient Greece to the present day.

This is an immense canvas for one volume and there can be no pretence of comprehensiveness or detail. The aim is to present as clear a picture as possible of the general evolution of style and taste in different areas, illustrating which trends, political, social, climatic, etc., influenced certain areas at certain times. I have given greater space in each chapter to the countries which were of paramount importance in leading certain movements and which produced the finest work of that age. The areas concerned vary from century to century: Greece and Rome in the classical world, France in the Middle Ages, Italy in the

Renaissance, Germany and Finland in the twentieth century. I have also given especial coverage to countries in eastern and northern Europe which tend to have been left out of books on European architecture.

Half the space is devoted to illustration, for architecture is a visual subject. My husband, John Yarwood, and I have travelled some 67,000 miles in Europe during the last nine and a half years, mainly by car, visiting each of the countries, many of them several times. My husband has taken over 25,000 photographs from which the illustrations, both line drawings and photographic plates, have been made.

In Europe, as on a smaller scale in England, great buildings are constantly in process of demolition and alteration. Few of the books available on European architecture provide a reliable guide to the present state of such monuments. I hope that at least for a few years, this book will provide an up-to-date guide on the condition and existence of interesting architectural work. In our travels we have encountered many discrepancies from written descriptions; a Renaissance church in a great city is now a sports shop, buildings referred to as intact were totally destroyed in the Second World War, others have been adapted, restored or altered. This is a continuous process and only constant study can present an accurate overall picture.

I hope that one of the uses of this book may be to encourage readers to go to see buildings *in situ*. With this in mind, I have not followed the common tradition of naming buildings and places according to the time of their construction, but have referred to them by the names used currently in their present countries, names to be found readily in standard atlases and guide books.

I should like to express my appreciation to colleagues and friends who have provided me with data and photographs for areas which I was not able to visit. These are Professor Robert Clothier for his photographs of Aigues Mortes in France, Miss Margaret Briggs for her work at Knossos in Crete and especially Mr. Vjachaslav Orelski and his colleagues from the Union of Architects in Moscow, who assisted me greatly in that city and provided me with material on the more remote cities in the Soviet Union which lack of time made it impossible for me to visit. I would also like to thank Miss Constance Waight, Mrs.

Elizabeth Bangham and Mrs. Jean Naylor for typing this long and demanding manuscript.

The author and publishers wish to acknowledge the kindness of Mr. Geoffrey Trevelyan of Chatto and Windus Ltd., for permitting the reproduction of some of my drawings from my *Architecture of Italy*, published by them in 1970. These are Figs. 157, 177, 187, 191, 195, 213, 215, 217, 223, 228, 255, 262. They also wish to thank the British Museum for permission to reproduce plates 2, 4, 5, 7, 8, Mr. A. F. Kersting, A.I.I.P., F.R.P.S. for plate 22, and Professor John Yarwood, M.Sc., F.Inst.P. for the remainder of the photographic plates.

Doreen Yarwood

Plates
The bold numerals indicate plate numbers; italic numerals in brackets indicate those pages between which plates appear:
1-3 (*12-13*); **4-7** (*26-27*); **8-11** (*34-35*); **12-17** (*46-47*);
18-22 (*86-87*); **23-26** (*134-135*); **27-32** (*142-143*);
33-38 (*178-179*); **39-44** (*204-205*); **45-48** (*232-233*);
49-53 (*238-239*); **54-58** (*296-297*); **59-62** (*318-319*);
63-66 (*325-326*); **67-70** (*346-347*); **71-74** (*362-363*);
75-78 (*376-377*); **79-81** (*382-383*); **82-85** (*400-401*);
86-89 (*410-411*); **90-95** (*422-423*); **96-99** (*488-489*);
100-103 (*502-503*); **104-107** (*548-549*).

PART ONE
ANCIENT CIVILISATIONS

I
Minoan and Greek: *c.* 3000–146 B.C.
Pre-Hellenic Greece: The Bronze Age *c.* 3000–1100 B.C.

Remains survive of Neolithic and Early Bronze Age building by the peoples inhabiting islands and mainland areas in the Aegean dating from about 3000 B.C., but these early constructions are not architecture and only provide architectural interest because of the influence which they exerted on later peoples. Greece is poor in material resources and timber for building has always been scarce and difficult to transport across mountain regions. The chief material, therefore, in those times was sun-dried brick, made in summer sunshine, and built upon a base of stone blocks with a floor of beaten earth. Even from early times these Mediterranean peoples used the trabeated constructional form of posts or

walls and horizontal lintels to support roofs or make openings.

The *chief centres of civilisation* in Bronze Age Greece were on the coast of Asia Minor, the islands, particularly Crete, and the later mainland developments of Mycenae. Building work of this culture is commonly divided into three parts: early, *c.* 3000–2000 B.C., middle, *c.* 2000–1600 B.C., and late, *c.* 1600–1100 B.C. The work is called by different names according to definition: Pelasgic after the race of people, Minoan after King Minos of Crete, Aegean after the area of occupation or Mycenaean after the later settlements. Archaeological study is still yielding new information, particularly in more accurate dating of the work; the whole subject of this period of development is comparatively recent in discovery, dating only from the original, magnificent achievements of Heinrich Schliemann at Mycenae and Tiryns and Sir Arthur Evans at Knossos in the late nineteenth century and early twentieth. The early peoples were intent on providing shelter and protection for themselves and, therefore, remains from the first period came from houses and fortifications. Later ages yield palaces, tombs and more elaborate walled towns with fortified gates. Types of walling are large scale in rough cyclopean blocks with small stones and clay in the interstices or later polygonal courses, while designs of columns, fresco decoration, jewellery and arms show influence of Egyptian and Assyrian culture, although unmistakably Minoan or Mycenaean. The later Hellenic peoples of Greece also borrowed much from their Bronze Age ancestors, particularly in ornamental forms. Columns characteristically taper inwards towards the base (there are two of these standing outside the museum at Eleusis (**20**), and there are also those from the Treasury of Atreus now in the British Museum (**59**). Roofs are often vaulted in triangular or barrel vault form. Stone blocks in horizontal courses are built to project inwards one above the other to form the vault. There is a fine triangular example at Tiryns (**9**) and the bee-hive tombs at Mycenae are dome-shaped. Openings from the earlier times are triangular headed with large blocks forming the openings (**6** and **11**) while later examples have horizontal lintel stones (**5** and **10**).

Minoan Architecture in Crete

Here there were a number of building periods, of which two produced a high standard of work: the first climax came in the middle Minoan period from *c.* 2000 to 1600 B.C. and the second in the late Minoan period up to 1100 B.C. In the first of these were built the palaces at *Knossos, Phaistos* and *Mallia*. This is presumed to be the era of King Minos, whose name has come down to us in Greek legends, and it is also the time of active foreign trading and a flourishing activity in building and the arts. The second climax brought larger palaces, wealth for the upper classes and spacious architecture which boasted adequate sanitation systems. Walls and ceilings were decorated with brilliantly coloured fresco paintings in their now characteristic ornamental forms of continuous scrolls (**64**), fret and guilloche and of lively human and animal forms, the former in vividly depicted dress. Examples, partly restored, can be seen in the National Museum in Athens. Here also discoveries were made in gold, silver, ivory, faïence and terracotta of sculpture and ornament from the tombs showing the characteristic Minoan forms which, like the architecture, owed something to Egypt but lacked its monumentality. The palace architecture of the best Cretan work illustrates an adaptation of Western Asiatic and Egyptian ideas and construction but employs the native means and proportions. Taken from Egypt is the central palace courtyard, but Cretan courts are more rectangular in shape, being twice as long on the north/south axis as on the east/west in order to gain the maximum sunshine in winter.

Palace of King Minos at Knossos

There were several periods of building here and they continued over a long time. The palace was originally excavated by Sir Arthur Evans, who was responsible for much reconstruction work. The palace was a remarkable construction covering nearly five acres. It was destroyed by fire, earthquake and invasion, like the other palaces of Crete, about 1400 B.C., and was not rebuilt. After this time the Minoan civilisation dwindled and the Mycenaean predominated.

The principal living rooms of the palace have been excavated and show the royal apartments grouped round the courtyard, which measures some 180 by 90 feet. The apartments were of several storeys, reached by stairways and the whole palace was interconnected by innumerable passages and stairs. The main palace entrance was on the south side, approached by a paved road, which crossed a ravine spanned by a large viaduct pierced to allow water passage. The external façade, like most Cretan designs, was stepped back sharply, especially on the west side. Walls were of rubble and brick with stucco facing and, near the base, faced with stone slabs. Apart from the royal apartments with their throne room suites and grand staircase there are also a number of halls, two other courts and many smaller rooms. One of the finest apartments is the

Hall of the Double Axes (so called because of the two-bladed axe carved repeatedly on the walls). This was a ground floor room with another hall above. It was colonnaded and open at both ends and could be divided into two rooms in winter by the fitting of four double doors. The two rooms, measuring 18 by 26 feet were then heated by charcoal braziers. The palace was fitted with a drainage system of terracotta pipes, bathroom and toilets, which had water closets with wooden seats. Throughout were magnificent painted ceilings and walls of which fragments remain although for the most part they have been taken to museums for safety (**1, 2** and **3**).

These peoples built citadels on carefully chosen sites, protected by cyclopean walls and fortified gates. Inside the walls were constructed the palace and other important buildings. The citadel of Mycenae itself is a clear example of such patterns for living. Smaller than the palace of Knossos it illustrates nevertheless the architectural layout and typical mode of life of these peoples. The Mycenaeans were seafaring peoples and took over the Minoan trade connections with Egypt. Their methods of building show a more advanced understanding of engineering principles than hitherto and illustrate something of the monumentality of Egyptian work.

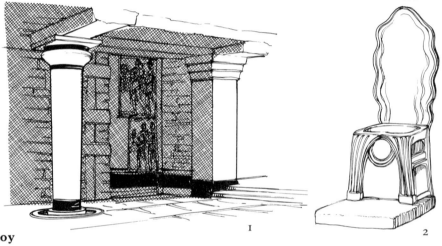

1   Palace of Knossos, The South Propylaeum, 1775–1580 B.C.
2   Minoan Throne
3   Grand Staircase

Troy

The Trojan civilisation on the coast of Asia Minor is a different branch of development as it owes much of its culture to the interior of Asia Minor rather than the Aegean area and its influence spread only to neighbouring islands. Like Mycenae it was also originally excavated by Schliemann, who doggedly persisted in his search for the city of Homeric legend despite the scepticism of his day. The buildings now excavated cover the period *c.* 2700 B.C. to the Sack of Troy in *c.* 1200. There is a palace with much interesting work surviving and, in the rest of the citadel, fortifications and houses.

Mycenae

The Minoan civilisation spread to the mainland and, with an intermingling of peoples from Asia Minor and the north, provided the nucleus for a new culture around Mycenae in the Peloponnese.

* *The term originated from the attitude of the Greeks, who found it difficult to believe that such vast blocks had been erected by man and attributed the construction to the Cyclops.*

The *citadel of Mycenae* is built on a small hill situated between two larger hills which rise above the plain of Argos near to the sea and the present day port of Nauplia. The citadel (**4**) was rebuilt about 1350 B.C. and is surrounded by walls of cyclopean* masonry in limestone boulders. The walls are 20–25 feet high and the upper courses are of sun-dried brick. At Mycenae there are also walls of fitted polygonal and square stones without mortar. The road from the plain winds up to the fortified main entrance, called the *Lion Gate*. The name is derived from the carved sculpture on the triangular relieving slab† above the lintel wherein are depicted two lions in bold relief, one each side of a column. The heads, which would have faced the visitor to the citadel were separate blocks dowelled in and have disappeared. The lions' paws rest on a plinth. The

† *The relieving or discharging arch or slab is constructed to prevent the weight above from crushing the lintel stone. Thus, in Mycenaean architecture both the arch and lintel form of construction was employed. It is thought that the triangular relieving arch came from Egypt as it is not known in Minoan architecture.*

column, like most Minoan and Mycenaean designs, tapers slightly towards the bottom. Its capital consists of a square abacus, an echinus and decoration of a row of circular disks. This is probably the most ancient carved sculpture in Europe* and the progenitor of pediment sculpture in Hellenic Greece. The gateway itself is constructed with two vertical jamb blocks and, horizontally across the top of these, a vast lintel block, all of dressed ashlar conglomerate. The lintel stone measures 15 by 7 by 3 feet and is estimated to weigh 20 tons. The doorway is 10 feet high and the sides incline inwards slightly towards the top. It had two wooden doors which

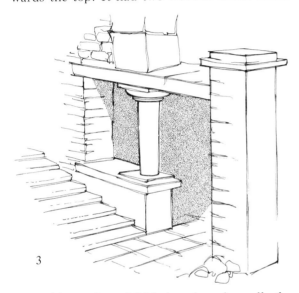

3

opened inwards and folded against the wall; the fitting holes are still visible (5).

After passing through the Lion Gate the visitor ascends a ramp and staircase to reach the palace which was constructed on top of the citadel. The ramp winds backwards and forwards to reach the top while the staircase provides a short cut. The *palace* is laid out on Minoan lines with a great court (which had a patterned floor and walls) and a megaron suite leading off it wherein the bases of the columns are still visible. Most of the rooms here were two-storeyed. Part of the megaron has now fallen into the ravine at the edge of the citadel, but the hearth with its raised rim is extant and was originally in the centre of the 40 feet square room. Much of the grand staircase leading down to a lower level can still be seen. A sketch plan of these rooms and a drawing of the staircase as it is today are illus-

* Another old and impressive sculptural scheme is the Lion Terrace on the sacred Isle of Delos (plate 1).

trated in Figs. **7** and **8**. On the north side of the citadel there is a gate in the fortified wall now called the *postern gate* (**6**) which has a triangular shaped roof and which leads towards a secret cistern outside the walls. The vault of this tunnel is formed in the triangular shape, as at Tyrins, with large stones. The exit is composed of horizontally bedded large stones each projecting slightly in front of the one below. This is typical of Mycenaean arches, none of which has radiating voussoirs.

Tholos tombs at Mycenae

These tombs are found primarily in the Peloponnese and consist of underground circular chambers covered with a mound of earth and approached by means of a dromos, which is a stone-faced passage. Inside, the tomb is faced with squared blocks of masonry set in horizontal courses which are corbelled to meet at a domed centre overhead. Such tombs are constructed by first cutting the open passage (dromos) into the hillside until the ground is rising high enough above it. After the last burial the dromos is filled in. Only the mound of earth is then visible and the tomb would last as long as the vault withheld the water from the earth above. Good examples have buttress walls encircling the vault to protect it and take the thrust. The best and most famous tholos tomb at Mycenae is that known as the *Treasury of Atreus* built *c.* 1330 B.C. This is finely constructed with dressed and curved, conglomerate blocks. Inside the dome each block overlaps and counterweighs the one below on a cantilever system. The blocks are wedge-shaped and the interstices are filled with clay and stone. The chamber is $47\frac{1}{2}$ feet in diameter and is 43 feet high. Its interior is intact except that the decoration has been removed. There is a rock cut chamber at one side with its own doorway. The dromos approach is 120 feet long and 20 feet wide and its side walls, made of blocks of dressed grey conglomerate, are regularly laid and rise in steps towards the doorway. This doorway is 18 feet high and inclines inwards, Egyptian fashion, while the entrance itself also slants inwards. The lintel blocks, inner and outer, are gigantic (each 26 by 16 by 4 feet and weighing 100 tons) and extend across into the walls of the dromos. The relieving triangle above is now empty, but originally it had a decorated faced slab parts of which, with the original flanking columns of green limestone, are now in the British Museum (**59, 60**). The columns, decorated by scroll pattern, are slender and taper towards the base. The doorway passage is paved with limestone slabs and there was originally a double wooden door (**10, 12**). This tomb, like that of Clytemnestra and others, was built for the burial of a king and his family. Tombs for other people were cut into the rock.

Citadel of Tiryns

The ruins here are of an early palace built on a ridge rising from the Argos plain nearer to the sea than Mycenae. Much of the citadel walls remain as does the layout of the palace on top of the acropolis. The cyclopean masonry is particularly large scale and well built. There are different periods of work here from *c.* 1400 to *c.* 1280. The palace itself was built in the thirteenth century B.C. and was of sun-dried brick with wooden columns. The most interesting remains are a long gallery which is covered along its entire length by large stones horizontally bedded to form a triangular shaped roof and this is in a good state of preservation (**9**). There is also a little postern gate nearby of similar construction (**11**).

These great Mycenaean settlements were destroyed by fire in about 1100 B.C., but the knowledge of them and their people lived on by word of mouth. The Homeric poems describe a picture of Mycenaean life—the age of Agamemnon, Clytemnestra and Troy—distorted by time and repetition but basically true. The Mycenaeans were conquered, it is believed, by the northern Dorians, but it is not yet established how close their connection was with their inheritors, the Greeks. Classical Greece was chiefly peopled by Dorians (centre Sparta) and Ionians (Athens) who were descendants of the Pelasgi.

Hellenic Greece *c.* 700–146 B.C.

Several centuries passed between the collapse of Bronze Age Mycenaean architecture and the rise of Hellenic art; a period of 'Dark Ages' ensued, and when Hellenic architecture evolved it was different from the work of its predecessors. The Greeks were strongly influenced by maritime contact with their neighbours: Egypt, Assyria and Persia. Their massive Doric Order, always the Greek favourite, has much of Egyptian monumentality in it as has their art something of the Assyrian richness of detail. Colour was as important to them as to all peoples who live in a sunny climate and they used it to adorn both exteriors and interiors of their buildings; this is a fact not always realised when studying the weathered ruins extant today. Indeed, both effort and knowledge are required in order to understand Greek architecture from these ruined buildings. None of them is intact; the sculpture has been almost entirely removed to museums; the wood and metal parts are missing and, most important from the viewpoint of appreciating the original appearance, they are roofless so that light enters where shadow once was and the whole balance of form is altered. It is a tribute, therefore, to the perfection of Greek form in building that these ruins should appear so satisfying and so moving to twentieth century beholders. The prime feature of Greek architecture is its intellectual quality. The Greeks did not create a variety of design or show great inventiveness or a desire for innovation. They developed to an intensely high degree a standard of perfection for the designs which they evolved. As the most important Greek buildings were temples (rather than palaces and tombs as in Minoan architecture), every effort was made to develop the finest possible harmony of their different parts and proportion and line of these individually and collectively. This ideal was pursued relentlessly by architects and artists who were not satisfied with less than perfection. This standard was reached at the zenith of the Hellenic style in the fifth century B.C. where buildings such as the Parthenon even today illustrate to the most uninformed beholder the intellectual beauty of line and proportion which can only be the result in human endeavour of tremendous study, effort and knowledge.

Greek architecture belongs to three chief periods: the archaic, up to about 480 B.C.; the early classical of the fifth and fourth centuries and the later Hellenic from then until the Roman Conquest in 146 B.C. Their buildings included temples, theatres, stadiums, agora (market places), town fortifications, palaistras and treasur-

CITADEL AND PALACE OF MYCENAE

4 LION GATE

PALACE

ENTRANCE

5

6

7

MEGARON

THRONE ROOM

GREAT COURT

PORCH OF THE MEGARON

VESTIBULE

HEARTH

ANTE-ROOM

DRAIN

CLIFF

GRAND STAIRCASE

8

4 *General view of citadel, c. 1350 B.C.*
5 *The Lion Gate*
6 *The Postern Gate*

7 *The Grand Staircase*
8 *Simplified sketch plan of the layout of the principal palace rooms*

ies. Of these the most common remains are of temples and theatres, though the latter were, almost without exception, altered in Roman times. Ancient Greece extended beyond the mainland and surrounding islands and remains of Greek buildings are found today in the Greek colonies of Sicily, Southern Italy and in Asia Minor. As the prime building material of Greece was marble, many of these buildings have endured without great surface damage until today. Their damage is due primarily to earthquake and destruction by man. Greek marble is of high quality and the Greeks so admired its fineness of surface grain that in areas such as southern Italy where limestone was used for building, as at Paestum, they made a stucco of powdered marble and coated the limestone to provide their usual high standard of finish. Greek architecture was suited to the climate and mode of life which was outdoor in character. Colonnades supported porticoes and roofs and these supplied shelter from the hot sun and sudden rainstorms but also cool air in their shade. Windows were unimportant but doorways were finely proportioned, simply designed and rectangular in shape. The style of architecture was entirely a trabeated form and composed of horizontal blocks upon columns and walls. Vaults and arches were comparatively rare and roofs were generally of timber and tiled above. Archaic work was severe and stark, generally with heavy columns and capitals. Gradually refinements were made and proportions became more elegant though still robust in construction. In fifth and fourth century work, for example, stability was increased as well as refinement achieved by extreme care in the fitting of blocks especially in columns and walls. Surfaces were rubbed down to fit perfectly and there was no need of mortar.

Greek Town Plans

Many Greek cities were built on natural hills and were surrounded by walls with fortified gates and towers. Remains of these fortifications exist as, for example, at *Syracuse* in Sicily where Dionysios built his forts and walls in the fourth century B.C. for protection against the Carthaginians. The city upon the hill was called the acropolis (a literal translation of this conception) and the principal buildings of the city were inside these

walls on top of the hill, while most of the houses were outside. Credit for invention of the orderly city plan on gridiron pattern is given by Aristotle to *Hippodamus of Miletus* who laid out *Piraeus*, the port of Athens, in the mid-fifth century. Streets were straight and wide and crossed one another at right angles. This is a pattern adopted later by the Romans and, in our own times, by the French and the Americans. Hippodamus had also planned the city of *Miletus* in Asia Minor about 470–466 which contained some hundreds of rectangular blocks in its layout. The central area was reserved for the agora and stoas, where business and commerce were carried out, while residential areas surrounded it. Other cities on similar lines were *Priene, Pergamon, Ephesos* and *Corinth*.

The Orders

All the countries in Europe as well as those in the New World have, for long periods in their architectural history, used a system of orders in classical architecture, a system first devised by the Greeks, adapted by the Romans and revived in Renaissance Europe. It is a formula which has survived for some 2500 years and was still being used, in modified form, in architecture of the earlier twentieth century. The term 'order' is given to the three styles in Greek architecture: Doric, Ionic and Corinthian. Each order consists of an upright *column* or support which has a *base* (optional) and *capital* and the horizontal lintel supported by it. This last member, called the *entablature*, is divided into three parts; the lowest member is the *architrave*, the centre member the *frieze* and at the top the *cornice*. Each order possesses specific relative proportions between its parts, also certain distinguishing features and mouldings peculiar to itself. The size of a building does not affect these proportions, which remain constant, and differing scale does not impair the perfection of such proportions. The Greeks never used a part of one order with a part of another or, except rarely, employed more than one order on a building façade though they might use one for the exterior and another for the interior. The proportions of the orders were developed by trial and error over a long period of time. Earlier examples of the seventh and sixth centuries have massive columns,

9 *The Gallery, Tiryns, thirteenth century B.C.*
10 *Treasury of Atreus, Mycenae, Interior of doorway,*
   c. 1330 B.C.

11 *Gateway to gallery wall, Tiryns*
12 *Treasury of Atreus, Mycenae, Exterior of doorway.*
   Columns and decoration restored as in British Museum

GREEK CLASSICAL ORDERS AND DETAIL

13 The Doric Order, The Parthenon, Athens,
    447–432 B.C.
14 The Ionic Order, the Erechtheion, Athens,
    421–405 B.C.
15 The Corinthian Order, the Monument of Lysicrates,
    c. 334 B.C.

16 Ionic capital, Delphi
17 Ionic base, Delphi
18 Entablature, Tholos to Minerva, Delphi, c. 390 B.C.
19 Corinthian capital, the Olympieion, Athens,
    begun 174 B.C.

20 Minoan Column at Eleusis
21 Base, the Erechtheion, Athens, 421–405 B.C.
22 Ionic capital, Erechtheion
23 The Parthenon, Athens, 437–432 B.C. (restored)
24 Ionic base, Temple of Athena Nike, Athens, 427–424 B.C.
25 Ionic capital, Temple of Artemis, Ephesus, mid-sixth century
26 Order, porch of the Tower of the Winds, Athens, c. 40 B.C. (restored)
27 Corinthian capital, Tholos at Epidauros, c. 360 B.C.
28 Proto-Ionic capital, Larisa, Asia Minor, early sixth century

capitals and entablatures, and the intercolumniations were narrow. Mouldings and curved forms became more refined as time passed. A clear example of this process can be seen by comparing the echinus in a Doric capital from the temples at *Paestum* or *Agrigento* with those of the *Parthenon* (**23, 48** and **50**). The former are more bulbous and semi-circular in section, the latter are of a most subtle, flattish silhouette. The Greeks preferred the Doric Order and used it particularly for large buildings and for exterior façades. The Ionic Order is seen more in eastern colonial areas, especially in Asia Minor and Aegean islands.

The Doric Order

This is the most massive of the Greek orders and the one upon which the Greeks lavished the most care. The columns are placed close together and have no bases but stand directly upon a three-step stylobate. As in all Greek orders the shaft is fluted in shallow, subtle curved sections divided by sharp arrises. The number of flutes per column varies; in the ideal design like the *Parthenon* there are 20, but a greater or smaller number is used according to material and proportion; for example, at *Paestum* in the *Temple of Hera* there are 24 while in the *Temple of Poseidon* at *Sounion* only 16. Including the capital, the column has a height of four to six-and-a-half times the base diameter, and, in general, the earlier the building the thicker the column. The *capital* itself consists of a square *abacus* at the top and below this a curved *echinus* and annular rings. The *entablature*, usually about a quarter the height of the order, has a plain *architrave* and a *cornice* which projects strongly and under whose soffit are flat blocks called *mutules*, set one over each triglyph and one between, which have each 18 *guttae* in three rows beneath. The *frieze* of the Doric Order is distinctive; it is divided into *triglyphs* and *metopes*. The triglyphs, each of which has vertical channels carved in it, are placed one over each column and one between except at the angles where, the columns being closer together, the external triglyph is placed at the extreme end of the frieze and not over the centre of the angle column. The metopes are the spaces between, rectangular in early examples and square in later ones. These are commonly decorated with sculptural groups, as in the

Parthenon, so many of whose metopes are in the British Museum or the Louvre in Paris. These metope sculptures together with the pedimental groups constitute the glory of the Doric Order which epitomises the ideal union of simple, perfectly proportioned architectural masses with sculptural decoration. The frieze is separated from the architrave by a narrow band called the *regula* with six guttae beneath each triglyph (**13, 18** and **23**).

The Ionic Order

This order is in general a later development than the Doric but early prototypes have been found, particularly in Asia Minor from where the Aeolian capital (from Aeolis in north-west Asia Minor) stems. This has two volutes with palmette between, flattened to fit the architrave. Below, the echinus is formed by a water-lily shape. This design is related to both Egyptian and Syrian capitals (**28**). The true Ionic capital dates from the late sixth century and has two scroll *volutes*, based upon a shell formation or that of an animal's horns, which face the front elevation, while below is an *echinus moulding* with egg and dart enrichment. The *necking* or astragal is sometimes, as in the Erechtheion, decorated by anthemion relief design. The order is differently proportioned from the Doric; it has a much slenderer column, of height about nine diameters, carved into 24 flutes of semi-circular section separated by fillets not arrises and it is completed by a moulded base which is also often carved. The *entablature* is narrower in depth, generally one-fifth of the whole order, and has an architrave set forward in a three plane, triple fascia, a frieze without triglyphs or metopes but often decorated by a continuous band of sculpture, for example, the Erechtheion, and a cornice of smaller projection than the Doric, without mutules, but generally with dentil ornament surmounted by a corona and cyma recta moulding. The order is graceful and well proportioned and was used by the Greeks for smaller buildings, interiors and, commonly, in Asia Minor (**14, 16, 17, 21, 22, 24, 25** and **28**).

The Corinthian Order

This order was used much less by the Greeks

Plate 1
The Lion Terrace,
Delos, Greece 7th
Century B.C.
Plate 2
Lapith and Centaur.
Metope Parthenon
Athens 447–432 B.C.

XXVII

Plate 3
The Acropolis of Athens viewed from the Hill of Filoppapos. Below the theatre, behind the
Hill of Lycabettos.

THE ACROPOLIS, ATHENS

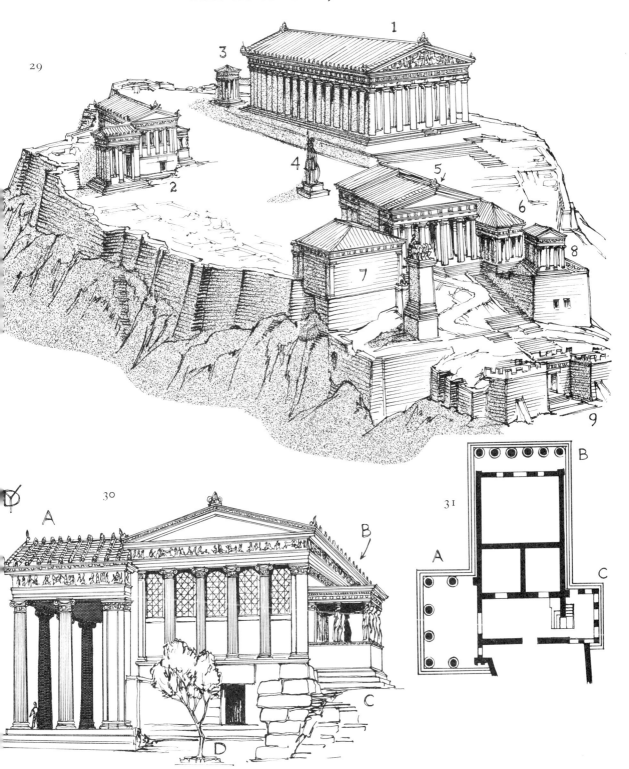

29 Sketch showing restoration of the principal buildings
of the Acropolis, viewed from the west.
1) The Parthenon
2) The Erechtheion
3) Ionic Tholos
4) Statue of Athena Promachos by Pheidias
5) The Propylaea

6) Southern wing of propylaea
7) North wing of propylaea, the picture gallery
8) Temple of Athena Niké
9) Main entrance to Acropolis
30 The Erechtheion (restoration), viewed from west,
421–405 B.C.
31 Plan, Erechtheion

than the other two orders and not many examples survive. The most common design, that adopted by the Romans, was similar to the Ionic Order in base, column and entablature, was richly ornamented and had a deeper cornice. The chief difference between the orders was in the *capital*, which was deep and had a four-faced abacus identical on all four sides. The capital below the abacus was in the form of a concave bell decorated by two tiers of acanthus leaves above which rose corner volutes supporting the angles of the abacus and central caulicoli or volutes also (**15, 19** and **27**). Another type of design had one row of acanthus leaves and, above these, a row of lotus or palm leaves with no volutes (**26**).

Building Materials and Methods

In early times the Greeks used sun-dried bricks, terracotta, wood and stone. Later, stone and marble were the chief *materials*; limestone and conglomerate were generally coated in marble stucco. Most of the temples in Greece itself are in marble which was used from *c.* 600 B.C. The best known marbles are Pentelic from Mount Pentelicus near Athens, Hymettian from Mount Hymettos also near Athens, Parian from the island of Paros and Eleusian from Eleusis. Pentelic marble is dazzling white and weathers well, as can be seen by the temples on the Acropolis in Athens even today. Hymettian marble is also white but has grey-blue markings; Parian is used predominantly for sculpture while Eleusian marble, as evidenced in the frieze of the Erechtheion, is dark grey and was used as a contrast material. Stone was more usual in the provinces, particularly in Italy and Sicily.

We have a good knowledge of *Greek building methods* in stone and marble from ruined remains, quarries and building inscriptions. The Greeks rarely used mortar but fitted their blocks with meticulous care, using metal dowels and cramps of bronze or iron set in molten lead to hold the blocks in position. This method is presumed to have been employed because of the earthquake hazard in the area. In particular, the drums of the columns were finely fitted so that the joints were barely visible even on close inspection. Bosses (ancons) were left on the sides of the drums for manipulation, as can be seen in the unfinished *Temple* at *Segesta* (**51**). Column flutes were

carved from top and bottom then completed when the column was *in situ*. Stone and marble walls were built in large blocks, without mortar, and the lowest course was generally twice as high as the others. Sometimes hollow wall construction was used in order to reduce weight or economise in material. Greek architecture is of lintel construction and the Greeks were slow or unwilling to develop new structural methods: they preferred to perfect their existing ones. This is particularly noticeable with regard to the arch and the vault—constructional means which the Romans were later to exploit. Greek roofing was by timber and the roof pitch was low (anything else being unnecessary in the Greek climate). Thus the pitch of the end pediments was determined by this rake and this gave the beautiful proportions which Greek pediments possess; comparison with Renaissance examples in Western Europe brings out this quality. The roof rafters were then covered by terracotta or marble tiles and interior ceilings were of coffered marble.

Refinements

These refinements of line, mass and curve are the factors that make all the difference between a good Greek building and a bad one and between the Greek original and the poorer Renaissance interpretation. The refinements used in the greatest periods of Greek architecture are so subtle as to be barely visible to the casual eye; indeed that is their chief purpose—to make the building appear correctly delineated and not curved, and to give it vitality and plasticity. The true horizontal or vertical line, particularly when silhouetted against a brilliant blue sky, appears concave to the human eye and, to offset this illusion the Greeks created a convex line and form so subtly and meticulously worked out as to appear to create a straight vertical or horizontal. Thus, taking the *Parthenon* as the finest illustration, all horizontal and vertical lines are in fact curved to counteract this visual illusion. This curvature applies to the stylobate (rise of $4\frac{1}{4}$ inches in a length of 228 feet, the entablature (curve 1 in 600), the columns (slanting inwards 1 in 150), and to the pediment. Columns diminish in diameter from bottom to top and, in addition, have an entasis whose widest point is about one third the way up from the base. Each flute curves in tune with the general entasis, which is to the order of about three-quarters of an inch to a height of 34 feet. In the Parthenon, the peristyle columns have a diameter of six feet two inches at base and four feet two inches just below the capital. Ionic and Corinthian columns, however, taper much less; in the *Erechtheion*, for instance, the difference is only six inches between the bottom and the top diameters. Also the inter-columniation (or column spacing) varies; the outside columns are closer together than the intermediate ones. At the Parthenon the differ-ence is two feet, from a six foot intercolumniation on exterior columns to eight feet elsewhere. Angle columns are also generally wider than their neighbours; this is because a silhouetted column appears narrower than one against a light back-ground. All the columns incline slightly inwards, as do the faces of the entablature and pediments, in order to lend a pyramidal form to the building. These refinements were costly to produce at their highest level and thus it is only such buildings as those on the Acropolis at the zenith of Greek architecture which achieved such a standard. These refinements are aesthetic in purpose as well as corrective, but since they are so subtly carried out the cost is proportionately great. On the Parthenon, for example, none of the correc-tions are arcs of circles but parabolae corrected down to the smallest members such as abaci.

Temples

The most important form in Greek architecture was the temple which was built not to house worshippers but the deity. The earliest examples were based upon the design of the Minoan megaron in the Bronze Age palaces and consisted of rectangular halls with frontal porches sup-ported on columns. The Greek desire for symmetry then created a porch at each end and enclosed a central naos or room to house the cult statue and later another smaller room behind to act as a treasury. From these beginnings evolved the varied designs of temple. However, even in the fifth century the variation in temples was not so much in form as in detail; they remained rectangular in shape, containing naos and trea-sury and with a portico each end and a surround-ing colonnade. According to whether the temple was large or small the number of columns

differed. Smaller temples had only four columns in their porticoes (tetrastyle form), larger examples had six (hexastyle), eight (octastyle), nine (nonastyle) or ten (decastyle). In each instance there were generally twice as many columns in the lateral peristyle as in the front and rear. The *Parthenon*, for example, is octastyle and has 17 columns at each side. All temples were raised on a platform (stylobate), generally of three steps. The entrance door was usually in the centre of the east wall behind the portico columns and designed so that the sunlight would fall upon the cult statue in the naos. Windows were rare. Light was admitted through the doorways or roof sky lights. Roofs were not flat but low pitched, with a ridge pole. The triangular space at each end of the temple was closed by a wall (tympanum) and protected by a raking cornice. The pedimental tympanum was generally filled with sculpture. The rafters were covered by tiles and these terminated at the sides in an antefix or gutter. Waterspouts, often in the form of lion's heads, were set at intervals to let out rain water. Acroteria decorated the three angles of the pediment.

Temples were designed for external effect, for the worshippers remained outside round the altar. Thus the naos was plain and solidly walled while the sculptural and painted decoration was on the exterior. It was usually confined to the pediments, frieze and acroteria. In large temples where the width of the naos was too great to be spanned by beams, interior columns were used to make nave and aisles. These were in two tiers and supported galleries over the aisles and the roof. Most of these second tier columns have vanished except in such examples as the *Temple of Hera* at *Paestum* (**44**) and the *Temple of Aphaia, Aegina* (see restored illustration **42**).

Temples on the Acropolis of Athens

Many Greek cities contained a hill which was the defensible part and where the important build-ings were constructed. In Athens there was an ideal natural hill with only one side, the west, which could be approached easily. It was in-habited by succeeding generations, but the ruined temples which now adorn it date principally from the fifth century when Athens, under the leadership of Pericles, experienced its great epoch (**29** and PLATE 3).

The Parthenon 447–432 B.C.

This temple, magnificent even in ruin, dominates the Athenian acropolis and is the finest of all Greek temples, marking the climax of the Doric style. The Parthenon had survived in good condition until 1687, when it was partially destroyed by an explosion during the Turko-Venetian war. From drawings made before this date we have a clear idea of what the pedimental sculptures looked like *in situ*. After the explosion the ruins deteriorated rapidly and in 1801–3 Lord Elgin removed much of the sculpture of the pediments, metopes and frieze to England, where it is at present beautifully displayed in the British Museum. It is a fallacy to suppose that Lord Elgin stole these sculptures or at least acquired them in a transaction of doubtful honesty. He was given formal permission by the lawful government of Greece (then the Turkish Empire) to remove the works. He did so with greatest care and later sold them to the British Museum for a much smaller sum than he had already spent. He had no means of knowing that Greece would become independent once more and if he had not acted when he did the sculpture would soon have suffered irreparable damage from neglect. Whether the British Museum or the Louvre should now return such work to Greece is another question.

The Parthenon was built of Pentelic marble on a limestone foundation over the site of an earlier temple. The architects were *Ictinus* and *Callicrates* and the chief sculptor *Pheidias*. It was the largest temple on the Greek mainland and had a peristyle of 17 lateral columns and octastyle porticoes. There was a naos which had interior columns on two storeys also a back chamber, presumably for use as a treasury. The temple was dedicated to the city's patron goddess Athena and was built on the highest part of the acropolis so that it was visible from the town. Near the west end of the naos stood the famous statue of Athena by Pheidias, made in gold and ivory and standing 40 feet high. Today the most prominent external features are the peristyle columns of which 32 still stand on their stylobate. The temple is so beautifully proportioned and refined that it is difficult, on sight, to realise its immense size, particularly as there is no other large building in the vicinity to give scale. In fact the columns are over 34 feet high and measure six feet two inches in diameter at base. The visitor only realises this when, sitting down gratefully on the stylobate for a rest in the shade after climbing up the acropolis, he leans his back against a column and finds that his shoulders neatly fit into one flute from arris to arris (**23, 29, 33** and **34**). Apart from the beauty of the Pentelic marble and the design and craftmanship of the Parthenon, its finest feature was its sculpture which, under the leadership of Pheidias, was of the highest quality of work by the greatest age of sculptors that Europe has so far produced. The two pediments represent, at the east end the Birth of Athena and at the west, the contest between Athena and Poseidon for Attica. A little of this work is *in situ*, the rest is in the British Museum, the Louvre and the Athens Museum. The metopes are about four feet five inches square and contained high relief sculpture which was originally brightly coloured (PLATE 2). The masterpiece of the Parthenon sculptures was the frieze which ran all round the temple inside the peristyle and high on the naos and porch walls. It was nearly 524 feet long and beautifully executed. Parts of it remain *in situ* but are difficult to see as the frieze is 40 feet above the ground and, owing to the narrow floor space between the naos wall and peristyle columns, one cannot step back to admire it. Indeed, it is much easier, if less moving, to view the long sections in the British Museum (PLATES 4 and 5). In order to assist the viewer from below the frieze was designed at an angle so that, while the face surface is vertical, the background tilts forward towards the top giving higher relief to the heads than feet.

The Erechtheion 421–405 B.C.

This is the best building in the Ionic order in Greece and is famed for its quality rather than its size. It stands on the acropolis north of the Parthenon on a sloping site; this factor, and because it housed three deities, account for its unusual plan. There are three façades, east, north and south, all at different levels. The eastern part was dedicated to Athena, guardian of the city; the ground slopes downwards towards the west where there is a basement room, with access on the west façade, while above this small doorway are four Ionic columns with bronze latticed windows between. The north porch is a large

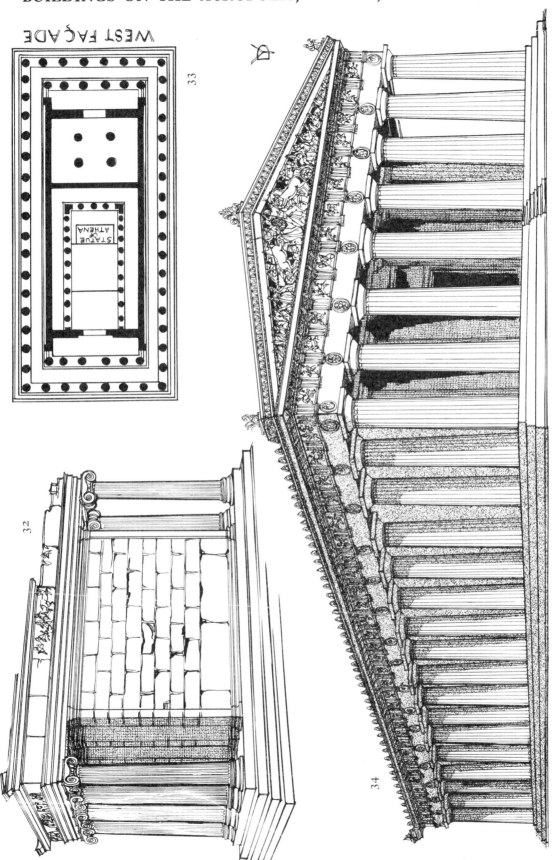

WEST FAÇADE

STATUE OF ATHENA

33

32

34

32 Temple of Athena Nike, 427–424 B.C.
33 Plan of Parthenon
34 The Parthenon from the north-west (restored), 447–432 B.C.

Ionic entrance and stands at the lowest level of the temple. Behind this portico is a magnificent carved doorway. The whole porch contains the highest quality of Greek decorative carving as can be seen in the capitals, bases and doorway details (**21, 22** and **65**). The south porch, on higher ground, has the six caryatid figures, each seven feet nine inches high, standing on a marble plinth and supporting a marble entablature and roof. The three western figures take their weight on the right leg, the eastern on the left (PLATE 6). The Erechtheion is built of Pentelic marble and was designed by *Mnesicles*. The decoration throughout is varied and shows exquisite detail and craftmanship; this is particularly apparent in the anthemion and guilloche ornament. The pediments are plain but the frieze of dark grey Eleusian marble was originally decorated its full length by white marble sculptured figures and animals attached by metal cramps. Gilt and colour were used also. The interior was destroyed when the building was converted into a church and later into a Turkish harem (**14, 21, 22, 29, 30, 31, 65** and **67**).

Temple of Athena Nike (Nike Apteros) 427–424 B.C.

This tiny building erected near the propylaea on the acropolis was designed by *Callicrates*. It consists of a single naos with four Ionic columns front and back and stands on a stylobate. It is only 23 feet high but beautifully proportioned and had some fine sculpture on the pediments and on the frieze, some of which remains (**32**).

Temples in Greece

Temples in or near Athens

The most complete Greek temple is that built on rising ground above the Athenian agora called the *Temple of Hephaistos* or the *Theseion*. Like the Parthenon it is of Pentelic marble, of similar date *c.* 449 B.C. and is in the Doric order. It has six columns to each portico and 13 lateral columns. The building was damaged by fire in A.D. 267; it originally had two storeys both in the Doric order but its inner colonnade was destroyed when the temple was made into a church in the fifth century A.D. and it was given solid walls and a barrel vaulted roof. Its preservation probably

resulted from this solid roofing. The sculpture, in Parian marble, consisted of high relief metopes illustrating the exploits of Theseus and a continuous frieze two feet eight inches high under the porticoes. Some of the metopes and the east end frieze are still *in situ* (**35** and **36**).

On a central space amidst the speeding traffic of Athens stand the 16 Corinthian columns which are all that remain of the immense temple of the *Olympeion* begun in 174 B.C. Dedicated to Olympian Zeus, it was built on the stylobate of an earlier Doric temple. It was designed by *Cossutius*, a Roman citizen, but whose work was essentially Greek. This enormous temple measured 135 by 354 feet and stood in a precinct (still marked out) 424 by 680 feet. The columns, each 56 feet high, are of Pentelic marble and have slender shafts and finely carved Corinthian capitals. It had a double colonnade of 20 lateral columns and three rows of eight columns at each end (**19** and **43**).

The Doric *Temple of Poseidon* (440 B.C.) has a magnificent site on the high southerly promontory of Attica at *Cape Sounion*. The white local marble columns can be seen for great distances especially from the sea. There were originally pedimental sculptures but no sculptured metopes. The columns, which have no entasis, have only 16 flutes to offset their slenderness. On the island of *Aegina*, the *Temple of Aphaia* also stands on a fine site on a ridge visible for miles out to sea. This hexastyle temple was built of limestone coated in marble stucco. The sculpture, of which a considerable quantity has been found, is in Parian marble. That from the pediments (now in a Munich museum) is an interesting example of late archaic work of about 480 B.C. Roof tiles on the temple were of marble and terracotta; those at the edge were of marble carved with lion's head water-spouts. There were fine antifixae and acroteria (**42**).

On a number of different sites on the *Greek mainland* and in the *Peloponnese*, Olympia, Delphi, Corinth, Epidauros, etc., are the remains of many temples. Most of these are fragmentary though the quality is high and enough remains for the original design to be apparent. Most interesting of these examples, which are all in the Doric order, are the temples at *Olympia*: the very ancient *Temple of Hera c.* 600 B.C. and the *Temple of Zeus c.* 470 B.C.; the *Temple of Apollo* at

THE GREEK AGORA, ATHENS

35 Ambulatory, Temple of Hephaistos
36 Temple of Hephaistos, c. 449 B.C.
37 Plan of part of Agora showing these buildings
38 The Stoa of Attalos, c. 150 B.C. Restored 1953–6 by American School of Classical Studies, Athens

BUILDINGS IN OR NEAR ATHENS

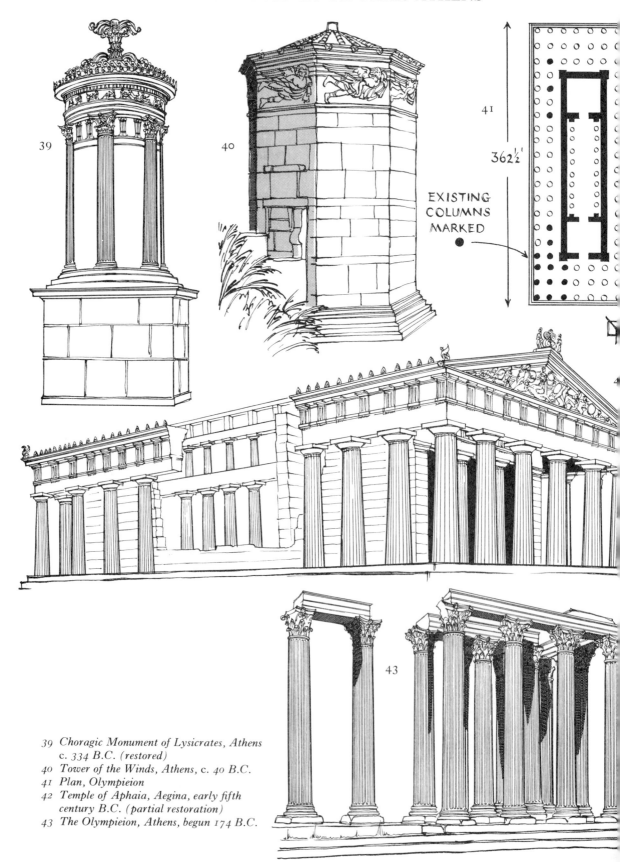

39
40
41
42

362½′

EXISTING
COLUMNS
MARKED
●

43

39 *Choragic Monument of Lysicrates, Athens*
   c. 334 B.C. (restored)
40 *Tower of the Winds, Athens, c. 40 B.C.*
41 *Plan, Olympieion*
42 *Temple of Aphaia, Aegina, early fifth*
   century B.C. (partial restoration)
43 *The Olympieion, Athens, begun 174 B.C.*

Corinth, also very ancient, sixth century B.C.; the *Temple of Apollo* at *Delphi*, fourth century B.C. and the *Temple of Ascelpios* at *Epidauros*, early fourth century B.C. At *Bassae*, near Andritsaina, in the Peloponnese, is the *Temple of Apollo* built *c.* 450 B.C. in which all three orders are used. It is a hexastyle temple with 15 lateral columns. Parts of the marble frieze and some metopes are in the British Museum. The temple was built in limestone by Ictinus, architect of the Parthenon, with the Doric order used on the exterior, Ionic inside and an early example of Corinthian capitals. These Corinthian remains have been lost, but the design can be perceived from drawings made at the 1811 excavations. They had two rows of small acanthus leaves and, above, pairs of tall leaves and volutes.

Temples in Asia Minor

These temples were mostly Ionic and larger than those in Greece but remains are fragmentary, only one or two columns standing in most instances. The Greek cities of *Ephesos* and *Miletus* contained a number of examples; for instance, the *Temple of Apollo Didymaeus* at *Miletus*, the *Temple of Artemis* at *Ephesos** and the *Temple of Athena Polias* at *Priene*. All of fourth century construction, these temples were large scale and had beautiful sculpture and decoration. There is little left because most of the material has been taken over the centuries to build Byzantine churches and other buildings. Capitals, bases and fragments of sculpture are displayed in European museums.

Doric Temples in Italy and Sicily

Here the remains are fairly complete, indeed much more so than in Greece, and are from early periods of building thus providing a contrasting source for study of the sixth and fifth centuries B.C. and for the differences between colonial architecture here and the more refined work in Greece itself. In *Italy* the chief group of remains is at *Paestum* in Southern Italy south of Salerno (the Greeks called it Poseidonia). There are three temples here of which two are large and in a good state of preservation. The best example is the *Temple of Hera*, popularly called *Temple of Poseidon*, built *c.* 460 B.C. Here all the exterior

* *No remains visible on site now.*

columns are standing and, inside, both tiers of the two storeys are represented. It is a hexastyle temple, 198 by 80 feet, built in travertine stone and originally coated with marble stucco (**44, 45, 46, 47** and **48**).

In *Sicily* there were a number of Greek centres which have remains of temples and theatres. At *Agrigento*, on the south coast of the island, there are several temples of which the *Temple of Olympian Zeus* is the largest. It was begun in about 485 B.C. but never completed owing to the Carthaginian invasion. Like other temples in Italy and Sicily it is built of coarse stone coated with marble stucco. An interior feature of its design are atlas figures about 25 feet high which probably stood between the columns. Another large *temple* at Agrigento is that of *Concord* which is well preserved probably because it was later converted into a church. It was built about 420 B.C., of local stone, and has complete gables as well as columns (**50**). There are further temples at *Selinunte* and at *Segesta* (**51**) while at *Syracuse* the *Temple of Athena* is now incorporated into the Baroque cathedral. The temple was hexastyle with 36 columns each 28 feet high and stood on a massive podium. In the seventh century A.D. the Byzantine bishop converted the temple into a basilica. Later the Normans further adapted it and in the eighteenth century the church was rebuilt after a series of earthquakes. The Greek temple is still there and 12 of its columns are visible in the north and south aisles of the present cathedral, still standing on their stylobate.

Tholoi

A number of buildings were designed on circular plan with concentric rings of columns. Some examples were used as council chambers, in other cases the use is unknown. There is a *tholos* at *Delphi c.* 390 B.C., partly reconstructed (**53**), and other examples at *Olympia, Epidauros*, the *Athenian agora* and on the *acropolis* in *Athens* (**29**). The *Delphi tholos* stands upon a stylobate and had an outer ring of 20 Doric columns inside which was the naos wall and inside this again 10 Corinthian columns. The external diameter was 48 feet. The roof over the naos was conical and there was a separate roof over the colonnade sloping at a lower level. This tholos was designed by *Theodorus* of *Phocaea* who set the pattern for these buildings which was followed by *Polykleitos the Younger* at *Epidauros*. This example, of which little remains, was larger, with an external diameter of 66 feet (**27**).

Other Buildings

Propylaea

The gateway to a sanctuary was sometimes a simple doorway called a propylon but in more important instances was a large construction combining several doorways called propylaea. There are remains of these at *Olympia* and *Epidauros* but the best known example is that at the *Acropolis, Athens*. This magnificent entrance on the western approach to the hill was built by *Mnesicles* from 437–432 B.C. but was never completed owing to the Peloponnesian War. Though roofless, much of it still stands as entrance to the acropolis. The design of Pentelic marble has a central mass with five doorways flanked east and west by a Doric hexastyle portico; the rear one being at a higher level than the former. At the sides, north and south, are wings, the northern wing containing two chambers including the picture gallery, but the southern wing was never finished. In the interior of the propylaea the Ionic order is used. The ceilings were richly decorated with marble beams, coffered, painted and gilded. The masonry is of high quality and the refinements excellent. The approach to the propylaea is very steep and was originally by means of a zig-zag path and ramp, suitable for sacrificial animals in the processions, which led to the central portico; later, this was replaced by steps (**29**).

The Tower of the Winds, Athens c. 40 B.C.

This weather guide and clock was designed by *Andronicus Cyrrus*. It is octagonal and under its cornice has a deep frieze of panels representing personified winds. On the north-east and north-west sides are porticoes with Corinthian columns and on the south side a circular chamber. The roof is of marble blocks originally surmounted by a bronze triton. The Corinthian capitals are interesting designs, having only one row of acanthus leaves, no volutes but a top row of tall, narrow leaves (**26**). This is the only surviving Greek horologium (**40**).

The Choragic Monument of Lysicrates, Athens, c. 334 B.C.

Erected by *Lysicrates* to commemorate the success of his company in the Choric dances, the monument is a circular pedestal of Pentelic marble standing on a square stone base. Its chief interest is the Corinthian order which is used in the form of six attached half columns surrounding the pedestal. These have very beautiful capitals designed with a lower row of lotus leaves, while above is a row of acanthus leaves and between them eight petalled flowers. The frieze is sculptured and the cornice is crowned with anthemion decoration. The roof, of one block, is slightly convex, ornamented by acanthus foliage and was surmounted by a tall bronze tripod—a replica of Lysicrates' prize at the festival. Although a small monument, almost hidden in modern Athens, it is of architectural importance because of its early use of such a beautiful example of the Corinthian order (**15** and **39**).

Treasuries

These small buildings are found in sanctuaries and were built by each community to house its offerings. Typical is the *Treasury of the Athenians* at *Delphi*, built originally *c.* 500 B.C. and reconstructed in 1907. It is a simple Doric building with a two-column porch surmounted by a pediment (**54**).

The Greek Agora

The Greek agora, like the Roman forum, was an open air meeting place for the transaction of business. Each town had one or more which comprised market place, business halls and temples. The long stoas were typical features of every agora. These were long colonnaded buildings, generally in two storeys, which contained shops and offices and enabled people to shop or carry out their business protected from sun and rain. In the *Greek Agora* of *Athens*, the stoa originally built by *King Attalos II of Pergamon* (159–138 B.C.), has been reconstructed by the American School of Classical Studies as a museum (**37** and **38**).

GREEK TEMPLES AT PAESTUM, ITALY

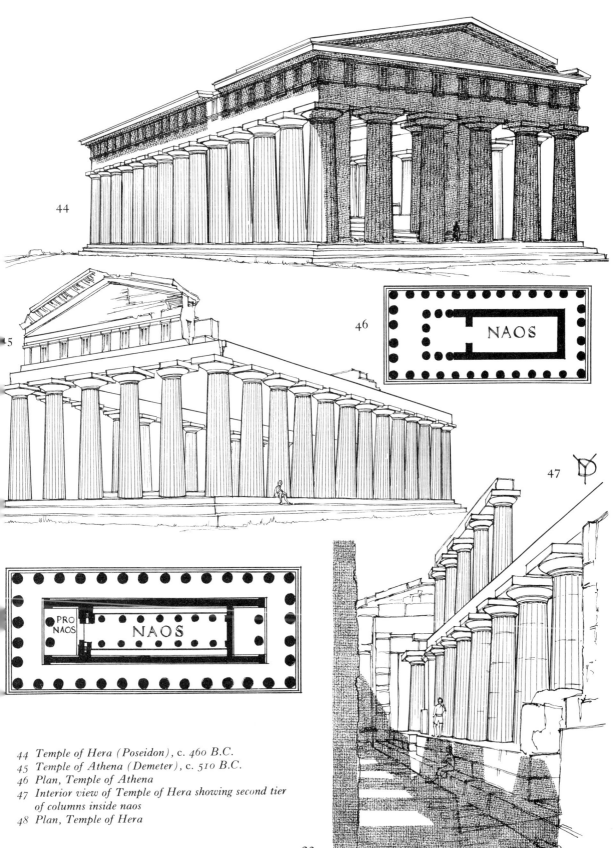

44   Temple of Hera (Poseidon), c. 460 B.C.
45   Temple of Athena (Demeter), c. 510 B.C.
46   Plan, Temple of Athena
47   Interior view of Temple of Hera showing second tier
      of columns inside naos
48   Plan, Temple of Hera

GREEK ARCHITECTURE IN SICILY

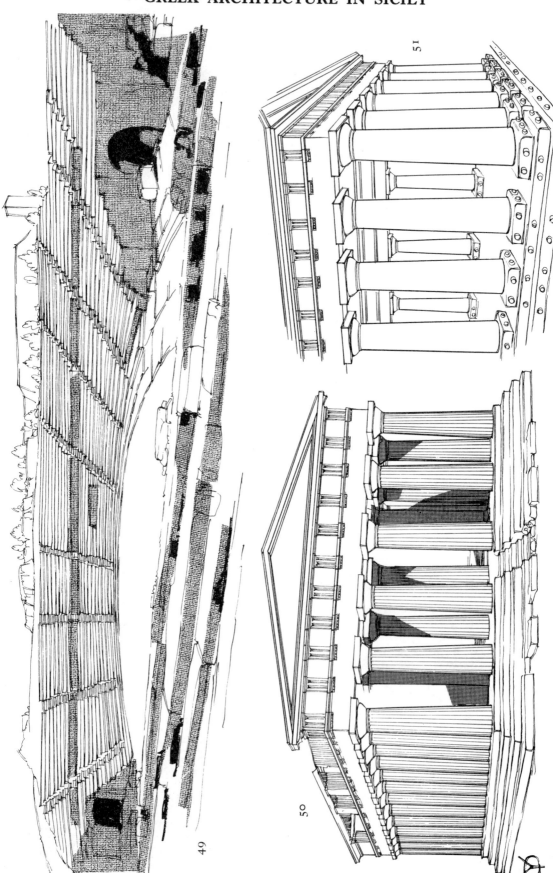

49 The theatre at Syracuse, third to second century B.C.
50 The Temple of Concord at Agrigento, late fifth century B.C.
51 Temple at Segesta, late fifth century B.C.

DELPHI

52 *The Theatre and Temple of Apollo, c. 510 B.C.*
   (altered later by the Romans)
53 *Tholos to Minerva, c. 390 B.C.*
54 *Treasury of the Athenians, c. 500–480 B.C.*

Theatres

The early Greek theatre performance consisted of dancing and chanting which told the story of the drama. The theatre design itself evolved according to these requirements. There was a circular space called the *orchestra*, meaning dancing place, and the *auditorium* was semi-circular in form and hollowed out from a curving hillside. It rose in tiers of seats cut into the rock which were sometimes marble-faced. As the drama developed and actors were introduced, a *stage* (skene) was added to provide entrance and exit accommodation also changing places for the actors (see plan **55**). Nearly all Greek theatres have been altered later by the Romans, who built a larger stage and reduced the circular orchestra to a segment of a circle. One example which retains its original form, though it has been partly restored, is that at *Epidauros*, one of the largest Greek theatres, measuring *c.* 390 feet across the top. It was designed by *Polykleitos the Younger* in *c.* 350 B.C. The acoustics are remarkable, as all visitors to the theatre know who have experimented for themselves. It is in present day use for drama and opera (**55** and **56**). In *Athens* the *Theatre* of *Dionysos*, built under the acropolis, is a smaller example. It was constructed in a number of building periods both in Greek and Roman times. The most interesting feature is its marble seats and central throne, in remarkable condition (**57**). The large theatre at *Syracuse* in *Sicily,* built third to second century B.C. has, like the one at *Taormina* nearby had its orchestra reduced to a semi-circle in later times, as also has the theatre at *Delphi*, built into the lower slopes of Mount Parnassos (**49, 52, 129**).

The Odeion

These were concert halls, also constructed for open-air performances. There is an interesting example in *Athens* near to the theatre of Dionysos under the acropolis hill. It was built in the fifth century B.C., altered by *Herodes Atticus* in A.D. 161 and has now been restored for present-day performances.

The Stadion

This was a foot race-course later used for general athletic competition. It was usually a stade in length (that is, 600 Greek feet) and was set into the side of a hill to provide seating for spectators. The ground had long straight parallel sides terminating at the far end in a semi-circle and at the starting end in a short straight side. The *stadion in Athens* was originally constructed in 331 B.C. but was rebuilt in marble in 1896 for the first Olympic Games of modern times and accommodates 50,000 spectators. There are several examples in a good state of preservation such as the one at *Delphi*, high up on the mountain-side above the theatre (**58**), also at *Epidauros*, *Rhodes*, *Miletus* and *Priene*.

Domestic Architecture

The remains in this field are scanty, and nothing equivalent to Roman work at Pompei or Ostia has been discovered. The most fruitful sites are on the *island of Delos* and at *Priene* in *Asia Minor*, where the houses are mainly fourth century and later. It appears that the Greek house was one-storeyed, designed with rooms grouped round a courtyard or garden which probably had a peristyle and perhaps porticoes. There were few windows which were small and placed high in the walls. A narrow passage gave access to the street. The house walls had stone bases but above this were of sun dried brick and wood, stuccoed and painted on the interior; roofs were tiled, floors of mosaic. There were living rooms and a bathroom; the latrine was in the court. Each house contained a place for worship with an altar.

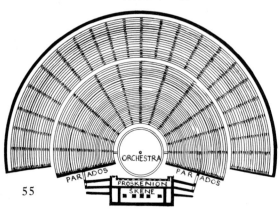

55

55 Typical Greek theatre plan, Epidauros, c. 350 B.C.

Plate 4
Heifers led to sacrifice. South frieze of the Parthenon, Athens *c.* 440 B.C.

Plate 5
North frieze, Parthenon Athens *c.* 447–430 B.C.

Plate 6
Caryatid figure, south
porch, Erechtheion,
Acropolis. Athens *c.*
421 B.C.
Plate 7
Nereid. Nereid
Monument Xanthos
Asia Minor *c.* 370 B.C.

GREEK THEATRES

56 *Theatre at Epidauros, designed by
    Polykleitos the Younger, c. 350 B.C.*
57 *Theatre of Dionysos, Athens, (below the
    Acropolis), various building periods, chiefly
    fifth and fourth centuries*

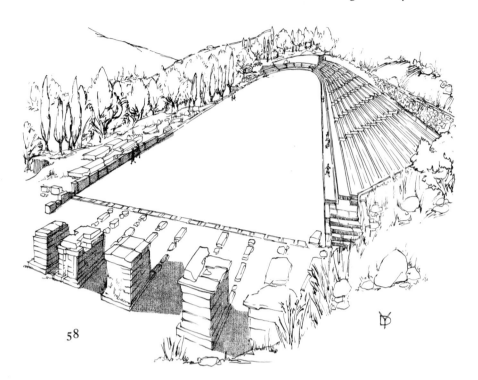

58

58 The Stadion, Delphi,
(a stade in length
i.e. 600 Greek feet)

Tombs

Mausoleum of Halicarnassos (Asia Minor)

Probably the most famous of all tombs, this monument was built for Artemisia in memory of her husband King Mausolos (hence mausoleum) after his death in 353 B.C. It was designed by *Pythius* and *Satyros,* but knowledge of its exact form is not definite as the building does not exist and the materials have been re-used. We have accounts from Pliny and Vitruvius, who base their descriptions upon the original designs. A number of conjectural restorations have been made, but these differ in form as well as detail. An interesting example of these is in the British Museum, carried out by Cockerell. Also in the Museum are parts of the sculptured frieze, horses and quadriga and statues of Mausolos and Artemisia. The monument, which was one of the wonders of the ancient world, stood on a square podium, was surrounded by a peristyle and surmounted by a pyramid with quadriga above. The base was about 100 feet square; the order was Ionic; the total height was 136 feet. One of the chief features of Halicarnassos was the sculpture, carried out by four of Greece's outstanding artists—*Bryaxis, Leochares, Timotheus* and *Scopas.*

Just south of Halicarnassos was *Cnidos,* famous for the *Lion Tomb* which was a similar monument but in the Doric order and surmounted by a colossal recumbent lion. Other interesting tombs included the *Harpy Tomb* at *Xanthos c.* 550 B.C. and the *Nereid Tomb,* (see PLATE 7). Sculpture from all these examples is on view at the British Museum.

Ornament and Mouldings

Greek *ornament* was of the highest quality and has never been surpassed in classical architecture. Designers used their decoration sparingly in order to enhance the architectural form. The motifs came from many sources: Egyptian, Assyrian, Minoan and Mycenaean, and were commonly based on natural plant and animal forms; the Greeks did not, however, use these realistically, but conventionalised them. Each moulding and part of the building was assigned its own ornament, all forms of which were characterised by simplicity of line, refinement and symmetry. Colour and gold were used to pick out the enrichments in carved marble. Among the natural motifs common to Greek ornament are the *acanthus leaf* (the spikier, *spinosus* variety) (**19, 26** and **27**), the *anthemion* or honeysuckle (**15, 16,**

59 *Flanking doorway column in grey-green limestone. Treasury of Atreus, Mycenae, c. 1330 B.C.*

60 *Frieze above doorway, as above, but in red marble*

61 *Tympanum decoration, as above*

62 *Anthemion ornament, Tholos, Acropolis, Athens, c. A.D. 14*

63 *Anthemion and bead and reel ornament, Delphi, late sixth century*

64 *Typical Minoan decoration, Knossos, c. 1500 B.C.*

65 *North porch doorway, the Erechtheion, Athens, 421–405 B.C.*

66 *Entablature and decoration, Tholos at Epidauros, mid-fourth century*

67 *Anta capital and decoration, east portico of the Erechtheion, Athens*

22, 23, 62, 63, 65, 66 and 67), the *palm*, the *rosette* (65 and 66), the *sphinx* and the *griffin* and *lion's head* (66). *Moulding decoration*, apart from the popular anthemion, included *egg and dart*, i.e. life and death (22, 25 and 67), *leaf and dart* (or tongue) (67), *guilloche*, like a plait (16 and 21), *fret* (66), *bead and reel* (16, 25, 62, 63 and 67), *dentil* (15), and the *scroll* (14, 16, 18, 22, 25, 27, 28, 59, 61, 63, 66 and 67).

Although *classical mouldings* are basically of the same form they vary in their usage and proportion according to country and period. The purpose of mouldings, apart from creating a projecting cornice to throw off the rain, is to define and beautify the lines of a building by means of light and shade. In Greece, where sunlight is brilliant, subtly curved and projecting mouldings are adequate; Roman ones are deeper and coarser while Renaissance examples in France and England are deeper still. In *Greek architecture* they comprise the *cyma recta* and *cyma reversa*, the former generally decorated by anthemion, the latter by leaf and tongue (67); the *ovolo*, with egg and tongue (67); the *fillet*, a flat separating moulding; the *corona* (23), the vertical face of the upper cornice often decorated by fret ornament; the *astragal*, with bead and reel (67); the *cavetto*, a hollow; the *torus*, a larger astragal often with guilloche enrichment (21); the *scotia*, a deeper hollow.

Sculpture

Little original Greek sculpture survives, whether *in situ* on buildings or in museums: the work in museums is predominantly copied or restored and most of that on the buildings is mutilated and any colour has gone. Despite these heavy handicaps the magnificence of the work comes through and makes plain the fact that sculptured decoration to the Greeks was an integral part of architecture. Thus, while their architecture was the finest and purest in classical style, their sculpture has also never been surpassed. It is fortunate that the Romans reproduced so much of the Greek work for it is due to their energies that we owe much of our knowledge of Greek sculpture. Some Roman copies are poor, but many are excellent and possession of these copies is far better than having no record of the originals at all. Much Greek sculpture was architectural in purpose and design. Figure sculpture was framed by the triglyphs and pediment mouldings. Much of it had religious inspiration and was used to decorate temples in the form of friezes, metopes, pedimental groups and cult statues. Subjects were commonly of two types; to illustrate the daily life of the period and the Greek legends. Life-size portrait sculpture belongs to the middle and later periods. The Greeks used stone, marble and bronze as their chief sculptural materials but most of the surviving work is in stone or marble; the bronze was mostly melted down later. Early bronze work was in plates fastened to a wooden core. Later examples were cast. The Greeks worked also in terracotta, especially for smaller items, possibly influencing later Etruscan work in this medium.

There are *four chief periods* in Greek sculpture: work prior to 450 B.C.; 450–400 B.C.; the fourth century and *c.* 340–146 B.C. *Early sculpture*, that prior to about 650 B.C., was generally of wood on a small scale. Subsequently, contact with Egypt and Assyria led to larger works in stone being attempted by the Greeks. The eastern characteristics in sculptural design are apparent in the Greek works of the seventh century. Figures stand stiffly, one foot slightly in advance of the other, arms at sides elbows slightly bent and heads facing front. The figures are generally nude and anatomical features are stylised. By the early sixth century attempts were made to study anatomy and movement and to fit the figures to the architectural shape, for example, the pediment. Animals, particularly lions and bulls, and sphinxes were used. The *first half of the fifth century* is the early classical period from which a number of architectural examples are available. From the *Temple of Zeus* at *Olympia* 465–457 B.C. are the pedimental sculptures and metopes. The *eastern pediment* has a centrepiece of five figures and a chariot; it illustrates sacrifice to Zeus and is still and forceful. The *western pedimental sculpture* is, in contrast, full of movement and depicts the struggle between Lapiths and Centaurs with a magnificent central figure of Apollo. There are a number of metopes extant, some showing the exploits of Hercules. From the *Treasury of the Athenians* at *Delphi c.* 490 the metopes illustrate the adventures of Hercules and Theseus. From the *Temple of Aphaia* at *Aegina* come pedimental sculptures. All these examples show more vigorous movement and realism than the archaic sculpture, also more naturalistic drapery, and are vivid in design and form.

450–400 B.C.

This was a prosperous time. Under the leadership of *Pericles* art and architecture flourished reaching the zenith of the classical style. The *Parthenon* represents all that is finest in Greek Doric temple building both architecturally and sculpturally. *Pheidias* was in charge of the sculptural decorations of the Parthenon and it is in the remains of this work that we can appreciate the wonderful quality of Greek art of this period and in particular the work of the greatest of Greek sculptors. Pheidias' contemporaries regarded his architectural sculpture as inferior to his great statues such as the colossal figures of *Athena Parthenos* in Athens and of *Zeus* at Olympia. We only possess copies of doubtful authenticity of such works but we can see considerable sections of the Parthenon sculptures—frieze, metopes and pedimental—in the national museums of Athens, Paris, Rome and London. Of the immense quantity of sculpture on the Parthenon, Pheidias carried out some and designed and supervised the remainder. There were over 50 large figures in the pediments, 92 metopes and over 520 feet of continuous frieze all carried out in 15 years. The quality of the work is magnificent, the drapery is lively and vivid, the horses, the bulls and the men are breathing, pulsing living beings, yet subtle and never overstated. In the frieze especially, the composition is always alive, never monotonous. The handling of the horses and bulls is in low relief yet distinguishing one horse behind another, with the four legs of each animal in recessive perspective giving the appearance of great depth of relief in reserve. The detail is fine and yet the unity of the whole frieze is intact. The subject is the procession of the Panathenaia, a sacred Athenian festival, depicting men and animals moving inexorably and perpetually forward round the building. Large sections of this frieze are now admirably displayed in the British Museum (PLATES 4 and 5). The metopes in high relief are mainly single combat groups between Greeks and Amazons or Centaurs and Lapiths. The part-bull part-man centaurs provide effective contrast to horse and man (PLATE 2).

Pheidias dominates the sculpture of Greece but in his own age there were a number of other fine sculptors. In architectural sculpture there are the famous caryatid figures of the *Erechtheion* south porch *c.* 420 (PLATE 6) (one of which is in the British Museum), the sculptured frieze and pedimental figures from the *Theseion, Athens*, in high relief, the frieze of the *Temple of Athena Nike* on the Athens acropolis *c.* 425 and the frieze from the great altar at *Pergamon* 168 B.C. representing a battle between Gods and Greeks.

2

Etruscan and Roman: 750 B.C. to A.D. 476
Etruscan Eighth Century B.C. to First Century B.C.

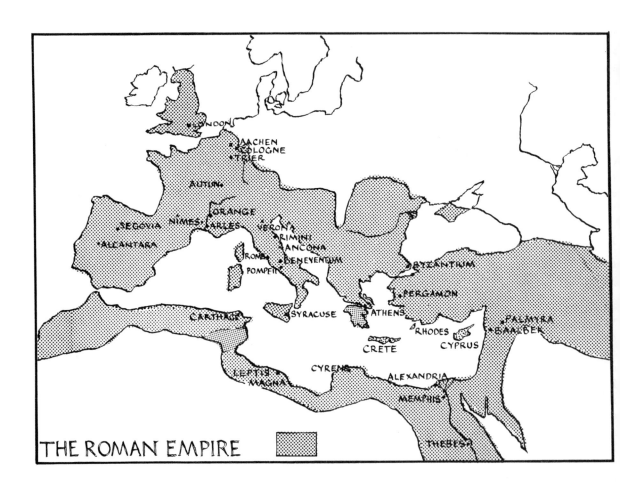

THE ROMAN EMPIRE

Despite archaeological discoveries which are still being made year by year and which throw more light upon the Etruscan civilisation, knowledge of these people, their origins, their way of life is still far from complete. It is generally accepted* that the Etruscans were of foreign origin, of a mixed Hellenic and Oriental culture, probably but far from certainly from Asia Minor, and that they established themselves in central Italy, in the area between the Arno and the Tiber, in the eighth century B.C. The civilisation appears to have developed and grown quickly and exten-

sively and, by about 700 B.C., the Etruscans were living an urban life in fine cities with wealthy citizens, and were capable of a high standard of building and visual and literary arts.

Although so far no one has succeeded in interpreting the Etruscan language we can fully appreciate their sculpture, painting and craftsmanship. No complete buildings are intact, but there are extensive remains in walling, gateways, arches and in tombs. It is in the tombs that so many fine works of art and crafts have been found. Few early peoples, apart from the

In Roman times there was one theory that the Etruscans originated in Italy.

Egyptians, have left to posterity so much workmanship quite undisturbed through the passage of time.

The Etruscans were great builders and in this respect they occupy a similar relationship to the Romans in the development of architecture as do the Pelasgic and Minoan peoples to the Greek. Etruscan builders fully understood the art of building in stone and used huge (cyclopean) blocks, generally without cement. They showed great skill in constructing polygonal block walling and introduced into Europe—though it is questionable that they invented it—vaulting by dressed stones. They constructed in this way true arches with radiating voussoirs, but a controversy exists as to whether the European origins here are Etruscan or Roman, as Etruscan examples all date from the later period of the third century B.C. onwards when Roman supremacy over the Etruscans was being established.*

Etruscan Remains

City Walls, Arches and Gateways

There are numerous hill towns in central Italy where can be seen extant remains of Etruscan city walling. Examples from the sixth century B.C. exist, generally of a cruder type of masonry at, for example, Volterra and Cortona. There are also, dating from about 500 B.C., gateways of the lintel and arched types. A famous lintel example is the *Porta Saracena* at *Segni*, originally part of the city wall, but now about a mile outside the modern town up on the steep hillside. This has a large lintel stone and the sides slope inwards towards the top (**69**). There is another gateway of this type at nearby *Arpino*, the *Porta dell'Arco*. An early arched gateway is in the town walls of *Ferentino* where the *Porta Sanguinaria* has radiating stone voussoirs; here the sides are vertical (**72**). A particularly good example is the *town gateway* at *Volterra*, of the third century B.C., which has cyclopean blocks fitted to make vertical sides, and radiating voussoirs which are exceptionally well prepared. The gateway is several feet in thickness but the outer face is in better condition (**71**).

The two best known Etruscan archways are both of later date: the *Arch of Augustus* at *Perugia* and the *Cloaca Maxima* in *Rome*. The Perugian

arch is called Augustan as the upper part was added by Augustus. The archway itself is in fine condition and dates from the third century B.C. It forms part of the Etruscan walls to the city and is the best extant example of Etruscan masonry. It is built of large blocks of travertine stone and the arch has two concentric rings of radiating voussoirs. Above this is a 'Doric' type frieze with 'Ionic' pilasters in place of triglyphs (**73**). Also in Perugia is the arch of the *Porta Marzia*, with a similar frieze and Ionic style columns at the sides (**70**). The *Cloaca Maxima* is a floodwater drain built by the Etruscans in the sixth century B.C. to drain the Forum Romanum. It was for many years claimed to be the earliest example of the true arch in Europe, but it is now recognised that it was constructed in the sixth century as an open drain and that it was only roofed over with its present stone vault of three concentric rings of radiating voussoirs in 184 B.C. Its exit into the Tiber can still be seen in Rome near the Ponte Rotto (**68**).

Etruscan Temples

Extensive remains of the foundations of such temples make it relatively easy to establish their plan, but reconstruction of the superstructure is more speculative as almost all the walls and trabeation have disappeared. Vitruvius provides a clear description of an example of the late period from which it seems that the temples contained three cells placed side by side and dedicated to three different deities. There was a portico, generally of wood, with posts supporting beams, and decoration was in terracotta. Larger temples generally had one or two rows of columns in front with wide intercolumniation. A smaller example from *Alatri* has been re-erected and restored in the Court of the *Villa Giulia* in *Rome*. It has a two columned portico and, behind this, a central doorway opening into the cella (**76**).

Etruscan Houses

Very little was known about these from actual remains until recent excavations at S. Giovenale by the Swedish expedition established plans from some foundations there. The layout of a seventh century B.C. example shows a large hall with entrance porch.

* *The Roman Conquest of Etruria is dated at about 280*

Etruscan Tombs

It is from this source that much has been learnt of the style of domestic building, the arrangement and designs of house interiors, of sculpture, painting and craftmanship in terracotta, metal and jewellery. The Etruscans put their burial places outside their cities, and due to the care with which they constructed the tombs many examples have been discovered intact, from the eighteenth century onwards. There are two chief types of tombs which date from the seventh to first century B.C. One type consists of a tumulus, or burial mound, of earth, circular in plan and surrounded at the base by a stone wall. There is a rectangular entrance and inside is the burial chamber(s). The other type is a rectangular tomb cut in the rock, where such rock—generally volcanic tufa—was suitably soft. In these cases the chambers are approached down a flight of steps. Tombs vary greatly in size and elaboration, from a nobleman's tomb with several chambers, richly decorated and furnished by household objects used in life, to simple, single-cell designs for an ordinary family. In the more elaborate tombs can be seen the manner of domestic interior design, for the rock has been hewn to imitate rafters and ridge-piece. Columns and piers of stone support the roof; these have carved capitals, some in voluted 'Ionic' designs (**83**). Many chambers have characteristic semi-circular headed windows and either semi-circular or square headed door openings with sloping sides (**78** and **81**). There are often wall recesses holding utensils and objects used in life such as helmets, swords, knives, kitchen pots and pans etc. Stone funerary beds are set on each side of the main chamber.

Two of the principal Etruscan cities which possess such examples in quantity are *Tarquinia* and *Cerveteri. Modern Tarquinia* (earlier known as Corneto but now re-named after the Etruscan Tarquinii) is built near to the original city. The enormous necropolis is adjacent and contains hundreds of tombs cut down into the tufa over a distance of two miles. The tombs are rock hewn chambers, many beautifully decorated by wall paintings in rich colours. They are mainly of the fourth, fifth and sixth centuries B.C. and illustrate episodes and customs in Etruscan life. Some of these are in exceptionally good condition.

Cerveteri is built near the extensive necropolis which served the Etruscan city of *Caere*, one of their largest towns, near the sea and only a few miles from Rome. The tombs represent a period of wealth and expansion in the sixth and seventh centuries B.C. Many of the finds in sculpture and decoration have been taken to museums, but the chambers remain. These are of several types but predominantly of the circular tumulus design with its stone base and decorative cornice (**80** and **84**). Later tombs here have no tumulus above but consist of a single large room cut into the stone. The room is reproduced as a house interior, furnished with benches, pillars, wall paintings and utensils. The larger tumuli are nearly 100 feet in diameter and contain several chambers as a house does rooms. The ceilings are coffered or have sloping beams and are supported by decorative pillars (**81** and **83**).

Sculpture and Ornament

Much of the extant Etruscan *sculpture* is in the form of sarcophagi in stone and bronze. The Etruscans are particularly noted for their terracotta work, a medium at which they excelled (**74, 75, 77** and PLATE 8).

Ornament also was commonly made in terracotta, often in the form of panels and friezes. Here the anthemion is a popular motif (**77**). *Moulding ornament* includes a version of egg and tongue, anthemion, leaves and flowers. There are several types of *capital* in which an 'Ionic' style predominates. Sometimes such a capital is also decorated with a head in high relief or with anthemion (**82** and **83**).

Roman 146 B.C. to A.D. 476

It is traditionally accepted that it was in about the year 753 B.C. that a tribe of people settled near the Tiber on the Palatine Hill. Here they built and established a walled city. They extended their domain and carried out raids upon neighbouring peoples. Until nearly 500 B.C. they were ruled by tribal kings. After this Rome became a republic which steadily expanded and absorbed the adjacent peoples and countryside. Piecemeal the country of Italy became a vassal state to the City of Rome: the Etruscans were absorbed; the Sicilians, Carthage and North Africa were

Plate 8
Etruscan Sarcophagus
from Chiusi, Italy *c.*
150 B.C.
Plate 9
Stucco wall relief,
Tepidarium. Forum
Baths, Pompeii, Italy

Plate 10
Detail, Trajan Column
Rome A.D. 114
Plate 11
Sculptured panel.
Arch of Galerius,
Thessaloniki, Greece

annexed and, in 146 B.C., Greece became a part of Rome. It is from this time onwards that the architectural style of Rome was developed and crystallised.

The expansion of Rome did not, however, cease at this point. In 30 B.C. Egypt was absorbed and campaigns were extended northwards and westwards in Europe, culminating in A.D. 43 with the successful annexation of most of Britain. For 400 years after this the Romans enslaved, organised and civilised the enormous area of their known world, which encircled the Mediterranean and stretched from Spain in the west to the Black Sea in the east, from Britain in the north to Egypt in the south. They first conquered the territories, then brought their rule of law, made roads, built cities and stayed to civilise with their arts, literature and industry. For, unlike conquerors before and after, the Romans did not only take from their subject peoples, they contributed also, and the result of these contributions in road communications, law and administration, heating systems, architecture and art has had a permanent effect in Europe despite the 1000 years which intervened between the collapse of the Western half of the Roman Empire and the rise of the Renaissance.

The republic of Rome was severely shaken in 44 B.C. by the murder of Julius Caesar. There followed a time of uncertainty and bloodshed which was eventually resolved when the republic developed into an empire with Augustus as its first emperor from 27 B.C. The Augustan period from then until his death in A.D. 14 was one of the great and successful ages of man and, architecturally, this is reflected in the many great buildings which were erected under the auspices of Augustus whose boast was that when he came to Rome it was a city of bricks but that he left it a city of marble. There is a basic truth in his assertion, for before his time the use of marble was rare in Roman architecture. It was from the first century B.C. onwards that the vast white marble quarries at Carrara were developed and that quantities of Greek marble were shipped to Italy from Hymettus and Pentelicus.

A number of the Roman emperors were great patrons of building and endorsed and encouraged extensive schemes of architectural development. Among the most outstanding of these were:

Augustus	27 B.C. to A.D. 14
Tiberius	A.D. 14–37
Nero	A.D. 54–68
Vespasian	A.D. 70–9
Titus	A.D. 79–81
Trajan	A.D. 98–117
Hadrian	A.D. 117–138
Marcus Aurelius	A.D. 161–180
Septimius Severus	A.D. 193–211
Caracalla	A.D. 211–17
Diocletian	A.D. 284–305
Maxentius	A.D. 306–12
Constantine	A.D. 312–337

It was in the Imperial age that the full magnificence and display of Roman architecture was reached. Before the first century B.C. little is heard of its quality. It was after the annexation of Greece that Rome began to take the place of the nation that she had absorbed and the civilisation which she had destroyed. But the Romans were never to replace the Greeks as artists. They excelled in and developed the arts of building, of engineering and of town planning. Their schemes, especially under the emperors, were extensive, grandiose, eye-catching, but never of the same meticulous quality of craftmanship and design that the Greeks had attained before them. The Romans did not try to compete in the sculptural and decorative field. They imported artists and artisans from Greece to carry out this work for them and to ornament their buildings; they also imported actual sculpture from Greece for the same purpose. It is, however, due to the large number of copies which the Romans had made of Greek masterpieces, some of them of high quality, that we owe our wide knowledge of such work today.

Extensive building schemes were projected not only in Rome and in Italy but all over the Empire. Wherever Roman civilisation went there were created cities, each with their buildings necessary to Roman life: the central fora, the basilicas, temples, baths, circuses and amphitheatres. The remains of these edifices in Italy, France, Germany, Spain, Yugoslavia, Greece, Rumania and Asia Minor give us a clear idea of their way of life as well as their modes of building and it is a much more complete picture than that which we have from the Greek civilisation because of its very complexity and variety. Greek remains are largely temples; Roman ones represent every facet of Roman life.

ETRUSCAN ARCHES AND GATEWAYS, SIXTH TO THIRD CENTURY

68 The Cloaca Maxima, Rome. Exit into the River Tiber
    near the Ponte Rotto, sixth century B.C. Roofed over
    184 B.C.
69 Porta Saracena, Segni, Town Gateway (now outside
    the present town)

70 Porta Marzia, Perugia (archway now blocked up)
71 Town Gateway, Volterra, third century B.C.
72 Porta Sanguinaria, Ferentino, Town Gateway
73 Arch of Augustus, Perugia, third century B.C. (only
    top arch is Augustan)

74 *Antefix, gorgon's head from Capua, terracotta, sixth century B.C.*

75 *Antefix, terracotta, Cerveteri, fifth century B.C.*

76 *Temple from Alatri (restored)*

77 *Terracotta decoration*

78 *Tomb doorway, Cerveteri, sixth century B.C.*

79 *Bronze griffin's head from Chiusi, 650–600 B.C.*

80 *Tumuli, Cerveteri, seventh-fifth century B.C.*

81 *Interior of Tomb of the Funerary Beds, Cerveteri, sixth-fifth century B.C.*

82 *Ionic style capital, Tomb of the Reliefs, Cerveteri, fourth-second century B.C.*

83 *Interior of Tomb of the Capitals, Cerveteri, sixth-fifth century B.C.*

84 *Tumuli, Cerveteri, seventh-fifth century B.C.*

In A.D. 324 Constantine moved his capital to Byzantium and a few years later the Empire was divided into two parts, eastern and western. Early Christian work began to influence the architectural style in the new Christian Roman Empire. In the fifth century Rome was attacked and sacked three times. Finally, in A.D. 476, the western part of the Empire collapsed, and in the eastern part with Byzantium as its capital, architecture developed in a different direction. Of this vast quantity of building which was achieved between 146 B.C. and A.D. 476 only a small fraction exists today and often this is in the best condition in the provinces of the Empire, despite the fact that the examples were generally less magnificent. Such well preserved works can be seen for example in Southern France and Spain, rather than in Italy, and particularly Rome, where greater toll has been taken by the use of marble for rebuilding and by barbarian invasions.

The Roman Architectural Style

The development of the classical style of architecture with trabeated construction belongs to the Greeks, who carried this to the highest possible standard of artistic perfection. The Romans also followed on these lines but adapted the construction to suit their more complex needs. They incorporated the arch and vault into their architectural style, using both lintel and arcuated construction, often in one building. The Greeks had perfected the lintel method of spanning an opening; the Romans adapted the arch from Etruscan designs and from their own development and thus led the way to later variations on this theme. They used the Greek orders, adapted them to their own taste, added two more variations and employed them constructively in temples and basilicas but more often, especially in later work, only decoratively when the arch mode of construction was used, for example, in the Colosseum and the Theatre of Marcellus. The Greeks had built predominantly in only one or two storeys; the Romans built up to four or even five, and the arched type of construction was more suitable for this type of work.

Roman workmanship is often criticised in comparison with Greek for its clumsy detail, as in capitals and mouldings, and for its less subtle proportions of columns and entablature. The Romans appreciated fine art but lacked the artistic sense of the Greeks. They never reached the standard of work evidenced by the Parthenon or the Erechtheion. Their outstanding abilities lay elsewhere and it is to their fine engineering achievements in vaulting such constructions as the Basilica of Constantine and the Baths of Diocletian, or in the building of amphi-theatres such as the Colosseum, or in layouts like the Palace of Diocletian in Split or the Villa of Hadrian at Tivoli that we can appreciate their genius for architectural effect and scale in planning.

Town Planning

Roman cities were planned as far as possible symmetrically on a grid system, although in the case of existing towns which they took over, or of hill sites, geographical problems made this difficult. The city would be encircled by its defensive walls pierced by town gates. The town was laid out in a military camp plan with a wide, straight road crossing the city centre from one side of the town to the other and similar roads intersecting the first at right angles. The town gates were set in the walls where these principal thoroughfares made their exit. The main forum was generally placed at the central cross-roads and round it were grouped the chief buildings of the town. The smaller streets criss-crossed on a grid pattern and the town walls surrounded an eight-sided city. This was considered to be the ideal layout and was followed where a new city was planned. Remains showing this design can be seen in a number of towns, especially where the city has since declined in importance and later building has not obscured the pattern.

Our chief source of information on Roman architecture for the first century B.C. is Marcus Vitruvius Pollio who wrote his famous work *De Architectura*, which he dedicated to Augustus, in 25 B.C. Vitruvius, as we call him, sets out his plans for an ideal Roman city in the first volume of his work.

The Roman Forum

In Roman life the forum corresponded to the Greek agora. It was a large open space surrounded by buildings and provided a meeting place and a centre for commerce and public life. Every town had a forum and large cities more than one. Under the republic the forum was both a market place surrounded by shops and a public meeting place. Under the empire, in large towns, the shops were cleared and it became the site for more magnificent buildings devoted to the administration of justice, bureaucracy and commerce, as well as for worship. There were many temples, set at different angles, not orientated like the Greek ones. The forum was planned symmetrically and was surrounded by covered colonnades to provide shelter from sun and rain.

Rome

At one period there were 17 fora in Rome. The largest of these was the *Forum of Trajan* but the oldest is the *Forum Romanum*, or as it is often called, simply 'the Forum'. Under Imperial rule, a number of emperors added their own forum bearing their name; one forum was not large enough for the needs of the whole city. Since Rome has been continuously inhabited ever since, and as Medieval, Renaissance and Modern cities have been built on the same site, very little is left of any of these fora except the excavated site and fragments of buildings.

The Forum Romanum owes its present layout largely to Julius Caesar, who replanned much of it. Originally the forum was a business centre and market place for the inhabitants of the three surrounding hills—Palatine, Capitoline and Esquiline. The great drain, the Cloaca Maxima crosses the valley from north to south and, after its construction in the sixth century B.C. the forum life began. By the second century B.C. it had become a large square surrounded by imposing buildings. A number of reconstructions were made from time to time, especially under Julius Caesar and Augustus. The body of Julius Caesar was burned near the Via Sacra and Augustus had built on the spot the Temple of Divi Julii to his memory. In the time of Augustus also were erected the Temples of Concord, of Castor and Pollux, and the Basilica Julia. The great Basilica of Constantine (Maxentius) was constructed along the Via Sacra in the time of these two emperors.

In the fifth century many buildings were destroyed in the Goth and Vandal invasions and,

later, Christians built churches in the temple ruins. Earthquakes assisted the destruction and the land silted up so that by the Middle Ages only the capitals of the columns stood above ground and the forum's name (Campo Vaccino) reflected its purpose—grazing land for cattle. A plan of the Forum Romanum as it is today is shown in Fig. **86** while a reconstruction of it as it was under Imperial Rome, looking towards Capitol Hill, is illustrated in Fig. **85**.

Building Materials and Construction

Unlike the Greeks, whose building materials were principally limited to marbles, the Romans were fortunate in the availability of a wide variety of materials in Italy itself. Much of their building was in brick and concrete faced, in republican times, chiefly with stucco and, under the empire, with marble. A useful selection of *stone* was also to hand; travertine, a form of hard limestone from the area near Tivoli, also tufa and peperino, both of volcanic origin. These were all used in large blocks for strong walling and arch voussoirs. *Bricks* were of two types, sun dried and kiln burnt, and these were widely employed, particularly in provincial work. The bricks were laid in alternate courses with stone or concrete, or were used only as a facing on a concrete core. They were about an inch to one and a half inches in thickness and nearly two feet square. The mortar joints between bricks were thick, generally about the same as the bricks themselves. The material which more than any other influenced the whole course and design of Roman architecture was *concrete* and this made the vaulting of huge spans possible. The exceptional strength and durability of Roman concrete was due to the substance *pozzolana*, a volcanic ash, found in quantity in the volcanic areas around Rome and Naples and named after the village near Naples where the best quality supplies were available. *Pozzolana* when mixed with the excellent lime from the local limestones formed an extremely hard concrete, to which base was also added brick and travertine fragments to provide a solid core for walling and vaulting. The concrete was poured between boards to make walls and over centering for arches and vaults.

Marble was not in general use in Rome until

the early days of the Empire. It was retained chiefly for decoration and facings to walls, floors and vaults. Marbles were imported from all over the Empire, particularly from Hymettus and Pentelicus in Greece, while Italian quarries were developed to provide, in particular, Carrara, Cipollino and Pavonazzo marbles. Granite and alabaster were also imported with precious materials such as porphyry to give richness and lustre to interiors. Roman columns were generally monolithic and unfluted. This method was more suited to hard materials like granite and cipollino marble and shows the veining to advantage. Despite the enormous quantities of marble used on buildings in Imperial Rome, little remains today as it was nearly all used in later ages for further building and decoration.

Metals such as bronze were generally retained for decorative use only and for sculpture, although there are individual examples of constructional needs, as at the Pantheon where the roof tiles and ceiling panels were of bronze.

For buildings which were not faced with marble or made of ashlar blocks, a marble *stucco* generally covered the brick and concrete walling. This material was most durable and the powdered marble imparted a brilliance to the finished surface. The stucco was applied in several coats to a thickness of up to three inches. Such work gave excellent protection to the wall surface. Much thinner coating was given to columns, capitals and other decorative features.

Methods of Construction

In Greek trabeated architecture the length of the lintel had determined the intercolumniation. As the Romans turned more and more towards arcuated construction, with the orders used in a decorative capacity there was no such restriction and the columns are sometimes separated by a distance as great as their height. In the buildings with a number of storeys they frequently used a different order on each storey, whilst the columns were lined up one above the other and the entablatures acted as string courses. The Colosseum shows the fine architectural effect which such a system can provide (**121**). In these circumstances the columns are placed on pedestals instead of just bases—a further breakaway from Greek tradition. Another instance of

this is seen in later examples of Imperial building where the entablature is continued round the arch or where free-standing columns (generally in interiors) possess their own entablature, often surmounted by a sculptured figure.

The Arch and Vault

In republican times and for smaller temples and basilicas the Romans followed Greek practice and roofed with timber covering. With the development of Imperial architecture and the need for large public gatherings in baths and basilicas the space was more often vaulted with brick and concrete. It is in this method of construction that the Romans made one of their greatest contributions to architectural development; their work was further adapted and continued in Byzantine and Medieval times. The supporting arches were made of brick and concrete or, more commonly, of stone. The supporting piers were massive, few in number in order not to obscure the interior vista but great in diameter and made into important features of the design. They were faced with beautifully patterned marbles in rich colours. The actual vaults were nearly always of concrete and it was the strength of Roman concrete which made it possible to cover the enormous spaces in this way. Many Roman vault spans were far greater than Gothic ones and were not equalled until the development of steel construction in the nineteenth century. This concrete provided a rigid mass covering the open space. There was, unlike Medieval stone vaults, no lateral thrust and this made possible great vaults such as the Pantheon dome, the largest example in the world. Indeed the tenacity of Roman concrete and mortar was so great that today, in the ruined buildings of the Empire, it can be seen that it is the stone which has fractured not the material which binds it. Some vaults were made with brick ribs and concrete filling while, towards the later days of the Empire, stone vaults were constructed, particularly in the provinces, as at Nîmes and in Syria. In design the vault was either barrel or groined. The barrel vault of semi-circular section was used for smaller buildings and was generally divided into rectangular compartments, with brick construction supported on wood centering and then filled in with concrete. For larger edifices the intersecting or

THE FORUM ROMANUM, ROME

85 *Forum Romanum (reconstruction) looking towards Capitol Hill*
   1) Tabularium   2) Temple of Concord   3) Temple of Vespasian   4) Curia   5) Arch of Septimius Severus
   6) Temple of Saturn   7) Imperial Rostra   8) Arch of Tiberius   9) Column of Phocas   10) Honorary Columns
   11) Basilica Julia   12) Basilica Aemilia   13) Temple of Divus Julius   14) Arch of Augustus   15) Temple of
   Castor   16) Temple of Vesta   17) House of Vestal Virgins   18) Temple of Antoninus and Faustina   19) Temple
   of Romulus   20) Basilica of Constantine   21) To Colosseum   22) Arch of Titus   23) To Palatine Hill   24) To
   Capitol   25) To Temple of Jupiter   26) To Temple of Juno

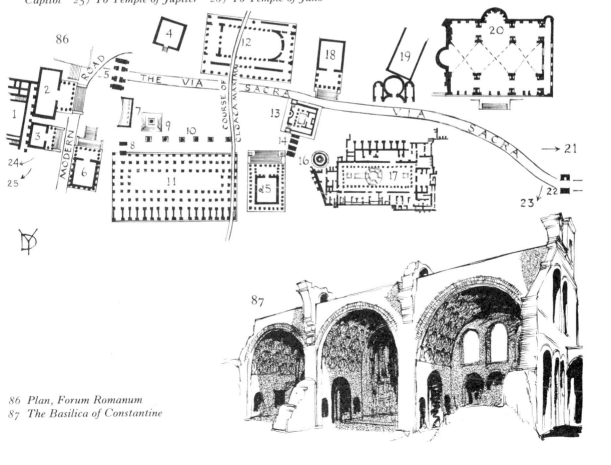

86 *Plan, Forum Romanum*
87 *The Basilica of Constantine*

ROMAN ORDERS AND DETAIL IN ITALY

88 *Triumphal column to Marcus Aurelius, Rome, Doric A.D. 174–80*

89 *Corinthian Capital and Entablature, Forum Baths, Ostia, second-fourth century A.D.*

90 *The Ionic Order, Temple of Fortuna Virilis, Rome, first century B.C.*

91 *The Doric Order, The Colosseum, Rome, A.D. 70–82*

92 *Ionic capital, Forum Basilica, Pompei, first century A.D.*

93 *Corinthian entablature, Forum, Pompei*

94 *Corinthian capital, Temple of Minerva, Assisi, first century B.C.*

95 *The Corinthian Order, Temple of Castor and Pollux,*
   Rome, A.D. 6
96 *The Tuscan Order, (reconstruction after Sir William*
   Chambers)
97 *The Composite Order, The Arch of Titus, Rome,*
   A.D. 81

98 *The Doric Order, The Baths of Diocletian,*
   Rome, A.D. 290–300
99 *Base, The Pantheon, Rome, A.D. 120*
100 *Capital, the Pantheon*
101 *Base and Pedestal, the Trajan Column, Rome,*
   A.D. 114

groined vault, which consists of two barrel vaults meeting one another at right angles, was used. If a long hall was to be vaulted by a cross or groined vault the room would be divided by piers into square bays each of which would be covered by a cross vault. Windows could then be inserted into the upper part of the walls. The Romans used the *dome* construction to a limited extent, but it was left to Byzantium to develop this type of covering to its logical conclusion. In Roman hemispherical domes, brick radiating ribs started at the springing and met at the apex. Semi-circular recesses were covered by half-domes. The interior surface of the vault was covered and decorated in various ways: by stucco, marble or stone facing, by mosaic or by paintings on the plain stucco. A characteristic Roman method was *coffering* such ceilings. The idea was suggested by the pattern made by timber roofed ceilings. The sunken panels or coffers used by the Romans as decoration were formed between the brick ribs or cut into the solid concrete. They were carved decoratively, painted and gilded (**87, 108, 123 and 150**).

The Orders

The Romans used the three Greek orders and developed two more of their own in addition. The proportions differed from the Greek prototypes, the mouldings and carved decoration were less subtle and, generally, more ornate. This is emphasised by the fact that the Doric was the favourite order of the Greeks and was used above all others for important buildings; to the Romans the Corinthian had a greater appeal. Vitruvius gives us a clear account of four of the Roman orders but, having lived in the days of Augustus, he was unable to describe the Composite Order.

Doric

The Roman Doric Order is less massive than the Greek but also less refined. It is often unfluted and, being slenderer, is given a base. The metopes which beautify the Greek frieze are frequently replaced in Roman work by bulls' skulls or garlands. The capital is much less subtle; the Greek echinus becomes a quarter round moulding and the three fillets replace the Greek necking mouldings. Among the best

examples are the Colosseum and the Baths of Diocletian, both in Rome (**91, 98 and 121**).

Tuscan

This is a simplified version of Roman Doric and is generally without flutes or any ornamented mouldings. No clear ancient examples exist, but the order was revived in Renaissance work with the assistance of Vitruvius' *De Architectura*, for example in the colonnade by Bernini in front of S. Peter's Basilica in Rome (**96**).

Ionic

This is the order which bears a closer resemblance to its Greek prototype than any other. Flutes are optional and in the capital angle volutes are often turned in order to present faces to both elevations. The mouldings are more richly decorated than in Greek examples. Among the best Roman versions extant are the Temple of Fortuna Virilis, the Temple of Saturn and the Theatre of Marcellus, all in Rome (**90, 119 and 127**).

Corinthian

One of the reasons for the popularity of this order with the Romans was that, since all four faces of the capital are alike, it presented an interesting view from different angles for the decoration of public buildings and triumphal arches. The shaft was fluted or left plain but the capital bell was strongly delineated, richly decorated and used the softer acanthus leaf design. In later examples all mouldings were enriched, thus somewhat defeating the purpose of the designers for there were no plain members to offset the decoration. Among the many examples, the Temple of Castor and Pollux, the Temple of Mars Ultor and the Pantheon, all in Rome, are very fine (**93, 94, 95, 99, 100, 102, 115, 123 and 124**).

Composite

This order, as its name suggests, was developed as a richer example than the Corinthian, but it is only in the capital that it differs materially. Here, the volutes are larger as in the Ionic order and the upper row of acanthus leaves is replaced by the egg and tongue and bead and reel mouldings

ROMAN ARCHITECTURAL DETAILS FIRST CENTURY B.C. TO FOURTH CENTURY A.D.

102 Corinthian capital and entablature, Maison Carrée, Nîmes, c. 16 B.C.

103 Walling at Ostia, opus reticulatum with brick, second century A.D.

104 Doorway, Temple of Romulus, Forum Romanum, Corinthian order, bronze doors, A.D. 307

105 Stucco wall decoration, tepidarium, Forum baths, Pompei, first century A.D.

106 Main doorway, the Pantheon, Rome, A.D. 120

107 Entablature, Forum, Ostia

108 Coffered vault, Basilica of Constantine, early fourth century A.D.

109 Decorated panel, Arch of Tiberius, Orange, c. 30 B.C.

110 Scroll decoration, Forum of Trajan, Rome

from the Ionic capital. The Composite Order was employed particularly on triumphal arches and its use on the Arch of Titus in A.D. 81 is the first recorded instance of its appearance (97 and 157).

Interior Decoration

Under the Empire interiors were rich and splendid. Floors were patterned in coloured mosaic and marble. Walls and ceilings were marble faced or decorated with paintings in fresco, tempera or caustic medium. Subjects included figure compositions or landscapes with architectural features introduced. A number of examples are extant at Pompei or have been removed to the Naples Museum. Sometimes the schemes lacked refinement but rarely richness, colour or magnificence.

Ornament

Roman ornament is a continuation of development from Greek and Etruscan work; it has solidity of mass and grouping, it is bold and vigorous, magnificent, but often lacks the Greek standard of refinement. Similar motifs were used, in particular the acanthus foliage, scrolls and anthemion. The Roman version of the *acanthus leaf* was usually based on the more rounded *acanthus mollis* plant rather than the Greek *acanthus spinosis*, which was spikier and more delicate. The Romans frequently used acanthus foliage in scroll decoration where spiral lines were clothed and decorated by foliage and sheaths with terminal rosettes. They also designed panels and borders with arabesques, mythological forms such as the chimera and griffin, as well as birds, animals and cupids. *Coffered ceilings* were panelled in square, hexagonal or octagonal coffers which had sunken borders enriched with egg and dart or water leaf mouldings and had a central rosette. In capitals, panels and friezes other foliage was also employed: water leaves, ivy, the vine or the olive leaf. All the Greek forms of *moulding enrichment* were used but in less refined form. Examples are illustrated in Figs. 89, 90, 93, 94, 95, 97, 98, 100, 101, 102, 105, 107, 108, 109 and 110.

Sculpture

Roman work in this field was not original but based on the Greek. The Romans imported a great quantity of sculpture—figures, groups and relief work—from Greece and Etruria and used it to decorate their buildings and homes. They appreciated realism and developed a style of figure sculpture clothed in the toga and also in the cuirass, which is effective and particularly Roman. A great number of equestrian statues must have existed but there are scanty remains of these. One outstanding exception is that of Marcus Aurelius now adorning the centre of Michelangelo's Piazza Campidoglio on Capitol Hill in Rome (page 318). This is the only example portraying a Roman Emperor which has survived intact from such an early age. Likewise the chariots and horses have disappeared from the triumphal arches, but good quality work exists here in the relief panels, especially in the Arch of Titus and, in another form, on the Trajan Column (PLATES 9, 10, 11, 12 and 13).

Buildings and Extant Remains

Basilicas

The Roman basilica was a hall of justice and a centre for commercial exchange. It was one of the most important of Roman buildings and wherever the Romans built a city the basilica would occupy a central position in or near the forum. The building was rectangular, generally twice as long as wide and had an apse at one or both ends. There were two chief designs. One type had a timber roof which was supported on two rows of columns which divided the hall into a larger, central area and two narrower, side aisles. Later and larger basilicas were roofed with concrete vaults which rested on a few, very large piers. The *Basilica of Trajan*, A.D. 98–112. in *Rome*, designed by Apollodorus of Damascus, was an example of the first type. The central space or nave was 280 feet long and 80 feet wide and the roof was supported on 96 granite columns. Of the basilica, which adjoined the Trajan Forum, there are only scanty remains, as there are of the enormous *Basilica Julia* in the Forum Romanum. The most famous basilica in Rome is the *Basilica of Constantine*, or Maxentius, as it is often called. The Emperor Maxentius began the basilica in A.D. 308 and the work was completed

Plate 12
Arch of Titus, Rome A.D. 81. Panel representing
the Emperor in Triumphal car

Plate 13
Carved marble mask. Theatre, Ostia, Italy.

Plate 14
Carved figure supporting seats. The Theatre, Pompeii, Italy

Plate 15
Floor mosaic, Piazzale delle Corporazioni, Ostia, Italy

Plate 16
Peristyle capital, Palace of Diocletian, Split, Yugoslavia, *c.* A.D. 300
This is the type of capital that Robert Adam used extensively in his designs.

Plate 17
Detail, mosaic pavement. Aquileia Cathedral, Italy, *c.* A.D. 320

by Constantine. It was one of the most imposing structures of the Roman world and its ruins, bordering the Forum Romanum, inspired Michelangelo in his designs for S. Peter's. Four massive, concrete piers, each 14 feet in diameter, supported a vaulted roof. The present remains comprise all one side of the basilica and part of the principal apse on the shorter side. In front of the main piers stood eight gigantic, marble columns, the last of which was removed by Pope Paul V and placed in front of the Church of Santa Maria Maggiore. There was originally a colossal statue of Constantine in the main apse, fragments of which are now in the courtyard of the Conservatori Palace. The basilica was badly damaged in the ninth century earthquake, and in Medieval days it was used, like the Colosseum, as a quarry for building. Due only to its immense solidity are the remains so adequate today. The coffered vault can plainly be discerned and some of the original stucco decoration is adhering to the deep, octagonal coffers (**86, 87** and **108**).

Temples

Roman designs are based upon the Greek and, more than any other Roman building, temples resemble the Greek prototype. The temple was built to house the deity, but the cella of a Roman temple was much larger than in Greek examples in order to accommodate the sculpture and treasures brought from Greece. Thus the Roman plan for rectangular temples was generally pseudo-peripteral, wherein the cella was widened at the expense of the peristyle, and often the side ambulatory disappeared and half columns attached to the cella walls lined up with those of the front portico; an imposing example of this design is the Maison Carrée at Nîmes (**113**). Circular temples were also built of which the Pantheon is the best known representative (**122–124**). Another feature of Roman temples was that they were generally raised on a podium instead of the Greek stylobate. The Romans considered the front aspect to be the important one and on this elevation the temple was approached by a flight of steps, more on Etruscan lines than Greek. On each side of the steps was a low wall decorated by sculptured figures. Most Roman temples are in the Corinthian order, a few Ionic but rarely Doric.

Rectangular Temples in Rome

There are remains of a number of these in the *Forum Romanum*. In a fragmentary condition, with three columns each, are the *Temple of Castor and Pollux* and the *Temple of Vespasian*. The former has Corinthian capitals, still beautiful despite their mutilation. The central volutes intertwine and a tendril and foliage breaks the line of the abacus between these and the angle volutes. The columns were part of an octastyle portico, each 48 feet high and standing on a 22 feet podium. The entablature has a small, plain frieze but a richly decorated architrave and cornice (**95** and **115**). The Temple of Vespasian (A.D. 94) stands near the *Temple of Concord* and both are now divided from the rest of the Forum by a modern main road.

The *Temple of Saturn* was an early building but was reconstructed in the 4th century A.D. It was large, on a lofty podium, and was fronted by a six-columned Ionic portico in grey granite. Its vaults housed the public treasury.

Two temples owe their better survival to later adaptation into Christian churches. The *Temple of Antoninus and Faustina* (A.D. 142) became the Church of S. Lorenzo in 1602 (**116** and **117**). Its portico of six Corinthian columns exists, as does the finely sculptured frieze of its entablature. Next door to it is the Church of SS. Cosmo and Damiano built in A.D. *c.* 307 as the *Temple of Romulus*. A miraculous survival here are the wonderful bronze doors still intact within the Roman doorway (**104**).

In the *Forum Boarium*, near the Tiber, survives almost intact the *Temple of Fortuna Virilis*. This remarkable example has been a source of inspiration for architects in Europe since the sixteenth century. The entrance hall at Holkham Hall in England is based upon it. It is a tetrastyle design, built in stone which was originally stucco-covered. It has a fine Ionic portico (**90, 118** and **119**).

The *Forum of Augustus* boasts the remains of the *Temple of Mars Ultor*, a Corinthian temple built in 2 B.C. by Augustus. It was a richly decorated example and still contains a coffered marble ceiling and part of the cella wall.

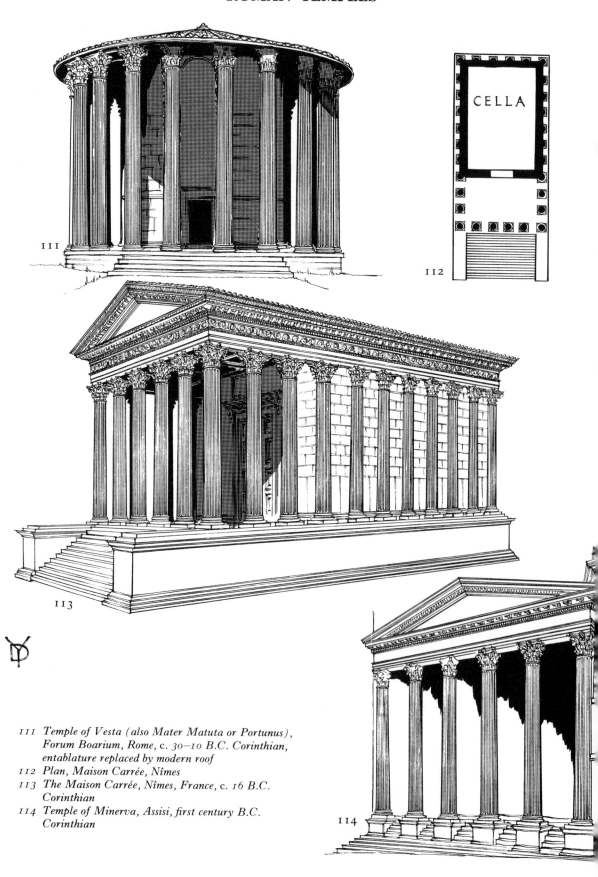

CELLA

111 Temple of Vesta (also Mater Matuta or Portunus),
Forum Boarium, Rome, c. 30–10 B.C. Corinthian,
entablature replaced by modern roof
112 Plan, Maison Carrée, Nîmes
113 The Maison Carrée, Nîmes, France, c. 16 B.C.
Corinthian
114 Temple of Minerva, Assisi, first century B.C.
Corinthian

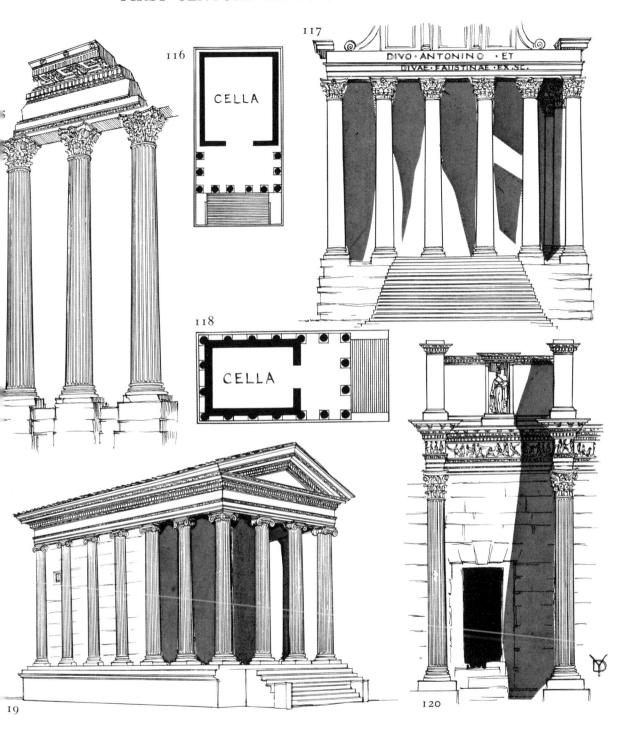

116

CELLA

117

DIVO · ANTONINO · ET
DIVAE · FAUSTINAE · EX.SC.

118

CELLA

19

120

115 *Temple of Castor and Pollux, Forum Romanum, Rome, Corinthian, A.D. 6 (capitals restored)*
116 *Plan and* 117 *General view of Temple of Antoninus and Faustina (capitals restored), Forum Romanum, Rome,*
  Corinthian, A.D. 142 (interior is church of S. Lorenzo)
118 *Plan and* 119 *General view of Temple of Fortuna Virilis, Forum Boarium, Rome, Ionic, 100–40 B.C.*
120 *Temple, Forum of Augustus, Rome, Corinthian, 27–14 B.C.*

Circular Temples in Rome

The Pantheon A.D. 120

This is the most famous of all ancient circular temples and, first as a temple, and later as a church, has been in continuous use since its building. It is a remarkable structure and a building of great beauty particularly in the interior. The inscription on the frieze of the portico—'M. AGRIPPA. L.F. COS TERTIUM, FECIT' (Marcus Agrippa, Son of Lucius, consul for the third time, built this)—for many years gave rise to misconceptions regarding the period of building of the Pantheon. For a long time it was felt that Agrippa was the builder, and later that his portico had been re-erected in the later building. Agrippa was the son-in-law of Augustus and an eminent town planner. In 27–25 B.C. he built a temple and baths on the site and called the temple the Pantheon, from the Greek word meaning 'to all the Gods'. Remains of these baths still exist on the south side of the Pantheon. In A.D. 120 the Emperor Hadrian rebuilt both temple and baths and, on the frieze of his new Pantheon, had repeated the original inscription. It was in 1892 that the French architect Georges Chedanne, when making examinations and excavations, discovered bricks, both below and above ground, dated A.D. 125 and 123. It was eventually decided that c. 120 onwards was the correct period of building and that the whole edifice was of one time although there were later restorations by both Septimius Severus and Caracalla, who added their inscriptions on the architrave of the portico below that of Agrippa.

The Pantheon is an unusual temple design. Here the principal emphasis is not on the exterior and the colonnade but on the cella, the interior. As a building it is composed of two parts: the portico and the circular cella. The Emperor Hadrian, who was a great lover of the arts and of Greek architecture in particular, supervised the work himself. Possibly due to his lack of professional knowledge, the exterior marriage of portico and cella is awkward. The porch itself consists of 16 monolithic columns, eight of which, across the front, are of grey Egyptian granite, and the rear columns, internally, are of red granite. The order is Corinthian and the capitals and bases are of white Pentelic marble. The en-tablature and cornice are decorated in a restrained manner and originally the tympanum was ornamented with a bronze relief of Zeus striking down the Greeks. Inside the portico is a well-proportioned doorway, 40 feet high and 20 feet wide, with two bronze-covered doors, each $26\frac{1}{2}$ feet high, between two bronze pilasters. The doors, which are the finest ancient examples in Rome, were originally gold plated. Above the doors is a bronze, openwork screen (**99, 100, 106** and **124**).

The interior of the circular cella is a masterpiece of construction and lighting effect. It is harmoniously balanced in form and mass. The dome, which is the largest ever built* has a diameter of just over 142 feet and is coffered in five concentric rings meeting in the centre in a large circular, unglazed oculus (142 feet from the floor) which is nearly 30 feet across and which is the only, but adequate, source of daylight for the temple. The construction of this dome was an outstanding feat. The material was poured on to hemispherical centering in which the coffered panels had been inserted. The dome diminishes in thickness from nearly 20 feet at the springing to almost 5 feet at the crown and it is built up in horizontal layers of brickwork and concrete where the cement mixture is varied so that the specific gravity diminishes with increasing height. The remainder of the construction is no less remarkable. Half the internal height is wall and half is dome. The walls give the appearance of inclining inwards from floor level. Relieving arches are incorporated into the walls to reinforce them and concentrate the load on to the eight massive piers. These arches are visible on the exterior wall surfaces. The marble floor is slightly convex (**122** and **123**). The Pantheon has survived many vicissitudes; first the barbarian invasions and later the despoliation by the Catholic Church. In A.D. 609 the temple was re-dedicated as a Christian Church to the Madonna and All Martyrs. It was venerated by succeeding Popes but had unfortunately been despoiled, first by the Byzantine Emperor Constans II who, in 655 removed the gilded bronze plates which covered the dome and replaced them with lead and later, in 1625, by the Barberini Pope Urban VIII who destroyed the portico roof in order to use the bronze beams supporting it for his own building schemes. This gave rise to the saying '*quod non fecerunt barbari, fecerunt Barberini*'.

* Comparative domes: S. Peter's Rome 140 feet, Florence Cathedral $137\frac{1}{2}$ feet.

ROMAN: THE PANTHEON AND THE COLOSSEUM, ROME

121 *The Colosseum, A.D. 70–82*
122 *Plan, the Pantheon*
123 *Interior, the Pantheon*
124 *Exterior, portico of the Pantheon, A.D. 120 onwards*

During the Renaissance and in later times the Pantheon has aroused the admiration of artists of all nations. Many were inspired by it, for example Raphael and Palladio, and the former is among the many famous men buried there.

The *Temple of Vesta* in the *Forum Romanum* was built in A.D. 205 as the sacred shrine in the city. There is little left of the circular cella which was surrounded by 18 Corinthian columns each $17\frac{1}{2}$ feet high.

More complete is the *Temple of Vesta* in the *Forum Boarium* (also known as Mater Matuta and as Portunus). Also in the Corinthian Order, it has an almost intact peristyle of 20 columns but the entablature has been replaced by a modern roof. The temple has a circular stylobate of marble steps and the columns of Parian marble are $34\frac{1}{2}$ feet high. The cella inside has a diameter of 28 feet. The temple, which was built c. 30 B.C. is Greek in the character of its capitals and columns; it is an outstanding example of the circular design (**111**).

Temples in Italy outside Rome

The *Temple of Minerva, Assisi*, was built about 40 B.C. There is a six columned portico raised on a podium. The Corinthian capitals are of Graeco-Roman design. The whole building is simple but effective (**94** and **114**).

At *Tivoli* are the remains of a number of temples, among which are the *Temple of Vesta c. 27 B.C.*, Corinthian in design and the *Temple of the Sybils* of the first century B.C. The latter has a circular cella and a peristyle of 18 columns, 24 feet high.

The *Temple of Vespasian* at *Brescia* is a triple-celled example on the Etruscan pattern. It has an entrance portico of 16 columns with projecting porch.

Temples outside Italy

The most important of such examples is also the most complete of all Roman rectangular temples, that now called the *Maison Carrée* at *Nîmes* in *France*. It was built about 16 B.C. and the fact that this area had once been a Greek colony probably accounts for its exceptionally fine detail and proportions. It is raised on a podium

12 feet high, approached by steps on the entrance façade. The order is Corinthian and the design pseudo-peripteral hexastyle. The well proportioned portico is three columns deep and shows Greek influence in its simplicity but the plan, with engaged columns on the sides of the cella, is indisputably Roman (**102, 112** and **113**). At *Split* in *Yugoslavia* there are the remains of two temples inside the Palace of Diocletian (see pp. 60–2).

The Roman Baths (Roman name thermae from Greek thermos = hot)

These were an institution which was an integral part of life in the days of the Roman Empire. Living conditions at home for those who were not well-to-do lacked space and comfort and the public baths provided free, or at least very cheaply, the daily means for the population to relax, chat, carry out business or social affairs, bathe, receive massage and medical treatment, eat and drink and take part in athletic sports and entertainment. In Imperial Rome alone, there are estimated to have been over 800 thermae of different sizes and accommodation. In the larger establishments there were restaurants, theatre, gardens and fountains, a sports stadium, rest rooms and large halls where poets and philosophers exchanged views and authors gave lectures or read their latest works.

In the bathing establishment itself the operation was long and often complicated. The bather began the process in the hot room (the caldarium); these were small compartments with hot water baths. He then received a rubbing down treatment which included scraping with a strigil. Afterwards he plunged into a cold water swimming bath (the frigidarium) and was then massaged and oiled. The baths provided warm rooms in winter, as in the large, moderately heated room (the tepidarium), and cool, shady gardens in summer, where strollers could walk or sit and relax under the roofed peristyles which surrounded the open courts.

The heating system was by hypocaust in which hot air from furnaces under the building was passed through hollow tiles and bricks in the walls and floor. The temperature could be regulated very exactly for the different needs of caldarium and tepidarium.

ROMAN THEATRES

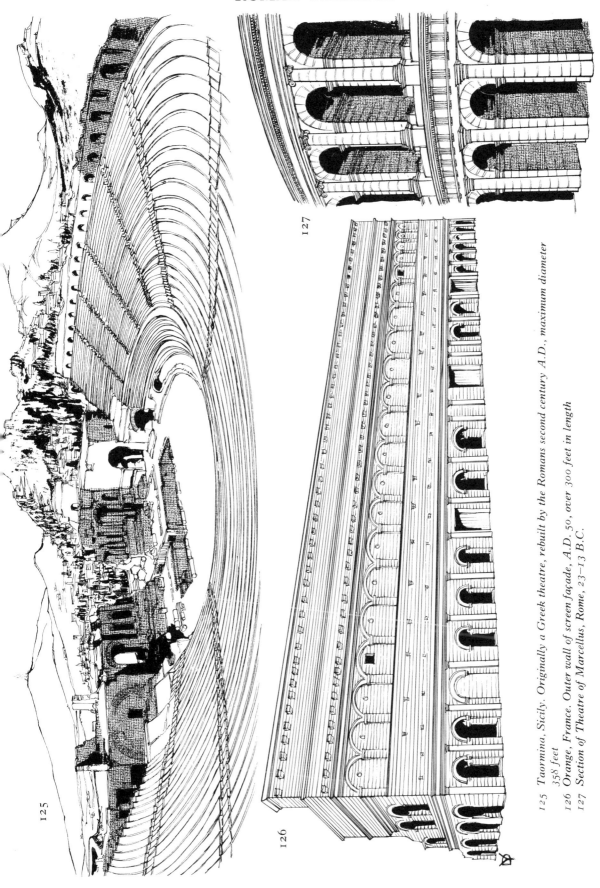

125 Taormina, Sicily. Originally a Greek theatre, rebuilt by the Romans second century A.D., maximum diameter 358 feet
126 Orange, France. Outer wall of screen façade, A.D. 50, over 300 feet in length
127 Section of Theatre of Marcellus, Rome, 23–13 B.C.

There are remains of many examples of thermae, particularly in Rome. Large establishments were built by most emperors, particularly Nero A.D. 60–71, Titus A.D. 80, Trajan A.D. 110, and Constantine A.D. 320. The most important remains are those of Caracalla A.D. 206–17 and Diocletian A.D. 284–304. These two famous examples in Rome illustrate the general layout of the extensive type of baths. There are a number of good reconstruction drawings of them and a clear idea of their appearance can be gained from the sixteenth century measured drawings by Renaissance architects like Palladio which were made when the remains were in a better condition than they are now.

The Baths of Caracalla, Rome A.D. 206–17

These thermae covered a very large area, greater than that of the Palace of Westminster, and stood upon an artificial platform some 20 feet high. Under the main buildings were vaulted cellars for storage and furnaces. Under the pavement of the baths was a lower floor upon which were built small piers of tiles about two feet high. These piers carried an intermediate concrete floor about one foot thick on which was a layer of broken and pounded tufa and ceramic. Upon this was laid a course of marble cement in which the mosaic pavement was bedded; alternatively marble slabs were laid. The furnaces were set lower still, below the hypocaust floor. The heated air passed under the mosaic floor and was carried by flues to the walls. In the caldarium flue pipes were laid all through the walls. The main building block of the Caracalla thermae is now in ruins but the plan and layout are still clearly to be seen. The area covered is 270,000 square feet of which the immense central hall occupied 79 feet by 183 feet. This is generally called the tepidarium but it is doubtful that it was in fact such a room for it would have been too immense to heat and no hypocausts have been discovered under it. The hall was covered by an intersecting barrel vault and was divided into three bays. It rose higher than the surrounding buildings and it was lit by clerestory windows below roof level. The vault was supported on eight massive stone piers fronted by granite columns 38 feet high. Next to the central hall was a smaller tepidarium and, beyond, the

caldarium which had a domed roof. The frigidarium was presumed to be open to the sky and contained a large open-air swimming bath. On each side of the bath, separated from it by a colonnade, were halls for spectators. Although the exterior of this building was plain in brick and stucco, the interior was magnificent in colour and decoration with marble faced walls and floors and a wealth of sculpture and relief ornamentation much of which was brought from Greece. During Renaissance excavations many examples were taken from here to museums in Rome and other European cities.

The Baths of Diocletian, Rome. A.D. 284–304

These thermae were larger than those of Caracalla and accommodated 3200 bathers; they were very similar in design.

They are, however, particularly interesting to us as they are not entirely in ruins, because in A.D. 1563 Michelangelo converted the tepidarium into the nave of his Church, Santa Maria degli Angeli and retained the circular caldarium as an entrance vestibule with its domical roof now decorated with caissons and central roses. The nave of three bays has also retained the original vault though the marble facing has gone. However, a good impression can be gained of the original chamber as windows have been inserted under the vault above the Renaissance entablature and provide a well lighted interior. The main buildings here, as at Caracalla, were surrounded by gardens and gymnasia.

Baths at Pompei

Three sites of public baths have been excavated here. They are smaller and less well equipped than the large Roman establishments but, being in a much better state of preservation, have provided invaluable material for study. The oldest layout at Pompei is the *Stabian Baths* built in the second century B.C. and remodelled later. The finest example is that adjacent to the forum, the *Forum Baths*. Here there is an open court with peristyle, the usual shops lining the site and the bathing rooms, ante-room and vestibule. The tepidarium is in a remarkable condition and still possesses a barrel vaulted ceiling with rich stucco decoration, stucco ornamented walls and, on piers surrounding the room, the figures of miniature Atlantes two feet high (PLATE 9). There was no hypocaust here; heating was by charcoal brazier. The frigidarium is small and circular in plan. The caldarium, also in good condition, had a hypocaust and wall flues; it is also barrel vaulted and stucco decorated (105 and 150).

Ostia

In the *Baths of Neptune* here there are some magnificent mosaic pavements in a fine state of preservation. There are two large examples, one in the entrance hall depicting Neptune driving four sea-horses surrounded by tritons, nereids, dolphins and other marine animals and, in the adjoining room, the mosaic shows Amphitrite with four tritons. There are remains of basins and columns in both tepidarium and caldarium. Next to the baths is the palaestra (gymnasium), which is a vast courtyard with surrounding colonnade and changing rooms. In the *Forum Baths,* on the other side of the town, the frigidarium is quite well preserved with remains of columns and capitals (89). Nearby is the public latrine with its 20 marble seats, washing facilities and holes in the entrance doorway floor for the two revolving doors (156).

Theatres, Amphitheatres and Circuses

Theatres

The Roman theatre, when built on a new site, differed from the Greek pattern in that it was generally constructed above ground and not hollowed out from the hillside. Concrete vaulting supported the tiers of seats as in an amphitheatre and under the vaults were corridors lit by outer arcades. The orchestra was restricted to a semi-circle in view of the needs of Roman drama and, in front of this was a raised stage. The auditorium was also lined up on a semi-circular plan (128). In a number of instances the Romans took over a Greek theatre (for example at Taormina) and adapted it to their requirements. Thus the theatre was still built into the hillside, but the stage was constructed and the orchestral area curtailed.

128 Typical Roman theatre plan (simplified)

Theatre of Marcellus, Rome, *23–13 B.C.*

This is the only ancient theatre left in Rome; its masonry is now in a poor state. It is built in the Roman manner on a level site and the auditorium seats are supported on radiating walls and concrete vaulting. Only two tiers of the wall arcade remain showing the use of the Doric Order below and the Ionic above. They are built of travertine covered with stucco. The proportions and detail of these orders are some of the best work of its type in Rome and illustrate clearly the Roman constructional method using arch and order together with the former bearing the load and the latter as a decorative feature (127).

Orange, France, A.D. 50

This theatre, which is in good condition, is partly hollowed out from the hillside and partly constructed. The diameter between the enclosing walls is 340 feet. The important remaining feature here is the massive outer façade screen wall, 324 feet long and 116 feet high, constructed of large, squared blocks, about three feet long and one foot six inches wide. Remains of the entablature and Doric pilasters are distinguishable in the ground arcade (126).

Taormina, Sicily

This was a Greek theatre, hollowed out of the steep mountainside and looking out over one of the finest views in the world, with the sea far below on one side and, in the distance, Mount Etna. The Roman superstructure replanning has largely obscured the Greek design. In the Middle Ages much of the marble was taken for building and nineteenth century restoration has

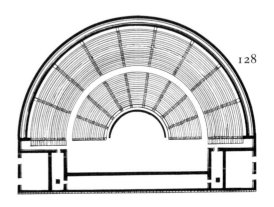

128

ROMAN AMPHITHEATRES

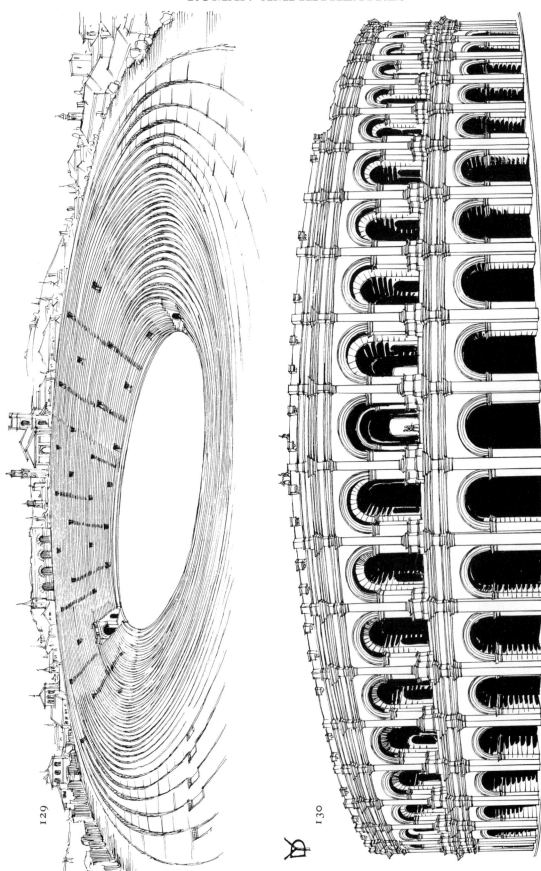

129 Amphitheatre at Verona, Italy, temp. Diocletian, c. A.D. 300, interior of arena viewed from back row, exterior measurement 498 ft × 404 ft

130 Amphitheatre at Nîmes, France, exterior arcade, exterior measurement 436 ft × 331 ft

129

130

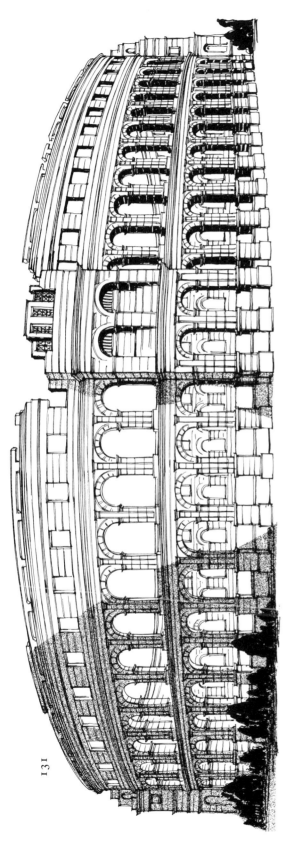

131

further confused the original layout. The Roman stage remains in ruined form and has curtailed the orchestra to a semi-circle, but the seating of the auditorium shows the Greek plan carved out of the hillside (**125**).

At *Pergamon* (Bergama) in Asia Minor is the beautifully situated Greek theatre. The scena still shows the three rows of square holes made to take the wood plank fittings when the moveable stage was in use. The Roman adaptation included the building of a large, permanent stage, 30 yards long, with accompanying terrace and porticoes 275 yards long. Among other interesting examples are those at *Mérida* in Spain (*c.* 18 B.C.) and *Verulamium* (S. Albans) in England (2nd century A.D.).

Amphitheatres

These were unknown to the Greeks and are peculiarly Roman constructions. Early examples were made of wood, but, due to fire risks, stone and concrete were used later. Most amphitheatres were very large and all important towns possessed their own which were used for displays of all kinds but particularly for gladiatorial combat and exhibitions. The plan is oval and rising tiers of seats are constructed round the elliptical area. The earliest known example is at Pompei and the largest is the Colosseum. There are a number of fine amphitheatres extant in a partly ruined condition and several of them are still used for performances of opera or for bull fights. Among them are those at Verona, Capua and Pozzuoli in Italy, Nîmes and Arles in France, Pula in Yugoslavia and Pergamon in Turkey.

The Colosseum, Rome, A.D. 70–82
(also known as the Flavian Amphitheatre after the Flavian Emperors Vespasian, Titus and Domitian under whose auspices it was built).

Even in ruin the Colosseum is a magnificent edifice of great structural interest and aesthetic splendour. The interior is in a poor state but much of the four tiers of the exterior arcade walling is intact and illustrates clearly the Roman building method of using arch and order, with the entablatures continuing in unbroken horizontal bands round the whole amphitheatre and the columns lined up one above the other. In this instance on the ground storey is the Doric Order and above this, in order of ascent, Ionic, Corinthian and Corinthian. The fourth tier was originally in wood and was rebuilt in stone in the third century A.D. Between the three-quarter columns are arched openings, 80 on each of the first three storeys, and in each was placed a statue. The top storey has no openings and the order is in pilaster form. Between these pilasters are still visible the corbels upon which were supported the masts of the velarium which was drawn across the auditorium. This was a covering curtain with a central aperture which left the arena open to the sky. The façade is built of travertine blocks without mortar but held by metal cramps. It is 157 feet high and the amphitheatre from wall to wall is 620 by 513 feet, the largest in existence.

The construction is interesting and throws light on the Roman methods of dealing with the problem of erecting such a structure on a level site to accommodate some 45,000 to 50,000 people. The solid foundations are largely of volcanic materials, the supporting walls of brick tufa and travertine and the vaults of more porous volcanic substance to reduce weight. Decoration seating and the orders are in marble. The supporting construction consists of wedge-shaped piers which are set to radiate inwards. These support concrete vaults which slope downwards towards the arena. The access to seats is well arranged by means of staircases built between the walls and by passages between the seat ranges. The arena itself, some 287 by 180 feet, was encircled by a wall 15 feet high. The floor was carried on joists and under this was space for storage, scenery, gladiators and animals.

The tremendous solidity of the construction accounts for the substantial remains today. In fact the Colosseum has suffered less from the depredations of the barbarians and the weathering of time than from its use in the Middle Ages as a fortress and later as a quarry by Renaissance builders (91 and 121).

Amphitheatre at Verona A.D. 290

The arena here is in an exceptionally fine state of preservation, with nearly all the seats intact, and it is frequently used for modern performances. However, only four bays of the upper section of the exterior screen wall are *in situ*. The amphitheatre measures 498 by 404 feet from exterior wall to wall (129).

Amphitheatres in France

At *Nîmes* the exterior wall, measuring 436 by 331 feet across, is in only two storeys above which is an attic used for supporting the masts of the velarium. The Doric Order is used on both stages, as three-quarter piers on the ground storey and as three-quarter columns above. In each case the entablature is returned at each column. Both the exterior wall and the auditorium seating are in good condition and the amphitheatre is in use particularly for bull fights (130). At *Arles* nearby the screen wall is not in such good condition; the design is similar but the Corinthian Order is used instead of Doric.

Yugoslavia

At *Pula* the exterior walling is in a fair state of complete preservation but the seating has disappeared; it was probably of wood. The masonry of the screen wall is rusticated and the orders are treated like those of the Colosseum, but in this case are less strongly defined. There are four projecting bays on the exterior with arcades in the ground storey and staircases in the upper storeys. The amphitheatre measures 450 by 361 feet (131).

Circuses

The Roman circus was used for chariot and horse races and was probably based, in plan, upon the Greek Stadium. There were many famous examples, but little is left of any of them except in such cities as *Rhodes*, where some twentieth century excavations and restoration have been carried out. The famous circuses were those built by different emperors in *Rome*, particularly those of Nero, Maxentius and Constantine. A very large example was the Circus Maximus, rebuilt by Julius Caesar and restored by later emperors. The circus built by Maxentius was called the Circus of Romulus and was 1620 feet long and 245 feet wide. The plan of this can still be determined.

132 Ionic circular portico of the 'Maritime Theatre'
      (Ninfeo dell' Isola), Hadrian's Villa, near Tivoli
133 Temple of Hadrian, Ephesus, A.D. 130
134 Caryatid figure, Canopus, Hadrian's Villa

Palaces

Rome

There are only scanty remains of any of the great palaces despite the quantity and richness of the building over several centuries. The favourite position in Rome chosen by the emperors was the *Palatine Hill* although, by the time of Constantine, it was necessary to search further afield because of lack of space. Augustus laid out the first Imperial residence in this part of Rome, followed by Tiberius, Caligula and Domitian; Septimius Severus built here on a very large scale. Nero constructed his Imperial Villa—the famous 'golden house'—which he began soon after the great fire of the city in A.D. 64. This colossal layout covered an area larger than the present S. Peter's and the Vatican gardens and had an imperial entrance approach from the Forum. The palace was destroyed after Nero's death to make way for later Imperial building and the Colosseum was erected on the site of its lake. Despite excavations on the Palatine Hill which have continued since 1863 and which have uncovered a wide area, it is still difficult to ascertain clearly the design of these palaces. Remains are scanty and conjecture has to take the place of evidence. The palaces were very large, richly decorated and comprised a temple(s), basilica, public rooms, banqueting hall, a throne room and magnificent gardens with peristyle and fountains.

Tivoli

Of greater interest for its extensive remains is *Hadrian's Villa*, which the Emperor began to build near here, in A.D. 118, over several square miles of terraced hillside. Villa is a misnomer, for it included several thermae, stadia, halls, theatres, magnificent gardens, terraces and fountains as well as the imperial apartments. Hadrian was an outstanding architect himself, and here he gave vent to one of his interests.

Most of the marble and treasures have gone—destroyed, re-used or now in museums—but a clearer idea can be gained here than elsewhere of what such Roman palaces were like. Especially interesting is the layout known as 'Canopus'. Hadrian based this on the Temple of Serapis and the Canal of Canopus in the city of that name near Alexandria, where the cult of the god Serapis flourished. In his villa, the Serapeum is a vast semi-circular hall covered with a half-dome, originally worked in white mosaic. Much of the sculpture found on the site has now been placed *in situ* by the archaeologists: for example, the caryatid figures along the Canopus canal, which were copies from the famous ones on the south porch of the Erechtheion in Athens (**134** and PLATE 6).

An adequate description of the Villa Adriana would need a fair-sized guide-book. The most complete, and therefore, more interesting remains, include the Maritime Theatre and the Library, the Hall with the square Doric pillars and the Piazza D'Oro or Golden Square. Leading from the Library, the visitor enters a circular building, about 45 yards in diameter with an outer Ionic portico. Inside is a circular canal enclosing a small island on which was built a fine pavilion with domed halls and a central fountain. It is believed that this was Hadrian's retreat, where he went to be quiet and enjoy his drawing, writing and music-making. The island was originally joined to the circular portico by two small wooden bridges of a revolving, pulley type. The present stone bridge is a modern one. The names of 'Maritime Theatre' and 'Island Nymphaeum' derive from the entrance hall decoration with motifs of tritons, nereids and other marine life (**132**).

The Palace of Diocletian, Split, Yugoslavia

In about A.D. 300 the Emperor Diocletian built a palace here and to it he retired in about 305. As Hadrian's villa is much more than a villa, so Diocletian's palace is more like a town and is also designed as a fortress. The north, east and west walls are protected by 16 towers, the south by the sea. The palace site is rectangular and comprises a large part of the original Medieval town of Split. It is about 700 feet long on the east and west sides and about 580 feet on the north and south. In the centre of each side is an entrance gateway, flanked by octagonal towers, of which the principal one is the Porta Aurea (the Golden Gate) on the north side (**138**). The Porta Argentea on the seaward, south side is connected to the interior of the palace by an underground passage way. On the east and west sides are the Porta

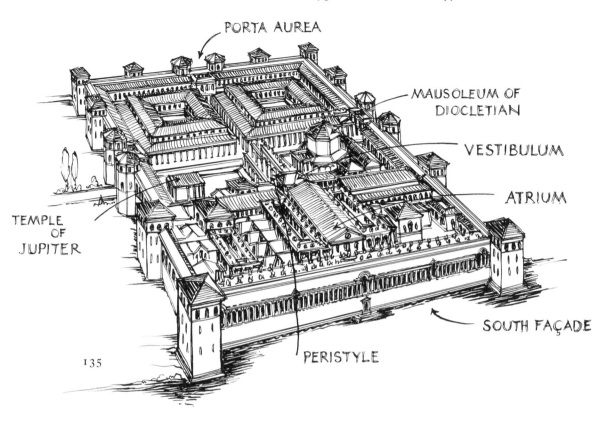

PORTA AUREA

MAUSOLEUM OF DIOCLETIAN

VESTIBULUM

ATRIUM

TEMPLE OF JUPITER

SOUTH FAÇADE

135

PERISTYLE

135 Suggested reconstruction of the Palace of Diocletian, Split

Aenea and Ferrea (bronze and iron) respectively. These gateways gave entrance to avenues with covered arcades on each side which led to the centre of the enclosure.

The Palace, a reconstruction of which is shown in Fig. **135**, was built of limestone in a little over 10 years. It was beautiful and luxurious and designed both as status symbol and for ease of living for the emperor himself. In the time of Diocletian the principal apartment was a long gallery on the south side facing the sea on whose façade a magnificent colonnade stretched along the Adriatic. Within the palace walls were temples, baths, living accommodation, reception halls and gardens. In the centuries between the collapse of the Roman Empire and the present time Split has lived under many regimes and nationalities. It is astonishing, considering this turbulent history, that the remains of the palace are so extensive today. For the layout shows a Roman palace left almost complete with much of the walls, towers and gates standing. Inside the walls among Medieval and later houses, are considerable remains of Roman buildings and

careful excavation in recent times is still disclosing more of the semi-underground parts of the palace itself.

To the visitor who approaches the south side of the palace today from the harbour of Split the once magnificent *south wall and colonnade* are disappointing and a clearer idea of the original splendour of this elevation can be gained from Robert Adam's drawing made in 1764 before the shops were built in front of it at ground level. However, after entering through the underground tunnel in this façade a clear idea of Roman construction can be gained from the restored vaulted chambers which now lead up into the peristyle courtyard. There is a complex layout of these *basement halls* which were built to support the upper storey state apartments. The latter were almost completely destroyed, but the basement halls, still being excavated, survived almost intact (except for their decoration) due to their use over the centuries as the city refuse dump. The halls vary in size and shape— circular, octagonal, rectangular, apsidal—but all are vaulted in dome, barrel or groined forms constructed in brick, stone and concrete. The walls are thick and have arches with radiating voussoirs in brick (**140**). The *peristyle* is in a remarkable state of preservation and much as Robert Adam saw it, as can be seen by comparing his drawing of 1764 with Fig. **141** drawn in 1964. The Corinthian Order is used throughout this open central court which gave access from the southern gate below to the state apartments above (PLATE 16). It also served as an open ceremonial hall. Next to the peristyle still stands the *Emperor's Mausoleum*, preserved by its transformation into the Cathedral in the early Middle Ages. The Cathedral has not obscured the Mausoleum; on the exterior the octagonal form remains with the surrounding colonnade of Corinthian columns. In places are fragments of the coffered roof which originally connected the colonnade to the building which rests on an octagonal plinth once flanked by sphinxes (one of these is still extant) (**136** and **137**). A Medieval campanile has been added to one end of the Mausoleum and a Choir at the other. The *interior* still retains its original brick domed roof though its mosaic inlay has gone. The brick relieving arches are still visible above the entablature. The interior walls are alternately recessed with square and semicircular niches and there are eight columns of the Corinthian order supporting an entablature, with, above, eight further columns of the Composite order. A frieze, richly sculptured, encircles the building in the upper entablature; included in the decoration are sculptured medallions of Diocletian and his wife. While the Mausoleum is on the east of the peristyle, on the west were originally a number of temples of which the *Temple of Jupiter* is the only one to have survived. Apart from the loss of its columns it is in fine condition and has richly decorated doorway (**139**) and, inside, a barrel vaulted, coffered ceiling, its caissons finely enriched with flowers and heads. It was later made into a Christian baptistery. Of the *external walls* and *gates* of the palace, the west wall is missing and a number of towers. On the north side, however, dominated by Meštrović's colossal statue of Bishop Gregory, the whole length of the wall is intact. Its gate, the *Porta Aurea* (Golden Gate) is in good condition. It is interesting to notice here indications of the decadence of the late Roman style in the relieving

arches accentuated over a lintel and columns supported on corbels (**138**).

Domestic Architecture

There are very few remains of this type of building in Roman cities, particularly in Rome itself. Therefore great reliance in these studies is placed on the excavated sites of Pompei, Herculaneum and Ostia where, due largely to natural causes, the site was abandoned, preserved, not rebuilt and excavated in more modern times. Of these, Pompei especially was a provincial town, but the chief difference between it and Rome would be in the materials and embellishments used rather than in the basic design.

There were three chief types of Roman domestic building: the *domus* or private house, the villa (country house) and the *insula*, the multistoreyed tenement. At Pompei and Herculaneum there are examples of the *domus* and the villa while at Ostia can be seen considerable remains of *insulae*.

Pompei

The story of the abrupt curtailment of life in Pompei by the eruption of Vesuvius in A.D. 79 and the subsequent preservation of the city, not only its architecture but of the stuff of life itself— bread, utensils, eggs and bodies of humans, dogs and birds—through the protection of its coating of lava and ash is a well known one and has been fully and vividly recounted many times from the eye-witness story of Pliny himself to the present day. It is an exciting and fascinating story and one which the visitor to excavated Pompei seems to re-live. From the architectural viewpoint the greatest importance of this site, now so excellently opened up and preserved, is that it has preserved for us a provincial Roman city at a certain point in time—A.D. 79—so that we can see for ourselves the buildings in which such citizens of the empire lived. No later buildings, no later civilisations with different ideas of development and design have pulled down, altered or erased the architecture remaining there.

Excavations have been continuing since the eighteenth century, and in the early years much was lost in plundering and in destruction by lack of knowledge of the work. In more modern times

THE PALACE OF DIOCLETIAN, SPLIT, *c.* 300 A.D.

136 *Mausoleum of Diocletian with surrounding colonnade (now Cathedral)*

137 *Corinthian capital from peristyle*

138 *The Porta Aurea*

139 *Doorway detail, Temple of Jupiter (now Baptistery)*

140 *Vestibulum. Underground approach to Peristyle —brick and stone barrel vaults*

141 *The Peristyle of the Palace*

142 The Great Palaestra
143 Street scene showing stepping stones
144
145 Plan, House of the Faun
146 Street scenes showing fountains
147

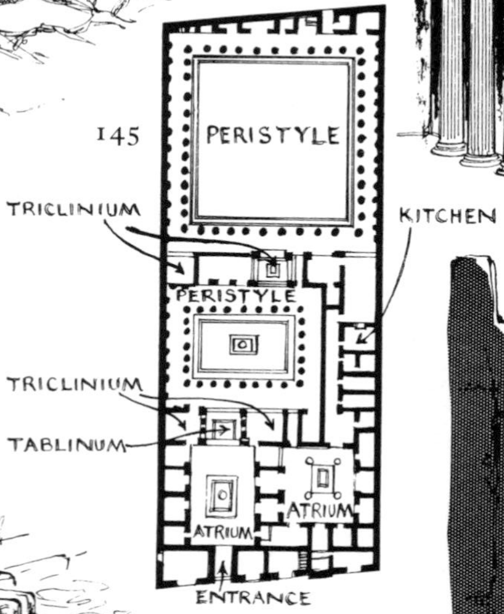

Plan labels:
PERISTYLE
PERISTYLE
TRICLINIUM
TRICLINIUM
TABLINIUM
ATRIUM
ATRIUM
ENTRANCE
KITCHEN
145

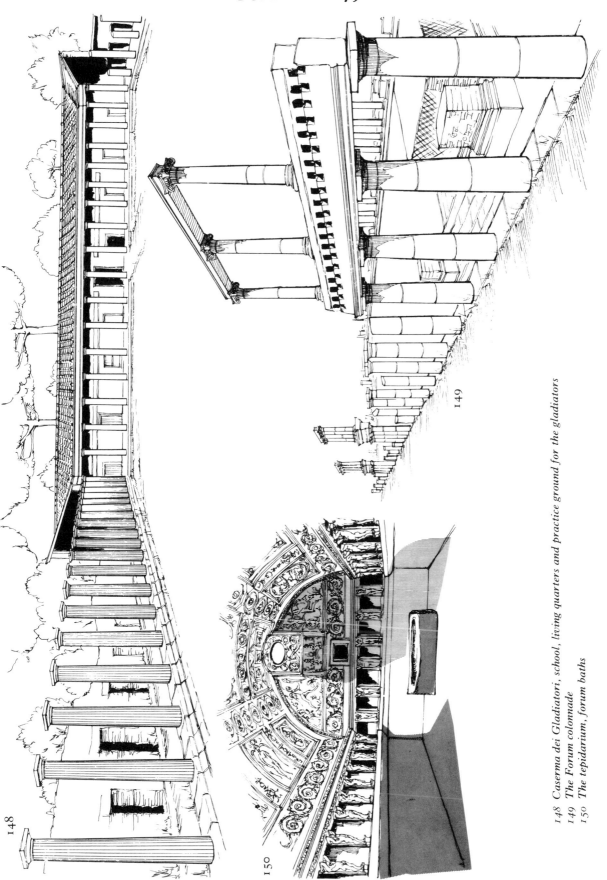

148 Caserma dei Gladiatori, school, living quarters and practice ground for the gladiators
149 The Forum colonnade
150 The tepidarium, forum baths

great care has been taken and it is a feature of Pompei that where possible, having regard to the safety of the work, sculpture, mosaics and frescoes have been left *in situ*, giving a clear picture of the interiors of houses and baths. The domestic gardens have also been recreated in their original plan and types of plants; many of the fountains are in working order.

The *city*, which had about 20,000 inhabitants, is irregular to plan and enclosed by stone city walls of double thickness with earth and stones between. There are towers at intervals for reinforcement and there are eight fortified city gates which were originally richly decorated with sculptural work. The *main roads* within the city gates are paved with dark local stone and have pavements and kerbstones. Large stone blocks are set as stepping stones for pedestrians to cross without becoming muddied. There are also street fountains at intervals (**143** and **146**).

Considerable remains of houses and public buildings exist and the layout is clearly defined. The *forum*, which is the most complete example in Italy, conforms closely to Vitruvius' account of ideal planning for a forum and its position in a city. It is a rectangle 520 by 125 feet, surrounded by a colonnade on three sides; this is in two storeys, the lower one Doric, the upper Ionic. At one end is the Temple of Jupiter built on a high podium; the Corinthian Order is used and the building was flanked by two triumphal arches. Opposite this, at the other side of the forum, was the Curia. Nearby are the remains of the *Basilica* which was the most impressive building here. It had a large nave with massive columns separating it from the aisles (**92** and **93**). Adjoining the forum is the Temple of Apollo which is the best preserved temple at Pompei; it had a portico of 48 columns and there is a fine statue of the god in the courtyard.

There are two theatres at Pompei and an amphitheatre. The *large theatre* was hollowed out from the hillside in the Greek manner and has a magnificent situation with mountain background. It was used for plays and mimes and seated about 5000 people. The *small theatre* or odeon was covered and adjoins the larger one. This is in a fine state of preservation and still retains two male figures carved in the tufa forming the head of the side parapets of the auditorium (**147** and PLATE 14). The theatre was built in

about 80 B.C. and accommodated 1200. It was used chiefly for performances of reading and music. The *amphitheatre*, constructed in 70 B.C. is a very early example and the first one to be built in stone. It is elliptical and very large—445 by 341 feet—and was used, as was the custom, for gladiatorial combat, dancing and animal baiting. The training grounds and living quarters of the *gladiators* (Caserma dei Gladiatori) are extensive at Pompei and adjoin the large theatre (**148**).

Houses

To facilitate the study of Roman houses the following list of common terms is given.

Atrium A large hall, lit by an opening in the centre of the roof called a *compluvium*. Rainwater ran from the eaves, through the gutters and spouted into a tank called the *impluvium*. Usually at one end of the tank was a sculptured figure from some part of which the water poured into the impluvium.

Bibliotheca Library.

Cubicula Sleeping apartments.

Culina Kitchen.

Exedrae Small rooms for reading and conversation.

Peristyle A large square or rectangular colonnaded space, open to the sky, and generally made into a garden with fountains and sculpture.

Pinacotheca Picture gallery.

Tablinum Large room generally richly decorated and sculptured.

Triclinium Dining room. Had couches on three sides; the fourth was for serving. The table was placed centrally.

It is in the field of domestic architecture that Pompei is unique; the houses are in a remarkable state of preservation and, apart from Herculaneum and Ostia, there is so little of such building extant. The Pompeian house does, of course, only depict the Roman home of up to the first century A.D. and in later years, as can be seen at Ostia, the plan was developed. The houses at Pompei vary greatly in size and elaboration, from two or three rooms to large buildings with many rooms arranged round courtyards. There are, however, a number of common features. The houses are entered from a narrow street façade

ROMAN: OSTIA FOURTH CENTURY B.C. TO THIRD CENTURY A.D.

151 *House of Diana (restoration)*
152 *Capital, Baths of Neptune*
153 *House of Diana, as it is today*
154 *Theatre, first-third century A.D.*

155 *Thermopolium (bar)*
156 *Public toilet facilities in the Forum Baths, facilities*
     also for washing, revolving doors at entrance,
     second-fourth century A.D.

often fronted by shops. Within they are generally planned on a narrow rectangular site, extending a long way back from the road. The rooms are all grouped around one or more peristyles. In a number of the houses the staircase has been preserved and much of the upper floors; only the roof is missing. Among the many examples the *House of the Faun* is often considered to have a typical layout. It is a large house and has two entrances, each leading into an atrium. From the atria one passes into the first peristyle which has an Ionic colonnade and a central fountain. A corridor from an exedra leads into the second, larger peristyle which had a gallery over the colonnade. The living rooms are arranged round the atria. The whole layout is well designed, spacious and suitable for the climate. The rooms were richly decorated with wall paintings, mosaics and sculptural work (**145**).

Among other outstanding houses at Pompei are the *House of Menander*, the *House of Pansa* and the *House of the Vettii*. In the last of these particularly, the peristyle has now been restored, as has the garden, and one gains a vivid impression of the original appearance (**144**). There are also a number of *villas* (country houses) at Pompei and here the plan is quite different. While the town house was completely enclosed in four walls on a rectangular plan to provide privacy from the streets, the villa was built in a less formal manner on a large ground plan and had terraced gardens overlooking the Bay of Naples. The *Villa of the Mysteries* with its two symmetrical, galleried wings is typical of these beautiful houses.

Herculaneum, the twin city to Pompei, suffered a similar fate but has proved more difficult to excavate. It was smaller, buried much deeper and the later town of Resina is built partly on top. There are some beautiful houses here, particularly those villas along the Bay of Naples where wealthy citizens (from other towns) wintered in a warm climate. These houses are laid out in terraces on the hillside with porticoes and colonnaded peristyles. There are also several storeyed tenements of the style excavated at Ostia and as were built in Rome.

Art in the form of sculpture, mosaics and painting has survived extremely well at Pompei and Herculaneum; the lava has protected the work from the invasions, wars and plundering suffered

by the rest of the Roman Empire after A.D. 476. Much of this work has been removed to museums for safe keeping, particularly to Naples. There are, however, a number of frescoes and mosaics *in situ* and they illustrate the Pompeian's love of rich colour and their knowledge of their craft. Mosaic, marble slabs, stucco and painted decoration covered a large area of the walls, ceiling and floor of each house. The work has vigour and good taste. It is strongly influenced by Greek and Etruscan artists and happily shows none of the degeneracy evident in some later Roman work (PLATES 9 and 14).

Ostia

The story of Ostia is less generally known than that of Pompei and Herculaneum. Yet, in many ways, events have created a similar situation: a town abandoned by humanity and then preserved by natural forces until excavation in modern times. The basic differences between them in respect of their value to architectural study is that Ostia was occupied and developed over a much longer period, from the fourth century B.C. to the third century A.D., and that it was not a provincial city but the port of Rome and, as such, became more important, as is evidenced by its buildings. The chief development period at Ostia was under the Empire, particularly under the Emperors Augustus, Tiberius, Claudius and Nero. The task of making Ostia into a large and suitable port to serve Rome with a tremendous quantity of goods, particularly salt and grain, continued over many years, and the building of harbours and dredging of the river were not completed until about A.D. 54. A fine city was then built, having a population of some 50,000 people, with well laid out streets, drainage system and many temples, public buildings, shops and houses. It was Constantine who transferred the municipal rights of the port of Rome to Porto and from this time onwards Ostia declined. By the fourth century buildings were neglected and the marble facings were being taken for building elsewhere. In the early sixth century the place was largely deserted and became a malaria infested area. In 1557 the Tiber changed its course and Ostia Antica (as it is termed to differentiate it from the modern Lido town) is now a few kilometres inland and not on the riverside any more.

Excavations are not yet complete at Ostia, but the main part of the town (though not the harbour) has been uncovered with its principal streets and buildings. The main street, the *Decumanus Maximus* is bordered by tombs until it reaches the city gate. Inside the gates it is flanked by colonnades and the principal buildings lie adjacent to it. This street is about a mile in length and runs from one end of the town to the other; it is ten yards wide. Sited by it are the *Baths of Neptune* (already described, see Baths, p. 52), the *Palaestra*, the *theatre* (**152, 154** and PLATE 13), and the *Piazzale delle Corporazioni*. This square is very large and was originally faced with 70 offices carrying on trade with the whole ancient world. The mosaic floors of each office depict the trade of the occupier (PLATE 15). In the centre of the square are the remains of the Temple of Ceres

It is in *domestic architecture* that Ostia provides the most interesting revelations for here are astonishingly well preserved remains of *insulae*, the *tenement blocks* which must have been constructed in quantity in Rome itself and, since Ostia is so near and as it had such close association with the capital, probably of a very similar character. It had long been thought that many seventeenth and eighteenth century blocks in Rome were of a type of construction essentially Medieval or Renaissance, but Ostia shows that the basic plan of these is Roman. Such blocks at Ostia were built in the Imperial period and housed a number of people. They were constructed up to a height of 50 feet in three or four storeys (height of buildings was limited by Roman law). Among examples of such apartment houses is the *Casa di Diana* in the street of the same name and that in the *Via dei Balconi*. Here is the typical layout of such blocks, which is quite different from the Pompeian house. At Ostia the block is much taller, generally four storeys high and the walls are brick faced. The entrances are marked by pilasters or engaged columns supported on a triangular gable. The decoration is in simple string courses and in painting of the doors and windows. Polychrome decoration is used also in the form of coloured brick and bands of pumice and tufa. The rooms are lit by windows on the exterior and in the courtyard walls and the rooms themselves are laid out much as in a modern flat. Some blocks

have covered arcades and shops on the ground floor and apartments above. Above the shops are projecting balconies which are supported either on wood or travertine corbels or are continuous along the whole façade. The interior courtyard is not like an atrium or peristyle. The windows, doors and staircases of the different storeys open on to it as in modern design. The staircases are of travertine with wooden treads. They descend into the courtyard or into the street. In the *Casa di Diana*, two storeys have been preserved; the street façade with shops on the ground floor, the second floor windows and above this the third floor balcony which projects along the length of the block. The interior courtyard has a fountain and there are fragments of terracotta and fresco paintings (**151, 153** and **155**). Nearby, in the *Casa dei Dipinti*, in the street of the same name some mosaic floors are still preserved and a hall painted with mythological scenes. The *domus* (private house) also existed at Ostia and examples resemble Pompeian houses. They have a narrow frontage to the street and are planned around an atrium and peristyle. Many have shops on the lower floor.

Greece and Turkey

There are extensive remains of Roman building in these countries, mainly where the Roman civilisation extended and altered earlier towns established under Greek culture. It is not always easy for the visitor to distinguish the Greek work from Roman in these instances, but in general much more Roman building survives than the earlier Greek.

In the second century B.C. the Romans had gained control of the Sacred island of *Delos* in the Cyclades and later established it as a commercial trading post in the Mediterranean. A forum, quays, harbours, villas, baths and theatres were constructed also a system of water conservation and control. Although the centre declined by the second century A.D., due largely to pirate raiding, the Roman remains are considerable.

In Asia Minor are a number of Greek towns which became Romanised and where excavation has revealed sites and building. *Ephesus* is one of the finest examples of these. There is a theatre, baths, the impressive library and an odeon mainly erected in the second century A.D. Like

SENATVS
POPVLVS QVE ROMANVS
DIVO TITO DIVI VESPASIAN
VESPASIANO AVGVSTO

157

158

SIC X SIC XX

IMP CAES ET CONSTANTINO MAXIM
QVOD INSTINCTV DIVINITATIS METIS
MAGNITVDINE CVM EXERCITV SVO
TAM DE TYRANNO QVAM DE OMNIS
FACTIONE VNO TEMPORE IVSTIS
REMPVBLICAM VLTVS EST ARMIS
ARCVM TRIVMPHIS INSIGNEM DICAVIT

157 *Arch of Titus, Rome, Composite, A.D. 81*
158 *Arch of Constantine, Corinthian, A.D. 312*
159 *Arch of Septimius Severus, Forum Romanum, Rome, Composite, A.D. 204*
160 *Arch of Tiberius, Orange, France, Corinthian, c. 30 B.C.*
161 *Porta Nigra, Trier, Germany, Town Gateway, Tuscan, early fourth century*
162 *Arch of Augustus, Rimini, Italy, Corinthian, 27 B.C.*

Pompei a number of streets have been uncovered, some marble paved and with remains on each side of shops, houses and public buildings. Two of these are the Via Arcadiana linking the theatre and the harbour and the Street of Kuretes which ascends the hill. The Temple of Hadrian is one of the buildings lining this thoroughfare (**133**).

Triumphal Arches and Columns of Victory

The arch is a typical form of Roman building and, in the design of monumental arches or town gateways, has survived better than any other feature of Roman architecture. The *triumphal arch* or, as it was earlier called the monumental arch, is the most typical of all the forms. Such arches were erected to commemorate important military or domestic happenings, or in memory and respect of generals and emperors. They were generally built astride a road and had one or three archways. The latter type provided a wide central opening for vehicular traffic and two smaller side ones for pedestrians. An order was used on the arch, usually with four columns or pilasters on each wide elevation; the common choice was Corinthian or Composite. The plinths below the columns, the arch spandrels, friezes and entablatures were enriched with carved ornament and sculpture. Above the cornice was an attic for the appropriate dedicatory inscription, while a large sculptural group surmounted the whole arch, usually in the form of a triumphal car with four or six horses flanked at the corners by statues. Several such arches were in the Forum Romanum and two remain, those of Titus and of Septimius Severus, while nearby, outside the Colosseum, is the Arch of Constantine. These are the most famous examples, in Rome but there are other excellent arches in Italy and other provinces at Ancona, Benevento, Rimini, Susa, Aosta and Orange.

The Arch of Titus, Rome (A.D. 81) is generally regarded as the finest of the extant triumphal arches, particularly of the single arched design. It is built across the Via Sacra at its summit, looking down on the Forum Romanum. It commemorates the capture of Jerusalem in A.D. 70 and in the two panels inside the central opening are represented the Emperor in his triumphal car and the spoils taken from the Temple (PLATE 12). The general design is a simple one and the standard of the sculpture and decoration is high. The Composite Order is used, the first known example of this (**97**). Since there is only one opening the base has a simple podium on each side instead of a series of pedestals. This gives strength to the design, which is also enhanced by the lofty attic, above which was originally a sculptured quadriga. The keystones are richly carved and the arch soffit is deeply coffered and enriched. The sides of the arch were destroyed in the Middle Ages when it was incorporated in the fortifications. Valadier restored them in 1821 in travertine which is distinguishable from the original marble workmanship (**157**). Also in the Forum Romanum is the *Arch of Septimius Severus* (A.D. 204); the best example of the three arched type triumphal arch. It was erected in honour of the Emperor and his two sons Caracalla and Geta for their victories in Mesapotamia. These events are depicted in four relief pictures above the side openings of the arch but are in a poor state of preservation. The arch spandrels are decorated by figures of winged victory and personifications of rivers. Originally the arch was surmounted by a six-horse chariot. The Composite Order is used; the columns stand on sculptured pedestals. The attic is large to accommodate the extensive inscription. Apart from the weathering of the sculpture, the arch has been well preserved due to the protection afforded in the Middle Ages from an adjacent church and fortifications (**159**).

The *Arch of Constantine* in *Rome* (A.D. 312) is a much later construction than the other two and is consequently larger and more richly decorated. The sculptural decoration, which is contemporary with the building of the arch, is cruder and poorer but much of the ornamentation was taken from earlier monuments in the period of Marcus Aurelius and Trajan. These Trajan and Antonine reliefs are of high standard. The arch has three openings divided by columns of the Corinthian Order based on sculptured pedestals; the entablature is returned over each column. The arch was built in honour of Constantine's victory over Maxentius (**158**).

In Italy, outside Rome, the *Arch of Trajan* in *Benevento* (A.D. 114) is a magnificent example which acts as a foundation for rich sculptural decoration which provides a pictorial history of Trajan's life and policy. It is a well preserved

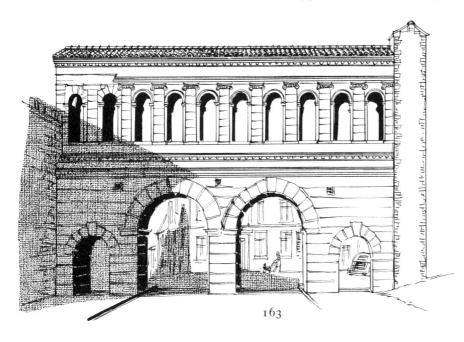

163

arch using the Composite Order. The *Arch of Trajan* in *Ancona* (A.D. 113) was set up at the harbour entrance astride a causeway. It is approached by a flight of steps and has a high podium. The sculptural group for which it was originally intended as a pedestal has now gone and the proportion of the arch appears too tall and narrow. The *Arch of Augustus* in *Rimini* (27 B.C.) is a very early and simple structure. It is a single arch with large voussoirs. The decoration is restrained and, apart from the Corinthian Order, is seen in the medallions in the spandrels. The arch was built to commemorate Augustus' restoration of the chief highways of Italy (**162**).

Outside Italy, one of the finest examples is the *Arch of Tiberius* at *Orange* in *France* (c. 30–20 B.C.). It straddles the main road into Orange, but a large roundabout has been constructed for the arch to stand serenely in a wide circular grass plot in the centre of the pounding traffic. This is a very early example of a three-arched design, in the Corinthian Order. The sides and arch panels are sculptured and there is a rich coffered vault under the central opening (**109** and **160**). The *Arch of Galerius* in *Thessaloniki* in Greece is also interesting (PLATE 11).

Town Gateways

There are a number of arches extant which were built as entrances to towns or bridges, or formed part of the fortified town walling. Most of these in Italy are in a poor condition as in Rome, Ascoli, Pompei, Ostia, etc. but the provinces have fared better. In *France* there is the *Porte de Mars* at *Reims* and two gateways at *Autun*. Here the *Porte S. André* has four archways, two larger ones for traffic and two smaller for pedestrians. It is surmounted by an arcaded gallery with Ionic pilasters. It is still in use as the town gateway as is the other example on the other side of the town which uses the Corinthian Order (**163**). At *Split* in *Yugoslavia* the *Porta Aurea* in the Palace of Diocletian has already been referred to (**138**), and in *Spain* at *Alcántara*, the Roman bridge still possesses its portal over the central pier (**167**). Probably the most interesting of these provincial archways is the *Porta Nigra* at *Trier* in *Germany* built in A.D. 275. It was part of the city walls but now, like the arch at Orange, stands in a protected island from the surrounding traffic. It consists of an outer and inner gateway with two storeys of arcading having engaged columns between in the Tuscan-Doric Order. It is flanked by two towers four storeys high (one of which has been damaged and has only three storeys left). Much of the interior remains and can be visited and explored. This archway is different from other examples and possesses a Romanesque quality rather than a Roman (**161**).

ROMAN BRIDGES

164 Bridge at Mérida, Spain, over River Guadiana. 60 arches over half a mile.
     The longest surviving example
165 Bridge and the two cathedrals at Salamanca, Spain. River Tormes
166 Ponte Fabrizio, Rome, 69–21 B.C. Spans half of River Tiber to the Isola Tiberina
     in centre of river

164

165

166

Columns of Victory

Like the triumphal arches these were erected in honour of victorious generals. The two most famous examples are in *Rome*: the Trajan Column and the Antonine Column. The *Trajan Column* was built by the Greek architect *Apollodorus* of Damascus, like the rest of the Trajan Forum, and was set next to the basilica there in A.D. 114. It is a remarkable column surmounted by a Doric capital which is in one block of marble 14 feet square and nearly five feet high (**101**). The column itself is decorated by a long relief frieze wound round from top to bottom and representing episodes from the Emperor's Dacian campaigns. It is over 800 feet long and contains some 2500 human figures. The standard of work is high as can be seen from a small section shown in PLATE 10. The *Antonine Column* to *Marcus Aurelius* erected in *c.* 180 is very similar in design and commemorates the Emperor's victory on the Danube. The Doric Order is also used and the column is the same height as the Trajan one, that is 115 feet. The sculptural work is vastly inferior and is so high in relief as to be almost in the round (**88**).

Bridges and Aqueducts

Roman bridges were well and simply designed and solidly constructed. Most surviving examples are in well laid, massive stonework, while more rarely concrete with brick facings is used. The roadway is level throughout. Examples can be found in different parts of the empire. In *Rome* there were originally 11 bridges over the Tiber; nearly all of these have been modernised or replaced. The oldest surviving example is the *Pons Fabricius* (Ponte Fabrizio) built 62–21 B.C. and spanning half of the river from the main bank to the Isola Tiberina, near the Theatre of Marcellus. There are two semi-circular arches and, between, an opening over the central pier for flood water (**166**). Also in *Italy* is the beautiful single-arched bridge at *Ascoli Piceno* and, at *Rimini*, the *Bridge of Augustus* (Tiberius) still bears the heavy traffic of the Via Flaminia over the River Marecchia. The latter was built in A.D. 14 and is the best preserved example in Italy. It has five arches with pedimented niches between and with a parapet above. In Spain are three famous bridges; one is at *Alcántara*, built in A.D. 105 by Hadrian over the River Tagus. This is a most impressive structure. In wild, rocky countryside, it is 650 feet long, with a level roadway throughout, over six arches in granite blocks superbly laid without mortar. A dam is now being constructed just upstream from the bridge. It intrudes on the isolation of the scene and reduces the Tagus flow but presents an

167 Bridge over the River Tagus at Alcántara, Spain, A.D. 105–6

168

169

168 *Pont du Gard, Nîmes, France. Built by Agrippa, 18–19 B.C.*

170 Roman Aqueduct at Segovia, Spain. Temp. *Augustus*

interesting contrast in engineering achievement, ancient and modern (**167**). Another example exists at *Salamanca* (**165**) and there is a very long, many-arched bridge at *Mérida* (**164**).

The Roman system of supplying water to cities by means of *aqueducts* above ground presented an engineering problem. Such monumental works that are extant in all parts of the empire are without decoration of any kind, but consist simply of arch after arch for miles across the landscape, presenting an impressive and significant spectacle of considerable aesthetic quality, as important in the study of Roman architecture as, for example, the Colosseum. The Romans attached great importance to an adequate supply of good water for their fountains, baths and domestic use. In Rome alone, it has

been estimated that over 340 million gallons a day were needed from the 11 great aqueducts which poured into the city. These were built across the Campagna and surrounding areas, many miles in length, simply yet grandly constructed. With slave labour they were cheaper to build than it was to provide the necessary lead or bronze piping for alternative means. The supporting arches were often in tiers, sometimes of great height, while the water ran in a cement-lined channel in the top. According to Vitruvius, a fall of six inches over every 100 feet was considered desirable and often long detours had to be made to avoid a too sudden descent.

Of the extant examples the best known in *Italy* is the *Acqua Claudia* (meaning the eighth) built A.D. 36–50 from Subiaco across the Campagna to Rome. It is 44 miles long and for nearly nine miles of this distance is borne on arches up to 100 feet high. A number of lengths remain in the Campagna.

The finest aqueduct is the *Pont du Gard* near *Nîmes* in *France*. This is a comparatively short section, in a beautiful setting, of an original aqueduct 25 miles long. It was constructed by Agrippa in 18–19 B.C. and consists of two tiers of arches each about 65 feet high and an upper tier of smaller arches 28 feet high. The water channel is four feet wide inside and is covered by slabs of stone over cemented sides. This section is *c*.

900 feet long and crosses the valley 180 feet above the River Gard. The main road still uses the bridge on the first tier and one can walk along the full length of the water channel (**168**). There are some fine aqueducts in *Spain* notably at *Segovia, Tarragona* and *Seville*. Those at Segovia and Tarragona cross deep valleys and are of great height in two tiers of arches, the lower tier being much taller than the upper. At *Segovia* the aqueduct bridge is 2700 feet long and 102 feet high formed with 118 arches constructed in granite blocks without mortar. The aqueduct is still in use (**169** and **170**).

PART TWO
THE MIDDLE AGES

3
Early Christian and Byzantine: 325–1453

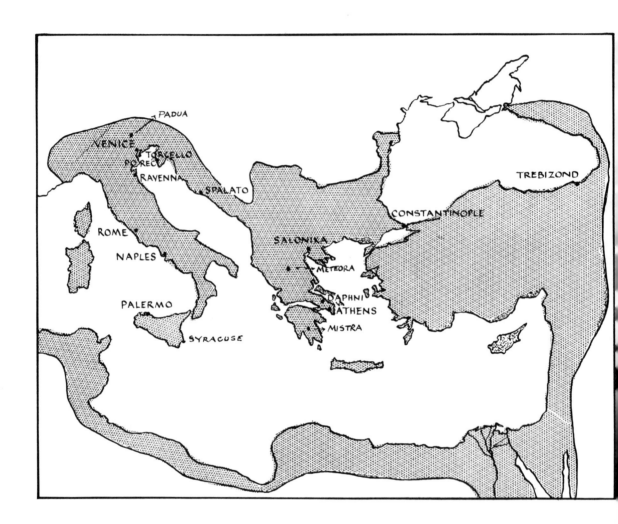

The interest and achievement of Byzantine architecture is in the wide spread of its influence in Europe and in its vital importance as a link, both structurally and aesthetically, between the work of Ancient Rome and the emergence of Romanesque. A glance at the sketch map above will show the general limits of the Byzantine Empire (which fluctuated greatly during this long period), but the influence of the style was exerted over a much greater area: north to Russia, north-west to southern France, east to Armenia and Georgia.

The *characteristics* of Byzantine design remained almost constant during this extended time but there were two chief phases of development, based upon the periods of expansion and wealth of the Empire. These were the fifth and sixth centuries, when Byzantine designs were forming themselves from early Christian patterns, and the tenth to thirteenth centuries when more elaborate buildings were erected in a new wave of expansion. To the earlier age belong the churches at Ravenna and those on the Istrian Peninsula and 'also Santa Sophia at Istanbul; to the later, many of the Greek, Serbian and Russian churches as well as the Cathedral of S. Mark in Venice. In this time, in the eleventh century, the Byzantine Empire flourished exceedingly and extended from the Euphrates to the Danube.

Extant remains of Byzantine architecture are largely in the form of churches and cathedrals and herein lies one of the chief differences between it and the preceding Roman epoch, which had produced much secular work as well as temples. The Byzantine Empire, with its capital at Byzantium (Istanbul), was strongly influenced by a number of contrasting elements: Christianity, which was the official religion; the Oriental factor from further east and the Hellenic force provided by a largely Greek population in the capital and surrounding area who, due to their heredity and training, provided the best craftsmen in building and decoration. The new culture of Byzantium, taking over from the dying Roman Empire, needed few secular buildings (except in the capital itself) for, although much had been destroyed, the population was greatly depleted. But the religion of the new Empire was Christianity and large numbers of churches were built, great and small, all over its domains, to the glory of God. Many of these were temples converted into Christian churches.

The structural link between Roman architecture and Romanesque was the Byzantine development of the *dome*. The Greeks had used the post and lintel principle—trabeated architecture; the Romans used the arch and vault together with the post and lintel and combined the trabeated and arcuated forms of construction. But they never fully developed the potentialities of the arch and rarely used the dome. When they did employ this form it was, as at the *Pantheon*, a dome set upon circular walls which did not present great constructional problems (**127, 128** and **129**). In Byzantine architecture was evolved the principle of the dome set over a square, first upon squinches which, built across the corners, provided an octagonal base for the dome, and later on pendentives. It is the pendentive which represents the great Byzantine contribution to structural form and enabled the large domed structures of Europe, from Russia to southern France, to be built. The construction of the pendentive is described on page 86 and illustrated

in Fig. **175**. It solved efficiently and finally the problem of how to construct a circular form upon a square one.

Early Christian Architecture

Until the early fourth century *Christianity* had been practised in secret in underground cellars and rooms. In A.D. 313 the *Emperor Constantine* issued the Edict of Milan which gave to Christians the right to practise their religion openly on an equal basis with other religions. In A.D. 325 the Emperor himself professed Christianity, which then became the official religion of the Roman Empire. It was from this time onward that Christian churches were built for the purpose of worship and a form of *Christian architecture* was begun. Until the fall of Rome in A.D. 476 such new churches were designed in Roman classical style and modelled upon the plan and construction of the *basilica*, the Roman hall of justice and administration. Such churches were, therefore, like the basilica, rectangular in plan, twice as long as wide and had two or four rows of columns set along the long axis, providing three or five aisles. At one end, generally the east, was an apse. The columns and capitals of the nave colonnade were frequently taken from ruined Roman buildings and are therefore different from one another and the capital does not fit its column or base. This colonnade carried a classical entablature and above was a plain wall (where the Medieval triforium normally is to be found) and above this a row of small clerestory windows. The ceiling was flat and of wood, simple but decoratively finished. The *basilican church* was generally built over the burial place of the saint to whom it was dedicated. The burial place was surrounded by the crypt and above it, in the church, was the high altar.

The term 'basilican' applied to churches and cathedrals is often loosely used and given to buildings of different plan and construction. A basilican church, like these early Christian ones, can be defined as one having the following features:

1. a rectangular not cruciform plan
2. therefore, no transepts
3. division into nave and aisles by columns not piers
4. an apse at one end of the nave called a *bema* (presbytery)

5. walls which are not reinforced and cannot bear a stone vault.

Early development of this basilican plan included the addition of a western *narthex* and a separate *baptistery*. In front of the church at the west end was built a portico or narthex which generally extended across the whole width of the façade. In front of this was usually the *atrium* or forecourt. The purpose of the narthex was to accommodate those, such as penitents, who were not permitted to enter the church, and to enable them to hear the service. Later designs further adapted the basilican plan with apses at both east and west ends and sometimes added short transepts. The baptistery was, in early Christian times, used only for the sacrament of baptism. At first only one or two were built in each city; they were large and generally on circular plan. By the fifth and sixth centuries they were set adjacent to larger churches, usually in the atrium facing the narthex.

Numerous *churches* were constructed in the fourth to sixth centuries after the establishment of Christianity as the official religion of Rome. Many of them were in Rome itself and many more in Italy and surrounding lands. Later, in the eastern part of the empire, the basilican plan gave place to Byzantine, Greek cross variations in layout, but in the west—Italy, France, England and Germany—basilicas continued to be built, even till today. Such churches were plain on the exterior but richly decorated inside. They were built mainly of brick but had columns, capitals, entablatures and wall coverings of marble and stone taken from the numerous ruined Roman secular buildings; most floors were of Roman mosaic. Such interior schemes were haphazard in design and sometimes incongruous but pleasantly and tastefully decorated.

Of the early basilicas, built in the second–fourth centuries A.D. none exists entirely unaltered, but sufficient survives or has been carefully rebuilt to the original pattern to give a clear idea of what such churches were like. *Rome* is the centre for most of these. The greatest examples have been lost completely: *Old S. Peter's*, built in 330 by Constantine, was replaced by the great basilica now standing on the same site and *S. John in Lateran* has likewise been rebuilt.

Of the other great churches, *S. Maria Maggiore* has been extensively altered outside but its interior, built 432–40, still retains much of the original features including the 21-bay Ionic marble colonnade with its gilded arabesque frieze. Above are Corinthian pilasters and a gold and white coffered ceiling, erected in the sixteenth century. The floor is of white and grey marble patterned with black circles and diamonds. The altar is at the west end* where the apse is decorated with rich gilt and coloured mosaics which cover the whole surface area and, in the conch, is depicted Christ and the Virgin Mary. In front is the great triumphal arch, also mosaic faced, and the Baroque baldacchino.

S. Paul-outside-the-Walls (S. Paolo fuori le Mura), built in 380, is so called, as is S. Lorenzo, because both great basilicas were built outside the city walls of ancient Rome. It was the largest of the Roman basilicas until its destruction in 1823. It was then rebuilt to the original design and today gives a clear picture of the layout and impressiveness of such churches. The vast exterior is fronted by a Corinthian colonnade and pavilions and, inside this, a very large atrium gives a magnificent view of the façade. The immense five-aisled nave is imposing with its 80 granite columns supporting the arches and cornice and, over this, is a row of circular medallions each with its painted portrait. The windows above glow because of their alabaster filling but make the interior darker than it would be with glass. The ceiling is deeply panelled, coffered and richly carved. The great triumphal arch is covered by mosaic as is also the apse (**173**). The whole interior, though doubtless closely based on the original, as can be seen by Piranesi's eighteenth century drawings, has, however, none of the early Christian or Byzantine atmosphere of the other Rome or Ravenna churches. It is vast, cold, magnificent but artificial, its detail mechanical, its mosaics pre-Raphaelite in feeling.

S. Lorenzo-fuori-le-Mura, which was made up from combining two early Christian churches, one dating from 432 and the other 578, was partly destroyed in World War II and restored in 1949. The restoration has been excellently carried out and the interior retains its early Christian feeling, with the long nave, Ionic colonnade and timber roof. The floor is at a higher level in the sanctuary where it is built over the enormous crypt beneath. A smaller example, but one which retains its original character, is the church of *S. Sabina*,

* *The apse contained the altar in early Christian churches from the earliest days but this was not necessarily orientated towards the east.*

EARLY CHRISTIAN CHURCHES IN ROME

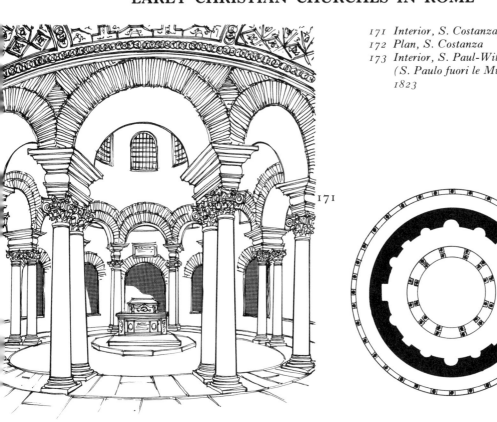

171 *Interior, S. Costanza, Rome, c. 340*
172 *Plan, S. Costanza*
173 *Interior, S. Paul-Without-the-Walls*
    (S. Paulo fuori le Mura), 380. Rebuilt
    1823

171

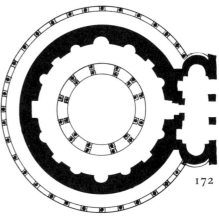

172

173

built 425, with apsidal mosaics dating from 822 (**174**).

Apart from those on basilican lines, a number of early Christian churches were centrally planned and developed from the Roman mausoleum concept. A remarkably complete example is the mausoleum of Constantine's daughter, Constantina, now *S. Costanza*, built *c.* 320–50 next to the narthex of the cemetery of S. Agnese in Rome. This is on concentric, double circle plan, with central dome and sloping outer roofs. Inside the brick walls have niches, originally with mosaic covering. The circular colonnade has Composite coupled columns. The mosaics (now restored) cover the vaulted ambulatory (**171** and **172**). *S. Stefano Rotondo* is similar but has an inner ring of Ionic columns supporting an entablature while, across the circle, is a pierced dividing wall supported on two Corinthian columns. The outer walls are painted with frescoes.

The Byzantine Church

From the fifth century onwards the Byzantine forms of church plan were evolved from the Early Christian examples. *Basilican churches* continued to be built for a long time but many variations of form developed, with one dominant theme: a dome, or domes over an open space below. The chief characteristic of the Byzantine Church is the *dome*; it represented the symbol of the vault of heaven and its builders developed constructional ability in domical form which enabled them to create many different types of design with it as covering and architectural feature. In general, in the west the basilican plan prevailed, with Rome as inspiration, but further east, in Syria, Armenia, Greece and Serbia Byzantium acted as the model and the dome was the dominant feature.

The *exterior* of Byzantine churches is plain and simple; its appearance is ceded to the glory of the *interior*. The windows are small and the

174 Church of S. Sabina, Rome, A.D. 422–32

vital characteristic is the mosaic covering to all interior surfaces. These brilliant vitreous squares of colour catch the limited rays of light from the high windows of the drum and create a shimmering effect which glows and is alive in the semi-darkness of the church. These mosaics are not only decoration; they are an integral part of the Byzantine scheme of architecture. There are few columns or piers in these domed forms of construction, thus leaving open spaces in the interior where wall, vault and ceiling pictures can be seen without interruption. On these surfaces are depicted in gold and brilliant colour the story of Christianity. The mosaics effect the same purpose as the Gothic portals in the great cathedrals: they tell the Bible story to a population which could not read. There was a tradition for the placing of such mosaics. Generally the central dome which represented the vault of heaven was covered with a picture of Christ Pantocrator (the Ruler of All) surrounded by angels and His apostles. In the drum there were prophets; on the pendentives evangelists. Each part of the walls and the rest of the ceilings received their appointed section of the Christian story.

The chief types of *Byzantine church plan* are as follows:

1. The *domed basilica* where there is a central dome with an extension on the long axis into two semi-domes, e.g. Santa Sophia, Istanbul. This is a plan typical of Byzantium and its surrounding area.
2. *Cruciform plan* with dome over the crossing and often over each arm also, e.g. S. Mark, Venice.
3. The *domed hall church*: rectangular plan to building.
4. A *dome-over-square* church where each of the four sides of the square ends in an apse. This is an eastern plan, e.g. Armenia.
5. *Cross-domed basilica* where dome is extended by barrel vaults. Related to No. 1.
6. *Circular* or *polygonal plan* with dome in centre, e.g. S. Vitale, Ravenna.
7. *Cross-in-Square.* This is the classic Byzantine form, particularly of the second half of the period. There is a central dome rising on a drum which has a cylindrical interior and polygonal exterior. The drum is supported on a circle made by four pendentives

between four semi-circular arches which in turn are supported on four piers or columns. The church has a cruciform plan where, in western areas, the western arm is longer than the others. There are many examples of this form, mostly small. It is essentially Byzantine and was used particularly in Greece, Serbia, Sicily and Istanbul.

All these churches have domes which cover a central area and are supported on pendentives. The entrance is generally at the western end and, opposite on the other side, is an apse where the altar is housed in the sanctuary. The space between is the open naos or nave. There is generally a narthex at the western entrance, sometimes crowned by a dome or domes. There is no bell tower; these, as in Ravenna, were added later.

Architectural Construction and Building Materials

The outstanding contribution of Byzantine builders to architectural construction was, as we have emphasised, their development of the pendentive. The *dome* is the most typical feature of Byzantine architecture as were the orders to the Greek and the steeple to the Middle Ages. Without doubt the chief reason for this is the eastern influence on the Byzantine Empire. It is still disputed where exactly the dome based upon pendentives originated, but its adoption for use in Christian churches is now accepted as being from eastern influence not, as was originally thought, from Imperial Rome. The *essential characteristic* of *Byzantine dome construction* is that such a dome is supported upon and covers a *square* form. The Romans made only tentative essays into building such designs but in the eastern Mediterranean and even further east—in Persia, Iran, Armenia, Syria—Christianity had taken root earlier than in Rome and churches were built of this type from the second century A.D. onwards. Long before this time wooden huts were made in these areas, by primitive peoples, which had domed structures built over square forms supported by means of planks set across the angles of the square thus making it into an octagon. Certainly Byzantine domical construction was evolved from wooden prototypes, but from exactly which area of the Middle East and eastern Mediterranean is not established. Early Christian centres have been found in Syria, Alexandria, Anatolia and Persia, to name a few, and, while after the acceptance of Christianity as the official religion of the Roman Empire in 325, churches were freely built in Rome and the west; these generally had flat, timber roofs in basilican style. Contemporary churches in the eastern part of the Byzantine domains were domed with vaults of brick or stone and such domes covered a square plan.

To understand the nature of the difference between Roman dome construction and Byzantine and the development of the latter, a series of sketches are given on page 87 in Fig. **175**. 'A' shows the normal Roman approach to covering a space with a dome. This, as at the Pantheon in Rome, is to support the hemisphere upon cylindrical walls. Here no great constructional problems are created. Apart from this type of building, attempts had been made in many countries to provide an adequate base for the circular section of the dome so that it could be set upon a square section building. Such schemes were of one of the following types:

1. To place a flat slab of stone across each angle of the square thus providing an octagonal basis. This is a direct transference to stone or brick building of the primitive wooden hut method mentioned earlier.

2. Courses of stone were corbelled out from the angles of the walls of the square, each projecting beyond the others below and carried upon them. This is an advance but not suitable to carry a larger dome.

3. The *Squinch*. Here an arch or series of arches are flung across the angles in a similar manner to (2). This is stronger still. (See 'B' and 'C'). The squinch had been known for some time and was used in Persia, Turkestan, Armenia and Asia Minor. The earliest western examples are in the Mausoleum of the Palace of Diocletian at Split (now Cathedral) (**136**), the fifth century baptistery at Naples and in S. Vitale, Ravenna (**194**).

The Byzantine contribution was the *pendentive* and this is not only a more satisfactory solution but will support large domes. The earliest extant example is the immense dome of *S. Sophia* at *Istanbul*. The term 'pendentive' is to some extent a misnomer since it appears to define a form which depends from the dome instead of, as it does, supporting it. In a pendentive method of construction the triangular spaces between the square section and the circular base of the hemisphere are built as if they are parts of a lower and larger dome so that their section is like that of an arch carried across the diagonal of the square space to be covered. This lower dome possesses a horizontal section which is concentric with the plan of the intended dome. As the lower dome is too large to fill the square space it is cut off in vertical planes formed by the four walls of the square. When the four remaining parts of the lower dome have been built high enough to form a complete circle within the walls of the square, this circle provides the basis for supporting the actual dome. The pendentive construction so far described is illustrated in Fig. **175** 'D' while in 'E' the dome is set in position above its lower dome (i.e. pendentives). Later, more complex constructions were built up further with a drum upon the pendentives, pierced by windows in the sides to light the building beneath, and the dome surmounted this drum ('F'). In pendentive construction the weight of the dome is transmitted via the four pendentives to the wall angles of the square and efficient abutment is needed at this point to offset the thrust. Given such abutment the construction is a stable and strong one. Such Byzantine domes are visible externally and are not obscured by timber roofing. Generally the dome roof is tiled.

Apart from the dome and pendentive construction, Byzantine methods and *materials* vary according to locality. In the main, building, particularly for churches, was in *brick*. This is true particularly of Greece, Italy, Egypt and southern Russia. *Stone* was, however, more common in southern France, Armenia, Georgia, Syria and on the Greek islands. In brick churches the whole construction was of this material, though interior wall facings, capitals and columns were of marble. On the exterior the brickwork was used for banding and in decorative patterns; bricks were laid at different angles in herringbone, chevron and fret patterns, for example. There are many fine Greek versions of this craft. Stone bands were also used to decorate the walls and arches. As in Roman times, the core of the walls was often concrete or rubble. White

Plate 18
Mosaic of S. George. Outer narthex, Church of
S. Saviour in Khora, Istanbul, Turkey, 13–14th
century
Plate 19 and Plate 20
Capitals, Poreć Cathedral, Yugoslavia, 535–43
Plate 21
Capital, Church of S. Vitale, Ravenna, Italy,
526–48

Plate 22
Apse, Church of S. Apollinare in Classe, Ravenna, Italy, 534–50

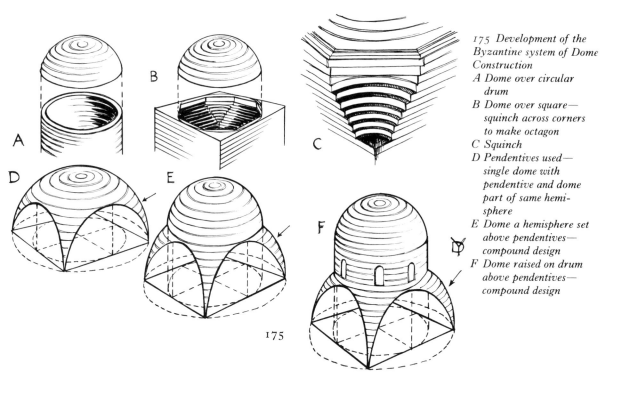

175 Development of the
Byzantine system of Dome
Construction
A Dome over circular
drum
B Dome over square—
squinch across corners
to make octagon
C Squinch
D Pendentives used—
single dome with
pendentive and dome
part of same hemi-
sphere
E Dome a hemisphere set
above pendentives—
compound design
F Dome raised on drum
above pendentives—
compound design

175

Greek *marbles* were used for interior work also coloured ones from Thessaly and areas near Istanbul. In important buildings the interior decoration was by *mosaic* over all surfaces; in poorer churches painted *frescoes* were substituted.

Openings : Arcades, Doorways, Windows

Openings were either spanned by a semi-circular arch which rested directly upon the capitals, without entablature, or by a lintel. *Arcades* of semi-circular arches were used in churches to support galleries. *Doorways* commonly had semi-circular arches but alternatively flat, segmental or horseshoe designs (**183**). *Windows* were small, partly to keep the interior cool and partly to provide the maximum plain wall area for mosaic pictures. They had semi-circular arched heads and were generally filled with alabaster or marble sheets or, sometimes, glass. Many windows were single lights; others were two or three light designs. Most of them had pierced openings for part or the whole of the light, either left open or filled with glass (**180** and **181**).

Capitals and Columns

Byzantine capitals show great variety of form and detail. Classical capitals were interpreted, particularly the *Corinthian* and *Composite* designs, and in this form the wind-blown acanthus was a typical variation (**186**). Both *acanthus spinosus* and *mollis* plant forms were used. Such Corinthian capitals were adapted to Byzantine use; generally the two rows of acanthus leaves were retained but the rosettes and volutes were altered in different ways (**182**). Some capitals were based on the classical *Ionic* pattern but the volutes were much smaller (**176**). The most typical Byzantine form is the *basket* or *cubical* capital. These were decorated in many ways; with plaitwork, leaves, circles and geometric scrolls. Their chief characteristics were the deeply incised lines and drilled holes giving a strongly defined black and white effect (**177, 178, 179, 184, 185** and PLATES 20, 21). Many Byzantine capitals were surmounted by a *dosseret* (pulvino). This is a larger block set between the arch and the capital to provide a broader supporting top for the arcade above. Such dosserets are cushion or cubiform and are often carved with a cross in the centre of each face or by a monogram (**177, 179, 182, 184, 186** and PLATES 19, 20, 21). They were used in Greece and Italy but rarely in Istanbul. *Columns* were in early times taken from ruined Roman buildings. Later Byzantine columns were monolithic and usually of marble.

Ornament and Mouldings

Decoration was nearly all of an *applied character* and in the interior. The lower parts of the walls were generally panelled or veneered with slabs of marble in white and colours. The upper parts, the vaults and domes were covered by mosaic. There were few mouldings to interrupt this pattern and few corners or sharp edges. *Carving* was shallow and often only incised. It was employed on marble and was usually confined to capitals, pulpits and fonts. Figure sculpture was not permitted and motifs were chiefly in plant and geometrical form. A feature which often occurred comprised the cross and circle used in an interlaced ornament with acanthus or vine leaves. Deep, small holes were drilled at appropriate points in the leaf and stem decoration. The guilloche ornament was also used. All Byzantine decorative form is a mixture of east and west treated in a symbolic rather than realistic manner (**187**).

Mosaic

The covering of most of the internal wall and vault surfaces by glass mosaic was the predominant feature of Byzantine churches. In the dim light the gold and strong colours glittered and glowed with rich intensity. These mosaics have suffered great damage through the ages, particularly in countries occupied for centuries by the Turks such as Greece and Turkey itself. Mosaics have been whitewashed, damaged and destroyed in fires, earthquakes and wars. It is in *Ravenna* that the most accurate impression can be gained of how such interiors looked in the Byzantine era. Churches like *S. Vitale, S. Apollinare Nuovo* and, nearby, *S. Apollinare in Classe* have suffered damage and restoration but still present remarkable workmanship and much of their original splendour. In S. Vitale, in particular, can be seen the typical combination of subjects in the Bible story depicted next to the Emperor Justinian, his Queen and his Court. The mosaics of the fifth and sixth centuries especially have a glowing richness of colour and a vividness of draughtmanship which complements their hierarchical treatment of figures and compositions. The simple drawing of figures and the conventional drapery are admirably adapted to this medium. Often the whole of the interior was covered in this way but the areas which received the most important designs and subjects were the dome, the apse, and the triumphal arch (PLATES 18, 22, 23 and 24).

Byzantium (Constantinople, or Istanbul)

In the fourth century A.D. Byzantium was a Greek city with connections with the Roman Empire. It had, indeed still has, a strategic position commanding the waters between east and west, between the Mediterranean and the Black Sea. It also had a good natural harbour and an established trade with the east and with Italy and France. The *Emperor Constantine*, impressed by the city's possibilities, transferred the Imperial seat of government there in A.D. 330 and began to build a great new city which he called New Rome. Later in the century the Roman Empire was divided into two parts, eastern and western and after the fall of Rome in the following century the eastern part ruled alone. Byzantium was renamed *Constantinople* after its first Christian Emperor and remained capital of a vast polyglot empire until its capitulation to Mohammedanism in 1453. Even before his death in 337, Constantine inaugurated many building schemes but, after him, one of the most famous names in building history of the empire is that of the *Emperor Justinian* who acceded in 527. He retook areas of land from the Goths and raised the empire to its greatest extent and power from Africa to Italy. He was also a reformer and builder; his reforms were far-reaching in administration and law while the arts flourished at a high level. He built fortifications, aqueducts, bridges, theatres and baths and planned whole cities. Many of his churches, which were numerous, still survive particularly in *Istanbul* and *Ravenna*. In the mid-sixth century under Justinian the Byzantine Empire reached its zenith of influence and

BYANTINE ARCHITECTURAL DETAIL: FIFTH to TWELFTH CENTURY

176 *Capital. S. Sophia, Istanbul, Turkey*
177 *Capital. Poreč Cathedral, Yugoslavia*
178 *Capital. S. Sophia, Thessaloniki, Greece*
179 *Capital. Poreč Cathedral*
180 *Cupola. Church of the Holy Apostles, Thessaloniki*
181 *Cupola. Church of the Virgin, Stiris, Greece*

182 *Capital. S. Apollinare Nuovo, Ravenna, Italy*
183 *West doorway. S. Sophia, Thessaloniki*
184 *Capital. Poreč Cathedral*
185 *Capital. S. Mark's Cathedral, Venice*
186 *Capital. S. Sophia Cathedral, Thessaloniki*
187 *Perforated decorative panel. S. Vitale, Ravenna*

greatness; it covered an approximate area of a million square miles.

The *city of Byzantium*, founded in 666 B.C. by the Dorian Greeks, situated on a hill above the Golden Horn, was too small to act as a capital city for the Roman Empire, so *Constantine* built new city walls enclosing a larger area. The new city, standing on seven hills and bounded by the Bosphorus and the Sea of Marmora, was easy to defend. It was laid out on Roman plan with six fora, the Imperial Palace, theatres, baths, hippodrome, etc. It was from this hippodrome that the four horses now on the façade of S. Mark's Cathedral in Venice were originally taken; they were set high above the track in Istanbul. Many churches were also built, after the adoption of Christianity, and *Justinian* in particular was responsible for the erection of the most famous of these. Between 410 and 1453 Constantine's *city walls* were extended to enclose a larger area and much of the walls still stand, encircling the city, as a monument to the importance of Constantinople during its 1123 years of rule as capital of the Christian Empire. There is an inner wall some 15 feet thick and an outer, thinner one. Towers were set at intervals and there was a terrace and deep moat. One of the main gateways was the *Porta Aurea* (golden gate), which was in marble in the form of a Roman triumphal arch with three archways and decorated with gilded sculpture.

Apart from these walls little remains today of the great Roman city laid out by Constantine and his successors. Warfare, which included the Crusades, and the neglect and decay since 1453 under Turkish rule, have destroyed the classical buildings and much of the ecclesiastical work. The churches were made into mosques and a number of these still stand, including the magnificent S. Sophia. During its years of power Constantinople was the largest city in Europe with a population of more than half a million. Arts, architecture and literature flourished and set a pattern for the whole of Europe. Its influence lasted in Western Europe and in Russia long after the collapse of the city.

S. Sophia 532–7

This great building is to Byzantine architecture what the Parthenon is to Greek. It was the prototype of Byzantine pendentive construction for large buildings and, despite its later adaptation as a mosque and present use as a museum for tourists, the greatness has been preserved and, like the Parthenon, forms no anti-climax but creates a deep impression of its immensity and magnificence.

S. Sophia was built on the site of two earlier churches of the same name, one by Constantine in 335 and one by Theodosius in 415. After a disastrous fire the new church was begun by *Justinian* in 532 and was built in the incredibly short time of six years, though the interior decoration was completed after this. The architects were *Anthemius of Tralles* and *Isodorus of Miletus*. In plan the church is nearly a square; at the west end is the narthex and at the east the apse. There is a large central space of 107 feet square under the dome, which is supported upon four massive stone piers, while east and west of this dome are continued hemi-cycles which have semi-domes; these assist in containing the thrust and counter-thrust within the building itself. This construction creates a vast oval nave measuring 107 by 225 feet and it is the open space under this airy dome which gives the unique impression of light and floating architecture which is the chief quality of S. Sophia.

On the *exterior* the church measures 250 by 220 feet (**188** and **189**). On the north and south are enormous buttresses to take the thrust of the great pendentives and the main arches of the piers. These were built after the earthquake of 1305. The exterior view is somewhat disappointing and not easy of access. Like most Byzantine churches it is unpretentious and lacking in colour. The four Turkish minarets were added in the sixteenth century. At the west end is the great atrium which leads to the outer narthex (the marble columns of the atrium have disappeared). Through the triple entrance of the outer narthex is approached the main narthex which is constructed in two storeys. It measures some 205 by 30 feet and extends almost the whole width of the building. The upper storey is in the form of a gallery for women which extends into the church.

The *interior* of S. Sophia is monumental; the architectural design is simple but the effect dynamic in its quality of light and open space. The central dome is 180 feet above ground,

188

189

190

188 *Plan*
189 *Exterior from the south-west*
190 *Interior, looking south-east*

supported on gigantic pendentives* which in turn stem from the four semi-circular arches and enormous, ground-standing piers. The dome is made of brick with thick mortar joints. It is lighted by 40 small, arched windows which pierce the lower part. All the wall surfaces and the piers were faced with marble in white, green, blue, rose and black. The floors are in coloured mosaic with a gold background and with figures of apostles, saints and angels upon this. The columns are in coloured marble; the capitals, of white marble, are tremendously varied, some from ancient Roman temples, others Byzantine basket or cubiform designs. Originally they were gilded and had blue backgrounds. The domes and vaults were decorated with mosaic. The whole interior gives a feeling of weightlessness and harmony. The design is unique but has influenced many smaller churches. It has never been equalled on this scale. It represents one of man's great architectural feats and was technically a major step forward.

The mosaics of S. Sophia have been covered by layers of painted plaster over the centuries; in most places it is two inches thick. This is being removed slowly and carefully and, in the gallery in particular, one can see the glittering beautiful mosaic emerging from its years of cocooning, brilliant as ever, preserved by its coverings. In the nine-bay narthex, the mosaics are mainly plain gilt with crosses in the tympana, except the central one which depicts Christ. The quadrangular bays of the ceiling have formal floral designs in colour on gilt backgrounds.

From the ground floor of the church the viewer absorbs the impact of the immense church. Dominating the interior is the vast, shallow cupola supported on its tremendous pendentives and flanked by the half domes on the two long sides. The marbles are still rich and some of the mosaics are visible, but in general the colour is disappointingly dark and dull, showing little of the brilliance it once had.

From the gallery, one gains a clearer understanding of the plan and construction (190). The cupola and pendentives descend to the great flat sides, pierced by semi-circular headed windows and the arcades below. The two levels of arcades continue all round the church and the gallery, at first floor level, is of vast width and dimensions. The tremendous variety of capital

forms can clearly be discerned up here.

Since its original building S. Sophia has survived many dangers. It suffered damage by earthquake in the sixth century and in the tenth, the greatest deprivations and despoliation came from those who should be expected to respect it— the Crusaders. In the Fourth Crusade especially, in 1204, the interior was looted and the gold and treasure carried away to western Europe particularly to the Vatican in Rome. This despoliation was greater than any perpetrated after 1453 by the Turks who, in general, cared well for the structure and revered it as a mosque. S. Sophia remains the supreme achievement of sixth century Byzantine architecture.

Churches in Istanbul

Such churches had a western narthex through which a tri-portal entrance led into the building. The eastern end was commonly tri-apsidal. Walls were usually of stone while vaults and domes were in brick. In later churches there were many domes raised on drums. These examples were less cubical in basic plan and more elegant in design. Chief among surviving Byzantine churches are: *S. Saviour in Khora, S. Irene, SS. Sergius and Bacchus, S. Theodore* and *S. Mary Pammakaristos.*

S. Saviour in Khora

This church represents many Byzantine building periods. It was begun in 413 outside the city walls (hence its name, hôra meaning meadow). It was restored by Justinian and again enlarged and altered c. 1050. After damage in the Fourth Crusade it was further restored and added to in the fourteenth century (192). Some of the interior mosaics are of an early date but the majority, especially those in the narthex and domes, are of thirteenth century work and are very fine and rich. They represent today the finest mosaics in Istanbul and are quite as good a quality as those at Ravenna. Parts are missing owing to damage by fire and water, but the existing remains are beautifully displayed and in magnificent condition. Most of them are in the outer and inner narthices, on the walls, lunettes and in the ceiling shallow domes and ribbed cupolas. They are very detailed, made with small tesserae with gilt grounds and subtle colouring tones. The tech-

* *These are the largest triangular pendentives in the world. Those at S. Peter's, Rome are of quadrangular form.*

CHURCHES IN ISTANBUL

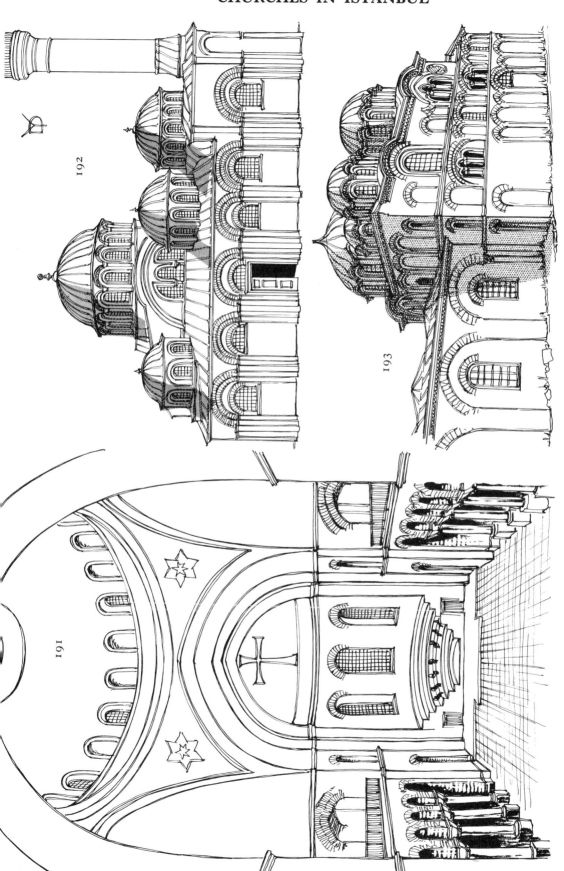

191 *S. Irene. Interior, looking east. Begun 532*
192 *S. Saviour in Khora. Built before 413. Restored by Justinian in sixth century, and again in thirteenth century*
193 *S. Mary Pammakaristos, eleventh and fourteenth century*

nique is free and realistic for such an early date. They are pictorial, with good drapery and expressive features to the figures. The whole scheme tells the Bible story in considerable detail (PLATE 18). Originally the church had one dome raised on a tall drum but in later periods further domes were added so that now there are six. This tendency in later Byzantine work to add more domes in order to make the exterior more impressive is parallel to the Medieval desire to add spires to Gothic churches.

S. Irene

The church was begun in 532. The exterior still shows the original form well but has lost all decoration. The plan is that of a cross-domed basilica with nave, aisles, eastern apse and western atrium. The dome is one of the earliest examples raised on a drum and pierced with windows. The interior shows the basic form much as it was built, though it has been stripped of its decoration. There is a flattish central cupola and a secondary domical vault at the opposite end. The gallery (viewpoint of Fig. 191), is arcaded in parts but solid in others.

SS. Sergius and Bacchus and Other Examples

This church is a classic example of the marriage between eastern and western Byzantine influences. It was built c. 527 by Justinian on a picturesque site on the shores of the Bosphorus. The construction is of Roman type, as is the masonry, but the decoration is Byzantine. In plan it is nearly square—109 by 92 feet. The exterior is uninteresting but the interior, now used as a mosque, is very fine. The central dome is vast. There are two storeys below it with a beautiful, rich, decoratively carved entablature on classical pattern and, below, Byzantine carved capitals of basket design and exceptional quality. Behind, in the ambulatory, are cubiform capitals of drilled hole type. The church is octagonal and has an apse on one face, opposite to the entrance.

Rebuilt in the twelfth century over a sixth century site the *Church of S. Theodore* is square in plan excluding a double narthex at one end and the *bema* at the other. It has five domes, the largest over the centre of the church and three are over the outer narthex; all are raised on high drums. The exterior is simple and typical of a small church; it is constructed of brick and stone in bands with coloured decoration and with arched window designs. The building is now a mosque. The minaret added to the present mosque is of brick and of a design to fit in with the rest of the church. The capitals in the wall arcade are bastard Composite and basket Byzantine.

The *Church of S. Mary Pammakaristos* (the All-Blessed Virgin) is a very fine late example mainly of the fourteenth century and is built on an interesting site overlooking the Golden Horn. It was converted into a mosque when the east end and dome were altered. The interior, especially the domed central space, is impressive. Part of the building is now used as a mosque and part as a museum. Only fragments of the mosaics remain but there are some interesting basket type leaf capitals surmounting the marble columns. The exterior is very like the Greek Byzantine churches, especially the examples in Thessaloniki (193).

The *Church of S. Saviour Pantocrator* (also later a mosque) is an unusual one in that it consists of three churches joined to one another and all of twelfth century date, but all have easy access to each other inside. Originally the decoration was in rich mosaic and marble but much of this has gone due to looting during the Fourth Crusade. The architecture is still in a fair condition and some of the marble facing remains.

The *Church of S. Theodora* originally belonged to a monastery; large cisterns found in the vicinity give credence to this theory. It is a small church with an exo-narthex covered by three small domes. The mosaics here date from the thirteenth or fourteenth century. The church itself dates from the fifth century but was altered in the fourteenth century. The exterior capitals are interesting and varied.

The *Church of S. John the Baptist* belonged to the monastery of Constantine Lipos. It is a simple building with two domes or drums and a long façade. The building is low but extensive.

One of the most interesting early structures in Istanbul is not a church but the famous *cistern* thought to have been designed by Anthemius of Tralles, one of the architects of S. Sophia. It is an underground cistern, still in fine condition and containing 336 columns mainly with Corinthian and cubiform capitals. The water level is lower than when it was in use but the level is sufficient to give reflections and provide an impression of what it was like. It was built in Justinian's day and measures 460 feet by 230. The ceiling is in brick, formed in groined vaults with barrel vaulted bays. The interior is now artificially lit and the appearance is impressive.

Italy and Sicily

Long before the fall of Rome Italy was suffering from barbarian attacks. The economy of the peninsula rapidly deteriorated and the seat of government of the western part of the Roman Empire was moved from Rome to different centres for safety. In A.D. 409 it was established at *Ravenna* and this area of the Adriatic coast from Ancona to the Istrian peninsula—designated the Ravennate—became the connecting link between Constantinople and the western half of its empire. Later in the fifth century Theodoric took over Ravenna as capital of the Ostrogothic kingdom but after his death in 526 Justinian recaptured the city and Byzantine control of the area was retained until *c*. 750. It is this part of Italy which today possesses the finest Byzantine architecture and art in the peninsula, in *Ravenna* itself, in *Venice* and the *Venetian Lagoon* and in *Istria*. In the south also Byzantine influence was strong from the seventh century until the Middle Ages. In *Apulia* and in *Sicily* the Saracens and Byzantine Greeks lived and worked, both giving to the region their style of architecture and high quality of craftmanship. Here Greek temples were adapted to become Byzantine churches— as at Syracuse (p. 21)—and new churches were built, particularly in Sicily.

Ravenna

The city of Ravenna was a naval port of Imperial Rome. Like Venice, it was built on a group of islands surrounded by marshes near the mouth of the river Po. Since that time the land has silted up in the river delta and the sea has retreated so the city, like Ostia, is now three to four miles inland. Because of the security of such a city the Emperor Honorius chose it as a refuge capital for the western part of the Roman Empire. Even today Ravenna is unique in the quality of its

Byzantine work, particularly the mosaics, most of it from the finest period of the fifth and sixth centuries. Some of the mosaics have been lost during the centuries but much remains and is carefully looked after by the Ravenna authorities.

There are three chief periods of work to be seen in Ravenna:

1. *The early fifth century*; the period when Honorius moved his capital from Rome (e.g. the Mausoleum of Galla Placidia and The Orthodox Baptistery).
2. *The Ostrogothic era*; Ravenna was taken by Theodoric in 493 and he ruled for over 30 years. He was a great builder and erected churches to the Arian religion (e.g. the Arian Baptistery and the Mausoleum of Theodoric).
3. *The Justinian era*; for over 200 years from 537 to the eighth century Ravenna was the seat of an Exarch, subject to Constantinople. The earlier part, under Justinian's influence, produced the finest work (e.g. S. Vitale).

Ravenna churches have a number of specific characteristics. They are Byzantine not Roman basilican. The eastern influence from Constantinople had merged with that of Italy to give a coherent style. They are built of red brick and are plain outside. The east end is apsidal, semicircular on the inside but, unlike the Roman, polygonal on the exterior; it is generally lit by three or five large windows. At the west end is the narthex and in later times a campanile has been added. Some examples have a baptistery near the church in the atrium. Inside, the columns are often from ruined Roman buildings but the capitals have been made specifically for the church and therefore the general interior scheme is more congruous than examples in Rome. The capitals, which are of varied Byzantine design, are superimposed by dosserets. The interior plan is commonly like the Roman basilican pattern with a timber roof and nave arcade of semicircular arches supported on columns, side aisles and mosaic decoration in the apse, triumphal arch and nave walls.

The Mausoleum of Galla Placidia, c. 430–40

This is a small cruciform building (33 by 39 feet), situated behind the church of S. Vitale, made of brick and covered by a central dome. The exterior is unpretentious but the interior is sumptuous. It is a very early example of both a cruciform construction and a dome upon pendentives and, because of its date, the dome and pendentives are part of the same hemisphere. The interior walls are lined with marble slabs and both dome and vaults still have their original mosaics which are of rich and exceptional quality. On the central part of the vault is a deep blue background decorated by stars arranged in concentric circles round a cross; at the corners are symbols of the four evangelists. In the lunettes are the apostles—figures in white and below, scenes from the Life of Our Lord. Particularly beautiful is the lunette of Christ as the Good Shepherd depicted as a young man seated with His sheep around Him. The lighting of this tiny interior is soft and gentle; it comes only through the alabaster panes of the small windows. Galla Placidia was the sister of the Emperor Honorius and died in Rome. This mausoleum was built to house her tomb but it is empty now.

The Tomb of Theodoric, c. 530

This original building which stands just outside the city was constructed by Theodoric, King of the Ostrogoths, as a mausoleum to house his ashes. It consists of two storeys and is decagonal in plan. The lower storey has thick walls while the upper one has thinner walls set back to form a terrace all round at first floor level. The upper part is circular, 30 feet in diameter, and is covered by a massive block of Istrian marble three feet thick and weighing 470 tons, which acts as a lid to the Mausoleum (**197**).

The Ravenna Churches

S. Vitale, 526–48

This is the most interesting and well preserved specimen of sixth century Byzantine church building in the west. The *exterior*, built of brick, is simple and plain but the interior is magnificent in its mosaic and marble decoration and its unique capitals. S. Vitale was founded by Justinian. It is octagonal in plan, with a diameter of 115 feet. Inside this octagon is another, with a diameter of 55 feet, having an apse on each side of the figure except the east. The church had a narthex set at an oblique angle to one of the outer octagon sides; it is believed that this was not the original narthex, which would have directly faced the eastern apse (**195**). The inner octagon is covered by a dome supported on squinches which are made (which is uncommon) of small earthenware pots fitted into one another and are, therefore, light in weight. The dome is protected by a timber roof and is tiled on the exterior. The view from above in Fig. **194** illustrates the plan and construction of the building and shows the present entrance door on the left and the eastern apses on the right.

Inside the church, where the lighting is subdued but not dim, the central dome is supported on eight piers. It is now decorated by eighteenth century frescoes. There are, however, most beautiful *mosaics* of which the principal area is in the sanctuary. The apse mosaics have a gold background and are of early type, being stiff and formal in design. In the centre is the Saviour attended by two archangels. Below are the two famous panels; on the left is shown the Emperor Justinian and his court while on the right is the Empress Theodora with her attendants. Not only are these mosaics of great beauty and rich colour but they provide accurate data of the costume and appearance of Justinian's period and illustrate the hieratic splendour of the Byzantine court. In the centre of the vault of the choir is the crowning of the Lamb on a strong blue background and below this are four angels, and beyond, four evangelists. On the lunettes and walls are further panels representing scenes from the Old Testament. The *capitals* of S. Vitale are unusual and varied. They are surmounted by dosserets, decorated by animals and birds, and are mainly of cubiform or Corinthian design. They are of high quality, finely carved and are Byzantine in treatment with deep undercutting and drilling (PLATE 21).

S. Apollinare Nuovo, 526

The main interest of this church is in its *interior mosaics* because much of the building has been

194 *Church of S. Vitale, 526–47*

195 *Plan. S. Vitale. (Parts marked with dotted line do not now exist)*

196 *Church of S. Apollinare Nuovo, 493–525. Campanile sixth century. Portico Renaissance*

197 *Tomb of Theodoric, 530*

altered in later times. It was built originally by Theodoric, on basilican plan, as his Arian Cathedral. It was completed by Justinian and dedicated to S. Apollinare the first Bishop of Ravenna. The exterior façade, which is pleasant and striking, is now composed of the campanile *c.* 1000 and the sixteenth century Renaissance portico (**196**). Inside, the basilican plan is retained, with a flat, panelled timber roof decorated in gold and blue. There are high clerestory windows and nave arcade with simple Corinthian type capitals and plain dosserets above (**182**). The mosaics which cover the nave walls are of two periods; the upper pictures date from Theodoric's time and represent scenes from the Life of Christ and the figures of apostles and saints. Below these are the magnificent pageant panels of Justinian's time showing, on one side a procession of saints advancing towards Christ from the town of Ravenna (PLATE 24) and, on the other, virgin saints led by the Three Magi moving towards the Virgin from the port of Classis. The figures of the saints are dressed mainly in white and are shown against a gold background with palm trees in between. The Magi are in rich colours particularly red.

The *Church of S. John the Evangelist*, built *c.* 425, is on basilican plan and has one of the earliest of the Ravenna bell towers. This is on a square plan and dates from the ninth century. Unfortunately the church was severely damaged in an air raid in 1944 but has now been rebuilt to the original design. The campanile was largely spared.

S. Apollinare in Classe, 534–50

This church stands about three miles from Ravenna at *Classe* (Classis) which was the port for the city in the days of Imperial Rome. It was begun by Theodoric and finished in 549–50. It is a large, three-aisled basilica, 150 feet long and 98 feet wide, with a timber roof, nave arcade of semi-circular arches and a deep, high eastern apse which is circular on the inside and polygonal outside. The chancel is raised over a crypt below. The church is constructed of thin bricks with wide mortar joints; its atrium has disappeared but the narthex remains. On the north side is a very early, circular campanile, detached from the main church (**216**). Inside, the columns of the nave arcade are of marble and the capitals, with dosserets above, are typical—acanthus decoration with drilled holes pierced deeply. Unfortunately the church was despoiled of its marble wall covering in the fifteenth century when Alberti used it to enrich the Cathedral of Rimini. The mosaics in S. Apollinare are confined to the triumphal arch and the apse (PLATE 22). They make up in quality for their comparatively small area. In the conch of the apse is a great cross within a circle and with a background of stars. On either side are the figures of Moses and Elijah.

In Ravenna also are two interesting *baptisteries* with their mosaic decoration. They are both octagonal in exterior form and inside are decorated by mosaic pictures illustrating, in the dome, the Baptism of Christ. The finer of these is the *Orthodox Baptistery* built to serve the *Cathedral* in 449–52. The dome mosaic here shows the Baptism of Christ by S. John the Baptist; the background is gold and Christ is half immersed in water which, in the mosaic medium, has an unusual visual effect. In a larger circle round the central picture are apostles and saints against a dark blue background. There is a further circle and, beyond this, arches all round the baptistery in two tiers. The lower storey is richly ornamented in the arch spandrels with further mosaics in gold and blue with central figures and arabesque patterns around them. The arches are supported on columns with Composite capitals. There is a central font with marble floor around it. The other, the *Arian Baptistery*, is similar but plainer. It was built in Theodoric's time in *c.* 500. The mosaics are not so fine and are more hieratic.

The Ravennate:
The Venetian Lagoon

Torcello

In the same manner and for the same reasons that Ravenna became the capital for the western part of the Roman Empire, the lagoons on the northern shore of the Adriatic became a refuge for people fleeing from barbarian attack. Communities which had fled from Rome and other cities established new centres of civilisation on these islands, which provided shelter and asylum from

ITALIAN BYZANTINE: THE RAVENNATE

the invader. One of the earliest of these settlements was on the island of Torcello on the Venetian Lagoon, and nearby Venice was established later. These new communities brought with them their tradition of culture and art and set up trading relations with Byzantium. The eastern capital, in turn, influenced the Venetian culture and the architectural form which developed here owes as much to Oriental bias as it does to Italy, particularly after the passage of two or three centuries.

Like Venice, *Torcello* was originally built on several islands and was a city with canal networks connecting these. Now it is only a small island with a few houses and the great cathedral with its accompanying church, S. Fosca. The *Cathedral* of *S. Maria Assunta* is a well-proportioned basilica with a tall campanile. It was built in the seventh century and after several restorations was finally reconstructed in 1008. Inside, the west wall is decorated by a mosaic representation of the Last Judgement. The capitals are all different versions on the Corinthian pattern and each has a double abacus, a straight sided one above and a curved one underneath; this is a later development from the dosseret and typical of Byzantine work of this date in Italy. The cathedral façade is decorated by tall, unbroken pilaster strips with blind arcading. A narthex extends across the façade and connects the cathedral to the neighbouring church of *S. Fosca* which is a small building with a portico which extends round the outside. This church was rebuilt in the twelfth century and is octagonal with an eastern apse (**198**). The buildings form an attractive group in contrasting Byzantine style and construction (**200**).

Aquileia and Grado

About halfway between Venice and the modern city of Trieste there is another island lagoon formation at Grado, where settlements were established at the same time as those in the Venetian lagoon. *Aquileia* was a Roman centre and the original basilican *cathedral* was erected early in the fourth century but was destroyed by Attila the Hun a few years later. Two basilicas were then built, side by side, the larger of which has disappeared. The other, after many restorations and additions, still exists and now has an eleventh century campanile and gabled west front with a low portico connecting this to the fifth century (roofless) baptistery. The interior is most interesting: it is large and has an 11-bay nave with varying classical capitals and columns. The mosaic pavement of the original church or c. 320 has now been laid bare; it is in magnificent condition and covers the whole of the nave and one aisle. Well illuminated, despite the tiny clerestory and aisle windows, the mosaic is in rich colours, particularly black and red, on a white background. The decorative scheme incorporates portrait Roman heads, animals, birds, fishes and Roman geometrical decorative forms. It is a wonderful example of a Roman Christian church pavement (PLATE 17).

Grado Cathedral, built on an island in the lagoon a few miles further south, is similar in design but the workmanship is not of such a high standard. It was founded in the fifth century and altered later. The atrium has gone, a campanile was added long afterwards and there is an early octagonal baptistery at the north-east side (**199**). Inside, the original mosaic pavement of the sixth century is very fine and the twelfth century pulpit is of unusual design. The columns and capitals are from different buildings and do not match one another. The lighting is soft and pleasing due to the marble sheets in the windows (**201**)

Istria

The influence of the Ravenna school of Byzantine architecture extended further east along the Adriatic coastline and included the Istrian peninsula in what is now *Yugoslavia*. The *Cathedral of Parenzo* is an important example of this work. Now called *Poreć*, this cathedral was built in 535–43 and displays a high standard of design and craftmanship in its layout, carving and mosaic, all of which are well up to Ravenna standards and better than the work at Grado or Aquileia. The plan is that of a Roman basilica in front of this is a covered atrium, finely preserved and with beautiful Byzantine capitals of varied form but high quality (**177** and **179**). In front of this again is an octagonal baptistery and further west still a later campanile. The eastern end of the church has an apse of Byzantine form that is, semi-circular inside and polygonal outside. Originally the cathedral was decorated al

BYZANTINE CHURCHES IN YUGOSLAVIA

202 *Interior, Poreč Cathedral, Istria (Parenzo)* 535–43,
Baldacchino 1277.
203 *Plan, Poreč*

204 *Plan, Gračanicá*
205 *Church of the Virgin, Monastery of Studenica,* 1183–91
206 *Monastery Church, Gračanicá,* 1321

VENETIAN BYZANTINE: S. MARK'S CATHEDRAL, BEGUN 1042

207 *The west façade, eleventh to fifteenth century.*
    Domes thirteenth century
208 *Viewed from campanile showing Greek cross pla*
    and siting of domes
209 *Plan*

over, inside and out, with mosaic, stucco painting and inlay. Much of this has been preserved or restored, particularly the west front of the building, above the arcaded atrium, and inside. The exterior work is largely restored but the interior decoration in the apse is mainly original and consists of marble, porphyry and mother-of-pearl inlay on the lower part of the walls and mosaic above this and in the semi-dome. The nave has 10 bays and single aisles. The columns are of marble and have varied capitals of high standard—basket, Corinthian, Composite, and Romanesque types (**184** and PLATES 19 and 20). The walls are plain and there are small windows at clerestory level and in the aisles. A mosaic paving of an early floor has been excavated in two sections. It is like that at Aquileia but not so extensive or of such quality (**202** and **203**).

Venice

S. Mark's Cathedral : begun 1042

There are two buildings in Byzantine architecture which are of supreme importance constructionally and in design and which are also superb architecture. One is S. Sophia in Istanbul, the other is S. Mark in Venice. S. Sophia is the prototype and representative of the early period in Byzantine art—the sixth century—and S. Mark of the later—the eleventh century. S. Sophia represents the eastern approach to the architectural form, in Constantinople and S. Mark the western, in Venice. Yet, despite the five centuries which passed between the creation of these two buildings and their different geographical location, they have much in common. This is partly because the Byzantine architectural style altered comparatively little in its long history and partly because Venice is not a typical western European or even Italian city; its roots, owing to to its extensive commerce, are as much in the east as in the west. Both Constantinople and Venice were, between the sixth and fourteenth centuries, cosmopolitan cities and thriving commercial ports with wide connections with all nations of the Byzantine world from the western Mediterranean to Russia.

S. Mark's Cathedral is the third church on the site. The present building was begun in the mid-eleventh century and incorporates an earlier one which was partly destroyed by fire in 976. It was built as chapel to the nearby Doge's Palace and was made into the Cathedral of Venice in 1481. The plan is in the form of a Greek cross with arms of equal length and it is based upon the design of the famous Church of the Holy Apostles in Constantinople which had been begun by Constantine and rebuilt by Justinian but which was destroyed in 1463. S. Mark's Cathedral appears to be a complicated building, not easy to define, either from the façade in the great piazza or from the interior, and it is not easy to view from other aspects as buildings crowd closely upon it. The main reason for this is that the simple plan and elevation of the original cathedral have become obscured by later work, for the cathedral was being continuously added to, altered and developed from the eleventh to the sixteenth century. The *exterior* form is most clearly apparent when viewed from the campanile: a drawing of this view is given in Fig. **208.** The Greek cross plan is visibly marked by the five domes, one over the crossing and one over each arm of nave, choir and transepts. To the west of this is the great narthex with, behind, the complex façade of pinnacles, mosaic decoration and sculpture. It is a beautiful front but, as can be seen from above, it is only a façade, not a constructional form. The east end of the cathedral is apsidal (see plan, Fig. **209**).

The *west front* closes the eastern end of the Piazza S. Marco; this façade shows the rich and vital contrast between dazzling white marble and sombre coloured mosaic recesses. The lower part is the narthex with its five arches, all two-tiered and with relief decoration in the tympana. Mosaics cover the half-domes of the niches but only the extreme left doorway—the *Porta di Sant 'Alipio*—has its original mosaic of the thirteenth century; this illustrates the transportation of S. Mark's body to the new church and shows how the church looked at about 1210, based upon Justinian's Church of the Holy Apostles (PLATE 23). Many of the marble columns and capitals on this façade came from the earlier church and other Byzantine buildings in Italy and elsewhere (**185**). Above the narthex, set back, is the cathedral façade whose central window, now glazed, was originally traceried in marble. In front of this window are the four bronze horses taken from the Constantinople quadriga (p. 90). The five ogee arches of this stage of the cathedral are carved with white marble foliage, saints, angels and pinnacles and present a fretwork skyline; these are of Gothic workmanship. The façade is a complex mixture of styles and periods of work from the eleventh to sixteenth centuries, but it presents a coherent whole which is unsurpassed, even in Italy, for richness of colour and materials (**207**). The other elevations of the cathedral are also decorated with marble veneer, carving and mosaic. The south front was reconstructed as late as 1870.

The great *campanile*, over 300 feet in height, was built between the twelfth and sixteenth centuries. It collapsed in 1902 but was rebuilt to the same design. It is simple, decorated only with flat, low pilasters in brick, and has a belfry and pyramid above. It is in sympathetic contrast of plain verticality to the riotous curves of the cathedral façade.

The five *domes* of S. Mark's (**207** and **208**) have no drums. The central one is larger than the others; it is 42 feet in diameter and the other four are each 33 feet. Inside, the central dome rises nearly 100 feet above the cathedral floor. It is supported by massive piers at the crossing, each of which is 28 feet thick and is pierced by two tiers of arches, one at ground level and the other at the gallery stage. These piers support pendentives, like those at S. Sophia, which carry the dome. The other four domes are supported in a like manner and short barrel vaults connect one dome to another.

The *interior* is lit partly by the 16 windows in each dome which are set above the springing line, but this has been less effective since the thirteenth century when the outer cupolas were constructed. Now the interior lighting is not adequate and comes mainly from the west and transept windows and the small apse and aisle windows. Despite this deficiency the splendour of the interior is apparent. The whole scheme is covered by *mosaic* and *marble decoration*. The mosaics extend continuously over the surface of the vaults and domes and illustrate the Story of the Creation, the Fall of Man, the Legends of the Saints and the Miracles of Christ. These are of different dates—of which the earlier works are the best—but all have a gold background. The mosaic *pavement* is very fine while the *pala d'oro*, the golden screen in front of the high altar, is one of the glories of the cathedral. It was made, also

altered, between 976 and 1345 and represents one of the superb achievements of the goldsmith and jeweller's art. There is a wealth of variety in the *capitals* in S. Mark's; most of these are of high Byzantine standard of carving and design; there are over 500 individual capitals in the cathedral (**185**). Some of the most beautiful mosaics are the thirteenth century pictures covering the vault of the great *narthex*. These represent over 100 scenes from the Old Testament; they have a gold background and are well lit. The great bronze *doors* of the central doorway, which lead from the narthex into the cathedral, were made in the early twelfth century and are decorated in silver.

Sicily

Byzantine work in this area is of high standard and dates mainly from the eleventh and twelfth century. It is, however, different in style from that of northern Italy due to the admixture of influences: Norman and Saracenic. The buildings are generally of solid, Norman construction with Saracenic arcuated forms while the decoration in mosaic, capitals, columns and carved ornament is a blend of Byzantine and Saracenic. This combination of differing cultures creates surprising and most successful artistic forms. Most of the work extant is in *Palermo* and its surroundings. In the city itself is the Cappella Palatina and the churches of La Martorana, S. Cataldo, and S. John of the Hermits while the nearby Cathedrals of Monreale and Cefalù contain beautiful mosaics and carved marble (see Chapter 4).

The twelfth century *Cappella Palatina* (the Palatine Chapel) was the royal chapel of King Roger II and part of the Norman palace in *Palermo*. It is not a large interior but is superbly decorated. It has a nave of five bays with stilted Saracenic arches; the dome is supported on squinches and at the east end are three apses. The entire interior surface is covered with mosaic and marble decoration. The gold background and coloured pictures glitter and glow in the subdued light which filters through the tiny round-headed windows and gives a sensation of unreality and fairy-like mysticism. The chapel is a fine illustration of the admirable blending of cultures: the construction and architectural design is Norman; the arches and carved stalactite

210 *S. Cataldo, Palermo, Sicily, 1161*
211 *Church of Gorgeopekos, Athens (or S. Eleutherios or The Little Metropole Cathedral), ninth-thirteenth century*
212 *Church of Kapnikarea, Athens, 875 and thirteenth century*

213 *Plan, Church of Gorgeopekos*
214 *Plan, S. Cataldo*
215 *Church of S. Giovanni degli Eremiti (S. John of the Hermits), 1132, Palermo*

BYZANTINE ARCHITECTURE IN FRANCE AND ITALY

216 *S. Apollinare in Classe, nr. Ravenna,*
   Italy, 534–9
217 *Basilica of S. Antonio, Padua, Italy, f*
   the north-west, 1232–1307, 7 domes
218 *Cathedral of S. Front, Périgueux, Fra*
   interior 1120–50
219 *Cathedral of S. Front from the south*
220 *Plan of Cathedral of S. Front*

216

217

219

ceiling vaulting are Saracenic; the mosaic is Byzantine. These mosaics stem from different periods; the earlier ones by Byzantine Greek craftsmen are the finest, the later Italian ones are less rich and vital.

The *Church of La Martorana* in *Palermo* originally belonged to the monastery of that name. It now stands alone and has a baroque façade is plain also, while the east end is apsidal Byzantine dome and drum with beautiful mosaic decoration on a gold background. The adjacent campanile is also interesting and is a combination of Norman and Byzantine work. Next door to La Martorana is the *Church of S. Cataldo*, built in 1161. It has typical Sicilian plain domes, three of them in a row, and a Saracenic parapet. The façade is plain also while the east end is apsidal (**210** and **214**). The interior is simple and has now hardly any painting or mosaic except on the floor. The three domes have deep drums and light the church by small, round-headed windows, pierced in Byzantine fashion with round holes. The capitals are Corinthian except for one which is in Romanesque animal form. It is a charming Norman interior reminiscent of S. John's Chapel in the Tower of London but also has an affinity with the small Byzantine churches of Greece.

Also built by the Normans in 1132–48 but containing Byzantine and Saracenic craftmanship is the *Church of S. Giovanni degli Eremiti* (S. John of the Hermits). The exterior has plain golden-coloured walls, a campanile and five, red simple domes like those at S. Cataldo. Each bay of the nave is covered by domes and there are further domes over the choir, south transept and north transept bell tower. Like many Sicilian buildings the windows are very small so as to exclude the hot sunshine (**215**).

Byzantine Influence in Southern France and Northern Italy

In these areas there exist a number of churches which are Byzantine in inspiration but which differ from the eastern pattern in their execution. They are buildings of the Romanesque or Gothic periods and possess strong Byzantine characteristics. In *France*, the region formerly called *Aquitaine* is principally where such churches are to be found, particularly in or near Périgueux (Dordogne in modern France). Here, the major

example is the *Cathedral of S. Front* in the town of Périgueux. Originally a Benedictine Abbey Church, which was destroyed by fire in 1120, it was rebuilt soon after this much on the pattern of S. Mark's in Venice and was made into a Cathedral in 1649. Like S. Mark, the cathedral is based on the Greek cross plan and has five domes, one over each arm and one over the crossing. These domes are carried on pendentives and are each 40 feet in diameter. The light to the interior of the Cathedral is low due to being provided mainly by four tiny windows in each dome. Also like S. Mark's, the domes are supported on massive square piers which are pierced at two levels by round arched passages. However, there are some differences between this western version and eastern Byzantine large churches. The domes are not hemispherical but spheroidal in shape and are elongated towards the top; the pendentives are also elongated and more in the form of squinches. In the late nineteenth century the cathedral was extensively restored and altered, particularly the main apse which is now disproportionately large, but much of the twelfth century work remains, especially inside. S. Front is similar in size to S. Mark but the workmanship is not so fine (**218, 219** and **220**). Other churches in the area which have similar Byzantine characteristics also differ mainly from the Constantinople pattern by their ovoid domes, elongated and double curved pendentives, their Romanesque fenestration and arcading; also these churches are built on the western style Latin cross plan. Such examples include the *village church* of *Tremolat* (Dordogne), that at *Paussac*, near Bourdeilles and the *church* at the village of *Brassac-le-Grand*. All these have several domes carried on pendentives and were built between the eleventh and thirteenth centuries.

South-west France, which was much further from the central sphere of Byzantine influence, showed, through trade influence, more evidence of church designs of this type than *northern Italy*, which was much nearer. There are, however, one or two examples and the chief of these is the basilica of *S. Antonio* in *Padua* (1232–1307). This is a large, pilgrimage church, also reminiscent of S. Mark's in Venice. The exterior is very fine and all the seven domes are visible; at the east end is an apse with chevet and nine radiating chapels; the west front has an upper, arcaded

BYZANTINE CHURCHES IN THESSALONIKI (SALONICA) GREECE

221 *Church of the Holy Apostles, c. 1315*
222 *Church of Our Lady of the Coppersmiths (Chalkaion), eleventh century*

gallery of pointed arches. Inside, the nave is in square bays which are covered by domes on pendentives. The other domes cover the crossing, choir and transepts. The general interior layout is magnificent, but later alterations have made the decoration of a lower standard. Most of the interior dome surface is now plain (**217**).

Greece

There are a large number of *Byzantine churches* in Greece especially in *Thessaloniki, Athens*, the area near *Delphi* and in the *Peloponnese*. They are of characteristic design and differ from those in other Byzantine regions. They are less ornate than those in Serbia and smaller and simpler than those in Constantinople. They are nearly all of the late Byzantine building period—eleventh to fourteenth centuries—and mostly have many domes raised on drums. The maximum possible wall and vault area inside is covered by mosaic or, in poorer churches, by fresco paintings. Most designs are based on the cross-in-square plan and have an apsidal east end, generally with three apses of which the centre one is larger and contains the altar. At the west end the narthex is commonly enclosed as part of the church which thus resembles a square in plan. Most of the churches are small.

Thessaloniki (Salonica)

Of all *Greek cities* this one was the most important under the Byzantine Empire and shows the closest affinity in art and architecture with Constantinople. In the later period, from the tenth century, it was the second largest city of the empire and its rich Byzantine heritage still shows this.

Cathedral of S. Sophia

This is one of the largest and earliest of Greek Byzantine churches. The exact date of its original building is disputed but it probably stems from the late fifth or early sixth century. It has been considerably altered, mainly under Turkish rule, and then later restored so that the exterior, in particular, is changed. It is a domed basilica with a tri-apsidal east end, a wide western narthex which runs round three sides of the

church like S. Mark's Venice, and a central dome, 45 feet in diameter, carried on pendentives. Some very fine original mosaics remain. In the dome is represented the Ascension with Christ seated on a rainbow and surrounded by a ring of angels and apostles alternating with olive trees. In the apse is an earlier mosaic—about eighth century—showing the Virgin and Child (**178, 183** and **186**).

Church of S. George, c. 310 onwards

This is an unusual building with a chequered history, having served as Roman temple, Christian church and Mohammedan mosque. Now, almost empty, it is a museum. It was built *c.* 310 as a Roman rotunda by the Emperor Galerius and, like the Pantheon, has eight great arches and entrances on the ground floor and a massive dome overhead. It is lighted by semi-circular headed windows above these. The dome, 80 feet in diameter, is based, Roman fashion, on walls of cylindrical plan which are 20 feet thick to support it. In the fifth century it was converted into the Church of S. George and the dome decorated by mosaics, few of which remain. The dome was covered on the outside by a flattish pitched roof, an ambulatory was constructed round the rotunda which became the nave and a chancel was added at the east side. The minaret is a souvenir from the Turks' use of the building as a mosque. In its present form it is more like the original Roman Pantheon and is a most interesting example of Roman brick arcuated construction (**223, 224** and **225**).

Church of the Holy Apostles, 1312–15

Situated on the hillside which rises above the port of modern Thessaloniki the Church of the Holy Apostles is not easy to find amidst the poorer districts of the town, but it is well worth the effort of searching. The exterior, especially, is a perfect example of its type in good condition. It stands in a small square, now some five feet below the present ground level, surrounded by cypress trees. The Turkish buildings which had adjoined its walls have now been removed and the church can be seen clearly. It is made of polychrome brick in richly decorated patterns in reds, browns and yellows. It has five domes on high drums with projecting cornices on each of their sides. The high quality of the brickwork is unique in the typical late Byzantine patterns of zig-zags, frets and diamonds (**180** and **221**). The interior has suffered seriously at Turkish hands and the frescoes have been badly damaged.

Church of S. Demetrius, late fifth century

This was one of the finest and largest churches here but, having survived much of the bombardment of the First World War, it was seriously damaged in the fire of 1917 when its wooden roof was totally destroyed and caused great ruination when it collapsed into the church. Now the building has been restored but with newer and different materials, mainly white marble and red brick. Only a few capitals and a little of the marble panelling and mosaic remain of the original decoration. These have been preserved and incorporated into the new, impressive church.

Athens

A number of churches here survived the Turkish occupation, but were lost in the nineteenth century when the capital of the newly independent Greece was re-organised and planned on broad lines. Those remaining include the *Church of Gorgeopekos*, the *Kapnikarea, S. Nicodemus* and *S. Theodore*.

The first of these, the *Church of the Virgin Gorgeopekos* (also called S. Eleutherios or the Little Metropole Cathedral due to its proximity to the great nineteenth century Metropolitan Cathedral) is the most interesting. It is a tiny building, only 38 by 25 feet, and now stands a little below the present pavement level. It has a central dome, nine feet in diameter, on a high drum pierced by small windows, which is supported on four piers. The church is built of white Pentelic marble and is decorated by sculptured slabs and panels mainly of decorated marble taken from other buildings, thus illustrating a mixture of Greek classical and early Byzantine work from egg and dart carving to signs of the zodiac and dragons (**211** and **213**). The *Church of the Kapnikarea*, built originally *c.* 875 and enlarged in the thirteenth century, now stands on a small island in the centre of Athens traffic.

It is of similar plan to the Little Cathedral but is larger; at the east end are three polygonal apses and there is a beautiful thirteenth century porch. The central dome is small—only six feet in diameter—and is decorated inside with gold mosaic (**212**).

The other two churches are less interesting due to alterations and restorations in later periods. *S. Theodore, c.* 1065, is situated in a pleasant square. It is built on Greek cross plan and has a small dome on an octagonal drum. It is of stone with thin bricks between. The east end is apsidal with three polygonal apses and there is a later bell tower at the south side. *S. Nicodemus* is the oldest of this group of churches but was excessively restored and altered in the nineteenth century when the campanile was built.

Monastery Churches

Daphni

Here is an eleventh century monastery church situated in a grove by the side of what was originally the sacred way from Eleusis to Athens (now a dusty highway with commercial traffic pounding from modern industrial Eleusis to the capital's port at Piraeus). The fine Byzantine church was considerably restored in the nineteenth century, but retains its original character. It is built of sandstone with red bricks set between courses. The east end has the three polygonal apses, the central one taller and larger, and the dome rises above an eight-sided drum and is capped by a flattish, tiled roof. Inside, the mosaics and frescoes are very fine especially those of the dome which illustrate the Christ Pantocrator in all His Glory (**229** and **230**).

S. Luke of Stiris (Osios Lukas)

The monastery buildings here are in a beautiful mountain setting between Levadia and Delphi where peace and solitude still remain, tourists apart. Architecturally the buildings form an unusual and interesting group consisting primarily of two churches joined together; the larger S. Luke and smaller church of the Virgin (**226** and **228**). The monastery takes the form of an open square in which the two churches stand. The *Church of S. Luke* has a central dome carried on 12 piers with squinches to transform the

BYZANTINE CHURCHES IN GREECE

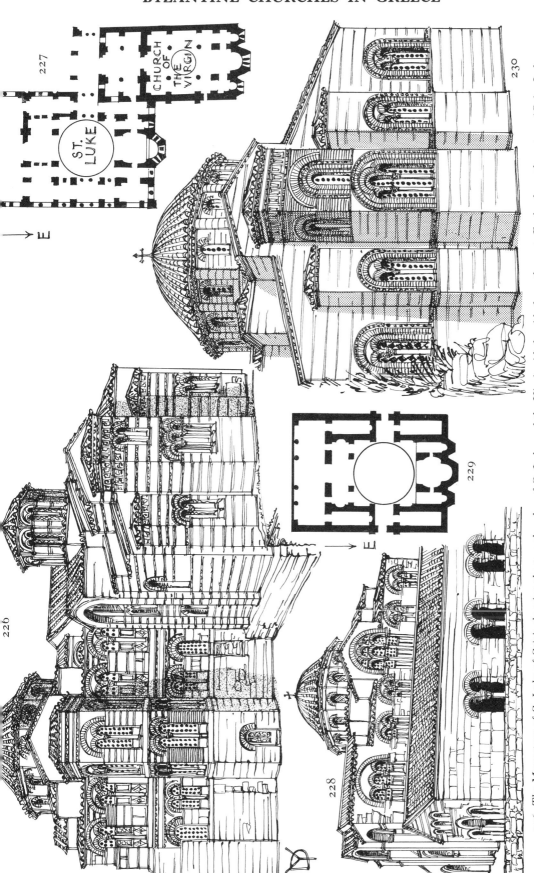

227 CHURCH OF THE VIRGIN · ST. LUKE

229

226 *The Monastery of S. Luke of Stiris showing the two churches of S. Luke and the Virgin side by side from the east. Early eleventh century (Osios Lukas, near Delphi)*

227 *Plan of the two churches*

228 *Church of S. Luke from the south*

229 *Plan. Monastery Church of Daphni, ninth century*

230 *Monastery Church at Daphni from the east*

square into an octagon while higher up are small pendentives which convert the octagon to a circle. The rest of the church is vaulted and the vaults, dome, squinches and walls are richly decorated with coloured marble and mosaic. The dome is raised on a drum which has 16 windows (some now walled up) while each arm of the cross has a half-dome. The east end is apsidal with a single polygonal apse. The mosaics in the narthex are in good condition, restored, in brilliant gold and colours. The floors through-out are of the original coloured marble while large portions of the windows still possess their original marble slabs. The smaller adjoining *Church* dedicated to *the Virgin* is also eleventh century and has a fine dome on an octagonal drum which is pierced by double windows which have slender, marble shafts between the lights. Between the windows the drum is richly panelled in carved marble slabs (**181**). Like the Church of S. Luke, the floor is of beautiful coloured marble and the walls and vaults are decorated by marble and mosaic. The eastern end is tri-apsidal, polygonal on the exterior (**226**).

Mount Hymettos

There have been several monasteries here on the mountain slopes above the city of *Athens*; they are now deserted and partly ruined. The largest of them is the *Monastery of Kaisarani*, which has a beautiful situation surrounded by cypress trees. The church dates from the eleventh century and is magnificently decorated by fresco paintings in the narthex, dome, apse and on the walls. The dome is supported on four columns which have Ionic capitals taken from a classical temple which earlier stood upon the site. Higher up the mountainside is another, smaller church of the *Monastery of Asteri* which is equally finely situated and has magnificent views of the hills encircling Athens and of Daphni.

Meteora

In these remote valleys of *Thessaly*, not far from the city of Larisa, are the remains of some of the most remarkable monastery churches. Originally, in the fourteenth century, there were 30 monasteries, now, only five or six remain. The churches are small, perched on the summits of

high, needle-like rocks which rise sharply from the valley floor and in which the monks lived and prayed in retreat from the world at large. Two of the most impressive survivors of these churches are those of the *monasteries* of *S. Barlaam* and *S. Stephen*. They are built on the Byzantine pattern, in small scale, and have painted fresco decoration.

Mistra

Much further south, near ancient Sparta in the *Peloponnese*, is the now deserted city of Mistra (Mystras). On a rocky hill, about 2000 feet above the sea, Mistra was developed in the late days of the empire from the fourteenth century and was, at that time, an important centre and therefore contained some large churches. Most of these are now desolate except for the fifteenth century *Church of the Pantanassa*, still a convent, and a few others such as the fourteenth century *Church of Evangelistria, S. Sophia, c.* 1350, and the fourteenth century *Church of Peribleptos*. The Church of the Pantanassa is particularly fine, sited on a hillside ledge overlooking the valley. It has five domes on drums and a belfry, also a loggia. Inside, there are frescoes in rich colour typical of the best of late Byzantine work. There were also a number of outstanding secular buildings such as the *Palace* with its great hall and courtyard, but much of the rest of the city is in ruins.

Asia Minor

Christianity spread here early and into Armenia and Georgia. Many churches were built but almost all are ruined or have disappeared. A number of examples were domed basilicas, particularly on the coast, while inland churches were small and of stone, usually with barrel vaulting. An important church is that of *Khodja Kalessi*, built *c.* 451, in *Southern Turkey* in the ancient region of Cilicia, but this is partly ruined. Remains of many churches still exist in and near the ancient city of *Ephesus* (Efes). The most notable are those dedicated to S. Mary and to S. John. S. Mary, the cathedral where the Council of Ephesus met in A.D. 431, is sometimes referred to as the 'Double Church' because of its different building periods. Only fragments remain

RUMANIAN AND BULGARIAN MONASTERIES AND CHURCHES

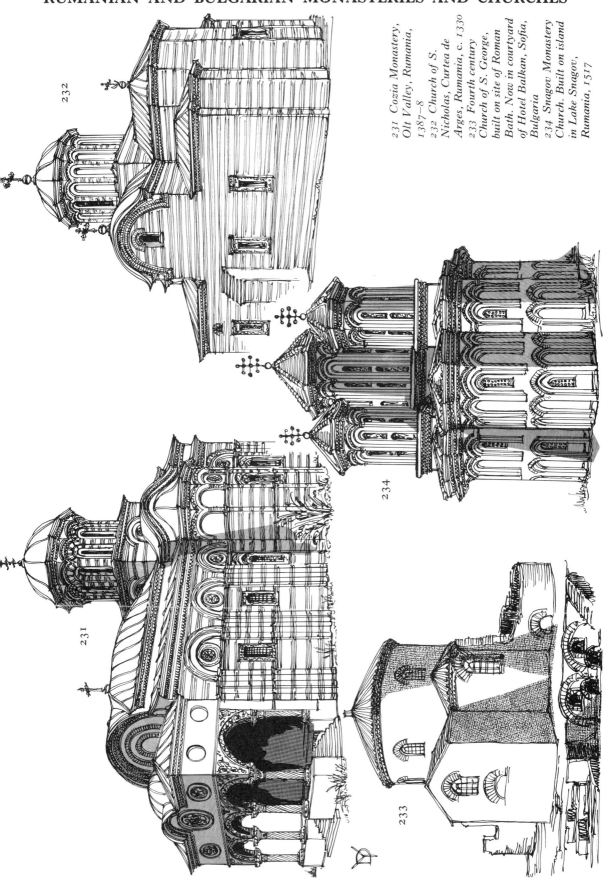

231 Cozia Monastery, Olt Valley, Rumania, 1387–8

232 Church of S. Nicholas, Curtea de Arges, Rumania, c. 1330

233 Fourth century Church of S. George, built on site of Roman Bath. Now in courtyard of Hotel Balkan, Sofia, Bulgaria

234 Snagov Monastery Church. Built on island in Lake Snagov, Rumania, 1517

but these show the immense size of the building, over 400 feet in length. The church of S. John was built in the early fifth century then re-built by Justinian about 565. This was a famous and magnificent building but only a small, well preserved, portion remains.

Armenia

Armenian Byzantine churches have something in common with Greek designs and date chiefly from the tenth to the thirteenth century. Those of the tenth century are the finest and richest. The churches are small in plan but tall in proportion. Ground plans are square or rectangular and the east end is apsidal, generally with three polygonal apses which are semi-circular inside. The domes are constructed on high drums but are hidden externally by steep conical, stone roofs. The most famous example is the *Cathedral* at *Ani*, the capital, now called Erivan (Yeŕevan) and under the jurisdiction of the U.S.S.R. This cathedral dates from 1010 and is of cross-in-square design but with longer east and west arms. It is in a ruined condition.

Yugoslavia

Many interesting examples of Byzantine work have survived in the territory which comprises modern Yugoslavia and they stem from either Italian or Serbian origins. The northern part of the Adriatic coast was under Italian influence, of which the best example is *Poreč* (Parenzo) already described on pp. 100, 103 (**202, 203**), while the mountainous central area extending as far as the southern part of the Adriatic coastline contains Serbian Byzantine churches. These are a relic of the independent existence of Medieval Serbia when this territory was of great importance in the Balkan Peninsula at a time when the Byzantine Empire was at a low ebb. For over 200 years, in the late Byzantine period, Serbia was strong and influential and built many monasteries and churches before succumbing to the Ottoman Empire. In architectural style these churches are generally tall, like the Armenian ones, but very richly decorated in brick and stone. They have numerous domes on tall drums. The surviving examples are almost all in or near tiny villages in remote mountain regions; among the

best are those at *Studenica, Dečane, Gračanica* and *Kruševać.*

The *monastic royal Church of Studenica* was built beside a river of the same name in 1183 in the central mountain area far from any large town, the nearest being Niš (**205**). Its walls are faced with white marble and the interior is richly decorated with fresco painting. The *Monastery of Dečane* is south of Studenica, in even wilder country near the Albanian border. It was built in the fourteenth century and shows Italian influence, being designed by craftsmen from Kotor (Cattaro) on the coast south of Dubrovnik where there is further Byzantine work. This Italian feeling is shown in the decorative bands of black and white marble and sculptured tympana which are Romanesque in type. However, the dome, general plan and interior frescoes are Serbian Byzantine. The *Church at Gračanica*, built 1321, is one of the most striking examples of Serbian Byzantine architecture. In the mountains not far from Dečane and near the present-day town of Prština, it lies just off the main road to Skopje. It has a tall central dome and smaller ones, also set on drums, over the angle spaces. The exterior has a fine, grouped massing of domes typical of the late Byzantine period and the brick decoration is rich and of high standard. Inside are fresco paintings (**204** and **206**). The *Monastery Church at Kruševać* is near to Studenica and part way between Niš and Belgrade. It is also a fourteenth century church and shows Romanesque tendencies in its sculptural decoration.

Rumania and Bulgaria

Like Russian Byzantine architecture, the best *Rumanian* Byzantine churches belong to a late period, in some cases, after the collapse of the Empire in Constantinople. In style, however, they are more usually like those of Serbia.

One earlier example is of the cross-in-square type with a dome over the crossing. This, the *Church of S. Nicholas* at *Curtea de Arges*, has a poly-sided drum. The exterior is built in simple brick and stone courses and, like the interior has been restored a number of times. Inside the decoration is remarkable. All surfaces—dome, drum, pillars, chancel screen and walls are covered in paintings, some of which belong to the fourteenth century building period (**232**).

RUMANIAN CATHEDRALS

235 *Patriarchal Cathedral, Bucharest. From the south-west, seventeenth century*

236 *Cathedral and royal mausoleum, Curtea de Arges. From the south-east, Early sixteenth century*

235

236

The more common Rumanian pattern is on trefoil plan with a square narthex at the west end. *Cozia Monastery Church* is an example of this design (**231**), with a dome over the central part. Traditionally Byzantine in the building materials and plan, it is more eastern in the decoration and treatment. The monastery has a beautiful situation, on the very edge of the river Olt in fine mountain country. The interior has painted surfaces all over; especially interesting are those in the narthex.

Two famous churches of early sixteenth century date are the *Cathedral of Curtea de Arges* and the *Monastery at Snagov*. The Cathedral is a remarkable building, richly ornamented inside and out. The exterior gleams in gold and colour and stands in a park amidst beautifully kept flower beds. It was built in 1517 as a royal mausoleum. The tombs are in the narthex which is large, almost half the building, and which is approached by a flight of steps. One large dome and two smaller ones with twisted columned drums are set over the narthex which has 12 columns to support them inside. The main church behind is small and high, with the largest dome over it. This building is on the typical Rumanian trefoil plan, with three apses round the square (**236**). The intricate decoration shows a variety of motifs and designs from Byzantine, Renaissance and Mohammedan sources. There are no mosaics inside but paintings on all surfaces. The columns are ornamented in geometrical designs but on the apses, domes and walls are depicted biblical scenes with the Christ Pantacrator, apostles and saints.

Snagov Monastery occupies a romantic and peaceful island site in the Lake of Snagov which is now a centre for boating, fishing and bathing, used at weekends and holidays for the city dwellers of near-by Bucharest. The monastery church is small and lofty, on cinquefoil plan and with four drums and domes very like their Serbian counterparts. One large dome covers the crossing, another the narthex and there are two smaller ones over the eastern apses (**234**). The church is built of brick (recently restored) and has narrow slit Byzantine windows. Inside four arches support the central dome with squinches rather than pendentives. Below the arches are fat, circular columns instead of the usual piers, and there are openings between

these and the apses. The chancel is barrel vaulted. The interior surfaces are painted with work dating mainly from 1815.

The Byzantine style of church building continued, as in Russia, for several centuries. Later larger buildings were more complex in plan and construction with a multiplicity of domes but often, basically on cross-in-square foundation. The *royal church* at *Tîrgoviṣte* not far from Curtea de Arges is one of these, built in the sixteenth century. Similar, but larger, is the *Patriarchal Cathedral* at *Bucharest*—dating from the seventeenth century and several times restored (**235**). This has a fine site, surmounting a hill in a park overlooking the busy, central Piata Unirii. The building has a large narthex extending the whole width of the church with three saucer domes over it. These and the walls are painted all over. The eastern end of the Cathedral is tri-apsidal and there are four domes on tall decorative drums.

Bulgaria also had a long history of Byzantine building of churches and monasteries but remains of original work are not numerous or of high quality. Earthquakes took a high toll, as at Turnovo, and some of the more famous examples, like Rila Monastery, near Sofia, have been rebuilt much later (see Chapter 8, p.499).

Serbian influence was strong in Bulgaria, as in the Turnovo churches, but more common were the aisleless halls, barrel vaulted and with two domes raised on drums, one over the centre and one the narthex. S. Dimitri at Turnovo was one of these.

Among the work still surviving is the *Monastery* of *Bachkovo*, near Plovdiv, which was built in 1083. Its early seventeenth century church is pleasing and interesting. *Rozhen Monastery*, near Melnik, is of early date. The Church of the Holy Virgin in the courtyard is of the fourteenth century and contains some fine wall paintings.

Most dramatically situated is the *Preobrazhensky Monastery*, near Turnovo. It is lodged on a shelf on the mountain gorge, high above the Yantra river with precipitous rocks falling steeply below it. The long, low church is decorated by paintings all over the exterior and interior walls openings and window frames. The roof is tiled and the cupola is of Greek Byzantine type. The monastic buildings surround the church and spread up the hillside above. Inside, the church is designed in three parts. The centre portion is the largest and is surmounted by the shallow cupola on an octagonal drum carried on squinches with four arches below. The naos has a painted barrel vault and the pro-naos a flat-timber roof. The paintings are all of biblical scenes with Russian Byzantine influence.

Russia

The Byzantine origins and influence dominated much of Russian architecture even into the sixteenth and seventeenth century. The Russians were interested in and finally converted to Christianity at the end of the tenth century and from this time onwards their ecclesiastical architecture was based on that of Constantinople while the churches were, in many cases, built and decorated by Byzantine craftsmen. After the collapse of the Byzantine capital it continued as inspiration for Russian architects and artists who gradually adapted the style to their own climate, building materials and taste. This was particularly so in the area round *Novgorod*, where the dome was altered to Russian designs and climatic needs and established the characteristic Russian church skyline. By the twelfth century the typical onion shape had emerged whereby the dome was increased in diameter above the springing then became more slender and steep above to throw off the rain and snow. The number of domes used increased and larger buildings had many, all on cylindrical drums and placed almost haphazardly on the building. The results were striking, especially when bright colour decoration was added as in the *Cathedral of S. Basil* in *Moscow* (**249**) which represents the culmination of the Byzantine style in Russia and shows also how far Russian Byzantine forms had diverged from Constantinople and the West.

Kiev

Byzantine architecture was introduced to three principal centres in Russia: *Kiev, Novgorod* and *Vladimir*. The earliest of these was at Kiev where, in 988, Vladimir, Grand Duke of Kiev was converted to Christianity and from this time onwards he and his successors encouraged commerce and cultural exchange between the area and Constantinople. Architects and craftsmen

came to Russia to build the first churches and to share their experience with the Russians. At that time Kiev was one of Russia's greatest cities and within half a century had a great cathedral and hundreds of churches. However, in 1239 the city succumbed to Tartar invasion and much of the Byzantine architecture was destroyed while church building developed further in areas which suffered less from barbarian attacks. It was the ambition of Vladimir and his son Yaroslav to create at Kiev a city as fine as Constantinople and they planned monasteries, churches and schools. Early buildings were in wood and have perished, but parts of later stone ones survive.

Cathedral of S. Sophia, begun 1037

This building was the first great Byzantine church in Russia and it set the pattern for innumerable smaller churches. It is difficult to define accurately what it was like for, although it still exists, it has been damaged, altered and restored so the original design has been obscured. Only in recent years, due to patient work, is its early form beginning to be discernible. It is a brick, cross-domed basilica, its plan clearly based on Constantinople pattern, and was originally nearly square in plan, with a central dome about 25 feet in diameter and 12 smaller domes (to represent Christ and his apostles). It had aisles and five semi-circular apses (**237**). Later, four more aisles were added, each terminating in a round apse, thus giving an east end with nine apses (**238**). It also gained two western towers and eight more domes. After the sack of the city in 1239 the cathedral fell into decay until the seventeenth century, but even in this ruinous state greatly impressed travellers of the period. In the eighteenth century it was restored and the domes added (**239**). Although based on Byzantine type plan, S. Sophia, even in the eleventh century, had acquired individual Russian characteristics. This was evidenced in the 13 domes and their arrangement. They were low domes set on tall, narrow drums, possibly based in design upon the wooden Cathedral of S. Sophia at Novgorod (destroyed by fire 1045). The church was also surrounded on three sides (except the east) by an open arcade on which a gallery was later built. Inside, the piers were massive and there were more of them than in examples further west. Also the interior was higher and narrower, both characteristics being necessary to support the 13 domes. Unfortunately, as elsewhere in the tenth and eleventh centuries, the Russians followed Byzantine building methods closely in, for example, laying the tiled roofs directly upon the vaults. This was suitable in a Mediterranean climate but fatal in Russia. The Russians learnt to adapt this system to their climate as they adapted roof and dome pitches for the same reason.

Today, the exterior of S. Sophia is very much like the eighteenth century model in the cathedral (**239**). The lower part is of the simpler Medieval Byzantine period while the domes and drums are more Baroque. The building is surrounded by walls and the visitor enters through the great bell tower gateway. Inside the cathedral there is more light than is usual in such great Byzantine churches. This is because there are so many domes and the lantern of each is pierced with windows. In addition there is a large western lunette window. An unfortunate ornate gilt altar screen obscures the simplicity of the vertical lines of the great eastern apse, but above is visible the mosaic in the conch depicting the Virgin against a gilt background; below are saints and apostles. In the crossing cupola are mosaics of the Christ Pantocrator with four angels around him. The great piers dividing nave and aisles and the smaller octagonal columns are fresco covered.

Not only did *Byzantine churches* in *Kiev* suffer from barbarian invasion in the Middle Ages, but damage to these fabrics in the Second World War was devastating. On the fringe of the city, now in the Botanic Garden of the Academy, still stands the *Monastery of Vydubitsky* which contains the churches of *S. Michael* and *S. George*. The latter dates from the eighteenth century but S. Michael was built in the eleventh century and much of it survives. Of the famous *Lavra Monastery* on the ridge of hills overlooking the Dnieper river on the outskirts of Kiev little exists from Medieval building. One enters by the gateway underneath the *Church of the Trinity 'on the Porch'*. This was a combined church and look-out gateway and was constructed early in the twelfth century. The interior, consisting of two lookout rooms on the ground floor, has been well preserved, and the church above with central cupola supported on four piers. The

exterior was decorated in the eighteenth century with Baroque frescoes (**865**). The masterpiece of the monastery was the centrally placed *Cathedral of the Assumption*, built in the late twelfth century and, due to its fine proportions and construction, used many times as a model to later churches. It had been redecorated in Baroque style in the eighteenth century, but its Medieval character had been retained until it was wantonly destroyed by order of the Germans in the Second World War. The remainder of the Lavra buildings are of eighteenth and nineteenth century construction.

At *Chernigov*, a few miles north-east of Kiev is the *Cathedral of the Transfiguration*, begun 1031 and the *Church of S. Paraskeva*, 1118. These two examples are of similar design; they are cross-domed basilicas with short western arms and apsidal east ends. The cathedral has five domes on drums, the central one supported on four piers. The building was richly decorated in marble and fresco but little of this remains.

Novgorod and Pskov

Novgorod (new town) was, despite its name, an old settlement which, by the tenth century, had become an important trade centre. It had regular contacts with Constantinople, notwithstanding its northern position (near the city of Leningrad) by means of the river Dnieper and the Black Sea. More important still, it was the only large town in Russia not ravaged by barbarian invasion in the thirteenth century, due to its marshy situation on the shores of Lake Ilmen, so it was able to expand and become wealthy. It was an artistic and cultural centre as well as a commercial one and retained its importance until the rise of Moscow in the fifteenth century. Its tenth century architecture was strongly influenced by that of Kiev. For nearly 500 years the people of this area built churches, cathedrals, schools and houses on the Byzantine model and, as time passed, adapted these designs to their own needs. Thus, while Kiev was the originator in Russia of Byzantine architecture, Novgorod was the district where this architecture became Russianised and indigenous. Building was primarily in wood, because of the quantity of timber in the area, but was also in brick and stone. The complex Kiev church plans were soon adapted to simpler

THE CATHEDRAL OF S. SOPHIA, KIEV, U.S.S.R.

237

238

239

37 The Cathedral as it existed in the thirteenth
    century. Drawn from a model now in the cathedral
38 Plan. Of the same date
39 Cathedral as it was redesigned in the eighteenth
    century and as it has been restored now. Model of
    eighteenth century version also in Cathedral

versions of four piers supporting one dome and with three apses at the east end of the church. Wall surfaces were covered with stucco and then painted white. Cornices and drums were decorated in brick with zig-zag and saw-tooth ornament. The climate of this region was largely responsible for the adaptation of Byzantine roofing methods. Low pitched Byzantine roofs and hemispherical domes were unsuitable for snow and rain so the people of Novgorod developed roofs of steeper pitch with onion domes. It is disputed whether these onion domes were a development indigenous to the area or whether the idea came from further east, but the former seems more likely on the weight of evidence; they were being built by the mid-twelfth century here and were designed in a great variety of shapes and in large numbers.

Cathedral of S. Sophia

The first cathedral of this name in Novgorod was built in wood soon after Vladimir's conversion to Christianity in 988. It typified the northern Russian timber interpretation of Byzantine architecture just as the cathedral at Kiev illustrated that of southern Russia in masonry. It was destroyed by fire in 1045 and a new cathedral was begun soon after. This time the building was in stone and was a simpler edition of its namesake in Kiev. It is smaller and has five aisles and three eastern apses. There are six lofty, tapering, bulbous domes on tall cylindrical drums. Inside, the great piers curve up the interior space and emphasise the verticality of the design. The twelfth century frescoes have now been restored.

There are a number of *churches* still surviving in the area. The twelfth century examples are simple and tall with nave, single aisles, three apses carried the full height of the building and a tall cupola covering the crossing supported on six piers. Some churches have further domes over the west end. The exterior form is tall, cubical and very simple and represents the beginning of a national style. Extant examples include the *Nativity of the Virgin*, 1117, in the Monastery of S. Anthony, *S. George*, 1119–30, in the Yuriev (George) Monastery and *S. Nicholas*, 1113. In the thirteenth and fourteenth centuries designs were further simplified and nationalised. Piers were reduced from six to four, the apse became shallower and often single, the aisles were

decreased in height and width. Many churches had four simple gables of equal size one on each face, surmounted by a central dome upon a drum. Examples of this style include the *Church of S. Theodore Stratilates*, 1360–2 and the *Transfiguration*, 1374, both in the commercial quarter of Novgorod. Later churches are represented by *S. Peter* and *S. Paul*, 1406, and the *Twelve Apostles*, 1450. Near to the town is also the *Church of the Annunciation*, 1179, at Lake Miatchine. One of the finest churches was that dedicated to the *Saviour at Nereditski*, 1198, which was completely destroyed in the Second World War.

Pskov, a town north-west from Novgorod, also established independent architectural expression in similar form, in the Middle Ages, but the work was simpler and cruder. The city remained free until the early sixteenth century but was less wealthy. A basic difference in the architectural construction was the use in Pskov of corbelled arches rather than pendentives to support the domes. This was partly due to economy and partly to inexperience. Examples of churches remaining include *S. Sergius*, *S. Cosmos* and *S. Damian*, all of the fourteenth century.

Vladimir

After the decline of Kiev, a new centre of power and influence was slowly established in the region of Moscow. Craftsmen had fled from Kiev and brought their architecture with them. Two such centres were *Vladimir* and *Suzdal*. The architectural style of the region was derived partly from Kiev but was also influenced by Novgorod and by Western Byzantine culture. Later in the twelfth century Vladimir became the capital and leading city of the area and continued so until it succumbed to the Tartars. Much of the finest building dates from the twelfth century. Churches were built of white sandstone, in contrast to brick at Kiev and wood at Novgorod, and followed a simple plan with one bulbous dome over the crossing supported on four piers and three round, high apses at the east end.

The *Cathedral of the Assumption* (Dormition) now called the Uspensky Cathedral, was built in 1158 but rebuilt after a fire in 1183. It was based upon the designs of S. Sophia in Kiev and is therefore, more elaborate in plan than is usual in

240

240 *Cathedral of the Assumption, Vladimir, U.S.S.R., twelfth century*

this region. It is a double-aisled church and has a central dome and four more over the angles. The central dome is supported on pendentives and the smaller ones on squinches (**240**). The interior was richly decorated with fresco paintings but much of this has been lost. The *Cathedral of S. Dimitri* was begun in 1194 and has a simpler plan with four piers supporting a single dome. It is a large, solidly built church and particularly finely decorated on the exterior by carved decoration on the upper walls and drums, also on the portals (one on each side) and corbel tables. It is a mixture of Romanesque and Byzantine designs, both in Russian style. The lower parts of the walls were restored in the eighteenth century and represent biblical scenes.

Outside the city, nearby, are some further examples. The *Church of SS. Boris* and *Gleb* was built in 1152 on the bank of the river Nerl near Suzdal in the village of *Kideksha*. Much of

the exterior, however, has beem damaged. At *Pereyaslavl-Zalesski* is the *Cathedral of the Transfiguration*, 1158, built in white stone, which is in better condition. It has a single dome (rebuilt in the sixteenth century) supported on four piers and a tri-apsidal east end. The roof rests directly on the church vaults. The *Church of the Protection and Intercession of the Virgin*, 1165 (the Church of Pokrov) is also near the river Nerl where it joins the river Klyazma. It is a well-preserved and particularly fine example and one of the four early churches extant. It has the single dome on four piers and three eastern apses. The walls are thick, pierced by splayed window and door openings. There is some of the earliest surviving Russian sculpture here; on the upper section of the three façades are carved relief figures and carved corbel blocks. These, together with the west doorway decoration, display a Romanesque quality.

MONASTERIES AND CATHEDRALS IN MOSCOW

241 *Cathedral of the Annunciation in the Kremlin, 1482–9, Pskov architects*

242 *View and* 243 *plan of the Smolenski Monastery Cathedral, c. 1525, bell-tower seventeenth cent Moscow*

244 *Cathedral of the Assumption (Dormition) in t Kremlin, 1475–9, Aristotele Fioravanti*

241

243

242

CHURCHES AND MONASTERIES IN AND NEAR MOSCOW

245 *Corner octagonal tower of the Church of the Decapitation of S. John the Baptist, Dyakovo, near Moscow, sixteenth century*

246 *Church of the Nativity of the Virgin in Putinki, Moscow, c. 1650*

247 *Monastery of the Virgin of the Don, near Moscow, 1593*

248 *Andronikhov Monastery. Church of the Saviour, Moscow, 1425*

245

246

247

248

Moscow

Until the fall of Constantinople in 1453 Russian Christian architecture had been directly inspired and assisted by artists and craftsmen from the Empire. In the late fifteenth century the new centre of power and culture in a unified Russia was being established in *Moscow*. The residence of the Metropolitan had been transferred here from Vladimir and Ivan III (the Great), 1462–1505, had the wooden buildings of the Kremlin largely rebuilt in more durable materials. After 150 years of Tartar domination Russia was recovering and, since the fall of Constantinople, architects and craftsmen came to Moscow to advise and build Ivan's now permanent city. In Western Europe this was the beginning of the Renaissance and the change from Medievalism to classicism; in Russia also there was a new era but not a Renaissance. It was an entirely new architectural age and one commonly called *Muscovite* since much of its force and inspiration came from the Princes of Moscow. The new *Moscow churches* still followed the Byzantine ground plan and inside were decorated with Byzantine style mosaic and fresco on walls with few interrupting mouldings, but outside Renaissance ornament made its appearance, introduced by the Italian craftsmen who brought their new style with them. Often, instead of a central dome, a tall steeple would be built; this was no Gothic spire, but a traditional Russian design in pyramidal form. Gradually, by weaving together all these different influences and ideas, a truly Russian architectural form was evolved which, by the sixteenth century, was entirely national and its chief example is the *Cathedral of S. Basil*.

The Cathedrals of the Kremlin

When Ivan III came to the throne the Kremlin hill was still covered with wooden buildings. The reconstruction he undertook was largely completed in his own reign. Much of this work was comprised in the cathedrals of the Kremlin. The first of these was the new *Cathedral of the Assumption* (Dormition), 1475–9, which was the primary church of Russia and the seat of the Metropolitan of Moscow (**244**). The cathedral was begun by Russian architects in 1471 but part of the building collapsed in the earthquake of 1472 so the work was handed over to an Italian architect and engineer, *Aristotele Fioravanti* from *Bologna*. His terms of reference were to design a building based on the Cathedral of the Dormition in Vladimir and which would be structurally sound. He carried out this commission and built a five-domed cathedral in cubical mass. It is, however, an unusual building in that, although it conforms to the Vladimir plan and Byzantine pattern, the architect introduced Italian fifteenth century building methods, using light bricks and tie rods in the arches and vaults. By his skill in design and execution he blended the Italian Renaissance with Russian Byzantine so that in decoration, particularly on the exterior, the roofing and lighting, the whole effect is more modern and classical than the Vladimir prototype. The Assumption in Moscow became the new prototype and was copied again and again all over Russia for many years as the orthodox pattern for such great churches.

The second *Cathedral* is that of the *Annunciation*, built 1482–90 by architects from Pskov (**241**). Here also the model was the Vladimir Cathedral but this design is much more in the tradition of Russian Byzantine architecture. It was built with five domes and three eastern apses and has entrances on three sides. In the sixteenth century further galleries and chapels were added.

In and near Moscow are a number of other monasteries and churches built between the fifteenth and seventeenth centuries, all of Byzantine character but displaying individually Russian features particularly in the domes and the stepped ogee, triangular and rounded shell formations (called *kokoshniki*)* which topped the main building and acted as a base for the tower or cupola drums. Such examples include the early *Church of the Saviour* (1425) in the *Andronikhov Monastery* in the city (**248**) and the *Monastery of the Virgin of the Don* (1593) which is on the outskirts (**247**). A most colourful version is a small but richly decorative church in the centre of Moscow, the *Church of the Nativity of the Virgin in Putinki* (c. 1650) which is now closed to the public. It is surrounded by modern blocks, but is nevertheless well preserved on the exterior (**246**).

On one of the hills but still in the city, is the *Smolenski Monastery*, built in 1524–5 as a memorial for the victory and return of the city of Smolensk to Russia (**242** and **243**). This is one

A kokoshnik is a traditional, feminine head-dress. The arches were thought to resemble this.

249

249 The Cathedral of S. Basil the Blessed, Red Square, Moscow, 1554–1679, Postnik and Barma

of the most ancient buildings in Moscow and a very early stone structure. The cathedral here bears considerable resemblance to the Assumption Cathedral in the Kremlin. Under it is constructed a sixteenth century mausoleum and behind (242) is the seventeenth century bell tower. The interior walls are entirely fresco covered. The five tall domes are supported on steeply sloping pendentives.

A few miles outside Moscow on a ridge of hills sloping steeply down to the river Moskva below is the *Church of the Decapitation of S. John the Baptist* at *Dyakovo* (245), which is only about a mile away across the trees and woods from the unusual *Church of the Ascension* at *Kolomenskoe* (Chapter 5, Fig. 560). S. John's Church is octagonal, with plain ribbed walls and four openings. One of these is the main doorway, one leads to the apsidal altar chamber and the others to side entrances. It is an immensely tall church, ascending to a diminishing lantern form with windows and with a tall steeple above. This main octagon is the central chamber or nave. At four corners are smaller octagons, replicas in design of the large one and all very tall. One of these is shown in Fig. 245. An ambulatory round the central octagon joins together the four chapels of the smaller ones.

A fitting finale to Russian architecture based on Byzantine form is the great *Cathedral Church of S. Basil the Blessed* (Vasili Blazheni) in the Red Square of *Moscow*. Begun by Ivan the Terrible in 1554, designed by two Russian architects *Postnik* and *Barma*, it was not completed until 1679. It is different from any Byzantine architecture in east or west but owes much of its fundamental character to the Byzantine style. It represents the logical conclusion to preceding buildings and is the expression of national culture; it stands for the essence of Muscovite Christianity in Russia and was the last great church of the movement in this architectural form. In plan it is simple and almost symmetrical but three-dimensionally it is complex: a bizarre, richly coloured building. The central part of the cathedral stands, like the Ascension Church at Kolomenskoe, on a high platform and has a tall octagonal tower. On the four main axes are set four large octagonal chapels, each with towers, while at the angles between these are four smaller polygonal chapels. These are all surmounted by bulbous domes, and in the seventeenth century the brilliant polychrome decorative colour was completed, giving the cathedral its characteristic Russian appearance (249).

4
Pre-Romanesque and Romanesque: Seventh Century to Thirteenth Century

With the gradual emergence of Europe from the disorders and chaos of the Dark Ages and the establishment of a Medieval society the story of architecture becomes more complex. In the preceding three chapters the styles of work and the surviving examples discussed came from different parts of Europe but, in each chapter, only one basic source of inspiration and culture was affecting building design and function. Thus, in studying the baths, bridges and temples of Ancient Rome, the differences between those in the Imperial city and remains from France, for instance, are noteworthy but not very great. Similarly, in buildings from Ancient Greece and those of Byzantine origin, the fundamental characteristics remain the same even though Sicilian Byzantine churches differ in several respects from Greek or Serbian Byzantine ones.

With Romanesque architecture and with its preceding movements in Saxon England, Visigothic Spain and Carolingian Germany, the situation is quite different. The collapse first of the Roman Empire in the fifth century and consequent withdrawal of protection and influence from the states of the Empire—England, France, Germany, Spain—and, later, the phased withdrawals of the Eastern half of the Roman Empire eastwards to Byzantium, left behind chaos, disruption and the total collapse of Roman civilised life in the countries of western Europe. The Dark Ages, once thought to be of extensive duration lasting until Norman influence established itself or even beyond, are now becoming less 'dark'. Through archaeological and other studies, buildings and other remains are yielding up information of centuries which were not, as thought by our grandfathers, representative solely of barbarianism and the negation of culture. The fifth, sixth and early seventh centuries are still scantily represented in remains and knowledge, but from then onwards more and more is being learnt. From about 1000 A.D. the true

Romanesque style of architecture shows itself and, since it emerged in many different countries of Europe which were not in all these years under the influence and direction of one empire, as previously, it developed in different ways. Thus, German Romanesque has various characteristics which define and distinguish it from French or Italian, for example. Climate was a decisive factor in establishing these differences as was the availability of building materials, the degree of culture of the peoples, their beliefs and needs. For the student, therefore, the story becomes a more complicated one. Not only does he need to understand features basic to the Romanesque style—a pre-requisite—but he will want to trace the backgrounds leading to the differing crystallisation of one country's Romanesque from that of another.

The process of development of architectural style, however, is a continuous one. It will be noticed that the dates of buildings covered in Chapter Three overlap with those in Chapter Four. Byzantine architecture indeed continued to expand and change in lands in Eastern Europe during the same centuries that Medieval architecture was spreading across western countries. There is no definite dividing line, either geographical or chronological, between Byzantine and Romanesque, pre-Romanesque and Romanesque or Romanesque and Gothic. These styles and modes of building merged and developed one into another at different dates in different countries. Thus, for instance, Italy began building in a Romanesque style earlier than most nations—for its emergence from Roman work was a natural corollary—continued it later, produced little Gothic work and then burst forth into the Renaissance a century and more before the rest of Europe. England, on the other hand, had a comparatively short Romanesque period of development following an extensive Saxon one but a very long and a unique building period in Gothic architecture emerging into a tardy Renaissance, nearly the last in Europe except for that of the Iberian peninsula. Germany's Romanesque work is extensive, of long duration and outstanding quality but her Gothic work is more restricted. France, in contrast, had some fine Romanesque architecture, especially of Norman character, but established Gothic construction very early, producing probably the finest quality of building in this style to be found anywhere in the world. The story, therefore, from the seventh century onwards becomes an increasingly complex one as more countries sought out individual ways of satisfying their own needs, techniques, modes of living and religious beliefs. To endeavour to simplify this complexity in each chapter from now onwards, a general description of the fundamentals and similarities of the style is given first and the contributions of each country are then dealt with individually. In each chapter, from 4–9 inclusive, a larger proportion both of text and drawings has been allocated to the countries whose contribution to that style has been most notable, for instance, France in Gothic architecture, Italy in Renaissance designs.

Pre-Romanesque c. 650–1050

Only some European countries possess remains of buildings, decoration, sculpture, pottery, burial and so on which enable us to trace the evolution of architecture during these centuries. This does not mean, of course, that the others did not have such buildings. They may have been of impermanent materials, such as wood, or the countries may have suffered greater devastation than their neighbours. Study and research into pre-Romanesque architecture is still comparatively recent and more is being found out each decade. At one time it was thought that the only inspiration for pre-Romanesque Europe was Ancient Rome and Byzantium. For Italy, Southern France and Dalmatia this is largely true. But in countries further west a stronger inspiration comes from indigenous sources. Examples of this tendency are the timber constructions of Scandinavia, Britain and Germany with their timber roofing (later leading to Romanesque stone vaults), the stone churches of Moravia and Croatia, and also the Visigothic churches of Spain displaying horseshoe arch forms long

before the arrival of the Saracens. Influences are very mixed and, though travel was not easy, ideas spread with remarkable speed. Specific features such as the horseshoe arch, vault designs, interlacing in ornamental carving and the circular church design appear in widely separated places —Scandinavia, Britain, north Germany, Yugoslavia, Bohemia, for example—and are not Roman features so they would, one presumes, have percolated through from northern Europe rather than southern. Equally, in central Italy, as opposed to Lombard Italy which shows similar influences to northern Europe, and in southern France the Ancient Roman pattern reigned supreme. Pre-Romanesque Europe produced buildings of considerable interest and capability and created methods of construction certainly not all due either to Roman, Byzantine or later Romanesque knowledge as our forefathers believed. This study has yet far to go and it would be unwise to be too dogmatic about sources and influences at this stage.

By the sixth and early seventh century civilisation in Europe had declined to its lowest point. Urban communities gave place to rural ones and the Roman influence became attenuated though the language at least did not perish. Christianity and the emerging monastic orders began to be a civilising, educating influence and, even after the twelfth century, culture and learning were the monopoly of these orders and centres. At the same time, different peoples, sometimes referred to as barbarians, began to establish themselves in different parts of Europe and evolve their own culture, sometimes Christian, sometimes not, but the former was not necessarily more civilised than the latter. The Goths, who came from Gotland in the late third century divided and merged with other peoples. They established themselves as Visigoths in Spain, Ostrogoths in Italy and, in further movements of peoples, the Merovingians became paramount in modern France and the Vandals in north Africa. In so far as this affects the contemporary architecture, the Ostrogothic work in Italy has already been discussed (see Chapter 3, Ravenna) but the Visigothic work in northern Spain was influential as was the effect of the Merovingian culture in northern France leading to the Carolingian dynasty in northern Europe under Charlemagne.

250 *Brixworth Church, England, seventh and tenth centuries, Saxon*

251 *Earl's Barton Church tower, England, early eleventh century, Saxon*

252 *Church of S. Donato, Zadar, Yugoslavia, early ninth century, Croatian*

253 *Interior, Church of S. Michael, Fulda, Germany, c. 820*

254 *Plan, S. Michael, Fulda*

255 *Plan, Palatine Chapel, Aachen Cathedral, Germany, begun 792*

Carolingian

In A.D. 800 Charlemagne (771–814) was crowned Holy Roman Emperor. Under his leadership northern Europe became more settled and a period of building activity was begun, though it was not of long duration. In style it owed much to Ancient Rome but was not only a copy of it; it showed Byzantine influence and also new ideas, adapting itself to its own period. Charlemagne himself was an energetic, cultured patron. Stone and brick buildings were initiated of which considerable portions exist. The *Monastery of Lorsch, Germany*, was begun in 774 (the three-arched gatehouse, 810, is extant); *S. Michael's Church* at *Fulda, Germany*, a monastic burial chapel, dates from *c.* 820 and is typical of its time, being a circular construction with ambulatory and based upon the Holy Sepulchre Church in Jerusalem. A strong Byzantine influence is visible here in the drilled hole capitals (**253** and **254**). Charlemagne's most famous building enterprise was the *Palatine Chapel* (part of the Cathedral) at *Aachen*, the seat of his court and site of his palace in *Germany*. Owing much in design to S. Vitale in Ravenna but on more elaborate lines, it was originally symmetrical and had a western entrance with atrium and two-storeyed gallery; the court-yard here was large and had a capacity of 7000. Apart from this it is not greatly altered, with its 16-sided exterior (105 feet in diameter) and octagonal interior. It is decorated in Italian mosaic and marbles and above has an octagonal, domical vault which, like much of the interior, is reminiscent of Rome at its most imperial. The cathedral has been enlarged in later times around this chapel which is now a central feature in the architectural mass (**255**).

Also a Palatine group was the lay-out at *Germigny-des-Près* in *France*, near Orléans, where in 806 a palace and church was built. The palace has almost disappeared and the church has been poorly restored and does not give a good impression of the original. Other examples of French work of the ninth century showing particularly early examples of the French contribution in apse development towards later chevet designs are *S. Germain* at *Auxerre* (crypt, 859) and *S. Philibert-de-Gardlieu*, 847.

256 *The Island of Reichenau, in Lake Constance, Germany. S. George, Oberzell. Interior towards western apse, ninth century and c. 1000*

257 *The Minister, Mittelzell, ninth century to 1048 (later belfry)*

Reichenau, Lake Constance, Germany
Of slightly later date are the three basilican churches on this island, part of the monastic centre here first established in 724. The *Minster at Mittelzell* is the chief church, built first just after 800 but added to and altered a number of times since (**257**). The *Church of S. George at Oberzell* and that of *SS. Peter and Paul at Niederzell* have more remaining from the early work. At S. George, which was a small abbey founded in 840, most of the present church dates from the ninth to tenth century with the ninth century crypt as the earliest part. The western apse is of about the year 1000 and the narthex is later. The church, like the others on the island, is a three-aisled basilica with its western apse extending the full height of the church. The choir is still raised over the vaulted crypt which contains primitive, baseless columns (**399**). Inside, the roof is of the nineteenth century but the fresco painting on the walls is one of the oldest decorative schemes in Germany, dating from *c.* 1000. The nave arcade is also very old, with green sandstone columns and Tuscan bases (**256**). At *Niederzell* the *Church of SS. Peter and Paul* was begun in 799. It is also basilican and parts remain of the earlier work. The nave arcade, with its capitals and columns, is the most interesting and dates from the eleventh century (**401**).

Italy
Here the pre-Romanesque examples are not numerous and much of the work is Lombardic, in the north. The basilican *Church of S. Vincenzo in Prato* in *Milan* dates from *c.* 833. This is more an early Romanesque church than a pre-Romanesque example, has three parallel apses and is vaulted with brick wall supports. Outside are pilaster strips and there are also arched corbel tables. Further south is the interesting *Church of S. Pietro* at *Tuscánia*, deriving from Roman and Lombard sources. Here is a very early crypt dating from the seventh century and a five aisled nave with varied finely carved capitals (**420**).

Scandinavia, Croatia, Moravia
Occurring in many, widely separated places is the circular planned, stone church, like that already mentioned at Fulda. Other examples include several on the *Island of Bornholm* in

Scandinavia (see p. 189) and the outstanding one at Zadar. These churches have a circular exterior and interior plan with an interior row of columns supporting a dome; some versions have eastern semi-circular apses. *S. Donato* at *Zadar* in *Yugoslavia* is an early church of this type from *c.* 812–876. Its inner row of granite columns supports a circular inner wall which is pierced by eight narrow high arches. There are three apses at the east end (**252**) and these contain niche recesses. The nave is barrel vaulted and on its north side a staircase leads to the upper storey which has a round gallery. The high, conical cupola above the centre is lit by small windows in the drum. This is a particularly complete example, though the decoration has not survived. Square planned churches also exist in these areas, though both designs are in a more fragmentary state in the western Slavonic districts. All examples show similar characteristics; they are generally stone vaulted—an unusual feature in so early a period and rare in southern Europe—the majority have cupolas supported on squinches and/or intersecting barrel vaults; the stonework is solid but crude; ornament generally includes interlacing in bands of carving on stone borders and the patterns are made up from circles, diamonds or zig-zags—the interlacing is like a prototype of the later Romanesque basket work patterns. Animals and birds are sometimes included in the interlacing.

England
Much of the Saxon work was in timber and was destroyed in Viking raids. A number of stone churches survive in whole or in part and these date from two different periods of building: the seventh to eighth century and the tenth to eleventh. These buildings show characteristics different from later Romanesque work. Generally they have thinner walls and are unbuttressed, having pilaster strips and long-and-short work quoins. The windows and doorways are distinctive with their round and triangular heads and baluster shaft openings to the former. Most churches are of basilican plan with semi-circular eastern apse (though the altar might still be at the west end) and a western or central tower standing on the ground. Roofs were usually of timber. Among the surviving examples are *Brixworth Church* (where Roman bricks have been re-used

but without radiating voussoir construction) (**250** and **392**), *Earl's Barton*, tower (**251**), *Sompting Church*, eleventh century tower, *S. Lawrence, Bradford-on-Avon*, tenth century, *Worth Church*, tenth century (**386**), also those at *Greensted, Barton-on-Humber, Escomb, Boarhunt* (**426**) and *Bradwell*.

Spain

It is ironic that the most interesting group of pre-Romanesque churches in Europe should be in a country largely taken over by the Moslems. In the eighth century the Moors moved rapidly over Spain from their base in North Africa and occupied the whole country except for a small area in the north-west, between the Cantabrian Mountains and the sea. The religious freedom of Christians in Spain, however, was not suppressed and they were permitted to retain their churches and worship in them. Moslem Spain was the most cultured society in Western Europe at the time. The peoples who survived in the north-west area gained greatly from the mixture of arts and race but retained their individuality also until the tide turned once more and the north-western island increased its influence eventually over the whole of Spain.

Visigothic architecture had established itself before the Moslem invasion and was flourishing from *c.* 450—720. A few examples are extant from this early period but most of these have been greatly altered. These include the *episcopal palace* at *Mérida* and the *baptistery* of the *Church of S. Miguel* at *Tarrasa*. The most interesting feature of Visigothic architecture is the use of the horseshoe arch, employed both construction-ally and decoratively. This early use shows that its introduction is owed here not to the Moslems, who arrived much later, but probably to Syria and Persia. (The Romans had used it also but only in decorative form.) Visigothic decoration is primarily Roman in character but in simplified form; cable borders, rosettes, circles, stars and types of Corinthian capitals were in general use. The finest Visigothic church extant is *S. Juan Bautista* at *Baños de Cerrato*, near Palencia, built in 661. (The date is inscribed over the sanctuary arch.) It is a three-aisled basilica of stone with a four-bay nave which has clerestory windows above the nave arcade and a timber roof. The sanctuary is covered by a horseshoe tunnel vault.

The columns and capitals are a mixture of genuine Visigothic versions of Corinthian capitals and of original antique capitals and columns taken from Roman building in the area (**258** and **393**). A later example is the remotely situated *S. Comba* at *Bande* of the eighth century, which is a granite church on Greek cross plan with a square chancel. It also has a horseshoe arch entrance to the sanctuary, but its decoration is poorer than that at S. Juan.

After the Moslem occupation was complete the small area left to Christian Spain consisted of the north-west mountain district in Galicia and Asturias. An interesting architectural style evolved here, generally called *Asturian*, which came from Visigothic designs but also embodied Carolingian features of construction. This small area was centred around Oviedo on the northern coast. Two particularly fine examples, very close together, are *S. Maria Naranco* (842—50) and *S. Miguel de Liño* (848). S. Maria was originally a church built adjacent to a palace and was part of it, which probably accounts for its extensive and unusual character. It consists of two rectangular halls one above the other, giving a lower and upper church. The lower one is barrel vaulted; the upper hall is approached via steps and lofty porches (the south one is now destroyed) and these porches gave a cruciform plan to the building. Inside, the upper part consists of a hall 35 by 14 feet, with a rectangular tribune at each end divided from the hall by double arcades—good examples of stilted arches and mixed piers and columns. The capitals are carved diversely with human figures, animals and dragons. Outside, buttresses decorate and support the double vaulted storeys and these extend the whole height of the building (**259**). *S. Miguel*, nearby, is also a fine example both in construction and decoration, but only the western end exists, consisting of a two-storeyed narthex and part of the nave. The decoration of windows, doorways, panels and nave capitals is exceptionally good (**260** and **381**). Both these churches illustrate the Asturian characteristics of the round-headed rather than the horseshoe arch construction (the Carolingian influence is evident), and Roman type decoration and capitals, though the Visigothic cable pattern is also used. Other nearby examples include *S. Julian de los Prados* (c. 830 (near Santullano), *S. Salvador de Priesca* (921

258 S. Juan Bautista, Baños de Cerrato, near Palencia.
Interior towards chancel. Visigothic, 661

259 S. Maria de Naranco, near Oviedo, Asturian,
842–850

260 S. Miguel de Liño, near Oviedo, Asturian, 842–850

261 S. Miguel de la Escalada, near Léon, Mozarabic,
also Roman and Visigothic, 913

(**400**), and *S. Salvador de Fuentes* (1023), both near Villaviciosa.

Towards A.D. 900 refugees coming north from Moslem-occupied Spain settled near *León* and established in that area an architectural style part Christian and part Arabic, called *Mozarabic*. The buildings were based upon late Roman designs but also displayed Oriental features especially in decoration and their use of brickwork in constructional and ornamental forms. A very good example here is the Church of *S. Miguel de la Escalada*, built as part of a monastery in 912–13. This basilica, overlooking the river Esla, is 70 feet long and has a five bay nave separated from the aisles by marble columns with mixed capitals —Roman, Visigothic and tenth century Mozarabic (these last-named are palm leaf designs as in the Cordovan Mosque). The nave has a wooden roof. It terminates in a magnificent chancel arcade of horseshoe arches. Outside, the beautiful 12-bay portico was added *c.* 930–40 (**261, 380** and **403**).

Romanesque *c.* 1050–1250

Although the regional and racial interpretations of the true, mature Romanesque style were varied, there are a number of basic features common to all Romanesque buildings. Those which have survived have, not unnaturally, been altered and added to in a greater or lesser degree and entirely Romanesque examples are not numerous. Nevertheless, in Europe as a whole, there is a great quantity of Romanesque work and much of it in buildings where a considerable portion is in the original style, though perhaps restored. The greater part of building in this period was, of course, wholly or partly in timber and little of this exists. Our knowledge is derived from work constructed in more permanent materials—stone, marble, mosaic, brick—and such buildings were naturally the more important ones and not necessarily typical of the whole. The overriding influence in the Middle Ages was a religious one and, in Europe, the religion was Christianity. The Church, both as an organisation and in its buildings, was of supreme importance to all European communities, not only for the spiritual but physical and intellectual succour which it provided. In return for this support in times of need, it demanded contributions from everyone, in labour and in wealth, although the latter was often payment in kind. The Church gave to every community, large or small, refuge from persecution and pillage, provided education and learning, medical aid and a basis for life by which were allayed the superstitious fears of the individual, which stemmed from his lack of experience and knowledge of health, life and death, understanding of the world and of man himself.

Appreciation of the vital place which the Church had in Medieval life is necessary to an understanding of the buildings which we have inherited from this time. In the eleventh and twelfth centuries to build in stone, granite or marble was a prodigious undertaking, particularly if the area concerned did not possess the materials close to hand. Early Medieval peoples were not as the Empires which had preceded them had been, living in slave states (though one people might be in subjugation to another). The vast constructions built up on slave labour by the Ancient Egyptians or Romans were therefore not possible in Romanesque Europe. Yet, with only a slowly emerging technical understanding of how to build on the large scale in durable materials and with immense difficulties of transport, lack of communications and inadequacy of power, vast buildings were erected and these cathedrals and churches of Romanesque Europe still stand as testimony to the determination of man when his spirit is sufficiently aroused.

From this period of time the great majority of extant work is ecclesiastical. These churches were built in honour of God and to provide shelter and succour in times of need. Everyone contributed to their building. The churches also carried out the function of education in spiritual guidance to a population largely illiterate. Though the extensive story telling of the Bible and Gospels was developed especially in Gothic architecture, in the great portals and walls, Romanesque work too tells this story. It is, however, not only a story of what happened in the Old and New Testament but also provides guidance on how to live, tells of the life to come and gives protection against spirits and devils. Romanesque capitals, in particular, abound with terrifying monsters devouring hapless victims—animal and human— and the different animals: lions, dragons, oxen etc., all have their appointed place and meaning in this mythology and language.

Plate 23
Porta di S. Alipio, façade, S. Mark's Cathedral, Venice, Italy. 13th century mosaic

Plate 24
Mosaic detail showing part of the procession of Saints. Temp. Justinian. Nave arcade, Church of S. Apollinare Nuovo, Ravenna, Italy

Plate 25
The prophet Isaiah. Church of S. Mary,
Souillac, France, c. 1130

Plate 26
Apostles. Portico de la Gloria, Cathedral of
Santiago de Compostela, Spain. 1166–88, Mateo

The differences in Romanesque style of various nations will be dealt with individually; the main reasons for the differences are climate and availability of materials. In general, in the north, roofs slope more steeply to throw off rain and snow, windows and doorways are larger to let in available light and walls thick to keep out the cold. In Mediterranean areas the openings are small to exclude the sun and roofs are flatter as a steep pitch is superfluous. Stone buildings abound in much of France, especially Normandy, also in England, the German Rhineland and southern Italy; in Sicily and central France volcanic materials are much in evidence; along the whole Baltic coastal plain, brick is the predominant material as building knowledge developed, and elsewhere timber was in prime use. The traditional building in these materials led to variations in style and construction. All areas have a few stone buildings which were of vital importance but, in a district like northern England or Normandy, where stone is easily accessible and in abundance, understanding of construction in masonry developed much earlier.

The dominant power behind the movement in church building lay with the *monastic orders* who developed their own individual style (on Romanesque patterns) to suit the needs of the order. These styles transcended frontiers and thus one Benedictine church is much like another whether in France, England or Italy. The *Abbey Church* evolved from the early Christian basilica and early examples still had the altar at the west end. Churches in southern Europe continued to be influenced by Roman methods of construction in style and even used parts of Roman buildings— capitals, columns, decoration, etc.—but further north a newer style was produced which was monumental, austere and strong. The plan was generally based on the Latin cross and roofing was of timber. The fire hazards of such roofs led to the rediscovery of how to vault in stone. Barrel vaults were developed first and remained satisfactory in the south where their immense thrust on the walls could be borne by the use of small windows to avoid weakening the structure. In the north, however, where larger windows were essential, the intersecting and later the groined and ribbed vaults were evolved at a comparatively early date and walls were thickened to solve this problem. Domical vaults developed in parts of

southern France and in Italy and the crossing was covered by a dome or tower. Bell towers were important features of most churches, serving as places of refuge, means of raising the alarm and giving notice of events.

Knowledge of architectural features of style was dispersed partly by the monastic orders and partly by the great pilgrimages. The cult of relics was important and great churches were built to house such relics. Pilgrims then came on foot and horseback for hundreds of miles across many countries to pay homage to these relics and churches were erected along the routes to such pilgrimage centres. The most famous instance is the great Church of *S. James* at *Santiago de Compostela* in north-west Spain, said to contain the remains of the apostle. Pilgrims to Santiago came from France, Germany, England, Italy and even further afield, from the tenth century onwards, along established pilgrimage routes across the Pyrenees. As a result there are pilgrimage churches right across northern Spain and on the main routes traversing France, Germany and Italy. Such *pilgrimage churches* tended to follow similar architectural patterns due to their similar needs. They are generally large to accommodate the pilgrims and resemble the church which was the pilgrimage goal. The richness of such churches, their decoration and sculpture, particularly the portals, is tribute to their important position on the routes. Famous *French* examples include such churches as *S. Trophîme* at *Arles* (**389**) or *S. Front* at *Périgueux* (**219**). The typical pilgrimage church has a long, aisled and galleried nave, wide transepts and a large sanctuary. Commonly the whole church is barrel vaulted at one height throughout and these vaults have transverse arches carried on piers. The aisles and galleries continue round the whole building. The crossing is covered by a dome or lantern. The use of the choir (if the church is monastic) is retained for the clergy while the pilgrims occupy the nave and transepts. The exterior is large, forceful in design and has an impressive façade with tall towers. The *Church* at *Santiago* itself, the pattern for the rest, is shown in Fig. **319** and *S. Madeleine* at *Vézelay* in **267**.

Apart from pilgrimage churches, most examples follow certain general lines. The nave is lofty and divided into nave arcade, triforium and clerestory. The middle stage is often arcaded but not often lit (its alternative name is the blind storey which is more descriptive). On each side of the nave is a single aisle (though this may be double in larger churches) and the divisions are made by arcades of piers or columns. The aisle is roofed at a lower level than the nave and the triforia have the function of masking the lean-to roofs which cover these vaults. In Mediterranean countries, particularly southern Italy, the triforium is omitted and replaced by solid wall decorated in mosaic or fresco painting. From the eleventh century onward the eastern arm was developed and extended, partly to provide more space for chapels and relics and partly to seclude the clergy from the laity. Such arms were generally apsidal in one or three apses and these designs led to the later development of the chevet, particularly seen in France; also, in order to retain their privacy, the monks re-established the nave altars east of the crossing, so confirming the eastern altar position. An ambulatory generally circumnavigates the whole of the east end of such churches, providing communication throughout the building with access to the nave aisles.

France

Alone of the countries of Europe during this time England presented a more or less single, unified group. Elsewhere, the modern names and regions are difficult to reconcile with the Romanesque ones. The area that is modern France displayed within its boundaries a great variation on the Romanesque architectural theme, since it was not one nation but a number of states whose buildings were influenced by climate, materials and purpose. Even with drastic simplification it is necessary to sub-divide the country.

Northern France

Taking the river Loire as a boundary the lands north of this reflected the *Norman* influence—that same influence which produced England's Norman architecture also that of Sicily and southern Italy. Here, in modern Normandy and Brittany, Roman remains were scanty and a new Romanesque style evolved. Stone, particularly of the Caen neighbourhood, enabled the techniques of masonry to be understood early. Churches are tall, monumental and austere. Norman architecture, owing something to Lom-

bardic influences, was the earliest to develop the true Romanesque—as opposed to Roman—style. The Northmen (Norsemen) settled here and by the early tenth century were converted to Christianity and began to build churches. Little of the early work—such as the original Abbey of Jumièges—survives, but in *Caen* itself exist among other work, the two famous churches of William I of Normandy (William the Conqueror of England). These are the *Church of S. Etienne* (L'Abbaye-aux-Hommes) and the *Church of La Trinité* (L'Abbaye-aux-Dames). *S. Etienne*, built originally 1066–77, has a magnificent exterior illustrating the best of Northern Romanesque grouping in masses and towers. The west front is vertical in emphasis with two tall towers capped by Gothic spires and with a plain façade decorated only by round-headed windows and doorways (**265** and **398**). The east end was altered in mid twelfth century by an early chevet design with turrets and flying buttresses which blends admirably with the earlier work (**264**). Inside, the long nave is vaulted in sexpartite fashion in the typically French vaulting manner, comprising one nave bay to two aisle bays, retaining the square compartment and with an intermediate transverse rib introduced to the springing from the aisle vaulting shaft, thus giving extra support to the vault. The church is lofty, with three stages and, over the crossing, has a lantern with its octopartite rib vault. *La Trinité*, founded in 1062 by William's Queen, Matilda, of Bayeux Tapestry fame, has retained its original pattern better. It is a massive, very Romanesque building with a monumental façade of twin western towers in arcaded stages and, between, a gabled centrepiece with deeply recessed round-headed doorway below; there is a square tower over the crossing with stumpy spire. The interior is finely preserved (**263**) and has a long nave, with barrel-vaulted aisles, broad transepts and a fine apse with groined vault. In the nave, the upper part above the ground arcade is a little later and has decorative triforium and arcaded clerestory. The sexpartite styled vault is of twelfth century construction. Fig. **262** shows the existing Romanesque parts of the nave of the *Abbey Church of Mont S. Michel*, not far away. The eastern part of this church is Gothic but this portion illustrates clearly the typical Romanesque wall pattern divided into its three parts of nave arcade, tri-

262

263

264

265

Abbey Church of Mont S. Michel, nave, 1022–1135
Abbaye-aux-Dames (La Trinité), Caen, looking
1063–1125
Abbaye-aux-Hommes (S. Étienne), Caen, from the
1066–1166
Abbaye-aux-Hommes, west front

forium and clerestory with wooden roof above. The piers, arches, aisles and proportions present here a good guide to the classic pattern of such interiors.

Burgundy

In Romanesque times this was a very large, flourishing province with a strong monastic influence in its ruling house. The Burgundians were great church builders, in varied style, but chiefly based on the design of the great *Abbey of Cluny*. The third building on the site here was begun in 1089 but has been demolished. Churches on this pattern have barrel vaults and particularly fine nave porches with narthex in front. Two particular examples are Autun Cathedral and the Abbey Church of S. Madeleine at Vézelay. The *Cathedral* at *Autun* was begun in 1120 and considerable parts of the Romanesque building remain. The two finest parts of these are the narthex and the nave interior. The west façade, flanked by two towers, is approached up a flight of steep steps into a magnificent, open narthex (1178) where is situated the west portal. This portal is famed for its rich, vivid sculpture by *Gislebertus*. The tympanum is exceptionally large and, with the lintel below, depicts the Last Judgement. In the centrepiece is Christ, seated on a throne, and the remainder illustrates with extraordinary clarity and detail the Romanesque conception of heaven and hell, with the celestial delights for the fortunate and the demons clawing upwards to capture the souls of the damned. Inside, the cathedral is barrel vaulted with transverse arches and the east end is triapsidal. The nave, still a fine example of Burgundian Romanesque, shows the influence of Ancient Rome on its classically fluted pilasters and piers (**266**). Many of the famous capitals, decorated by animals, biblical scenes, demons, etc., have been removed for safety from the vibration of the bells to an upstairs museum where they can be studied at leisure and at a more accessible height. Copies have replaced them in the cathedral nave.

Like Autun, the *Abbey Church* of *S. Madeleine* at *Vézelay*, has a magnificent narthex and western porch. The exterior portal has been restored with modern sculptural decoration but inside the narthex the original work of 1128–32 survives; this has three bays and is a very early, typically Burgundian example. This church is

situated on the summit of a hill; its façade ha only one western tower complete and, between is a gable containing a fine, five light, sculptured window with portal below. Inside is a palely polychrome effect with the striped semi-circular transverse arches separating the quadripartit vaulting bays. The church is high and light s that the vista from narthex to eastern apse is clea and uninterrupted. The capitals display amazing vividness and variety in subject and handling neo-Corinthian, animal, bird and human sub jects (**267, 411** and **412**).

Central France

In this broad extent a number of influences ar apparent from the domed churches of Périgor with their Byzantine inspiration to the richly coloured buildings in volcanic materials in th Auvergne. In the northern part of the region th *Abbey of Fleury*, now *S. Benoît-sur-Loire*, pre sents a fine, mature example. This large monaster was begun about 1070 and, though the abbe buildings have gone, the church remains. I

266 Interior, Autun Cathedral, France, 1120–1140

266

267

268

269

57 *Abbey Church of S. Madeleine, Vézelay, Burgundy, nave, c. 1104*
58 *Basilica of S. Benoît-sur-Loire, choir, 1070–1130*
59 *Pilgrimage Church of S. Sernin, Toulouse, from the north-west, 1080–1150. Tower and spire 1250–1435*

possesses a most interesting tower porch (*clocher-porche*) originally three-storeyed but now only two as the bell chamber has disappeared. The upper storey is now a disused chapel but below is an unusual and magnificent entrance porch. It has four rows of four columns and piers, each with different capitals, representing biblical scenes with human figures, monsters, demons and a type of Corinthian design. The original purpose of this large porch was to shelter pilgrims. The church itself, now partly restored, is cruciform with a quadripartite nave vault (Gothic) and barrel vaulted choir. There is no triforium to the nave but in the eastern arm is a stubby triforium arcade and a fine apse with ambulatory and radiating chapels. The clerestory continues all round the church. The central dome is raised on squinches above the wide pointed crossing arches (**268**). The *Cathedral* at *Angers* is a good example of the massive, domical building of Anjou, though parts of it were rebuilt in Gothic times. It retains, however, its Roman simplicity, particularly in the interior which is large scale and spacious. The cathedral was begun in the eleventh century and completed in the thirteenth. It is aisleless, cruciform and the nave is of the twelfth century with three large domical vaulted square bays in ashlar construction and is very wide, having a vault spanning 54 feet and which is 80 feet high—a remarkable achievement for so early an example. The transept and crossing have Angevin rib vaults in octopartite divisions.

Further west in the area from the Loire down to Périgueux are a number of well-known churches and cathedrals of the domed and domical vault type. Still on the Loire is the impressive *Abbey of Fontevrault*, founded in 1098 and originally covering a tremendous area with four convents and supporting buildings of which a number remain. The abbey church is a magnificent example of these domed churches; it is 275 feet long. Like most other examples of this type it has no aisles but a short, wide nave, covered by four domes. These are replacements but are still carried on the original pendentives. At the crossing is a domed covering under the tower, supported on high piers. The transepts have barrel vaults and the east end a semi-circular vault. Round the eastern end is an ambulatory with radiating chapels. Though further north than the other churches of this type, it is a perfect

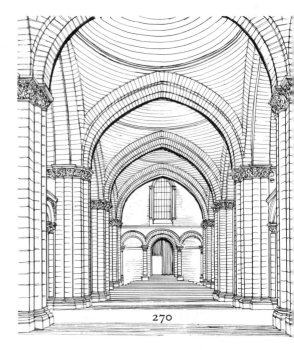

270 *Interior of nave, Abbey Church of Fontevrault, France, 1104–1150*

example of the style (**270**). Probably of greate[r] renown than the church is the great *kitchen* her[e] with its eight oven shelters each containing [a] central fireplace and with a great vault in th[e] middle. On the exterior (**276**) is the high pyrami[d] surrounded by smaller ones all covered with th[e] scaled roofing tiles so typical of the region. I[n] *Poitiers* are two churches in particular: *S. Hilair[e]* begun 1025 and rebuilt 1165 and the mor[e] famous *Notre Dame La Grande* (**271**) whic[h] dates from 1130. This is the richest of the in[-] digenous churches of the district where limeston[e] is plentiful and masonry developed early. Th[e] façade is decorated all over with carving an[d] sculpture; the recessed doorway is enclosed i[n] four orders of short columns and the arche[s] have carved, decorative voussoirs. On either sid[e] are arcades capped by a sculptured corbel tabl[e] and above is a further arcading and a centra[l] window. The other regional feature of th[e] exterior displayed here is the fish-tail roofing o[f] turrets and lantern, which has an oriental appear[-] ance and is like that at Fontevrault kitchen (**276**) and Angoulême Cathedral (**273** and **376**), als[o] the Spanish Cathedral of Zamora (**316**). Poitier[s] was on one of the pilgrimage routes to Santiag[o] and the interior of Notre Dame shows this in it[s]

ROMANESQUE IN FRANCE: THE BYZANTINE INFLUENCE

271 *Church of Notre Dame La Grande, Poitiers, from the south-west, eleventh and twelfth centuries*
272 *Abbey Church of Solignac, near Limoges, c. 1145*
273 *Angoulême Cathedral from the east, 1100–1128 (restored nineteenth century)*

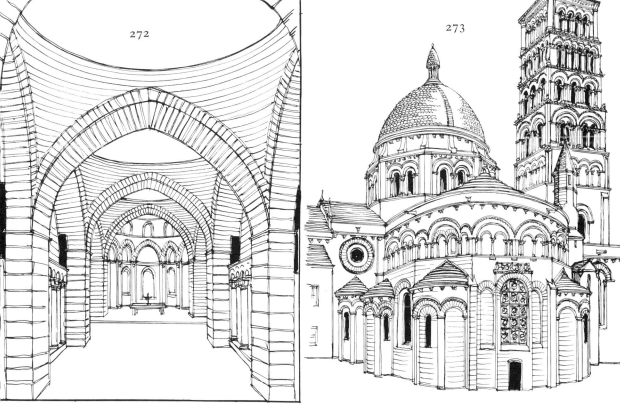

layout and barrel vaulted roofs. There is neither triforium nor clerestory; the crossing dome is conical and unusual.

Further south are some of the outstanding examples of the Byzantine influenced Romanesque churches of France. *S. Front* at *Périgueux* has already been described (Chapter 3, p.107), but at Angoulême and Solignac is further work. The *Abbey Church of Solignac* is a large building in a small village; it was also on one of the pilgrimage routes. Built on Latin cross plan, it has a polygonal eastern apse with three smaller apses and there are two more on the transepts. The interior, built of large blocks of reddish stone, is wide and spacious, its nave covered by two plastered domes and others over the crossing and one transept (while a barrel vault covers the other). The domes are carried on pendentives and below are rectangular piers without capitals. The wide pointed arches have no mouldings. There are no aisles or triforium (**272**). The *Abbey Church of Souillac*, now chiefly famous for its magnificent Romanesque sculpture, is nearer to Périgueux. The best of these are now set on the interior of the west wall (PLATE 25). The *Priory of Moissac* (further south still) is likewise best known for its beautiful sculpture in figures and carved decoration, chiefly on the portal. The *Cathedral at Cahors* is also a domed, Byzantine type structure with its domes supported on pendentives, but the building in general is now a mixture of styles with a largely Gothic façade. The north doorway has a remarkable tympanum deeply set in the porch like that at Autun.

The two most outstanding examples of this Byzantine-Romanesque style are *S. Front* at *Périgueux* and *Angoulême Cathedral*. The former is based on Greek cross plan and has been included in Chapter 3 but *Angoulême*, despite its layout and domes, is fundamentally Romanesque. The domes, like the others of this area already mentioned, are pointed in form and are supported on pendentives. The construction and the pointed shape are Byzantine, but the Aquitaine versions possess a type of curved silhouette indigenous to the region. The cathedral is on Latin cross plan with projecting transepts; these are square ended with towers over them (though the upper part of one of these was destroyed in the sixteenth century). The east end is apsidal with four smaller apses grouped round the centre one (**273**). The church is domed over the nave and crossing (though only the latter dome can be seen from the exterior as the others are covered by timber roofing) and the chancel and transepts have barrel vaults. The façade is beautifully decorated all over with Romanesque carving, representing the Ascension and Second Coming in arcading and sculpture, and the remaining tower is similarly decorated (**376** and **422**). Inside, the nave has no aisles; it is covered by three stone domes and the crossing dome is raised on a drum which has 16 windows. The cathedral, which stands in a commanding position on a hill overlooking the wide valley below, was begun in the early twelfth century. It has been extensively restored but retains much of its original form (**273** and **384**).

Auvergne Churches
In this volcanic region the Byzantine influence is shown not so much in construction as in decoration, which displays diaper designs and striped polychrome inlaid in lava and red and white stone. Like the southern Italian and Sicilian Norman churches, there is also an eastern influence seen in the use of horseshoe arches often with trefoil and cinquefoil cusping. Two interesting examples are the cathedrals at Issoire and Le Puy. *S. Austremoine*, the *Cathedral at Issoire*, is, like a number of churches in the area, based on hall pattern (with nave and aisles of equal height). There is a tall nave arcade and no clerestory. Round arches are used throughout, as are barrel vaults. The interior is simple, its chief decoration being in colour and in variation of capitals like those at *S. Pierre* in *Chauvigny* (PLATE 27). These capitals at Issoire are also very large, painted all over and represent animals, human figures and foliage. The columns and arches are painted in diaper and other patterns in indian red, black and white. The east end is apsidal and the church is blockish, building up in an impressive composition to an octagonal tower (**275**). The *Cathedral of Le Puy* is unusual in its setting and layout and reflects Moorish influence strongly. The volcanic area is formed into steep cliffs with outcrops of rock and the cathedral is perched on a ledge near the top of one of these, above the town, which clings to platforms on the hillside (**274**). One approaches the west façade of the cathedral up steep flights of steps and the triple

Plate 27
Choir capital. Church
of S. Pierre,
Chauvigny, France,
12th century
Plate 28
Exterior carving.
Urnes stave church,
Sognfjord,
Norway, c. 1125–40
Plate 29
Kilpeck Church,
England. South
doorway
detail, c. 1140

Plate 30
Wheel window of marble plates
Troia Cathedral, Italy
Plate 31
Doorway capital detail, Bitonto Cathedral, Italy
1175–1200
Plate 32
Column support, west doorway. Church of
S. Nicola, Bari, Italy, 11th century

ROMANESQUE IN FRANCE: LOIRE, PUY-DE-DÔME, AUVERGNE

274 *Le Puy Cathedral from the south-west,*
twelfth century
275 *Cathedral of S. Austremoine, Issoire,*
twelfth century
276 *The kitchen, Abbey of Fontevrault, from*
the eleventh century
277 *The cloisters, Le Puy Cathedral*

entrance porch leads, not into the nave due to the steepness of the hillside, but below it and one must ascend further steps inside to reach the nave above the porch. The façade, like the rest of the building, is built of red and black granite and decorated in lava and coloured stone in shades of pink, grey and black. Inside, the nave vaults are octagonal domical shape and the central dome is carried on pseudo-pendentives rather like squinches. On the south-east side of the cathedral is a fine porch (*porche du For*) of Transitional design with the same polychrome decoration and interesting capitals. On the north side is an exceptional cloister in black and white stone with walls above the arcade decorated in lozenge mosaic patterns in red, black and white. The capitals are mainly foliated and are varied (**277**). The cathedral, which was begun in the eleventh century, shows clearly its Moorish influence throughout in its zebra striped patterns, lozenge and diamond inlay and cusped arches. Nearby is the unusually situated *Chapel* of *S. Michel de l'Aiguilhe* on top of its pinnacle of rock. It is built of the same materials and shows the same Moorish features of decoration and construction (**415**). The interior is unusual with columns set on circular plan but with flatter, straight sides to the exterior walls. It is reminiscent of circular interiors like S. Michael at Fulda in Germany.

Southern France
At *Toulouse*, towards the Pyrenees, is the famous pilgrimage church of *S. Sernin*, which is one of France's largest, barrel vaulted churches. It was begun about 1077, the first construction being at the east end, so that the nave is early twelfth

century and the façade a little later. It is cruciform with a long, double-aisled nave, aisled transept and a central, octagonal tower over the crossing the steeple is mainly thirteenth century with spire, 215 feet high, built in 1475 (**269**).

In *Provence* the Romanesque architecture different from that in most other parts of France Here, the influence is from Ancient Rome no Normandy or Byzantium. The classical tradition as in Italy itself, never died and the churches this region, though indubitably Romanesque have a classical interpretation of the style and us classical columns, capitals, mouldings an decoration often, as in Italy, incorporating actu Roman fragments from ruined buildings. Th façades, especially the entrance porches, and th cloisters show the magnificent decoration of suc churches at its best. Two particular examples a S. *Trophîme* at *Arles* and S. *Gilles* nearby. S. Trophîme the Roman influence is very stron in the west porch, which is based on a Roma triumphal arch. The Romanesque developmen shows, however, in the deeply recessed moulding and jambs and in the columns which stand lions' backs. The sculptural decoration here very rich in figures and picture carving. Th tympanum represents Christ as Judge of th World and, below, the architrave has a row sculptured figures above the larger figures saints which alternate with the columns (**389** an **419**). The cloisters are equally fine and on th north side date from 1170 like the portal. The have round arches and varied, beautiful carve capitals. The *Church* at *S. Gilles-du-Gard*, ne Arles, possesses the most impressive of the portal entrances in Provence, this time in trip

278 *Le Pont du Benezet, bridge over the Rhône at Avignon, 1177–1185 (originally 22 arches now only 4)*

arched design, connected by colonnades. The church was part of a great Cluniac priory and a pilgrimage centre. The façade dates from 1140 (**391**).

Among the few secular constructions of the Romanesque period in France is the famous *bridge* in Provence at *Avignon*, the *Pont S. Bénézet*, built in 1177–85 by the Sacred Guild of Bridge Builders across the river Rhône. It is a good example of construction in masonry though it now possesses only four of the original 22 arches which spanned the river. S. Nicholas' Chapel still remains at the end of the existing structure (**278**).

Italy

Even more than French, Italian Romanesque architecture was subjected to varied influences in different parts of the peninsula. In the north, building design had much in common with northern Europe and primarily evolved from Lombard styles; in central Italy, particularly Tuscany, coloured marbles were used as veneers in decoration both on the outside and inside of the buildings giving a colourful rather than plastic effect to the decoration. Southern Italy was under Norman domination and architecture here has much in common with Norman buildings in France and England, taking into account the different climatic conditions and needs of the area. Sicily is, like southern Italy, especially rich in Romanesque work, but in this region the Norman style, which was dominant, was tempered by the mixed heritage of the island—Saracenic and Byzantine, in particular—and the architecture is an exciting and enchanting amalgam of these influences and a unique study in its own right.

In general, however, Italian Romanesque architecture has, as in other European countries, common features. As in Provence in southern France, links with the Roman tradition were never wholly severed so that arches, arcades, entablatures, columns and capitals tend to approach the classical form more than the Medieval. In churches, the basilican plan is most common while stone vaulting is the rarity rather than the rule. The Roman technique of timber roofing to nave and choir, with lower, sloping, timber coverings to the aisles, was commonly

adhered to. Likewise, the early Christian ground plans and arrangements had a strong influence. The altar remained at the west end in a number of cases. Separate baptisteries continued to be built for many years and separate, free-standing campaniles were the general rule; these features acted as watch towers and were symbols of local importance. Many examples were very tall—up to 250 feet high. In a constructional sense the arch never dominated Italian Romanesque work as it did in northern Europe; it remained as in Roman times, more decorative than constructional in its purpose. It is simple and rarely deeply moulded. Arcading, using round arches, is a popular feature in Italian Romanesque buildings but it is always decorative in its application except in a number of instances in northern Italy. The elevation of Italian churches, unlike those of northern Europe, is low, with the emphasis on the horizontal lines. Inside, the triforium is often omitted or is just a decorative band, while the nave arcade is of great importance. Over the crossing, a cupola raised on a drum is more usual than a tower, particularly in Lombardy and Tuscany. Italian Romanesque architecture is of a very high standard of craftmanship and beauty, differing from French, English or German examples but in general, ahead of these on contemporary development. Churches such as S. Miniato in Florence, built in 1013, show a sophistication unknown at this early date in northern Europe.

Northern Italy

The Lombard Plain is a natural corridor flanking the river Po at the foot of the Alps. The Teutonic race of Langobards (Lombards) were conquered by Charlemagne in 774. They were then unskilled builders but quickly developed in technique and understanding. Most of the existing remains are of the eleventh and twelfth centuries though built on sites of earlier buildings from the eighth century onwards. The natural communications of the region, the navigable Po and the Alpine passes, made this a suitable area for an exchange of ideas with Germany, France and Spain; architecturally a movement was established here which led the way for other regions. By the eleventh century a number of towns existed along the valley and important civic and ecclesiastical buildings were erected. *Milan* was

ITALIAN ROMANESQUE

279 *Trani Cathedral, Apulia, from the south-east,*
begun 1094
280 *The Baptistery, Parma, 1196–1296*

281 *Church of S. Miniato al Monte, Florence, 1013 to*
thirteenth century
282 *Old Cathedral of S. Corrada, Molfetta, Apulia,*
twelfth century

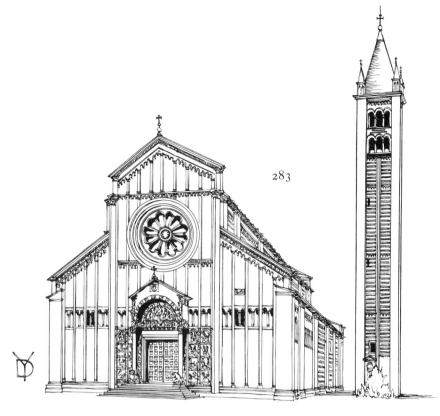

283

283 *Church of S. Zeno, Verona, Italy, from the west, c. 1140*

one such centre; others included *Parma, Cremona, Como, Pavia* and *Ferrara*. Brick was the regional building material, with stone or marble facing, though a few buildings were entirely of stone. Two particular characteristics of regional building style were the tall towers—either for churches or civic buildings—and the development of the rib vault which, in Italy, was unusual. The towers were very tall, unbuttressed and were decorated by pilaster strips and corbel tables. Usually, as in most Italian towers, the window and belfry openings increased in number of lights as the stages ascended—commonly from one to five. Good examples exist at *Pomposa Church* 1063 and at the *Cathedrals* of *Ivrea* and *Aosta*. Twin towered churches in German style are found in the lower Alpine areas, as at *S. Abbondio* in *Como* which is an outstanding specimen of a stone church begun in 1063.

Vaulting was being developed all over Europe by the later eleventh century, but in Italy the wooden roof and/or the domical covering were the usual method. In Lombardy, however, the rib vault was experimented with and a number of examples were built. The usual church design had aisles which were half the nave width and there was an intermediate column between each pier. Thus, nave and aisles could be vaulted on

square bay pattern. Generally the vaults have replaced the original wooden roofs in the churches here and so are later than the rest of the building. Octagonal cupolas covered by flat pitched roofs were still normal crossing space covering.

A particular feature of northern Italian churches was the façade projecting porch built in two or three stages. It was vaulted and this vault was carried on columns which in turn were supported on the backs of animals—lions or oxen. Above the porch was usually a decorative circular window in the façade gable which lit the nave behind.

One of the best of early Romanesque churches in this region is *S. Ambrogio* in *Milan*, which set a pattern for Lombard churches. It was built in brick over a long period; the east end dates from the ninth century and the west from the tenth and eleventh while the vaults are mainly twelfth century. In front of the west façade is a large cloistered atrium and the narthex is flanked by towers, an older one on the south and a typical twelfth century pilaster strip one on the north side. Inside, the building is well lit by the ring of windows in the later, central, octagonal lantern. The nave is covered in double bays of domical rib vaults supported on piers while the aisles have groined vaults.

There are a number of *cathedrals* along the Po

284 Palazzo Loredan, Venice, Italy, twelfth century

valley with similar characteristics to one another, particularly those at *Parma* and *Cremona* which each comprise the basic threefold group of buildings—campanile, baptistery and cathedral —all separate. At Parma, the twelfth century cathedral exterior is of brick in simple design. It has continuous loggias all round the building and panelled walls and apses; there is a low octagonal cupola with small lantern. The façade is gabled with towers (only one completed) and three open loggias. The campanile, nearly 200 feet high, is later, 1284, and is of brick with stone faced pilasters at the corners. It is topped by a cone. The baptistery stands separately at the south-west corner of the cathedral and was begun in 1196. It is faced with stone on the outside and red marble inside. It is octagonal (16-sided on the interior) and has fine, carved sculpture and decorative doorways by *Benedetto Antelami* (**280**). At *Ferrara* the cathedral has been much altered, but the façade remains with its lower part Romanesque and the upper stages Gothic. The three Romanesque doorways are magnificently carved and the centre one has a typical projecting

porch of the twelfth century with infedels supporting the columns and vault. *Modena Cathedral* also has an impressive façade with wheel window in the gable (**383**) and porch below, on either side of which are four panels by *Wiligelmo* depicting the Bible story from the Creation to the Flood (**390**). The magnificent 300 feet campanile—the *Torre Ghirlandina*—dates from the thirteenth century. The interior is in simple, brick design with high vaults and brick piers and marble columns. The pulpit and gallery are beautifully sculptured; the columns are supported on infedels and lions—the latter devouring their prey and possessing a sad but demoniac appearance. *Piacenza* is another interesting Cathedral.

Among the churches of the region, *S. Zeno* at *Verona* and *S. Michele* at *Pavia* are exceptional. At *S. Zeno Maggiore* the façade is simple but very impressive. It is beautifully proportioned with central, projecting porch, its columns supported on the backs of crouching lions, and with marble, sculptured panels on either side of the magnificent bronze doors by *Niccolo* and *Gugliemo*. Above is the gable wheel window which lights the nave. The whole façade is decorated by pilaster strips connected by corbel tables. Beside the church is the free-standing, lofty campanile, also beautifully proportioned. It has no buttresses and has alternate courses of marble and brick. The bellchamber provides the only openings near the top which is surmounted by a high, pitched roof (**283**). The interior of the church has no triforium and only a small clerestory. The choir is raised high above the crypt in which, according to the early Christian custom, the saint's tomb is placed immediately underneath the altar in the choir above. *S. Michele* at *Pavia* (**424**) shows Byzantine influence in its east end and central cupola, but the façade is a cliff-like gable wall with fine Romanesque carving on three doorways (**408**) though, unfortunately, this is now somewhat weathered. The gable is wide and typically Italian in its stepped arcade following the gable angle. Below are shafts and dosserets which form shallow buttresses.

Venice

Venetian Romanesque architecture was dominated by the city's eastern contacts and Byzantium continued to have more influence than Lombardy or Pisa. Mosaic decoration was more usual than carved stonework and this type of ornament was still carried out predominantly by Byzantine Greek craftsmen. Not many buildings of this period survive unaltered; the *palace* in Fig. **284** shows a Grand Canal façade of the time with cubiform capitals and stilted as well as semi-circular arches, while the finest complete example is the *Cathedral* of *SS. Mary and Donato* on the *Island* of *Murano* in the Venetian Lagoon. This building is more Romanesque than other works; it is cruciform and has a particularly fine galleried and arcaded apse dating from about 1140.

Central Italy

In this region exists the finest Romanesque architecture in Italy in quality and development. It is also an area which produced several variations in style from the Pisan school centred on Pisa and Lucca to the work in Florence with its coloured marble facings and the districts further south in Assisi and Rome where contacts with the Lombard style are notable. There was no shortage of excellent building materials from varied marbles to stone, brick and volcanic substances.

The climate is good, not too hot but with brilliant sunshine to set off the vivid colouring and give shade and modelling to the arcaded treatment of façades. Vaulting is unusual, most roofs are timber spanned, windows are not large, walls unbuttressed and roof pitches shallow. The influence of Papal Rome largely prevailed and the basilican church plan was usual. The campaniles were separate but not generally as tall as Lombard ones.

The Pisan School

Here developed in the eleventh and twelfth centuries a centre for the arts which attracted artists and craftsmen from all over Italy. The typical Tuscan church of the region has exterior arcading and open galleries over its façades, often all round the building. The arches spring from low projection pilasters and engaged shafts. The façades are rarely, as in Lombardy, divided into bays and masses but are evenly decorated all over with arcading, up to four or five rows on the west side.

The most outstanding example of this type of work is the Pisan complex, the *Piazza dei Miracoli* in the city (**285** and **286**). This consists of four separate buildings: the baptistery, the cathedral, the campanile and the cemetery (this last, the *Camposanto*, was badly damaged in the Second World War but is now largely rebuilt apart from the beautiful frescoes which were for the most part beyond repair). The building of the complex spanned a long period, from the foundation of the cathedral in 1063 to the completion of the campanile in 1350, but the whole group is one stylistic unit. All the buildings are faced with marble panelling and decorated with arcading which still gleams white and sparkling in the sunshine. The basilican *Cathedral* has a double-aisled nave, transepts and apsidal east end. The oval dome over the crossing is supported on squinches and shallow pendentives. Apart from the interior triumphal arch, which is pointed, the other arches are semi-circular. The façade is very fine, with typical Tuscan arcading in four rows to the top of gable while below are three doorways set in a marble panelled and inlaid front. The columns and capitals derive from classical rather than Romanesque sources. The original doors of 1180 by *Bonanno* were replaced

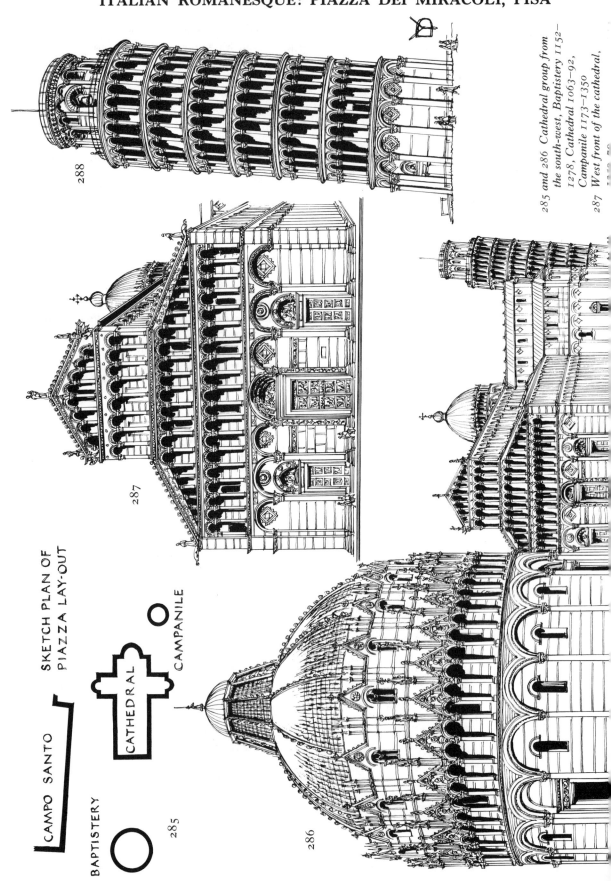

285 and 286 Cathedral group from the south-west, Baptistery 1152–1278, Cathedral 1063–92, Campanile 1173–1350
287 West front of the cathedral,

288

287

285

286

SKETCH PLAN OF PIAZZA LAY-OUT

CAMPO SANTO

BAPTISTERY

CATHEDRAL

CAMPANILE

in the seventeenth century. His work on the transept doorway is, however, still extant (**287**).

The *baptistery* is circular, 114 feet in diameter, and is covered by a later cupola. The truncated cone, which extends upwards through this cupola, is the original roof. The interior consists of two concentric, circular forms, the outer walls in white marble, banded in grey and black and, inside these, an inner circle of Corinthian columns and piers. The classical influence is even more marked here (**414**). The pulpit of 1260 by Nicola Pisano is a masterpiece. It is hexagonal and stands on seven columns; the central one has a base of human figures and animals while the others are supported on the backs of lions.

The *campanile*, the famous leaning tower, is cylindrical, 52 feet in diameter and, like the cathedral, is marble faced and arcaded up to six storeys. It settled even while building was in progress and the fourteenth century bellchamber was differently angled in an attempt to right the inclination. The tower is nearly 180 feet high and over 13 feet from the vertical at the top (**288**).

The Pisa group is so superb that it overshadows the rest of the work in this district. Also, it is so situated, in a piazza on the fringe of the town,

that it can be appreciated without the distraction of heavy traffic and commercial buildings. The very fine work in this same style at *Lucca*, for example, should not be missed, for it is of high quality and is equally typical Tuscan Romanesque. There are three outstanding churches in the city: the cathedral of S. Martino and the churches of S. Michele and S. Frediano. The *Cathedral*, begun 1160, has a beautiful Romanesque façade (1196–1204) with a narthex, galleried and arcaded with screen gable and, beside it, a tall bell tower with typical Italian openings, increasing in number of lights towards the top. There is some fine carving and inlay decoration on this façade. Inside, the cathedral is Gothic. *S. Michele* (**289**) is the best of the three. It was begun *c.* 1140, but the impressive arcaded façade dates from the early thirteenth century. Like the others, it is covered with white and coloured marble sheathing with marble carving and decoration. *S. Frediano*, 1112–47, which is similar, is noted for its striking mosaic on the gable façade; the church shows a Byzantine and Roman influence.

Further south the Romanesque architecture is traditional but strongly tinged with classical

289 Church of S. Michele, Lucca, Italy, begun c. 1140, façade c. 1239

forms from Rome. The *Cathedral* of *S. Rufino* at *Assisi*, begun 1144 (now overshadowed by S. Francesco) has a beautiful façade, very simple and dominated by its circular windows and sculptured doorways. Of the three windows, the large central one is carried on carved figures, an unusual design, which has much in common with the façade at *Spoleto Cathedral*, of similar date, but with a later porch in front. *S. Maria in Cosmedin* in *Rome* still has its elegant tower of *c.* 1200 in seven storeys, each of which is arcaded, and has a brick cornice. The tower is the least altered part of the church where the interior, especially, has been much restored, but it is still interesting and retains its ancient atmosphere. It is a basilican church which incorporates the original building on the site—a Roman corn hall. Like most Roman churches, the building is of brick and is fronted by a porch and open narthex. South, on the coast, are two interesting cathedrals

at Amalfi and Salerno. *Amalfi Cathedral* has been partly rebuilt but still has its beautiful campanile and eleventh century façade doors (**377**). At *Salerno* the original rectangular atrium fronts the cathedral with its Saracenic styled arches and Roman capitals and columns. The Porta dei Leoni, the eleventh century entrance, is still intact.

The Tuscan work of the *Florence* School is a separate study because its characteristics are so different from those of Pisa or Rome despite its geographical nearness. The *Church* of *S. Miniato al Monte*, perched on a hill above the city is an early but mature and perfect example. It incorporates three influences: Roman, Byzantine and Romanesque. Antique Roman columns and capitals have been used, in some cases of ill-matching sizes, in the nave. The Byzantine influence is seen in the mosaic decoration inside and out and in the marble facing patterns while

290 The Baptistery, Florence Cathedral, viewed from campanile—black and white marble, fifth-thirteenth century

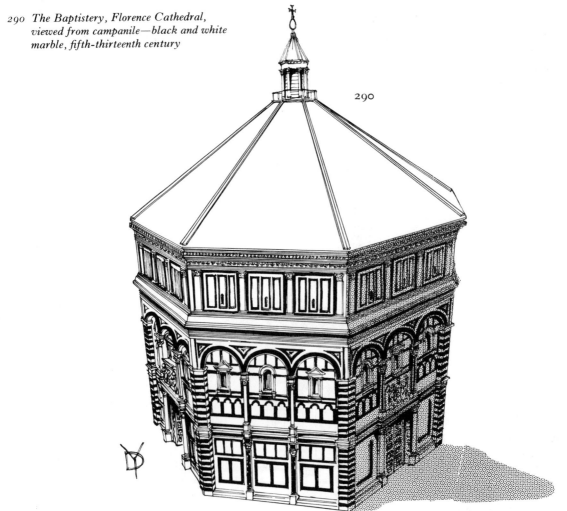

290

he Romanesque provides the general constructional layout. The façade, begun in 1013, is faced in white and green marble, with five arches on the lower part supported on composite columns. Above is a gable with window and mosaic decoration. The whole façade is faced with coloured marbles. Inside, the same vivid colour treatment is used on walls, columns, roof and pavement. The apse is mosaic-covered in its semi-dome above the decorative arcade. There is a beautiful, marble pulpit (**281**). The *baptistery of Florence Cathedral* shows the same marble decorative treatment. Partly Byzantine and partly Romanesque, it was altered in the Gothic period by Arnolfo di Cambio when he was working on the cathedral. The exterior view (**290**) is still primarily Romanesque; it is octagonal, 90 feet in diameter, and covered by an internal dome, 103 feet high. The façades are in three stages in black and white marble, surmounted by a low roof and lantern.

Apart from the ecclesiastical buildings of northern and central Italy, there are many *towers* surviving from the Romanesque and Medieval periods when they were places of refuge, fortresses and, later, status symbols. Many towns were a forest of such towers but most of these have now been demolished. S. Gimignano, near Siena, is the outstanding instance where a number of towers still survive and these date from the twelfth and thirteenth centuries. They are square in plan and rise sheer to varying heights without ornament, abutment and with few openings. Two particular towers remain in Bologna, the *Asinelli Tower* of 1109, 320 feet high and the *Garisenda Tower* of 1110. Both of these are inclined, from four to ten feet out of plumb, but they remain intact, the city traffic milling round them. They are survivors of about 180 such towers in Medieval Bologna.

Southern Italy

Although Calabria has always been a poor region, *Apulia*, in the years from the ninth to twelfth century, was rich. It was a large area, with its capital at Bari. From 870 to the mid-eleventh century it was a Byzantine colony where the Eastern Emperors held power despite Saracen attacks. In 1040 the Normans took over the area and its great cathedral churches date from the

succeeding 100 years. Apulian Romanesque architecture is individual; it has the Norman characteristics of power and solidity but also Saracenic arch construction and Byzantine decoration. Because of the brilliant hot sun, windows are small, roofs flat and walls thick. Buildings are of the plentiful stone from the district and the sculpture is of as high quality as in the north of Italy at this time. The churches have short naves with high clerestory but (no triforium), single aisles, triapsidal east end, timber roofs and, on the exterior, large twin towers and one or more cupolas over the crossing, nave and transepts. The eastern and Byzantine influence is also noticeable in the lack of portrayal of the human figure in decoration; façades are ornamented with plant and geometrical forms. The great stone Cathedrals of Apulia have suffered from neglect over the centuries of impoverishment since the Norman civilisation crumbled, also from alterations and additions in eighteenth century Baroque work. In a number of cases, though, their magnificent bronze doors remain. These are often of solid cast bronze rather than bronze plates fixed to wooden doors as was more common in the north. Among such examples are those at Trani, Troia and Ravello, all of late twelfth century date and still in good condition.

Trani Cathedral was a large pilgrimage church built by the edge of the sea in a setting which appears to have changed little over the centuries. It was begun in 1084 and built over a seventh century church which now forms a crypt. It is tall, of golden stone and has a powerful, lofty eastern central apse with two smaller ones on either side of it, all lit by high windows (**382**). The transepts have large circular windows. There is only one tower (recently restored) at the southwest corner; the façade is arcaded and has three doorways, the central one finely sculptured. The bronze doors are by *Barisano da Trani* and have 33 panels decorated with foliage, animals and figures, depicting mythological and biblical scenes (**279**). *Troia Cathedral*, begun in 1093, is built high up in the small hill town and is visible for miles as it stands out of the surrounding flat plain. It is not large but is of high quality. One of its unusual features is the later window in the façade which is filled with decorative marble plates instead of glass (PLATE 30). The sculpture here, inside and out, is very fine and vigorous;

the bronze doors are unusual and interesting. At the east end the main apse is decorated by two rows of free-standing columns.

Other noteworthy cathedrals in Apulia include that at *Canosa* (now unfortunately somewhat derelict), the Old Cathedral at Molfetta (so-called to distinguish it from the Baroque one) and Bitonto Cathedral. *Molfetta Cathedral* has a fine site on the edge of the harbour. It has two tall Lombardic towers and three domes over the nave. It dates from the twelfth century and reflects the essence of Norman power and strength in architecture (**282**). *Bitonto* is different but equally massive. It has a gabled façade with wheel window at the top and two-light windows below. The central of the three portals is sculptured in a masterly manner with birds above the capitals (**417** and PLATE 31) and with columns supported on the backs of crouching (rather worn) lions. The nave is long and aisled with the aisles projecting to transept width. The interior is most noteworthy. The stone church of *S. Nicola* at *Bari* is one of the few ancient buildings in the city to survive. It is the oldest important church in southern Italy and was the prototype for many others. It was planned as a pilgrimage church with a large crypt for the relics and with stairways leading to it from the aisles. It was built mainly between the late eleventh century and 1197. The gable façade has three portals, the centre one of which (**388**) has columns supported on the backs of oxen (PLATE 32). Inside, the transept opens behind a triumphal arch which frames the apse with its altar. The famous Bari (Bishop's) throne is here; this is a magnificent piece of sculpture, 1098, by *Gugliemo* (**425**).

Sicily

The great cathedrals here, particularly those at Cefalù, Palermo and Monreale, are also of Norman origin but, owing to the mixed ancestry of the island's peoples, illustrate varied influences. Both Byzantine and Saracenic civilisations left their mark here, the former in decorative mosaics and carvings and the latter in the construction of stilted, horseshoe and pointed* arches and stalactite vaulting. The standard of craftmanship in these fields was high especially in glass mosaic design and application. Some of the Sicilian interiors glow with rich colour like

the greatest of the Byzantine ones. A favourit[e] exterior wall decoration here is with lava an[d] coloured stone inlay giving a cream, red an[d] black scheme in geometrical shapes of lozenge[s] and zig-zags like the volcanic decoration in[-] fluenced by Byzantine work at Le Puy in Franc[e]. Decorative motifs in Sicily, however, wer[e] immensely varied from Byzantine lozenges t[o] Norman billet, Roman acanthus and Gree[k] key patterns. The important cathedral founda[-] tions on the coast were begun between 1130 an[d] 1200. *Palermo Cathedral*, begun in 1135, is th[e] largest of the Norman royal buildings on th[e] island but it has since been much altered. Th[e] façade and south porch are now Gothic and th[e] interior and cupola were transformed in th[e] eighteenth century. Only the east end remain[s] typical of Sicilian Romanesque work, with inter[-] laced arcading on the apses decorated ornatel[y] in inlaid lava and coloured stone. At *Cefalù* th[e] *Cathedral*, built 1131–48, is impressively site[d] on the side of a mountain overlooking the sea[;] it appears to be growing out of the mountainsid[e] (**292**). Like Apulian cathedrals, it has a massiv[e] stone exterior with apsidal east end and tin[y] windows, also western towers. The choir an[d] transepts are immensely lofty with the main aps[e] rising to the full height of the building but th[e] nave is considerably lower. The façade is fronte[d] by a narthex which is supported on Norma[n] columns and capitals. Inside, the most spectac[-] ular part is at the east, where the apse and vau[lt] are covered by high quality Byzantine mosai[c] pictures, showing the form of the Pantocrat[or] with angels above and the Virgin, archange[ls] and apostles below. The cloisters are fine an[d] have varied and original carved columns an[d] capitals.

Monreale is the most notable of the Norma[n] monuments in Sicily, situated in the hills abov[e] Palermo. It is a mixture of influences: Norma[n], Christian, Byzantine, and Oriental Saraceni[c]. The cloisters (1172–89) of the abbey church ar[e] beautiful; they are enclosed on four sides b[y] coupled columns of stone and marble, inlai[d] with brilliantly coloured glass mosaic in patter[ns] on the shafts and have richly varied carve[d] capitals. The main doors of the cathedral are th[e] original bronze ones, 1186, by *Bonanno of Pis[a]* which have 42 sculptured panels depicting th[e] Old and New Testament; they are similar to th[e]

---

* *The pointed arch was used here long before it appeared in early Gothic buildings in Europe.*

ROMANESQUE CATHEDRALS IN SICILY

291 *Monreale Cathedral, begun 1174. Apsidal east end. Limestone inlaid with black lava, marble shafts*
292 *Cefalù Cathedral from the south-east, begun 1131*

291

292

ones which he did later on Pisa Cathedral (p. 149). The exterior of the cathedral, particularly the apses of the east end, are incredibly decorated in coloured stone and inlaid lava in arcades, rosettes, strips and lozenges (**291**). The interior, which presents the most striking Sicilian example in Romanesque church building, is decorated largely by mosaic pictures on walls, apse vault, capitals and columns. The lower part of the walls is marble faced and the open roof is of painted and gilded wood. The mosaics cover an enormous area and tell the Bible stories in detail and at length.

England

English Romanesque architecture is generally called 'Norman' after the dynasty established by William I of Normandy in 1066. English Norman architecture has much in common with its prototype in Normandy but, as the child will often outpace his father, so the English branch reached greater heights than its progenitor. No other European country produced such magnificent and varied Romanesque architecture and none other possesses such a quantity of that heritage extant. These remains are not only in large cathedrals; all over the country exist many parish churches, abbey ruins and remains of fortifications and castles. Most of the cathedrals and churches have later alterations and additions but, in many cases, Romanesque work is present in quantity; perhaps due to the depredations of Henry VIII, English abbeys and priories, instead of being given Baroque face-lifts, have survived, more or less, as ruins from the Medieval period (PLATE 34).

English Norman architecture was, in the case of important buildings, constructed from stone, often Caen stone imported by William from Normandy. The style is massive, austere, finely proportioned and intensely durable. Builders tended to underestimate the strength of their work and walls, in particular, are of tremendous thickness as at, for example, the Keep of the Tower of London. In cathedral building the pattern developed differently from the Continental one. The nave is often very long, as at Norwich with 14 bays and Ely with 13, while Continental examples are much shorter. In distinction, the eastern arm in England is shorter and, after the earlier Norman work, terminated

more often in a square rather than an apsidal end. The cruciform pattern on Latin cross plan was retained, with much lower vaults than on the Continent. This led to the ability to span roofs with stone vaulting at an early date—a field in which England led the way—and, also, to provide a sound basis for supporting a massive central tower which, in later times, also carried a spire. On the Continent a central cupola was more common or, if a tower were intended, it was usually never built as the high vaults would not bear it. Few English cathedrals still have Norman vaults; they either retain a timber roof as at Ely, or more commonly were re-vaulted in the Gothic period; there are, however, numerous examples of Romanesque arcades supporting later vaults—a tribute to Norman constructional ability.

England is the only country of Europe where Romanesque building does not vary greatly in style from district to district. This is due to William of Normandy who created the foundation of a nation—the first in Europe. Of course, certain differences occur, due to varied needs and the availability of materials. Timber was used for building where stone was rare or expensive to transport but, for important building in abbeys, cathedrals and castles, the same style and stone material was employed whether in London or elsewhere.

Cathedrals

The English heritage is rich and, of these buildings standing all over the country, many retain a considerable Romanesque portion. One cathedral is paramount in this respect: *Durham*. Sited magnificently on steep rocks overlooking the river Wear, it was built in this commanding situation not only as a monastic centre but as a fortification (**294**). The exterior has been altered many times and now only the lower parts of the western towers and the main nave and choir show Romanesque work. Inside, though, the whole interior is of one Romanesque scheme. Durham was a very early example in Europe to be stone vaulted over such a wide span. The choir has since been re-covered, but the nave high vault survives in its original form, which was completed in 1133. The Durham vaults are quadripartite ribbed constructions—a great advance over the more usual barrel and domical

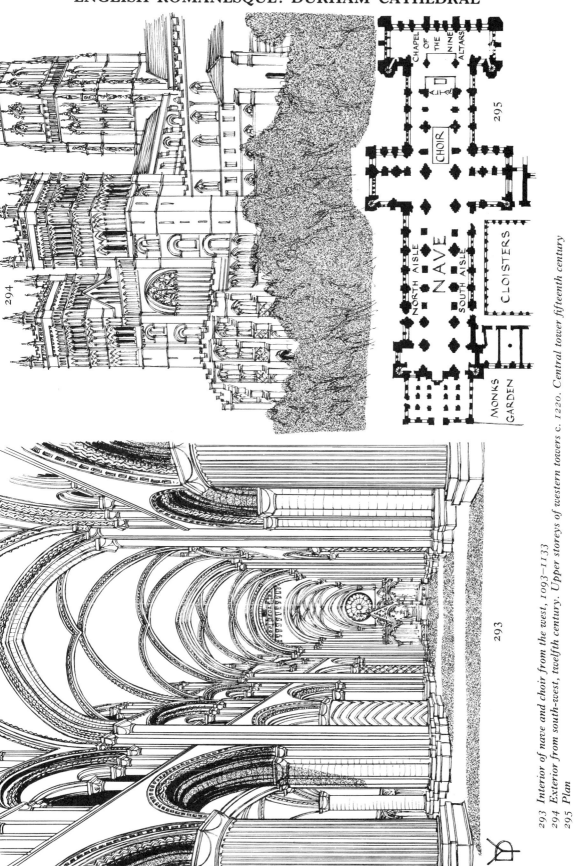

293 *Interior of nave and choir from the west, 1093–1133*
294 *Exterior from south-west, twelfth century. Upper storeys of western towers c. 1220. Central tower fifteenth century*
295 *Plan*

designs of France or Italy. The ribbed vault is a lighter construction and so does not place the same enormous stress upon the walls and arcades supporting it. At Durham also, flying buttresses were put in to take some of the thrust of the vault but these are not visible, being hidden under the triforium sloping roofs (293). Durham Cathedral was begun in 1093 on cruciform plan (295) with a low, central tower (since rebuilt) and two western towers. The great columns of the nave, with their varied chevron and fluted decoration and their cushion capitals, alternate with piers which have shafts extending upwards to support the vault. The aisles are also rib vaulted as can be seen in Fig. 293. The cathedral has the traditional triforium arcade with two round arches under one larger one per bay and clerestory windows above. Durham is one of the very few ecclesiastical buildings in England to retain its original clerestory windows (as can be seen in Fig. 294 of the exterior). Most churches had larger windows inserted later to give greater light to the interior, but the Durham examples were not so small as usual. The interior certainly does look light, though it is assisted in this respect by the Cathedral eastern Gothic rose.

A good idea of how the great Norman towers looked when they were built is provided by the large, pilgrimage church at *Southwell* (296). The

stubby spires here which surmount the western towers are not ancient, but they replace the originals in the earlier style and are the type which Durham would have had in the eleventh and twelfth centuries. Southwell Minster is a very beautiful building, much of its exterior unchanged from Norman times but also with its unique thirteenth century interior work (Chapter 5).

The eastern end of *Norwich Cathedral* (298 and 299) is one of the few English examples which retains the apsidal termination—in this case, tri-apsidal. As indicated in the drawing, the spire, Lady Chapel and clerestory of the choir are later work in Gothic style but the remainder, giving a basis of design and construction, is Romanesque. Among the many cathedrals with Norman remains, it is most usual for the nave to

296 Southwell Minster from the north-west. West front c. 1130, later perpendicular windows. Chapter House c. 1290

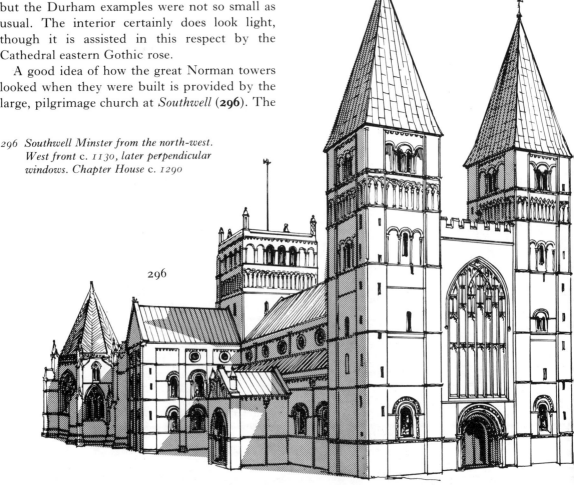

296

ENGLISH ROMANESQUE CATHEDRALS

297 Ely Cathedral, towered transept, begun 1083
298 Norwich Cathedral, plan (dotted line represents original Lady Chapel)

299 Norwich Cathedral from the east, 1096–1120, clerestory 1362–9, spire c. 1464–72, Lady Chapel c. 1930

be unaltered—the eastern arm and transepts were generally enlarged later to provide more accommodation. Outstanding *cathedrals* still possessing such naves include *Ely, Rochester, Gloucester, Peterborough, Hereford* and *S. Albans*, also the *Abbey Churches* of *Tewkesbury* and *Waltham*, though most of these have undergone one or more restorations since the original building. *Lincoln Cathedral* still retains a Romanesque lower section to its west front with a remarkable portal (**395**). *Exeter* has Norman transeptal towers (an unusual design) and many cathedrals have Romanesque *central towers—Winchester, S. Albans* and *Tewkesbury*—while a number of *abbeys*, ruined and in use, have Norman remains, for example *Fountains, Buildwas, Leominster* (**405**) and *Malmesbury* (**413**). At *Ely* (**297**) is a particularly fine example of Transitional work, that is, the style which evolved from Romanesque and preceded a complete transference into Gothic. This is in the surviving transept and towers. Another instance of the type of work which generally includes both round and pointed arches in one building is in the *Church* at *New Shoreham*. Here, the round arches are predominant on the lower storey of both nave and tower and pointed arches above.

Parish Churches

Norman work surviving among these is too numerous to list. Every county has many such churches with a Norman nave, tower, west doorway or south porch, sculptural decoration and other features. *Iffley Church*, illustrated in Fig. **301** is a good example with typical, beautifully carved doorways and window openings showing Norman ornament of chevron, billet and dentil. Of particular interest, in sculpture, is the Herefordshire School, of whose work *Kilpeck Church* is the outstanding example. The south doorway here, for instance, of reddish sandstone, is beautifully carved (**407** and PLATE 29). *Barfreston Church* in *Kent* also has a richly carved doorway and corbels and a number of churches like *Eardisley*, also *Herefordshire*, have interesting Romanesque basket plaited fonts. In general, though, English Romanesque was not noted for its sculpture. The decoration is often rich, but more commonly of geometrical or plant form as at Lincoln (**391**).

Castles and Fortifications

William I of Normandy took over a new countr and, to unite it and to bring peace and prosperit to it in accordance with his ideas, he had to sho strength. To this end he built many castles. A first these were of timber, on motte and baile pattern, but gradually during the eleventh an twelfth centuries the wooden keeps were re placed, in important places, by stone ones. Man such keeps survive, in a ruined condition, as Rochester, Colchester or Castle Hedingham or, sti in use as at Dover and London. The Tower London was William's first and most importar care and in 1080 he built the stone keep no called the White Tower. This is a classic examp of the Norman design. It has four storeys an rises to over 90 feet in height. Its walls are massiv (up to 20 feet thick at base) and its openings at small and well protected (302). Of particul interest in the White Tower is the survivir Chapel of S. John, which presents an excellet impression of Norman work. It has a simple na with aisles in the wall thickness and continue round the east end with an ambulatory behir the altar. The columns are circular, very thic and have cubiform capitals. Above the na arcade is a clerestory but no triforium (300). Th keep of Rochester Castle, though ruined and wit its floors missing, still gives a clear impression what living in such keeps was like. This castl built c. 1130, is of stone and is about 125 feet hig and based on a plan 70 feet square. The walls at 12 feet thick and have passages, garderobes an bedchambers in them. The arrangement accommodation is typical; the floors, of timbe were divided vertically by walls giving two roon per floor. The second floor is the principal on comprising the great hall and the dividing wa here is pierced by arches and piers to make on large room. Each of these parts has its own fir place. Among the smaller examples Oakha Castle in Rutland still possesses its Great Ha which is famous for its windows, doorways an Transitional style capitals; it dates from 1190 an is now used for Assize Court sittings.

Spain and Portugal

It is sometimes stated that, due to the occupatio of the Iberian Peninsula by the Moors until 145 there is almost no Romanesque architecture her

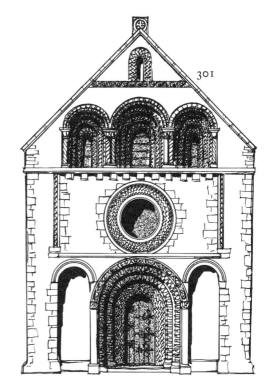

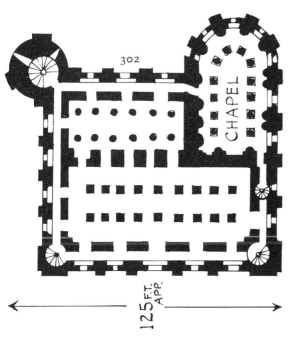

*300 S. John's Chapel, White Tower, Tower of London,
        c. 1080*
301 West front, Iffley Church, Oxfordshire, c. 1170
302 White Tower, plan of third floor of keep
*303 Gloucester Cathedral, nave looking east, c. 1100–60,
        vault c. 1242*

Anyone who takes the pilgrimage route to Santiago de Compostela from the Pyrenees and along the northern route via Pamplona, Logroño, Santo Domingo de la Calzada, Frómista and León will find that almost the opposite is true. It is a fact that, due to Moorish occupation, Christian buildings exist mainly in the northern half of the country in a broad band stretching from the Pyrenees down the Mediterranean coast to Tarragona and across to the west coast at Santiago, but, because of the Moslem domination, the Christian opposition in Spain was warlike and strong and Romanesque architecture reflects this spirit. The war of reconquest against the Moors got under way in 718 in the north-west near Oviedo and, over the years, Christian Spain forced a Moslem retreat south-eastwards, reaching Toledo by 1085. Because of its remoteness behind the Pyrenean mountain barrier and because of Moslem dominance, architectural ideas were slower to reach Spain and develop there. As a result, Romanesque architecture lasted much longer than in Italy or France or England, indeed it was more on a par with Germany in this respect, but, equally, Gothic architecture when it arrived, also lasted much longer, delaying the Renaissance till the late sixteenth or early seventeenth century.

Indicative of its militarism was the Christian forcefulness and enthusiasm for the *pilgrimage* to *Santiago*. The Apostle S. James was made Spain's patron saint and according to legend, was brought by sea from Palestine and died martyred. After burial at Santiago, a church was built over the relics. Later, in 1077, the great pilgrimage church was begun and, all along the route from the French frontier, Romanesque pilgrimage churches were built to give shelter and succour to the thousands of pilgrims. Today, the pilgrimage still takes place, now by air or car for many, but for 1965, the last pilgrimage year, the Spanish government made strenuous and successful efforts to restore and clean these famous churches (and also provide hotels for tourists) on this traditional route.

Spanish Romanesque architecture is subject to a number of influences, in particular, the mixture of Christian and Mohammedan sources —the basis of the country and its people for hundreds of years—and European sources, especially from France and Lombardy. At this time the Moors had a higher standard of culture which included art and architecture. Their buildings were more finely finished and decorated and were certainly more beautiful. In contrast, the Spanish Romanesque is rougher, more austere, more solemn than not only Mohammedan architecture but also Romanesque work from elsewhere in Europe. There are two periods of Romanesque in Spain: the basic Spanish product, of buildings erected before the great southward expansion in the late eleventh century and a transitional style of Late Romanesque of twelfth and thirteenth century work, resulting both from this expansion and from the French influence coming in from the north-east.

From the tenth and eleventh centuries, as the church established itself in northern Spain, the French seized the opportunity and set up monastic centres in the region under the Cluniac Order. In the twelfth century came a wave of Cistercian expansion to add to and replace the earlier foundations. Thus, in the northern coastal districts and also particularly in Aragon, Navarre, Castile and across to Galicia, French influence on Romanesque architecture was paramount. In the central regions the Mohammedan and Mujédar example was stronger and resulted in beautiful construction and decoration in brick, while in Catalonia, with its Mediterranean mercantile trade, the Lombard ideas percolated most strongly. In Portugal the French influence was strongest, led by Burgundy, and craftsmen and artisans had reached as far south as Lisbon by the mid-twelfth century. Despite all these outside influences, Spanish Romanesque architecture remains individual and nationalistic, being fundamentally a marriage of the two parts of the population: Spanish Christian and Spanish Moslem.

Catalonia and the North-East

In this area, due to the maritime trade with Italy from the Catalonian ports, Lombard Romanesque had the strongest effect. Many churches were built, generally small but stone, barrel vaulted and with Roman detail in ornament, columns and capitals, many probably taken from ruined Roman buildings. The layout is a solid one with thick, cellular walls and tall buttresses with chapels between. The whole exterior has a blockish appearance and the

304 *Monastery Church of S. Maria, Ripoll, Spain, façade c. 1160, restored nineteenth century*
305 *The Old Cathedral (Sé Velha) Coimbra, Portugal, east apsidal end, 1162–1300*
306 *Meira Abbey Church, Spain, interior looking east, twelfth century to 1258*

308 *Interior looking east, Church of
S. Martín de Frómista, 1066*
307 *Church of S. Martín de Frómista,
Spain, from the south-east, 106[6]*

...teriors are easier to comprehend. *Perpignan Cathedral* (then in Spain) is a good example of these churches. Lombard influence shows chiefly in the bell towers. These have many storeys, are unbuttressed and have no batter. Pilaster strip decoration is usual and small windows, increasing in size towards the top. Many small churches of the period survive, but few important ones and these have been greatly altered, e.g. Gerona and Tarragona Cathedrals and Ripoll Abbey. The Benedictine *Abbey Church* at *Ripoll* was rebuilt in 1020 and was the Catalan equivalent of Santiago. It was drastically restored in the late nineteenth century from a ruined condition and with the aid of drawings. It was originally inspired by Old S. Peter's in Rome and is a cruciform church with double aisles and seven apses. It had magnificent vaults based on the conceptions of Imperial Rome and was one of the great abbeys of its age. The west portal and arcade with its twelfth century sculpture, representing scenes from the Old Testament, still remains, but the sculpture is now in a crumbling condition. There is still a fine, two-storeyed cloister dating from *c.* 1125 (**304**). *Tarragona Cathedral* was begun in 1171 and has mainly pointed arches, but is predominantly Romanesque in its heavy construction and masonry though some of it has been rebuilt later. The interesting cloister is of late twelfth century design and part of the west front is Romanesque. Some of the portal sculpture here is Gothic in date but Transitional Romanesque in its solid character.

Castile and Central Spain

The main *pilgrimage route* from the Pyrenees to Santiago extended across this area and, mounted by the Cluniac Order, the pilgrimage was

309 *Church of S. Esteban, Segovia, Spain, eleventh to thirteenth century*

309

ROMANESQUE IN SPAIN

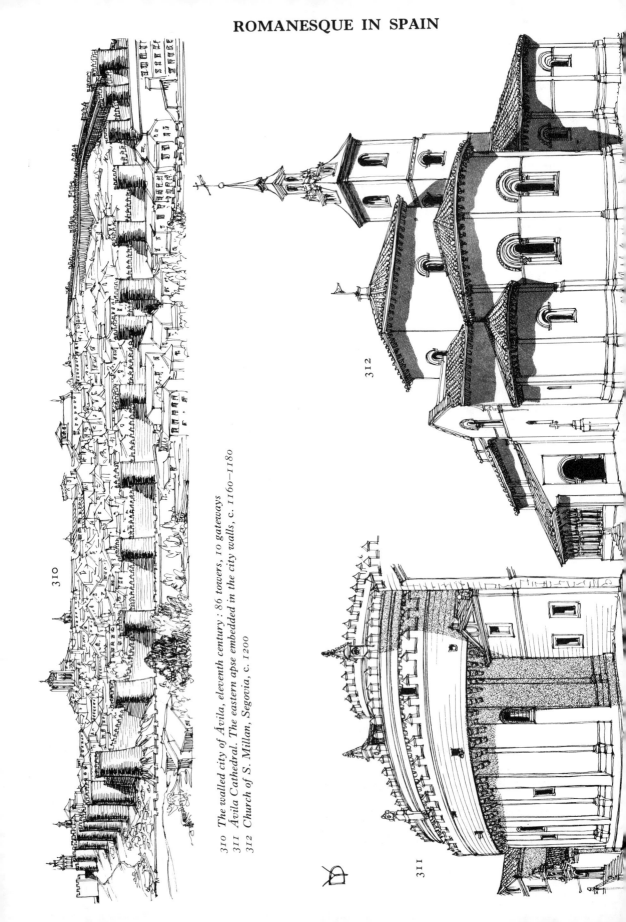

310 *The walled city of Ávila, eleventh century: 86 towers, 10 gateways*
311 *Ávila Cathedral. The eastern apse embedded in the city walls, c. 1160–1180*
312 *Church of S. Millán, Segovia, c. 1200*

310

312

311

established on a large, international scale and churches were built. The usual route was through Pamplona, Logroño, Santo Domingo de la Calzada, Burgos, Frómista, León and Astorga; bridges were constructed where necessary and information given to pilgrims to assist their journey, which generally took 14 days from Roncevaux in the Pyrenees. The Romanesque churches built along this route were, therefore, monastic and French in origin. Characteristically, they had a nave and aisles of similar height, and, as a result, no triforium or clerestory. The choir arm was short, ending in three parallel apses which abutted directly on to the transepts. The central, larger apse was used as a sanctuary and the choir was then moved westwards into the nave. The classic surviving example of this pattern is the *Church of S. Martín* at *Frómista*, which is roughly half-way between Burgos and León on the route. Fig. **307** shows the church from the south-east with its three apses, octagonal lantern over the crossing and twin, circular turrets at the west end. The aisled nave has four bays and the church is barrel vaulted throughout at almost the same height—there is neither triforium nor clerestory. The church, which was built in 1066, is as finely proportioned and designed as any in France of this period (**308** and **404**).

There are three interesting Romanesque churches in *Segovia*: S. Martín, S. Estéban and S. Millán, all of twelfth century origin. *S. Estéban* has a later tower (**309**) and *S. Millán* is the most unusual and striking. It has the normal tri-apsidal east end but the most interesting feature is the arcaded entrance (**312**). Nearby is the ancient town of *Ávila*, now comparatively small, but of great importance in the Middle Ages and, still surviving here, are the remarkable *city walls* and *gates*, the *cathedral* and the *Abbey Church* of *S. Vincent*. This last-named was begun in 1090 in the style of S. Martín of Frómista but was completed later under Burgundian auspices. It was a pilgrimage church and follows the classic Spanish pattern for such designs. The *city walls* are the best examples in Europe for their completeness and lack of alteration. Unlike Carcassonne in France they have not been extensively restored and compare more closely with Aigues Mortes (Chapter 5, p. 212). At Ávila the walls are of granite and there are 86 towers and 10 gate-

ways (**310**) all dating from the eleventh century. There is a battlemented parapet walk-way round which is very extensive (like that at York in England). The *Cathedral* apse provides a bastion in the city walls and this part of it was built 1088–91. The apse contains an ambulatory in this vast semi-circular projection (**311**).

Galicia, West and North-West Spain

In the western area the most interesting examples are at Zamora, Salamanca, Toro and Ciudad Rodrigo. *Zamora Cathedral* was begun in 1152. Typical of late Romanesque in Spain, the pointed arch is used predominantly and vaults are quadripartite in pointed barrel design. One of the most interesting features here is the central lantern which has eastern fish-tail covering like the examples in France at Poitiers, Angoulême and Fontevrault (**316**). The *Collegiate Church* at *Toro* (**318**) was built in 1160–1240 and has much in common with Zamora Cathedral; its vaults are almost entirely of pointed barrel type. The *Cathedral of Ciudad Rodrigo* (1165–1230) has domical octopartite vaulting and shows French influence on the Poitiers pattern. *Salamanca Old Cathedral*, so-called because it forms one unit with the much larger New Cathedral, was built in 1120–78 (**165, 379**). It is particularly noted for its dome with high drum, supported on pendentives and pierced with two rows of windows and crowned by a stone ribbed cupola (**313**). On the exterior is an octagonal spire, called the *Torre de Gallo*, after its weathercock. The only access to the interior of the Old Cathedral now is through the New.

The great *Church of Santiago* (S. James) *de Compostela* is a fitting climax to the end of the pilgrimage road. This is the greatest Romanesque church in Spain. The town itself, not very large, has been preserved in the centre and the traffic diverted round the outside. Inside the walls it is still, today, a haven of pilgrimage and peace. The exterior of the church is now largely Baroque, rebuilt in the eighteenth century, but the interior remains Romanesque on pilgrimage church lines. It was largely based on the design for S. Sernin in Toulouse and was started after but completed earlier than the French church (**423**). The nave has single aisles and is very long; it has a barrel vault while the aisles are cross-vaulted

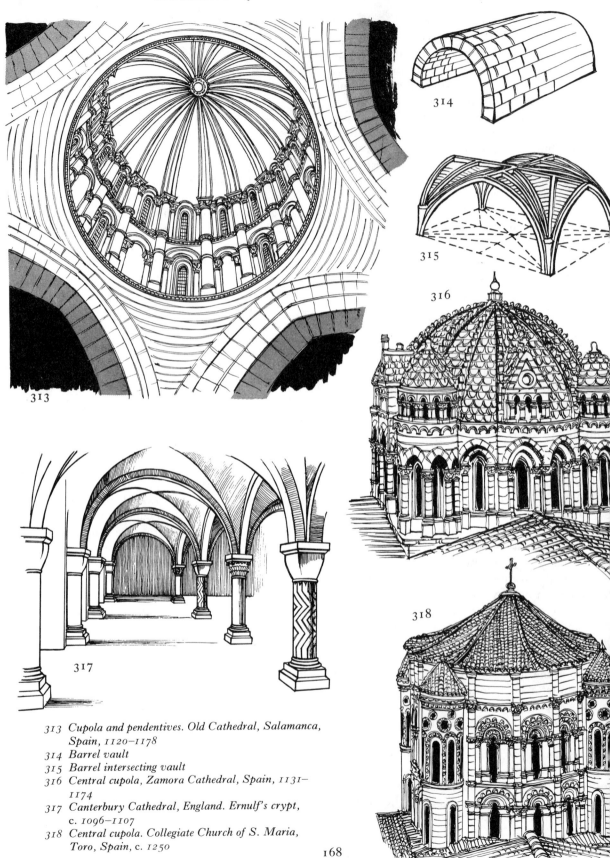

313 *Cupola and pendentives. Old Cathedral, Salamanca, Spain, 1120–1178*

314 *Barrel vault*

315 *Barrel intersecting vault*

316 *Central cupola, Zamora Cathedral, Spain, 1131–1174*

317 *Canterbury Cathedral, England. Ernulf's crypt, c. 1096–1107*

318 *Central cupola. Collegiate Church of S. Maria, Toro, Spain, c. 1250*

319

19   The nave looking east. The great pilgrimage church of S. James, Santiago de Compostela, Spain, begun 1077

(319). There are transepts and a French style chevet, with ambulatory and five radiating chapels. Apart from the interior, the south transept portico remains from the Romanesque period; the portico—*la Puerte de las Platerías*—was built in 1103; it has some fine sculpture of 1116 (396). The outstanding part of the building sculpturally, however, is the *Portico de la Gloria*, originally the façade but now approached via the classical stairway on the west front, from the square below. This Romanesque triple portico is sculptured by *Master Mateo* (who is buried in the church) and who worked on it from 1168—88. The statue of S. James the Apostle decorates the trumeau and on each side are statues of apostles, prophets and elders. The whole portico tells the story of Man's Trials and Salvation. It is one of the great examples of European Romanesque art (PLATES 26 and 36).

The Cistercian Abbeys

The important Benedictine Order had become wealthy and more worldly all over Europe and in Spain as in England, the Cistercian Order was founded and flourished with the aim of re-asserting the vows of poverty, austerity and dedication to a monastic life devoted to the original humble origins. The Cistercian Order in Spain, as in England, played an important part in establishing Gothic architecture. In England are abbeys such as Fountains and Rievaulx. Spain has many examples too. A number of them were largely built in the late Romanesque style and of these some survive in whole or in part. The churches are large, very simple and austere and have little of the richly carved doorways, capitals and mouldings of other Romanesque work. Among the more interesting examples are the *Abbeys* of *Moreruela*, 1169, near Zamora, which is ruined but retains a complete chevet, of *Veruela*, 1170, in Aragon and the famous *Abbey of Poblet*, 1151—96, in Catalonia. This has been altered greatly in later times and was neglected in the nineteenth century. Parts of the buildings, particularly the church interior and cloisters, are still very fine. The drawing in Fig. 306 shows the interior of the *Abbey Church* at *Meira* in Galicia. This church, *c.* 1190—1258, follows closely on its Burgundian pattern and is extremely austere. It is remotely situated in this small town high in the

mountains. The Romanesque is of Transitiona type, with wide pointed arches and barrel vault a clerestory but no triforium. On the façade, th portal still possesses the original and unusua doors and above is the typical circular window (378).

Portugal

The French influence here was even greater tha in Spain and in the eleventh century the norther region had broken free to become a satellite o Burgundy, though later it became independent There is, however, little Romanesque wor existing. Surviving examples include the *Churc* of *S. Salvador* at *Travanca*, the *Cathedral* a *Evora* and the *Church* of the *Convent of Christ* a *Tomar*, all twelfth century but with considerabl alterations in later periods. The best and mos typical Portugese example of Romanesque is th *Old Cathedral (Sé Velha)* in *Coimbra*, begu 1162. The east end (305) is tri-apsidal, there is square tower with cupola, which has Byzantin type coloured ceramic tiling, and the west faça has a fine portico, approached up a flight of step (388). The cathedral has a castellated, fortifie appearance and obviously incorporates Mosler features. The façade, in particular, is severe an in sheer, block form; it is impressive in it austere simplicity. The interior is very Roman esque. There is a barrel vaulted nave wit transverse arches and a triforium which has wide ambulatory supported over the full widt of the aisle vaults. The square tower is rib vaulte and its windows give good light to the cathedra

Germany

Romanesque architecture developed early i Germany. It was clearly related to the Lombar style of Northern Italy owing to the politica links between the two countries under the Hol Roman Empire. These ties were particularl strong during the Hohenstaufen dynasty in th twelfth and thirteenth century. The predominan characteristic adopted by the Germans fron Italian patterns was the conception of arcadin as an all-over pattern, especially on the apse The Germans developed their own style late and this was eminently suited to the character o the people, producing buildings which wer

GERMAN ROMANESQUE CATHEDRALS

320 Worms Cathedral from the south-west, c. 1110–1200
321 Speyer Cathedral from the north-east, c. 1110
322 Limburg Cathedral from the north-west. River Lahn in the foreground. c. 1215–35
323 Plan. Worms Cathedral

324 *Abbey Church of the Monastery of Maria Laach from the north-west, c. 1112 to thirteenth century*
325 *Plan. Maria Laach*

326 *Mainz Cathedral from the north-east, 1085–1239 (central tower completed 1361)*
327 *Interior, Mainz Cathedral looking east*

strong, dignified, austere, with limited decoration and fine masonry. A peculiarly German Romanesque feature is the church planned with an apse at each end of the building, west as well as east. Many important buildings have this characteristic, though the western apse was generally single and the eastern might be triple. This feature, which is thought to have developed from a desire for an apse and altar both for abbot and his monks at the east end, and for the bishop and laity at the west, gave no opportunity for masons and sculptors to decorate a deeply moulded western porch, as was usual in France or England. The entrance doorway on such churches as *Mainz, Worms* or *Speyer Cathedrals* are usually lateral transeptal ones. A second feature which characterises German Romanesque churches is the dramatic skyline pattern created by the multiplicity of towers, cupolas and turrets. It was common for larger churches to have one or two cupolas, often polygonal, over the crossing and nave (or choir) and four towers, two at each end. These towers were transeptal or set just behind the apses and were polygonal or circular in form. Circular towers are unusual in the Romanesque architecture of other European countries, except in northern Italy, but they are a common feature of German ones as at, for instance, *Worms Cathedral* (**320**). The German helm type of covering to the square or polygonal tower was especially typical of the Rhineland, of which the *Church of the Apostles* in *Cologne* is a notable example (**328**).

Romanesque architecture in Germany lasted very late, as it did in Lombardy. There are many examples which date from well into the thirteenth century in a style not much altered from 100 years earlier. Having established this effective, impressive mode of building, so suited to their race, the Germans seemed unwilling to abandon it. The majority of surviving buildings are in stone but there were originally a vast number of timber and half-timber (*Fachwerk*) constructions. All along the Baltic region brick building began early, owing to the lack of stone materials, but such work has mostly been altered later, in the Middle Ages, or was destroyed in the Second World War.

The external walls of the churches are decorated simply by pilaster strips and corbelled string courses with arcading, as in Lombardy.

Inside, the layout and execution are simple and austere. Stone vaulting developed fairly late and most of these vaults are replacements of the timber roofs. When vaults were used, the square bay pattern was adopted, with one nave bay being equal to two aisle ones as at *Worms Cathedral*. Some examples have a western atrium as at *Maria Laach Abbey Church* (**324**).

The Rhineland

Although most of the great churches and cathedrals of this area suffered greatly from damage inflicted in the Second World War, the region still possesses some impressive examples of German Romanesque architecture. The three famous cathedrals of Worms, Mainz and Speyer were all severely damaged, but are all now largely restored and rebuilt once more. Apart from wartime damage, *Worms Cathedral* is the least altered of the three in that it retains its Romanesque plan and general layout (**323**). It has east and west apses and there are two large, and four staircase, towers which break the skyline. It is a highly typical example of German work in its restrained, symmetrical severity. The entrances are in the aisles. Exterior decoration is by pilaster strips and arcading which continues round the church. The interior is completely vaulted on square bay pattern, one nave bay to two aisles (**320**).

Mainz Cathedral is immense and was altered in later periods when the crossing towers were rebuilt in different styles and houses were constructed abutting on to and becoming part of the cathedral flanks. Despite this, the vast red sandstone bulk of the cathedral towers above the severely damaged and consequently modern city, the impression it creates little affected by the trolley bus wires which cross the tourists' line of vision. The eastern end (**326**) illustrates the original German design, its apse surmounted by a gable end flanked by two towers. The interior (**327**) is plain and dignified.

Like Mainz, *Speyer Cathedral* is very large. Its west façade was rebuilt in the eighteenth and also in the nineteenth century. The remainder (except for parts devastated by war and now being renewed) retains its Romanesque characteristics and is accessible and attractively sited amongst the trees in a park (**321**). The crypt is the

328 *Church of the Apostles, Cologne, Germany. East end*
c. 1190–1200. (N/W tower missing)
329 *Church of S. Gereon, Cologne. East end c. 1160*
(west end severely damaged in second World War)

330 *Plan. Church of the Apostles*
331 *Interior. Church of Romainmôtier,*
Switzerland, c. 1000

earliest extant part of the cathedral, c. 1030, and is remarkable. It is large, with stout columns and cubiform capitals supporting a heavy groined vault. The nave is wide and long, with immense piers supporting a very high domical, groined vault. At the crossing, the vault is higher still (the loftiest Romanesque example in Europe) and has a great octagonal tower built on squinches. The nave arcade is high but there is no triforium between it and the round-headed clerestory windows.

Further north, but near the Rhine, is the magnificently preserved and untouched *Monastery* of *Maria Laach*. The *Abbey Church* was begun in 1093 and was built slowly over many years but all in one style. There are six towers, two large and four smaller, and three apses on the east side and one on the west, with an atrium in front of it. The narthex has 82 small columns and some beautifully carved capitals as well as a western doorway. Built of local stone, the church is simply and typically decorated by pilaster strips and corbel arches (**324, 325** and **410**). Inside, the church is austere and serene. The groined vault is carried on grouped piers.

Also on the Rhine are a number of interesting churches in and near *Cologne*. These all suffered damage, in the Second World War, varying from partial to total destruction. The most famous, that dedicated to the *Apostles*, was fortunately damaged least. Here is the classic pattern for the region, based on Lombard design, with trefoil, cruciform plan. There is a semi-circular apse at each transept and a further apse at the east end. The crossing is covered by a low, octagonal tower while the two staircase towers on either side rise higher still. The whole eastern end is arcaded round all the apses. The main towers (not all existing) are completed in German (Rhenish) helm roof style, a type of roofing rare outside Germany though there is an example still on the Saxon tower of Sompting Church in England **328** and **330**). Of the other Cologne Romanesque churches, *S. Martin* was destroyed but is now largely rebuilt while *S. Gereon* was badly damaged but the exterior is preserved at the eastern end. This view shows the wide semi-circular apse flanked by two tall towers, decorated by arcading **329**).

Apart from the Rhineland, Romanesque examples are scattered throughout Germany. Not far from the Rhine are the churches in Soest and Freckenhorst. In this area, the façades, like the Dutch churches of the period in Maastricht, are fortified castle wall exteriors. *S. Patroklus* in *Soest* has small corner towers and a tall gable with a vast western tower. *Freckenhorst Abbey Church* (**332**) is typical, with flanking, circular western towers and a cliff-like central mass with a tiny doorway at the bottom, tiny windows above and surmounted by a tall roof and turret. Behind this vast, *westwerk*, a long nave and aisles lead to a transept and two further, eastern towers. The masonry is good but rugged and the whole ensemble is imposing. Inside is a fine Romanesque font, c. 1130 (PLATE 33).

Also not far from the Rhine is *Limburg Cathedral* on the river Lahn. It is smaller than those of the Rhineland but is characteristic nevertheless. It is sited on top of a hill in an attractive old town overlooking (and reflected in) the river. Like Durham, it appears to grow out of the rocks above the river bank. It has seven towers, attractively grouped. The octagonal crossing tower rises high with its spire. The nave is short and the other towers make a compact composition. In date and style it is a Transitional or late Romanesque building and shows a French influence in its choir ambulatory (**322**).

The *Church* of *S. Quirin* at *Neuss* also has a cliff-face façade, arcaded and gabled, while above it rises the large, square tower; a typical, interesting example (**333**).

Further south, on the river Moselle, is *Trier* where the *Cathedral* and the *Liebfrauenkirche* form a group. The town was an important Roman centre and the cathedral incorporates a Roman building which occupied the site in 1019 when the cathedral was begun (**334**). The Liebfrauenkirche is of early Gothic date and makes a group side by side with the cathedral in a tree-lined square. In Bavaria the town of *Regensburg* on the Danube possesses the interesting *Church* of *S. Jakob* (the *Schottenkirche*) which has an elaborate portal, finely sculptured (**394** and **402**). The church is basilican with triapsidal sanctuary but has no transept.

In the north, on the borders of East Germany towards Berlin, is the *Abbey Church* of *Königslütter*. The carving and sculpture here is outstanding, particularly the apse corbelling and arcading and the cloister capitals and columns

332 Freckenhorst Abbey Church, Germany, c. 1130. Viewed from the south-west
333 Church of S. Quirin, Neuss, Germany. West front, begun c. 1209. Tower c. 1230

333

332

334

334 Trier Cathedral, Germany. From the west, 1016–47

335 Imperial Palace (Kaiserpfalz) Goslar, Germany, eleventh century (restored)

(**406** and **416**). Inside, the apse has painted decoration of a very high order. At *Hildesheim*, not far away, the town was badly damaged during World War II and the famous *Church* of *S. Michael* has had to be almost entirely rebuilt. Its magnificent sculptured bronze doors still exist but are now on view inside the church, hung on the inner side of the west portal. There are 16 panels depicting high relief figures on a low relief and incised background. The standard of craftmanship is remarkable for bronze work of this date, 1015. At *Goslar*, in the region of the Harz Mountains, the *Kaiserpfalz* here was restored in the nineteenth century on its original pattern, 1132. The main hall of the palace is built over a large undercroft and has twin naves with columns supporting a timber roof. A balcony opens from the hall on to the façade through a triple arched opening. The building includes a two-storeyed chapel and the imperial apartments (**335**). Nearby is the site of the cathedral which is now destroyed but whose narthex still remains, with its original entrance (**409**).

Austria

Remains are scarce as most of the work has been rebuilt at a later date. *S. Stephen's Cathedral* in *Vienna* still has a Romanesque wing though it was built in the mid-thirteenth century. The Giant's Door here is finely carved with notable multi-column jambs, foliated capitals and typically Romanesque sculpture (**336**). In the *Cathedral* at *Gurk* there is a vast crypt possessing 100 columns which support a groined vault dating from 1160.

The round columns have cubiform capitals and moulded bases.

Switzerland

A number of small country churches exist with remains of this period. *Romainmôtier Church* was originally part of a Cluniac Monastery, built in the early tenth century. The present building dates from about 1000 and is basically in Lombard style. The interior shows many original features such as the columns, capitals, nave arcade and apsidal end (**331**). In the *Church* of *S. Jean* at *Grandson* the nave capitals are of varied Romanesque design, depicting animals, birds and demons. The vault is in stone, in barrel form (**418**). The *Church* at *Zillis* has the most remarkable painted wooden ceiling, illustrating in panels, scenes from the New Testament in rich

336 Detail of the Reisetor (West Portal) S. Stephen's Cathedral, Vienna, 1258–67

Plate 33
Detail, font. Freckenhorst Abbey Church,
Germany, 1129
Plate 34
Cloister garth lavatory cistern. Much Wenlock
Priory, England, *c.* 1160
Plate 35
Column support, porch. Trogir Cathedral,
Yugoslavia, *c.* 1240. Master Radovan
Plate 36
S. James. Portico de la Gloria, Cathedral of
Santiago de Compostela, Spain. 1166–88, Mateo

Plate 37
South portal arch
mouldings. Lund
Cathedral, Sweden
Plate 38
Painted ceiling, Zil
Church, Switzerlan
Scenes of the New
Testament. 12th
century. Restored
19th and 20th
centuries

ROMANESQUE CHURCHES IN THE LOW COUNTRIES

337 *Tournai Cathedral, Belgium. From the north, 1066–1338. Nave (right side) Romanesque, Transepts (centre) Transitional, Choir (left side) Gothic*

338 *S. Mary's Church, Maastricht, Holland from the east, tenth century and later*

339 *Interior of apsidal transept, Tournai Cathedral, twelfth century*

colours. The ceiling has been restored in the nineteenth and twentieth centuries (PLATE 38). *Basle Minster* was originally Romanesque but much of it is now Gothic. The east end retains its Romanesque characteristics and the *Galluspforte* (the portal named after S. Gall) is a twelfth century design with elaborate sculptured decoration. The Minister has a magnificent position on the top of the hill above the town and with a steep hillside descending on its east side towards the river Rhine (**385**).

Belgium

In comparison with Germany, France, England or Italy, little Romanesque architecture survives in the Low Countries, in Scandinavia or in Eastern Europe. In Belgium the outstanding example is *Tournai Cathedral* which, although added to and altered later, is certainly one of the finest Romanesque buildings in Europe. It is large and tall and difficult of access and to view due to its position in the centre of the town, closely hedged in by other buildings. The east end of the Cathedral is Gothic, but the long nave

is still Romanesque and the transepts are in a Transitional form of the style; the two parts of the cathedral form a marked contrast, particularly inside the building, and a useful study. The cathedral exterior, largely built of black Tournai marble, has a large central tower and spire and four spired towers grouped around it and flanking the north and south apses (though it was originally designed for nine towers). The towers, like the semi-circular ended transepts, are Transitional. The nave dates from 1110; it is lower than the Gothic choir and still has its original fenestration (**337**). The interior of Tournai Cathedral is magnificent. The nave is simple Romanesque, the transepts in Transitional style (**339**) are higher, having a tall tower arcade, a shallower triforium arcade with a smaller sub-triforium above, before reaching the clerestory, giving lofty arms to the interior and suitably connecting without awkwardness the long, low nave and short high choir. The crossing has very tall piers and arches under the central tower.

There are a number of *castles* in Belgium with work dating from Romanesque times. In *Antwerp* the castle in the port area, called the Steen, dates

340 Antwerp Castle (The Steen), Belgium, tenth century onwards

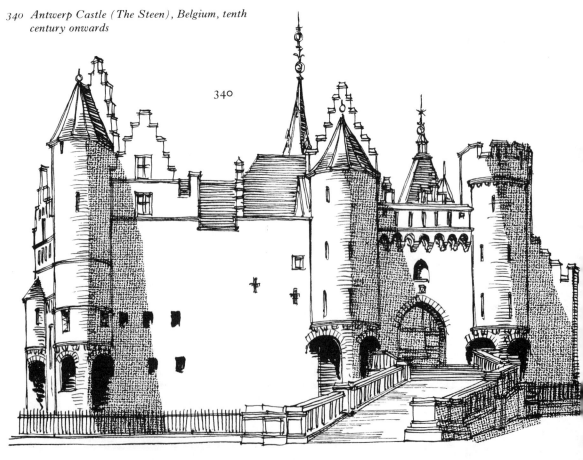

ROMANESQUE ARCHITECTURE IN YUGOSLAVIA

341 *Zadar Cathedral, west front, twelfth and thirteenth centuries*
342 *S. Grisogono, Zadar from the south-east,* c.
343 *Trogir Cathedral from the east,* 1206–59
344 *Trogir Cathedral plan*

from the tenth century onwards and still has Romanesque doorway and window openings inside (**340**), while in *Ghent* the *Gravensteen Castle*, which belonged to the Counts of Flanders, has interesting remains. The hall dates from the ninth century and is divided in the centre by a row of four circular columns with simple leaf capitals, like the design in S. John's Chapel in the Tower of London (**300**). The entrance barbican has a Romanesque doorway and window openings. In the exterior walls prison chambers still survive which are of Romanesque date, while the audience chamber possesses a fine wall-fireplace.

Holland

The chief Romanesque work here is in *Maastricht*, which was at the centre of a prosperous region in the twelfth century. The *Church of S. Servaas* has a Romanesque east end with apse and twin towers. *S. Mary's Church* is like Freckenhorst Abbey Church on the west front and has *west-werk* pattern in the form of a formidable fortified wall with small twin towers. At the east it has a large semi-circular apse and Rhenish capped towers (**338**). The interior is simple and also in German style.

Eastern and Central Europe

Most contemporary building here was in timber and has not survived. The tradition in this region was, as in pre-Romanesque times in Western Europe, to build in solid wood, not half-timber work as was the western European method during the Middle Ages. In the east the forest reserves were so vast that solid timber construction was possible in quantity.

In *Yugoslavia*, particularly on the Adriatic Coast, the Italian influences led to Italian-style stone churches and cathedrals of which a number survive. In *Zadar* the Cathedral and the *Church of S. Grisogono* are good examples, the latter especially showing strong Italian influence; both Lombard and Pisan (**342**). The *Cathedral* has much in common with contemporary Norman cathedrals on the Italian southern Adriatic coast opposite. Begun in 1105, the east end is Lombard but the west front has a tower like that at Trani (**374**) and Tuscan type arcading on the gable

façade and the three Romanesque doorways (**341**). *Trogir Cathedral*, despite its late date, 1240, is Romanesque in style and has a magnificent entrance portal by *Master Radovan*, the Slav sculptor who had been trained in Apulia (PLATE 35). The church is basilican and has three apses at the east end (**343** and **344**). It is stone vaulted throughout, with massive piers to support the vaults.

The Lombardic influence also extended to *Hungary* and the monastic orders. Benedictine and, later, Cistercian, built a number of abbeys and churches. Many of these have been rebuilt, like the *Cathedrals* of *Esztergom* and *Székesfehérvar*, although some original sculpture survives in both these examples. The chief monument in the country is the *Cathedral of Pécs* (Fünfkirchen), rebuilt about 1150 and restored mainly in the nineteenth century. This, the oldest cathedral in Hungary, is of a German pattern, like Bamberg, with four corner towers and arcading decorating the whole building. The east end is triapsidal and the choir is raised high above the superb crypt. The cathedral possesses some fine capitals and sculpture. A smaller Romanesque church survives at Lébeny, near Györ. This is a remarkable example in its purity of style; it was restored to the original design in the nineteenth century (**345, 346**) and inside the tall nave has a lofty, stone barrel vault. The clerestory windows are small and there is no triforium. The nave arcade has round arches behind which are lower aisles. The semi-circular chancel is covered by a semi-dome. The *Church of the Premonstratensian Abbey* at *Zsámbék*, near Budapest, is one of the oldest in Hungary. It was built in the later twelfth century and altered again about 1258. The architect, a Frenchman, is said to have based his church on the Cathedral of Notre Dame in Paris. This impressive stone building has a commanding sight on a hill above the surrounding plain. The interior is partly ruined but there is a fine Romanesque façade (**347**). Among other Romanesque churches are the decorative example at *Ják*, with its richly sculptured doorway and chevron ornament and the interesting churches of *Század*, *Ócsa* and *Karcsa*.

In *Rumania*, the *Cathedral of Alba Iulia* (Gyulafehérvar) was completed about 1239 but reconstruction was necessary after the Tartan invasion of 1242 (**348** and **349**). Some of it is now

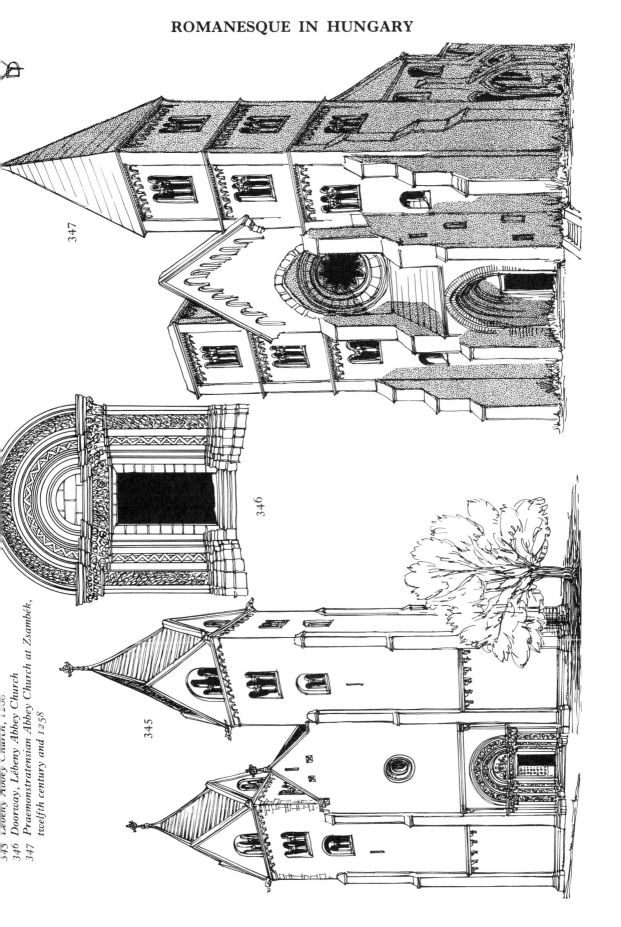

345 *Lébeny Abbey Church, 1208*
346 *Doorway, Lébeny Abbey Church*
347 *Praemonstratensian Abbey Church at Zsámbék,
    twelfth century and 1258*

348 Façade of the Cathedral at Alba Iulia, Rumania.
Re-built in Romanesque style 1272–91. Gothic and
Renaissance additions
349 Plan of cathedral

Gothic and later, but the Lombard/German plan is still distinguishable, as are the nave supports of alternating columns and piers. There are two western towers with a high, open vaulted porch between (Chapter 5, p.301).

Further north, in *Poland*, extensive Romanesque work in stone and/or brick was carried out, but much of this has been altered through the centuries and the limited remains suffered damage in the Second World War.

The capital of the north-central area, and its cultural centre, was *Gniezno*, a not very large town about 30 miles south-east of Poznan. Pagan until the tenth century, Gniezno became the seat of the first Polish archbishopric in A.D. 1000, when the stone, rotunda building there became the Metropolitan *Cathedral*. This was replaced by a second Romanesque cathedral in 1097 which, in turn, was largely demolished when the present Gothic cathedral took its place (**262**). Remains of both the earlier cathedrals can be seen in the walls of the present building, while the magnificent bronze doors from the second cathedral, with their twelfth century Romanesque sculpture in 18 relief panels representing the life of S. Adalbert, are now displayed in one of the chapels of the choir. These are in low relief and are fine examples.

The *Cathedral church* of *S. Mary* at *Plock* (north-west of Warsaw), a twelfth century granite structure, which also had some fine bronze doors

(now in Novgorod Cathedral in the U.S.S.R.), is typical of such Romanesque structures in that it retains little of the original work. Better preserved are the *Collegiate church* of *SS. Peter and Paul* at *Kruszwica*, which has a Baroque interior, the circular *Church of S. Procopius* (*c.* 1160) and the *Church of the Holy Trinity*, both in *Strelzno*. These small towns are in the Gniezno region. The *Abbey Church* at *Trzebnica*, on the outskirts of Wroclaw (Breslau), still has some of its Romanesque (1219) exterior, but the interior is entirely Baroque (p. 446).

A number of Romanesque structures were built in *Cracow* on *Wawel Hill*, where a royal castle and church were erected, surrounded by a walled, fortified town. The city developed chiefly after 1040, when the residence of the kings was transferred from Gniezno to Cracow, and stone buildings began to replace the wooden ones. The earliest Romanesque structure was the Rotunda *Chapel* dedicated to the *Virgin*, built in the tenth century. In circular form, with a surmounting cupola, it had four adjacent apses, each with a semi-circular roofing. In its simple manner it is like other contemporary examples in Germany, Yugoslavia, Italy or Greece, and the building style resembles some Anglo-Saxon structures in England (**351**). Later called the Chapel of SS. Felix and Adauctus, its walls are incorporated in the later palace.

The first Romanesque *cathedral* was then begun (*c.* 1020) (**350**) and this was largely replaced in the early twelfth century by another, larger one. It was designed on German lines, with four large towers in the angles of the cruciform plan. Remains of this building exist in the present structure, of which the *crypt* of *S. Leonard* is the chief part. It is situated under the cathedral nave and has a typical vault supported on rows of columns (**352**).

Not far from the Wawel Hill in Cracow is the *Church* of *S. Andrew* (1086), which, despite a Baroque interior, is a fairly well preserved Romanesque building, especially in its fortified, massive walls.

In *Czechoslovakia* Romanesque structures were being erected from the early tenth century, in the form of castles and churches. Remains are, in many cases, little more than fragmentary, as in the *cathedral* on *Castle Hill* in *Prague*. The present, fine Gothic building (p. 245) replaced

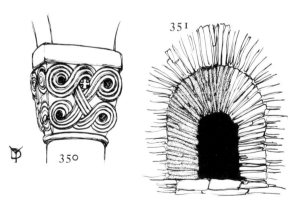

350 Capital from the first Romanesque cathedral on Wawel Hill, Cracow, Poland, early eleventh century

351 Window opening from the Chapel of the Virgin (S.S. Felix and Adauctus)

352 *S. Leonard's Crypt from the Romanesque cathedral at Cracow, 1090–1115. Situated under present cathedral*
353 *Basilica of S. George, Castle Hill, Prague, Czechoslovakia, from 1142*

two earlier Romanesque ones. These are now only visible in the foundations excavated and preserved under and near the cathedral. The nearby *castle* retains Romanesque portions, like the barrel vaulted Romanesque hall and parts of the mural towers, but the chief surviving building from this period on Castle Hill is the *Basilica of S. George*, built originally in 920, but the Romanesque church dates from its rebuilding in 1142 after a fire. The façade is now Baroque, but inside it retains its simple Romanesque form, though it was extensively restored in the late nineteenth century (**353**).

Remains exist of one or two stone Romanesque rotunda churches in *Prague*, but these are in poor condition and are, in general, small and primitive. A typical example is that of *S. Longinus*.

Scandinavia

For the majority of building, wood was the chief material and little has survived, though rebuilding has often been in similar traditional style. Masonry was used for important, ecclesiastical work, especially in the south and some of this work is extant. In this material Scandinavia was strongly influenced by foreign designs and workers, in general, Denmark by Germany,

France and Holland, Norway by England, and Sweden by all sources.

Denmark

In this flat country building materials available were, apart from timber, limestone, brick and flint. Masonry developed traditionally at the same time as Norman England, but most of the buildings have been altered. Amongst surviving examples are the cathedral at Ribe in South Jutland, begun c. 1130 and Viborg Cathedral in North Jutland, of granite, from c. 1140. The large *cathedral* at *Ribe* is situated in the centre of the small, old market town. Like Lund Cathedral in Sweden, it is a mixture of Rhineland and Italian Lombard designs. The exterior is severely Romanesque with a gabled façade, transeptal towers and spires and an apsidal east end. The interior, though restored, is based on the original pattern, though with later vaults and enlarged clerestory windows (**354**). *Viborg Cathedral*, though still on original lines, is extensively restored and so possesses that machine finished appearance typical of Scandinavian nineteenth century work. It has twin west towers and gables with similar eastern towers flanking the apse.

Several large *abbey churches* survive, mainly built in brick, and all carefully restored. The two

354

354 *Ribe Cathedral, Denmark, begun* c. *1130*

ROMANESQUE IN DENMARK AND SWEDEN

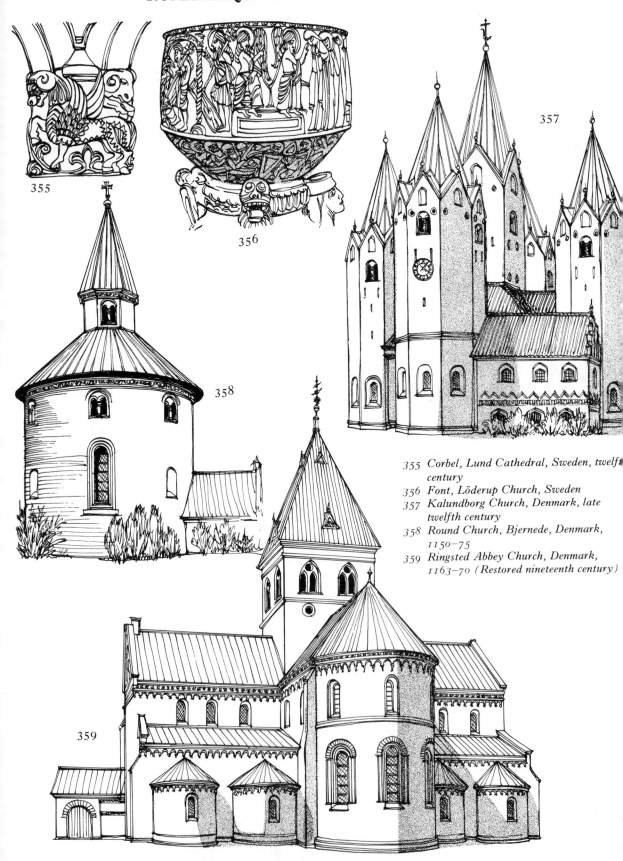

355 Corbel, Lund Cathedral, Sweden, twelfth century

356 Font, Löderup Church, Sweden

357 Kalundborg Church, Denmark, late twelfth century

358 Round Church, Bjernede, Denmark, 1150–75

359 Ringsted Abbey Church, Denmark, 1163–70 (Restored nineteenth century)

chief examples are close together on Zealand: Ringsted Abbey and Sorø Abbey, both of brick. The *Abbey Church* of *S. Benedict* at *Ringsted* is on Latin cross plan with apsidal east end and a later crossing tower (**359**). Inside, it is more Scandinavian than Ribe. It has no triforium and small, round-headed clerestory windows. *Sorø Abbey* has a very similar interior treatment but outside it is large, long and low.

The most original and interesting Romanesque building in Scandinavia is the *Church* at *Kalundborg*, north-west of Sorø on Zealand. Also of brick, it is large and imposing and, despite restoration, has a Medieval feeling still. On Greek cross plan, it has one square tower over the crossing and an octagonal one over each of the four arms (**357**). It is a centralised structure, a Scandinavian version of a Byzantine theme. There are four simple columns supporting the crossing; all arms are barrel vaulted.

There is a tradition in some parts of Denmark for *round churches*, probably based on Eastern European origins. This is particularly so on the *Island of Bornholm* where these distinctive buildings were used sometimes as fortresses. They have single, central piers supporting conical roofs. The best examples are at Østerlars, Ny, and Nylar. In *Zealand* the example at *Bjernede* survives (**358**). The lower part is of stone, the upper of brick. Inside, four large stone columns on torus moulding and square bases support a quadripartite ribbed vault on their cushion capitals, while groined vaults cover the encircling ambulatory.

Sweden

Timber was the chief material and the stave churches of the later Medieval period were influenced by this tradition. Christianity gained a hold here later than in Denmark but was established by the twelfth century and the Cistercians began to found monasteries soon after, as at *Varnhem* and *Alvastra*. The early Christian influence came from England from the tenth century onwards and its principal centre was at *Uppsala*. Architectural influences from outside were strong and, apart from England, included France, Russia and Byzantium. The work in Sweden was simple, sometimes crude but not unattractive. The outstanding *cathedral* of the

period to survive is at *Lund*, in Skåne, which was begun about 1080. Built in limestone, it was extensively restored in the nineteenth century when the Rheno-Lombardic west front took its final form. The apsidal east end, which resembles Speyer in Germany without the flanking towers (**355** and **360**), is largely in its original design, as is also the south portal (PLATE 37) and the crypt. This is very fine, groin vaulted throughout and supported on cushion capitalled columns with varied shafts (**368**). The interior, despite restoration, has a Romanesque effect (**362**). It is severe and built on monumental lines. There is no triforium and clerestory windows are tiny. The choir is on a higher level than the nave built, in Italian Romanesque fashion, over the crypt.

Most of the Swedish Romanesque stone churches are tall, with semi-circular eastern apses, lofty nave and choir and tall towers. The churches are wide and are generally vaulted. Typical examples include the late Romanesque *Church* at *Lärbro* on the Island of Gotland. Of German, fortified type, like Freckenhorst, is the *Church* at *Husaby* in Skaraborg. This was originally a stave church. In 1057 an immense stone tower was added. This square tower has circular turrets on each side, the whole making a fortified place of retreat. About 1090, the stave church was demolished and the stone church added to the tower (**361**).

While the fortified tower façade at Husaby shows German influence, the body of the church is more English in derivation. Also English in pattern are the remains of the three Romanesque churches at *Sigtuna*, near Lake Mälar. *S. Olav* is the most complete of these stone churches (**369**); *S. Per* shows a square tower and part of the nave but *S. Lars* is only fragmentary. They were all made of large, irregularly cut stone blocks and of simple cruciform structure.

Swedish Romanesque churches, like their English counterparts, are noted for their carved stone *fonts*. Outstanding examples are those at *Löderup Church* in Skåne (**358**) and *Varnhem Abbey Church* near Skara (**366**).

As in Norway, the first churches from the early days of Christianity in Sweden were of wood. These were generally of log structure, with corner joint method or timber framed with in-filling of boards. The commonest type, also as in Norway, was the stave church, but few examples

ROMANESQUE IN SWEDEN

360

361

362

360 *Lund Cathedral from the e*
   from c. 1140
361 *Fortified Church at Husaby*
   from 1057
362 *Lund Cathedral nave*
363 *Font, Varnhem Abbey Chu*
   thirteenth century

36

survive in Sweden. One is the *stave church* at *Hedared* in Västergötland. It is small, consisting of nave and chancel. Restored, it is in good condition and retains its later, eighteenth century furniture and wall paintings. The staves rest on a wood sill.

The little wooden *church* of *Sôdra Råda*, remotely situated in rural surroundings near the vast inland sea of Lake Vänern, dates from about 1300. The exterior is shingled and very simple, but inside, the nave and chancel roof and walls are painted all over. It is reminiscent of the Swiss church of Zillis (p. 178), showing circles filled with figure compositions depicting biblical scenes. The style of work too is much like Zillis, though these are mainly fifteenth century paintings and less restored. The work is very fine.

Norway

Architectural influence here is not notable since timber has been for centuries the traditional building material. Most of the work is of later date, though building styles changed only slowly. It is a remote country with difficult communica-tions, climate and geography. These factors created an original architectural form which was less closely related to the rest of European development than work in Denmark or southern Sweden.

Contacts and connections with the British Isles were close and the *stone churches* show this influence. From about 1100 such churches were built, very much in Norman style. *S. Magnus' Cathedral* at *Kirkwall* in Orkney (then under Norse control) shows a close relationship to English Norman cathedrals, as does also *Stavanger Cathedral,* which was begun *c.* 1130. It still has a Romanesque nave with large circular columns; these have varying types of cushion capitals, and chevron decoration remains on one or two of the nave arcade arches (**364** and **366**). There is a large, semi-circular headed chancel arch leading into the Gothic choir, which is at a higher level than the nave. The cathedral is all of stone, quite small, but despite restoration a good example of Anglicised Norwegian Roman-esque building and the finest in Norway.

The smaller stone churches are generally very simple and most have been greatly altered. *S.*

364 The nave, Stavanger Cathedral, Norway, 1125–50. Modern roof and seventeenth century pulpit

364

ROMANESQUE IN NORWAY AND SWEDEN

365 *Stave construction, Lom Church, Norway,*
thirteenth century
366 *South doorway capital, Stavanger Cathedral,*
Norway, twelfth century
367 *Doorway detail, Borgund Stave Church*
368 *Crypt column, Lund Cathedral, Sweden,*
twelfth century

369 *Plan, S. Olav's Church, Sigtuna, Sweden,*
twelfth century
370 *Dragon finial, Borgund Church*
371 *Borgund Stave Church, Norway, from the*
south-east, c. 1150
372 *Nave capital, Urnes Stave Church, Norway, c. 1125*
373 *Dragon finial, Gol Stave Church, Norway*

Mary's Church in *Bergen* is one example. It has a plain exterior with two western towers. The interior is mainly in plain, massive Romanesque style with nave arcade and triumphal arch to the chancel; there is a triforium but no clerestory. The homogeneity of this monumental Norman workmanship contrasts with the crude, over-decorated Baroque pulpit, altar and other, later decoration.

Wooden Churches

The *mast* or *stave* churches of Norway are now unique in Europe and were built during the whole of the Middle Ages from the eleventh century to the Reformation, after which timber churches based on the Eastern European pattern were more usual. There were, at one time, over 500 of these churches extant; now only a handful survive and these are largely restored. The method of construction is different from that of Romanesque stone building. Here, the roof is not supported on the walls, but each part of the church is separately supporting. The walls (the stave screens) are self-contained units and rest upon the ends of timber sleepers but do not take the weight or thrust. The whole church is based on a skeleton framework, the supporting roof poles are placed on top of the intersecting ground sills and there are cross beams on top of the poles. The design is based on the timber ship building pattern in which each section is a self-sufficient unit. The most advanced type of stave church has another row of poles or pillars inside the four which frame the external wall and this row supports its own part of the divided roof. The interiors of these churches are tall and dark and bear strong similarities to inverted ships.

The finest, least altered examples of these churches are at Borgund and Urnes. *S. Andrew's Church* at *Borgund* is inland from the end of the Sognfjord, near Laerdal (**371**). It dates from mid-twelfth century and is nearly 50 feet high, built in six stages. Its height is the striking feature and this is emphasised by the spire. The highest roofs terminate in dragon's heads (**370**) (the Viking art

symbol). The construction is based on 12 'masts', or posts of wood, standing on four sleepers or sills under the floor which enclose the plan. The name 'mast' comes from these pillars and the alternative 'stave' derives from the name given to the wall screen sections. The masts extend upwards to support the central roof and are joined together with three stages of horseshoe timber arches and timber boarding. At the east end is a rectangular choir and later apse. The inside is plain; the interior of the steeple is not roofed over so the construction is visible. Outside is a richly carved doorway (**367**).

The *Church* at *Urnes* (Ornes) is at the top of a small village built on a hill overlooking the Lusterfjord, which branches northwards from the end of the Sognfjord. There is no road link with Laerdal, Kaupanger or Årdal and the only means of access for visitors is by hiring a small boat across the Lusterfjord from Solvorn. In this fine, lonely situation, the little church is in good condition. It is a combination of two old structures, one of about 1130–50 and the other rather older. Despite some later rebuilding it still possesses much work from the oldest stave church in Norway. Of especial interest are the exterior carvings on the north portal and the carved capitals inside (**372** and PLATE 28).

Other surviving (though much reconstructed) examples remain at Lom, Kaupanger, Fantoft and in the Oslo Museum. *Lom Church* has a fine mountain situation near Gudbrandsdal. It is a large stave church with later transepts and spire. Of especial interest is the interior stave construction (**365**). This type of S. Andrew's cross structure can also still be seen in the *stave church* in the Norsk Folkemuseum at Bydøy Park across the ferry from Oslo. The church comes from *Gol* in Hallingdal and dates from 1200; it was re-erected in the museum in 1885. The exterior is very picturesque, though reconstructed, and still has dragon finials and carvings (**373**). The examples at *Kaupanger* (Sognfjord), built *c.* 1200 but rebuilt in 1862, and at *Fantoft*, near Bergen are simpler but also of considerable interest.

ROMANESQUE TOWERS

374 Zadar Cathedral, Yugoslavia, thirteen[th] century

375 Canterbury Cathedral, England, Norm[an] tower, south side, c. 1100

376 Angoulême Cathedral, France, west to[wer,] twelfth century

377 Amalfi Cathedral, Italy, campanile, twelfth century

WINDOWS: SEVENTH CENTURY TO 1200

Meira Abbey Church, Spain
Salamanca Old Cathedral, Spain
Church of S. Miguel de la Escalada, Spain
Church of S. Miguel de Liño, Spain
Trani Cathedral, Italy

383 Modena Cathedral, Italy
384 Angoulême Cathedral, France
385 Basle Minster, Switzerland
386 Worth Church, England
387 Castle Rising Church, England

388 West porch, Church of S. Nicola, Bari, Italy, 1098
389 West porch, Church of S. Trophime, Arles,
France, 1150–80

390 West porch, Modena Cathedral, Italy, twelfth cen
391 West portico, Abbey Church, S. Gilles,
France, 1140–1195

392 Brixworth Church, England
393 Church of S. Juan, Baños de Cerrato, Spain
394 Church of S. Jakob, Regensburg, Germany
395 Lincoln Cathedral, England
396 Pilgrimage Church of Santiago de Compostela, Spain
397 Sé Velha (the Old Cathedral), Coimbra, Portugal
398 Abbaye-aux-Hommes (S. Étienne), Caen, France

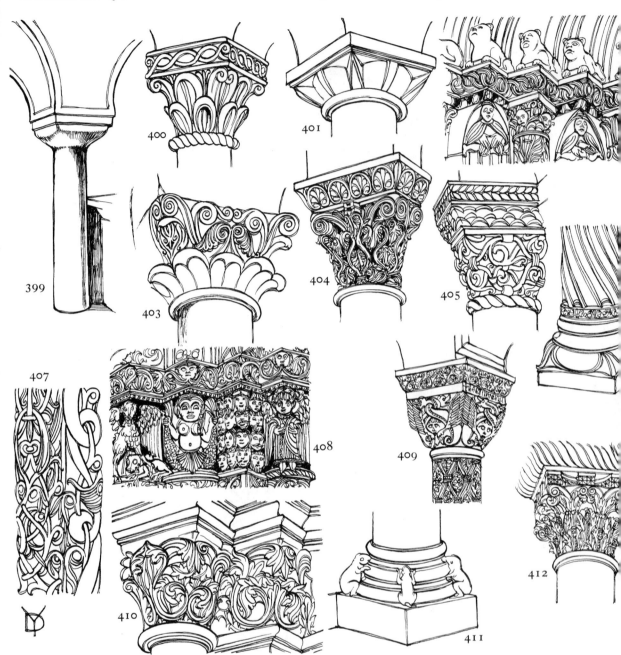

399 *Crypt, S. George, Oberzell, Reichenau, Germany, ninth century*

400 *S. Salvador de Priesca, Villaviciosa, Spain, Visigothic, 921*

401 *S.S. Peter and Paul, Niederzell, Reichenau, Germany, 1050*

402 *S. Jakob, Schottenportal, Regensburg, Germany, c. 1180*

403 *S. Miguel de la Escalada, Spain, Visigothic, 913*

404 *S. Martín, Frómista, Spain, 1066*

405 *Leominster Priory Church, Norman, England*

406 *Cloister, Königslütter Abbey Church, Germany, c. 1135*

407 *Kilpeck Church, England, c. 1140*

408 *S. Michele, Pavia, Italy, 1188*

409 *Narthex, former cathedral at Goslar, Germany, c. 1150. Built on to the 1050 cathedral. Cathedral demolis 1819, narthex remains*

410 *Abbey Church of Maria Laach, Germany, c. 1220*

411 *and* 412 *Abbey Church of S. Madeleine, Vézelay, France, 1120–30*

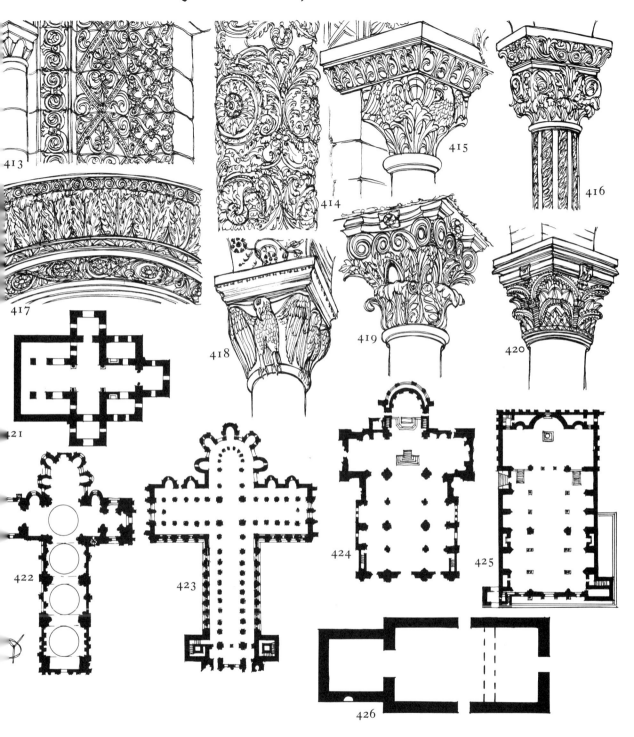

413 Porch, Malmesbury Abbey, England
414 Column, baptistery, Pisa, Italy
415 Doorway capital, S. Michel d'Aiguilhe, Le Puy, France
416 Cloister capital, Königslütter Abbey, Germany
417 West doorway voussoirs, Bitonto Cathedral, Italy
418 Nave capital, S. Jean, Grandson, Switzerland
419 West portal, S. Trophîme, Arles, France
420 Nave capital, S. Pietro, Tuscània, Italy
421 Plan, S. Pedro de la Nave, Spain, Visigothic
422 Plan, Angoulême Cathedral, France
423 Plan, Santiago de Compostela, Spain
424 Plan, S. Michele, Pavia, Italy
425 Plan, S. Nicola, Bari, Italy
426 Plan, Boarhunt Church, England

5
Gothic: 1150–1600

It is a truism that artistic endeavour is influenced by current fashion. So the designs of one era are often rejected by another, usually in reaction and because of the human need for change. Such reaction gave birth to two at least of the names applied to architectural styles. These are Gothic and Baroque; both misnomers. They were coined in a later age as terms of disapprobation, even contempt. It was Giorgio Vasari who applied the word 'Gothic' to Medieval architecture. Vasari, a sixteenth century Mannerist architect and historian, was only expressing the thinking of his time in equating Medieval architecture with barbarism. To a post-Renaissance intellectual, the Middle Ages had advanced only a small way beyond the sixth century Goths; it was the Renaissance which brought greatness to architecture.

Similarly, the term 'Middle Ages' was applied to this period in the seventeenth century by a German scholar. He likened it to an intermediate era between the collapse of the Roman Empire in 476 A.D. and the re-birth of classicism in the Renaissance ideals of the fifteenth century. To him also it represented a period of barbarism and decline.

Seen from a more distant perspective, we can appreciate that Gothic architecture (for the term is now synonymous with Medieval building) was a great art form in its own right. It emerged from Romanesque into a specific style, different from but no less fine than the works of the Renaissance. Its conception and inspiration were totally dissimilar from the later classical form but, diverse and richly variable as it is throughout Europe, Gothic architecture is characteristically definable wherever it is to be found.

The all pervasive influence during the Middle Ages was Christianity. By 1200 its dominance extended over most of Europe when the Western church from Rome had met and joined the Greek centre from Constantinople. Churches and cathedrals, in stone, brick and timber were built in increasing numbers all over Europe from Scandinavia to Sicily and Portugal to Russia. The Church was the essence of being to Medieval peoples whether in town or village. Portal sculptures, wall paintings and mosaics created in each church a pictorial record of the Bible stories and teaching. To an illiterate population they gave tangible reality to their beliefs. Despite the happenings of the 400 years which have passed since the last of these buildings were being constructed, the quantity which exists in all European countries is testimony to the ability of the builders and the truly vast numbers of structures which were put up between 1150 and 1550.

Though the Church was the great patron of the Middle Ages, the rising wealth of the merchant classes, especially in the fourteenth and fifteenth centuries, led to the erection of many fine secular buildings: town halls, trade and guild halls, palaces, manor houses, town mansions and bridges. Castles and towns were still fortified but, in the later Middle Ages, as prosperity and a greater peacefulness spread to many parts of Europe, the fortification diminished and both towns and individual buildings were extended and elaborated.

It is difficult to pinpoint the exact beginning of a new movement. Gothic architecture evolved from the Romanesque style but its characteristics are different. The feature usually described as predominant in Gothic buildings is the use of the pointed arch in place of the semi-circular one which had been employed in both Roman and Romanesque structures. In the past it has been stated categorically that the originator of the Gothic style was France. Late nineteenth century historians, either French or French orientated scholars in England or Germany, asserted this clearly. It is undoubtedly true that the earliest buildings completed in the Gothic style come from the Île de France, a small area in the neighbourhood of Paris, and that the classic pattern of northern Gothic cathedral was established here, witness such famous examples as *Notre Dame, Paris, Reims, Amiens* and *Laon*. It cannot be argued so categorically that this was the sole source of the style in the twelfth century or that it would not soon have developed in a similar manner elsewhere if the Île de France had not then produced it.

Great movements in all subjects—arts, sciences, medicine—begin and establish themselves because the climate is ready to receive them. The need is there and so is the ability to create the new development. In the case of Gothic architecture, the pointed arch was evolved because it became the key to constructing buildings which were then desirable. The low pitched timber roof of the basilica type church had to be replaced by stone vaults for safety and durability, and extension of size of the vaulting system itself (see p. 202) depended on arched support of a specific type and adequate wall abutment. This led in turn to larger and higher buildings, extended window and door space and a complexity of design for exterior and interior undreamed of in Romanesque architecture. The pointed arch was not new. It had long been used in the Middle East and, in Europe, was employed in areas subject to Moorish influence like Spain, Sicily and even Provence. Its use was being developed in these areas in the twelfth century. Northern France, though, was more suited to the establishment of a new style, being an area less troubled by warfare and of more stable economic climate.

The stability of the region led to the creation of schools of artists and craftsmen which spread to other suitable places, southern England and Flanders, for example. These craftsmen then travelled widely to execute commissions. The transition from Romanesque to Gothic proceeded at a variable speed in differing countries. Some, like parts of Germany, Italy and Spain, felt an affinity with Romanesque building. The style expressed their mood and artistic ideas and they clung to it well into the thirteenth century. Others, like England, Flanders, Northern France and the Baltic region adapted quickly. Transitional work can be seen in all these countries, with parts of a building in one style and other parts in newer forms.

As in Romanesque work, climate was an important factor. Northern Europe eventually established a Gothic style which was different from that in the warmer countries south of the Alps and the Pyrenees. In the north, the emphasis was on height, of steeples, buttresses, roofs and on large windows with richly coloured glass and large doorways with equally rich sculptural adornment. Further south where the sun was stronger and the rain and snow less damaging, roofs were flatter, the horizontal line predominated, window and door openings were smaller, stained glass rarer and decoration was more by painting, mosaic and other coloured media than by three-dimensional sculpture.

Whereas certain countries, in particular, Spain, Portugal, Germany and Scandinavia, were slower to adapt to Gothic forms, these same countries were, in the main, also slow to abandon Gothic for the Renaissance and classicism. An exception was Italy which slowly and reluctantly adopted Gothic tenets but, in contrast, was the originator of the Renaissance, establishing its forms nearly two centuries before England, which was another exception. England had been one of the first countries to adopt Gothic designs but was one of the last to relinquish the style which passed into a Perpendicular phase unique to the British Isles.

As the Gothic period advanced, buildings became larger and higher, window and doorway openings increased in size so the churches were flooded with light. The knowledge of structure in masonry was extending quickly and with this advance in technique came the means to erect buildings which were mere shells of stone ribs and pillars. The area of solid wall became less and the design correspondingly more complex. Each individual member of the building became more attenuated. Heavy columns and solid piers were replaced by slender, lofty piers encircled with clustered column shafts, terminating in small moulded or foliated capitals. Some shafts rose the full height of the wall to support the vault springing, others ended at the nave arcade. Towers became slenderer and many had elegant spires set on them. These became taller and steeper as time passed. The exterior became a forest of vertical stone pinnacles, stretching up into the vaults of heaven; the interior a mystic chiaroscuro in stone, gently illuminated by shafts of sunlight gloriously coloured by their transition through the cathedral glass.

This miracle of immense stone buildings

pierced by great openings and carved into tracery was only made structurally possible by the engineering development of the stone vault and its consequent abutment. Both of these stem from the original adoption of the pointed arch. As mentioned earlier, this type of arch was not new but its replacement of the round one led to the variations and complexities of *Gothic vaulting*. The semi-circular arch presents great problems in vaulting a church. This is because the nave or choir and their aisles often have different widths and heights. Vaulting is made in bays and the semi-circular arch lends itself to a square bay. The bay is decided by the positioning of the supporting piers or columns. In Romanesque cathedrals the bay was transversed at roof level by two ribs which curved in diagonal line from nave pier to nave pier. As the diagonal ribs were longer than the four ribs connecting the four sides or faces of the bay, it was impossible for all these ribs to be semicircular in section unless the vault were domical (dome-shaped), thus creating an uneven ridge line, or the side arches were stilted. Alternatively two bays had to be treated as one. Further problems arose because the aisles were narrower and lower than nave or choir, and it was difficult to reconcile these variations with the use of a semicircular arch. The pointed arch provided a more flexible system since it could be varied in proportion of width to height in order to accommodate different spans and roof levels. The French aptly term this arch the *arc brisé*, the broken arch, which gives a clear picture of its function.

The basis of a structure with the pointed arch supported on piers led, over many years, to great variety in vault design. The Gothic vault is a framework of stone ribs which support thin stone panels filled in later over the centering. Early ribbed vaults are *quadripartite*, that is, each bay is divided into four compartments by diagonal ribs. The French then developed a *sexpartite* vault, wherein the intermediate pier is carried up as a vaulting shaft to carry a rib which transfers the vaulting compartment into six. The English introduced extra (*tierceron*) ribs into their quadripartite vaults. These spring from the same points as the diagonals and divide the four large compartments into smaller ones. The next stage was the *lierne* vault where many small lierne or tie ribs (so-called after the French word *lier* = to

bind) are used at different angles to connect the main ribs to form an intricate geometrical pattern. The *star* vault is a version of this. The final stage, a peculiarly English one, is the *fan* vault (p. 222). Decorative bosses are superimposed at the intersections of all rib vaults. They are to be seen in the late lierne examples as the boss covers the awkward junction of differing diameter ribs and creates a decorative design on the roof covering.

The Gothic *buttress* is the complement to the vault. As the latter progresses and becomes higher, wider and more complex, so does the abutment. The structure of a Gothic church, its arches, piers and vault, exerts an outward and downward thrust upon the walls. In order to avoid thickening the whole wall area, as the Romanesque builders had done, the Gothic mason provided extra reinforcement in the form of a stone buttress at the point on the wall where it was most needed. This point is just below the springing line of the vault. Early Gothic buttresses were simple designs. Slowly they became more complex. Pinnacles were added above the parapet level. These pinnacles are decorative but also functional in that the weight of the pinnacle above the arch springing exercises a vertical pressure which helps to counteract the vault's outward thrust. The buttresses themselves became larger, heavier and richly ornamented with carving and panelling. The final stage was the *flying buttress*, developed especially by the French, and to be seen in all its decorative glory on the chevet of many a French cathedral; *Le Mans* and *Reims* are two outstanding examples. A flying buttress transmits thrust rather than resisting it. Thus, starting high on the nave wall, between the clerestory windows, the buttresses progress downwards in arches and pinnacles, conducting the thrust, in stages, from the upper wall to the ground. Because of the flying buttress sytem, it became possible to construct thinner walls as time passed instead of increasing the thickness to offset the large windows and higher vaults.

Window design is also a characteristic feature of Gothic architecture. In general, window openings became wider and larger. At the same time, the window area was subdivided by more numerous stone ribs; the horizontal transoms and the vertical mullions. The window head was decoratively designed by stone ribs into varying

FRENCH GOTHIC CATHEDRALS

427 Notre Dame, Paris, from the
south-west, 1180–1330

428 S. Julien, Le Mans, from the
east showing the chevet, 1217–54

427

428

patterns; this was called tracery. The designs differed from country to country, but the general trend was from geometrical shapes—circles, triangles, quatrefoils—in the earlier period, to curved flamboyant forms in the later years. English designs of the fifteenth century were in Perpendicular tracery, which resembled panelling, and echoed the wall decoration. The circular window, the Gothic rose, evolved from the Romanesque wheel window. The rose designs were divided by tracery into geometrical and flowing shapes, instead of the radiating wheel spokes used before. Many windows were filled with magnificent coloured glass, ranging from those of the simple parish church to the wonders of *Chartres* or *León Cathedral*.

The affinity between the fellow craftsmen at work on great buildings grew closer during the Gothic period. The rapport among masons, glaziers, painters, mosaicists and metal workers was complete and satisfying. No craftsman was of more vital importance than the sculptor. It was the golden age for carvers and modellers, who enjoyed a freedom of expression and an architectural surface upon which to create and experiment never equalled before or since. The Gothic cathedral façade was here the supreme vehicle. The pattern was established in northern France in the early thirteenth century of a twin-towered façade with central rose window and a triple portico at base, spreading, like a Roman triumphal arch, across the full width of the elevation. The whole façade was decorated with symbolic sculpture, but these portals, encrusted all over, were the three-dimensional focal centre of the design. Jamb and trumeau figures, tympanum scenes, archivolt groups, gargoyles and cresting, all played a part in relating the Bible story from Old and New Testaments, in rich, full, glorious sculptures. French sculptors were supreme and they travelled all over Europe, showing other nations how to enrich their cathedral façades. As the Middle Ages advanced, sculpture changed from its Romanesque origins. The mysticism and incarnations of devilry gave way to realistic graceful expression, especially in treatment of the human figure and its drapery. By the fifteenth century portraiture in figure statuary was evolving and German sculptors began to challenge the French supremacy.

France

In the Middle Ages France was still not one nation. The country was large, by Medieval standards, the climate and peoples differed greatly from one region to another. Architecture reflected these differences. The contrast, architecturally, between north and south is especially marked. In the north, particularly in the area of Paris, Gothic developed early, before 1150, in buildings notable for their verticality, vigorous bold plasticity, hand-in-hand with delicate, finely detailed ornament. In the south, Roman traditions made Romanesque architecture a natural style while, later, the climate made more suitable a greater affinity with Spanish and Italian Gothic forms than those of northern France.

In northern and central France a stupendous number of cathedrals and large churches were constructed in the thirteenth century. The majority of these, unlike their English counterparts, were not monastic foundations but new cathedrals purpose-built for the town they served. Paris was the focal centre of the Île de France region, which produced the early and most famous examples which set the pattern for the whole of northern Europe. One of the very first examples of Gothic architecture was the *Abbey Church of S. Denis*, built in the decade from 1135 by the Abbé Suger. Now in a Paris suburb, most of the church has been restored or rebuilt, but part of the original choir exists, while the reconstructed west front still shows the early mixture of round and pointed arch heads. *Sens Cathedral* of similar date has common features with S. Denis. Other examples followed. The establishment of the Gothic cathedral pattern began with the building of the Cathedral of Paris in 1163.

Cathedrals

The world famous cathedrals of the Île de France all built between 1150 and 1300 (though parts were added to or altered later), are similar to one another. The Cathedrals of Paris, Laon, Reims, Amiens, Chartres have all been likened to the Parthenon in Athens in that they, collectively and individually, present the greatest contribution to the architecture of their time—Gothic—and became prototypes for churches all over Europe. They have a common form. The plan is cruci-

Reims Cathedral, France
Plate 39
Angel in the Annunciation, central portal, façade,
c. 250–60

Plate 40
Virgin on trumeau, central portal, façade, 13th century
Plate 41
Jamb figure, central doorway, façade, c. 1240

Chartres Cathedral, France
Plate 42 Tympanum, centraldoorway, façade,
c. 1150–5

Plates 43 and *44*
Jamb figures, central doorway, façade, *c.* 1150–5

form, with an apsidal eastern arm, slightly projecting transepts and a longer nave. All are lofty with high vaults supported by flying buttress schemes. Numerous chapels are set in or added to the walls but the chief area for this is the *chevet*. This is a French innovation and refers to the apsidal east end which has an interior ambulatory behind the high altar, giving access all round the church usually at least at choir and triforium levels. Between the bays are set semi-circular chapels giving an exterior appearance of a gladiolus corm growing its smaller new corms around its base. Between the chapels radiate the forests of flying buttresses. The façade design is a classic one. *Notre Dame* in *Paris*, built 1163–1235 (**427**) is one of the early examples which set the character. There is a triple portal (**512**), sculpture filled across the width of the base of the elevation, above, a gallery of sculpture (here, the *galerie des rois*), then the central rose window.* Apart from the two flanking west towers, the architectural emphasis is horizontal.

All these cathedrals were intended to have many towers surmounted by spires. Few of the towers, apart from the western ones, were built and even fewer spires. Partly this was due to cost, but mainly it was because French cathedrals are so vast and so lofty, with high vaults of great span, that a steeple became too great an engineering hazard. As it was, some high vaults collapsed before towers were added, as at Beauvais. The lack of spires is one of the chief differences between French and English cathedrals.† The latter are smaller and lower and could bear the weight of a tall spire as at Salisbury (**450**). In France, a very tall but lightweight flèche was erected over the crossing.

French cathedrals are often difficult to view as few have any open space around them. They were built for and of the town and were surrounded, up to their walls, by houses and civic buildings. Only in the last 150 years have a number of these buildings been demolished, but even so it is only in Paris, Chartres and few other instances that an open space in front of the building offers a clear view. This is in contrast to the English monastic foundations which surround the cathedral with close and cloisters.

All these Île de France cathedrals are store-houses of magnificent craftmanship. *Notre Dame* in *Paris* suffered greatly in the Revolution of

1789 when much of its sculpture was badly damaged and had to be replaced by Viollet-le-Duc and others. It is chiefly famous for its architectural qualities of exterior and interior. *Laon*, built 1160–1225, is noted especially for its west façade, a masterpiece, which is less static than Notre Dame, and for its magnificent towers and rose window. High up the towers are sculptured bulls which commemorate the original animals which carried the building stones up to the top of the hill from the flat plain below.

Reims is the richest and most glorious, as befits the cathedral built as the Coronation Church for the Kings of France. The present structure was begun in 1211. Despite a long building period, both interior and exterior are remarkably homogeneous (**430**, **600** and **610**). Its glory is its sculpture, especially that on the triple western portal (PLATES 39, 40 and 41). There are 500 statues here, as well as richly decorated gables. The cathedral suffered grievi-ously in the First World War, being bombarded mercilessly for four years, during which time it suffered 300 direct hits. Only its solidity and quality of construction saved it from total destruction. Today it is a tribute to the French architects and craftsmen who have been restoring it so faithfully ever since.

Amiens is the latest of the group and was built over a comparatively short period (1220–88). It has, therefore, a unity of design like its con-temporary, Salisbury. Amiens is the classic cathedral on the Île de France pattern and typical of the French Gothic tradition. It has progressed beyond the Paris model and its façade (**431** and **464**) is more plastic with the horizontal emphasis more broken and sophisticated in handling. Its portal sculptures and great carved choir screen are Medieval masterpieces (PLATE 45).

Chartres Cathedral is of the same pattern as the others but is given a different appearance by the spires on the western towers (**433**). They are non-matching spires, the north, the *Clocher Neuf* being rebuilt in 1506–13 in contrast to the *Clocher Vieux* of 1145–70. The two superb features of Chartres are the remarkable coloured glass (**457**) and the exterior sculpture. There are 130 beautiful windows and 2200 sculptured figures. The latter, particularly those on the west front, are of especial interest on account of their transitional quality. They are unique in their

---

* *At Notre Dame it is still of wheel design.*

† *Norman cathedrals, like Coutances, are exceptions and set the pattern for English tradition.*

early period and are prototypes for later work. The drapery still has a formalised austerity of line, while the figures are serene and of a stylised, elongated proportion (PLATES 42, 43 and 44).

In northern and central France several outstanding cathedrals were built in the thirteenth century. These developed variations from the Île de France pattern. *Bourges*, in central France, built mainly 1190–1275, is of homogeneous design with an exterior and interior in simple Gothic. Sculptural decoration is restrained, as is the coloured glass and other ornamentation. It is an architectural cathedral, long and low on the exterior with geometrical traceried windows and simple flying buttresses. The interior is exceptionally fine, giving long vistas of ascetic Gothic forms (**434**). Further north is *Le Mans*, famous for having the finest chevet in France (**429**). The eastern arm was rebuilt in the thirteenth century on to a Romanesque nave. The chevet has 13 chapels radiating round the apse (**428**). The sophisticated scheme of abutment to this immense choir built on sloping ground is not only a remarkable engineering achievement for its day but a creation of great aesthetic beauty.

In *Normandy* are two interesting cathedrals at Bayeux and Coutances. Both are typical of Norman Gothic. They are severely simple with tall towers and spires and lancet or geometrical window design. At *Bayeux* the choir was rebuilt in the thirteenth century on to an earlier nave, presenting a fine composition from the east (**432**). *Coutances* is notable for its unity of design, internally and externally. The severe tall west front is finely proportioned (**469**), as is the contrasting eastern chevet showing the central tower above (**452** and **615**). The inside, like Bourges, is a masterpiece of superbly handled simplicity.

Of richer High Gothic phase are some widely separated examples, notably Rouen, Strasbourg and Beauvais. *Rouen Cathedral* suffered serious war-time damage in 1944, but is now largely restored. The building represents many construction periods from Romanesque to late Gothic. Of especial interest, apart from some fine sculpture on the north transept portal, is the *rayonnant* period work on the north and south transept façades, the magnificent west window and the early *flamboyant* gables above. The south-west tower is a wonderful instance of late Gothic

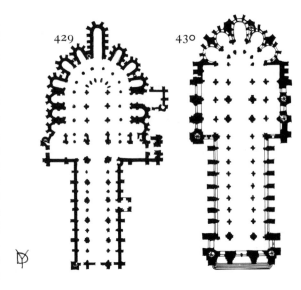

429 French Cathedral plans : Le Mans
430 Reims

work. It is 252 feet high in contrast to the older *Tour de Romaine* on the other side of the façade and is called the *Tour de Beurre* because money was provided for its erection from payments for dispensations given permitting consumption of butter during Lent (**471**). The 512 feet high flèche is a nineteenth century metal replacement.

Strasbourg Cathedral is a typical product of Alsace. It is a combination of German and French sources. It is basically a German cathedral as it was mainly built by Germans, but it clearly owes a great deal to the influence of French cathedral design. The western part of the cathedral was erected in the thirteenth century and culminated in one of the most beautiful façades anywhere in Europe. On traditional French pattern, it has a triple portal, a wonderful rose window and two towers. A lop-sided appearance is given by the fact that the north-west tower received its spire in 1399, but the south-west one was never built. The existing spire clearly shows the German origins of the building, with its openwork tracery designed by Urich d'Ensingen. The sculpture on the portals and the interior is magnificent, very French in treatment but German in expression; the wise and foolish virgins, for example. Damage to the sculptures during the Revolution was considerable, but the restoration has been excellently done (PLATE 46).

FRENCH GOTHIC CATHEDRALS

431 *West front, Amiens, 1220–88*
432 *Bayeux from the south-east, thirteenth century, central tower fifteenth century*
433 *West front Chartres, twelfth-sixteenth century*
434 *Interior, Bourges, early thirteenth century*

431

432

433

434

Beauvais Cathedral in northern France was an ambitious project of the High Gothic period. Begun in 1247, it was designed on a tremendous scale. The choir, completed 1272, has the highest Gothic vault in Europe (of 157 feet), with accordingly strong flying buttress reinforcement. The attempted creation of such an immense building led to problems. The roof collapsed in 1284 and the 500 feet high spire fell in 1573. The building has never been completed and, though the existing arm is of magnificent quality and proportions, with beautiful coloured glass and a fine chevet, it is still a truncated church, impossible to view as its builders intended. Even for the miraculous Gothic age its dimensions were excessive for the engineering accomplishment of that time.

In the *south* of France, and especially the south-east, the legacy of Ancient Rome represented the overwhelming influence on Gothic architecture just as it had on Romanesque here before this. A in Italy, pure Gothic never flourished. Th tendency was for buildings with a horizonta rather than a vertical emphasis, with few piers o columns or any obvious constructive members Nave and choir were wide and low, vaulting bay square and flying buttresses uncommon; indeed the abutment was often internal and invisible.

There are a number of fine cathedrals in thi region, at *Narbonne, Perpignan, Béziers, Carcas sonne* and *Rodez*, for instance. The most unusua and interesting, as well as the one displaying th area characteristics most, is the *Cathedral a Albi.* It was begun in 1282, built of warm pinkis brick on massive lines, fortress-like and remini scent of a Castilian castle. The only exception t the rounded, impregnable exterior is the richl carved stone porch, added in the fifteenth centur to the south side. The cathedral shares no com mon denominator with those of the Île de France

435 *Le Mont S. Michel, Normandy, France, tenth-thirteenth century*

435

FRENCH GOTHIC CATHEDRALS

436 *Vendôme Abbey Church, begun 1306*
437 *S. Pierre, Caen, from the south-east,
      1308–1545*
438 *S. Ouen, Rouen, west front, 1318–1515*
439 *Church of the Jacobins, Toulouse, twin
      naves, 1230–92*

436

437

438

439

Its origins are closer to Catalan, and especially Barcelona, Gothic. There are no transepts and no western doorways; all the entrances are lateral. The building is a rectangular hall, nearly 60 feet wide and 100 feet high. The buttresses, also of brick, project outwards only slightly, but more into the interior, giving a thickness of 15 feet. Between them are the tall, narrow, round-headed windows. The interior is spacious and finely proportioned though the illumination level is low on account of the slit-like fenestration (**461**). The walls and wide, quadripartite vaults are in polychrome. All round the church are chapels at two levels, set between the buttresses and in the immense thickness of the walls. At the upper stage, windows are recessed into the quadripartite vault ceiling. At the west end is a 300 feet tower in the same architectural mode and crowned by a fine octagon.

Churches

Among the monastic foundations in France, the *Abbey Church* of *Mont S. Michel* occupies one of the most picturesque sites. It is perched on top of a rock just off the Normandy coast and is connected to the mainland by a causeway (**435**). It is a fortified monastery, restored in the nineteenth century but still containing a beautiful Romanesque nave (see p. 136 in Chapter 4) and taller Gothic choir. Much plainer, but one of the best monastic examples in France is the *Church of La Chaise Dieu* in the Auvergne (*c.* 1344), while in *Toulouse*, the *Church of the Jacobins* is a quite different interpretation of Gothic from the north. Of brick and stone construction, it was built *c.* 1300 with twin naves of equal height divided by a central row of columns (**439**).

The fifteenth century saw the final phase of Gothic architecture in France, when many richly ornamented buildings were erected in the *flamboyant* style. These show the basic French Gothic characteristics of verticality, abutment and good proportion, but the flying buttresses are more slender and more decorated than before, the windows are larger with complex curvilinear tracery in the head, ogee arches and mouldings are found on all members. The *Abbey Church* at *Vendôme* is a good monastic example. Both west façade and eastern chevet are outstanding here, while the interior is simpler (**436**). In Normandy,

S. Pierre at *Caen* is a late example with an ornate eastern arm (**437**). In *Rouen* nearby are two particularly fine churches of this time, *S. Maclo* (1437) and *S. Ouen* (**438** and **470**). In *Abbeville* the remarkable classic of *flamboyant*, *S. Wulfram* largely built 1488–1534 but never finished (**516**).

A unique building, *La Sainte Chapelle* in Paris (the Chapel of the French Kings here), was built earlier, 1244–8. The design has gone beyond the style of the Île de France cathedrals. The fenestration is larger, breaking up the wall area into strips with buttresses, so that the impression is of coloured glass framed by masonry. The chapel has a high stone vault and is apsidal at one end.

Civic Building

Early Gothic work in this field was unpretentious and overshadowed by ecclesiastical architecture. By the fifteenth century the growing wealth of towns was reflected in the municipal buildings. These had all the Gothic characteristics of vertical emphasis and elements of decoration and structure, but were more symmetrical and dignified. Some had tall towers and steeples like the *Town Hall* at *Arras* (restored in 1919). Many of these buildings which survive are in northern France and suffered bombardment in the First World War, but all are well restored to the original design. The *Town Hall* at *Compiègne* is shown in Fig. **440**. That at *Dreux* has a tall uncompromising donjon appearance, while the one at *Saumur* has a simple façade with rectangular windows bordering on Renaissance patterns. The famous *Palace de Justice* at *Rouen* is now largely rebuilt after its severe damage in the Second World War. It was erected originally in 1493, an important building reflecting the wealth of the city. The late Gothic façades are surmounted with steeply pitched roofs containing tall dormer windows.

Fortified Structures

Until nearly the end of the Middle Ages fortification was still necessary, for monasteries (Mont S. Michel, for example), for castles and palaces and even for bridges. The *Pont Valentré* at *Cahors* an impressive instance (**444**). Towns were also fortified. These were often built on top of a hill like an acropolis in Ancient Greece. *Avignon* still has remains of such a town in buildings like the

FRENCH MEDIEVAL HÔTELS AND CHÂTEAUX

440 Hôtel de Ville, Compiègne,
1502–10
441 House of Jacques Coeur, Bourges,
courtyard, 1443–51
442 Château at Chaumont, 1465–
1515
443 Château at Sully-sur-Loire,
fourteenth century keep, later
additions

440

441

442

443

444 Pont Valentré, Cahors, France, 1308–80

fortress *Palace of the Popes* (1316–70), but the two most complete towns are Carcassonne and Aigues Mortes. The city of *Carcassonne* retains its picturesque setting. Built high above the river Aude, it constitutes a museum of military architecture extending from fifth century Visigoths to the sixteenth century. Much of the building is of the thirteenth century and comprises encircling outer and inner curtain walls incorporating over 50 towers. Inside the walls are narrow Medieval streets, shops, houses, the castle and the cathedral of S. Nazaire. Unhappily the city fell into partial ruin in the eighteenth and early nineteenth century, but restoration has been carefully continuing since it was begun by Viollet-le-Duc in 1844 (**445** and **447**). Though Carcassonne is more picturesque, *Aigues Mortes*, built in the thirteenth century at the mouth of the river Rhône near Montpellier, retains much more of its original work. The ramparts, with their mural towers, enclose a rectangular town which was built to house both maritime and fluvial ports. The characteristics of the landscape differ from Carcassonne. Here is a flat estuary region, but the town is as impressive in its individual manner (**446**).

Castles were built throughout the Middle Ages in all European countries. In France they were strongly fortified till after 1453, when the Hundred Years' War ended and the English retired from the soil of France. After this time

existing castles were added to and adapted as palatial residences. The Loire valley region is especially noted for its châteaux as the fifteenth century court was not yet fixed in Paris and this hunting area was a favoured one for the royal house, who visited loyal subjects in their castle homes. The river was generally utilised to make water defences and it is these which give to the châteaux the picturesque quality which so many possess. Architecturally, the French castle has much in common with Scottish ones; the round towers with their pyramidal roofs, for instance. There was a close link between Scotland and France and the two countries tended to join forces against the English aggressor.

A late fifteenth century example is *Pierrefonds*, near Compiègne; a truly massive pile, fortified, its skyline broken by numerous towers and high pitched roofs. It was accurately but extensively restored in the mid-nineteenth century by Viollet-le-Duc. A beautiful castle of the same period is the *vieux château* at *Sully-sur-Loire* (**443**). The entrance (1304–8) of *Fort S. André* at *Villeneuve-les-Avignon* is another massive fortification. Even larger and more impregnable are the immense mural towers at *Angers*, while the fourteenth century keep of *Saumur* château rises above the river and the town, dominating the landscape.

Later fifteenth century châteaux show the beginnings of the transformation from fortress

FORTIFIED MEDIEVAL TOWNS IN FRANCE

445 *Entrance façade, the castle, Carcassonne, twelfth century*
446 *Town walls and gateway. Porte de la Reine, Aigues Mortes, thirteenth century*
447 *Outer walls and towers, Carcassonne, thirteenth century*

into palace. *Chaumont*, on the Loire is an impressive example. It has a commanding site and entrance (**442**) and the main courtyard is entirely domestic, containing a fine stone, Medieval staircase. A similar courtyard exists at *Montsoreau* nearby, while the Gothic Court at *Blois* is entirely palatial. Among other interesting châteaux are *Langeais* (Loire, 1465) and the beautiful façade of *Josselin* in Brittany.

Houses

Though the country house was still a semi-fortified château, the French town house, the *hôtel*, was evolving a specific late Medieval pattern suited to its smaller site. The *hôtels* which survive are not numerous and are the larger examples built by well-to-do merchants or church dignitaries. The finest of these is the house of *Jacques Cœur* in *Bourges* (**441**). It is in the classic pattern for the fifteenth century *hôtel*; built round a courtyard and with an entrance doorway leading up to the Medieval stairway in the centre of the court façade. High pitched roofs contain the typical ornamental dormers. Similar, though more simply decorated are two examples in Paris, the *Hôtel de Cluny* (**514**) and the *Hôtel de Sens* (**458**), both late fifteenth century and both retaining finialled dormers and *flamboyant* window tracery. A number of half-timber houses still exist. There are examples in *Chartres* and a few have survived the devastation in Normandy of the Second World War at *Lisieux, Caen* and *Rouen*.

England

The quality of Gothic work here is as fine and abundant as in France. England also developed the Gothic style early; in a transitional form at first, but, by 1200, all the characteristics of the Gothic form were fully evolved. The progress of the style was different from the French model, due largely to the island status of the country. During the Middle Ages, indeed for long after, the surrounding narrow strips of sea were sufficient to impede the easy spread of ideas. Thus Britain was isolated from Continental thought and evolved national characteristics in architecture as in other fields. Nevertheless, England was a maritime nation and had enough contact

with the Continent, commercially, to acqu new techniques and influences.

The British climate was suited to the north Gothic forms as established on the Île de Fran more than adequate building materials w available, stone, granite, clay for bricks a timber so the development of the new style v rapid and complete. A much smaller coun than France, English work in the Gothic m varies much less from region to region. T climate differs less from north to south a distances are shorter. The only notable facto determining regional differences was the ava bility of building materials. Transport of st was difficult and costly so areas with availa stone—mainly the north and south-west of country—used this freely, while others like E Anglia and Cheshire, built in timber and bri The types of building were much the same.

The Gothic style of architecture in Engla was employed from about 1170–1560; a l period, possibly longer than that in any ot country. The style was adopted early and rel quished late; the former because it suited country and its people, the latter because li with Renaissance ideas were slow to percolate to the isolation from the Continent. Henry V in the 1530s, had begun to encourage Renaissa work by importing Italian craftsmen, but break with the Pope over his religious and mar problems postponed the arrival of the Ren sance in England for nearly a century. Got architecture in a pure form flourished into reign of Elizabeth I. There were four disti phases in this evolution. The first three, Tra tional, Lancet and Decorated, ran parallel French development but the last, Perpendicu was uniquely English and lasted from about 1 till 1560.

Ecclesiastical Architecture

Cathedrals, Churches, Chapels and Abbeys

As in France, Gothic buildings in England w at first *Transitional*, incorporating features of new style into Romanesque work. The comm expression of this phase was the appeara of pointed and round arches together in structure, in windows and vaults especia *New Shoreham Church*, Sussex is an example a

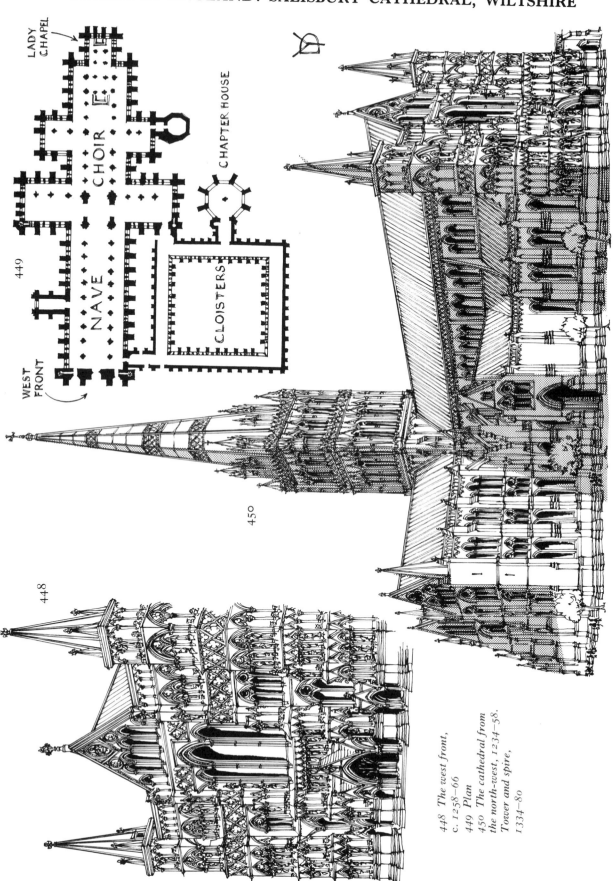

LADY CHAPEL

CHOIR

NAVE

WEST FRONT

449

CHAPTER HOUSE

CLOISTERS

450

448

448 The west front,
c. 1258–66
449 Plan
450 The cathedral from
the north-west, 1234–58.
Tower and spire,
1334–80

451

453

454

455

451 *Lantern and Octagon, Ely Cathedral, England,*
452 *Lantern, Coutances Cathedral, France, early*
    thirteenth century
453 *La Seo Cathedral, Zaragoza, Spain 1498–1520*
454 *Nave fan vault, Sherborne Abbey, England,*
    c. 1475–1500
455 *Cloister, S. Juan de los Reyes, Toledo, Spain,*
    c. 1470

GOTHIC WINDOWS

456 Carlisle Cathedral, England, fourteenth century
457 Chartres Cathedral, France, plate tracery, 1196–1216
458 Dormer, Hôtel de Sens, Paris, 1475–1507
459 Casa de la Conchas, Salamanca, Spain, (Palace of the Ambassadors), 1475
460 S. George's Chapel, Windsor, England, 1485–1509

461 Albi Cathedral, France, 1282–1390
462 Mechelen Cathedral, Belgium, begun 1341
463 Church of the Nativity of the Virgin in Putinki, Moscow, 1649–52
464 Amiens Cathedral, France, fifteenth century
465 Palacio del Infantado, Guadalajara, Spain, begun 1461

ENGLISH GOTHIC CATHEDRALS

466 Canterbury
Cathedral from the south
west. Nave, 1378–1405;
south-west tower, 1423–
34; central tower, 1490–
467 Canterbury
Cathedral, plan
468 York Minster,
interior looking east,
1291–1341 (Organ
omitted)

466

467

BECKET'S
CROWN

LIBRARY

N.W.
TRANSEPT

S.E.
TRANSEPT

CHAPTER
HOUSE

CHOIR

S.
TRANSEPT

CLOISTERS

NAVE

S.
PORCH

TOWER

TOWER

WEST FRONT

468

Buildwas Abbey, Shropshire. The outstanding instance is the choir of *Canterbury Cathedral*, rebuilt by William of Sens (so-called because of his work on that French Cathedral) in 1175–84.

From 1200–75 the *Lancet* or Early English style was fully developed. Ribbed quadripartite vaults are characteristic of this period, narrow, pointed arched windows arranged singly or in groups of three or five lancets, slenderer towers generally capped by spires, larger windows and stronger abutment. The vertical emphasis was strong, shown in a higher vault supported on taller nave and choir piers which, like the French ones, were slender and with clustered shafts encircling the central pier.

The supreme example of the style is *Salisbury Cathedral* (**448** and **450**). This is the only English Gothic cathedral to be built largely in a single operation and, therefore, single style. On a new site, the cathedral was begun in 1220 and by 1258 was virtually complete; the tower and spire were a little later. The cathedral is surrounded by a beautiful green-swarded close. Apart from its situation and its unity of style, Salisbury is also remarkable for its high standard of craftsmanship. Built on traditional cruciform plan, the tower and spire over the crossing is the tallest in England (404 feet). Inside appears the three-storeyed division of ground floor arcade, triforium and clerestory. The windows of the latter are of typical Early English design. The west façade is more richly decorated with sculpture than is usual in England (**448**). Other fine examples of Early English work are the nave of *Wells Cathedral*, the façades of *Peterborough Cathedral*, *Ripon Minster* and *Wells Cathedral*, much of *Lichfield Cathedral* and the *Abbeys* of *Glastonbury*, *Tintern*, *Fountains* and *Bolton*.

This first main stage of Gothic architecture in England is often likened to the springtime of the style. It was fresh and almost severe in its classic simplicity, comparable to Bourges and Coutances Cathedrals in France. The hundred years between 1275 and 1375 was the high summer or second stage. Windows are larger, stained glass richer, tracery more complex. There is a smaller area of wall, broken by more extensive abutment. Vaulting becomes more complex with rib and boss decoration. Exteriors and interiors have become more exciting, more three-dimensional. The ever-expanding knowledge of the builders led to these

forms. The comparative French work in the fourteenth century of *rayonnant* and *flamboyant* styles is similar. It is in this period that English and French work come closest together.

The designers experimented with new ideas in spatial forms and lighting. The work at *Ely Cathedral* (1323–30) is one instance. Here, the old central tower over the crossing was replaced by the unique octagon and lantern. From the interior, in particular, the effect is three-dimensional and remarkable; the tall piers at the crossing, with their alternating arch openings and windows, support the ribbed vault, which extends upwards on all eight sides of the panelled lantern. From directly underneath the view is of a star pattern in the centre of a radiating web of ribs, which culminate in the rich stained glass and curvilinear tracery of the windows (**451**).

In both window tracery and vaulting designs there are, despite many variations, two distinct types of pattern. The earlier style in window tracery is usually *Geometric*, based on the circle and its component parts and shapes, and the later style, *Curvilinear*, is composed of curved lines sweeping in all directions, based mainly on the ogee curve. This is a similar evolution to the contemporary French patterns (**456**). In *vaulting*, quadripartite designs spread to tierceron patterns, with intervening ribs as at *Exeter Cathedral*, and then to lierne vaults as in *York Minster* (**468**) or *Gloucester Cathedral* choir.

Two fine Decorated Gothic* west façades can be seen in *Exeter* and *York Cathedrals*. Exeter has a small but impressive sculptured screen. At York, the towers are later, but the façade fenestration is typical fourteenth century work. Other examples include the Angel Choir at *Lincoln Cathedral* (**608**) and several central towers as, for example, at *Hereford*, *Wells*, *Worcester* and *Lincoln* (**474**).

From about 1360 onwards, English development of Gothic architecture began to diverge from that on the Continent and the *Perpendicular* style was evolved. This, as its name suggests, was an exercise in vertical lines but there was also a new emphasis on the horizontal. The three principal features in this work are panelled decoration all over the building, in windows, wall and buttress alike, an increasing area of window space and consequently development of the flying buttress (much later than in France) and

* *This was the English name for this style of work.*

GOTHIC TOWERS AND SPIRES

469 *Coutances Cathedral, France, thirteenth century*
470 *Church of S. Ouen, Rouen, France, 1318–1515*
471 *Tour de Beurre, Rouen Cathedral, France, late Gothic*

472 *Cimborio, Burgos Cathedral, Spain*
473 *Church of S. Maria Maggiore, Rome, Italy, 1377*
474 *Lincoln Cathedral, England, 1240–1311*

roofing by means of the fan vault. The finest Perpendicular examples are not confined to cathedrals and abbeys but are to be found in parish churches, chapels and houses. In the cathedrals, Perpendicular work is mainly limited to replacing towers, vaults or windows rather than large scale alterations. The best and most extensive work here is at *Canterbury Cathedral* where the nave, south-west and central towers, cloisters, transepts and Lady Chapel are in Perpendicular style (**466** and **467**).

Of buildings entirely in fifteenth century style, the chapels are supreme: outstandingly *Eton College Chapel* (1441), *King's College Chapel, Cambridge* (1446–1515), and *S. George's Chapel, Windsor* (1475–1509). In all these chapels the plan is rectangular and simple. There are many large windows, separated by finialled flying buttresses, leaving a small wall area. At the ends are gigantic multi-light windows (**460**). Both windows and walls are panelled alike, whether in traceried glass or in stone.

Similarly traceried are the *fan vaults* which roof these magnificent buildings. This peculiarly English design was evolved from the desire for a vault which would accommodate ribs of different curves as they sprang from the capital. The radiating ribs of a fan are of equal length and the bounding line is in the form of a semicircle. The whole group of ribs is made into an inverted concave cone. The radiating ribs are crossed by lierne ribs and the whole surface is then, like the windows, walls and buttresses, panelled and cusped (**454**).

The chapels mentioned are masterpieces of their period, entirely English and representing the climax of craftsmanship and design in the Gothic style, achieving a harmonious balance of mass and form. Also magnificent are many of the large parish churches, some of almost cathedral size, reflecting the wealth of the period in a number of centres. Many of these have tall towers, sometimes with spires, generally set at the west end. They were most common in flat landscape areas, on the eastern half of the country, where they are visible for many miles. Typical is *S. Botolph's Church, Boston*, in Lincolnshire, called colloquially the 'Boston Stump' because its top storey was added so much later than the rest of the church and for many years the tower had a decapitated appearance (**476**). Other

examples include *Louth Church*, Lincolnshire (**477**), *S. Mary Redcliffe, Bristol* and *Thaxted Church*, Essex. Among the less lofty towers are those of many remarkable churches like the richly decorated *Lavenham Church*, Suffolk, *S. Mary's, Taunton, S. John, Glastonbury* (**475**) and *S. John, Cirencester* (**478**).

Contemporary with the fan vault was the equally English development of the *timber roof*, used to cover church naves, guild and domestic halls. These evolved from the simple, massive tie and collar beam designs of the thirteenth and fourteenth centuries to the more complex, beautifully carved versions of the fifteenth and sixteenth. The outstanding example here is that covering *Westminster Hall* in London, designed by Hugh Herland and built *c*. 1395. There are many others, like those of the great hall of *Hampton Court Palace*, 1535, the great hall of *Eltham Palace*, and the more domestic type of *Rufford Old Hall*, Lancashire, 1505.

Until the death of Henry VIII, architecture in England held tenaciously to the Perpendicular Gothic style. Henry VIII himself, having heard and seen something of Renaissance art in France, tried to attract French and Italian craftsmen to England. Among those who came was *Pietro Torrigiano*, who designed the tomb of Henry VII and his queen in the new *chapel* at at *Westminster Abbey*. The chapel itself (1503–19) is a masterpiece of panelled, fan vaulted Perpendicular Gothic art, but the tomb, finished in 1518, is classical. After Henry VIII's break with Rome, England's tenuous links with Renaissance Italy were broken and the English Renaissance was postponed. Its form was also altered; Torrigiano's monument is Italian classical, the Elizabethan Renaissance forms are 'Mannerist', from Flanders and Germany (p. 336, Chapter 6).

Bath Abbey is the outstanding ecclesiastical example of Tudor Gothic. Designed all in one style, it displays an exceptional unity (**480**). *Hampton Court Palace* is its domestic equivalent. It is built in brick and has some fine Tudor gateways in this material which have the flattened, four-centred arch, typical of the later Perpendicular period. Though parts were altered in the seventeenth century, the Tudor Great Hall, entrance court and river façade remain as a tribute to Cardinal Wolsey's foresight and taste.

ENGLISH GOTHIC CHURCHES

475 S. John's Church, Glastonbury, c. 1485
476 S. Botolph's Church, Boston, Lincolnshire,
1350–1509
477 S. James's Church, Louth, Lincolnshire, 1465–1514

478 Church of S. John the Baptist, Cirencester.
Tower c. 1400 ; porch, 1500
479 S. Patrick's Church, Patrington, Yorkshire,
fourteenth century

80 Nave and choir, Bath Abbey, Somerset, 1501–39, Designed Robert and William Vertue

481

481 *Monnow Bridge with military gateway, Monmouth, late thirteenth century*

Fortified Building

Fortification was necessary also in England, particularly in the twelfth and thirteenth centuries. The years 1275–1350 are noted for the building of the Edwardian castles, mostly in Wales and Scotland, so-called because King Edward I erected many of them to establish his rule. These castles differ from Norman ones in that they are built in concentric rings of walling, studded with mural defence towers, with an open space in the centre. Here was constructed the domestic accommodation, while the space between the mural defences housed stabling, garrison buildings, cattle and villagers. The pattern was like a miniature Carcassonne. A number of these castles exist in Wales, such as *Caernarvon, Caerphilly, Conway, Harlech* and *Beaumaris. Bridges* were also fortified at this time and the *Monnow Bridge* in the Welsh border region is a survivor (**481**).

As in France, fifteenth century castles were part defensive and part palace. The fortifications were slowly curtailed, and the living accommodation became more spacious and comfortable. *Herstmonceux Castle* in Sussex survives from this period (**482**), as does the later moated house of *Oxburgh Hall* in Norfolk (1482).

Domestic and University Building

Most numerous surviving examples come from the fifteenth and sixteenth centuries. There are stone manor houses from the twelfth century onwards, like that at *Boothby Pagnell*, Lincolnshire (*c.* 1180) and the early brick house, *Little Wenham Hall*, Suffolk (*c.* 1270). Fourteenth century houses were larger and less strongly fortified. They comprised a great hall of two storeys open to the roof timbers, solar, storage accommodation and bedchambers. *Penshurst Place*, Kent is a fine example, as is also *Ightham Mote*, Kent and *Markenfield Hall*, Yorkshire.

England possesses many such houses from the fifteenth and early sixteenth centuries, built in different materials; stone, brick or half-timber. Some are large and spacious like *Compton Wynyates Manor House*, Warwickshire, *Hengrave Hall*, Suffolk and *Horham Hall*, Essex, a

482 *Herstmonceux Castle, Sussex, c. 1440*

482

483

483 Tudor parlour, c. 1530. Oak and plaster panelled ...om

484 The Feathers Inn, Ludlow, Shropshire, c. 1520–30; timber-framed

...rly sixteenth century. Others are less grandiose, ...ch as *Paycocke's House* at *Coggeshall*, Essex ...d *Great Chalfield* and *South Wraxall Manor ...ouses* in Wiltshire (**483**).

Though she suffered from aerial bombardment ...ngland was spared the devastation caused by ...ilitary engagement and occupation in the ...econd World War. Consequently, unlike Ger-...any, France and Italy, who lost such a wealth of ...eir Medieval *timber framed buildings*, England ...ill possesses a fair number. One of the several ...ns of this type still in use is illustrated in Fig. **484**. ...ivic building in this medium also exists, as at the ...uildhall in Lavenham and there are many ...uses like the Priest's House at Prestbury and ...ufford Old Hall in Lancashire. All these date ...om the fifteenth century.

Both *Oxford* and *Cambridge Universities* con-...in fine work from the fifteenth and sixteenth ...nturies. There is Magdalen College, Oxford, ...gun in the mid-fifteenth century, whose tower, ...en to advantage from the river, is of particular ...auty. The front quad of New College, Oxford ...ustrates clearly the usual quadrangle method of

484

GOTHIC PORCHES AND PORTALS

485 *S. John's College, Cambridge, England, early Tudor*
486 *Coronation Church of S. Matthias, Budapest,*
Hungary, fourteenth century

487 *Central façade portal, Orvieto Cathedral, Italy, from*
488 *Central porch, Regensburg Cathedral, Germany,*
fourteenth century

Medieval layout which was retained for so long by those universities. In Cambridge are a number of typical gateways, as at Jesus College and S. John's (**485**). Both show the four-centred arch with carved decoration above.

Belgium

The Low Countries, or Flanders as they were termed in the Middle Ages, were subject to varied artistic influences from different sources. Sandwiched between the Latin peoples of France and the Germanic peoples to the east, the architecture reflects both sources as well as some Spanish influence due to conquest. But in general the architecture of the area divides itself clearly in the period 1200–1600 into two main types. The country which is now Belgium was primarily French orientated and present day Holland was Germanic. The work in the Netherlands is therefore considered here with that of the Germanic Baltic group with which it has much in common.

Belgium was a wealthy area in the Middle Ages, particularly during the later years. In the fourteenth century, while France was being drained by constant warfare, the artistic centre of this part of Europe moved from Paris to Belgium, where Brussels and Antwerp were able to attract artists of fame and quality. The architectural style was mainly French. Important buildings were constructed in stone and have lofty towers and spires and great richness of sculptural and carved decoration. The fifteenth century saw an emancipation of Belgian architecture from the French. Bruges became the northern centre of the Hanseatic League and other important commercial centres grew up in Ghent, Antwerp, Louvain and Ypres. The rich merchants contributed to the magnificent civic building which arose in those years; the town and guild halls, exchanges, municipal belfries, warehouses and city houses. No other country in such a small area possesses as rich a heritage of this type of work from such an early date.

Ecclesiastical Building

The strongest influence on the design of these buildings was northern French. This is seen in the eastern chevet and the width of the churches, with double or triple aisles. A number of façades,

like those of Brussels and Antwerp Cathedrals, have twin western towers and portico below. German influence is evidenced by the churches with a single western tower and spire, like the Cathedral of S. Bavon in Ghent. These and other sources of style were welded by the Belgians into a characteristic mode of their own and many of the cathedrals and larger churches have the same features repeated again and again. Particular examples which show these features are *Mechelen* (Malines) and *Brussels Cathedrals* and the *churches of S. Jean, Louvain* and *S. Jean and Notre Dame in Mechelen* (**462**). These characteristics are the use of large columns to divide nave and choir from the aisles; piers are used only at the crossing and then have slender clustered shafts. The nave arcade is high and its columns are topped by foliated capitals and, below, are life-size sculptured figures attached to the column. There is no proper triforium, only a continuation of the clerestory window mullions downwards in blind form. Vaults are quadripartite. Interiors are light owing to the large clerestory and aisle windows. The east end is apsidal and has an ambulatory vaulted over pointed arches narrowed to accommodate the curve. The interior of Mechelen Cathedral shown in Fig. **491** is typical of this style. On the exterior, Mechelen has a flèche over the crossing, but a single tall western tower, one of the most beautiful in Belgium of this type.

Similar interiors can be seen at the *Church of S. Pierre, Louvain* (**489**) and the *Cathedral of S. Bavon in Ghent*. But in these cases, the cylindrical columns are replaced by slender vaulting shafts with tiny or no capitals and arcade piers with no break of any kind before the arch. *Ghent Cathedral* has brick vaults and walls. Stone is used only for ribs, piers and windows. The vault is most effective in its brick and stone colouring. Designs vary in the cathedral; the choir and nave are quadripartite with intermediate ribs, on the English pattern, and the aisles and crossing have lierne vaults which are not common in Belgium.

Brussels Cathedral (**490**) was built over a long period. The choir, begun 1226, is the earliest Gothic work in Belgium. It has an apsidal termination but no complete ambulatory; there are large flanking side chapels ending before the apse, and the ambulatory encircles only the end

GOTHIC CHURCHES IN BELGIUM

489 Church of S. Pierre, Louvain, from the east, 1425–97

490 West front, Cathedral of S.S. Michael and Gudule, Brussels, 1226–80. Towers 1518

491 Interior, Cathedral of S. Rombaut, Mechelen (Malines) begun 1341

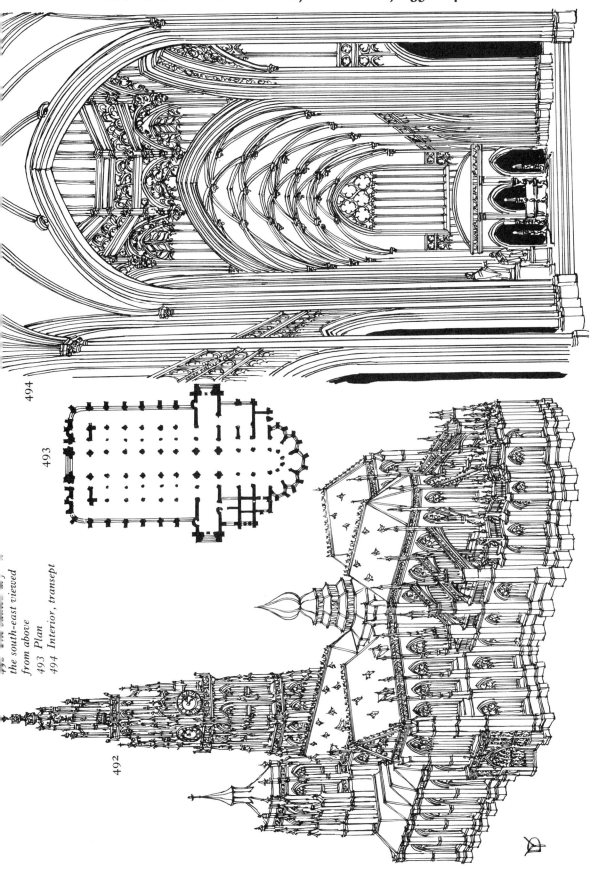

492 ...

the south-east viewed
from above
493 Plan
494 Interior, transept

494

493

492

495

GOTHIC CIVIC BUILDING IN BELGIUM

496 Town Hall, Oudenaarde, *1525–9*
497 Town Hall, Louvain, *1448–63*
498 Trade Hall 'La Vieille Boucherie,'
    Antwerp, *1501*
499 Maison des Franc-Bateliers, façade, *1531.*
    (Caravelle relief over front-door). Quai-
    aux-Herbes, Ghent

part. The nave was built 1425–75 and is of the classic Belgian pattern as illustrated in Fig. **491**. The cylindrical columns support statues of the apostles (**612** and PLATE 47). The façade of 1518 is on Île de France pattern.

Antwerp Cathedral, a rich example of late Gothic, is the most impressive in Belgium. It was begun in 1352 at the east end, the choir being completed in 1411 and the nave by 1474 (**493**). The façade is richly decorated with a central sculptured portal and large window above. The twin towers are on French pattern, but one spire was built, the north one. This is graceful and finely proportioned, rising to 400 feet in height. The whole cathedral shows a greater French influence than elsewhere in Belgium. Apart from the façade, this can be seen in the chevet, transept portals and the triple aisles (**494**). The strange lantern over the crossing is an unfortunate relic of Spanish occupation. Apart from the west end, Antwerp cathedral is exceptionally difficult to view. It is surrounded by buildings, the houses being built on to it at the eastern apse. The best viewpoint is from above, from the tall modern buildings nearby some of which have suitable access. This view is shown in Fig. **492**.

Civic Building

In the fifteenth and sixteenth centuries in particular, the wealthy merchants were independent and organised members of society and had greater freedom than in many countries. They used some of their wealth to build the magnificent trade and town halls of the Belgian cities. These are unique in Europe for their quality of craftsmanship and richness of decoration and design.

Three typical *town halls* are illustrated; the somewhat restored *Brussels* example (**495**), the most richly ornate at *Louvain* (**497**) and a more provincial but very typical one at *Oudenaarde* (**496**). The *town hall* at *Bruges*, built 1377, is one of high quality, as befitted the town's importance as centre for the Hanseatic League. There is a fine hall inside on the first floor which has a pendant timber roof and modern frescoes round the walls. *Ghent* illustrates the metamorphosis from Gothic to Renaissance forms since the right-hand part of the building is in an exception-

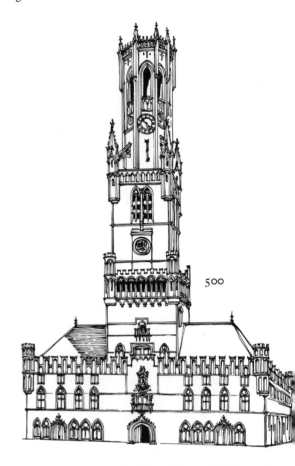

500

500 Halles and 279 ft. belfry, Bruges, Belgium, 1280

ally ornamented Gothic with a quantity o figure sculpture and the left portion is full classical in a façade using three superimposed orders. The Medieval section dates from 1518–3; and the Renaissance 1595–1622.

The *guild halls* are equally fine and probabl more varied in design. The most impressive an the greatest example of secular Medieval archi tecture in Europe was the *Cloth Hall* at *Ypres* built 1200–1304. It was destroyed in 1915 durin action in the First World War, then was rebuil after 1918 to the original design. The exterio front elevation is in a low, unbroken façade, 44 feet long, simple in design but richly detailed There is an immense square tower in the centr and a high pitched roof on either side of it. Th later town hall, next door, is completely eclipse in scale and dignity.

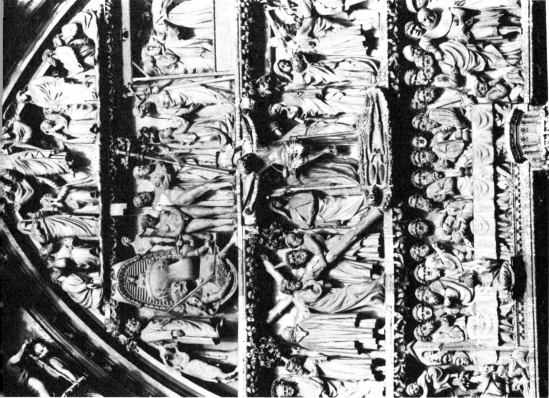

Plate 46
Tympanum, central portal, façade, Strasbourg Cathedral, France, 1276–1318

Plate 45
Madonna Portal, south transept, Amiens Cathedral, France, *c.* 1280

Plate 48
Façade doorway detail. Plateresque. Salamanca New Cathedral,
Spain, 15th and 16th century

Plate 47
Nave columns. Cathedral of S. Gudule, Brussels, Belgium, 1425–75

Of different design, simple but also of classic proportions, are the *Grande Boucherie* in *Ghent* (1408) and the *Vieille Boucherie* in *Antwerp* (1498). Both of these have stepped gabling, but the Antwerp example is tall and the Ghent one long and low. More ornate and late Gothic in treatment are the *Ghent Maison des Francs-Bateliers* (1499) and the *Cloth Hall* in *Mechelen*. There are two outstanding municipal *belfries* in Belgium. The one at *Ghent* (1300–39) is 400 feet high and stands uncompromisingly four square, surmounted by an elegant spire. The building known as the *Halles and Belfry* at *Bruges* is unique. It has the same monumental simplicity as well as the fine proportions of the Ypres Cloth Hall (500).

Large *squares* were laid out in many city centres. Several still exist with some Medieval, some Renaissance and part later building. Among those which retain their unity of treatment are the Grandes Places in Brussels and in Antwerp. Here are narrow buildings with ornate, stepped and curving gables, topped by sculptured finials standing side by side, each one different but creating a homogeneous whole. Even where restoration and modernisation has taken place, it is discreet, as in the Grande Place in Antwerp.

The Germanic Influence

Germany, Switzerland, Austria, Hungary, Czechoslovakia

Germany

Medieval Germany was not a nation but a collection of states of differing sizes which covered much of central Europe. Architecturally the German influence extended from the Baltic coast to the Alps and from Alsace to modern Hungary. The building pattern of the northern part was dominated by the Hanseatic League and this work, together with areas to the west (Holland) and the east (Poland) along the Baltic are considered on p. 251.

In the remainder of the region now comprising East and West Germany Gothic development took a different form from that encountered in France, England and Belgium. In these countries the Gothic style evolved steadily and naturally from the Romanesque. In Germany Romanesque architecture had been so successfully adopted,

and suited the needs and character of the peoples so well, there was reluctance to change it. German builders tended to adopt the Gothic vault and the pointed arch to go with it, but little else. Till virtually the end of the thirteenth century building was on Romanesque style, as at *Bamberg* and *Naumburg Cathedrals*. Bamberg (501), in particular, is typical. It was rebuilt on the foundations of an earlier Romanesque cathedral in the early thirteenth century and largely completed by 1237. But it is still basically Romanesque, with its four terminal towers, polygonal ends, lateral entrance and round-headed window and doorway openings. Only the interior ribbed vaults are Gothic, and the abundance of fine sculpture both on the exterior and inside. This largely dates from the late thirteenth century (PLATES 50 and 54).

The House of Hapsburg came to power in 1273, and soon afterwards Gothic architecture made its appearance. But it did not develop from German Romanesque. The need for change was felt strongly, so builders cast their eyes at the ready-made style in neighbouring France and based their ideas of Gothic upon French schemes, especially Amiens Cathedral which, at that time, was the exemplar in western European architecture.

A number of important cathedrals, minsters and churches were begun in the late thirteenth century in emulation of the French prototype. The cruciform plan was adopted, a high vaulted nave and choir, with one or more flanking aisles, an eastern chevet and richly ornamented west façade. Some of these façades have twin western towers, but many retain a German preference for a single one. A particular German characteristic was the treatment of the towers and spires. Finials and crockets were profusely employed and the spire itself was a fretwork of stone with light shining through from all sides. These spires were masterpieces of craftsmanship and engineering. *Strasbourg Cathedral* is an example already discussed (p. 206).

Typical of the twin-towered façade type are *Cologne* and *Regensburg Cathedrals*. The building history of Cologne is probably the longest of any great Medieval Cathedral (504). It was begun early, in 1248, on the eastern arm, which is almost a replica of that at Amiens. Both exterior and interior are imposing in scale and detail.

GERMAN GOTHIC CHURCHES

501 Bamberg Cathedral from the
    north-east, 1205–37
502 Church of S. Elisabeth, Marbu
    from the south-east, 1235–83
503 The Frauenkirche, Nürnberg
    (Nuremberg), hall church,
    1354–61

501

502

503

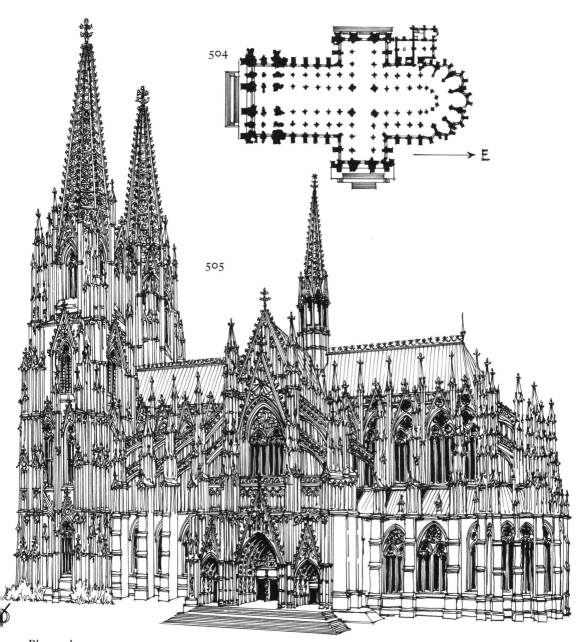

504 *Plan and*
505 *View from the south-east of Cologne Cathedral, Germany. Choir, 1248–1322; transepts begun 1325; west front*
completed to fourteenth century designs but work not finished until 1880

The chevet has an ambulatory and seven radiating chapels, which are polysided; they are separated by great double arched flying buttresses. The choir was consecrated in 1322, transepts and nave were begun but the money ran out and the fabric slowly began to decay. Today, only the eastern arm is Medieval. The rest of the cathedral was completed in 1824–80, to the original designs, but nineteenth century stonework and craftsmanship was more mechanical than its Medieval prototype. The west front, with its two vast steeples, is harder in treatment than the east end. Cologne Cathedral is of immense size, the largest in northern Europe. It is 468 feet long and 275 feet wide; the nave vault of 150 feet is nearly the height of Beauvais and this is a complete building. It is French in inspiration, the essence of High Gothic yet still characteristically German, lacking the elegance of French prototypes (505).

Regensburg Cathedral (506) occupies a pictur-

GOTHIC CATHEDRALS IN GERMANY

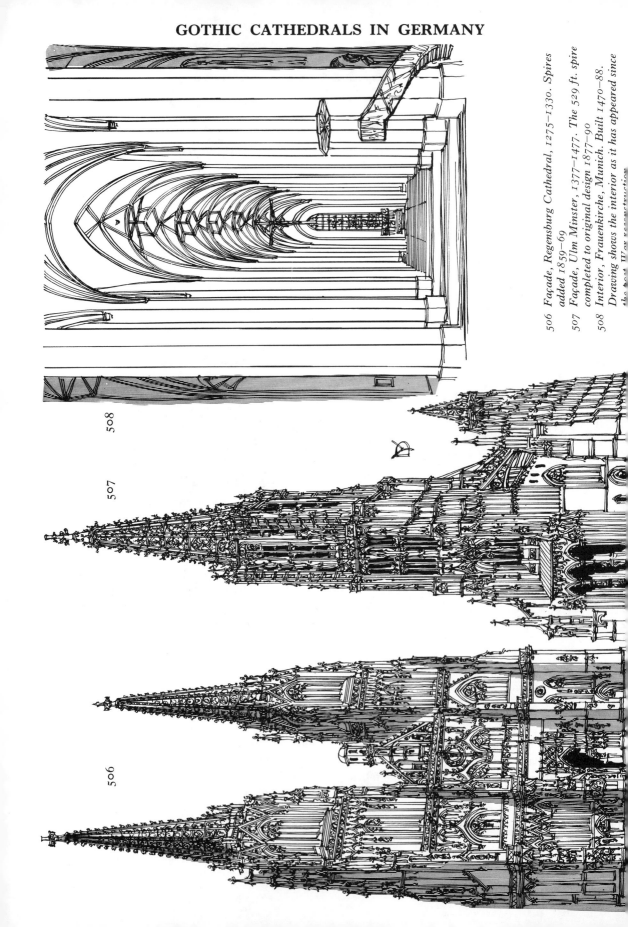

506 Façade, Regensburg Cathedral, 1275-1330. Spires added 1859-69

507 Façade, Ulm Minster, 1377-1477. The 529 ft. spire completed to original design 1877-90

508 Interior, Frauenkirche, Munich. Built 1470-88. Drawing shows the interior as it has appeared since the post-War reconstruction

508

507

506

509

510

511

509 *Town Hall (Altes Rathaus), Brunswick, 1393–1468*
510 *Half-timber house, Dinkelsbühl,* c. *1440*
511 *S. George's Church, Dinkelsbühl, hall church design, 1448–92*

esque position on the Danube in Bavaria. It replaced a Romanesque cathedral on the site and was begun in 1275. The façade has twin towers of which the spires were added in the 1860s. The elevation is slenderer, less weighty than Cologne and, being Medieval, has greater quality of craftsmanship in its stonework and glass. An attractive and unusual feature is the central porch, which is triangular (**488**). The eastern arm is polygonal-ended. It is simple and less obviously buttressed than French counterparts. On the exterior, but more particularly inside, is some fine figure sculpture (PLATE 51).

Beautiful examples of the single-towered west façade are the *Minsters* at *Ulm* and *Freiburg*. Ulm was begun in 1377; it is like a parish church on an immense scale, particularly at the west end. The lofty tower was completed in the sixteenth century, its spire was added, to the original design, in the nineteenth. It reaches 529 feet above ground. It almost overwhelms the building (**507**). The exterior is richly carved, with ornamented buttresses, fenestration and spire. The triple porch is especially noteworthy. The church interior is less successful; its proportions make it too high and dark. The glory of the interior are the carved wood choir stalls. German woodcarving was of a very high standard in the fourteenth to the sixteenth century, and these examples, together with those at Munich, are among the finest.

Freiburg Minster is somewhat smaller, but also on parish church pattern. Begun as a Romanesque basilica in 1200, it was completed at the west end in Gothic style about 1350. The façade has a 380 foot tower and spire; an early example of the open traceried type. In front of the main doorway, which has a fine sculptured tympanum, is the 'Golden Gate'. A Gothic choir was begun in the fourteenth century to a design similar to the contemporary one at Augsburg Cathedral, but was not completed till 1513 for lack of funds.

The cathedrals and churches just described are mainly in the French tradition of Gothic architecture. Much of the work in Germany was not like this: these buildings were an import of a foreign pattern. The Germans naturally excelled at a style developed by themselves; most commonly this was a simplification of Gothic features. Abutment was reduced to a minimum, transepts were often not built and the plan became a simple rectangle. From these ideas evolved the most usual form of German Gothic, the Hallenkirche or *hall church*. Apart from the features just mentioned, the important characteristic of a hall church is that the vaults of nave, choir and aisles are of the same height. This means that the building is, however richly ornamented, a simple hall. The nave and choir can have no triforium or clerestory so must be lit by exceptionally large aisle windows. Hall churches often have beautiful interiors. The tall slender piers support a high vault and there is no triforium or clerestory wall to obstruct the vista from end to end and from side to side of the church, only a forest of delicate piers. The vaults show a variety of quadripartite and lierne designs. The interiors are well illuminated, simple and finely proportioned. The hall church is only rarely found outside the realms of Germanic influence. There are two or three in Italy, as at Perugia and Todi.

The best instance of a hall church in Germany is the *Marienkirche-zur-Wiese* at *Soest*, dating from c. 1340. The exterior has a twin-spired façade on a large scale, like Regensburg Cathedral. Inside, immensely high piers ascend to the vault without any break for capitals. Both nave and aisles continue the same quadripartite vault, though the former is in square bays and the latter rectangular. There is no crossing or separation of nave and choir; tall windows continue all round the building including the apsidal east end. They are three- and four-light with decorated traceried heads and very fine coloured glass, especially in the apse. The whole simple interior is of great beauty.

Two other excellent hall churches are S. Elisabeth, *Marburg* and S. George, *Dinkelsbühl* (**502**, **511** and **613**). S. Elisabeth has a plain quadripartite vault; the one at Dinkelsbühl is more complex and resembles lattice work. Two other famous examples suffered in the Second World War. The *Frauenkirche* in *Munich*, now the cathedral, was begun in 1470, replacing a Romanesque basilica. It was built quickly, being completed, including the strange onion-dome towers on the façade, in 1512*. It is a large, brick hall church, 358 feet long, and has a nave over 100 feet in height (**508**). The interior received unsuitable eighteenth century classical additions, then nineteenth century Gothic Revival alterations. It was severely damaged in 1945, but today

* *The Church of S. Ulrich at Augsburg, built 1467, has one similar tower.*

Plate 49
S. George and the
Dragon. Wood
sculpture by Bernt
Notke from Lübeck.
Storkyrka, Stock-
holm, Sweden, 1489

Plate 50
The Prophets.
S. George's Choir.
Bamberg Cathedral,
Germany, 1220–30

Plate 51
Pier figure,
Annunciation.
Regensburg
Cathedral, Germany,
1280

Plate 52
Pulpit. Siena Cathedral. Nicola Pisano, 1265–9
Plate 53
Chapter House window. Convent of Christ, Tomar, Portugal.
Manoeline, early 16th century. Diogo de Arruda

GOTHIC DOORWAYS

512 Central façade portal, Cathedral of Notre Dame,
   Paris, 1200
513 North transept, Barcelona Cathedral, Spain, 1300
514 Courtyard, Hôtel de Cluny, Paris, 1483
515 Frauenkirche, Nuremberg, Germany, 1354–61
516 Façade, S. Wulfram, Abbeville, France, 1483–1534
517 Cathedral of the Saviour, Andronikhov Monastery,
   Moscow, 1425

has been well restored, almost to its original glory. The famous carved choir stalls, completed in 1502 by Erasmus Grasser, were tragically not stored with the other interior decoration during the war. By great good fortune, some of the half length figures have been preserved and are once more *in situ*. The *Frauenkirche* at *Nuremberg* was also badly damaged. The exterior is now fully restored (503) but the interior is partly modernised. The unpretentious but ornamental façade faces the market place. It has an elegant, carved, square porch, very richly ornamented and, above, a finialled stepped gable (515).

Until 1939 Germany possessed many good examples of *civic architecture* from the fourteenth and fifteenth centuries. Like Belgium, there were ornately carved stone town and guild halls as well as brick and half-timber versions. Sadly, the Second World War took a heavy toll, especially in cities like Cologne, Ulm, Hildesheim and Lübeck. Many of these halls have been restored but, though the craftsmanship is good and great care has been taken, the task was too extensive to permit the finance necessary to restore the buildings to the standard of richness that they had originally. Several notable examples remain. The *Altes Rathaus* at *Brunswick*, built in stone and now restored, survives (509). This is a particularly outstanding town hall. Of simpler, provincial type is the stone *Rathaus* at *Goslar*, in the Harz mountains region. This is much smaller and less pretentious, but it has good geometrical window tracery above a ground floor arcade. There is a finialled, gabled roof. Inside is a fine decorative chamber.

Castles and *houses* have also suffered greatly from war-time damage in Germany. Before 1939, the country probably possessed more half-timber Medieval structures than any other. Now there are few. There is one at *Dinkelsbühl* (510) and there is the *Kaiserworth* (now a hotel) at *Goslar*. Probably the finest surviving instance of a fortified town is at *Rothenburg-ob-der-Tauber*, which still retains its picturesque walls and towers. Heidelberg possesses some of these, but most of the work here is of a later date or has been replaced. The timber and stone houses which made towns like Brunswick, Nuremberg, Frankfurt and Hildesheim so attractive have nearly all disappeared.

Switzerland

Swiss Medieval architecture is much like that in Germany though, in general, rather plainer, especially on the exteriors. The finest of the *cathedrals* is that at *Basle*, which has a picturesque situation on the Rhine. The west façade is fifteenth century and typical of Swiss Gothic work (519). *Berne Cathedral* is mainly of late fifteenth century construction. The architecture of *Lausanne Cathedral* is mainly thirteenth century Gothic, very simple, with plate tracery in the rose windows and lancet aisle windows all round the building. The west doorway, richly decorated with sculptured figures, is in late Gothic style, but was not constructed till the seventeenth century. The interior is simple and austere and has much in common with English cathedrals of this date. Pointed arches are used throughout. There is a tall nave arcade, a short arcaded triforium and a clerestory of one lancet window to a three arcade group. The glass is of good quality.

Fribourg is a small town built on a picturesque hilly site on a bend of the river Sarine. It retains many of its late Medieval buildings and much of the atmosphere of a town of this period. The *cathedral* is the largest monument. It has a fine Gothic tower (520) which was completed in 1490. The western porch below, surmounted by its rose window, is sculptured. There are apostles flanking the doorway also angels and prophets (520) and a Last Judgment tympanum. Nearby is the sixteenth century wooden *Pont de Berne* and the *Town Hall* of 1500–22.

Austria and Hungary

Austria also closely reflects the German Gothic style. Its supreme monument is *S. Stephen's Cathedral* in *Vienna* (521). It has two late Gothic towers, separated by the width of the church but, like Strasbourg, only one was surmounted by its spire, which is a graceful, ornate one. S. Stephen's is a hall church, thus having no triforium or clerestory. The interior is dark and full of Medieval atmosphere. It has an exceptionally lofty nave arcade whose pointed arches reach almost into the vault. The roof is vaulted in square bays in stellar pattern, as are also the aisles, but the chancel is quadripartite. Some of the original coloured glass is still in the windows.

518

519

520

518 *Kapellbrücke, Lucerne, 1333*
519 *Façade, Basle Cathedral,*
fifteenth century
520 *Fribourg Cathedral from the*
west, 1470–92. Tower 250 feet
high

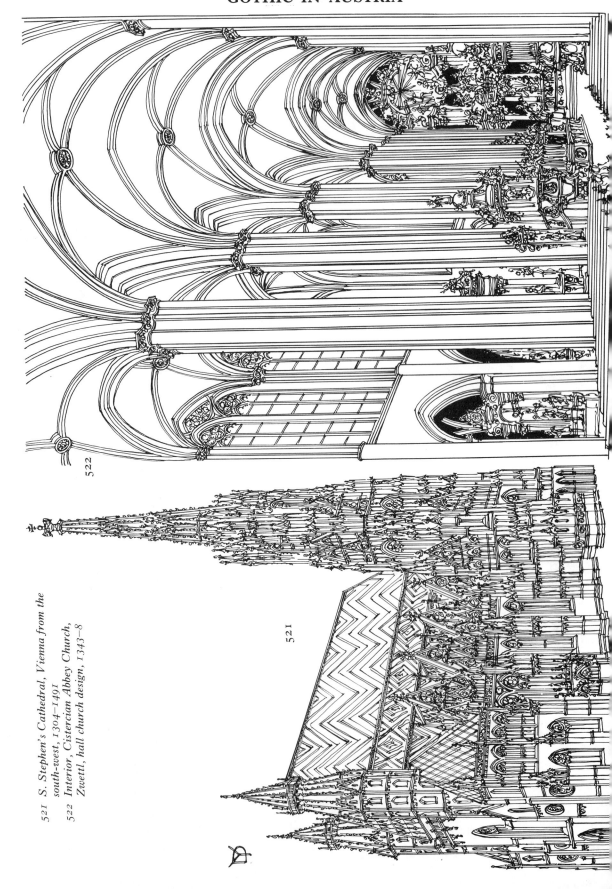

521 S. Stephen's Cathedral, Vienna from the
south-west, 1304–1491

522 Interior, Cistercian Abbey Church,
Zwettl, hall church design, 1343–8

522

521

river Tagus, Portugal, 1500–22.
Francisco de Arruda
524 Great hall, Salzburg Castle,
Austria, 1502
525 Town gateway, Rhodes, fourteenth and fifteenth centuries
526 Castle walls, Salzburg

524

526

523

525

It is beautiful, but both the light and view are partly obscured by a later altar. The rest of the glass is mostly modern. There is some good sculpture and an especially interesting Medieval pulpit, traceried and carved with heads.

527 *Church of S. Matthias, Budapest, Hungary. Reconstructed 1255. Tower 1470*

The *Cistercian Abbey Church* at *Zwettl* is a superb fourteenth century work. The façade and steeple are rebuilt in Baroque style, but the interior is a classic hall church. The tall, grouped piers ascend to tiny, foliated capitals. The vaults of nave and aisles are of the same height and both are quadripartite. The windows are in simple Gothic style. Baroque altars and pulpits of great ornateness provide a foil to the severe grey and white Medieval interior (**522**).

The *castle* at *Salzburg*, impregnably and romantically situated on top of the hill Hohensalzburg, is a Medieval one. It is now partly a museum and partly a private residence. It has been restored but not altered a great deal in modern times. The central keep dates from the early twelfth century but concentric walling with mural towers was added during the Middle Ages, bringing its fortification up to date (**526**). The state apartments are interesting. The best of them, the great hall and the golden room (**524**) date from the early years of the sixteenth century. There are brightly coloured and gilded, patterned wood ceilings, curved columns, richly carved doorways under ogee arches and fantastic metal and ceramic stoves.

527

Medieval remains in *Hungary* are few. The best were in the city of *Budapest* which is divided by the river Danube into the hilly right bank where Buda is situated and the flatter lands opposite of Pest. The main population of the city has always lived in Pest but after the Mongol invasion of 1241, a citadel was built on the hills opposite, since known as castle hill. A whole Medieval fortified town was established in Buda, as it came to be called, named after Attila's brother. Here, before the destruction of the Second World War, were narrow streets and houses, mural towers and walling. There was also a seventeenth century Town Hall and the immense Royal Palace, with S. Stephen's Chapel.

The only great Medieval building to survive here is the *Coronation Church* of *S. Matthias* (**527** and **486**). This was originally a Romanesque building but was gradually turned into a Gothic one in the fourteenth and fifteenth centuries. During the Turkish occupation the church was used as a mosque and later became a Jesuit monastery. It was restored in Gothic manner under the Emperor Franz Josef in the nineteenth century and once more used as a coronation church. The damage caused in the Second World War has been repaired on the exterior, which now looks well. Inside, much remains to be done, especially to restore the frescoes which cover all surfaces of walls, vaults, piers and capitals, as at Chauvigny in France. It is a three-aisled church with triforium and small round clerestory windows.

Sopron, near the Austrian border, has several Medieval churches but they are mainly in a poor state of preservation. There is the *Church of the Holy Ghost* (1421), *S. Michael* (1484) and the *Cathedral, S. George*, a larger fourteenth century building.

Czechoslovakia

In contrast with Germany, there was no strong Romanesque tradition here and Gothic architecture, spread by the monastic orders, was soon accepted and established. Unfortunately, due to the troubled times in this area of central Europe, little survives of early Gothic building; the great Czech monuments of the Middle Ages are of the fourteenth and fifteenth century, and even later, and are, in consequence, in the richer, more decorative Gothic style.

The Cistercian and Praemonstratensian Orders were especially active in the building of *abbeys*. Many were designed by French builders but carried out by the local craftsmen. Few such churches remain in anything like their former state. A thirteenth century Cistercian doorway survives from the *Klôšter Hradištĕ* (near Mnichovo Hradištĕ), now part of the walls of a modern building, while at the Benedictine Monastery at *Sázava*, which stands above the river of the same name, a tributary of the Vltava, the Gothic church was never completed and only part of the nave exists. The best preserved Cistercian Abbey Church is that on the river Vltava south of České Budejovice at *Zlatá Koruna*. Founded in 1269, most of the building was of the fourteenth century, though it has been extensively restored after damage in the late Middle Ages.

From the fourteenth century onwards considerable building was carried out in the Gothic style. The chief city was *Prague* which, despite energetic later construction in the Baroque form, still possesses much of its Gothic heritage. Most of Czechoslovakia, and Prague in particular, was spared the devastation of the Second World War suffered by neighbouring countries. The great buildings of the country have, unfortunately, partially succumbed to a slower, more insidious destructive process; that of time and the decay wrought by lack of restoration when needed. Prague before 1939 was a beautiful city. Now, the signs of that beauty are still discernible but tend to be offset by the layers of crumbling stucco, stone or woodwork resulting from too many years of neglect. Specific buildings, notably those on Castle Hill, including the cathedral and palaces, are restored and in good repair. Elsewhere, the condition of many of the great monuments ranges from shabby to ruinous.

The *city of Prague* is built on both sides of the beautiful river Vltava. It is of ancient foundation though few Romanesque monuments survive (p. 186). Much of the great Gothic work is on the narrow hill ridge (**530**) on the north-west side of the river. Here on *Castle Hill*, the Hradčany, grouped around the courtyards, are the buildings of the castle-palace, the cathedral and S. George's Basilica (p. 186) (PLATE 56).

Outstanding, and the finest Gothic building in Czechoslovakia, is *S. Vitus' Cathedral*. It was designed and begun by *Matthias of Arras*, who

GOTHIC ARCHITECTURE IN CZECHOSLOVAKIA

528 Town Hall and houses in the Market Place, Tábor, fifteenth and sixteenth centuries
529 Convent Church, Market Place, Tábor, fifteenth century
530 View of Prague showing river Vltava, Charles Bridge, Castle Hill (Hradčany), with cathedral, castle, Church of
      All Saints and S. George's Basilica

531

532

533

534

31 Vault, Church of S. Barbara, Kutnà Hora, fifteenth
nd sixteenth centuries
32 and 533 Interior and exterior of the choir, S. Vitus'

Cathedral, Prague, 1344–85. Lower part Matthias of
Arras, upper part Peter Parler
534 Plan

GOTHIC IN CZECHOSLOVAKIA

535 *Façade, Church of S. Barbara, Kutná Hora, early sixteenth century*
536 *Façade, Tyn Church, Prague, 1365–1511*
537 *Vladislav Hall, Prague Castle, 1487–1500, Benedikt Rejt*

came to Prague in the 1340s from the court of the Popes in Avignon. As would be expected it is, therefore, on French Gothic pattern (**534**). The architect died in 1352 and his place was taken by *Peter Parler* from Cologne, who was invited to come from Schwäbisch-Gmünd to work on the cathedral. Parler brought with him the influence of the Cologne school and, though only the choir and chapels with part of the south façade were completed at this time, it is interesting to compare, both on exterior and interior, the work of Matthias on the lower part and Parler on the upper (**532** and **533**). Parler's influence can especially be seen in the vaulting, most particularly in the stellar designs of the Sacristy and Wenceslaus Chapel. The choir vault was completed in 1385 (**532**).

S. Vitus' Cathedral is cruciform and much in one style in the interior though the nave (the west end) is of nineteenth and twentieth century construction. There is a lofty crossing and short transepts. The interior vista is very fine, the vault throughout at one level with flanking, lower aisles. The vaulting shafts run up to the full height of the building. Both clerestory and triforium openings have glass. The east end is apsidal with ambulatory and chapels (**532** and **533**).

Peter Parler's work in Prague extended beyond the cathedral. From its commencement in 1357, he was in charge of the building of the *Charles Bridge*, which spans the Vltava and leads to Castle Hill (**530**); also of the entrance tower on the bridge (1376–8). It is a fine, Medieval bridge, guarded at each end and fortified as befitted its position as the sole river crossing and approach to the castle. It was of great length for its period, nearly 2000 feet from tower to tower. It was decorated by 30 sculptured figures on the parapet, created over the years from the fifteenth century onwards, but mainly of the eighteenth and nineteenth century date. Most of these are now being replaced as the soft sandstone from which they are carved has become seriously eroded.

Peter Parler was also responsible for the choir of *S. Bartholomew's Cathedral* at *Kolín* (1360–78), which is a fine example of his work. The Parler family was an architectural one, the members of which had a great deal of influence on Gothic architecture both in Czechoslovakia

and further afield to Vienna and Milan. The family architects included Peter's brother Michael and his sons Wenzel and Johann; indeed, work on Prague Cathedral was a family affair.

The *castle-palace* near the cathedral on the Hradčany in Prague has several Medieval interiors. Of these, the *Vladislav Hall* (**537**) begun in 1487, is of particular interest. The interiors here are of a later date and were designed or influenced by *Benedikt Rejt* and *Matthias Rejsek*. The vaulted ceilings of the palace interiors are unusual, as can be seen in the plaited swirls in the Vladislav Hall and in the Old Diet Chamber. Other interesting late Gothic buildings in Prague are the *Powder Tower* completed by Rejsek, the *Old Town Hall*, the restored *New Town Hall* in Charles Square, which is only a little later, and the *Týn Church*. This was built over a long period—both Peter Parler and Rejsek worked on it. Standing in Town Hall Square in the Old Town, it is fronted at the base by seventeenth and eighteenth century gabled houses, while behind is the Renaissance Týn Court with Doric loggia. The stone church is well proportioned and has a fine exterior which can be clearly viewed from the Old Town Hall tower opposite (**536**). Inside, it is a tall, aisled church without transepts, Medieval in structure but with Baroque decoration and furniture.

Outside Prague there are a number of outstanding later Gothic churches. One of these is *S. Jakob* (S. James in English) in *Brno*. The exterior is plain and undistinguished but with a tall, elegant tower. Inside, the hall church is very fine and in good condition. The stone nave piers are grouped columns which soar up to tiny capitals and then to the beautiful vault which springs from them (**538**).

In *Kutná Hora* there are several interesting churches of which the most notable is that of *S. Barbara*, which is large and imposing and in a fine state of repair. The west façade, which is the later part of the building, shows the complex flying buttress system on either side (**535**) which extends all round. Inside, the five-aisled church is immensely tall, its piers extending up to the complicated stellar and geometric ribbed vaults of nave and choir. The nave arcade has tall pointed arches above which is a gallery whose columns support aisle and nave vault (**531**). The choir has an ambulatory behind the lancet-

538 Church of S. Jakob (James), Brno, Czechoslovakia, 1480–1500

pointed arches of the arcade. The church is very light because of the large, decoratively traceried windows. It is a stone building, constructed over a long period and one of the richest Czech Gothic ecclesiastical structres. Also in Kutná Hora is the Medieval *Church of S. James*, which has a tall western tower and apsidal eastern termination. It is a hall church, simple and a good stone example. There are no capitals to the nave arcade which supports the quadripartite vault over naves and aisles. The eastern windows are obscured by a vast Baroque alterpiece.

At *Košice* (Kassa) the *Cathedral of S. Elizabeth* is a magnificent Gothic building of the fourteenth and fifteenth centuries. It was begun in 1380 but the tall tower was not built until after 1500. Some of the fine craftmanship was carried out by Viennese artists. Other notable examples include the *Church* at *Znojmo* and *S. Maurice* at *Olomouc*, though the latter has been much altered on the exterior; it has a hall church interior.

Secular remains of Gothic architecture in Czechoslovakia are fewer. The *town hall* at *Olomouc* dates from the late fourteenth century. Though it has been altered in later periods, it retains some Gothic features. *Znojmo*, which is a town listed as an ancient monument, needs a good deal of restoration but its *town hall* of 1445 still possesses its tall, elegant steeple. The *town hall* at *Brno*, on the other hand, which had a fine late Gothic pinnacled portico, is now rebuilt, showing only the decoration above the doorway.

Tábor retains its late Medieval aspect best in the market square and castle. The *market square* is attractive and homogeneous. There is a late Gothic *church* (**529**), which has a wide, short, dark interior on hall church pattern. The octagonal nave piers have no capitals and ascend to carry the reticulated nave vault above. The choir vault is of radiating, lierne design. Nearby are some gabled *houses* and the *town hall* (**528**). The latter is now much restored in nineteenth century Gothic style as a museum. The whole group of buildings in the square present a charming provincial ensemble. The town is still largely encircled by its fortified walls, at one point of which stands the *castle*, overlooking the river gorge.

The Baltic Region

Holland, Northern Germany, Poland and Northern U.S.S.R.

It is convenient to discuss the architecture of this area separately, although it cuts across the geographical frontiers of a number of present day countries. This immense stretch of Europe, extending over 1200 miles along the North Sea and Baltic coasts from Bruges in Belgium to Novgorod in the Soviet Union, displays a close unity of architectural style. There are two chief reasons for this: first, the control and wealth of the Hanseatic League, and second, the paucity of building materials which caused brick to be most commonly used for Gothic buildings. This is a limiting material for design purposes, so it was inevitable that a strong similarity of form should prevail.

The Hanseatic League* was originally a German federation, primarily concerned in trade, protection from piracy then rife in the northern seas and promoting successful commercial interchange as a result of close co-operation between towns and guilds. There was sometimes a political element in the League's activities, but this was subordinate to the commercial projects. Exact beginnings are not clearly known but by the mid-thirteenth century Lübeck and Hamburg in Germany were co-operating together and soon other German towns were joining: Lüneburg, Wismar, Stralsund, Soest and Dortmund. Utrecht in Holland became a centre, Bruges in Belgium, and even London was drawn in. Scandinavia co-operated, as did Danzig (Gdansk) and Novgorod. The corridor of land administered by the League extended as far south as Cracow, Göttingen and Cologne. Its power continued till the fifteenth century, after which it declined in face of competition from new trade routes opening up.

This wide coastal belt is a generally flat plain, only partially wooded, containing little building stone. Brick was the material developed and used almost universally for permanent buildings, timber for some other structures. This forced on builders a simple form of Gothic architecture. Brick is unsuitable for spires, finials, flying buttresses and carved ornament is impossible. Thus, walls, vaults, piers were all plain. Buildings were large and barn-like.

* *From* hansa, *an old high German word for company or guild.*

539 *Church of S. Jan, Maastricht, c. 1450*

540 *Tower of Utrecht Cathedral, 1321–82*

541 *Steeple, Nieuwe Kerk, Delft, 1383–96*

542 *S. Peter's Church, Leyden, 1339–1426*

By the thirteenth century a need for decorative additions was felt. This was provided by polychrome or coloured brick surfacing. Black, yellow and white bricks were introduced to give a pattern, as were also small quantities of other materials. Ceramic polychrome was introduced and coloured tiling for roofs. Builders became expert in providing plastic forms in brick. Panelling was achieved on walls, giving blind recesses of differing shapes. Windows in the later period were very large and had ornate geometric or curvilinear tracery. Sometimes brick tracery was used, sometimes the small quantity of stone needed was found for important buildings.

Holland

Dutch Medieval work is very typical of the Baltic area, though it is generally plainer than that of neighbouring Germany. *Cathedrals* and *churches* tend to be large, with lofty nave, choir and transepts, but with few projections such as porches, portals or buttresses. *Utrecht* and *Haarlem Cathedrals* are of this type. Utrecht is in warm coloured brick, barn-like in general form but having very fine large traceried windows. Now the nave has gone, only choir and transepts with cloisters are left, separated, by a space where the nave stood, from the great fourteenth century tower. The latter was a prototype design for many other Dutch towns (**540**). Haarlem is a fifteenth century cathedral and very similar. It has a lantern tower over the crossing. The *Cathedral* of *S. Jan* at *'sHertogenbosch* is an exception to the usual plainness of Dutch Gothic design. Perhaps because it is situated not far from the Belgian border where stone is more readily available, it is a richly decorated late Gothic cathedral, definably Dutch in treatment but Belgian or French in design. It is a fifteenth century building with some sculpture dating from early in the sixteenth century. It has transepts and an enormous ornately decorated south porch, a central and western tower and forests of flying buttresses (**543**).

543 *Cathedral of S. Jan, 's Hertogensbosch, Holland, 1419–1529*

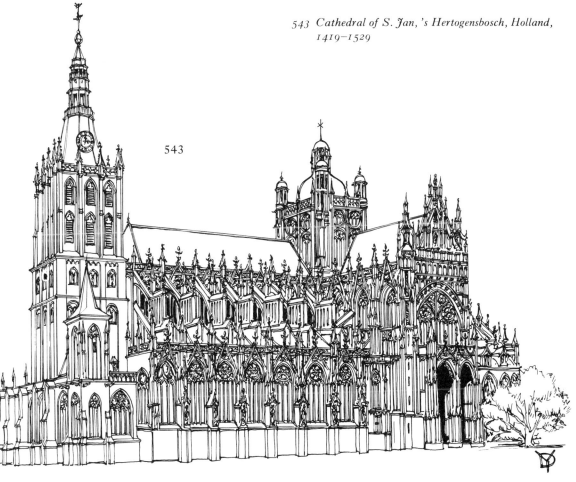

543

The *Oude Kerk* in *Amsterdam* and the *Nieuwe Kerk* in *Delft* (**541**) are typical of some of the fine Dutch steeples as is *S. Jan* in *Maastricht* (**539**). The steeples are often in a later style, partly Renaissance and reminding the onlooker of Wren's designs of the city churches of London. The Oude Kerk in the centre of Amsterdam was begun *c.* 1300 and is a large, many-gabled church with simple fenestration. Building continued till the later sixteenth century and the steeple is typical of this period. One of the greatest and most typical churches in Holland is that of *S. Peter* in *Leyden* (**542**). This has no tower. It is a large, spreading, brick church of the fourteenth and fifteenth centuries. Inside, the crossing piers are cut back and a wooden barrel vault extends across all four arms of the cross. The interior walls are also of plain brick with stone arches and columns and particularly fine late Gothic traceried windows. Large columns with foliated octagonal

capitals are used throughout the church, supporting an arcade of pointed arches which narrow round the choir ambulatory. This eastern termination is polygonal. There is a blind triforium and large clerestory windows above which brightly illuminate the whole church.

Equally typical is the simple and remote *Grote Kerk* at *Brouwershaven* in south-west Holland on the north coast of the Island of Schouwen-Duiveland. The fourteenth century choir is very fine, with its columns, capitals and pointed arches in similar style to S. Peter's in Leyden. Here also is the lancet-arched, blind triforium with geometric clerestory windows above, the whole roofed in wood (**544**).

Remains of a number of fortified buildings exist in Holland, also constructed in brick. The *Amsterdamsche Poort* at *Haarlem* is a fine town gateway (**546**) and the thirteenth century moated castle at *Muiden* is a picturesque solid structure (**547**).

544 Choir and ambulatory, Grotekerk, Brouwershaven, Island of Schouwen—Duiveland, Holland, early fourteenth century

544

MEDIEVAL CASTLES

545 Bran Castle, near Braşov, Rumania, fourteenth century
546 Amsterdamsche Poort. Town Gateway, Haarlem, Holland, 1488
547 Muiden Castle, Holland, thirteenth century
548 Hunedoara Castle, Rumania, fifteenth century. Later restorations

Northern Germany

All along the coastal plain bordering the North Sea and the Baltic, stretching from the Dutch frontier to that of the U.S.S.R., the towns suffered years of bombardment from sea and air during the Second World War. The devastation of these Hanseatic towns, where the best of this type of Gothic architecture had survived remarkably well until 1939, extended up to 150 miles inland. Such towns, which had magnificent brick cathedrals, churches and civic structures, included Hanover, Hamburg and Lübeck in West Germany, Wismar, Prenzlau and Stralsund in East Germany and Szczecin (Stettin) and Gdansk (Danzig) in Poland.

Four great Gothic monuments survive in

Lübeck, though considerably restored and rebuilt the Marienkirche, the Petrikirche, the Cathedral and the Holstentor. The *Marienkirche* (S. Mary's Church) is the finest of these and forms an architectural group with the *Town Hall*, round the market place. Built mainly in the thirteenth and fourteenth centuries, it is a typically German brick, Hanseatic church. It is large, with tall twin western towers and spires, nearly 400 feet high. The east end is polysided, with ambulatory radiating chapels and flying buttresses. There are no transepts (**549**). Severely damaged, the church is now largely restored and in the interior, which is virtually complete, the work has been beautifully done. The building is lofty and light in its tall nave and choir, with the shafts of the ribbed vaults ascending unbroken between the high clerestory windows. The aisle vaults are lower but are also ribbed and painted (**550**). The neighbouring town hall is also now rebuilt; it is part Gothic, part Renaissance (**549**).

The *Petrikirche* (S. Peter's Church) is restored on the exterior but inside the work is only partly advanced. It is a five-aisled hall church, entirely of brick and with a single, very tall western tower and spire. Inside, the vaulting is quadripartite throughout and all of one height. It is supported on octagonal ribbed piers with tiny foliate capitals. All round the church are tall, geometric

549 *S. Mary's Church and part of the Town Hall in the Market Place, Lübeck, Germany. Viewed from the bell tower of S. Peter's Church*

549

550

550 Interior, S. Mary's Church, Lübeck, Germany, 1251–1302

cally traceried windows. The *Holstentor*, which is still the town gateway though the walls have partly disappeared, is now fully restored. It is a fine example of Baltic patterned brickwork (**552**).

Lübeck Cathedral is an immense building

which is still under restoration at the time of writing. Originally built in Romanesque style, a Gothic choir and aisles were added in the fourteenth century, making it into a hall church. It has tall, twin western towers and spires and a long

GOTHIC ARCHITECTURE IN NORTHERN GERMANY

551 Hanover Town Hall, thirteent*
century (left), Marktkirche,
fourteenth century (right)
552 Holstentor, Lübeck, fifteenth
century
553 Town Hall, Stralsund, late
fourteenth century

GOTHIC IN POLAND AND NORTHERN GERMANY

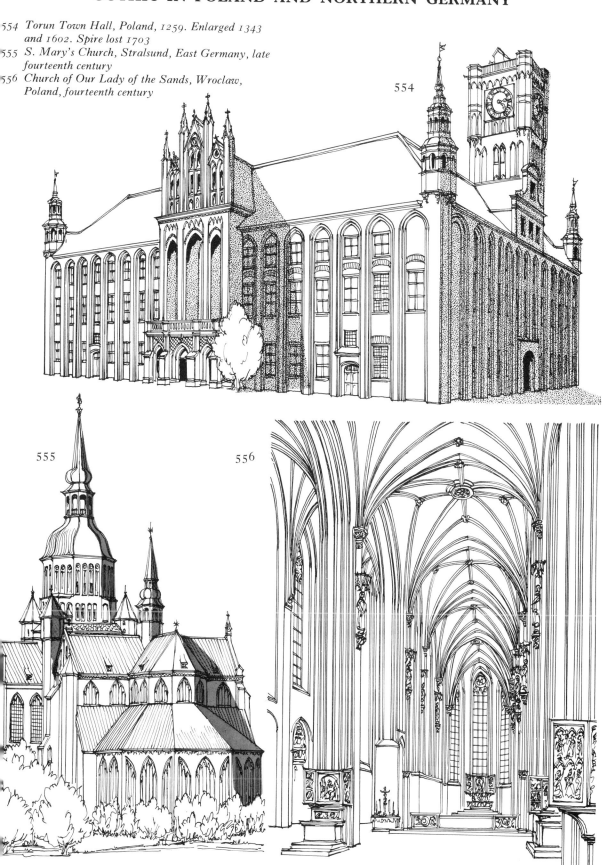

554 *Torun Town Hall, Poland, 1259. Enlarged 1343 and 1602. Spire lost 1703*

555 *S. Mary's Church, Stralsund, East Germany, late fourteenth century*

556 *Church of Our Lady of the Sands, Wroclaw, Poland, fourteenth century*

554

555

556

nave and choir. Inside, the west end, nave and crossing are now restored though the woodwork is all modern. The Romanesque nave is domical barrel-vaulted, in square compartments supported on great square piers, all in whitewashed brick. The aisles of the same height are in Gothic design. The east end, still partly unrestored, is apsidal, with ambulatory encircling the great, round, Romanesque brick piers.

In *East Germany*, the great churches such as S. Mary's Church in *Wismar*, S. Mary's Church at *Prenzlau* and the *Szczecin* churches are still mainly roofless shells. *S. Mary's Church* in *Stralsund* is in fair condition but needs considerable repair. It is an immense brick church, dominating the town, with its octagonal tower and steeple and tall west façade, nave and choir (**555**). The beautiful, richly decorated brick façade of the *Town Hall*, adjoining the great Church of S. Nicholas, still exists (**553**), but is also badly in need of restoration. The gables are a façade in a literal sense, only sky being visible through the tracery.

The great West German city of *Hanover* was the target for countless raids in the Second World War. Not surprisingly little of its pre-war architecture survives, but the fine monumental group of the *Marktkirche* and the *Town Hall* (**551**) survived in shell form and both are now fully restored. The thirteenth century Town Hall is a great gabled rectangular building, panelled and decorated entirely in typical Hanseatic style brickwork. The Marktkirche was built in the fourteenth century, adjacent to the Town Hall. Also in brick, it has a tall, German-roofed western tower, a lofty nave and apsidal choir, but no transepts. The hall church interior is very fine. It is simple and monumental, its tall, round, brick columns, without capitals, supporting a simple quadripartite vault.

Poland

Over much of the country a fine Gothic heritage, largely in brick building, survived until 1939, but after 1945, all the major Polish towns, except Cracow, had been severely damaged or totally devastated. Progress towards rebuilding has been slow. The great Medieval buildings are now, one by one, being rehabilitated and these, where the work is completed, illustrate (as in Germany) a very high standard of workmanship, faithful to the Gothic traditions, spirit and design. Two of the cities which had the finest heritage, Gdansk (Danzig) and Wroclaw (Breslau), suffered the greatest destruction.

Gothic architecture was brought to Poland by the monastic orders, firstly the Cistercian, then the Dominicans and Franciscans. In general, Romanesque style work continued late and Gothic design was slow to develop. The majority of new churches and cathedrals were monastic settlements. Over much of the country brick was still the building material. Typical examples of the monastic churches include the *Dominican Monastery* of *S. Adalbert* in *Wroclaw* and the *Dominican Church* and *Franciscan Church* in *Cracow*. All these have suffered from rebuilding. The Wroclaw example was largely destroyed in the Second World War. The monastery has gone, but the church is now rebuilt. A large, brick building, it has a tall nave, choir and transepts and apsidal choir termination. Inside, it is simple and lofty, with a fine vault and traceried windows in the choir. The Dominican Church in Cracow has a Medieval Baltic, brick façade with decorative gable. Much of the church was rebuilt in the nineteenth century and both Cracow churches have lost some of their Medieval character.

The German pattern of *hall church* spread widely in Poland and there are still a number of large brick examples. One is the *Church of the Assumption* at *Chelmno*, entirely Gothic on the exterior but, inside, the Baroque features overpower the simplicity of the brick vaults and columns. Others include the *Church of S. John* in *Torun* and the *Collegiate Church of Our Lady* in *Poznan*. There are two fine examples in *Wroclaw*: the *Church of the Holy Cross* and the *Church of Our Lady of the Sands*. Both of these were badly damaged in the War. The former is of unusual design as it was built in two storeys (largely in the fourteenth century), one church above the other. It is therefore a tall but also slender building, all in brick, with a high, elegant south tower and spire. The interior is still in ruinous condition though the exterior is fairly intact. Both this church and the Church of Our Lady of the Sands (na Piasky) have *Piast vaults*.* These are unusual in design, being tripartite but divided into nine, panelled compartments. The Church of Our Lady of the Sands is still very battered on

*As do also a number of famous Polish Medieval churches, particularly in Wroclaw, Szczecin and Torun.

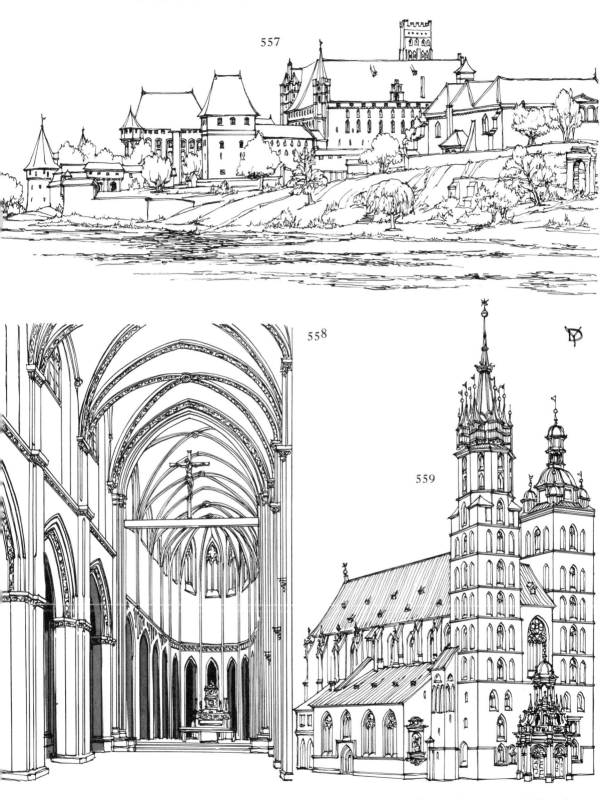

557

558

559

557 *Castle of the Teutonic Knights, Malbork (Marienburg)*, c. *1400. From the river bridge*
558 Gniezno Cathedral, mid-fourteenth century

559 *S. Mary's Church, Cracow, fourteenth and fifteenth centuries, Baroque porch*

the exterior but the interior has been beautifully restored (556). It is a hall church, with soaring, ribbed nave piers. The nave and choir have the usual Gothic ribbed vault but in the aisles the Piast vaulting can be clearly studied. The choir is apsidal with very fine modern glass in the windows. The whole interior is in red brick, partly whitewashed.

Among the most outstanding Medieval ecclesiastical building in Poland are the Cathedrals of Wroclaw, Cracow and Gniezno and the two churches dedicated to S. Mary, one in Cracow and one in Gdansk. The *Cathedral* at *Wroclaw* was heavily damaged in 1945 but is now reconstructed, apart from the western spires. It is a brick building with a long nave which has simple, rectangular plan piers, without capitals, supporting a pointed arched arcade. There is a short, square-ended choir and almost no transepts. *Cracow Cathedral* was based on a similar design but, being later, is of more advanced Gothic form. Built on the site of two earlier Romanesque cathedrals, it is situated on the crown of Wawel Hill (p. 185). The dramatic, fourteenth century exterior shows to advantage on this site and, despite its Renaissance and Baroque towers and chapels, presents a homogeneous whole. The interior is less satisfactory; it is muddled and confused by a multiplicity of bric-à-brac in a variety of periods. The choir, with its carved wood stalls and Gothic vault is the most impressive part. *Gniezno Cathedral* is also built on the site of two earlier Romanesque ones (p. 185). It is mainly a fourteenth century building though its western towers are Baroque. A simple, monumental structure, it has no transepts, but an apsidal-ended choir with ambulatory and chapels round it; an unusually French design for Poland. The interior is plain. The large nave piers have simple capitals and above is a pointed arched arcade. There is no triforium. Both nave arcade and clerestory windows continue uninterrupted, but in narrowing form, round the choir apse.

The *Church of S. Mary* in *Gdansk* (Danzig) is the largest Gothic church in Poland. It was built in the later fifteenth century and was seriously damaged in 1944, but is now excellently restored. It has one large, tall tower and a number of turrets. Inside, it is a hall church, all of whitewashed brick. Octagonal piers divide the nave from aisles; these piers have no bases or capitals.

The nave arcade has tall, stilted arches. The rectangular vaulting bays are mostly star vaulted in many different designs. The tall aisle windows illuminate this beautiful stellar vaulting. The *Church of S. Mary* in *Cracow* is the town church built in the market place in the fourteenth and fifteenth centuries but with the addition of Renaissance cupola and a Baroque western porch. The church has lofty western towers also a tall nave and choir. It is on basilican plan (559). The interior is dark due to the coloured glass in the narrow windows, the wealth of Baroque ornamentation and the deep colours of blues, reds, brown and gold with which vaults walls and arcade are painted. Like most buildings in Cracow, the church escaped war damage, but badly needs cleaning and repair.

Many fortresses and *castles* were built in the Middle Ages in Poland. Struggles for power within the country and attacks from outside were violent and sustained. Earlier structures had central keeps surrounded by walls and moat. After the thirteenth century larger schemes were built of stone but, more often in the north, in brick. There are examples of large castles at Niedzica, Czersk and Mir (now in the U.S.S.R.) but one of the greatest was the vast complex built as the headquarters for the Teutonic Knights, on the river Norgat, an arm of the Vistula, 35 miles south of Gdansk. It was called Marienburg (now *Malbork*). One of the most powerful fortresses in Europe, it has many parts, built at different times. Still extant, and now repaired after war damage, are some impressive Gothic rooms like the *Grand Refectory* and *Capitular Chamber*, which have rows of columns supporting fine vaulted ceilings, and two immense *court yards*, that of the Middle Castle and that of the High Castle. The latter has an upper gallery which goes round the whole court, providing impressive vistas through the traceried openings. The large church is still under repair. Especially notable is the approach view from the road bridge where the vast pile can be seen rising from the banks of the great river. Even to twentieth century eyes it is a symbol of power (557).

In *Cracow*, sections of the city walls survive from Medieval building. The city had been walled and moated since the thirteenth century. It had a number of fortified gates, of which the barbican and *S. Florian's Gate* exist.

MEDIEVAL BUILDING IN THE U.S.S.R.

560 *Church of the Ascension at Kolomonskoe,*
     near Moscow, stone, 1532

561 *Wooden Tower fortification from the*
     White Sea, 1690. Now at Kolomonskoe

562 *The Kremlin, Rostov, seventeenth century*

563 *The Kremlin, Pskov. Showing buildings*
     inside the fortified walls, sixteenth and
     seventeenth centuries

There are a number of examples of civic Medieval building still in Poland. *Torun Town Hall* has retained most of its Gothic character. It was begun in 1259, though Renaissance gables and turrets were added in 1602. The tall spire was unfortunately lost in 1703 but the building remains a good example of a Medieval town hall (**554**). In *Cracow*, the tower of the fourteenth century *town hall* survives in the Market Place, while the richly decorated example at *Wroclaw* in the Rynek, the central square of the town, though altered later, is still in Gothic style; it has a tall tower and ornamental gables. The *Town Hall* at *Gdansk* has an exceptionally lofty tower and elegant lantern. The building is brick and dates from the fourteenth century, though with later fenestration and entrance doorway.

The *University of Cracow* was founded in 1364. The buildings were rebuilt from about 1500 in stone and brick and survived until 1837, when the architect K. Kremer was commissioned to enlarge and adapt the university, called the Cracow Academy. In recent years, further restoration has been carried out and, though the work is obviously of the nineteenth and twentieth century, a Medieval spirit has been retained. The courtyard behind S. Anne's Street and Jallegonska Street gives a good impression of how the small Medieval court would have looked.

Northern U.S.S.R.

There is very little Gothic architecture in the Soviet Union. The Byzantine style dominated important building, particularly in the ecclesiastical field, until the seventeenth century (see Chapter 3, p. 124). There are some Byzantine buildings with Gothic fenestration and detail (**463** and **517**) and later, there are similar buildings with Renaissance features (Chapter 6, p. 362). But in the Baltic area, in *Lithuania, Latvia, Estonia* and right round to the coastal strip of the White Sea, there are brick and timber buildings which have much in common with those found in the Baltic region of eastern Germany and Poland. The example illustrated in Fig. **561** is a purely timber log structure of the type built all over eastern Europe till long after the Middle Ages. Whole logs are used in such heavily wooded areas, not just timber planks as in western Europe where wood was less plentiful.

This structure, from the White Sea area, is similar to some churches in the Carpathian mountains in Rumania (**643**). Fig. **563** illustrates a brick and timber construction. It is a Kremlin, that is, the fortified citadel of the town. Here shown are the defensive walls and towers and, inside, the Byzantine style churches.

Two towns on the Baltic coast where some good Medieval buildings survive are Riga in Latvia and, further east, Tallinn in Estonia.

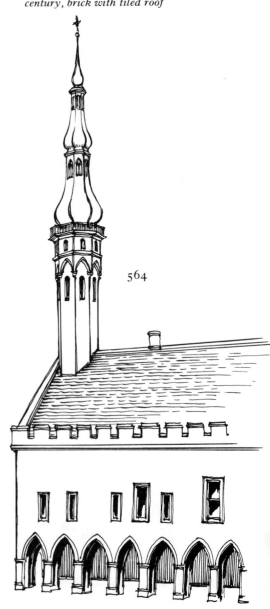

564 *City Hall, Tallin, Estonia, U.S.S.R., fourteenth century, brick with tiled roof*

564

In *Riga* are some stepped gable façades in brick with pointed and round arched windows together and a deeply recessed pointed arched doorway below. In *Tallinn* there is a fourteenth century town hall of brick with battlemented parapet and steeply pitched roof above. Although typical of the Hanseatic area, the pointed arch ground arcade and the tall, elegant tower are reminiscent of Italian Medieval town halls (**564**). Here also are some fine Medieval façades with tall pointed gables, decoratively recessed in brick and with two rows of windows above the street arcade. These date from the fifteenth century. Nearby is a solid, fortified fourteenth century Knight's Castle, built on a mound. It is similar to Castilian examples in the strength and solidity of its exterior brick walls and towers.

There are some churches in the area; some are of hall church pattern, others have an English influence from commercial contacts with sea-faring traders.

Scandinavia

In the Middle Ages architectural development was not in accordance with the existing geographical boundaries of the four countries; it was determined by climate, distance from the main European influence, terrain and available materials. In the south, that is Denmark and southern Sweden, the influence was from the Baltic: Holland, northern Germany and Poland. This was the most prosperous area with the best climate, richest land and closest proximity to European influence. The style was, therefore, chiefly in brick building with decorative brick-work on gables, fenestration and doorways, though a limited French and Belgian influence existed. In Norway, in the west, the land was poorer, the terrain mountainous and difficult of access, the climate inhospitable. Here the building was chiefly of wood, retaining the national craft styles already established. The few stone buildings showed English and Scottish influence above all. In the east, in northern Sweden and in Finland, building was in brick, stone or timber; the two former in larger centres, the latter in the villages.

There is, however, apart from these regional differences, a similarity about most Scandinavian Medieval architecture. It never reaches the heights of drama, of aesthetic beauty, of religious experience that is felt and seen in the contemporary cathedrals and churches of France, Germany and England. There is a poverty of architectural splendour which reflects the poorer regions in which these churches were built. But the question is not only one of poverty but of social and natural development. In the chief centres of Europe in the Middle Ages the cities, the universities and the monasteries were being established. Christianity was the moving, living force of life. From vitality of faith sprang the great cathedrals of France and England. In Scandinavia, at this time, development was slower, the cites poorer and smaller, universities late to appear and the prime force in life was commercial, seen chiefly in dependence on the Hanseatic League.

The great cathedrals and churches are therefore only copies from those in the main centres of civilisation. Technically the buildings are as good as some of those in central and western Europe, but the Medieval spirit is missing. In architectural terms this is evidenced in the smaller, narrower windows, lack of intricate tracery or coloured glass, the almost total lack of development of the flying buttress system, the poverty of decoration in sculpture and carving. There are exceptions but these are few. Because of the inadequate fenestration later Gothic buildings, in particular, are dark inside compared to their equivalents elsewhere. In view of the northern latitudes, the windows should, logically, have been larger, not smaller.

Denmark

Here, as elsewhere in Scandinavia, the chief buildings to survive are ecclesiastical; some are based on the French or English pattern but most are of Baltic design, in brick, with decorative gables and on hall church pattern. Denmark has three important *cathedrals*: Roskilde, Odense, Aarhus. *Roskilde* was an important town in the Middle Ages, a royal residence, and the cathedral was used as the burial place for the Danish kings. The present structure was built from 1190 in brick, though its slender, western spires were seventeenth century additions. This is the least Hanseatic of Danish cathedrals. It clearly shows a·French influence in its triple-aisled plan, while

GOTHIC BUILDINGS IN BRICK IN DENMARK

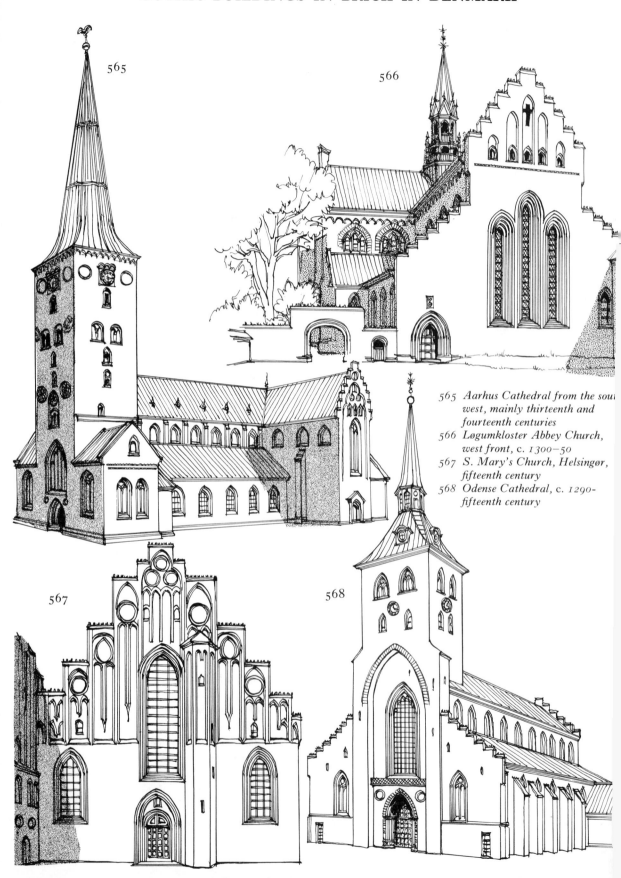

565 *Aarhus Cathedral from the sou[th] west, mainly thirteenth and fourteenth centuries*
566 *Løgumkloster Abbey Church, west front, c. 1300–50*
567 *S. Mary's Church, Helsingør, fifteenth century*
568 *Odense Cathedral, c. 1290– fifteenth century*

the choir resembles that of Tournai Cathedral in Belgium.

The *Cathedral of S. Knud* (Canute) at *Odense* is one of Denmark's finest Medieval buildings. Re-built in Gothic style from 1247 in brick, it is large, simple and spacious. The exterior, with its tall, single, western tower and spire is dignified and solemn (**568**). *Aarhus Cathedral* is even larger, also with a lofty western steeple. This brick building replaces a stone Romanesque cathedral and dates from the thirteenth century onwards (**565**). Inside, the nave and choir are also lofty, the brick walls and ribbed vaults whitewashed with painted decoration on the vaulting. Though sometimes described as a hall church, it is not one. The choir is of hall pattern, with aisles of the same height as the central area, but the tall transepts are aisleless and the nave aisles are barely half the height of the nave itself.

Decorative brickwork is seen more on smaller churches and abbeys. Developed from the Romanesque craft, it has much in common with Dutch, northern German and Polish examples. Blind openings, window surrounds and especially gables are decorated with arcading, saw-tooth courses and herring-bone brickwork. The mullions of traceried windows are also in brick.

After the Reformation the *monasteries* were largely destroyed or fell into ruin. As in England, a number of abbey churches have survived and remained in use, while the abbey buildings have disappeared. A fine example of this type of *abbey church* is that at *Løgumkloster*, founded in 1173 by the Cistercian Order. The eastern part of the church was rebuilt from *c.* 1200, in Romanesque style, but the later western end is in early Gothic with tall lancet windows and stepped gabling (**566**). The fine brickwork has simple mouldings and decoration. The church is cruciform, in three stages, nave arcade, blind triforium and clerestory, showing an English influence. Inside, the lofty crossing is on square plan, a wide pointed arch on each side supported on ribbed brick piers. The night stairs to the cloister remain in the transept. *S. Mary's Church* at *Helsingør* survives from the Carmelite Convent. This has a Baltic style decorated brick, stepped gable façade (**567**).

The simple *Church* at *Bogense* is a typical example of gable decorative brickwork on a less ambitious level. It has two projecting gables with stepped and panelled decoration. The church dates from 1406; it has an unpretentious, white-washed interior.

Norway

The mountain barrier between Norway and Sweden was so impassable in the Middle Ages that the easier exit from the country to the outside world was by sea, and the nearest important neighbour was the British Isles. This influence is shown especially in the larger stone churches in Norway. The square rather than apsidal eastern arm is usual and the style of vaulting and proportions of vault, tower and spire are English. *Stavanger Cathedral* (p. 191) was built in Romanesque design, but its fine choir is late Gothic.

The chief monument to the Gothic style in Norway is *Trondheim Cathedral* (a town which, in the Middle Ages, was called Nidaros). The cathedral was built between 1130 and 1290 but, due to several fires and other hazards, suffered damage and was extensively restored and rebuilt in the nineteenth and twentieth centuries. It is still an imposing structure and Medieval in concept (**571**). The central and western towers are heavy and solemn and the façade, though finely sculptured, is of recent restoration. It is a large cathedral and its interior retains a Medieval sense of spirituality. The choir is encircled by a stone screen with an ambulatory behind. The choir arcade piers are grouped with large carved foliated capitals. Over the crossing is a lantern, supported on lofty grouped piers with small, foliated capitals. The transepts are Romanesque and contain fine, round-arched arcading on the walls of triforium and clerestory. The arches are decorated with chevron ornament. The nave is of later style, loftier, and with grouped, shafted piers and moulded capitals. The triforium reminds one of the Angel Choir at Lincoln Cathedral in England. The clerestory has a passage also, in front of the Decorated Gothic windows. The façade rose window is very fine, in flamboyant style like that at Reims Cathedral in France (**570**). In general, the cathedral is dark but impressive inside. It is much the most imposing in Scandinavia. It is of typically northern design and finish, very much after the manner of buildings in northern England and Scotland.

Among the other Medieval, stone buildings

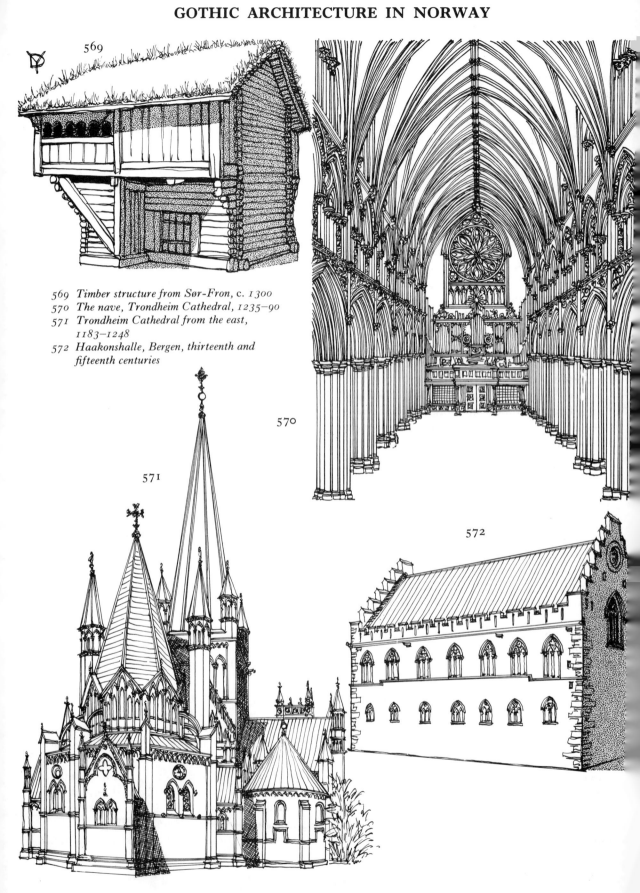

569 Timber structure from Sør-Fron, c. 1300
570 The nave, Trondheim Cathedral, 1235–90
571 Trondheim Cathedral from the east,
   1183–1248
572 Haakonshalle, Bergen, thirteenth and
   fifteenth centuries

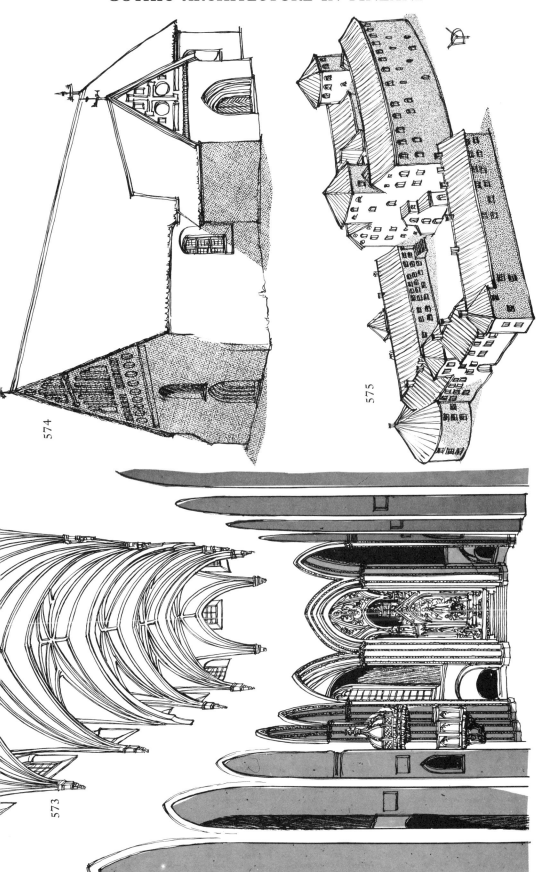

573 Turku Cathedral. The choir, thirteenth and fourteenth centuries
574 Pernä Church (Pernaja), late fourteenth century
575 Turku Castle, late thirteenth century (restored)

in Norway are the Archbishop's Palace at Trondheim and the Haakonshalle at Bergen. The *Trondheim episcopal palace* adjoins the cathedral and dates from the twelfth century. Like the Kaiserpfalz in Goslar, it is a Medieval palace in two storeys, with nearby gatehouse. The *Haakonshalle* in *Bergen* is part of the Bergenhus fortress group of buildings (**572**). The lower floor is early Gothic in style, with deep set windows and a groined vaulted roof. Above is the larger, later Medieval hall with plate traceried, deep-set windows along one side and larger windows at each end. At one end is the minstrels' gallery and, at the other, the daïs with high table and sedilia. The whole interior has been extensively restored.

Most of the building in Norway was still in *timber*. Structures were built of logs, the ends cut and dovetailed. Moss and cloth were laid between the logs to make the walls air and water-tight. The standard of craftsmanship was good and many such structures have now been re-erected in the Oslo Folk Museum at Bygdøy Park on an island near the city (**569**).

Finland

In the Middle Ages, Finland was a land on the north-eastern fringe of Europe to which architectural styles percolated slowly, and had then to be adjusted to suit national and climatic needs. Only the south-western, chiefly coastal part of what is now modern Finland was inhabited. Despite the distance from the centres of European culture, the inhospitable climate and the small population of barely a quarter of a million, Finland possesses, apart from one Medieval cathedral, a number of large churches. Those which survive are of stone and brick. The majority had been of wood and most of these were lost through fire.

Christianity was introduced to Finland via Sweden and the Åland Islands. The capital was Turku (in Swedish Åbo), on the coast in the south-west corner of the country. *Turku Cathedral* survives, though greatly restored and rebuilt, having been damaged and battered in its long history. It is of red brick and simple in style, with a massive western tower on square plan, now surmounted by a nineteenth century lantern. The cathedral was begun in the early thirteenth

century and building continued till after 1300, while a later choir and chapels were added as late as 1520. Inside, there is a tall nave and choir on classic three-aisled pattern, with lofty vault, many times restored. Despite so much rebuilding, Turku Cathedral, like that at Trondheim, retains its Medieval character as well as a national one. It has a fine site, near the river and surrounded by trees. The interior is very simple, in brick, with square piers and no capitals in the nave and octagonal piers with small capitals in the choir. The vault stretches uninterruptedly along the whole length of the cathedral (**573**).

There are a number of surviving *churches* around Turku and along the coastal area eastwards towards the Soviet border. These mainly have an easily recognisable national character. They are fairly large hall churches on three-aisled plan. Vaults have generally replaced the original timber roofs in the later Middle Ages and most churches have a detached, later campanile. The buildings are generally of stone with brick used for the decoration of the gables window and doorway surrounds and interior piers and vaults. Many examples still have paintings over much of the vault and wall surface area and attractive, though rural, carved wood church furniture, especially pulpits.

Among the best examples with elaborate brick gable ornamentation and fine interior painting and carvings are *Hollola Church, Porvoo Cathedral* and *Pernå* (Pernaja) *Church*. Hollola is a fine country church with decorative gables and detached, classical bell tower added in 1848. Inside, it is a hall church on a two-aisled rectangular plan with a central row of square brick pillars supporting the deep, pointed arched ribbed and star vault. There is some good wood carving and ironwork also (**576**).

Porvoo Cathedral was built *c.* 1415 and stands on high ground on the outskirts of the town. The exterior is like a larger version of Hollola Church and it also has a separate campanile and richly decorative brick gabling. The interior is more elaborate, but has also been more altered in later ages. *Pernå Church*, nearby, is much like Hollola on the exterior (**574**); this simple pattern of three aisled, rectangular, hall church is more attractive and appropriate in the smaller country buildings than on the cathedral scale of Porvoo.

There are some beautiful vault and wall paint

ings inside Pernå Church and some outstanding instances of this work in the two small churches of Lohja and Hattula. The *Church of S. Lawrence at Lohja* (between Helsinki and Turku) has a large, simple, stone exterior with brick gable ornamentation. Inside, it is decorated all over walls and vault with biblical scenes, the figure groups and panels separated by arabesque banding. It was built in the fifteenth century and the paintings date from *c.* 1520; it is a very fine

example indeed. *Hattula Church* is very small. Standing in fields on the outskirts of the hamlet of Hattula, near Hämeenlinna, the exterior is unpretentious and rural. Inside, it is on three-aisled, rectangular plan with Medieval vaulting and walls painted all over in figure compositions. There is also a carved and painted wood pulpit with high relief figure decoration. The whole interior is of primitive, peasant standard and style, its colour and drawing charmingly handled;

576 Hollola Church, Finland, c. 1480

576

a superb example of the period. Another remote country *church*, near the sea and not far from Turku is that of *Inkoo*. It has a separate, wooden bell tower standing on a stone base, and decorative brick gabling. Inside, the two-aisled, hall church is vaulted and covered by paintings, but these are not so fine as those at Lohja and Hattula.

Many *castles* were built in Finland in the Middle Ages, for defensive purposes. Most of these have largely disappeared and the two chief examples surviving are those at Turku and Savonlinna. *Turku Castle* was built in the thirteenth century in a strategic position on the harbour. It was enlarged in the later Middle Ages and, in the sixteenth century, state rooms were incorporated. It is a large castle, strongly fortified and with small window openings high up on the massive walls. The interior has been excellently restored after damage caused in the Second World War, though it has been done in a modern, simplified manner. The exterior still retains its Medieval appearance. The drawing in Fig. **575** incorporates its existing state with that of the original structure as shown in the model in the castle.

The most complete Finnish castle is the *fortress* of *Olavinlinna*. It was built as a defence against the Russians, on whose border it still stands. It occupies a small rocky island in the Kyrönsalmi Strait, which is swept by rapid currents; the town of Savonlinna grew up around it between the two lakes. The castle is named after S. Olav and was built in 1475 by Erik Axelsson Tott. It has a strategic and romantic site and was, in its day, a modern fortress built on mural, concentric plan rather than the old central keep system. It was extensively restored in the nineteenth century; the courtyards are now used for staging dramatic spectacles.

Sweden

From the fourteenth century onwards the Church grew richer and more influential. The great cultural influence came from the monastic settlements, where the Cistercian Order was most active. After the Reformation these buildings fell into decay but, as in England, some of the churches were retained and enlarged as parish or cathedral churches. They were nearly all altered in the seventeenth and eighteenth centuries, then restored to their Medieval appearance in the nineteenth or twentieth.

Among such examples are the abbey churches at Varnhem and Vadstena, S. Mary's Church at Sigtuna and the Riddarholm Church in Stockholm. *Varnhem Abbey Church* in Västergötland was of the Cistercian Order. It was rebuilt after a fire in the thirteenth century, altered and restored in contemporary style in the seventeenth but returned to its former state in the 1920s. It is a simple, cruciform stone church with tall western, fortified towers. The interior is monumental and most interesting. It is broad and low with wide, pointed, quadripartite stone vaulting, the vaults being supported on columned corbels with foliated capitals. The nave piers are plain and square, without capitals. The nave arcade is round-arched, simple and unmoulded. There is no triforium, but above are round-headed clerestory windows. The apsidal east end with ambulatory is the best preserved part of the original church.

The Cistercian *Abbey Church* at *Vadstena* on Lake Vättern was founded by S. Bridget and the church begun about 1368. The building has been carefully restored and in the process has lost its Medieval atmosphere, but it still retains a remarkable vault, supported on rows of octagonal piers, which covers the whole hall church interior. The seated statue of S. Bridget (*c.* 1440) survives and is displayed in the church with other sculptural fragments.

S. Mary's Church at *Sigtuna* is typical of the Scandinavian brick church design, based on Baltic influences from northern Germany and Holland. Such buildings are often large; they are wide and low, rarely having towers, except when of cathedral status. S. Mary's Church was part of the Dominican monastery. It is a hall church with typical Baltic decorated gabled façade in ornamental brickwork. Inside, the church has three aisles separated by brick piers without capitals. Above is a wide, pointed arched, quadripartite vault. It is a simple church, well built and very Nordic. Similar are the *Convent Church* at *Ystad* on the southern coast of Sweden and the *Church of the Holy Trinity* at *Uppsala*. The Ystad church has a particularly fine Baltic brick gabled façade (**577**), while Holy Trinity Church is more interesting inside. The simple nave arcade is of moulded brick in wide pointed arches. The quadripartite vault is higher than usual (this is not a hall church) and both nave and aisle vaults are painted.

There are one or two *cathedrals* on a similar but slightly larger, more ambitious scale; *Västerås* and Strängnäs, both on Lake Mälar, are two of these. *Strängnäs Cathedral* has a large square western tower, though its apsidal east end presents the finest exterior view of the building. It is a simple structure, a larger version of the churches just described, but it is impressive and well proportioned. Inside all is brick, piers, columns and quadripartite vaults. It is a five-aisled church, not of hall type, with a wide, lofty nave and ribbed vault. The aisle vaults diminish in height towards the outer walls. Because of this and the consequently small aisle windows which provide the limited nave lighting, the interior is darker than is usual in churches of the kind. The tall apse windows give better illumination to the east end.

In *Stockholm*, the *Riddarholm Church* survives from the Franciscan Abbey, founded in the thirteenth century. Originally it had no towers and was aisleless, but extensive additions in the fifteenth and sixteenth centuries made it into a three-aisled church with a tall tower. It became an important building as the burial place for the

kings of Sweden. Despite later additions of classical chapels and high altar, the Riddarholm Church retains a strong Medieval atmosphere with its wide, low, quadripartite vault and fine, arched nave arcade. Also in the city is the *Storkyrkan*, the church of S. Nicholas, founded in the early thirteenth century and rebuilt about 1306. It has been substantially altered in later periods and has a largely classical, dull exterior. Inside, though, remains a fine lierne vault over the main nave and choir while, in one of the aisles, is a magnificent example of Medieval sculpture, S. George and the Dragon (1489), carved in wood. Painted and over life-size, this is a vivid composition by the Lübeck sculptor, *Bernt Notke* (PLATE 49).

An important centre in the Middle Ages was the *Island of Gotland*, regained by Sweden at this time from control by the Hanseatic League. Its strategic value lay in its situation, ideal for commercial use of the trade routes to England and France in the west and Russia and Europe to the east. Its capital was Visby and both here and in other centres, architectural proof of its Medieval importance lies in the richness and quality of its Gothic buildings, constructed in local stone. After the Middle Ages, trade routes changed and the island lost is importance. Many of the churches are, unfortunately, largely ruined.

577 Convent Church, Ystad, Sweden, façade, fourteenth century

577

GOTHIC IN SWEDEN

578 Uppsala Cathedral, interior looking east, 1270–131
579 Skara Cathedral from the south-west, c. 1300
580 Kalmar Castle, late Gothic

578

579

580

As in Finland, in country areas, Sweden retains some small but beautifully *painted churches*. That at Södra Rådå has already been referred to (p. 191). There is also an example in good condition at *Härkeberga*, a tiny village southwest of Uppsala. The exterior is very simple and unpretentious, but the interior is painted all over: piers, vaults and walls. The colours are soft, mainly browns and greens, on a gold and white ground. The subject is the Bible story.

In a purely Gothic and less Scandinavian manner, are the important *cathedrals* of Sweden: Uppsala, Skara and Linköping. Here is seen less of the Baltic brick approach and more a derivation of French and English design. *Uppsala* is the finest, despite a hard and heavy restorative hand by the nineteenth century

contemporary of Viollet-le-Duc, Helgo Zettervall. Though begun in *c.* 1270 on an English plan, the cathedral soon developed on French lines under the Frenchman Étienne de Bonneuil. It is very much a cathedral of one building operation and retains a Medieval impression despite the mechanical quality of its restoration. On the exterior it is tall, its two western towers and spires reaching high into the sky. The apsidal east end, with attendant chapels, is very French, as is the flèche over the crossing. Inside, it is impressive and lofty. Its height, its vault and fine proportions remind one of Bourges Cathedral as does the detail of the clustered columns and dainty capitals (**578**).

Skara Cathedral in Västergötland (**579**) is more English than French. Here is a stone, tall,

581 Interior looking east of Linköping Cathedral, Sweden, 1260–1412

581

well-proportioned cathedral, with western towers and spires, built on classic Latin cross plan. Inside, the tall nave is divided by piers with clustered shafts and foliated capitals. The shafts extend to the vault springing. There is an arcaded triforium below small clerestory windows. The vaulting is ribbed throughout, lofty and well-proportioned. The east end is rich in its coloured glass. The exterior of *Linköping Cathedral* is unimpressive. Inside, the hall church pattern is paramount and magnificent in its proportions and in the elegance and chiaroscuro of its vault (**581**). It is the least restored Gothic cathedral in Sweden, especially in its east end where the choir ambulatory, its star and lierne vaults on supporting pillars and the traceried windows are of great quality and beauty.

The majority of Medieval remains in Sweden are ecclesiastical. Most domestic building was in wood and has perished, but some of the great mural fortresses survive. Of these *Kalmar Castle* (**580**) presents a dramatic, fortified silhouette, picturesquely situated on a promontory on the eastern sea coast. It has a moat, drawbridge and surrounding ramparts with four corner towers. Originally it had gates and walls further out to sea. *Gripsholm Castle* is built on the edge of Lake Mälar, not far from Strängnäs. It is large and also picturesquely sited in a park. Built in 1537 of brick, it has immense circular mural towers and massive, impregnable walls. It is now used as a school.

Europe South of the Alps, Pyrenees and Carpathians:

Italy, Yugoslavia, Rhodes, Spain, Portugal

Climatic influence has produced specific features common to all Gothic architecture in the southern part of Europe. Unlike the Baltic zone, however, the similarities are far outweighed by the differences. The Gothic style in Italy developed hesitantly and was short-lived because of the country's overwhelming classical tradition. In Spain, on the other hand, development was late but, having arrived, became deep-seated, and slow to be altered in favour of Renaissance forms which were as alien to Spain as Gothic was to Italy. The other countries under discussion in this section were influenced by either Italy or Spain.

The sunny, warm climate of the Mediterranean countries made certain features desirable whatever their interpretation of Gothic architecture. These features are mostly to be seen in central and southern Italy, the Dalmatian coast and central and southern Spain. Colour is used far more than in northern Europe; in marbles, mosaics, and frescoes on the outside as well as the inside of buildings. Window and door openings are smaller to keep the interior cool. The horizontal emphasis is greater than the vertical and, in these countries, it is only in the northern, cooler regions that tall steeples, flying buttresses, traceried large windows and rich, carved decoration in finials and crockets are to be seen. Roof pitches are lower and timber coverings were often preferred to stone vaulting.

Italy

The climate apart, the circumstance which made Italian Gothic architecture different from that in France, Germany or England was the classical tradition. It is sometimes said that there is no Gothic architecture in Italy or that the Italians have never understood the fundamentals of the style. Neither of these statements is true for they exaggerate the reality. Typically Italian Medieval work was still based on Roman or Romanesque designs, examples of both of which existed in quantity all over the country.

The exception is in the north and in monastic structures. The outstanding example is *Milan Cathedral*, as near northern Gothic as the Italians ever reached. Sheathed in white marble (over a brick structure), pinnacled and sculptured, the cathedral has some of the finest stained glass in Europe in its eastern windows. Like Cologne, Milan Cathedral is only really Medieval in its eastern part. Begun here in 1385, the west façade was not completed till the nineteenth century. The majestic polygonal eastern apse is the finest part of the building (**582**). There is a vast quantity of decorative sculpture, carved in white marble and carried out between the fourteenth and nineteenth centuries. Statues and gargoyles on turrets and pinnacles are all over the building, up to the topmost finial. Sculptors came from Italy, France and Germany to carry out this work, but the bulk of the structural and architectural achievement was due to German workers.

582 *Milan Cathedral from the east, 1387–1410.*
Spire 1750
583 *Milan Cathedral interior, fifteenth century nave*
and choir

584 *Florence Cathedral (Santa Maria del Fiore) from*
the east, 1296–1421. Dome, 1420–37
585 *Florence Cathedral, plan*

The cathedral interior (**583**) is lofty and austere in contrast. The nave, especially, is not richly decorated. An unusual ornamental feature is in the niches containing standing, sculptured figures, set above the capitals and below the vault springing. Despite its pinnacles, buttresses and vaults, even Milan Cathedral lacks the northern Gothic verticality; the emphasis is on the horizontal and the design is geometrically based—a fundamental Italian approach.

Some of the abbey churches belonging to the monastic orders follow a traditional Gothic pattern. One is the *Cistercian Abbey* at *Fossanova* in thirteenth century Burgundian style. A more famous example is the early Franciscan double church of *S. Francesco* in *Assisi*. This has a plain traditional Gothic exterior, but inside are mosaic and fresco decoration.

The Italians in general retained the basilican plan to their cathedrals and churches. They built a tall nave arcade and clerestory, but rarely a triforium. They retained the timber roof where possible; if a vault was used, they kept to a square bay compartment over nave and choir. They used brick faced with marbles. Sculpture was more often in relief than in the round. These features, it will be realised, were all Roman or Romanesque practice. The concession to the needs of Gothic design was in the partial use of the pointed arch, the tall campanile and the screen west façade. The screen was indeed, in literal terms, only a façade. Behind its great gable, which masked the aisle roofs, was a church whose construction and interior bore little relationship to its façade. The west wheel window was the chief connecting link between exterior and interior.

Most surviving Medieval work is north of Rome. The Eternal City lay neglected, its Popes in exile in France, while in the south, the long Sicilo-Norman rule and culture gave place to Angevin, centred on Naples not Palermo; Lombard work was still very Romanesque, strongly influenced by its long, powerful tradition. The best Medieval architecture is in Tuscany, south towards Rome and, of completely different derivation, in the expanding empire of Venice. Characteristic are the pointed arch (side by side with the round one), vivid decoration in marble, mosaic and paint, carved white marble tracery and relief sculpture. Ornament and detail were primarily classical; even capitals were Corinthian

more than Gothic, while incorporating Medieval figures and animals. Windows never reached the vast size of northern European ones. The deeply recessed, sculptured portals of France had no counterpart in Italy. Here, the portals were shallower and decorated more by mosaic tympana, relief, bronze door panels and marble sculpture at the sides. The timber nave roofs and lower side aisle vaults needed less abutment and fewer pinnacles. Towers were still separate and a cupola generally covered the crossing.

The finest *cathedrals* are those of *Florence*, *Siena* and *Orvieto*, all typifying this Tuscan approach. At Florence (**584** and **585**) the original pattern has been altered by later work, the Renaissance dome and the nineteenth century façade. Much of the east end, the plan and parts of the interior are Medieval and the work was in fact begun by Arnolfo di Cambio in 1296. On the exterior, the marble inlay and veneer creates an essentially classical feeling imposed on Gothic apsidal form, while the campanile, designed by Giotto and built 1334–87, is a unique composition in marbled harmony with the group.

Siena cathedral is the most outstanding, clad all over, exterior and interior, in black and white stripes of marble. It is carved richly with white marble and further ornamented with coloured mosaic, bronze sculpture and, on floor and ceiling, marble veneer; it is a glowing, gleaming master-piece (**588**). The building displays a tremendous sense of space and light inside (**587**). The sculptured pulpit by Nicola and Giovanni Pisano (father and son) stands out even among so much beautiful workmanship (PLATE 52). They were also responsible for much of the façade.

The hill city of *Orvieto* rises abruptly out of a flat plain and its cathedral is sited on top; a glorious colourful building, reminding the visitor of the days of the city's greatness. The three gable façade dominates the piazza in a riot of colour, gilt bronze sculpture and white marble. It is two-dimensional constructively and decoratively. The rest of the exterior is in plain black and white striped marble (**586** and **487**). Inside the cathedral is simple, spacious and impressive. It is more cohesive than Siena. The magnificent west, rose window is dominant and sheds a golden glow over the whole interior in the evening light.

In contrast is the *Cathedral of Palermo*. Begun in 1185 under Norman Romanesque auspices,

ITALIAN GOTHIC CATHEDRALS

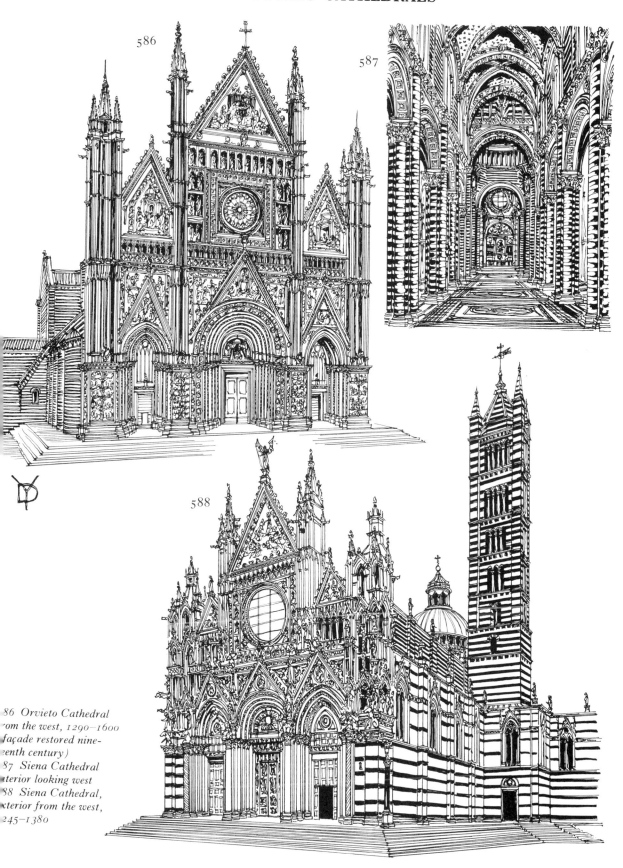

586

587

588

586 Orvieto Cathedral
from the west, 1290–1600
(façade restored nine-
teenth century)
587 Siena Cathedral
interior looking west
588 Siena Cathedral,
exterior from the west,
1245–1380

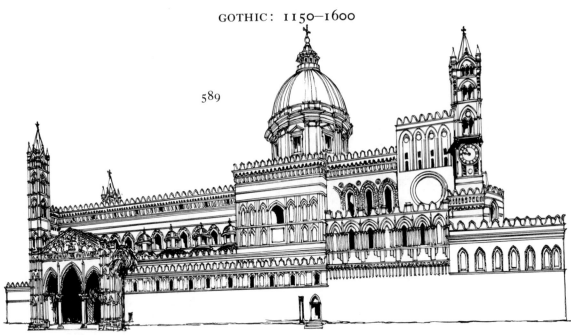

589

589 *Palermo Cathedral, Sicily from the south-east, 1170–85. Porch, 1480; cupola, eighteenth century*

it was continued till after the end of the four-teenth century. The south façade (**589**) is the prime example of Sicilo-Norman style, richly arcaded and crested. Especially beautiful is the open porch, built *c.* 1480, with its Saracenic style arches and decoration. The west end is more Saracenic in character. It is connected across the street to the Archbishop's Palace. There are two slender minaret towers balancing those at the east end. The interior was rebuilt in 1780 in Baroque style, when the cupola also was added.

Italian Gothic churches are less interesting and many have been altered later. In the Tuscan carved marble, coloured mosaic tradition is the beautiful little *S. Maria della Spina* at *Pisa* (1230–1323). Much plainer brick churches with only marble decoration and facings are the thir-teenth century *SS. Giovanni* and *Paolo* and *S. Maria Gloriosa dei Frari* in *Venice*. In *Florence* are *S. Maria Novella*, to which Alberti gave a new façade in 1460 (p. 312) and *S. Croce*, also both of the thirteenth century. Of interest are the hall churches of Perugia and Todi. The *Cathedral of Perugia* is typical of the hall church pattern, wide and high inside, with nave and aisles of equal height. The interior is darker than is usual with German examples as the aisle windows are much smaller and are all filled with coloured glass. The apse is especially beautiful in the colouring. The quadripartite vault is ornately painted in a later style.

Italy has many Medieval palaces, civic build-ings, castles and bridges. The finest *palaces* are in *Venice*, mainly fronting the Grand Canal and of these the *Ca' d'Oro* is of the classic pattern (**590**). This can be seen in the white marble ogee arches, the tracery, elegant balconies, arcading and roofline. The *Palazzo Franchetti* is another example (**593**). World famous is the *Doge's Palace*, begun in the ninth century; the present façades to S. Mark's Square and the Grand Canal waterfront date from 1309–1424. In pinkly glowing patterned brickwork and brilliant white carving and arcading, these elevations are the essence of Venetian Gothic architecture at its best. Stylistically they represent a fusion of Constantinople, the Orient, classical Rome and Medieval Gothic, resulting in a unique harmony (**594, 602** and **605**).

Medieval Italy produced a wealth of *town halls* originally the seats of government for the city states of the peninsula, though the scale varied according to importance. That at Siena (**592**) with its slender, tall tower, castellated roofline and Gothic fenestration is typical. Others include the Palazzo Vecchio, Florence (**591**), the Palazzo dei Priori (or del Municipio), Perugia (1281), the Palazzo dei Priori, Volterra (thirteenth century) the Palazzo Pubblico, Montepulciano and the Palazzo dei Consoli at Gubbio (1332).

Fortified castles and bridges reflect the general western European trend. The *Ponte di Scaliger*

590

591

592

593

590 *Palazzo Ca' d'Oro, Venice, 1421–36*
591 *Palazzo Vecchio, Florence, 1298–1344. Restored sixteenth century (viewed from cathedral campanile)*

592 *Palazzo Pubblico, Siena, 1288–1309*
593 *Palazzo Franchetti, Venice, c. 1430*

594

594 *Doge's Palace, Venice. Piazza San Marco façade, 1343–1438*

at *Verona* is an example (**595**). The *Ponte Vecchio* in *Florence*, over the river Arno, is a civil bridge with houses and shops on it. Two early castles belonged to the Emperor Frederick II, who incorporated Roman military symmetry into the Medieval concentric defence system. One is the *Castel del Monte* in Basilicata (1233–50) which has a classical entrance doorway, and the other the larger, thirteenth century castle at *Prato*. Of the moated, castellated, machicolated, strongly defensive, massive structures, the *Castello degli Estense* in *Ferrara*, is a fine fourteenth century example. There is also the *Castello Nuovo* in *Naples* (1279–83) and the immense, fourteenth

century stronghold on the hill at *Volterra*. In Apulia, at *Lucera*, remains exist of a fortified hill town of brick walls and towers with stone quoins and openings.

Yugoslavia

As in the U.S.S.R., the Medieval work in the southern and inland areas such as Serbia and Macedonia is in Byzantine style. Gothic architecture is to be found down the Dalmatian coast, and this is Venetian owing to the extensive spread of the influence of Venice in this direction. Much of the Gothic work was in continuation of

595 *Medieval fortified bridge, Ponte di Scaligero, Verona, 1335*

595

GOTHIC IN YUGOSLAVIA

596 Ćipiko Palace façade, Trogir,
fifteenth century
597 Šibenik Cathedral, south-west
façade, 1440–1540
598 Wheel window, Šibenik
Cathedral
599 The Rectors' Palace façade,
Dubrovnik, fifteenth century

596

598

597

599

GOTHIC ARCHITECTURAL DETAIL

600 *Nave capital, Reims Cathedral, France,*
thirteenth century
601 *Cloister capital, Poblet Monastery, Spain,*
thirteenth century
602 *Adam and Eve, Doge's Palace, Venice, Italy,*
fourteenth century
603 *Cloister detail, Jeronimo Monastery, Belém,*
Portugal, from 1500

604 *Cloister Capitals, Convent of Christ, Tomar,*
Portugal, late Gothic
605 *Corner Capital, Doge's Palace, Venice*
606 *Pier base, Batahla Abbey, Portugal, 1515–34*
607 *Tomb detail, Cartuja de Miraflores, Spain, from*
608 *Choir Capital, Lincoln Cathedral, England, from*
609 *Choir Capitals, Southwell Minster, England, c. 1*

GOTHIC ARCHITECTURAL DETAIL

10 *Apse flying buttresses, Reims Cathedral, France,
1210*

11 *Doorway head, Casa de las Conchas, Salamanca,
Spain, 1475–83*

12 *Nave pier base, Brussels Cathedral, Belgium,
fifteenth century*

13 *Tympanum, S. Elisabeth, Marburg, Germany,
1257–83*

14 *Manoeline Tower window, Belém, Portugal,
1515–21*

15 *Apse flying buttresses. Coutances Cathedral, France,
thirteenth century*

610

611

612

613

614

615

Romanesque schemes; the tower at *Trogir Cathedral*, for example, and the choir stalls at *Zadar*. The work of *Šibenik Cathedral* is of Gothic origin (**597** and **598**), as is the *palace* at *Trogir* (**596**). In *Dubrovnik*, the local authorities began a new palace for the rectors (**599**). Though restored, this is still an interesting example; particularly noteworthy are the arcade capitals.

Rhodes

Military and fortified domestic Medieval architecture spread through the south-east Mediterranean. The island of Rhodes, near the Turkish coast, was occupied from 1309–1522 by the Knights Hospitallers of S. John of Jerusalem. In the capital (Rhodes) during this time, they built great *mural defences* to the town, especially round the harbour, the *Palace of the Grand Master*, the *cathedral* and the *streets of Inns* of the different countries belonging to the Order. The city was taken by the Turks in 1522. In succeeding years, much of the Gothic work fell into ruin or was destroyed. The Italians, when they occupied the island between 1912–43, restored a number of streets and buildings and rebuilt the destroyed cathedral outside the city walls.

Much still remains to be seen today. There are the city walls, massive gateways (**525**), and the *Hospital of the Knights* (now a museum), with its open courtyard and staircase. On the first floor is a huge room which housed 30 beds. Near each bed was a small room for the servant of the Knight so that he could sleep near his master. The room is well preserved and has a chapel and altar. In the *Street of the Knights* are many Medieval Inns, now restored. There is the Inn of France, of Provence, of Auvergne, of Spain and of Italy. These inns acted as a club for the Knights speaking the appropriate language. Food and drink were provided.

Spain

Development of Gothic architecture in the Iberian Peninsula had something in common with Italy and even more with Germany. The similarities to Italian forms were due to climate, especially in central and southern areas. Here, the large traceried windows and high vaults with consequent flying buttress schemes were unsuitable. Spain preferred smaller windows and larger wall areas to keep out the brilliant sunshine, thick walling, flattish roofs and cloistered shady arcades. As in Italy and Germany, Gothic architecture came late to Spain, partly for the same reason that Romanesque architecture was slow to change but mainly because of the Moorish occupation. In this matter, Iberian development differed from the rest of Europe. The effect of the retreat of the Moors and the advance of the tide of Christianity was discussed in Chapter 4, p. 162. This movement affected Gothic development also. Since Moorish occupation of the peninsula did not fully end until the abandonment of Granada in 1492, Gothic architecture in the south was late to evolve.

The most traditional Gothic work developed in the northern region. Here, rather as in Germany, builders found by the thirteenth century that their Romanesque work was internationally out of date and began to adapt themselves to Gothic. But the process started, as in Germany, not as a gentle evolution from national Romanesque, but by an import of fully developed Gothic from France. Monastic orders spread their influence south and west from France and French masons and builders were invited to create imposing cathedrals in Spain. As time passed, German builders also were asked to help so one can see León Cathedral, for example, on French lines and Burgos nearer German (**616** and **617**).

The Catalan area, around Barcelona, developed a style which had more in common with southeast France. Albi was the inspiration here, with heavy walling, into the thickness of which were built chapels with buttresses between, giving barely any exterior projection.

As in England, Gothic architecture in Spain lingered, but whereas in England the final stage was Perpendicular Gothic, Spanish late Gothic is decorative and richly ornamented and carved. Fifteenth and sixteenth century cathedrals, like Segovia and Salamanca are typical of this. The Spanish love of surface decoration found expression, especially in central and southern areas, in using Moorish forms of ornament. In the final stage of plateresque, whole areas of buildings were covered in surface decoration, both outside and in the interior. The

SPANISH GOTHIC CATHEDRALS

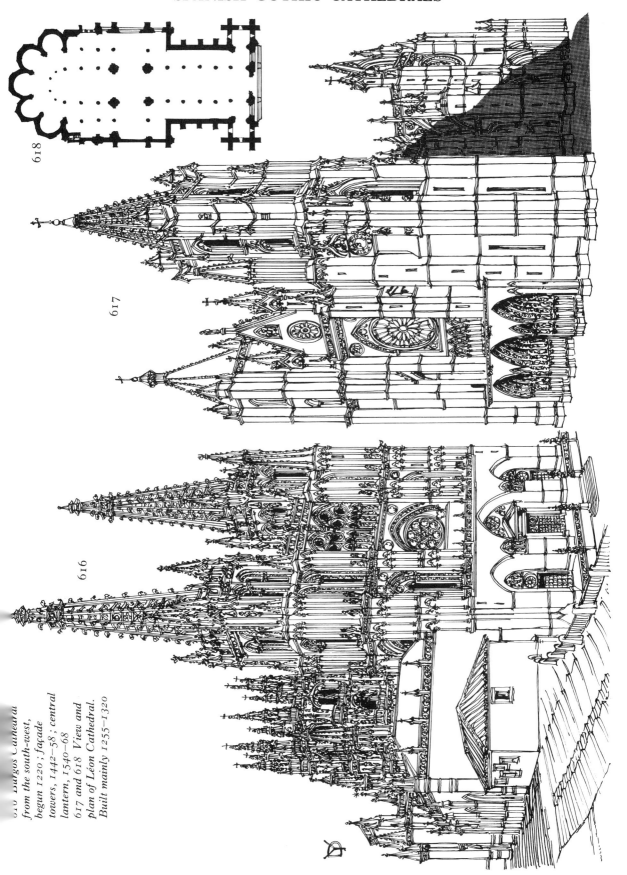

616 Burgos Cathedral,
from the south-west,
begun 1220; façade
towers, 1442–58; central
lantern, 1540–68
617 and 618 View and
plan of Léon Cathedral.
Built mainly 1255–1320

616

617

618

ornament, though rich, was controlled and rarely vulgar. Motifs were predominately Moorish in intricate geometrical and flowing patterns with pierced stone tracery and the use of varied arch shapes. In the south, especially, the horseshoe arch is used, but the pointed arch had been employed here even before it arrived in the Île de France.

Ecclesiastical Building

Cathedrals and Churches

These were nearly all built in stone, a material in ample supply in the mountainous Spanish terrain. Volcanic material was incorporated for polychrome decoration. Also Roman brick construction was employed with wide mortar banding. There was little timber building as forest areas were inadequate. Church plans were usually wider and shorter than in northern Europe, generally on basilican plan but with the *coro* (choir) situated west of the crossing and divided from the altar by an elaborate screen. There were numerous chapels in large ecclesiastical buildings, all round the church. Until 1936, the majority of Medieval cathedrals and churches were in good condition, inside as well as on the exterior, but a tremendous amount of damage was wrought in the Civil War years of 1936–9, particularly in the regions of Madrid, Toledo and Barcelona.

As in France, Spain still possesses a great number of fine cathedrals. Four of the most outstanding, representing different patterns, are León, Burgos, Toledo and Barcelona. *León Cathedral* is on the French model of the best Île de France type. It was built largely in the thirteenth century (**617** and **618**) on a plan similar to Reims. This is in Latin cross form with single aisled nave and double choir, which has a polygonal end and five chevet chapels with double arched flying buttresses. The glass and sculpture make it the Spanish equivalent of Chartres. The façade and transept portals are sculptured. There is some good work, especially in the tympana, but it is not up to French or German standard. The magnificence of the interior is in the vast quantity of coloured glass in the large windows which fill the wall space from vaulting shaft to vaulting shaft. Much of this glass dates from the extensive nineteenth century restoration,

but it is of fine quality and merges well with the original work, presenting a worthy challenge to Chartres. Despite the area of glazing (triforium as well as clerestory) the level of illumination is not high. The impression is of a luminous Byzantine quality in the rich coloured light. The stonework is effectively simple; there is little sculpture or decoration; all the glory is in the glass.

Burgos Cathedral (**616**) is quite different. Whereas León is not impressive on the exterior, lacking the soaring quality of Gothic, Burgos is striking outside, with its classic façade, central lantern and pentagonal, eastern chevet. The building period is a long one and the style of work varies from the early lower part, begun 1221, to the very rich sixteenth century lantern. The cathedral is wide and fairly low, apart from the façade towers which were completed with their fine German style openwork traceried spires in 1486 by Hans of Cologne. The very rich late Gothic *cimborio*, the octagonal central lantern, followed in 1568. Inside this has a magnificent eight-pointed star vault (**472**). The choir is in the usual Spanish position west of the crossing, reducing the nave to a mere vestibule. There are some beautiful late Gothic side chapels, of which the Capilla del Condestable (1482) is superbly ornamented.

Toledo Cathedral, though based on the French model, is very large and very Spanish. It is one of the finest Gothic monuments in Europe. Started in 1226 at the east end, the façade is fifteenth century and later, as is also the unusual and imposing north-west tower (**619**). There are some fine sculptured porches here of different styles and periods; the north with a typical fourteenth-century tympanum, the south, with the richly sculptured, almost plateresque *Puerta de los Leones* (1452) and the triple façade portal on the French pattern. Apart from the façade and interesting cloisters, it is the nave interior which is the glory of the Medieval part of the Cathedral. It is simple, majestic, lofty. The nave arcade has tall multi-shafted piers and foliated capitals carrying the pointed arches. The central shaft rise to the high vault, which is quadripartite. The clerestory windows have geometrical tracery and still a quantity of their original fine glass. There is also a beautiful rose window. The high altar screen is a Gothic masterpiece, representing hundreds of figures and groups scenes from the life of Christ. The great central space of the cathedral interior is devoted to the choir with its magnificent (later) choir stalls. The whole is enclosed in a Gothic style stone carved screen of great complexity and richness.

Catalan Gothic, which is admirably represented by Barcelona and Gerona Cathedrals, is quite different. The fourteenth century saw the opening of an era of prosperity in Catalonia based on trade with France, Italy and the Balkans, largely through the port of Barcelona. The architectural influence was French from the south-east region and, in particular, examples such as the cathedrals of Albi, Toulouse and Perpignan. The churches are aisleless or with a wide central nave and narrow side aisles. Buttresses are internal, immensely strong and projecting, like those at Albi, inwards into the church. The chapels were built between them.

619 Façade, Toledo Cathedral, Spain, 1400–52

619

The exterior wall was therefore plain and un-interrupted. Inside, Catalan churches are dark. Windows are small, long and narrow, triforia rare and vaults quadripartite.

Gerona Cathedral is based on this pattern. It is immensely wide, with aisleless fifteenth century nave spanned by a 73 foot wide vault. Inside, chapels are situated between the huge internal buttresses which are 20 feet deep and rise to the full height of the building as at Albi. The east end is aisled and has a chevet, a fourteenth century example based on that at Barcelona. The baroque façade rises above a great exterior staircase.

Barcelona Cathedral is the Catalan Gothic masterpiece. On classic Catalan pattern, it was begun in 1298 and largely completed by the early fifteenth century, apart from the façade which is neo-Gothic. The east end is the finest part of the building. It is on the French model of a seven-sided apse with ambulatory and radiating chapels. On the exterior, these chapels are deeply set into the ring of massive buttresses which are con-nected by flying arches to the clerestory wall, each one set between the circular windows. The cathedral interior is magnificent, giving a vivid impression of Medievalism. It is dark, the light shining in through a quantity of richly coloured glass in windows which are narrow and not very large. The nave arcade is high, with a shallow triforium and clerestory above. There is an octagonal lantern over the crossing. Adjoining the cathedral are the fine mid-fifteenth century cloisters with 22 chapels round them (**513**).

Many Spanish cathedrals still have beautiful *cloisters* and a number of these are of the thirteenth century early Gothic style. Of two particularly interesting examples, one is the *Monastery of Las Huelgas* in *Burgos* (**620**). The work is plain with double columns and foliated capitals, all different from one another. At *Poblet*, near Tarragona, the monastery has recently been restored from a damaged state. The thirteenth century cloisters, however, largely escaped the fire and sack of 1835 and the original work is in fair condition. The ribbed quadripartite vaults extend round the four sides of the cloister. The open arcade is carried on multi-shafted piers with grouped capitals of extraordinary variety and richness (**601**).

The fifteenth and sixteenth centuries in Spain produced many fine late Gothic monuments; among them three great cathedrals: Seville, Segovia and Salamanca. *Seville Cathedral* was the earliest of these, built over a long period beginning in 1402 at the west end. It is the largest Medieval cathedral in Europe and, on a roughly rectangular plan, measures 430 by 247 feet. The cathedral was not finished till *c.* 1520 and much of it is in the late Spanish Gothic style but, since it is in Andalusia where Moorish influence was strong till nearly 1500, both decoration and layout reflect eastern modes. The plan was controlled by its being built on the site of the Moorish mosque and the slender 'giralda' was its minaret. This was built in the twelfth century, of brick, with typical, high quality Moorish brick decoration in trellis patterned panels (**622**). The belfry, which is Renaissance, was added in 1568 and surmounted by the bronze figure which revolves, hence the name 'giralda' from *girar*—to turn round. It is certainly one of the most beautiful bell towers in the world.

Seville Cathedral is impressive, partly because of its immense size. The apsidal end is shown in Fig. **622** and this is the most interesting view. Much of the remainder is restored or altered and the flattish roofs and near horizontal flying buttresses are neither interesting nor very Gothic. Inside, the vista is breathtaking. The nave is very wide, with four broad aisles and surrounding chapels. It also is very high, with a quadripartite vault 130 feet above ground, supported on immense, clustered piers with tiny foliated capitals. There is no triforium, but stained glass clerestory windows with rich curvilinear tracery. The central lantern, rebuilt in 1882 after collapse, has an interior star vault. Despite its long building period and mixture of styles, the interior at least of Seville Cathedral has unity, richness and fine proportions. It represents an imposing penulti-mate achievement in the Gothic movement. But it was by no means the last.

Both Segovia and Salamanca are sixteenth century buildings and, being in central Spain, are less influenced by Moorish design and decoration. They are purely late Spanish Gothic. *Segovia* was built between 1520 and 1577 on a fine hill site on symmetrical plan. It has a seven-chapel chevet with gently sloping flying buttress-es and ornate crocketed pinnacles. The interior is very wide and high with slender, clustered shafts supporting characteristic late Gothic vault-ing (**621**).

early Gothic
621 South aisle, Segovia Cathedral, 1521–91
622 Seville Cathedral from the east, 1432–67. Tower
(the Giralda) 275 feet high, 1184–98 and 1568

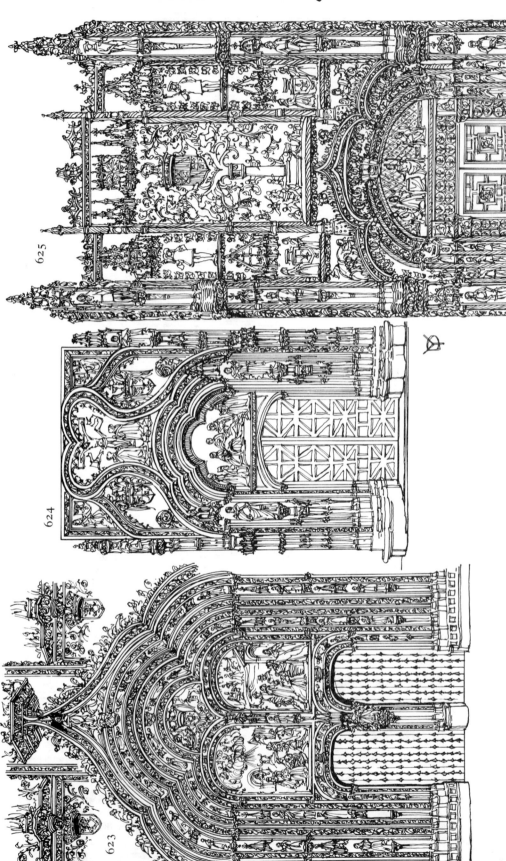

623 Principal doorway, façade, Salamanca New Cathedral, 1515–31

625

624

623

Salamanca Cathedral is exactly contemporary with Segovia. It is built next door to the Romanesque Cathedral (Chapter 4, p. 167) on the hill above the river Tormes spanned by the Roman bridge (**165**). It is much like Segovia, especially in its nave and Renaissance-inspired towers with cupolas and lanterns. It has a square east end, though, instead of a chevet and the exterior decoration, especially on the west façade, is of incredible richness (PLATE 48). This is a good example of what is termed *plateresque ornament*. It was named thus, in a later period, as a term of disapprobation in reference to its affinity with silverwork (*platería*), which was a major Spanish industry at the time. The name emphasises the entirely surface character of the ornament, which had barely any relationship with the architectural form beneath. Indeed,

since it was applied all over doorways, portals, even façades, it tended to blur the architectural lines with a complete carpet of decoration. Motifs, making up this ornamental covering, were varied; they included heraldic forms, Gothic features, human and animal figures, plant and bird life. Sculptural panels, often in high relief, were framed in the total design. The west façade at Salamanca Cathedral, of 1513–31, by Juan Gil de Hontañón, is a prime example (**623** and PLATE 48).

The period of excessive surface ornamentation on both exterior and interior of large buildings lasted through the fifteenth and sixteenth centuries and beyond. It reflected the wealth of the country as well as the love of ostentation and decoration felt by the Spanish people. The academic simplicity of early Gothic or Italian

626 *Cloisters, S. Juan de los Reyes, Toledo*, c. 1470

626

Renaissance was never fully acceptable to Spain. The plateresque form of decorative treatment continued from Gothic into Renaissance; only the motifs changed. Gothic Plateresque is sometimes referred to as Isabelline because the work largely emanates from the reign of Isabella. Other outstanding examples of the style can be seen on the façade of the *Church of S. Cruz in Segovia* (**624**) and the amazing façades in *Valladolid* of the *Church of S. Pablo* (PLATES 57 and 58) and the *College of S. Gregorio* (**625**). The last of these is a riot of ornament, with twisted columns, strange figures and Moorish elements.

Among the varied types of *churches* in Spain, one of the most beautiful is *S. Juan de los Reyes* in *Toledo*. Here are magnificent two-storeyed cloisters with traceried openings and sculptured statues in late Gothic style (**626** and **455**) which also prevails on the exterior of the church. Inside

is a fine late star vault under the *cimborio* and som beautiful plateresque decoration on the walls i the choir. The church was a masterpiece b Juan Guäs. Also in *Toledo* is the quite differen *S. Maria la Blanca*, which is a five-aisled churc on rectangular plan with the roofs at differin levels. The decoration of the capitals and wa arcades as well as the horseshoe arches sho strong Moorish influence (**627**).

Further variation in design can be seen in th hall churches of the very late period. These ar mostly from the sixteenth and seventeent centuries and are Gothic buildings with classica décor, like *S. Maria la Redonda* in *Logroño*. Ther are also the Catalan Gothic types on aisleless pla and with fourteenth and fifteenth century decora tion, like *S. Maria del Pino* and *S. Maria de Mar,* both in Barcelona.

627 *S. Maria la Blanca, Toledo. Built twelfth century as a synagogue. Consecrated as a Christian church 1405. Now a national monument*

627

SPANISH MEDIEVAL ARCHITECTURE

628 Coca Castle, north west of Segovia
629 Interior of the Silk Exchange (La Lonja de la Sede), Valencia, 1482–98
630 Castle of La Mota, Médina del Campo, 1440

629

628

630

Domestic and Civic Buildings

One of the most remarkable palaces in Gothic plateresque style is the *Palacio del Infantado* in *Guadalajara*. This was built 1480–92 by Juan and Enrique Guäs (architects of S. Juan de los Reyes) in an interesting mixture of Gothic and Mujédar forms. The interior, including the picturesque court, was destroyed by bombing in 1936, but the exterior façades remain to the full height of the walls and restoration is now taking place (465). There are similar, smaller examples at Baeza in southern Spain. Faceted and decorative stonework façades can still be seen at Segovia and Salamanca. The *Casa de los Picos* in *Segovia* is like the Palazzo dei Diamanti in Ferrara. The

Casa de las Conchas in *Salamanca*, also fifteenth century, is covered in sea-shell decoration. There are also some beautiful windows and grilles (611 and 459).

The *Palacio de la Andiencia* in *Barcelona* has been altered, but still retains a Gothic pointed-arched court with exterior stone staircase. There also still exist some of the exchanges which were so typical of Medieval Spain. The *Silk Exchange* in *Valencia* is the finest of these. It has a long stone façade with rich Gothic fenestration and doorway. Behind is a vaulted hall on hall church pattern, 130 by 75 feet, divided into nave and aisles by spiralled columns (629). The *exchange* at *Zaragoza* has now been restored. The exterior is dull but the hall is magnificent. This, like so

631 The Exchange (La Lonja), Zaragoza, c. 1550. Gothic with Renaissance detail

Plate 54
The Bamberg Horseman. Bamberg Cathedral,
Germany, *c.* 1220–30
Plate 55
Cloister detail. Batahla Abbey, Portugal. 14th
and 15th century
Plate 56
S. George and the Dragon. Castle Hill, Prague,
Czechoslovakia. Jiří and Martin of Cluj, 1373

Plates 57 and 58
Façade. Church of S. Pablo, Valladolid, Spain, 1276–1463

632 Bridge of S. Martín, Toledo, Medieval

632

Fortified Structures

Spain is more noted for its Medieval castles than any other European country. Castile, the immense area in the centre of the country, had so many that it was named from them (*castillo*). Medieval castles are in all styles: Romanesque, Gothic, Moorish, Renaissance. Many are now ruined, but a number of outstanding examples remain in good condition. One of the best is the *Castillo de la Mota* at *Medina del Campo* (**630**). There is a deep ditch all round, spanned by a bridge, reaching to the double, outer, windowless walls. The castle is austere, large and impressive, built in brick on a hill above the town.

One of the largest castles in Spain is that at *Olite*, near Pamplona, built in 1403. It was damaged by fire in the nineteenth century but 15 vast, mural towers remain. Near the Pyrenean frontier, it was partly of French construction and once had large halls, chambers and extensive gardens. Most of the best remaining castles date from the fifteenth century and are situated in

many of the sixteenth century exchanges, is a mixture of Gothic and Renaissance forms. The vault is Gothic, with Medieval bosses, but the supporting columns have Ionic capitals and Renaissance putti and shields. The hall is now used for exhibitions (**631**).

León or Castile. There is the large, interesting example at *Valencia de Don Juan*, ruined and romantically reflected in the waters of the river Esla below; the gaunt 150 foot pile of *Torrelobatón*, an impregnable castle in fine condition; and *Turégano* near Segovia, ruined part castle, part church. Not far away is *Castle Coca* (**628**), an immense mass of pinkish brick towers and turrets set within a deep, enclosing moat.

In large towns it was customary to build an alcázar, a fortified palace. Most of these have been rebuilt, as in Madrid, or much restored. The *Alcázar* at *Segovia* is one of these. It was transformed from a fortress into a fortified palace in 1455 but was rebuilt in more recent times after a disastrous fire in the nineteenth century.

A number of town gateways which were originally part of the city walling have fared better. In good condition are the *Puerta del Sol* at *Toledo*, dating from *c.* 1200 and with horseshoe arches and Moorish decoration, the *Puerta de Serranos* at *Valencia*, 1349, a typical octagonal towered, Gothic structure and the *Puerta de S. Maria* in *Burgos* which is Medieval with Renaissance decoration and sculpture.

Medieval *bridges* in Spain have suffered considerably but the bridge of *S. Martín* at *Toledo* survives (**632**). This is a fine example, spanning the rocky gorge of the River Tagus which almost encircles the town; it has defence gateways at

GOTHIC IN PORTUGAL

633 *The façade, Monastery Church, Batahla, 138*
1415
634 *Batahla, the cupola vault, Founder's Chapel,*
1415-34
635 *Interior of the Cistercian Abbey Church of*
Alcobaça, 1158-1220
636 *Batahla, cloister opening*

633

635

634

636

637

638

637 Façade, church and part of monastery
638 Cloisters

each end. The *Puente de Pietra* in the centre of *Zaragoza*, a stone example of 1401, has been somewhat altered and spans the river Ebro.

Portugal

Although no geographical barrier separates Spain from Portugal, and although the early history of Moorish occupation was similar in both countries, the artistic development differs. The two peoples are totally dissimilar in character and personality and they have been separate entities for hundreds of years. Not a great deal survives in Portugal from the Gothic era. Partly this is because so much Medieval work was lost in the great earthquake of 1755 which destroyed the city of Lisbon. Three outstanding buildings exist in the pure Gothic style, all abbey churches: Batahla, Alcobaça and Belém.

The *monastery of Batahla*, near Leiria, was founded in 1397. Built mainly in the fifteenth century, it is a fine architectural group. The façade, recently restored and cleaned, is now easy to view as a vast space has been cleared in front of it. The illustration (633) shows the square, richly decorated façade, the flying buttress scheme of nave and choir and, on the left, the remarkable cloister. These have individual and unusual arcade openings (636 and 606) in Manoeline style (PLATE 55). The church itself is cruciform, with apsidal east end and tall lancet windows. The interior is simple, contrasting with the façade and chapels. Its soaring, multi-clustered piers rise to a quadripartite vault. There is a clerestory but no triforium. Very fine, and especially richly decorated, is the octagonal founder's chapel. This has a magnificent star vault (634) carried on an octagonal drum with eight two-light windows and eight piers with cusped arches below. The capitals, like those in Wells and York Cathedrals, are of vine leaf design. It is a tomb chapel and all round the walls are tombs under rich Gothic canopies.

The *Cistercian Abbey Church* of *Alcobaça*, nearby, was built 1158–1223. It now has a Baroque façade in golden stone (Chapter 7, p. 406), but its interior presents a contrast. This is a large but simple Medieval hall church in white stone (635). The vaulting shafts of the tall piers are unusual in that they do not descend to the ground but are supported on corbels. (This can also be seen in Fossanova Abbey Church in Italy.) Nave and aisles are of uniform height and vault design. The aisle walls are plain, pierced only by round-headed windows set high, just under the vault. The east end is apsidal with an ambulatory. It has narrow lancet windows and round, Romanesque type columns instead of piers. The whole interior is of one scheme and design.

The *Jeronimo Monastery* at *Belém*, now a suburb of Lisbon, was the last great Portuguese Gothic structure (637). It was built in the early sixteenth century. The church is a rich example of late Gothic work with a fine sculptured portal and ornamental fenestration. Inside, it is again a hall church type. The nave has a remarkable lierne star vault; the remainder is almost a fan design. The columns supporting the nave are carved all over with late Gothic ornament. The window surrounds continue this decorative form. The whole church is in carved stone. As at Batahla, one of the glories of Belém is the cloisters. These are two-storeyed (638 and 603) with traceried, cusped openings and lierne vaults roofing each storey. The carved decoration of column and pier shafts is rich and varied.

Of an earlier Gothic style, in *Lisbon*, are the remains of the *Carmo Convent*, begun in 1385 and partly destroyed in the earthquake, now retained and preserved as the archaelogical museum. The former nave, open to the sky, still shows its fine design and structure. Later Manoeline and Renaissance ornament appear on windows and other details.

The *Manoeline* style represents, to a certain extent, the Portuguese equivalent to Spanish Plateresque. It is so called after Dom Manoel I who reigned 1495–1521, during the period when Portugal was establishing her new sea routes and her great navigators were exploring the world. Manoel was a patron of the arts and helped to encourage the rich decoration of fine buildings. The style, like plateresque, is essentially one of surface decoration. The buildings were late Gothic but rich ornament, chiefly round windows and doorways, was carved in motifs which were a wonderful collection of sea-shells and twisted ropes intermingled with exotic oriental forms. The cloister openings at Batahla are of this type of design, also Belém and some of the doorways at Alcobaça. The *Tower of Belém*, built opposite to the monastery, on the spot at the edge of the Tagus estuary where the navigators sailed from, is a fine example (**523** and **614**). Another building with some fine Manoeline carving is the Templar's Monastery, the *Convent of Christ*, at *Tomar*, north of Lisbon. The monastery is on a hill above the modern town. The round twelfth century church leads into the late Gothic portion which includes the chapter house. There are two remarkable windows here, a circular one on the church and an ornate, rectangular window in the chapter house. This has a frame displaying a riot of decorative forms carved in stone, including all kinds of marine motifs: seaweed, coral, cables, fishing nets mixed up with heraldry and plant life. The window is by Diogo de Arruda (PLATE 53). There are seven cloisters; an interesting Gothic one (**604**), some mixtures of styles and an excellent Renaissance example (Chapter 6, p.361).

Eastern Europe

Rumania

It is difficult for the student to trace specific buildings in eastern Europe as frontiers here have been moved a great deal during the twentieth century and especially since 1939. In consequence, the names of places are completely altered. This is particularly true of Rumania and Hungary. Present day Rumania is much larger than it used to be, and comprises much of what was Hungary, while the U.S.S.R. possesses some of the lands which were Polish and Rumanian. In this book monuments will be found listed under their present day Rumanian nomenclature, not Hungarian, as is common practice.

Rumania today is a large country which possesses a wealth of architecture from the Medieval period. Much of this, as in the U.S.S.R., continued to be Byzantine in form till well into the seventeenth century. This work is described in Chapter 3, p.114. The remainder is derived from differing sources and influences so is varied in style. Buildings are of stone or timber and a few are in brick. The country is partly mountainous and there is an abundance of both stone and wood. The most pure Gothic structures are not very common. They are chiefly of stone and follow mainly a middle period Gothic style which is not heavily ornamented. The modern

main road through Rumania from the Hungarian border at Oradea to Bucharest runs through the Carpathian mountains and also through the towns where most remains are situated: Cluj, Alba Iulia, Sibiu, Braşov, Sinaia. Sighişoara and Bran are not far from this road.

S. Michael's Church in *Cluj* is one of the best examples of pure Gothic design in Rumania. It was built during the fourteenth and fifteenth centuries, but has a nineteenth century tower, and has been excellently restored recently (**640**). It is a hall church with an apsidal ended short chancel which has tall, geometric traceried windows. The graceful piers extend upwards to the quadripartite and star vaults without any interruption from capitals. It is a finely proportioned, simple church of considerable size.

Alba Iulia Cathedral was described in Chapter 4, p.182.It was given a Gothic chancel in 1320–56 which is apsidal with lancet fenestration. There are several Gothic buildings in *Sibiu*, which is a remarkably unspoilt Medieval town. Several town gateways remain, as in the Piata Republica and, nearby in the Piata Grivitá, is the tall, Gothic style church with its six pointed gable façade.

Further east is the larger town of *Braşov* which still possesses a number of Gothic monuments. The *Black Church* is the best known. It is a tall, plain building on the exterior with narrow, geometric traceried windows. The east end is apsidal; at the west is a tall tower. The best view is from the hillside opposite (**639**) as the church is hemmed in in the centre of the town. The interior is in good repair and of unusual design. The nave is two-storeyed with cusped, ogee arches supporting a gallery. The one-storeyed choir rises to the considerable height of the church. Here are tall, octagonal piers with strange voluted capitals set up near to the groined vault. Also in Braşov is the *town hall* (**641**) and the Greek Orthodox *Church* of *S. Nicholas*, begun in 1595 but not completed till 1750.

Also in Gothic style are some of the many fortified structures in Rumania. In the romantic vein of a Carpathian castle are the mountain strong-holds at Bran and Hunedoara. *Bran Castle* is perched on top of a wooded hill, impregnable and difficult of access, not far from Braşov (**545**). Just south of Deva is the fifteenth century *castle* of *Hunedoara*, which is even more unapproachable

GOTHIC IN RUMANIA

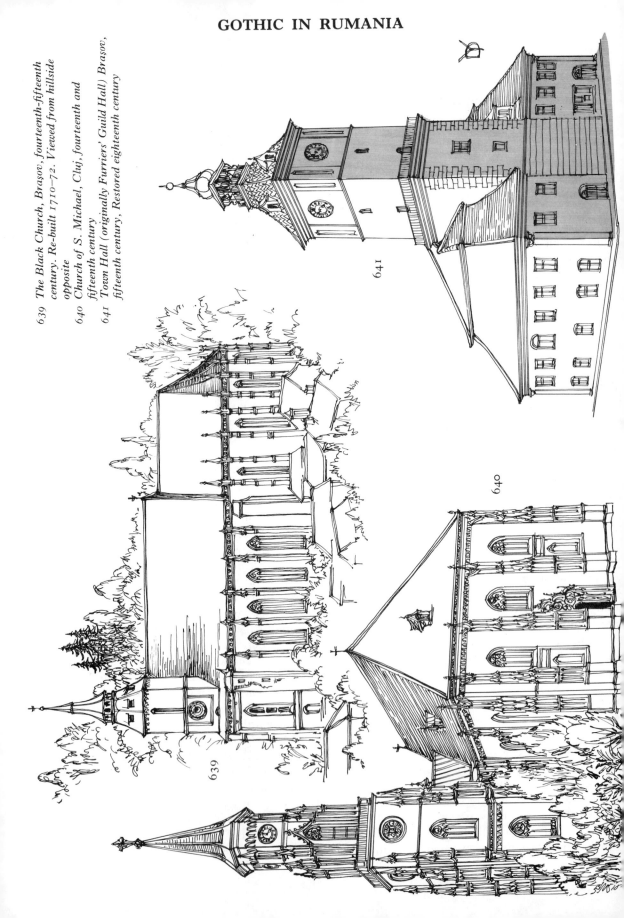

639 *The Black Church, Brasov, fourteenth–fifteenth century. Re-built 1710–72. Viewed from hillside opposite*
640 *Church of S. Michael, Cluj, fourteenth and fifteenth century*
641 *Town Hall (originally Furriers' Guild Hall) Brasov, fifteenth century. Restored eighteenth century*

641

640

639

(548). There is a fine fifteenth century chapel and hall; extensions and alterations were made in the seventeenth and nineteenth centuries. At *Sighişoara*, north-west of Braşov, is the fifteenth century fortified *church*.

The fifteenth and sixteenth centuries also saw the construction of fortified *monastic settlements*. Most of these have been altered or added to in later ages. Especially interesting examples are those of *Dragomirna, Putna* and *Suceviţa*. They are all fortresses as well as monasteries and are surrounded by buttressed walls with mural defence towers. Inside the rectangular court is built the church and other monastic structures. The fortifications are Medieval but the buildings within, good examples of their type, stem from Gothic, Renaissance and Byzantine sources and were added at different periods.

These monasteries are all in *Moldavia* in the north-east part of Rumania, the most remote from centres of population and sharing a border with the U.S.S.R. This is the least known region of the country but, architecturally, the most interesting, for here are the unique Moldavian *painted churches. Suceviţa monastery* contains one of these churches, built 1548. Others include *Voronets* (**644**), *Neamţ* (**642**), *Moldoviţa* and *Humor*. They all stem from the fifteenth and sixteenth centuries and are covered in fresco paintings on the exterior as well as inside. Like the French cathedral portals, they tell the Bible story and are teachers of Christianity to an illiterate population. Apart from their beauty and originality, they are also a mystery. It is still not known how these exterior frescoes have lasted in a severe central European climate for 400 years. The freshness of the colours is remarkable. All that is known is that the lime applied to the walls was kept in pits filled with water for three years before use and that the apprentices daily skimmed a film from the water, removing the impurities from the lime. *Suceviţa* and *Voronets Churches* are the finest examples. They are aglow with glorious colours. Voronets is only a tiny church but Suceviţa is large. On the exterior are frescoes showing vividly Heaven, Earth and Hell in a multitude of figures and scenes. The work is two-dimensional; there is no perspective, yet these are masterpieces of great quality.

In *Iaşi* (Jassy), the ancient capital of Moldavia, is a most original Medieval church, built as late as the seventeenth century, but a Gothic/Byzantine structure with all-over decoration on the exterior of an eastern type reminiscent of the giralda at Seville (**645**). This is the *Church of the Three Hierarchs* and is carved in stone lacework pattern intermingled with Medieval arcading.

There is also the tradition of *timber architecture*, typical of all the heavily forested countries of eastern Europe. These have been mentioned with regard to the U.S.S.R. (p. 264). Rumania possesses more surviving examples of this type of structure than elsewhere and a vast quantity continued to be built until the early nineteenth century in rural areas. Though there are still examples scattered throughout the country, we are indebted for their extensive and varied collection to the magnificent *Village Museum* in *Bucharest*. Here, almost in the centre of the city, in the park surrounding the beautiful Lake Herăstrău, are 15 acres of an open air site. This is planted with trees and shrubs and laid out with grass and paths, with an extensive selection of structures from all over Rumania, re-erected here to their original manner. There are churches, houses, farmsteads, cattle stalls, wells, workshops, portals and many other structures. Mainly they are constructed with solid timber logs, dovetailed and set on a stone or brick base. Roofing is by wooden shingles and these are extended to cover a variety of tall steeples and belfries. Many of the solid wood structures are beautifully carved, for example window frames, furniture, balconies, entrance portals. Some structures are of brick with mud and whitewash facing and many have thatched roofs. Some houses are built with the lower part for animals and the upper for the family. Others are constructed three-quarters underground with a sloping passage downwards from the front door which is at thatched roof level.

The *churches* are the most striking buildings in this medium. The typical layout can be seen in, for example, an eighteenth century church from *Turea* near Cluj and another of 1722 from *Dragomireşti* in Moldavia. Both have a pro-naos, a naos and chancel. Inside, they are subdivided by vast beams of solid timber. The tall steeple is

REGIONAL MEDIEVAL IN MOLDAVIA AND THE CARPATHIANS

642 *Neamț Monastery Church, Moldavia, 1497*
643 *Village timber Church, Rucar, near Brașov, c. 1650. (Church now at Tekirghiol)*
644 *Painted Monastery Church, Voroneț, Moldavia, sixteenth century*
645 *Three Hierarchs Church, Iași, Moldavia, 1639*

et up over the pro-naos. Upright baulks of wood lean slightly inwards towards the narrow steeple, supporting cross beams on an X pattern. Floors are of wood. Wood shingles cover the roofing and steeple. There are wide eaves for heavy snow. In the Dragomireşti Church, the naos is barrel vaulted in wood. The chancel screen is richly carved and all the walls and roof are painted in bright colours. Windows are tiny. The eastern end is apsidal, in pentagonal form. The great timbers are dovetailed into one another to turn the corners.

The example illustrated in Fig. **643** is not in the Museum but in *Tekirghiol*. This is a small spa on the Black Sea near Constantza. The church belonged to the Carpathian mountain village of *Rucar* and was given to Tekirghiol because, in 1930, so many people from Rucar had been cured of their ailments by the waters and mud treatment of the spa at Tekirghiol, that they decided the only thing they could give to express their gratitude was their most precious possession— the village church. It now stands, 400 miles from its birthplace, on the hillside above the restorative Lake Tekirghiol, the only building in the town of any architectural merit. It has been erected in the courtyard of a holiday home for priests of the Greek Orthodox Church. It is a tiny but beautiful example of craftsmanship. In layout it is similar to those in the Village Museum in Bucharest, with pro-naos, naos and chancel and wood partitions between. The chancel is painted all over inside, as is also the naos barrel vaulted roof, with biblical scenes.

U.S.S.R.

There was, as mentioned earlier (p. 264), little Gothic architecture in the Soviet Union. Two examples are illustrated; the *Kremlin* at *Rostov* (**562**), which is still largely Byzantine (Chapter 7, p. 447) and the remarkable *Church of the Ascension* at *Kolomonskoe* (**560**). This is a building which still defies classification by scholars. It is a brick church, immensely tall, of octagonal structure, bearing a great weight on the lower galleried arcades. It possesses the Gothic quality of verticality but is not Gothic in design or form. It is nearer to the tall, wooden tent churches of northern Russia but, though this has been suggested, concrete evidence is lacking for its dependence, in brick, on these wooden forms. This is a votive church, built in 1532 as part of the Tsar's country residence near Moscow (Basil III). If this unusual and fine building were in western Europe, situated as it is in open country so near to the capital and alongside the river (Moskva), the surroundings would have been landscaped with lawns, flower beds and paths as a place to visit. Here, in addition, are the Church at Dyakovo (126) and other later buildings of Byzantine style, but the place is untouched country, undeveloped and visited by few.

PART THREE
CLASSICAL ARCHITECTURE
1420-1800

6
Renaissance and Mannerism: 1420–1650

The Italians say '*Rinascimento*', the Spaniards '*Renacimiento*', the Portuguese, '*Renascença*'. The Germans and Dutch, like ourselves, use the French term '*Renaissance*'. The nations of Europe so describe this unique force which overwhelmed, like a restless tide, the thought and spirit of Medieval man. The words differ but the meaning is synonymous: re-birth.

The word is a literal description of what occurred at this time. Everyone has heard of the Renaissance, especially in relation to its transformation of the arts. We know that it was a movement towards Humanism from the hierarchical interpretation of Christianity; that there was a leaning towards the classical forms of literature and in the visual arts away from the Medieval. We also know that the movement began in Italy in the fourteenth century and that it spread westwards, first to France, then to Germany, England and the Iberian Peninsula and that its eastward influence, apart from Hungary and Poland, was negligible, due to the strength of the Turkish and Byzantine traditions.

But why did this movement arise in the fourteenth century? Why did it begin in Italy? Why, indeed, did a force of such power and surging life, sweeping all before it, begin at all?

It is impossible to overstress the importance of the effect of the Renaissance on architecture and its sister visual arts. As its ideas took hold in one country after another, the fundamentals of these arts were transformed. To gain an understanding of the character of this metamorphosis, it is essential to try to discover the answers to these questions. Perhaps it would be best to consider first the last query, for this is the essence of the matter. Why did the Renaissance come at all and what was its meaning?

After the collapse of the ancient classical world of Greece and Rome, mankind had slowly emerged from a barbaric state into the Middle Ages. The motivation of the rise in spirit and quality of living was religious, founded on Christianity. As has been described in Chapters 4 and 5, this religion in Europe, its form differing only marginally from east to west, had been the foundation of all life. Intellectual thought and culture had been provided by the Church.

The seeds of the Renaissance are to be found in the questioning of this Christian dogma by men of high intellectual stature. They questioned, not the importance of Christianity as a faith and way of life, but man's interpretation of it which, until then, had stressed his unimportance and impermanence. These Renaissance scholars, studying with fervour and absorbed interest the literature of ancient Greece and Rome, envisaged a concept of man as an individual human being, important in his own right. This view conflicted with the existing theological ruling that man's life on earth should be secondary to his future life after death. Despite the excitement and fears engendered by the questioning, after hundreds of years, of such established doctrines, the scholars continued their exploration. They set in motion intense desire for knowledge and a realisation of the need for expansion of learning in universities not subject to the jurisdiction of the Church. Their source of study was the ancient classical world. It is not surprising therefore that, rediscovering the greatness of its culture and art buried, often literally in the case of architecture, for 1000 years, they identified the new humanist thoughts with classicism.

The spirit of the Renaissance arose from man's vital spark of curiosity and his need for change which has always been present, and which distinguishes him from the animal world. It also, to a lesser extent, separates the man of intellect from the majority of mankind in whom resides resistance to change. Resistance to these new concepts was expressed, as is usual, most forcibly by older members in the community.

The Renaissance began in the fourteenth century because it was not until this time that the climate of opinion and the studies and understanding of the leaders of thought were ripe for such theories. Medieval society had largely gnored the remains—architectural, artistic and literary—of the classical world. The dissatisfaction with Medieval life, especially in regard to its religious concepts, combined with man's curiosity about himself and his historical development, led to the discovery of what had been. That the beginnings of this interest in the classical past should have manifested themselves first in Italy was a natural corollary of the fact that here had been the centre of the great Roman Empire. It was in Italy that the major part of the remains existed which came to be the basis for the dominant theme of the Renaissance.

The Renaissance began in the world of literature, and bore fruit in the writings of Petrarch, Boccaccio and Dante. It found expression in university expansion and continued in sculpture and painting with the work of artists like Nicola Pisano, Cimabue and Giotto. Architecture came later. Brunelleschi, in Florence, was the first outstanding architect to develop the classical style and this was more Tuscan and Romanesque than of classical Rome. The discovery of the manuscripts of Marcus Vitruvius Pollio (usually called Vitruvius) in 1414 led to the later, purer style developed under Bramante in Rome. Vitruvius was a Roman architect and engineer who had lived in the first century B.C. and in his books, which cover a wide field ranging from medicine to painting and mathematics to sculpture, are included detailed data on the correct proportions, rules and style of classical architecture as practised in his day. These books were to have a far-reaching influence on the classical architecture of Europe until the end of the eighteenth century. They were translated into many languages and certain architects and schools of architecture relied heavily upon them, notably the Palladian School in England.

Indeed, it was a characteristic of the Renaissance period of architecture and decoration that artisans and architects all over Europe gained much of their information from books of all types, published mainly in Italy and later in France, Flanders and Germany. Medieval craftsmen and designers had passed on their knowledge primarily by word of mouth and by example. In the Renaissance, leading architects and designers published their designs for buildings and ornament in what were termed pattern books. These drawings and descriptions led to a much faster spread of knowledge of the new styles than had ever been possible in the Middle Ages. Architects in England or Spain, for instance, came to erect buildings based on the designs in such books though they had never seen either an ancient classical building or a Renaissance one.

Meanwhile, in Italy, the early fifteenth century works of Brunelleschi and Alberti were followed by the pure High Renaissance designs of Bramante. Christianity was still the basis for designs in art, but the treatment, especially in sculpture and painting, was less hierarchical. Renaissance forms were vigorous, lively interpretations of nature in human and animal shape as well as plant life and landscape.

With the Renaissance, in Florence, came a change in the artist's status and also in his versatility. The artist, whatever his medium, became an important member of society. He was revered for his skill and paid well for his work. He was in demand by wealthy men of rank: to write about them, build churches and palaces for them, and to decorate these in the prevailing mode. The artist recognised this status and would not demean himself by working for a patron who did not follow his advice or appreciate his work. If the artist was good he could pick and choose. At the same time he was expected to produce a remarkably high standard of work in different media. All the great Renaissance artists were practised in more than one visual art form, though they might prefer to work in one rather than another. For instance, Giotto, a painter, was appointed architect to Florence Cathedral. Alberti, the famous Renaissance architect, was also a mathematician, writer and scholar. Michelangelo was not alone in excelling as painter, sculptor and architect, indeed he held the opinion that a complete, mature artist should have proved himself with commissions in all three arts, in that order, so that by the time he was 50–60 years old he might, after such experience, become a good architect. Renaissance artists created works of superb mastery, but they were never narrow specialists.

Italy continued dominant in architecture until the seventeenth century. The great centres of design shifted to Milan, Venice and other cities— but always with Rome to the fore. In the sixteenth century artists, once more seeking change and variety, moved from pure Roman classicism to Mannerism. This word Mannerism, which was coined about 50 years ago, is applied to the transitional type of work which differs from both the purer High Renaissance classicism and the full Baroque of the seventeenth century. It is characterised by a restlessness of feeling and motif and a reluctance to follow too closely the classical rules and traditions. Architects such as Raphael, Peruzzi and Michelangelo used its forms to a greater or lesser degree in different buildings.

Although all Renaissance architecture has fundamental characteristics which render it clearly recognisable wherever it is to be found, outside Italy there were many variations on the theme. These were created partly by national ethos, partly by climate and available building materials, but also by the distance separating the countries from Italy, the source of the style. This factor also governed the period of time which tended to elapse between Italy's fifteenth century work and the first pure examples appearing in England, Spain or Scandinavia as late sometimes as the seventeenth century, by which time Italy had gone on to Baroque.

France was influenced earliest by Italian example and possesses the purest building style. Germany and its neighbouring countries of Poland, Czechoslovakia and Holland based their earlier Renaissance work on pattern books, many of them Flemish in origin. The designs, having been thus copied and transmitted from Italy to France to Flanders, altered *en route* so that the style of building used by German, Dutch and English architects was not like the Italian prototypes. When the national characteristics and building traditions were also incorporated in the work the results became a Flemish Mannerism which is totally different from the Italian one. English work of this type is Elizabethan or Jacobean, characterised by all-over decoration, imperfect understanding of the orders, and buildings which are still basically Medieval with a clothing of Renaissance ornament superimposed. In few cases is Renaissance structure employed. This effect can be seen also in sixteenth century Polish, German, Dutch and Spanish work. In Spain it took the form of Renaissance Plateresque. This, like its predecessor Gothic Plateresque (see Chapter 5), is an all-over surface decoration of Renaissance forms in rich and intricate manner. Decorative motifs used in such Man-

nerism in all these countries is generally in high relief and includes a bewildering variety of forms human, animal, plant and bird life, cartouches, strapwork, obelisks and grotesques of all kinds.

None of this Mannerist work is pure Renaissance. In the past it was often deemed crude and barbaric. It is certainly not to everyone's taste but it always displays vigour and pulsating life though sometimes it may be vulgar; it has originality and reflects with uncanny accuracy its country of origin. For these reasons it is usually appreciated today on its own merits, not as a derivation, and for its own interest, though it would not be considered of the same high aesthetic quality as S. Peter's in Rome or the Florentine palaces.

Not all the countries of Europe possess remains of pure Renaissance architecture. Some, like the U.S.S.R., Bulgaria and Rumania, largely missed out on this period and retained their Byzantine tradition very strongly till the later seventeenth and eighteenth century. Other countries went direct from Mannerist designs to Baroque, but some, notably France, Spain and England created, later than in Italy, a pure Renaissance pattern of building. In England this movement was initiated by Inigo Jones and in Spain by architects like Juan de Herrera.

Classical architecture in different guises remained the fundamental form of building till after 1900.* There were countless variations but all subscribed to the basic theme: the use of columns as support and/or decoration, the orders and a trabeated form of building allied to a greater or lesser extent to the arcuated one. For the greater part of this 500-year period the inspiration was from ancient Rome but, in the eighteenth and nineteenth centuries, a proportion of the work was based on the civilisation of ancient Greece.

Confusion is sometimes created by the similar terms classical, classicism and classic, all in use to refer to the work of these years. Classical is the adjective describing designs and characteristics of the antique world of Greece and Rome and their later derivations. Classicism is the appropriate noun. Classic has a wider adjectival meaning. It is used to refer to designs of different species, provided that they are based on a proven early, original style; and this might be classical but could equally well be Romanesque or Byzantine.

*In the nineteenth century, eclecticism also explored Byzantine and Medieval avenues.

646
647
648
649

646 *S. Maria Novella, Florence. Façade, Alberti, 1470*
647 *The dome of Florence Cathedral, Brunelleschi,*
   1420–36; lantern, 1461
648 *Interior, S. Lorenzo, Florence, Brunelleschi, from 1420*
649 *Façade, S. Andrea, Mantua, Alberti, begun 1472*

311

Italy

Early Renaissance: Fifteenth Century Florence

Filippo Brunelleschi (1377–1446) was the first Renaissance architect. He had been both goldsmith and sculptor and had also studied mathematics and spent some time in Rome making measured drawings of ancient Roman buildings. His early work, like the *Ospedale degli Innocenti* (the Foundling Hospital), begun 1419, was Tuscan and Romanesque in derivation. Nevertheless, such designs showed the new classical approach, a desire for symmetry, proportions carefully related in one part to another and the adaptation of the new-found science of perspective to architecture.

In his commission to build a *dome* to the unfinished Medieval *Cathedral*, Brunelleschi had to bring all his knowledge of mathematics and of the structures of ancient Roman vaults. The practical problem for this date (1404) was considerable; how to construct a dome to span the 138 feet diameter space. This was too great a distance to support on available timber centering. Brunelleschi, like all classical architects, knew that a hemispherical dome would be aesthetically most desirable. He dared not build one on to the existing octagonal drum, which had no external abutment. So he compromised and proceeded carefully, step by step. His dome is constructed on Gothic principles with ribs supporting a later, light infilling. It is taller than a hemisphere to offset the thrust. To retain his exterior and to reduce weight, he made two domes, one inside the other. The lantern, though designed by Brunelleschi, was built after his death. It is weighty and impressive; a fine finial (**647**).

Brunelleschi built several churches and chapels. The outstanding ones are similar; *S. Spirito* (1436) and *S. Lorenzo* (*c.* 1420) (**648**), both of which are basilican and display a feeling of light not found in Medieval churches. His unfinished *S. Maria degli Angeli* (1437) is one of the earliest examples of the centrally planned church; a concept which has intrigued classical architects until the present century. This one is a 16-sided regular polygon; eight chapels open from the octagonal central area. His *Pazzi Chapel* (S. Croce) (1433) contains some magnificent ceramic work by *Luca della Robbia* (1400–82).

Fifteenth century Florence was one of the wealthiest of the city states so it is not surprising that the finest of the early *Renaissance palace* were commissioned here by the merchants and ecclesiastical families. Because of the early date and the still troubled times, such palaces are distinguished from later examples by their protective lower storeys, which are rusticated and almost undecorated and unpierced by window openings. These lower floors were used as warehouse and shop accommodation, while classical windows lit the living quarters above. A strongly projecting cornice was developed at the roofline. Inside the building was a square, open courtyard its light elegant arcaded colonnades contrasting with the forbidding exterior elevations. Most of these palaces were astylar. Typical is the *Strozzi* (1489) by *Benedetto da Maiano* (**651**), the *Medici Riccardi* (1444–60) by Michelozzo, the *Pazzi Quaratesi* and the later *Gondi* (*c.* 1490) by *Giuliano da Sangallo*. The *Pitti Palace*, begun 1458 and enlarged *c.* 1550, has a vast main elevation and is one of the best known. One or two palaces had façades with orders, such as *Alberti's Palazzo Rucellai* (1446). These are in pilaster form and the vertical strips make an effective break to the horizontal rustication bands. This set a new pattern with was followed increasingly later.

The Fifteenth Century outside Florence

Leon Battista Alberti (1404–72) was the second outstanding architect of this period. A Genoese he was a different type of man from Brunelleschi; he was more academic and scholarly and his book on architecture spread Renaissance ideas and classical designs far beyond the borders of Italy. Like Brunelleschi though, he had been a sculptor and mathematician. While the former turned his abilities to solving the problems of constructing the Florence Cathedral dome, Alberti tackled the age-old question of how to reconcile, in church façade design, the differing heights of nave and aisles by an architectural feature. The Medieval period had dealt with this problem by fronting the cathedrals' western end by a façade unrelated to the structure behind it, as at Orvieto and Siena. Alberti made a feature of it in his prototype, the new façade to *S. Maria Novella in Florence*; he inserted side scrolls to mask the junction (**646**). Here is pure Tuscan decoration

RENAISSANCE PALACES IN ITALY

Ducal Palace Courtyard, Urbino, Laurana, 1465–9
Strozzi Palace, Florence, Benedetto da Maiano, 1489
Farnese Palace Courtyard, Rome, Antonio da Sangallo before 1514; after 1546, Michelangelo
Doorway, Ducal Palace, Urbino
Palazzo Massimi alle Colonne, Rome, Baldassare Peruzzi, from 1532

654

653

652

RENAISSANCE ITALY

655 S. Pietro in Montorio. Chapel in courtyard called 'Il Tempietto', Bramante, 1500–2

656 S. Maria delle Grazie, Milan, Bramante, 1492–7 : (Gothic nave 1470)

657 The Capitol, Rome, including the Palazzo Capitolino, Palazzo Senatore and the Palazzo Conservatori, 1540–1644. Designed by Michelangelo

656

657

655

in coloured marble strips and veneer but correctly classical in its detail and proportions; it is a Renaissance version of the Romanesque S. Miniato al Monte (**281**).

Alberti also designed *S. Francesco* in *Rimini* (1446) and *S. Sebastiano* in *Mantua* (1460), but his masterpiece, also in Mantua, is his *S. Andrea*, begun 1472 (**649**). This is a prototype far ahead of its time, from the triumphal arch façade to the handling of the interior spatial concepts.

Among the palaces of this century outside Florence, the finest is the *Ducal Palace* at *Urbino* (**650** and **653**), set on a hill top. The courtyard especially is elegant and finely proportioned. *Venetian palaces* were still more Medieval than Renaissance in design, differing little from the Ca' d'Oro (**590**), though fenestration and detail slowly changed. The *Palazzo Vendramin-Calergi c.* 1500 by *Lombardo* is typical.

Lombardic work of this time is also apart from the main stream of the Florentine Renaissance. It is nearer to English Mannerism in its rich surface decoration all over the façades. It differs from the English in that the decorative medium is coloured marble rather than carved wood or stone. The *Colleoni Chapel* at *Bergamo* and the *Certosa di Pavia* façade, both of the 1470–80 period and by *Amadeo*, are typical.

The High Renaissance : Sixteenth Century

This century, the *cinquecento*, was the great age of the Renaissance in Italy. Architects of note and stature were numerous and the quality of the work produced in building and decoration was superb. This was the time when the majority of men of high intellect, talent and initiative became artists, for it was in this field that both monetary and human satisfaction were to be gained.

Among the wealth of talented artists, three stand supreme above the others for the originality of their contribution, its quality and their outstanding personalities: Bramante, Raphael and Michelangelo.

Donato d'Agnolo Lazzari (1444–1514), generally called *Bramante*, was born in Urbino and, after some time spent as a sculptor and a poet, began work as an architect in Milan. Here, he quickly established a reputation for Renaissance building, which for the first time was based on the pure Roman form. His *cloisters* at the *Monastery of S. Ambrogio* show this. He reconstructed the tiny *S. Maria presso S. Satiro*. It exists still, overshadowed by towering modern buildings in the centre of Milan. At *S. Maria delle Grazie** he added an eastern arm to the Gothic church (**656**). This had only recently been built, but Bramante's great polygonal drum with its attendant apses is in marked contrast. The feature was imitated widely by other architects.

Early in the new century Bramante went to Rome and here became the leading architect of his day. Like Brunelleschi before him, he was attracted to the classical symmetry of the centrally planned church. In this he was also influenced by Leonardo da Vinci's drawings showing such buildings on Greek cross plan, perfectly symmetrical and with radiating members. Bramante experimented with the theme in a small chapel erected in the courtyard of *S. Pietro* in *Montorio*. It has achieved a reputation quite disproportionate to its size and is generally regarded as the most perfect monument to the High Renaissance in the world (**655**). Typically Renaissance in his unconcern over combining Christian and pagan influences, Bramante's *tempietto* is built on the supposed site of S. Peter's crucifixion, but in design is based on a circular Roman temple. It is plain, with a Doric peristyle on a stylobate surmounted by a drum and dome within a parapet. Small though it is, the proportions are in such perfect harmony, it could be enlarged greatly without detriment.

Other architects followed Bramante's lead in centrally planned churches. There are many fine examples, notably *S. Maria di Loreto, Rome*, by *Antonio da Sangallo* (1507), *S. Maria della Croce, Crema*, by *Battagio, S. Maria delle Carceri, Prato* by *Giuliano da Sangallo* and, finest and most perfect of all, *S. Maria della Consolazione* at *Todi, c.* 1520.

Bramante carried out a great deal of other work in Rome during his stay there. This included the *cloister* at *S. Maria della Pace*, the *Vatican Courts* and *S. Peter's*. In the famous basilica, Bramante was given his great opportunity to design a large church on centrally planned lines. In 1503, the newly elected Pope Julius II had to face the problem of what to do about the 1200-year-old basilica, founded by the Emperor Constantine, but now in a seriously dilapidated condition. Courageously, he decided to destroy and rebuild

Noted for its possession of Leonardo da Vinci's Last Supper.

the Mother Church of the Roman Catholic faith. Bramante's completely symmetrical design on Greek cross plan, with central dome and apses on each arm of the cross, was approved (**658**). The first stone was laid in 1506, but when the architect died in 1514, little had been achieved and the four crossing piers proved inadequate to support the enormous projected dome and had to be rebuilt by his successors.

Raphael (Raffaello Sanzio, 1483–1520) had a short life but was responsible for a prodigious quantity of work. In the last decade of his life especially, in Rome, his output as a painter was tremendous. Some of his frescoes decorate the ceilings of the loggia in Peruzzi's beautiful *Villa Farnesina* on the banks of the Tiber (1509–11). In the architectural field Raphael was Surveyor to the fabric of S. Peter's after Bramante and he built a number of palaces and a villa. His earlier work is in Bramante's style, but later he turned to Mannerist forms. Sadly, little of this remains unaltered, though in some cases the building still exists. He built the *Palazzo Vidoni-Caffarelli* (1515) and the *Branconio dell'Aquila*, both in *Rome*, and the *Pandolfini* in *Florence*. His most ambitious and impressive work was the *Villa Madama* on the outskirts of Rome (1516). He based this on Nero's 'Golden House' and designed it for Cardinal dei Medici.

Michelangelo Buonarroti, 1475–1564

In a book devoted to architecture covering 3000 years in the 23 countries of Europe, space does not permit more than a brief mention of any one architect. Michelangelo must always be an exception. More has been written about him than any other artist the world has known, but this giant among Renaissance geniuses was unique. It is not usual for great artists to be praised in or just after their lifetimes. Again, Michelangelo was an exception. In common with a small group of creative artists, his reputation has never wavered nor has the praise abated. While he lived he commanded, despite his prickly, unbending personality, idolatry from his patrons, fellow artists and the public at large. In all three of the visual arts, painting, sculpture, architecture, he led the field while he lived. He himself preferred the medium of sculpture but when, under pressure, he carried out commissions to cover

great walls and ceilings with paintings, the qualities were still of superb genius. The Sistine Chapel ceiling and the wall covered by his Last Judgement bear testimony to this.

Much of Michelangelo's work in architecture was done late in life; S. Peter's and the Campidoglio, for instance. In *Florence* his work came earlier and some of it is in High Renaissance pure style though later, as in Rome, his tendency was towards Mannerism and even Baroque. But, with Michelangelo one cannot apply labels with any accuracy. His work was of his time or slightly ahead of it but it was always so personally Michelangelo that it defies classification. His architecture, like his painting, always possesses a sculptural quality. It is plastic, forceful, controlled, an undefinable mixture of tortured movement and immemorial peace. The contrast between this and Alberti's and Bramante's classicism is very marked. Michelangelo was responsible for two main works in Florence, both in *S. Lorenzo*. The first is his New Sacristy (so-called to differentiate it from Brunelleschi's). This is the *Medici Mausoleum* which Michelangelo designed in 1521, wherein both architecture and sculpture are his. It is a square interior, the walls of which are strongly articulated in High Renaissance manner. Above is a dome supported on pendentives. The tombs of both Lorenzo and Giuliano Medici are here and respectively adorn two sides of the room. They dominate the scheme. Each has a central sculptural portrait figure of the Medici and below are the symbolic designs representing Dawn and Twilight and Night and Day (PLATE 60). In the *Laurenziana Library* nearby, Michelangelo turned further towards Mannerism. This can be seen in the large coupled columns in recesses, bearing no load and flanked by blind windows. The power and tension in the narrow hall is noticeable contrasting with the controlled, ordered library above. Entrance hall, staircase and library are one complete, complementary unit.

Michelangelo's greatest work is in the *Basilica of S. Peter* in *Rome*. He spent the last 30 years of his life here and himself regarded his work on the basilica as his most important commission refusing any salary and working on it till his death at the age of 89. He was an admirer of Bramante and liked his plan. He had to modify it for practical reasons, simplifying the small

THE BASILICA OF S. PETER, ROME, 1506-1612

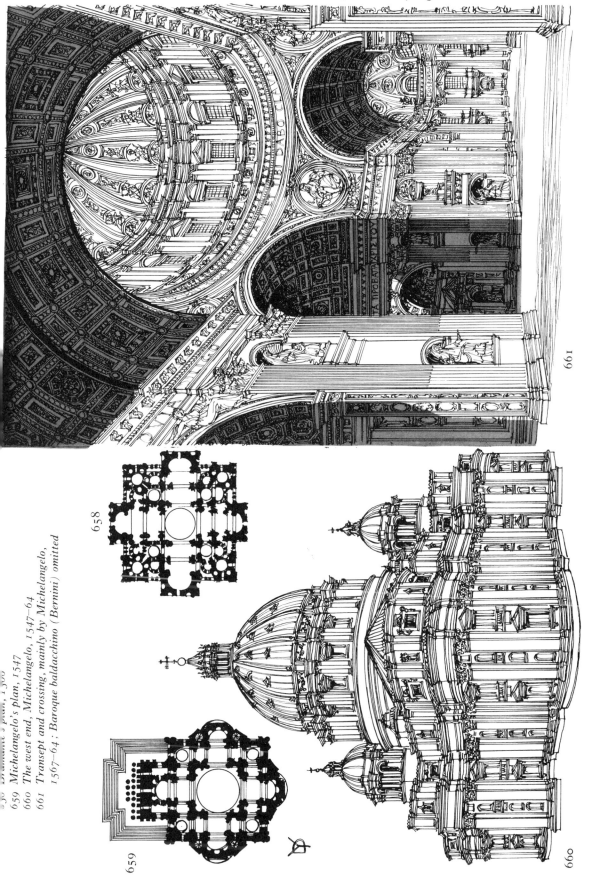

658 *Bramante's plan, 1506*
659 *Michelangelo's plan, 1547*
660 *The west end, Michelangelo, 1547–64*
661 *Transept and crossing, mainly by Michelangelo,*
  1567–64; Baroque baldacchino (Bernini) omitted

compartments into larger ones and making the building stable by increasing the size of the crossing piers. His plan is shown on p. 317, next to Bramante's (**659** and **658**). Michelangelo's S. Peter's is vast but is so beautifully proportioned that the visitor does not appreciate its size till he compares the height of a pier, for example, with the people in the basilica. Most of the present exterior (apart from the east façade) is Michelangelo's building. It is surrounded by Corinthian order pilasters in giant form, each 100 feet high, surmounted by a 32 feet attic. The whole forms a podium on which the great drum and dome rest. There are three apses, one at the choir (westerly end) and one to each transept. This view of the building, difficult of access because of the Vatican grounds, is shown in Fig. **660**.

About the evolution of the dome of S. Peter's scholars differ. Michelangelo designed a hemispherical one as Brunelleschi had wished to do in Florence and, like him, created an inner shell, but also in hemispherical form. This was based on ancient Roman ideas but, whereas the Romans in the Pantheon had supported the dome on circular walls, Renaissance architects had to raise it on four crossing piers and pendentives. The thrust involved is so great that at that time such a dome was not a feasible structural possibility. When Michelangelo died, the building was largely complete apart from the eastern arm and the dome above the drum. This dome was completed in 1587–90 by Giacomo della Porta and Domenico Fontana, but the exterior form is taller than a hemisphere and is not concentric with the inner one 20 feet lower. The conjecture is whether the final work was based on Michelangelo's altered designs or on those of della Porta and Fontana. Available evidence comprises Michelangelo's one-fifth size scale wooden model of the dome, made in 1561 and in hemispherical form and a taller version shown in a drawing by Michelangelo, now in the Ashmolean Museum in Oxford but not verified as intended for S. Peter's. Historians are divided on this point which is, no doubt, academic. The dome is constructionally sound and on both exterior and interior the most aesthetically satisfying in the world. Its span is 157 feet and the cross rises to 452 feet above the ground.

The interior of S. Peter's as it is seen today is also largely due to Michelangelo. It is architecturally simple. Four arms of the cross are barrel vaulted and decorated by coffers and panels. They meet at the crossing where the drum and dome rise on richly decorated pendentives. Despite the lengthening of the nave in the seventeenth century (Chapter 7) from Greek cross to Latin cross pattern, the interior is basically of one period and design. This is an incredible feat for a building begun in 1506 and completed in 1612. Not a small part of the success is due to the overriding genius of Michelangelo (**661**).

Michelangelo also interested himself in early town planning schemes. His chief contribution here is in the re-designing of *Capitol Hill in Rome* (Piazza del Campidoglio). This was designed in 1540. It had been the site for the centre of government since the days of ancient Rome and when, in 1538, the equestrian statue of Marcus Aurelius was moved here (under the impression that it was of Constantine), it was decided to make a worthy setting for this rare Roman monument. Michelangelo designed a piazza on trapezoidal plan, with palaces on three sides and steps approaching the narrow side up the steep hillside from the road below. He designed an oval pavement (which does not now exist) to emphasise this. The important feature of the architecture of the palaces is that it is the first recorded use of Michelangelo's giant order wherein the columns spanned two storeys. This was an innovation, giving dignity and unity to a façade, which was copied extensively in later work, not only in Italy but in France and England. The whole complex is on Mannerist lines and one of the few layouts existing from this century which comprises the handling of more than one building in a scheme (**657**).

Sixteenth-Century Palaces, Villas and Churches

The sixteenth century Roman palace differed from its fifteenth century prototype in Florence. Land in the city was costly so wealthy patrons tended to have a town palace on a smaller site then a more spacious suburban villa in which to relax. The town palace had a High Renaissance street façade and a small courtyard behind. Such palaces were designed by famous architects and tended, during the century, from Renaissance towards Mannerist. Chief among such architects

Plate 59
Florence, Italy
Detail door panel.
Porta di Paradiso.
Baptistery, Ghiberti,
1425–52
Plate 60
'Dawn', from Tomb
of Lorenzo dei
Medici. Medici
Chapel, Church of
S. Lorenzo.
Michelangelo, begun
1531

Plate 61
Neptune fountain detail. Piazza della Signoria, Florence, Italy.
Ammanati, 1569–75

Plate 62
Neptune Fountain detail, Bologna, Italy. Da Bologna, 1563–7

were Raphael, Peruzzi, Vignola, Romano and Antonio da Sangallo II. *Baldassare Peruzzi's* Villa Farnesina has already been referred to. Another of his town palaces is the *Palazzo Massimi alle Colonne* (654). This, built in 1532, is an early Mannerist work, designed for twin brothers. The façade is subtly curved and breaks many of the classical rules of proportion and the handling of orders, forming a sophisticated elevation, with a fine courtyard behind. The *Farnese Palace* is one of the most magnificent examples. Now the home of the French Embassy, it was built by *Antonio da Sangallo II* on High Renaissance lines. The finely articulated courtyard (652) is carefully based on the Colosseum principles with superimposed orders—Doric, Ionic, Corinthian. The top storey was added by Michelangelo.

The second half of the sixteenth century brought a new group of architects: Giorgio Vasari, Giacomo Barocchio (generally called da Vignola after his birthplace), Giulio Romano, Giacomo della Porta, Bartolommeo Ammanati. *Vasari's* famous work is the *Uffizi Palace* in *Florence* (1560–74), now the home of the great art gallery; this is severely Mannerist. *Vignola* worked with Vasari and *Ammanati* on the *Villa Giulia* in *Rome*, built for Pope Julius from 1550 but now the Museum of Etruscan Antiquities. He also designed the fine *villa* at *Caprarola*. *Della Porta* built the *Villa Aldobrandini* at *Frascati* near Rome, a beautiful Mannerist design with fine gardens and fountains.

Giulio Romano is particularly known for his *Palazzo del Te* at *Mantua*, in which city he also worked on the Cathedral and the Ducal Palace. The Palazzo del Te is planned round a central courtyard with a magnificent loggia (662) and garden façades.

The Veneto: Sixteenth Century

This area of north-east Italy, under the domination of the Venetian Republic, had always differed from the rest of the country in its artistic expression. Its close mercantile ties with the east gave to its architecture a mixed heritage. Eastern and western influences merged into a unique style. It had been so in Romanesque and Gothic periods; it continued so under the Renaissance. Fifteenth century palaces have been mentioned. In the sixteenth century the pattern continued.

Examples like the *Scuola di San Rocco* (1520–50 and now the City Hospital) and the *Church* of *S. Zaccaria* (1485–1515) illustrate this. But after the collapse of Rome in 1527 several artists came here from elsewhere and the style was brought into line with that of Rome and northern Italy. Two particular architects were Jacopo Tatti, called Il Sansovino (1486–1570) and Michele Sanmichele (1484–1559). *Sansovino* was a Florentine. He was sculptor and architect and a disciple of Michelangelo. Among his outstanding works in *Venice* are the *Library of S. Mark*, the *Mint* (Zecca) and his *Loggia del Campanile*, all in the region of S. Mark's Square. He also built a number of palaces, notably the *Palazzo Cornaro*, now the Prefettura. *Sanmichele* was a Veronese and he returned to his native city after years at Orvieto and Rome. He was in charge of the town's fortification scheme, building town walls and gates, and he designed many *palaces*, for example, the *Canossa*, the *Pompei* and the *Bevilacqua*. Both architects designed in plastic form, showing Michelangelo's influence in their power and chiaroscuro.

The pre-eminent architect of this area in the later sixteenth century was *Andrea Palladio* (1508–80), born Andrea di Pietro della Gondoa. Palladio reverted to the principles of Vitruvius and ancient Rome. He made hundreds of drawings *in situ*, not only in Italy but in Dalmatia and Provence. He published his own designs and ideas in several works of which two, 'I Quattro Libri dell' Architettura' and 'L'Antichità di Roma' were translated into many languages and spread his theories all over Europe. The Palladian school of architecture in eighteenth century England is, of course, named after him. Palladio's own work was a mixture of those sources allied to the classicism of Bramante and the Mannerism of Michelangelo and Vignola. Most of his work is in Vicenza and Venice. It comprises churches, palaces and villas, as well as civic works like the replanning of the *town hall* of *Vicenza* (663), where he established a pattern in his handling of two superimposed orders (Doric and Ionic) with entablatures broken forward over each column instead of giving the uninterrupted horizontal emphasis as in Sansovino's Library.

In his many palaces and villas he followed what he thought would have been the ancient Roman theme, but as Roman domestic remains are

662 *Palazzo del Te, Mantua, Giulio Romano, 1526–34*

663 *Town Hall (Basilica Palladiana), Vicenza. Re-clothed by Palladio from 1549*

663

fragmentary, he had to base them on temple design. Two particular examples illustrate his ideas; his *Palazzo Chiericati* in *Vicenza* and the *Villa Capra* (the Rotonda) outside the town. This was copied on at least two occasions in Palladian England, by Lord Burlington at Chiswick House and by Colen Campbell at Mereworth Castle. The Villa Capra is the domestic equivalent to Bramante's 'Tempietto' or S. Maria at Todi. It is the centrally planned villa with central domed hall and the whole *piano nobile* raised on a square podium with four identical porticoes with entrance steps on each side.

In his *churches*, Palladio also used what he thought to be the Roman temple pattern. He developed a type of façade design which incorporated two or more interpenetrating orders differing in scale. He employed this method to solve the old problem of relating the façade to the different height of nave and aisles (see Alberti p. 312). Palladio made his nave order larger and higher than that of the aisles. His two outstanding churches are in *Venice*, standing at the water's edge: *S. Giorgio Maggiore*, 1565, and *Il Redentore*, 1577–92.

In the second half of the sixteenth century the work of certain artists heralded the Baroque. Michelangelo's contribution at S. Peter's has been mentioned. Also in architecture came *Vignola's* Roman church of *Il Gesù*. This was the Mother Church for the Society of Jesus, which had been founded in 1540. The church design set a pattern for Jesuit churches all over Europe. It was begun in 1568. Vignola's terms of reference were to build a church which could hold a large congregation, all of whom could hear and see the preacher. So the architect must eschew columns, arcades and the nave with aisles pattern. He did so and created a precedent. Il Gesù has no aisles or colonnades; its short broad nave and choir with shallow transepts have side chapels leading off them. To compensate for the lack of side aisle lighting, the large dome has a fenestrated drum which floods the whole church dramatically with light and so gives a unity and space lacking in any Gothic or Renaissance church on the Latin cross plan. Vignola died in 1573 when the church had reached cornice level. Giacomo della Porta built the façade and the interior was altered later in the seventeenth and nineteenth centuries. Despite this it remains the sixteenth century prototype

for churches, especially Jesuit ones, all over Europe and marks the crossroads between Mannerism and Baroque. Similarly, in sculpture, *Giovanni da Bologna's* work, as in his *Neptune Fountain* in *Bologna* (1563–7) tends in the same direction (PLATE 62).

Yugoslavia

Remaining buildings of Renaissance style are not numerous. Most of them are in towns boardering the Adriatic coast and show the strong influence from Italy and especially the Venetian Republic. The purest work is in *Dubrovnik*. Two buildings here, in particular (though later restored), have survived the earthquake of 1667 which destroyed so much of the city. The *Rectors' Palace** had been built in the fifteenth century in Gothic style by *Onofrio Giordano della Cava*, but in 1463 the fine Renaissance portico was added. This contains the unusual and varied capitals carved by della Cava, George of Šibenik and Michelozzo (**665** and **666**). Next door is the *Sponza Palace* which served as both custom house and Mint. It was built by Paskoje Miličević and has a fine Renaissance courtyard (**668**). The street façade, like the Rectors' palace, has a ground floor, Renaissance loggia and Gothic fenestration above.

In a less pure, more Mannerist form, are one or two buildings further north. At *Trogir*, opposite to the cathedral in the main square, is an attractive *loggia* with primitive Corinthian style capitals. At one end of the building is a solid square tower. One of the town gateways at *Zadar* has a Renaissance clock tower. This blends with the earlier lower section (**667**).

France

France was the only major European country outside Italy to build in Renaissance form before the seventeenth century. Even here, however, it was not until after 1550 that such work was to be seen. In the earlier sixteenth century buildings erected were basically Gothic in structure and classical only in detail. This ornament was applied without proper comprehension of classical form; buildings were Mannerist. Ecclesiastical structures were especially treated in this way until the early seventeenth century, as at *S. Étienne du Mont* in *Paris* (**670**).

* *A Rector was elected regularly as head of the city government.*

RENAISSANCE IN YUGOSLAVIA AND HUNGARY

664 *Detail, Chapel of Archbishop Thomas Bakócz, Esztergom*
665 *Capital and* 666 *Base of Rectors' Palace, Dubrovnik, Yugoslavia, 1463*
667 *Porta Marina, Zadar, Yugoslavia; upper part 1571, lower part Roman*
668 *Sponza Palace (Custom House and Mint), Dubrovnik, 1516–21*
669 *Chapel of Archbishop Thomas Bakócz in the Cathedral of Esztergom, Hungary, 1507*

664

666

665

667

668

Though France had close contacts with Italy in the early sixteenth century, both economic and in warfare, and though French designers took easily to using Italianate decorative forms such as orders, scrolls, shells and putti, the Medieval tradition of building persisted. Architecture was slow to follow classical lines until the second half of the century, when architects like De l'Orme and Lescot adopted the new style. Most of this work was in palaces and châteaux where wealthy patrons wished to build in the latest mode. Francis I, almost exactly a contemporary of England's Henry VIII, was the first to show the way. He established a great court, determined to build his culture on Italian lines. He attracted many Italian artists and craftsmen to France, even the great Leonardo da Vinci.

At *Blois*, at *Fontainebleau* and soon in *Paris* (671 and 677), Francis built on Renaissance pattern. Others followed suit and French architects, having understood and developed the new

670 *Church of S. Étienne du Mont, Paris, 1517–1618*

670

style, took to it with pleasure. French Renaissance work is not the same as Italian. It is often more academic, less warm-blooded, monumental or plastic, but much of the later work of the sixteenth century, like Lescot's range in the Cour Carrée in the Louvre (679), is of high quality. It quickly established France as a leader of Renaissance design in her own right.

Early Sixteenth-Century Palaces and Châteaux

One of the first instances of Renaissance influence can still be seen in Francis I's wing at the *Château of Blois*. A whole court was planned, but under Francis I's aegis only this range was completed. It contains the famous staircase which, though constructed spirally on Medieval pattern, is classical in appearance and decoration. This range represents the chief contribution of the French court to the early establishment of Renaissance building in France (677). It provides an interesting contrast to the adjoining wing of Louis XII, built only a few years earlier but completely Medieval.

Francis' second venture was the immense *Château of Chambord* (674). Work was begun in 1519 on a building intended as a hunting lodge. The project grew and was enlarged and altered until the seventeenth century. The original design is thought to have been by the Italian architect *Domenico da Cortona* but, as interpreted by local masons, is very French in character. Chambord is vast, built at the waters' edge and still surrounded by acres of parkland. The château comprises an immense main block with traditional French circular corner towers and with further wings and towers extending at the sides. The wall articulation is simple and Renaissance but the roofline is a riot of chimneys, cupolas, pinnacles and dormers, having much in common (though Gallic in its Mannerist drama) with the Elizabethan great houses of England.

The château interior, based unusually on a Greek cross plan, is noted for the early development in France of the Italian method of arranging the rooms, grouped in suites (*appartements*). These are self-contained and more convenient than the Medieval design of corridor rooms. The double staircase is an outstanding feature of the internal plan. It rises spirally the full height of the building, to a lantern above.

The many châteaux built before 1550 display a varied proportion of Medieval to Renaissance features. Some are entirely Medieval in layout and structure but show classical detail and ornament. They remain fortified, often with moat or surrounding lake, and retain the picturesque French style of roofs, gables and dormers. Very much of this type is the finely situated *Rigny-Ussé*, with its profusion of turrets and chimneys. Also very Medieval is *Amboise*, rebuilt from 1501 by Italian craftsmen. This influence is reflected in the Renaissance detail of dormers and finials in particular. *Azay-le-Rideau*, like Chenonceaux, is among the most picturesque examples, reflected in the encircling spreading waters. It is small, built on simple L-shaped plan, with circular corner towers. The wall articulation and dormer decoration is Renaissance, but Medieval machicolations support the parapets. The frontispiece on the entrance side (**676**) is classical in treatment; a narrow structure with Gothic vertical emphasis. *Chenonceaux*, begun in 1515, based on the Medieval square keep plan, was extended later in the century by *De l'Orme* and *Bullant*. The château is built on the foundations of a mill set by the River Cher and it rises directly from the river. De l'Orme added a terrace across the river upon which Bullant later built his two-storeyed gallery to enlarge the château accommodation. It is interesting to compare the different stages of work from that of the early sixteenth century to the Renaissance and Mannerist style of building (**675**). A merging of Gothic and Renaissance styles can be seen in the two adjacent wings at *Fontaine-Henry* in Normandy. The lower wing is of fifteenth century origin while the taller block added on the left of the façade is Renaissance in its orders and fenestration. An immensely tall roof surmounts this part. A much later example (1606), but still completely Mannerist, is the *Château* at *Brissac*. It has Medieval circular corner towers but a richly articulated Mannerist façade. It is an illustration of how long had to elapse, even in France, before completely classical design replaced Gothic structures.

One of the architectural landmarks between the buildings just described and the more correctly classical ones of the later sixteenth century, is the *Château* at *Ancy-le-Franc*. This is the only surviving building in France by *Sebastiano Serlio*, the Italian architect and writer.

Serlio came to France in 1541 and his influen on French Renaissance design was far-reachir This was due primarily to his publicatio (p. 309), which guided French architects Italian and Roman classical design. His buildin in France were few. The Château at Ancy-Franc has been altered and its design is not Serlio originally intended. His first idea was a more Italianate structure, with façades of Do pilasters above a rusticated lower storey. T was too advanced for its time in France and w rejected in favour of the existing, more innocuo scheme of great corner blocks and walls artic lated only by low relief Doric pilasters. T entrance porch is richer (**673**) and the interi court displays more variety.

The Palace of Fontainebleau

The building history of Fontainebleau is lo and complex. It extends from the Mediev castle to manor house, to a larger château a eventually Napoleon's palace. It has been altere added to and restored many times. Its importan in Renaissance work lies in its development Francis I and the architecture and decoration the Italians Rosso and Primaticcio.

Francis I decided to enlarge the Mediev castle in 1528. The master mason *Gilles Breton* was in charge. He refaced the courtya of the old castle, called the Cour de L'Ova and added a fine porch. He built a new entran to the court, the Porte Dorée. This has thr storeys topped by a tall, French style roo Francis continued his enlargement and altera tions and his successors followed on. The Co du Cheval Blanc was begun. This is the immen entrance courtyard of the present palace. It w enlarged in Napoleon's time and is now cal the Cour des Adieux in memory of the Empero farewell to his Guard on his departure to exile the Island of Elba. The original name referred the copy of the equestrian statue of Marc Aurelius in the Capitol in Rome (p. 318).

The finest views of the exterior work of sixteenth century are the main entrance foreco of the Cour du Cheval Blanc (**671**) and the vi across the lake of the Cour de la Fontaine, w its fine wing by Primaticcio, the Aile de la B Cheminée.

FRENCH RENAISSANCE CHÂTEAUX

671 *Fontainebleau. Cour du Cheval (later Cour des Adieux), Gilles le Breton, 1528–40*
672 *Gateway, Anet, Philibert de l'Orme, 1548–52*
673 *Entrance doorway, Ancy-le-Franc, Sebastiano Serlio, begun 1546*
674 *Chambord, begun 1519*

Plate 63
Wall decoration. The King's Staircase. Château of Fontainebleau, France. *c.*1541–5, Primaticcio
Plate 64
Detail Outside pulpit. Prato Cathedral, Italy. 1434–8, Donatello

Plate 65
Courtyard, Episcopal Palace, Liège, Belgium. Mannerist. 1525–32
Plate 66
Detail. Schöner Hof, Plassenburg, Kulmbach, Germany, 1551–69

Inside, despite thorough restoration in the nineteenth and twentieth centuries, there still remain some excellent decorative schemes and galleries. The best, dating from the sixteenth century, comprise the Francis I gallery, the King's Staircase and the Henry II Gallery. The Francis I gallery is of typical long gallery proportions: 200 feet in length by only 17 wide. The lower part of the walls is panelled in wood, carved and gilded to the original designs. Above, are stucco sculptured figures and decorations framing the paintings. This type of interior décor was carried out by the two Italians, Giambattista di Jacopo, called *Le Rosso* (1494–1540) and *Francesco Primaticcio* (1505–70). Rosso, a Florentine, came first to Fontainebleau in 1530 and worked on the gallery for nine years, Primaticcio came soon after. He had worked at the Palazzo del Te in Mantua under Romano (p. 319). The decoration of this gallery by these two artists is very fine. It brought a new form of décor to France but, though Italian in origin and in vigour, this mixture of wood carving, stucco sculpture and painting is unmistakably French in its lightness and elegance.

The King's Staircase stands on the site of the bedroom of the Duchess of Étampes, Francis I's mistress. The architect, when he constructed the staircase, retained Primaticcio's magnificent stucco wall groups of slender maidens which frame the frescoes (PLATE 63). The ceiling is deeply coved. This cove is decorated with a riot of Mannerist strapwork and sculpture. The rectuangular centrepiece is painted. The Henry II gallery (or ballroom) is of later construction and has been much restored. It was completed under the architect *Philibert de l'Orme*, and decorated with sculpture and paintings by Rondelet, Primaticcio and others. It is a large, well-proportioned room, beautifully lit with large windows along each side. The walls are painted and panelled, the wood ceiling deeply caissoned and carved. At one end of the hall is a double-stage fireplace; at the other, a musicians' gallery.

Châteaux of the Later Sixteenth Century

After 1550, several architects were developing a more correct Renaissance building style. The chief of these were *Philibert de l'Orme*, Jean Bullant, Jacques Androuet du Cerceau and Pierre Lescot. De l'Orme's work at Fontainebleau has been mentioned. He was Superintendent of the King's Buildings and worked there for some years. He also designed the terrace across the river at Chenonceaux and worked at S. Germain. His principal contribution was at the *Château of Anet* (**672**) where he worked from 1547 to 1552 for Diane de Poitiers, favourite of Henry II. Much of the château has been destroyed but the gatehouse and chapel exist. The entrance screen and gatehouse provide one of the first Renaissance structures with the orders and proportions correctly understood and utilised.

De l'Orme, born in 1520, was one of France's first professional architects (as Inigo Jones became later to England). He designed, then supervised, the complete construction of a building. The son of a master mason, he studied for some years in Italy, making measured drawings in Rome and becoming fully conversant with the classical theme and grammar. His screen at Anet shows clearly his comprehension. Apart from his buildings, a number of which have now been lost, he published much written work. His major book was 'Premier Livre de L'Architecture', published in nine volumes in 1569.

Jean Bullant was also born *c.* 1520. He also worked for a number of years in Rome. His style is vigorous, classical but more Mannerist. Typical is his work at the *Château of Écouen*, his bridge and gallery at *Fère-en-Tardenois* and his gallery at *Chenonceaux* (p. 324).

He is thought to have built the *Petit Château* at *Chantilly*, about 1560. This stands on an island in the lake adjacent to the main château, which is of later design due to the destruction at the time of the Revolution. The Petit Château (**678**) escaped, and illustrates Bullant's Mannerist style. This is not the same type of Mannerism as the early French Renaissance work of the 1520–50 period. Then the classical rules were broken because they were not understood. Bullant adjusted the rules of proportion and handling in a similar manner to the great Italian Mannerist architects like Michelangelo and Raphael.

Du Cerceau (the elder) was the father of a family of architects. He was born *c.* 1520 and also studied in Rome. He published many volumes of engravings both of decoration and of

RENAISSANCE CHÂTEAUX IN FRANCE

675 Chenonceaux, 1515–76
676 Frontispiece, Azay-le-Rideau, 1524
677 Blois, Francis I range and staircase, 1515–24
678 Petit Chateau (left), Chantilly, Jean Bullant, c. 1560

679 *The Cour Carrée, Louvre. Range left of clock pavilion by Pierre Lescot, 1546–55. Sculpture largely by Jean Goujon (restored nineteenth century)*
680 *Place des Vosges (originally Place Royale), 1605–12*

architectural design. Almost nothing of his building work survives.

The fourth of these architects, *Pierre Lescot* (born *c*. 1510 or 1515 *d*. 1578), has become the best known probably because of his work at the Louvre, which is the only one of his major works to survive intact. The initiative for the rebuilding of the Louvre in Paris was due to Francis I. The original thirteenth century royal palace was a *donjon* fortification which existed until the sixteenth century. It had been altered and enlarged but remained Medieval, gloomily brooding over Paris.

Francis commissioned Lescot in 1546 to demolish the tower and court and rebuild on modern lines. Francis died, but his successor Henry II confirmed the commission and Lescot carried out the demolition and built a new west wing (**679**) and part of the south. This west wing of the Cour Carrée, the central courtyard of the Louvre, still remains and the range left of the clock pavilion is Lescot's work. He created here, for the first time in France, elevations on Italian palace courtyard lines. There are three storeys, treated as one façade, broken only by projecting frontispieces. The scheme is Italian but the treatment is French and individually Lescot. Here was a French architect who, though lacking early on-the-spot study in Italy, fully comprehended Renaissance architecture and adapted it to national and personal needs—as Sir Christopher Wren was later to do in England, on a much wider scale. Lescot's façade is correctly classical in proportion and handling; it is not Italianate, as is shown by his use of Composite and Corinthian orders rather than Doric and Ionic and the employment of pilasters throughout the elevation, columns being reserved only for the frontispiece pavilions. Much of the sculptural decoration is by *Jean Goujon*, the great French sculptor of the day. Of particular interest are the exterior ground floor figures and attic reliefs; also, inside, his gallery caryatid figure work. This work was done between 1549 and 1553, though it was extensively restored in the nineteenth century.

Civic Building in Paris and Elsewhere

In the last years of the sixteenth century Henry IV began to reconstruct the centre of Paris after the years of warfare and struggle. The city was impoverished and in need of large-scale development. The king initiated this work and was the first in France to envisage planning by streets and squares rather than solely by individual buildings. Only Italy had built such schemes before, as at Pienza, Venice and Rome (p. 318). Henry's two main achievements were in the area of the Île de la Cité and the Place des Vosges. The *Pont Neuf* (now the oldest bridge in Paris), had been begun in 1578 but left incomplete. Henry simplified the scheme and built a new, wide thoroughfare, paved and—most unusual at that time, without houses upon it—which spanned the western tip of the *Île de la Cité*, thus linking it to the north and south banks of the Seine.

681

681 *Paris:* '*Île de la Cité, Pont Neuf, 1578–1604 and Place Dauphine, begun 1607*

The *Place Dauphine*, situated on the triangular piece of ground at this end of the island, was developed as a well-to-do residential neighbourhood and an equestrian statue of the king was set up as a focal centre where the square joins the island section of the Pont Neuf. The Place Dauphine was planned in 1607 and named after Henry's heir. It, and the bridge, still stand, though only house number 14 dates from the original development (**681**).

The king also planned two other squares, the *Place Royale* and the Place de France. The former, begun in 1605 (**680**) and now called the *Place des Vosges*, was completed. It was also intended as accommodation for the wealthy and was a fashionable quarter for many years. The *Place de France* was begun in 1620 but not finished in this period. Henry's town planning on the pattern of squares was in advance of its time in Europe. Covent Garden, developed later in the century under Inigo Jones' direction, was a similar scheme. Other countries followed suit but, in general, not until the later seventeenth or eighteenth centuries.

The town hall of *La Rochelle*, on the western coast of France is an attractive example of provincial civic Renaissance work. Here, the exterior façade is Gothic but the internal courtyard is classical, built 1595–1607.

Churches
The Gothic tradition lingered in ecclesiastical building much later than in secular work. In France so many churches had been built in the Middle Ages that few more were needed and, without the spur provided by the Reformation,* as in England, Holland or Germany, the function remained unchanged and, thus, the design. The usual pattern in the few new churches constructed was that of a Medieval building, especially in the interior, and the introduction of classical motifs and decoration on the façade or chevet. These were applied often haphazardly in Mannerist form, with little understanding of the tenets of classical architecture. *S. Pierre* in *Caen*, built 1530–40 (p. 210), is one of these. It is an almost entirely late Gothic church. Another, *S. Eustache* in *Paris* was begun in 1532 but completed much later, while its façade is eighteenth century. *S. Michel* in *Dijon* has considerable Renaissance decoration on its façade but the interior is

* *Vigorously suppressed in France.*

entirely Gothic. Built 1537–40 the church has a Mannerist quality attractively merged with Medieval work. The most important example of purer Mannerist development is *S. Étienne du Mont* in *Paris* (**670**). This shows mainly on the façade (which was not built till the early seventeenth century) in the entrance portico and frontispiece. In Medieval manner, however, this incorporates, above the portal, a central rose window.

England

During the two centuries from 1420 onwards covered by this chapter, the development of Renaissance building in England was totally dissimilar to that in Italy and had little in common with France. It has been described in Chapter 5 how King Henry VIII, in the 1520s, began to encourage Italian craftsmen to come to England to work and teach local artists and masons the new decoration and architectural forms. This was in line with Francis I's similar efforts in France at the same date. But, whereas Francis was more successful in attracting Italian craftsmen and continued in this pattern, Henry's break with Rome delayed any change of style. The direct link having been cut, the geographical barrier of the Channel, together with the traditional insularity of the English, put off till the early seventeenth century the appearance of pure Renaissance architecture.

Perpendicular Gothic continued till about 1550. Under the Tudor dynasty it acquired slightly different characteristics, like the four-centred arch, an increasing use of brick, larger window openings and flat ceilings rather than open timber roofs. Elizabethan England saw great changes. A form of the Renaissance came to the country; not the pure Italian version based on Bramante or even Brunelleschi, but a Flemish Mannerist type. The design and pattern books which appeared in England, printed mainly in Flanders and Germany, a few in France, presented the English craftsmen with a garbled version of classicism and, since such artisans had never seen a classical building, they tended to accept it as the genuine article.

This Mannerist style was much the same as that employed in Germany and the Low Countries. The orders were used, but decoratively not structurally. The actual buildings, whether in stone, brick or half-timber, were constructed in much the same way as before. But, applied to the surface, often all over exterior façades, were pilasters, columns, strapwork, cartouches, animal and human figure derivations, both caryatid and grotesque. Skylines were a confusion of decorated chimneystacks, cresting and curved gables; the last of these was a specifically Flemish derivative. Building in Elizabethan and Jacobean times, from 1550 to about 1620, was largely domestic. Few churches were built and there was little civic or university work. It was a thriving, bustling age with a rising middle class and a wealthy aristocracy. This wealth was transmitted into the building of great mansions on the country estates throughout the land. Many, like the châteaux of the Loire in France, were built by noblemen to attract the visits of the sovereign and her entourage on the summer tours.

Some of the houses were traditionally English in that the design was monumental, the decoration restrained and the materials of local stone or half-timber. *Longleat House* in Wiltshire (1550–80), *Hardwick Hall* in Derbyshire (1591–7) and *Montacute House* in Somerset (1588–1601 (**682**) were of this type. Other versions were more striking and original but often over-decorated. The orders were used for entrance porches and for flanking window openings but Flemish strapwork and cresting abounded. The English Perpendicular Gothic form of window design persisted; it was of rectangular shape, divided by mullions and transoms and of casement design. A glorious mixture of styles, such houses were robust, lively, sometimes graceless but never dull. Of this type is *Wollaton Hall* (**686**), a square pile with turreted corners, surrounding a square court with a taller hall block.

In the Jacobean period in the early seventeenth century came *Audley End* in Essex where, somewhat altered, the hall remains with its fantastic carved screen—a testament to the Flemish pattern book (**687**). In the grand manner is *Hatfield House*, Hertfordshire, of the same date. This is most impressive, especially on the south, garden front, where the combination of red brick and grey stone is effective. Here the turreted terminal blocks are simple and the rich decoration is reserved for the central porch with its orders and Mannerist ornamentation.

Hatfield is typical, as is Montacute, of the Elizabethan house plan. The old courtyard of the Medieval layout had slowly been abandoned in favour of an 'E' or 'H' shaped plan where there was a central, rectangular block with side wings which projected forwards and backwards in the case of the 'H' and only forwards in the 'E'. The central projecting porch provided the middle stroke of the 'E'.

Half-timber houses were common in stoneless areas. They were picturesque, handsome houses, built in different sizes from cottage to mansion. They had projecting and overhanging gable roofs with carved wooden barge boards and richly decorated porches with corner posts. The same ornamental motifs appeared as in the stone houses. *Little Moreton Hall* in Cheshire is a famous example (**683**) as is also *Speke Hall* in Lancashire (1598) and *Rumwood Court*, Kent (late sixteenth century).

Three particular features of the house were the long gallery, the staircase and the entrance porch. The long gallery extended along one whole side of the longer elevation of the house. It was a narrow apartment, sometimes more than 150 feet in length and it was lit by windows at the ends and along one whole long side, while fireplaces were set opposite. Especially fine examples can be seen at Montacute House, Hardwick Hall, *Haddon Hall*, Derbyshire and Little Moreton Hall. The staircase was only just beginning to acquire importance in the layout. Elizabethan examples were of richly carved oak, massive and spacious, generally built round a large well. Jacobean staircases, like those at Hatfield, *Knole*, Kent or *Ham House*, Surrey, are magnificent structures, the focal centre of the house interior. Of similar importance outside was the entrance porch, or frontispiece as it was generally called. Set in the centre of the façade, it was the recipient of the main decoration of the building. Orders were superimposed in gay disregard for proportion and suitability.

It was *Inigo Jones* (1573–1652) who brought the Italian Renaissance to England. Although few buildings which he designed survive and much of his work on great schemes, such as Whitehall Palace, never reached fruition or was destroyed, his importance in the history of English architecture is vital. He brought a stylistic revolution to architecture. Before him,

ENGLISH RENAISSANCE

682 *Montacute House, Somerset, 1588–1601*
683 *Little Moreton Hall, Cheshire, half-timber,*
 1559–80
684 *Gateway, Chiswick House, Inigo Jones, c. 1621*
685 *Clare Bridge, Cambridge, Thomas Grumbold,*
 1639–40

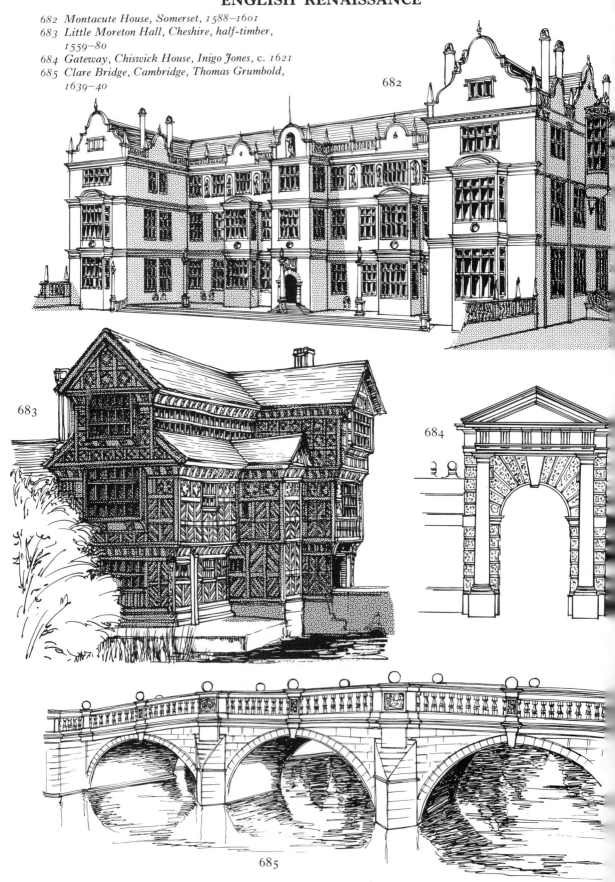

682

683

684

685

686

686 *Wollaton Hall, Nottinghamshire, 1580–5*
687 *The hall, Audley End, Essex, 1603–16*

687

in England, no one figure had acted as designer and overall supervisor of a building scheme. Each group of artisans—masons, carpenters, glaziers and sculptors—had their own master who was responsible for their section of the work.

Inigo Jones was appointed early in the seventeenth century as Surveyor to the Royal Family. He had the opportunity to travel to France and Italy to study personally Renaissance buildings about which he had read. He was away about 18 months, during which time he made measured drawings of original ancient Roman building remains and Italian and French Renaissance work based upon them. This first-hand study was a revolutionary idea to English builders. They had so far been content to use the second- or third-hand pattern book source.

Inigo Jones had been impressed, while still in England, by Palladio's books and also Vitruvius' works. He was interested, while studying *in situ*, to find himself often in agreement with Palladio's interpretation of ancient classical work. Nevertheless, when he returned home and began to design his own building in Roman classical manner, his schemes were his own, not copies of Palladio or Vitruvius. He was always an original architect.

His two outstanding public buildings still exist: the *Queen's House* at *Greenwich* and the *Banqueting Hall* in Whitehall. One can see immediately, in comparing these (**689** and **688**) with the Elizabethan and Jacobean works, the revolutionary change which he had brought to English architecture. Here, at last, was the pure Roman classicism. The orders were used correctly in proportions laid down and worked out by the ancient civilisations. Decoration is restricted to small specific areas of the elevations. It is in traditional classical form. The Banqueting Hall has two orders, Composite superimposed above Ionic. The building is rusticated and the window openings on the *piano nobile* have alternate round and triangular pediments. The Queen's House is even plainer, with Ionic columns confined to the centre portion and the remainder of the rectangular block broken only by rustication on the lower storey and by simple window openings.

Fragments of two town planning schemes by Inigo Jones exist in London. In *Lincoln's Inn Fields*, Lindsey House is thought to be by him and to illustrate his ideas on terrace town house

architecture. Here is a giant Ionic order spanning two floors. The whole façade is strictly symmetrical. He also designed a piazza for *Covent Garden* with S. Paul's Church and houses with classical elevations round the remainder of the square. The original work has been lost though the church has been rebuilt in the same style.

Towards the end of his life Inigio Jones rebuilt part of *Wilton House* in Wiltshire. He was responsible for the south front and the two cube rooms inside. The Double Cube Room (**690**) is a rich, magnificently proportioned interior. Its superb classical detail in white and gold is in contrast to the modest exterior façade.

Although Inigo Jones brought the Italian Renaissance to England and this had a lasting effect on architectural development, its influence until 1650 was small. Mid-seventeenth century building was plainer than Elizabethan or Jacobean and it was nearer Renaissance forms, but it still reflected Flemish gabling and brickwork more than Italian classicism. Brick was a popular material at this time. It was cheap and durable but builders discovered, as Medieval builders in the Baltic coastal regions of Europe had found in the fifteenth century, that it is not a suitable material for rich or precise decoration. So, like the Medieval builders before them, English and Flemish brick workers developed their own limited forms of expression in the medium, this time in classical not Gothic idiom. A fine example in England is *Kew Palace* in Kew Gardens (1631).

The Low Countries

Although part of the land mass of the continent of Europe, development in this northern region had much in common with that of England. Gothic building continued until the early sixteenth century, after which Renaissance decorative forms were used as all-over surface ornament to structures still fundamentally Medieval. Sources of knowledge for this decoration were the same pattern books used in England, though the results were often more ornate, so illustrating the Flemish love of rich decoration as well as their flat strapwork designs. A strong influence in this field, not only in the Low Countries, but further east as far as Germany and Poland, was *Vredema de Vries* (1527–1606). He was born in Frieslan

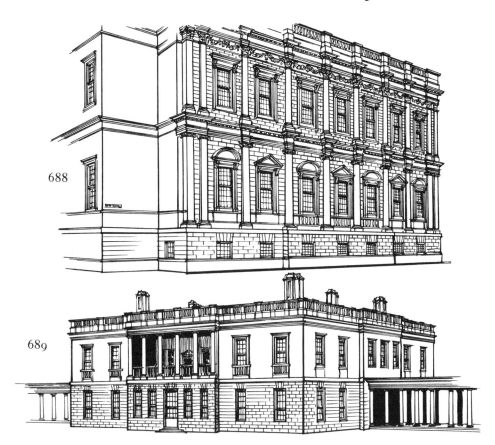

688

689

690

8 *Banqueting Hall, London, 1619–22*
9 *The Queen's House, Greenwich, south side, 1616–35*

690 *Double Cube Room, Wilton House, Wiltshire,*
      1647–53

and studied architecture at Antwerp which, in the sixteenth century, was still very much the cultural centre for the region. De Vries published his own books of architectural ornament, based on sources such as Vitruvius and Serlio. The best known of these was his 'Architectura', published in 1563. It includes designs for orders, strapwork, cartouches and animal and human figure details, including caryatids and grotesques. His designs were widely employed in conjunction with the orders, although, as in England, there was no basic understanding of their classical use.

Typical of the earlier sixteenth century work based on these decorative forms is the *Palais de Justice* at *Bruges* (1535–7). Here are superimposed orders with strange capitals, Gothic style fenestration, rich banded decoration between and tall, ornate, curving gables with high relief tympana and finials in human and animal shape. Of similar date is the vast courtyard of the *episcopal palace* at *Liège* (**693** and PLATE 65). This is still basically a Medieval court with its finialled pointed gables and widely pointed arched arcade, but the strapwork-decorated fat arcade columns are Flemish Mannerist.

The outstanding building of the sixteenth century is *Antwerp Town Hall*, built 1561–5 by *Cornelius Floris* (**694**). This is the chief monument to Flemish Mannerism. It shows a greater comprehension of classicism than contemporary works such as the *Old Town Hall* at the *Hague* (1564–5) or the Renaissance part of *Ghent Town Hall*, but is still totally unlike Italian Renaissance work. As in the case of such English houses as Longleat and Hatfield, it is indigenous yet has ceased to be Medieval. It is a large rectangular building with an arcade below the roof. It is symmetrical and has an impressive centrepiece, extending the full height of the façade and further into a three-storey gable. This centrepiece has a vertical emphasis contrasting with the horizontal lines of the side portions.

As in England, it was the seventeenth century which brought a purer classical style to the Low Countries, where Dutch architecture began to emerge as the dominant sector while Antwerp as a centre declined in importance. This Dutch architectural prominence was mainly confined to the large towns; the political centre at the Hague and the commercial one at Amsterdam. Two architects particularly are associated with this renaissance: *Lieven de Key* and *Hendrik* de *Keyser*. De Key (1560–1627) worked mainly at Haarlem and Leyden. He designed the *Leyden Town Hall* in 1597 (**698**) and the *Butchers' Trade Hall* at *Haarlem* in 1602 (**692**). Like Antwerp Town Hall, these are both Mannerist buildings with ornate, curving gables, decorated by obelisks and strapwork, but the windows in the town hall for instance, are purer Renaissance as is the Ionic entrance portal and rusticated staircase approach. Most of the Dutch building up to this time had been in brick. De Key introduced into these structures the combination of stone decoration and dressings on brick buildings as used at Hatfield in England.

De Keyser (1565–1621) was centred on *Amsterdam*. He developed a Renaissance style of house from the Medieval one. The city was being enlarged and developed in the early seventeenth century when the famous canals—the Herengracht, Prinsengracht, Keizergracht, etc.—were being planned and laid out. The terrace architecture flanking such canals has a specific individual character. Each house is tall and is surmounted by a lofty gable. Medieval ones had been stepped. Renaissance examples had scrolled sides, strapwork decoration, finials and a pediment at the apex. De Keyser developed a two- and three-stage type of gable, linked by scrolls at each step and with different pilasters to each stage. His façades below were symmetrical, divided into bays and were decorated by orders.

In civic architecture de Keyser designed the *Amsterdam Exchange* (1605) and the *Delft Town Hall* (1618). His most original contribution was in church building. In Amsterdam he built the Zuiderkerk (**695**), the Westerkerk (**697**) and the Noorderkerk. The *Zuiderkerk* was the first church to be built here after the Reformation and de Keyser had to plan a new type of design suitable for a Protestant church. This, like his *Westerkerk*, is a traditional plan, but is very tall and with a lofty tower. De Keyser, like Sir Christopher Wren in England, was noted for the variety of successful, elegant designs for his towers. Apart from these two, the *Mint Tower*, also in Amsterdam, is a landmark (**696**).

In his church design de Keyser shared some characteristics with Brunelleschi in Florence. The relationship and proportion between one part and another, especially in the interior,

RENAISSANCE IN THE LOW COUNTRIES

Campen, 1633, (remodelled, c. 1718)
692 Butchers' Guild Hall, Haarlem, de Key, 1602
693 Courtyard, Episcopal Palace, Liège, Aart Van der Mulcken

691

692

693

carefully calculated. His *Noorderkerk* is a small church but interesting as a centrally planned design. He adopted this as appropriate for Protestant needs, just as the Roman Catholics had found it so in Italy. It is on Greek cross plan and quite symmetrical. On the exterior it is a plain brick church, most unpretentious and quite different from the domed Italian counterparts as at Todi or Crema. However, the Noorderkerk proved a successful design and became the prototype of many other Protestant examples throughout northern Europe.

The beginnings of a pure Renaissance style came in the second quarter of the seventeenth century in the *Hague* with the advent of Dutch Palladianism. This, as its name suggests, is strongly influenced by Palladio but, just as Inigo Jones at the same date was introducing Palladianism into England, with his Banqueting Hall, neither the Dutch nor English examples are copies of the Italian architect's work. They are both nationally individual. The chief example in Holland is the *Mauritshuis* at the *Hague* (**691**), designed by *Pieter Post* (1608–69) and *Jacob van Campen* (1595–1657). This, like the nearby *Constantin Huygens' house*, also designed by

Post, in 1633, but later destroyed, had much [in] common with Inigo Jones' work, and also wi[th] the English architect Hugh May's later Eltha[m] Lodge. The plan is simple, in a rectangular bloc[k] Giant Ionic pilasters frame the simple, classic[al] windows and swag decorated doorway, which [is] approached, on the *piano nobile* by entrance step[s.] The two chief façades have a central pedime[nt] and, behind, rises the Dutch style hipped roof[.]

The Region of Germanic Influence:

Germany, Austria, Switzerland, Czechoslovakia[,] Hungary, Poland

Germany

The sequence of development in this area w[as] similar to the Flemish and English patter[n.] Medieval work continued till after 1500. Duri[ng] the sixteenth century buildings were mainly [of] Mannerist designs with the use of decoration a[nd] orders based on pattern books, the classic[al] structure being imperfectly understood. In Ge[r]many the work is vigorous and robust. T[he] strapwork and cartouche ornament covers lar[ge] areas of the building but, though in high reli[ef,] is ornamental not structural in character. T[he]

694 Antwerp Town Hall, Cornelius Floris, 1561–5

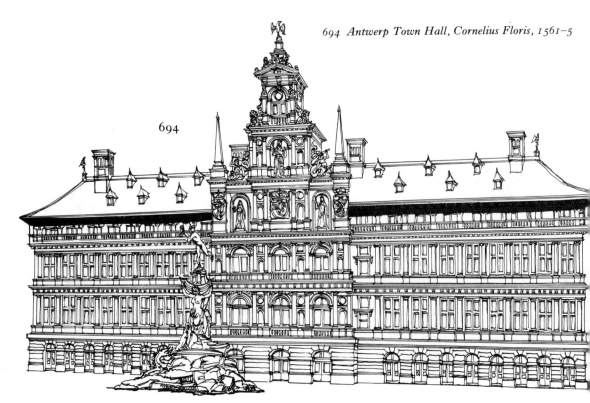

694

695 Tower, Zuiderkerk, Amsterdam, de
     Keyser, 1614
696 Munttoren (the Mint), Amsterdam, de
     Keyser, c. 1620
697 Westerkerk, Amsterdam, de Keyser, 1620
698 Town Hall, Leiden, de Key, 1597–1603

same motifs appear in carved stone or wood. Much of the considerable quantity of high quality half-timber work possessed by Germany until 1939 was destroyed in the Second World War. This was especially so in cities like Hildesheim, Bremen, Hanover and Frankfurt. In smaller, more remote towns, examples still exist as at Dinkelsbühl and Goslar. The *Bürgerhaus* (Willmann House) at *Osnabrück* (1586) has some typical carved detail, and is an interesting gabled façade.

Like the Flemish, the Germans specialised in the sixteenth century in the tall multi-storey gable, ascending in stages, with scrolls and strapwork, fenestrated and ornately decorated. There are a number of houses in *Lemgo* like the *Hexenbürgermeisterhaus*, 1571 (**700**), which are typical. The façades of the sixteenth century houses in many German towns were like these. The frontages were narrow but the houses tall, with orders used on five or six storeys, one above the other. The *Town Hall* in *Lemgo* has two very fine such porticoes with both strapwork and sculptured decoration (1565–1612).

With the seventeenth century, as in Flanders and England, came a purer Renaissance style. German *town halls* from about 1500–1700 show this development clearly. Typically German in the sixteenth century style is the façade and courtyard of the town hall at *Konstanz*. The doorway and window openings, in particular, have the typical pattern book decoration in carved stone as well as painted form. A simple, unpretentious example can be seen also at *Heilbronn* (1535–96). There is a different type of sixteenth century design at *Rothenburg-ob-der-Tauber* (**703**). A Renaissance wing was added to the old Medieval town hall about 1572. The Renaissance part, on the corner of the street, is a lower, long elevation with emphasis on the horizontal courses, in contrast to the older tall gabled building with a lofty tower. Here are the beginnings of comprehension of classical principles. Decoration is more restrained and articulation is clearer. The rusticated loggia was added in the seventeenth century. A more advanced design existed in the loggia of the *Cologne Town Hall*, built in 1569 by *Wilhelm Vernuiken*. This was a more Italianate structure, but became a casualty to war-time bombing. It is now rebuilt but in a much simplified form.

The understanding of purer classical design came with *Elias Holl*'s plain, finely proportioned buildings in *Augsburg*, notably the town hall and the arsenal. Both these show first signs of a Baroque quality, particularly the earlier one, the *Arsenal* (Zeughaus) (1602–7) (**705**). This is partly due to the articulation of the central section and the side scrolls, but more especially to the dynamic sculptural group above the portal of S. Michael and the Devil (PLATE 67). This is the work of *Hans Reichle*. No other European country could compete with the quantity and superb quality of sculpture created by Renaissance and Baroque artists in Italy. Sixteenth century Germany, however, developed a talented school of sculptors of whom Reichle was one: an outstanding artist whose style is clearly personal, always vigorous and displaying a powerful clarity.

The *Augsburg Town Hall* was Holl's masterpiece. Built 1615–20, it had a dignified, timeless quality, astylar, finely proportioned and fenestrated. The façade was rebuilt to the original design after damage in the Second World War. Elias Holl had travelled in Italy and was an admirer of Palladio and Sansovino. His own work, though, was much more severe than the approach of either of the Italians. This was perhaps a reaction from the ornate richness of the sixteenth century German façades so that, like Herrera in Spain, his establishment of the purer classical strain was even more restrained in contrast.

Several large scale *castles* and *palaces* were built in the sixteenth and early seventeenth century. These bore no relationship to the fifteenth century Florentine designs, though rather more to the courtyards of later Roman palaces. *Heidelberg Castle*, lying on a shelf of the mountainside above the river Neckar, has a romantic setting. It is very large, partly ruined and most impressive. Built over the period 1531–1612, two wings of the schloss, in particular, show a contrast of structural and decorative styles. The Ottheinrichsbau, built in 1556–9 and named after the Elector, its builder, is the earlier and finer part (**701**). Here is rich, powerful German Renaissance building, harmoniously proportioned and with finely carved ornament and sculpture. The whole façade is sculptured but the central, multi-storeyed portal is the focal point of the four-storeyed composition. The range is magnificent, even in ruin. The later, Friedrichsbau range is heavier and more pedestrian, though more correctly classical. This was restored from its ruinous condition in 1900.

The main courtyard, the 'Schöner Hof', at the *Plassenburg* above the town of *Kulmbach*, is a fine example of German palace courts of the mid-sixteenth century. The arcades are in three storeys, of which the upper two are richly sculptured in high relief after the Lombard style of treatment (**704** and PLATE 66). There are some interesting, richly sculptured doorways in this court also, while in the Kasernenhof the main doorway is equally typical of the later bold style in the early seventeenth century.

Aschaffenburg Castle, though a later structure (1605–14), is more Medieval in concept. It is an immense, severe, fortified square block of red sandstone with a tower at each corner (**699**). Its west elevation rises from the banks of the river Main. Inside is a square courtyard, all four sides identical except for a tower set centrally in the wall opposite to the entrance. The whole castle is plain and massive, the walls broken only by Renaissance fenestration. There are no orders, but in the centre of each side is a tall Flemish-style gable. Small staircase towers are set one in each corner of the court. The main entrance is imposing, with rusticated, coupled Doric columns flanking the richly carved strapwork doors.

One of the best examples of pattern book German Renaissance work of the sixteenth century is the entrance gateway to *Tübingen Castle* (**702**). Here is the classic form of orders and ornament of this type with some vigorous and characteristic sculpture and strapwork ornamentation.

One of Germany's largest town palaces is the *Munich Residenz*, built over several centuries from c. 1550 but badly damaged in 1944. In the centre of Munich, many ranges of buildings are grouped around six courtyards. The two Renaissance, early ones suffered least from war damage. These are the Antiquarian Court, built 1559 and altered by *Friedrich Sustris* in 1586–1600 and the Grotto Court (Grottenhof), also by Sustris (1581–6). This is a quiet, restful courtyard in Florentine style with a Perseus fountain in the centre, based on that by Benvenuto Cellini in Florence (**706**). The Munich

fountain is by the Dutch sculptor *Hubert Gerhard*, who carried out so much fine work in Augsburg, especially in the fountains (PLATE 68). The unusual grotto decoration of grotesques and shells is by *Ponzani* (1588).

As in Flanders and England, the sixteenth and seventeenth centuries were not years of extensive building of *churches*. There are one or two examples of the earlier German Renaissance style, where the building is fundamentally Medieval, based on the hall church pattern, then decorated with pattern book Renaissance detail all over the façades. A good example of this type is the *Stadtkirche* at Bückeburg (1611–15) (**708**). Another hall church design but with a purer classical façade is the *Hofkirche* (S. Michael) at Neuburg on the Danube (**707**).

A very early Renaissance building is the *Fugger Chapel* in the *Church* of *S. Anna* at *Augsburg*. This, like the Medici Mausoleum in S. Lorenzo in Florence, is the mausoleum for the Fugger family of the city. The chapel was begun in 1509. It was still designed with a Gothic star vault, but on the wall behind the altar are pilasters framing the four relief panels depicting the Fuggers and based on drawings by Dürer. The sculptured *pietà* by *Hans Dancher*, 1518, stands in front. It has survived, though the chapel was badly damaged in the Second World War.

The outstanding Renaissance church in Germany is *S. Michael* in *Munich*. This Jesuit church in the middle of the city was built 1582–97 by *Wolfgang Miller* and *Friedrich Sustris*. The exterior is a mixture of German gable design and Italian orders. It is plain apart from the sculptured figures in niches and the twin doorways on the façade with, between them, *Hubert Gerhard*'s magnificent S. Michael vanquishing the Devil. The interior, damaged during the last war but now restored, is cruciform with shallow transepts. The chancel is narrower than the wide nave and is apsidal-ended. The whole scheme is white and plain. It is classical, with the Corinthian Order used in pilaster form. The Jesuit plan* has the typical three bay nave with chapels leading off it but no colonnade. The barrel-vaulted ceiling is decorated in strapwork bands enclosing panels. The chief focus is the three-tiered high altar, rich in colour and classical decoration (**709**).

* *The pattern was set in the first Jesuit Church in Rome, Il Gesù (see page 321).*

GERMAN RENAISSANCE

699 *Aschaffenburg Castle, Ridinger, 1605–14*
700 *Hexenbürgermeister House, Lemgo, 1571*
701 *Heidelberg Castle, Ottheinrichsbau Wing, 1556–9*
702 *Tübingen Castle gateway, sixteenth century*

GERMAN RENAISSANCE: CIVIC AND DOMESTIC BUILDING

703 *Town Hall, Rothenburg-ob-der-Tauber, Gothic wing (left), Renaissance wing added 1572–8 (right). Balcony and staircase, Jakob Wolff*
704 *Doorway, Schöner Hof, Plassenburg, Kulmbach, 1551–79*
705 *Zeughaus (Arsenal), Angsburg, Elias Holl, 1602–7*

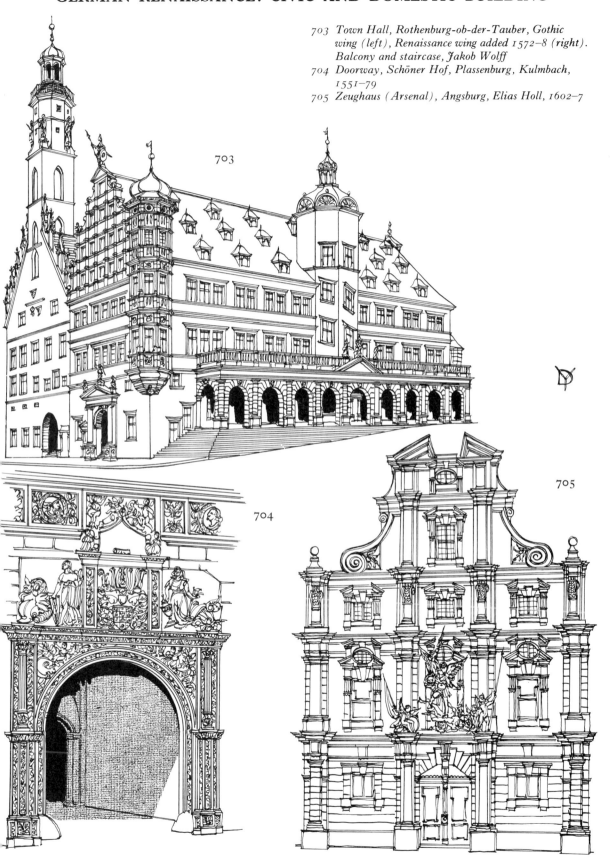

Austria

Not much Renaissance building survives in Austria. The chief examples are some very fine courtyards on a grand scale belonging to castles and civic structures. There is a two-storeyed one with caryatid figures all round the upper arcade at *Schallaborg* (1572–1600) and another, purer Renaissance type in the *Castle Porcia* at *Spittal-an-der-Drau* (c. 1530) which is in the centre of the town. The rectangular courtyard has three storeys of galleries round three sides. The orders used are Ionic on the ground floor, then Composite and Corinthian. On the fourth side the sturdy, decorative Ionic ground floor colonnade is continued unbroken, but above is solid wall pierced only by windows. A staircase in one corner of the court gives sloping balustraded galleries at each level. Another impressive excellent example is the court of the *Landhaus* in the centre of *Graz* (1557–65). This pure classical construction was damaged during the Second World War but is now beautifully restored. A three-storeyed arcade extends round four sides of the central courtyard, supporting a heavy cornice and deep roof with dormers. There is an attractive turreted stairway leading from the court up to the second and third arcade levels (**711**).

Switzerland

Here, the principal surviving building in the purer classical style is the *Spieshof* in *Basle*. This is in four storeys with superimposed orders—Doric, Ionic, Ionic—in engaged column form. The top storey has scrolls instead, supporting the projecting cornice (**710**). Less purely Renaissance, and largely Medieval in structure with sixteenth century detail and fenestration are the *Fribourg Town Hall* and the *Altes Rathaus* in *Lucerne*. The former is of sixteenth century date, the latter seventeenth. The *Basle Town Hall*, in red sandstone, retains its early sixteenth century form, with rectangular, mullioned and transomed windows and tall tower, though it was extensively restored in the late nineteenth century. The paintings all over the façade were restored at the same time.

Czechoslovakia

The Renaissance came late to Czechoslovakia and, since the time was one of strife, only a few buildings have survived unaltered. In *Prague* there are one or two exceptions to this rule. In the early sixteenth century, the Emperor Ferdinand had succeeded in attracting some Italian artisans to his court. The *Royal Summer Palace* (the Belvedere, **712**), was built by Italian

706 The Grottenhof, Residenz, Munich, Sustris, 1581–6. Fountain, Perseus, Gerhard

706

GERMAN RENAISSANCE CHURCHES

707 Church of S. Michael
(Hofkirche), Neuburg-an-der-
Donau, Vältlin and Alberthal,
1607–27
708 Stadtkirche, Bückeburg, Hans
Wolf, 1611–15
709 Interior, S. Michael, Munich,
Miller and Sustris, 1582–97

artists and its design clearly derives from Brunelleschi's Foundling Hospital in Florence (p.312), as can be seen in the simple, round-arched arcade which extends round the building. The *Archbishop's Palace*, also on Castle Hill, was built in 1561, but this was redesigned in 1765 with Rococo decoration. An interesting late instance of Renaissance architecture in the city can be seen in the more Mannerist design of the loggia to the *Valdštejn Palace* (713). Also an Italian scheme, this time by *Andrea Spezza*, it derives from Romano's Palazzo del Te at Mantua (662). The remainder of the palace in Prague, though of similar date to the loggia, is Baroque in treatment.

The small town of *Tábor*, just south of Prague, is Medieval in the centre but, due to several fires in the sixteenth century, a number of houses in the *Market Square* and the *Pražská Ulice* which leads into it were redesigned or redecorated in Renaissance character. The gabled house shown in Fig. 714 is one of these and there are several houses with ornamental, stepped gables in the Pražská Ulice (Prague Street), numbers 220–3 for example. Others in this street have painted decoration also, number 210 and, with extended, painted relief, pictorial panel, number 157.

Further south, in the centre of the town of *České Budějovice*, the *Market Place* retains a homogeneity and atmosphere of several centuries ago despite the varied periods of buildings which surround it. The houses are of sixteenth to eighteenth century origin but the round-arched arcades which extend all round this immense square give a coherence to the whole design. The town hall whose façade fronts the square is in Baroque style, as is the Samson fountain in the centre, while the cathedral interior is more neo-classical. The great belfry tower in the north-east corner of the square (from whose gallery a fine view can be obtained) is Medieval, but its gallery is supported on Tuscan columns and the cupola is also of Renaissance design.

Hungary

In *Esztergom*, on the Danube, there is one of the earliest surviving Renaissance works north of the Alps. This is the *Chapel of Archbishop Tamas Bakócz*, now part of the interior of the later cathedral. The work dates from 1507 and is based directly on Florentine Renaissance origins

(664 and 669). Italian Renaissance forms we[r]e established in Hungary at an early date [a]s Italian artists were being employed in Buda fro[m] the fifteenth century. Little else survives, u[n]fortunately, and the Italian influence was on[ly] short-lived in this turbulent area of Europ[e.] Also of interest are some of the houses, dati[ng] from sixteenth and seventeenth centuries [in] *Beliannisz Square* in *Sopron*, near the Austria[n] border. This is a picturesque square with simp[le] façades divided by ornamented pilasters and wit[h] simple, classical windows and porticoes.

Poland

As in Buda, Italian influence made itself felt earl[y] in Poland. Italian artists were employed first [in] *Cracow*, where some of the earliest Renaissan[ce] work outside Italy can still be seen. The roy[al] castle on *Wawel Hill*, which had been extende[d] during the Middle Ages, suffered considerab[le] damage by fire in 1499. It was decided to rebuil[d] and King Sigismund commissioned the Italia[n] *Franciscus Italus* to design him a Renaissan[ce] palace. On Italus' death in 1516 another Italia[n,] *Bartolomeo Berecci*, took over the work when th[e] courtyard was enlarged into a great quadrang[le] surrounded on all four sides by a three tiere[d] loggia. This courtyard is immense, about 2[30] feet square, and is one of the earliest examples [of] such courts outside Italy. The two lower store[ys] are arcaded in Florentine Renaissance design b[ut] the third floor is characteristically Polish, bein[g] unusually high and having distinctive column[s] and capitals; it is based on national, tradition[al] timber structures (717). Restoration of interi[or] rooms is still continuing and their condition is n[ot] yet as good as that of the exterior court, but the[re] are some fine ceilings of deeply caissoned woo[d] design enriched with gilt and colour, also so[me] interesting frescoes and tapestries. The Amba[s]sador's Hall dates from 1535 and the souther[n] wing was built from 1565.

Nearby on Wawel Hill at the *cathedral*, th[e] King in 1519 also commissioned the *Sigismu[nd] Chapel* as a mausoleum. It adjoins the cathedr[al] on the south side (720) adjacent and to the east [is] the seventeenth century *Vasa Chapel*, which ha[s] a similar exterior appearance though its interi[or] is in marbled Baroque. The Sigismund Chap[el] set the pattern in Poland for Renaissan[ce] chapels* as a centrally planned structure wit[h]

The Royal Palace courtyard similarly set the patte[rn] for palace courts.

Plate 68
Augustus Fountain detail, 1587–94, Gerhard

Augsburg, Germany
Plate 67
S. Michael and Lucifer. Façade, Zeughaus, 1603–6. Reichle

Plate 69
Doorway cartouche detail. The Armoury, Gdansk, Poland, 1605
Plate 70
Detail, Boim Chapel, L'vov, U.S.S.R., 1609–17

RENAISSANCE IN AUSTRIA AND SWITZERLAND

710

711

712 The Belvedere, Summer Palac[...]
of Prague Castle. Designed de[...]
Stella, built by Spatio and de[...]
Pambio, 1535–63

713 The Loggia, Valdštejn
(Wallenstein) Palace, Prague[...]
Andrea Spezza, 1621–8

714 House in the Market Place,
Tábor, mid-sixteenth century

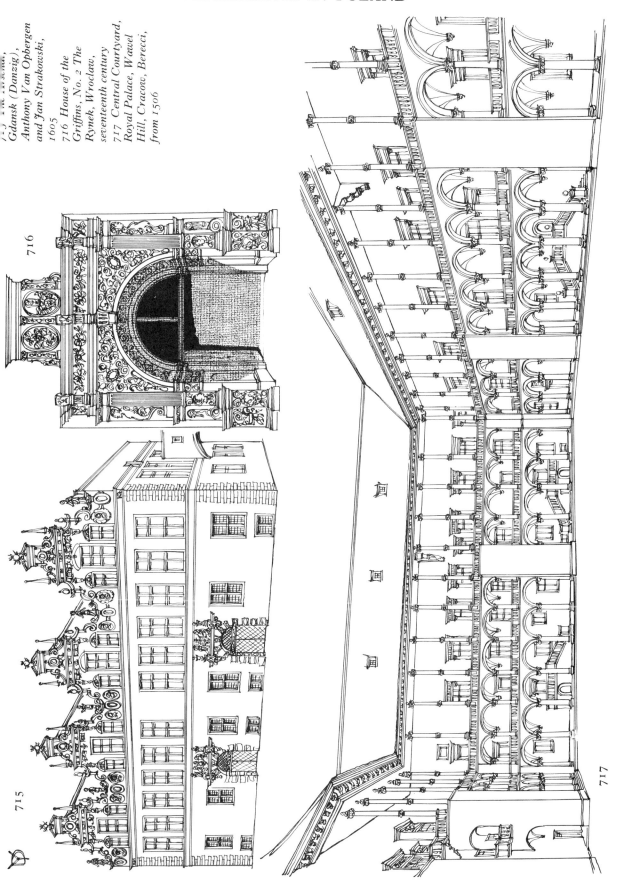

715 The Arsenal, Gdansk (Danzig), Anthony Van Opbergen and Jan Strakowski, 1605

716 House of the Griffins, No. 2 The Rynek, Wroclaw, seventeenth century

717 Central Courtyard, Royal Palace, Wawel Hill, Cracow, Berecci, from 1506

716

715

717

RENAISSANCE IN POLAND

718 *Façade, Poznan Town Hall, di Lugano, 1550–61*
719 *Chelmno Town Hall, 1555–69*
720 *Wawel Cathedral, Cracow, from the south, from 1320. Sigismund Chapel, 1519–33; Vasa Chapel, seventeenth century, spires; eighteenth century*

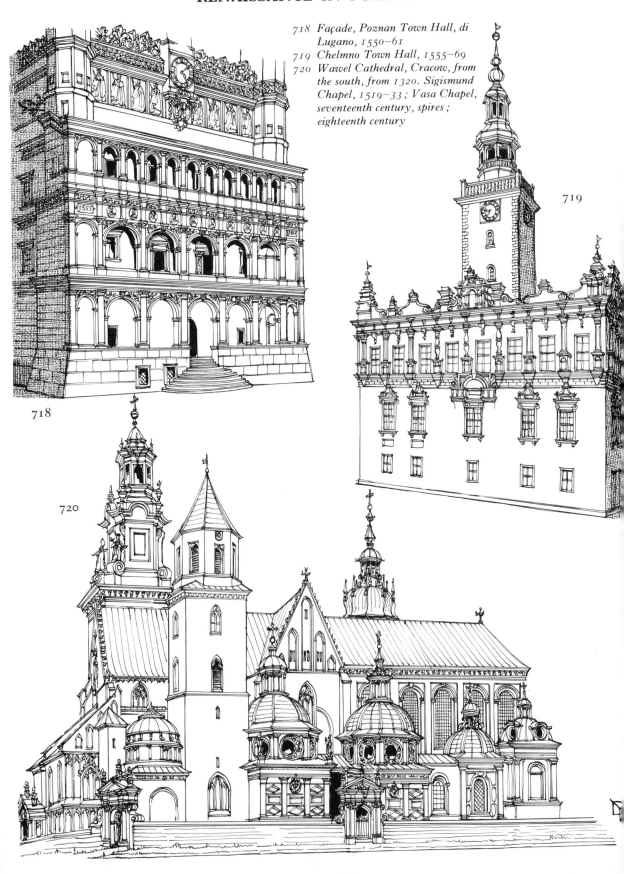

718

719

720

POLISH RENAISSANCE ARCHITECTURE IN L'VOV (NOW U.S.S.R.)

721

722

723

724

721 Doorway, Church of the Benedictines
722 Façade, Boim Chapel, 1609–17
723 Church of the Benedictines, 1578

724 The Anczowski House, Market Place, Peter
    Krasowski, 1577

dome and lantern. Built 1524–33, mainly by Italian artists, it is of stone, with an oak panelled and coffered interior dome supported on brick pendentives; the dome exterior is sheathed in copper. The interior lighting is from the circular windows in the drum. The walls below are articulated with Tuscan order pilasters, with panelling between. Rich sculptured and carved Renaissance tombs surround the walls.

Other chapels which followed, based on this prototype at Cracow, include the Renaissance chapel on the south-east corner of *S. John's Cathedral, Wroclaw* and the *Boim Chapel* at *L'vov* (now U.S.S.R.). The Wroclaw example is on Italian lines but that in L'vov (Lemberg) combines these characteristics with the essential L'vov style of building and decoration. The entire façade is carved in high relief sculpture, depicting scenes at the Crucifixion framed by orders and, below, portrait roundels, strapwork, lions' heads and floral designs, so interwoven that the decorated columns of the order are barely discernable (**722** and PLATE 70).

This blend of Italian Renaissance forms with south-eastern Polish decorative style can be seen elsewhere in L'vov, especially in the buildings grouped round or near the Market Square. The *Black Palace* by *Pietro Krasovsky* is in the same diamond-studded, faceted form as the Palazzo dei Diamanti in Ferrara in Italy (begun 1492) and the Casa de los Picos in Segovia (sixteenth century). The Black Palace in L'vov also has some vigorous, high quality carving on the doorway and window frames (**724**). There are interesting buildings all round the market square. Some are sixteenth century, others seventeenth and eighteenth. The earlier façades are Elizabethan in character.

Nearby is the *Church of the Benedictines*, 1578, which is a mixture of Italian Renaissance and Byzantine form. The domes are Byzantine, but the doorway is richly and beautifully carved in Renaissance style (**721** and **723**). The tall steeple is Italianate. The *Bernadine Church* in the town is typical of the later period in the early years of the seventeenth century. Here is a Gothic interior with a façade in late Renaissance Italianate form. It was mainly designed by *Paolo Romano* with contributions by *Przychylny* and *Bemer*.

There are several Renaissance civic buildings of note in Poland. The *Cloth Hall* at *Cracow* stands in the centre of the large market place. It was first built in the thirteenth century as a street of stone market stalls and about 1400 a market hall was constructed above. Destroyed by fire in 1555, in 1559 *Giovanni Maria Padovano* reconstructed it, adding classical parapets, gables and ornament. Unfortunately the structure has been altered in later years and was comprehensively restored in 1875.

The town halls of Poznan and of Chelmno retain far more of their original form and are more Renaissance in character. The *Poznan Town Hall* was also a Medieval building but, after fire damage in 1536, it was rebuilt from 1550 by *Giovanni Battista Quadro di Lugano* who constructed a Renaissance loggia in front of the Gothic façade (**718**) and added a classical steeple of diminishing stages, extending to 320 feet in height. The upper part was later lost and it was rebuilt to a different design. *Chelmno Town Hall* is a charming, simple Renaissance design (**719**). Symmetrical, with a square central tower and Renaissance steeple, it stands in the centre of the vast market place in this attractive small town.

More in the German and Flemish Mannerist Renaissance style are some of the surviving buildings in *Gdansk* (Danzig) on the Baltic coast. The finest of these which escaped the Second World War devastation of the city, is the *Armoury* (**715** and PLATE 69), built 1605. It has characteristic strapwork, sculptured and panelled gables, as well as richly decorated doorways.

There are many *town houses* on Renaissance pattern surviving in Poland, but some of them are now in poor condition. In *Cracow* the usual design was for a central courtyard surrounded by arcaded galleries. Typical are those in Kanonicza Street, built about 1550. Most of the examples in *Warsaw* have been lost but one or two good Flemish style Renaissance houses survive in *Wroclaw*. No. 2 in the main square, the Rynek, is one of these. Called the House of the Griffins, it has a stepped, curved gable, with painted reliefs of animals and birds at each stage of the gable. The doorway is typical of this type of work in Poland (**716**).

The Iberian Peninsula: Spain

Spain is rich in examples of buildings which are influenced decoratively or wholly by Renaissance ideas. A comparatively small proportion of these, however, are in a pure classical style based on Italian development. As in Germany and Flanders, the Roman High Renaissance concepts were slow to penetrate, partly due to the distance separating Italy from Spain but also for religious reasons. In England, the Renaissance was retarded because of the Reformation; in Spain, paradoxically, it was the strength of Roman Catholicism which held back the spread of humanist ideas.

There are three principle stages of Renaissance development between 1500 and 1700 in Spain. These overlap, as different areas adapted themselves to the new forms earlier than others. The first stage is termed *Renaissance plateresque*. This corresponds to the pattern book type of Flemish Mannerism which affected England, Flanders and Germany. Characteristically and similarly, the buildings are still Medieval structurally and only display Renaissance features in their decoration. The Spanish version of this decoration differs from the northern European one. The national love of ornament in Iberia comes to the fore and, exactly as in the Gothic plateresque works of the fifteenth and early sixteenth centuries, the whole surface is covered by carved or stuccoed ornament. The difference is that the motifs are now Renaissance not Medieval. There are many superb examples existing of this style of work in many parts of Spain. They date from any time in the sixteenth century and a few are early seventeenth century. Among the finest of these are the *University façade* at *Salamanca* (1516–29) (PLATE 73), the *Palacio Municipal* at *Baeza* in southern Spain (1559) and the *Casa de las Muertes* (House of the Dead) at *Salamanca*. One of the most successful architects in this style of work was *Enrique de Egas* (d. 1534). He built the great *Hospicio de los Reyes Catolicos* at *Santiago de Compostela* (1501–11), now one of Spain's largest luxury hotels, next to the cathedral (PLATE 72). His masterpiece is the *Hospital of S. Cruz de Mendoza* at *Toledo*, begun in 1504. The entrance portal is a beautiful plateresque feature. The interior court, with its carved stone staircase, is more Italianate and nearer to purer Renaissance work of the fifteenth century (726).

The second stage of Renaissance development was still partly plateresque in its rich surface decoration but shows a tentative comprehension of classical principles and construction. The orders are sometimes used structurally and are more correctly proportioned and detailed. Similarly, many fine examples of this type of work survive in varying districts of Spain. For instance, the *Town hall* (Ayuntamiento) at *Seville* (728, 729) by *de Riaño* and the *Luna Palace* (now the Audiencia) in *Zaragoza* (1537–52). This has a simple, Medieval-type façade with an interesting sculptured doorway, but the interior courtyard is reminiscent of Roman palace patios.

Two of the outstanding sixteenth century artists of this stage of development were the sculptor *Alonso Berruguete* (c. 1486–1561) (PLATE 71) and the architect and sculptor *Diego de Siloé* (1495–1563). Both studied in Italy and, on returning to Spain, developed a Spanish style based on Italian High Renaissance themes. One of de Siloé's famous works in his *Escalera Dorada* in *Burgos Cathedral* (1524) which, in its symmetry and handling, shows his appreciation of Michelangelo's Laurenziana Library. He worked for many years on *Granada Cathedral*, especially on the chevet and crossing. He was restrained here from developing a full, classical theme as he had taken over a partly-built Gothic structure begun by Egas. This had a five-aisled nave and chevet with radiating chapels. The result is thus less satisfactory than it might have been. It has power and a Renaissance sense of handling of space but became a hybrid Spanish/Italian composition. For example, inside, Roman orders are used in a Medieval manner. The crossing piers have engaged Corinthian columns on high pedestals, supporting classical entablatures from which, in turn, springs a Medieval lierne vault.

From this middle stage of development came a number of Renaissance courtyards which still exist and show varying stages of understanding of Italian High Renaissance principles. A beautiful example is at the *Tavera Hospital* in *Toledo*, designed by *Bartolomé Bustamente*, a priest who had studied in Italy. It is a vast rectangular building, 350 feet by 260 feet. The entrance façade is plain, with rusticated quoins and window openings and a three-stage classical entrance

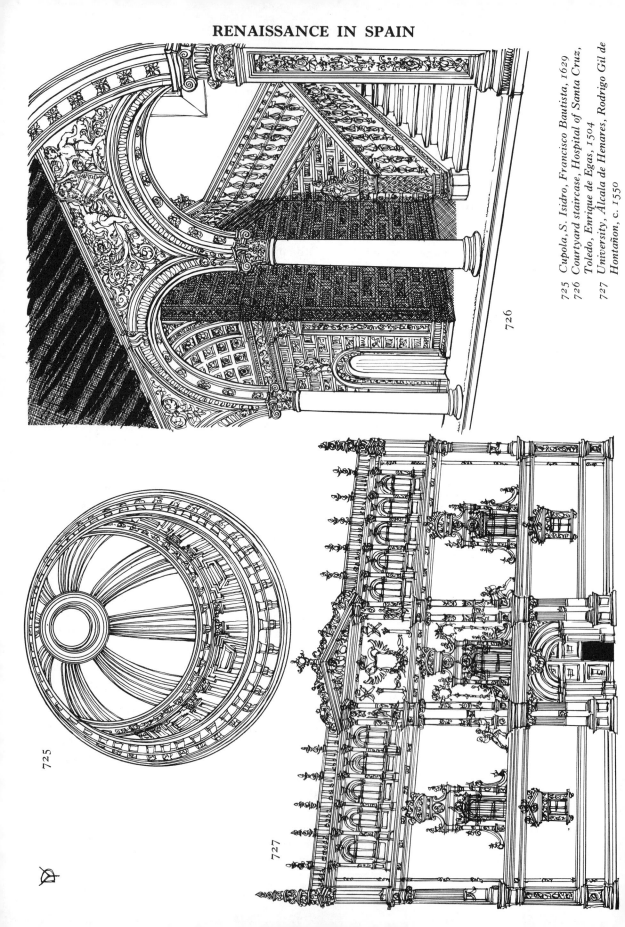

725 Cupola, S. Isidro, Francisco Bautista, 1629
726 Courtyard staircase, Hospital of Santa Cruz, Toledo, Enrique de Egas, 1504
727 University, Álcala de Henares, Rodrigo Gil de Hontañon, c. 1550

portal. The courtyard behind is two-storeyed, Doric below, Ionic above and is divided down the centre by a two-storeyed gallery (**731**). The church is more severely classical, with a giant Doric order all round in pilaster form, broken only by a Corinthian altarpiece. There is a dome over the crossing inside an octagonal tower. The *Alcazar*, also in Toledo, still dominates the town. Enlarged many times from its twelfth century origins, it was built in Renaissance style under Charles V by *Alonso de Covarrubias*. The work was continued by several architects and completed by Herrera. His south front and *de Villalpando's* grand staircase in the patio were outstanding. The Alcazar was left in ruins after the Civil War but is now almost rebuilt.

In 1540, *Rodrigo Gil de Hontañón* was commissioned to rebuild the façade of the *University of Alcalà de Henares*, near Madrid. This is still a middle period Spanish Renaissance work. The symmetrical façade has three storeys, flanked by lower wings. The portal definition is carried up to each storey by coupled columns, but these have more in common with a Jacobean frontispiece than a High Renaissance Roman doorway. The fenestration is classical and the decoration restrained. It is a good 'compromise' achievement (**727**).

The third stage, that of a purer classical style is mainly represented in late sixteenth and in seventeenth century work. There is one early exception. This is the Renaissance part of the *Alhambra Palace* at *Granada*, added by Charles V and built by *Muchaca* (1527–50) (**732**). Based on designs from Hadrian's Villa at Tivoli, the courtyard is circular, surrounded by a two-storeyed pure classical colonnade. It is plain, almost severe, and in strange contrast to the Moorish Palace adjacent to it. The Renaissance palace was never completed and it was many years before such correctly classical building was again attempted in Spain.

The architect who established the genuine classical style was *Juan de Herrera* (c. 1530–97). He studied in Italy and Belgium. His work in Spain is always severe, correct, monumental. There is little ornament and the interiors of his churches, for instance, are chilling. Herrera's influence, however, was considerable. By the later sixteenth century, Spain was ready for a change from over-decoration and a number of seventeenth century architects followed on the more correct classical lines, though not in Herrera's individualistic style.

Herrera's earliest and most famous work is the *Escorial*. This great monastic palace in the hills near Madrid is a memorial to Philip II. It was his retreat and displays the asceticism and almost fanatical religiosity of the King. He intended a monastery, a royal palace and a mausoleum for Charles V on one site, remote from any other civilisation. This he achieved, though in the twentieth century, civilisation has crept close to the gates of the Escorial in the form of tourist shops, reataurants and villas for wealthy Madrid citizens. The first architect of the Escorial was *Juan Bautista de Toledo*, who designed it in 1559. After his death in 1567, Herrera was commissioned to complete the work, which he did in 1584.

The palace and convent are in the form of a vast rectangle, 670 feet by 530 feet, of grey granite, hewn from the Guadarrama mountains, on whose lower slopes it stands; a magnificent desolate site. The long, severe exterior walls are unbroken save for rectangular window openings and four corner towers. It is a vast structure, enclosing the monastery and church and having 16 courtyards (**733**). Philip spared no expense. He supervised every detail of the construction. He told Herrera that the work must be noble, simple and severe, without ostentation. Herrera did as he was asked. The last part of the work was the great *Church of S. Lawrence*. He based it on a central, Greek cross plan, like Michelangelo's S. Peter's, but the nave arm, also like S. Peter's, was later extended, here with an entrance vestibule or narthex. Like the convent, this is also severe. The Doric Order is used throughout; in column form on the pedimented, entrance portico and in pilasters on the twin western towers and in the interior. The church is in grey granite. There is no colour or decoration. The interior is, nevertheless, most effective, though too cold for some tastes. Plain pendentives support the large dome and drum over the crossing. The whole interior is flooded with light from the large windows in the drum, enhanced by the position of the church on the mountain slopes (**734**). The mausoleum, the *Pantheón de los Reyes*, was built in the early seventeenth century for the Hapsburg monarchy by the Italian *Giovanni Battista Crescenzi*. This

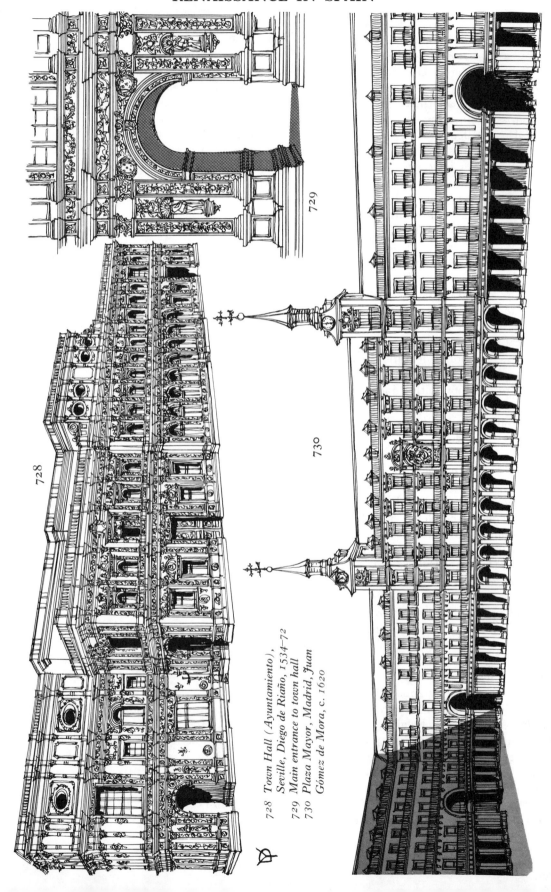

728 *Town Hall (Ayuntamiento),*
    Seville, Diego de Riaño, 1534–72
729 *Main entrance to town hall*
730 *Plaza Mayor, Madrid, Juan*
    Gómez de Mora, c. 1620

731 Double patio, Tavera Hospital, Toledo, 1541–79
732 Courtyard, Palace of Emperor Charles V, Alhambra, Granada,
     Pedro Machuca, 1526–50

732

is a domed octagonal chamber, set under the sanctuary of the church. The whole room is in grey and red marbles, decorated in gilt. The rich colouring is in contrast to Herrera's church above. Coupled Corinthian pilasters are set round the walls, in which are the Hapsburg marble tombs placed on shelves.

Herrera worked on many other projects, though little survives from some of them. At the *Royal Palace* of *Aranjuez*, south of Madrid, he again succeeded Juan Bautista de Toledo. He began a new design in 1567 on Italian High Renaissance villa pattern. The palace was not finished till the eighteenth century and Herrera's designs were considerably altered. His drawings, however, remain. In 1582 he designed the *Seville Exchange* and in 1575 the *Toledo Town Hall*. He worked for many years on *Valladolid Cathedral*. This is typical; plain, large, ascetic.

It is less well lit than his church at the Escorial because it remained incomplete after the architect's death. He intended a huge cathedral on basilican plan of 450 by 300 feet, with equal length nave and choir, corner towers to the façade and a dome over the crossing. At his death only the nave was complete and part of the façade. The latter was finished by Alberto de Churriguera, but the rest was never built so only the unlit, vast, barrel vaulted nave and monumental façade exist.

One of the leading architects of the earlier seventeenth century was *Juan Gómez de Mora* (1586–1647), a follower of Herrera's style and a prolific designer. One of his best known layouts is the *Plaza Mayor* of *Madrid*. This was originally planned by Herrera but de Mora carried out the scheme between 1617 and 1620 (**730**). It is a large square which retains its homogeneity on all

733 The Escorial, near Madrid, south front, Juan de Herrera, 1559–84

733

734

734 *The crossing, Monastery Church of the Escorial,*
  Juan de Herrera, c. 1584

four-storeyed sides with arcaded shops on the ground floor and dormers in the roof above. The north side with its twin towers is the focus of the scheme. The square is closed to traffic and reserved for pedestrians, cafés and shops.

Among de Mora's other works are the *Encarnación Church* (1611–16) and *Town Hall*, both in *Madrid*, and the *Jesuit Church* at *Alcalá de Henares* (1625). The Encarnación Church has a simple, narrow, classical façade. Inside it is light and well-proportioned. There is a dome over the crossing and coffered barrel vaults covering the four arms. There are no side chapels to the nave; the walls are articulated with Ionic pilasters with paintings and sculpture between.

Padre Francisco Bautista (1594–1679) based his style on Italian Mannerist examples. His work is to be found in Jesuit churches, chiefly in Madrid and Toledo. His important achievement is the *Cathedral of S. Isidro el Real* in *Madrid*. Here he followed Vignola's plan and form of Il Gesù in Rome, but the Madrid example was Herreran in its cool, grey treatment. The cathedral was sacked and the interior damaged by fire in 1936. It has now been rebuilt and redecorated (**725**).

Among other interesting seventeenth century surviving works are *Sebastian de la Plaza's*

735 Renaissance cloister (Gothic Plateresque church behind), Convent of Christ, Tomar, Diogo de Torralva, 1557

735

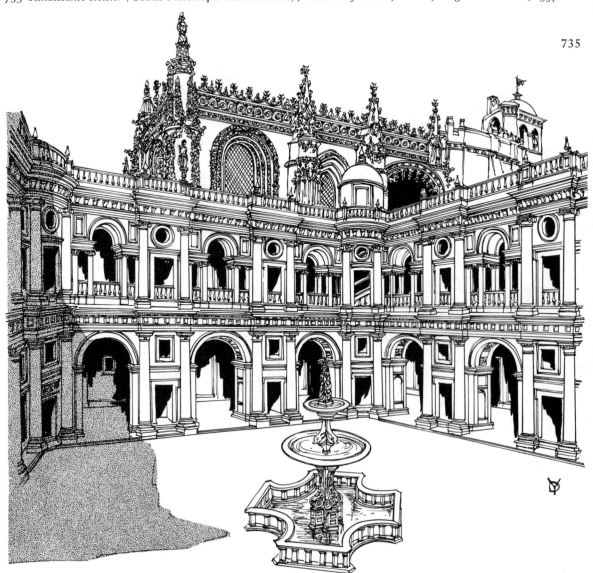

Portugal

Unlike Spain, Portugal possesses some pure Italian Renaissance buildings from early in the sixteenth century. This is due to *Diogo de Torralva* (1500–66), for the surviving examples are all by him. His first work was the *Church of La Graça in Évora* (1527–37). Though in poor condition externally today, the architect's intentions are clearly visible. Less purely classical than his later work, the façade has Mannerist features, especially in the upper storey of the portico, with its over-sized sculpture breaking the cornice line and giant rosettes set between the over-tall Ionic columns.

At *Tomar*, however, de Torralva surpassed himself. His beautiful, classic Renaissance cloisters at the Convent of Christ are superb. This cloister, the finest of the seven, has giant Ionic columns superimposed over Doric with, between, the smaller scale ordered openings: an insistent reminder of Michelangelo's Campidoglio palaces in Rome (**735**). Part-way up the hill that leads from the present day town of Tomar to the Convent of Christ is his small *Chapel of the Conception* (Conceição), built about 1550. Outside it is unpretentious and of pure classical design. The inside is in the manner of Brunelleschi but is now in poor condition.

Apart from de Torralva's work, most sixteenth century examples in Portugal were of more hybrid form, as in Spain. The *Cathedral* at *Leiria* is typical. A large barn-like building, it has great stone buttresses rising the full height of the façade, and impure, stodgy, windows and doorways.

The late sixteenth century saw a tentative approach towards Italian Mannerism and Baroque. An example is the *Sé Nova* (New Cathedral) at *Coimbra* (**736**). Here are side scrolls and curved and broken pediments. The interior is very plain with stone coffered barrel vaulting and a central dome on Pantheon lines. The plan is a Latin cross and the order throughout, in pilaster form, is Doric. The ornate Baroque altarpieces in the choir and transepts, decorated in gilt and colour, provide a rich contrast to the grey stone interior. *Filippo Terzi* (1520–97) came to Portugal from Italy in 1576 and increased the momentum towards Italian Baroque. He introduced the Jesuit style, based on the prototype, Il

736 *Sé Nova (New Cathedral), Coimbra, façade, Baltasar Alvares, late sixteenth century*

Bernardas Church in *Alcalà de Henares* (1617–26), which presages the Baroque with its oval nave surrounded by four chapels after Bernini; the Italian High Renaissance styled *Disputación* in *Barcelona*—a rectangular block with Doric porch and sculptured group above (1596–1617) by *Pedro Blay*—and *Jaén Cathedral*. This cathedral was built over a long period so that although the façade belongs to the Baroque style and period, the interior and the remainder are Renaissance. It is mainly the work of *Andrés Vandelvira* 1509–75), a pupil of Diego de Siloé, and he began work at Jaén in 1546 and continued until his death. It is built on hall church pattern, with lightly projecting transepts and a square east end, without ambulatory or radiating chapels. The interior has much in common with Granada Cathedral. There are similar nave piers of clustered Corinthian columns, standing on tall pedestals, with separate entablatures above which in turn support complex Gothic lierne vaults. The decoration of the cathedral is Renaissance and the aisle chapels are coffered and vaulted.

Gesù in Rome by Vignola. His chief work on this pattern is *São Vicente da Fora* in *Lisbon* (**737**). The interior is fundamentally similar to Il Gesù but the façade is more classical.

737

737 Church of S. Vicente da Fora, Lisbon, Filippo Terzi, 1582–1627

Northern Europe: The U.S.S.R.

Apart from some isolated instances, mainly in Moscow, the influence of the Italian Renaissance did not penetrate here; Byzantine trends were two strong. In the existing examples, Renaissance features are entirely decorative in character, acting as a covering upon a building, which was still Byzantine in structure and form. The emblems of classicism can be seen in the fenestration, the doorways and orders composed of pilasters supporting entablatures where neither the mouldings, proportions or capitals were of pure design. In this respect, Russian Renaissance buildings are a parallel to Elizabethan ones in England or pattern book Flemish in German and Poland. But since in the Soviet Union th basis was Byzantine not Gothic, the variation differed.

The purest Renaissance building is in th *Moscow Kremlin*, the *Cathedral* of the *Archange Michael* designed in 1505, not surprisingly b the Italian *Alevisio Novi*, who had worked fo some years in Russia. He was asked to build a: imposing church which would act as a restin place for the tsars and he was expected to follo the Vladimir type of structure, using also idea from the existing Kremlin Cathedral of th Assumption (p. 124) which had also bee designed by an Italian, Fioravanti. The interio of Novi's cathedral is on this theme, but on th outside he introduced, for the first time in Russi Renaissance detail: orders, pilasters, Composit capitals, arches. This is entirely decorative an bears little relationship to the building forn though the results are attractive. A particula feature of this external design is the shell decora tion in the upper row of arches above the entabla ture. This addition is ornamental but meaningles structurally (**741**).

This cathedral and the other two described i Chapter 3 (p. 124) are all in a central group insid the Kremlin walls. Also in the centre, nearby, i the *Faceted Palace* (Granovitaya Palata, *c.* 1490 which, like the Black Palace in L'vov and th examples in Italy and Spain (see p. 352), has i façades covered by diamond studding, broke only by decorated classical window opening flanked by Corinthian columns supporting en tablatures. It was built by two Italians, *Marc Ruffo* and *Pietro Antonio Solario*. The ecclesi astical buildings are kept now as museums. Th later Great Palace and other large buildings ar used as government offices. There is only on modern building inside the walls, the Palace o Congresses (1961, Chapter 9, p. 557). The *Towe of John the Great* (Ivan Veliki) is also inside th walls. This was a fine belfry, but was rebuilt afte 1812 in a less vigorous and decorative version o the original structure. Fig. **739** shows it as it i now. The photograph in PLATE 74 shows th belfry and the cathedral and palaces of th Kremlin viewed from the river Moskva, as they are today.

Surrounding the Kremlin are massive wall with towers and gatehouses set at intervals. Thes

Plate 71
Retablo 'Visitation of
the Virgin'. Museum
of Santa Cruz,
Toledo, Spain. 16th
century. Alonso
Berruguete
Plate 72
Façade detail,
Hospicio Real.
Santiago de
Compostela, Spain,
1501–11
Plate 73
Façade detail,
Salamanca Univer-
sity, Spain, 1516–29

Plate 74

RENAISSANCE IN MOSCOW, U.S.S.R.

738 Kremlin walls and Spasskaya
Tower, c. 1624
739 Kremlin. Tower of Ivan the
Great 1505–1600 (rebuilt after
1812)
740 Cathedral of the Archangel
Michael, Andronikhov
Monastery, seventeenth and
eighteenth centuries
741 Cathedral of the Archangel
Michael, Kremlin, Alevisio
Novi, 1505–9

738

739

740

741

date from different periods and several are of interest. The rebuilding of the walls from their original wood to red brick was begun in 1485 under Ruffo and Solario and completed in the early sixteenth century. Parts have been altered, but the general impression is still Italianate, reminding the viewer of those in Ferrara or Verona. The towers are a mixture of styles and dates, including Gothic, Byzantine, Renaissance and Baroque features. Among the most interesting are the *Spasskaya* (**738**), the *Nikolskaya*, the *Borovitskaya* and the *Troitskaya*.

The *Cathedral of the Archangel Michael* at the *Andronikrov Monastery* in *Moscow* illustrates a typical Russian adoption of Renaissance decorative forms on to a Byzantine church (**740**). Here, the corner columns and fenestration are classical, the remainder is traditionally Russian giving an uneasy appearance of fancy dress covering.

Scandinavia

There is little Renaissance architecture in Scandinavia, except in Denmark. In Norway, Finland and Sweden, this was a period of decline in architecture and in the arts in general. The Reformation led to the disbandment and demolition of monastic settlements. Not many new churches were built. Construction was primarily in defences and fortified houses, but few of these structures showed Renaissance features.

Denmark

The nearest part of Scandinavia to the rest of Europe, this country absorbed Renaissance ideas chiefly from Holland and also from Germany and England. Building was in the form of palaces and houses, still partly of a fortified nature but, with royal patronage, several large scale structures were erected. The work has mostly been extensively restored in the nineteenth or twentieth centuries but retains much of its original character.

The Renaissance style in Denmark closely resembles that of Holland and England. Much of it is in brick, with stone reserved for dressings and sculptured decoration. The gabling, chimney-stacks and doorways are very Dutch, the decoration and handling of the orders impure in the same sense and manner as English Elizabethan design.

King Frederick II was the moving spirit behind two of the great fortified palaces of the age. The earlier of these is *Kronborg Castle* at *Helsingør*, original of Shakespeare's Elsinore in 'Hamlet'. It was rebuilt from the early 1570s by Flemish masons in Mannerist style. The Renaissance character is seen in the horizontal emphasis of the elevations, though ornament and gabling are Flemish Mannerist. This large castle is built on a square plan on a headland overlooking the sea; the corners marked by tall, polygonal towers; it is surrounded by earth and brick ramparts. Inside, is an impressive, large, three-storeyed courtyard of grey sandstone with green copper sloping roofs, interrupted by decoratively gabled dormers. The fenestration, ground storey orders and frontispiece doorways are like those of Elizabethan English great houses.

At *Hillerød*, inland between Copenhagen and Helsingør, Frederick II began his second great palace. He acquired the estate at Hillerød, on islands in the lake, in 1560 and replaced the existing manor house with a castle which he re-titled *Frederiksborg*. Christian IV, born there in 1577, demolished much of it and rebuilt once again, from 1602, on a grander scale. This palace remained the chief residence of the Danish kings until 1859, when tremendous damage was done to the interior by a great fire. It was carefully restored and rebuilt by Medahl (p. 505). Much of the exterior, however, belongs to the original Renaissance palace.

Frederiksborg is an impressive group of buildings, certainly the first Renaissance palace in Scandinavia. The palace is approached through a tall, spired gatehouse, which leads into the great outer court. In the centre of this is the *Neptune fountain*, a good copy of the original one by *Adrien de Vries* (1623), removed by the Swedes in 1659 and now at Drottningholm (p. 461). Behind the fountain is the bridge leading to the magnificent Renaissance screen, decorated with its Flemish Mannerist sculptured niches, set in a wall articulated with a Doric arcade. The two storey gateway is ornamented by high relief sculptured panels and, above, a strapwork crested cartouche. The brick walls contrast attractively with the stonework ornament.

Behind this entrance screen rises the main structure of the palace, built round three sides of an inner court, reached by passing through the

742

743 Frederiksborg Castle, Hillerød, entrance court 1602. Rebuilding 1861–75 after fire damage

742

743

archway in the centre of the screen (**743**). Though laid out on the French *cour d'honneur* type of plan, this was the only concession to Renaissance symmetry. The buildings are romantically grouped round the courtyard, the elegant towers set asymmetrically, the gables, the turrets and dormers breaking the skyline like a Dutch or English great house of the period. The fenestration is classical, as is the two-storey entrance screen, but the use and handling of the ornamentation and orders are purely decorative rather than functional in the way that they would have been in Italy or France at that date. The restoration has been carefully done, closely following the available original drawings and, though a hardness of finish reminds one of the nineteenth century work here, the whole impression is of a remarkably coherent and homogeneous Danish Renaissance palace.

Christian IV was an influential architectural patron and was especially interested in town planning. Impressed by the ideal town planning schemes put forward by the Italian Renaissance architects, he envisaged a suitable layout for the centre of *Copenhagen*. Personally he drew up plans for an octagonal focal point with surrounding buildings. This scheme was not realised until the eighteenth century planning of the Amalienborg (p. 457), but the *palace of Rosenborg* was built from 1606 onwards and still stands much in its original form. It was designed as the summer palace and was built in brick and stone in similar style to Frederiksborg, but stands on a smaller ground plan, extending vertically rather than horizontally (**744**).

The most impressive Renaissance building in Copenhagen is the *Exchange*, constructed 1609–30 as a trading centre. It is an immensely long two-storeyed building with gabled ends and an unusual central tower with a spire made up of entwined dragons' tails (**746**). Although on Flemish Mannerist pattern, as shown in its row of tall, gabled dormers and sculptured caryatid decoration, the three-storeyed frontispieces on the two end elevations are of correct classical handling in the Doric Order.

A number of *manor* and *town* houses for the nobility and wealthier citizens were built in the sixteenth and early seventeenth centuries. Manor houses were still partially fortified, generally surrounded by a moat and approached via a drawbridge. Most of these were of brick and were still largely designed on Medieval pattern, though Renaissance features in gabling, fenestration and decoration were now being incorporated. The finest example is *Egeskov*, built 1545 near the village of Kvaerndrup, on the island of Funen, south of Odense. Magnificently sited in parkland on the edge of the lake, it is a structure based on the two-house principle, these houses adjoining one another and standing on a foundation of oak piles driven into the lake bed. The wall dividing the two houses is six feet thick and contains, in its thickness, stairways, small chambers and passageways. Egeskov has not been altered greatly over the centuries (**742**), only its gables and turrets were rebuilt in the nineteenth century and an iron suspension bridge built to replace the drawbridge approach. The gatehouse was altered in the same period.

A number of *town houses* survive from this period. A fine example is No. 9 Østeraagade in *Aalborg*, in the north of the Jutland peninsula. Built 1623–4 (**745**), this is a large, brick house with stone facings and decoration. It has a three-gabled facade to the street, an elegant oriel window and a finely sculptured doorway. In the High Street (Stengade) in *Helsingør* is a plainer example, at No. 76. Built in 1579, this has pedimented classical windows and a Mannerist gable. In *Aarhus*, the open air museum 'Den Gamle By', contains many buildings re-erected from the city and nearby towns and villages, preserved from different periods of architectural development. There are a number of examples—houses, shops, workshops and warehouses—from the sixteenth and seventeenth centuries, which are mainly of timber construction with brick or plaster infilling, like the English half-timber work. These are in traditional building style and are more Medieval in design than Renaissance. The windows are small and latticed the roof pitch steep and the upper storeys overhang the lower. Only in the doorway surround and lintels is there a sign of impure classical decoration.

Norway

In this period, until the later seventeenth century few buildings of note were erected in Norway an true Renaissance work is almost unknown.

744 *Rosenborg Palace,*
Copenhagen, 1606–17
745 *House doorway at*
No. 9 Østeraagade,
Aalborg, 1623–4
746 *The Exchange,*
Copenhagen, Lorenz and
Hans Steenwinckel,
1619–30. Spire 1624–5,
Ludwig Heidritter

745

744

746

country still disturbed and unsettled, the chief buildings in permanent materials were castles and fortifications and these showed Renaissance features only in fenestration and ornament. Typical is the *Rosenkranz Tower* in the Bergenhus fortress in *Bergen*, built 1562–8. This was erected by Scottish craftsmen, as were a number of other such buildings at this time. The *Akershus Fortress* in *Oslo* had been established in 1270. Rebuilding and extension work continued intermittently through the centuries, particularly in the years 1588–1648, but little of it exists unaltered today.

Of the *manor houses* built at this time, few survive. One of these is the *Austråt Manor House* in the Trondheim Fjord, built 1654–6. The house was constructed round a quadrangle, of which the existing Medieval chapel was the focal centre. There is a stone entrance wall and gatehouse which leads into a square court lined by a wooden gallery supported on columns. On the first floor, carved and painted wooden figures hold up the roof; these are replacements of originals destroyed in the fire of 1916.

Several Norwegian towns possessed fine timber buildings dating from these years, but repeated fires have destroyed the majority of them. The chief building material was wood, even in towns, until the early years of the twentieth century, and towns such as Trondheim and Bergen have lost nearly all their beautiful structures dating from earlier than the later eighteenth century.

Finland

Almost no churches and few houses of note were built here in the sixteenth and seventeenth centuries. The architectural influence was Swedish and there is no Finnish Renaissance style.

Sweden

Remains here are fragmentary and chiefly in castle-palaces. The best and most complete example is *Vadstena Castle* (**747**), picturesquely situated on the eastern shore of the immense Lake Vättern. Begun in 1545, the castle has a medieval fortified exterior appearance with round corner towers and the walls lapped all round by water. Inside is the palace, which is Renaissance in its symmetry and fenestration. The interiors are richer and more decorative.

747

747 Vadstena Castle, Sweden, sixteenth century

7
The Changing Face of Classicism: 1580–1800

It is appropriate to discuss in one chapter the tremendous quantity of work created in Europe during these two centuries because, apart from isolated tendencies, the architecture is all classical in derivation. It is based upon the Roman then, later, Greek classic structure of orders, columns, capitals and pediments, interwoven skilfully with arched openings and vaults.

Though it is convenient to consider together such a long period of energetic endeavour, it should not be presumed that the architecture of this extensive area and time was all similar. The variations on the classical theme were widespread, depending upon national characteristics, religious beliefs, climate, available building materials and, paramount, the overall European development of thought and style. As with previous architectural forms, different countries entered new phases at differing times. Italy continued as the leader and creator of prototype designs until the early eighteenth century, by which time France took her place as arbiter of architectural fashion. Meanwhile, other areas were dominated by alternative sources. The German influence was widespread; the southern designs being popularised in Czechoslovakia, Switzerland, Austria and Hungary, while the northern approach had more in common with England, the Low Countries and Scandinavia.

These years were the most fruitful architecturally for nearly all countries, even those most distant from Italy and France, such as Russia and Scandinavia. Only eastern areas still under Turkish domination, such as Greece and southern Yugoslavia, were exceptions to the movement towards greater building activity in classical form.

The predominant styles were Baroque, Rococo and Neo-classicism. Of these, the most vivid and strongly marked was the Baroque. In past ages this type of work was thought of as a late Renaissance art form, and it is less than 100 years since it was recognised as a style in its own right.

The word, which derives from the Portuguese *barroco* (Spanish *barrueco*), meaning an ill-formed or grotesque pearl, was first applied in a derogatory sense, just as 'Gothic' was first introduced (see p. 200). This was a reference to the strange curving, sometimes bulbous shapes to be seen in this type of architecture which, in the nineteenth century were thus deprecated.

Baroque art and architecture, like those of the Renaissance, originated in Italy so that, while other countries in Europe were beginning to adopt Renaissance forms, the Italians had moved on from these to Mannerism, then to full-blooded Baroque. The underlying force of the movement was, like that of the Renaissance, based upon a new process of thinking, this time not towards Humanism but from Humanism towards the Catholic Church. A deep feeling had arisen for a re-introduction of spiritual values; evidence of man's need for belief in something greater than himself. Among other Orders, the Jesuits were instrumental in re-establishing a Christian way of life more suited to the modern world than the outgrown Medieval concept. The Roman Catholic Church seized the opportunity and attracted people back to its fold with gaiety and pageantry in its buildings. Bernini, the greatest of Baroque artists, was a master of the dramatic form and lighting effects so typical of the Baroque interpretation of the current Christian approach.

From Italy the Baroque architectural forms spread throughout Europe, but it was suited chiefly to southern, Latin peoples of Roman Catholic faith. This was partly for its religious significance and partly because it is an extrovert, rich, colourful style. In the greyer north—in England, northern Germany, Scandinavia—it gained only a foothold; there, classical architecture remained cool and aloof, in straight lines and pure tones. Apart from Italy, therefore, we find Baroque architecture in its more vigorous and characteristic manner in southern Germany,

Austria, Switzerland, Czechoslovakia, Hungary, Spain and Portugal. One of its predominant features is a free use of curves (within the classical framework of orders and ornament). These curves, often of whole walls and ceiling, move from convex to concave. It was Robert Adam in England who, describing Baroque design as a feeling for 'movement', quoted S. Peter's in Rome as the prime example. He refers to the balance and contrast of the convexity of Michelangelo's dome in relation to Bernini's concave piazza colonnade. Another important feature of Baroque architecture, especially the interior, is of dramatic lighting effects in painting, sculpture and architecture, since all three arts are always fused in the Baroque into a unified design. The favourite plan is oval as this lends itself to a maximum feeling for movement. Rich, sensuous vitality in colour, form and light is the keynote of all Baroque work in all media.

The Rococo theme was predominantly French in inspiration though it is to be found also in other countries, such as Austria and Scandinavia. This is again a theme of movement, but here more on a decorative, two-dimensional plane than the Baroque. The orders tend to be omitted or reduced in importance and Rococo decoration surrounds window frames, doorcases, mirrors and paintings as well as providing a framework to ceiling painting. The decorative forms are still curving and sinuous, but now become gayer, lighter, less sensuous and in low relief.

The northern European approach to classical architecture was predominantly neither Baroque nor Rococo. Countries such as England, Holland, northern Germany, Scandinavia tended to keep to Renaissance and Palladian themes, then later to neo-classicism. This was less colourful and, with its emphasis on orders, based more directly on Roman than on Greek traditions. The architecture of these countries is, in many instances, of high quality, dignified, well-designed and often impressive, but it was never as colourful, richly ornamented or breathtaking as that of the Latin South.

Italy

Early Baroque in Rome

In the last years of the sixteenth century several architects in Rome began to break away from the academic Mannerism which was dominating the architecture of the city. Chief of these was *Carlo Maderna* (1556–1629), who became architect to *S. Peter's* in 1603. He was commissioned to complete the basilica which had been in course of building since Bramante's original design (p. 315): little had been done since Michelangelo's death in 1564. It fell to Maderna to alter Michelangelo's centralised plan by lengthening the unfinished nave arm to the form of a Latin cross. Maderna was most reluctant to do this, but was overruled by the Pope who wanted the extra space thus provided. History repeated itself 50 years later at S. Paul's in London when Wren was unwillingly overruled for the same reasons. In both cases the clergy were responsible for putting expediency before aesthetics. In Rome, S. Peter's was lengthened by three bays. As a result, the view of the dome from the piazza is truncated and the basis of the design thus thwarted. Maderna did his best to minimise the aesthetic loss; he retained Michelangelo's articulation inside the nave and faithfully echoed vault and wall design. His façade is bold and well-planned and, again, the giant order and articulation are maintained (**749**).

With the Counter-Reformation came a new wave of church building in Rome. The Mother Church of the Jesuit Order, *Il Gesù*, was one of the first to be built (p. 321). Following this came *S. Susanna*, to which Maderna added the façade in 1595–1603. This was a true Baroque elevation and one which set the pattern for many others in years to come. Next door is *S. Maria della Vittoria* (1624–6) by *Giovanni Soria*. Maderna designed the interior here apart from Bernini's famous Cornaro Chapel sculpture of S. Teresa Maderna also completed and enlarged *S. Andrea della Valle* in 1608. This is his best work, with a majestic dome over the crossing (**750**).

High Baroque in Rome

The two great architects here were Bernini and Borromini. Acutely contrasting both in personality and architectural approach, between them they set a standard impossible for their followers to excel. *Gianlorenzo Bernini* (1598–1680) was a genius whose qualities would have risen to the surface whenever he had lived. His particular abilities and personality were, however, mad

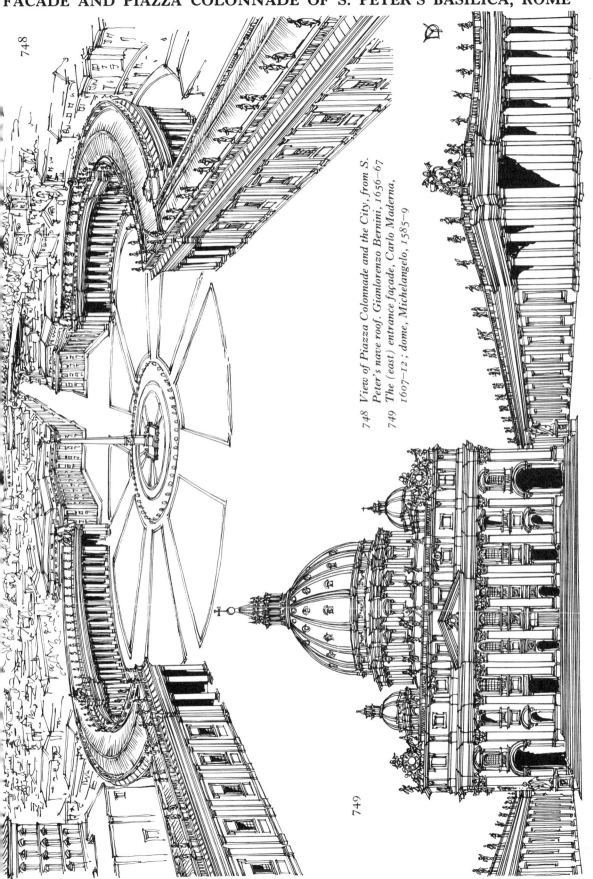

748 *View of Piazza Colonnade and the City, from S. Peter's nave roof. Gianlorenzo Bernini, 1656–67*

749 *The (east) entrance façade, Carlo Maderna, 1607–12; dome, Michelangelo, 1585–9*

748

749

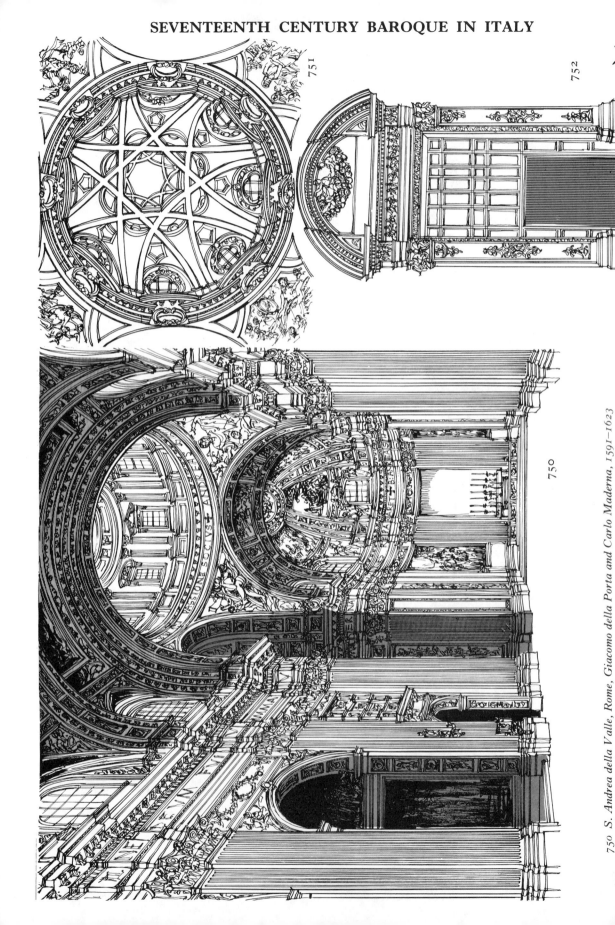

751

752

750

750 S. Andrea della Valle, Rome, Giacomo della Porta and Carlo Maderna, 1591–1623

o measure for the period. He dominated his world for 50 years, towering far above all other artists of his time, creating achievement after achievement with consummate ease, concentration and energy. Only Michelangelo was ever respected and revered more by his contemporaries. Bernini was to the Baroque what Michelangelo had been to the Renaissance. The two giants had much in common. Both were strong personalities and of great religious conviction. Both lived long lives, master of their own artistic circle, to the end. Both were painters, architects and poets, but regarded sculpture as the most rewarding of the arts. They were both perfectionists, magnificent craftsmen, and would permit nothing to turn them away from the work in hand. In personality they were opposites. Bernini was a Neapolitan with all the charm and gaiety of his race. He was a happy husband and father and got on well with everyone; a contrast to the proud, introspective Michelangelo.

Bernini entered upon the challenge of the Counter-Reformation with zest. The drama and vividness of his work was essentially suited to this need. His sculpture especially portrayed an expression of instantaneous movement as in a snapshot, held it and perpetuated it as in life. He led a school of artists—architects, painters, sculptors—and kept Rome the centre of European art, cradle of the Baroque and inspiration of the Roman Catholic faith.

His architecture, like that of Michelangelo, was always sculptural in its handling of mass, but he displayed an exuberance and sensuality never to be seen in Michelangelo's work. Like his predecessor, his great work was at *S. Peter's*, where he became architect in 1629. His first work here was on the baldacchino and some sculptural groups, but his chief contribution was the designing of the piazza colonnade on front of the basilica. The problems of this layout were immense—aesthetic, practical, liturgical. It needed a man of Bernini's stature and artistic authority to solve them. He created a symbol of the Mother Church of Christendom embracing the world with his vast elliptical colonnades. The western ends adjoin the basilica façade with two long corridors. The piazza successfully provides space for the immense crowds who came to see and hear the Pope give his blessing to the city and the world from the façade loggia. Architecturally

the colonnades have made history. They are not arcades like most Ancient Roman examples; the continuous Ionic entablature rests directly upon the Doric/Tuscan columns which stand four deep, 60 feet high, surmounted by a procession of saints, extending outwards from the façade parapet of S. Peter's all round the piazza (**748** and **749**). All over Europe for 200 years these colonnades have been emulated, on large and small scale, in places as far apart as England and Russia. Bernini also adapted and re-designed the ceremonial entrance staircase, *the Scala Regia*; it is one of his masterpieces. It was so hemmed in by the existing walls as to appear a narrow dark well. The architect could not alter the physical situation but, by his wall articulation and adjustment of the stair flights, he contrived an impression of spaciousness. This was further enhanced by his Baroque treatment of the lighting and his elaborate coffered vault above. It is one of the great staircases of the world.

At the age of 60, Bernini built *S. Andrea al Quirinale* (**753**). This became a prototype for Baroque churches all over Europe. It is designed on centralised plan in oval form. The exterior is monumental with a tall curving porch, but the small, perfect interior is in contrast with its magnificent handling of lighting, colour and sculpture. The darkness below draws one's attention to the heavenly dome above with the figure of S. Andrew as centrepiece.

Bernini is also well known for his extensive work on *Roman palaces* and, in his capacity as sculptor and town planner, for his *fountains* in Rome. His monumental style is evident in the former but in his fountains, in particular, can be seen his breakaway from the Florentine Renaissance tradition into a powerful style, full of movement and vigour. The *Triton Fountain* in the Piazza Barberini shows this clearly, but his masterpiece is the layout in the *Piazza Navona* (PLATE 78). The unusual shape of this square is due to its following the exact pattern of the Roman Emperor Diocletian's stadium. The church of S. Agnese is built on one of the long sides and three fountains are equally spaced along the piazza's major axis. Bernini designed two of these, the Moro and the Fiumi. The latter, the fountain of the rivers, dates from 1648; it is the perfect centrepiece for the piazza. It sets off the church behind, showing it to advantage but

BAROQUE CHURCHES IN ITALY

753 S. Andrea al
Quirinale, Rome,
Gianlorenzo Bernini,
1678
754 and 755 View and
ground plan, S. Carlo
alle Quattro Fontane,
Rome, Francesco
Borromini, 1638–40
756 S. Maria della
Salute, Venice,
Baldassare Longhena,
1631–87

753

756

755

not competing for effect. The fountain represents the essence of Bernini's contribution to Baroque sculptural purpose in street architecture. It is a living, pulsating composition, the flowing water used as an integral part of the design to give vitality to the sculpture. The action is caught at an instant of time. It is not static but is about to continue the movement at any moment.

Francesco Borromini (1599–1667) was a contemporary of Bernini and a great contrast. He was a recluse, a neurotic, unhappy man who eventually took his own life. His work was quite different from that of the Neapolitan but, in his individual manner, also brilliantly original. He went much further than Bernini in challenging the concepts of classical architecture as they inherited them. Bernini was original in his handling of design, sculptural form, dramatic lighting and was a master of portraying the human spirit. He did not, however, contradict the basis of Renaissance thought; he adapted it to Baroque interpretation. Borromini went further. He cast aside the concept of classical architecture tied indissolubly to the proportions of the human figure as enunciated by Leonardo da Vinci. Borromini's concepts were of a classical architecture dependent on engineering thought rather than human sculpture and nearer to Medieval structure than Renaissance ideas. Despite these fundamental differences, Borromini's work is as indisputably Baroque as Bernini's. His contribution was almost entirely in ecclesiastical design, in an original form that had lasting and widespread influence.

S. Carlo alle Quattro Fontane (1638–40) was his first church. It caused an immediate sensation (**754** and **755**). It combines the fundamentals of several different types of design. On Greek cross plan, the walls are Baroque, in undulating form, and the oval dome is supported on pendentives. Borromini's structural unit basis is the triangle not the classical module pattern. The church is not large but, inside, appears of much greater volume than it actually is due to the sensation of movement from the alternately convex and concave wall surfaces. The lighting, in true Baroque manner, is controlled from one source, the dome, and accentuates the billowing quality of the wall design. The exterior façade was not built till nearly 30 years later and shows the architect's more mature approach. It is equally original and composed of undulating curves.

Borromini followed with his University Church, *S. Ivo alla Sapienza*, in 1642. This also is based on a triangular unit; an equally original structure, full of curves. In 1646 he was asked to restore the Cathedral of Rome, *S. John in Lateran*, an early Christian basilica, then in a poor state of repair. He was not permitted to rebuild, so he carried out the difficult task of making it structurally sound and re-clothing the interior in Baroque manner. He encased the columns in pairs and faced these piers with a giant order of pilasters extending the whole height of the cathedral. Between these he set arches containing large sculptured figures. He intended to vault the whole interior, but was not allowed to do this; the sixteenth century wooden ceiling was preserved, newly painted and gilded (**759**). Another of Borromini's triumphs is the fine Baroque exterior which he carried out on Rainaldi's church, *S. Agnese* in *Piazza Navona* (1652–6). This scheme was finished with an imposing dome flanked by twin Baroque towers. This became the basis for church façade design all over Europe.

Venice

The outstanding architect here was *Baldassare Longhena* (1598–1682), whose masterpiece is the church of *S. Maria della Salute*, built in thanksgiving for deliverance from the plague in the city in 1630 (**756**). Magnificently situated at the head of the Grand Canal, nearly opposite to S. Mark's Cathedral and the Doge's Palace, it is, apart from its picturesque exterior and position, one of the most interesting structures of the seventeenth century. The church is based on a mixture of themes; the centrally planned buildings of Ancient Rome like S. Costanza and the Byzantine pattern of S. Vitale. It is octagonal in plan with a surrounding ambulatory. The interior is plain in contrast to the flamboyant exterior, which has peculiarly Baroque giant scrolls which, supported on the ambulatory arches, provide abutment for the dome.

Northern Italy

Two gifted and contrasting architects in *Turin* created some magnificent architecture in these years. *Guarino Guarini* (1624–83) was the chief seventeenth century architect and had much in common with Borromini. He was also original and worked on Medieval and mathematical principles. He too used the triangle as his unit basis and clothed such structures in Baroque dress. His chief works in Turin were the *Church of S. Lorenzo* (1668), with its unusual cupola made up from 36 arches in triangular pendentive construction (**751**), the Baroque *Palazzo Carignano* with its undulating façade (**757**) and his *Sindone Chapel* in the *Cathedral* which was built to house the Holy Shroud. This chapel also has an unusual cupola. It is a complex Medieval structure, carried on pendentives set on the diagonal axes, which transform the octagon into a Greek cross at this level.

Turin continued to be a great architectural centre in the first half of the eighteenth century. Then *Filippo Juvara* (1678–1736) was the leader. He continued the development of the city where Guarini had finished and in his 20 years there achieved a prodigious quantity of work in churches, palaces and street layout. He varied his style according to the commission and four of his outstanding works illustrate this: the Church of S. Cristina, the Palazzo Madama, the Superga and Stupinigi. He added the façade to *S. Cristina* (1715–28)—a church which had been begun in 1639 as one of the twin churches in the Piazza San Carlo. This is Roman Baroque in style. His *Palazzo Madama* is a rich town palace with a superbly elegant staircase. The so-called hunting lodge at *Stupinigi*, outside the city, is an immense country palace with wide-spreading wings extending on each side of a monumental Baroque centrepiece. This contains the beautifully decorative curving, rococo hall.

Juvara was a Sicilian but much of his life was spent in Turin, from where he also travelled a great deal to build large-scale structures in other countries—Spain, for example (p. 404). His masterpiece is the immense royal burial church of Piedmont on the fringes of Turin. Entirely Baroque in concept, the *Basilica di Superga* represents the final great achievement of the Baroque era in Italy. It is fronted by a monumental Corinthian portico. The large central drum and dome, rising above the octagonal nave, are flanked by fine western towers. Here is Italy's last word on the centrally planned church theme which had intrigued classical architects since the days of Brunelleschi.

Southern Italy

A different form of Baroque architecture flourished in the seventeenth and eighteenth centuries here and in Sicily. It reflected strongly the Spanish rule in the area, so the buildings are more richly ornamented than those of Roman or northern Italian Baroque origins. They have much in common with their equivalents in Andalusian and Central Spain (p. 403). The two outstanding architects of *Naples* were *Cosimo Fanzago* (1591–1678), whose work is mainly ecclesiastical, like his cloisters at *San Martino*, and *Luigi Vanvitelli* (1700–73), who is best known for the vast *royal palace* at *Caserta*. This immense building, 16 miles from Naples and still dominating the town of Caserta, was built as the summer residence for the Bourbon monarchy. Its extensive gardens echo Versailles and are immensely long, rising slowly for two miles from the palace in fountains, cascades and stairways to culminate in two fountains on a grand terrace below a steep cascade (PLATE 75). The water for these in this hot, dry region, comes via the aqueduct constructed by Vanvitelli from mountains 20 miles away. The palace is regular and dignified on the exterior. The interior is different; it is of Baroque splendour, especially in the state rooms and grand staircase, whose scenic quality is breathtaking.

Further south, to *Apulia*, the seventeenth century once again brought energetic building activity. Half forgotten since the great Norman empire of the twelfth century, these new forms were Baroque, but, as with the Norman work, different from interpretations elsewhere. This was due to the same racial mingling which had been effective 500 years before (p. 153). This time the foreign dominance was Spanish instead of Norman, and the Medieval and Byzantine Greek traditions mingled with Saracenic decoration, Spanish plateresque forms and southern Italian gaiety; all were fused into a strangely stable theme which imposed the rich decoration on the surface only of a Baroque classicism beneath. The small town of *Lecce* was the centre of this type of building and still possesses many

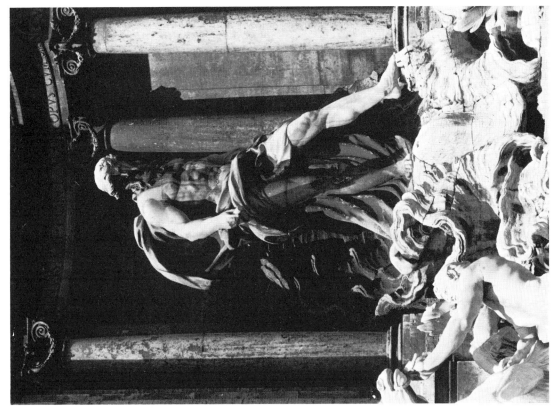

Trevi Fountain, Rome, Niccolò Salvi, 1735–72. Sculpture, Bracci

Garden sculpture. Royal Palace, Caserta, Italy, 1760s

Plate 77
High Altar 'The Ascension'. Stiftskirche, Rohr, Germany, 1723, Asam bros.

Plate 78
Fountain detail, Piazza Navona, Rome. 1653, Bernini

CLASSICAL ARCHITECTURE IN ITALY

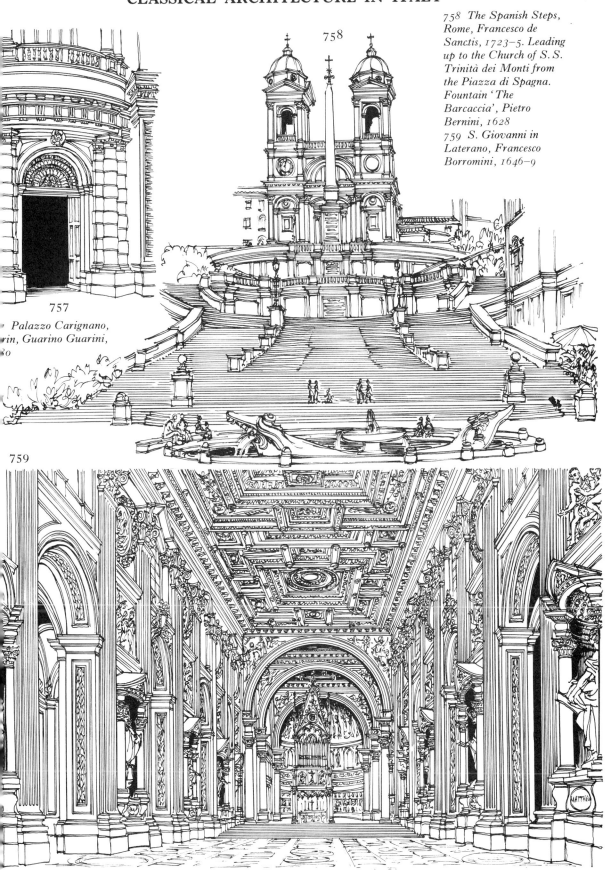

758

758 *The Spanish Steps, Rome, Francesco de Sanctis, 1723–5. Leading up to the Church of S.S. Trinità dei Monti from the Piazza di Spagna. Fountain 'The Barcaccia', Pietro Bernini, 1628*
759 *S. Giovanni in Laterano, Francesco Borromini, 1646–9*

757
Palazzo Carignano, rin, Guarino Guarini, o

759

examples built over a long period in the seventeenth and eighteenth centuries by many architects. Of particular note are the *Church of S. Croce*, the *Cathedral* façade and the adjacent *Seminario* (**752**).

Sicily

This area too possesses a rich Baroque heritage, much of it from the seventeenth century. It is different again from the Apulian work in that it is less riotously ornamented and is more a vigorous, Spanish-Sicilian form of northern Baroque. Buildings in *Palermo* such as the *Quattro Conti* and the *Arsenal* are typical; outstanding is the *Cathedral of Syracuse*. This will be remembered (p. 21) as unusual in incorporating a Greek temple in its nave, where the columns are still visible.

Town Planning by Streets and Grouped Buildings

Limited schemes by one or two individual architects had been essayed in the sixteenth century (p. 318). Larger scale plans were carried out in the seventeenth and eighteenth, but still by individual architects and clients. In *Rome*, the Piazza del Popolo, the Spanish Steps and the Trevi Fountain were such layouts. The *Piazza del Popolo* was the first Baroque scheme in Rome, a prototype of the later French development of the *rond-point* theme. The Porta del Popolo is one of Rome's entrance gateways and leads into a large piazza from which, opposite, three streets radiate to different parts of the city. There is an obelisk in the centre of the piazza and facing it are two island sites dividing the three roads. On these sites stand two Baroque churches— *S. Maria di Montesanto* and *S. Maria dei Miracoli*, built 1662–75 by *Carlo Rainaldi* and *Carlo Fontana*. They are not identical churches and the sites differ in size and shape, but they are sufficiently similar to complement one another and to act as focal centres for the view of the piazza from the Porta.

The *Spanish Steps* sweep in triple ascent, dividing as they go, up the steep hillside from the Piazza di Spagna to *Alessandro Specchi's* elegant church of *SS. Trinità dei Monti*. At Easter the Steps are one of the sights of Rome with colourful flowers banked up the sides of each staircase

(**758**). The *Trevi Fountain*, built 1735–72 b Niccolò Salvi is, apart from its romantic associa tions with coin-throwing, a remarkable com position and engineering feat. The classica palace façade in the form of a Roman triumpha arch acts as a backcloth to the sculptural dram in front (PLATE 76).

In the north, the idea of designing palaces i streets instead of individual buildings was deve loped in *Turin*, where Carlo Emmanuele employed his architect *Carlo di Castellamente t* lay out the *Piazza San Carlo* and the beginning of the *Via Roma* (1638). Work was continue throughout the seventeenth and eighteenth cen turies under Guarini and Juvara. Similarly, i *Sicily*, *Giovanni Battista Vaccarini* replanne *Catania* after the earthquake of 1693, making it Baroque city. The fine buildings of the Cathedra the Palazzo Municipale and the Churches of S Agata, S. Placido and S. Chiara were chie buildings in the scheme.

France

After Italy, France produced some of the fines architecture in Europe at this time, particularl in the seventeenth century, but only a little of i was in the Baroque style. This type of design wa foreign to French artists, who preferred some thing less flamboyant, more correctly classica and with delicate decoration. This is not to sa that there is no Baroque in France, only that i was not the fundamental style that it became i Italy.

The chief architect of the early seventeent century was *Salomon de Brosse* (1571–1626). H designed, like Philibert de l'Orme, in bold plastic manner, largely on Renaissance pattern He was concerned with the architecture mor than the decoration and his use of orders wa correct and classical. He built three great château and two palaces. Of the latter, the Parlement o Brittany at Rennes (near the Palais de Justice) which he built in 1618, remains fairly unaltered Its simplicity and fine classical detail are notable It has a rusticated lower storey and, above, ar Doric columns and pilasters below a high gable roof. His *châteaux* included that at Coulommier (1613) (mainly demolished), Blérancourt (1619 and Luxembourg (1615). The *Palace of Luxem bourg* in *Paris* built for Marie de' Medici was

SEVENTEENTH CENTURY CHURCHES IN PARIS

760 *Church of Val de Grâce. Begun F. Mansart, completed Lemercier, 1645–65*
761 *Church of the Sorbonne, Lemercier, 1635*
762 *Church of S. Sulpice, begun Le Vau, 1655*
763 *Church of S. Gervais. Façade, de Brosse, 1616–21*

760

761

762

763

château, but has since been extended and turned into a large town house. At *Blérancourt* only a fragment exists in the entrance screen with gateway and bridge. These have been restored and maintained, fronting a museum, and clearly show the architect's style and intentions. The work is crisp, clear and well-proportioned; very classical and French.

In *Paris*, de Brosse also worked on two *churches*, the more important being *S. Gervais* where he added the façade in 1616–21 (**763**). This is a Renaissance rather than Baroque façade, far earlier in style than Maderna's S. Susanna in Rome of 1605. However, de Brosse was fronting a Gothic church and so needed a tall façade. He provided a three-storey structure with super-imposed orders; a satisfactory answer to his problem.

The middle years of the seventeenth century saw the rise of a number of great French architects—Lemercier, F. Mansart, Le Vau, Perrault and J. H. Mansart. *Jacques Lemercier* (*c.* 1585–1654) became the chief architect to the Crown after de Brosse and worked largely for the King's chief Minister, Cardinal Richelieu, for whom he built a château (later much altered), the town which adjoins it and the Church of the Sorbonne in Paris. The *town* of *Richelieu* is still much as it was built, small, unpretentious, homogeneous. It is planned on grid-iron pattern, with two main streets at right angles to one another and with two squares at intersections. There are gateway at the four entrances to the town; these and th houses are all of stone or brick with plaster an have rectangular window openings and dormer in the gabled roofs. Time seems to have stood sti since the seventeenth century in the peacefu Grande Rue of this little 'new town'.

The *Church* of the University of Paris, th *Sorbonne*, was commissioned by Richelieu an is Lemercier's best work (**761**). There are tw fine façades to the street and to the universit court. Both are of Roman design with two storey of superimposed orders, pediment and sid volutes linking the central portion to the aisl stages. The dome is impressive on the exterio and also inside where there is an interior she giving a different, more suitable silhouette withir

In 1646 Lemercier took over the completio of the *Church* of the *Val de Grâce* from Mansar designing one of the finest domes of Paris (**760** He also continued work on the Cour Carrée of th *Louvre*, repeating Lescot's wing on the north side

François Mansart (1598–1666) was a mor original architect than Lemercier and imparted t French architecture a national leadership whic gave it a certain independence from Rome Mansart had worked abroad and, in France, unde de Brosse. His originality and qualities as a architect were offset by his personality, whic was prickly and arrogant, losing him commission such as the Val de Grâce Church, where h

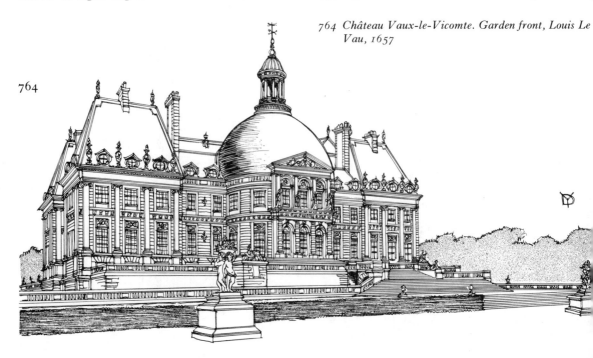

764 *Château Vaux-le-Vicomte. Garden front, Louis Le Vau, 1657*

764

carried out much of the work but which was left to Lemercier to complete and take credit for.

Mansart designed several *châteaux* of which the one at *Balleroy* in Normandy is typical and exists today. Begun in 1626, it is a tall, well-planned, dignified country house built in local yellow stone with white ashlar facings and surmounted by high gabled roofs. It has a tall central pavilion with cupola and lower side blocks. At the *Château de Blois*, Mansart planned large-scale alterations and enlargements, but only part was built. The central block (1635–8) and quadrant colonnades are in Baroque style, towards which Mansart veered in his middle years. His best surviving work, and that which shows his mature ideas is the *Château de Maisons* (1642–50) (called Maisons-Lafitte since its purchase by Jacques Lafitte in 1818), near Paris. The surrounding gardens and estate are now curtailed by villa building, but the château itself stands altered only in part by nineteenth century development. Although not extensive it is impressive since it is one free-standing block, with short wings, built in stone with high slate roofs. It is the only one of his châteaux where the interior decorative schemes survive, and its hall and staircase are of great beauty. Both are vaulted, articulated with orders and decorated with carving and sculpture.

Mansart designed a number of *churches* of which the best is the *Val de Grâce* in *Paris*. This he carried out up to the first cornice line before Lemercier was commissioned to complete the work (though the whole plan was Mansart's). The interior is Baroque, and similar to Il Gesù in Rome; though structurally like the Italian church it lacks its warmth and colour. The vaults are panelled and decorated all over but not painted; high relief Baroque sculpture breaks the guilloche banding. There is a large, well-fenestrated dome and, below, a vast Bernini-style baldacchino.

French Baroque Architecture: Le Vau and J. H. Mansart

The second half of the seventeenth century was a great period for building and the visual arts in France. Louis XIV presided over an autocratic régime and thus dictated firmly the style that state artists should follow; if they did not do so

they did not receive further commissions. This type of rigid autocracy in the arts has, in many ages as, for example, in the Soviet Union today, had a restrictive, devitalising effect. This is because the state so often is dictating the course for political reasons and without insight and knowledge as a patron of the arts. Louis XIV's policy no doubt lost him the services of some gifted artists, but he was a great builder and an enlightened, cultured patron. The result, for France, was a time of spectacular success in such arts. Jean Baptiste Colbert was the King's chief advisor from the 1660s; he controlled artistic appointments as well as others and employed artists prepared to give their best for the greatness of France. He appointed *Charles Le Brun* to be in charge of the artistic activities of the Academies of France and Le Brun brought

765 *Church of S. Louis des Invalides, Paris, J. H. Mansart, 1679–1756*

together teams of artists: sculptors, painters, architects, craftsmen of all kinds.

In architecture, the official style was more Baroque than hitherto: Louis XIV liked its positive, theatrical quality. It developed in France on more restrained lines than in Italy, with less ornamental exuberance but the curving, plastic massing on buildings was seen more in the 40 years after 1660 than at any other time in French architectural history.

The two architects who adapted themselves best to this style were Le Vau and Mansart. *Louis Le Vau* (1612–70) was, in contrast to François Mansart, a pleasant, able, vigorous man who carried out successfully a large number of commissions in a style very near to Italian Baroque. Like Wren and Adam in England, he gathered a team of fine craftsmen around him, who decorated his buildings, which are chiefly large houses, with work of high quality. In Paris he built several hôtels such as those of the Île de S. Louis. The *Hôtel Lambert** was the best known of these; it still exists, but has been restored extensively and denuded of all exterior decoration.

France's most Baroque building is the *Institut de France*, built by Le Vau from 1661 as the Collège des Quatres Nations. This was the building, standing on the banks of the Seine, with its drum and dome rising above the central mass, which with its contrastingly concave colonnades so impressed the young Wren on his short visit to France. It is a classic Baroque layout, but with refined French style handling of orders and decoration. The sweep of these concave curves from the terminal pavilions to the domed centrepiece is viewed best from the Pont des Arts opposite (PLATE 79). The interior of the *Church of S. Sulpice* is also by Le Vau (1655); it is Italian in its decorative handling (**762**).

Louis Le Vau's most outstanding work is the *Château de Vaux-le-Vicomte*, begun in 1657 (**764**). This was commissioned by Nicolas Fouquet; and is the finest house of its day in France, forerunner of Louis XIV's Versailles. It is not an immense house; it is a free-standing block with tall, corner pavilions, built on a parapeted platform surrounded by a moat which encircles the house and inner court. The garden front has a convexly curved, pedimented centre-piece and dome to accommodate the cupola-

* *This is attributed to Le Vau as stated on the façade plaque.*

covered oval saloon inside. The gardens, la[id] out by *Le Nôtre*, are extensive, with fountain[s] grottoes, cascades, all foreshadowing Versaille[s] The interior decoration of the château is ve[ry] fine, in stucco, sculpture and painting, main[ly] under the leadership of *Le Brun*. The saloon [is] the impressive room here; the lower part of t[he] walls is articulated with Composite pilaster[s] with doorways and windows between in eac[h] bay. The doorways are on the entrance si[de] leading from the hall and the windows face t[he] garden. Above the entablature is a further sta[ge] of rectangular windows separated by caryati[d] sculptured figures and ornamented entablatu[re] above. Only the painted ceiling by Le Brun [is] not there, but his designs are shown on an eas[el] in the saloon.

Fouquet, like Cardinal Wolsey at Hampto[n] Court in England, paid the price for creating to[o] magnificent a house while in the service of a[n] autocratic, acquisitive monarch. He entertaine[d] the King and Queen and all the Court at Vaux-le[-] Vicomte in 1661 to show off his château with [a] suitable banquet, ballet and firework displa[y] He was too successful. Within weeks he wa[s] arrested, imprisoned, his château and his tea[m] of artists taken over by royal decree.

J. H. Mansart was born Jules Hardoui[n] (1646–1708), but later took the family name of hi[s] great-uncle François Mansart. His work soo[n] showed him to be the successor to Le Vau rathe[r] than of his great-uncle and he became the mos[t] prolific, controversial and Baroque architect o[f] France. Apart from his extensive contributio[n] over long years at Versailles, his other work[s] include the Church of Les Invalides, famou[s] squares in Paris and the Château de Dampierr[e.]

The great structure of *Les Invalides* had bee[n] built 1670–7 by *Libéral Bruant* to house dis[-] abled soldiers.* It is a severe but impressiv[e] layout planned in courts. Bruant built a chape[l] but Louis XIV wanted a more impressive one Mansart was commissioned to design it. Th[e] result, the *Church of S. Louis des Invalides*, i[s] the most outstanding classical church of Paris more Baroque than any other, especially in it[s] stepped façade of grouped columns and it[s] superb dome (**765**). It is designed on Greek cros[s] plan, with circular chapels at the corners. Th[e] interior is very light and plain in contrast to th[e] gilded richness of the dome and drum.

* *The Royal Hospital, Chelsea was inspired by the ide[a] of Les Invalides. It was built by Sir Christopher Wre[n] 1682–92.*

Plate 79
Institut de France (Collège des Quatres Nations), Paris, begun 1662, Le Vau *Paris, France*

Plates 80 and 81
Fountain, Place Stanislas, Nancy, France, 1760

Mansart rebuilt the *Château de Dampierre* in the early 1680s. He designed a large central rectangular block with recessed, pedimented front and advancing side pavilions. There is an extensive forecourt flanked by arcaded ranges. It is a pleasant, well-designed but not pretentious country house.

The Paris squares of the *Place Vendôme* and the *Place des Victoires* were laid out 1685–1700. The latter has been much altered, but the Place Vendôme still gives some idea of Mansart's Baroque street architecture. Its houses were built 1702–20.

The Palace of Versailles

Like most of the great royal palaces of Europe, Versailles was not the work of one architect or artist and, because of succeeding alterations, it is not the masterpiece it might have been. Many English visitors are disappointed in the palace itself. It is so famous yet it lacks vitality in its monotonous horizontal lines. What is superb are specific interiors, like the Hall of Mirrors, and the fountain layouts nearer the palace. The architectural importance of Versailles is that it is principally the *chef d'oeuvre* of one king— Louis XIV—and that it became the prototype for subsequent palaces in all of Europe. Other countries did not copy Versailles but used it as a model: Spain, in Madrid and La Granja, Portugal, Queluz, Austria, Schönbrunn, Russia, the S. Petersburg Peterhof, etc. Only England has no Versailles.

Built over a long period from the early seventeenth century to the later eighteenth, Versailles is principally the work of three architects—*de Brosse, Le Vau* and *Jules Hardouin Mansart*. The palace, as a masterpiece, was probably created by Le Vau, but Mansart, on the King's insistence for greater accommodation space and impressiveness, made alterations and extensions which impaired the originality and character of Le Vau's palace. Mansart did not agree with what he had to do, but he was a court architect. *De Brosse* began Versailles for Louis XIII in 1624, *Le Vau* took over in 1661 under Louis XIV. In 1678, after Le Vau's death, *Mansart* was put in charge.

Today, the entrance front faces the vast Place d'Armes. From here, three roads radiate:

the centre one, which leads direct from the King's bedroom, goes to Paris, 20 kilometres away. Turning one's back on the Place d'Armes, one enters the wrought iron gateway into the Cour d'Honneur, in the centre of which is the equestrian statue of Louis XIV. From here one comes to the Cour Royale and the Cour de Marbre; the state rooms are here. The Cour de Marbre is the oldest part of the present palace, parts of it surviving, though altered, from the Louis XIII building. It is now mainly the work of Le Vau, who extended the palace in a long rectangular block, adding on each side of the original court, leaving this still open on the main front but enclosed and with a terrace on the garden façade.

Mansart, when commanded to extend the accommodation and create a new impressive room, filled in Le Vau's terrace on the first floor, creating the Galerie des Glaces here and added further wings at each side, providing an immense 600 metre frontage on the garden side, monotonous in its repetition of Le Vau's articulation and unbroken horizontal skyline; there are no curves and no gabled roofs (**768**).

Apart from the fine buildings which Mansart constructed—the chapel, the stables, the orangery and, on the other side of the park, the Grand Trianon—he also designed some magnificent interiors, many decorated by Le Brun: the Hall of Mirrors and the chapel for instance. It is these and the extensive garden and parkland layout which have a breathtaking quality at Versailles. André Le Nôtre laid out these from 1665; there is a gradual descent from the garden elevation of the palace by means of terraces, sculptured cascades and fountains to the circular Apollo fountain at the end of the vista a kilometre away.

Mansart's Church of the Invalides and his *Royal Chapel* at *Versailles* are probably the most Baroque structures in France and the last before the eighteenth century developed along different lines. The chapel was begun in 1689 and completed in 1710. It is a tall, two-storeyed building, the lower floor for the courtiers and the public and the first floor, connecting with the King's apartments, for the royal family and guests. The exterior is richly articulated, and inside are painted ceilings and apse and colonnades of Corinthian columns, with an ambulatory all round at both levels. It illustrates the limits to

PALACES AND CHÂTEAUX IN FRANCE

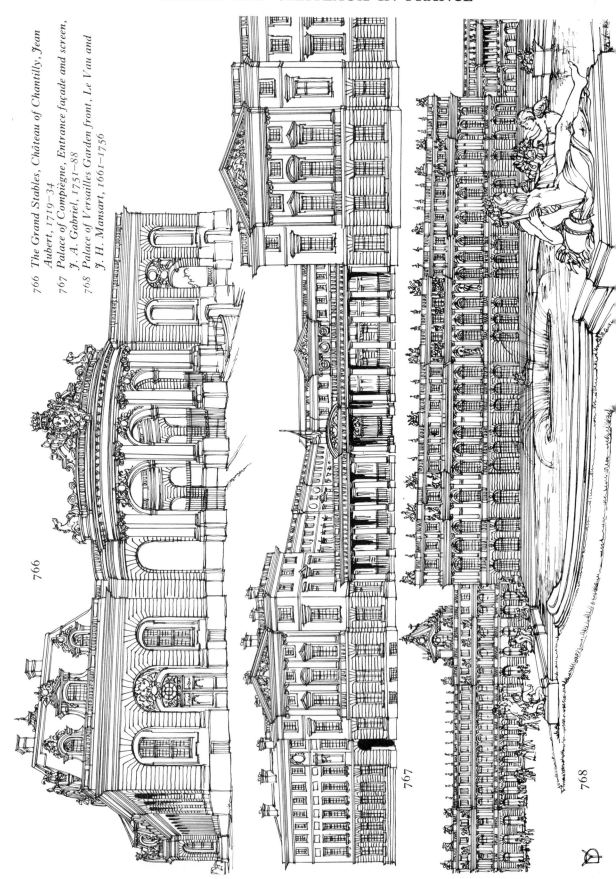

766 *The Grand Stables, Château of Chantilly, Jean Aubert, 1719–34*
767 *Palace of Compiègne, Entrance façade and screen, J. A. Gabriel, 1751–88*
768 *Palace of Versailles Garden front, Le Vau and J. H. Mansart, 1661–1756*

766

767

768

EIGHTEENTH CENTURY PLANNING AND DECORATION IN FRANCE

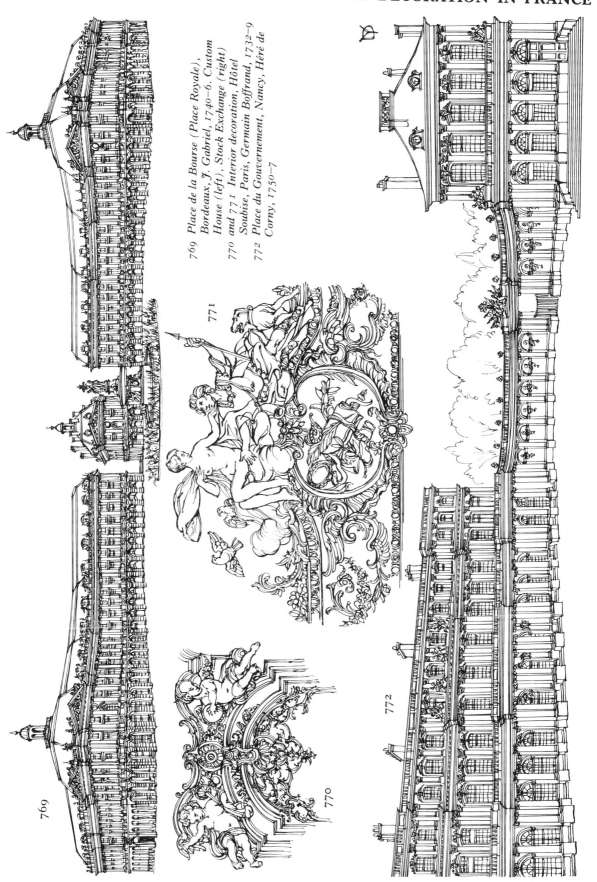

769 Place de la Bourse (Place Royale), Bordeaux, J. Gabriel, 1740–6. Custom House (left), Stock Exchange (right)

770 and 771 Interior decoration, Hôtel Soubise, Paris, Germain Boffrand, 1732–9

772 Place du Gouvernement, Nancy, Héré de Corny, 1750–7

which the French were prepared to go in their emulation of the Italian Baroque theme. There are few curves, entablatures and pediments are unbroken and rich colour is in the ceiling paintings only.

At this time also it was decided to complete the royal palace in Paris, the *Louvre*. Le Vau, who was building the Institut de France opposite, on the other side of the Seine, in the early 1660s, and who designed a bridge to connect the two buildings, was an obvious choice. He had already followed Lemercier in work on the east side of the Louvre in the 1650s. Colbert preferred to go elsewhere and at first asked François Mansart, then approached Italy. Bernini made several designs upon request, at first large-scale Baroque and later, in response to French preference, he designed an immense palace without curves. The plan was never fulfilled and Bernini did not trouble to hide his low opinion of French taste, architecture and craftmanship. Eventually the east façade of the Louvre was built 1667–70 as a three-man committee plan: *Le Vau*, *Le Brun* and *Charles Perrault*. There has always been discussion about who made the largest contribution. It is generally thought to have been Perrault—a writer, physician and amateur architect—and moreover, assistant to Colbert, perhaps the most important qualification of all.

Eighteenth Century French Classicism

Louis XIV died in 1715 after reigning for 72 years. His prolific, vigorous architect Jules Hardouin Mansart had died in 1708. A new style was ushered in, under Louis XV, which was in reaction from the majestic, imposing structures of the previous century. This style was Rococo and soon its popularity was spreading to other European countries, to Germany, Austria, Scandinavia, even to parts of Italy. The Italian dominance of the architectural and artistic world which had been unbroken since 1420 had passed and France became the leader of European fashion.

The style of Rococo is seen chiefly in the interiors and in decoration rather than structure. Exteriors were fairly plain, strictly classical and rather like work of the early seventeenth century. Inside, all was lightness, elegance and gaiety. Gone were the heavy gilding, the large painted schemes, the dark coloured marbling and the orders. Rococo

architecture tended to eschew the orders. The decoration which surrounded window and door openings and enclosed ceiling and wall panelling was in low relief and dainty with ribbons, scrolls, arabesques, wreaths of flowers, volutes, seaweed and shells replacing the Roman classical motifs. The term Rococo comes from the French *rocaille coquille*, the former appertaining to rocks or stones and the latter to shells. Colour schemes were also light, white being preferred for areas of wall with pastel shades and light gilding for decoration. Mirrors adorned the walls to increase the effect of light and to reflect the candelabra.

The chief architect of the years 1700–35 was *Robert de Cotte* (1656–1735) who built and decorated a number of Paris hôtels with his team of craftsmen. Another notable architect was *Jean Aubert* (d. 1741) who enlarged and redecorated the *Château de Chantilly* from 1719. He also built the fantastic stables there (**766**), the most impressive accommodation for horses in the world, and he redecorated in Rococo style Bullant's Petit Château adjoining the larger one (**678**). The main château was largely demolished in the Revolution and rebuilt in the later nineteenth century, but the stables remain.

Germain Boffrand (1667–1754) designed a number of hôtels and châteaux in these years. The latter include one at Lunéville and another at Craon. His best Rococo decoration is in the *Hôtel Soubise* in *Paris* (now the Archives Nationales). On the second floor, the Salon Ovale and the adjoining bedchamber were decorated by him in the years 1732–9. They are typical of high quality Rococo decoration and colouring (**770** and **771**).

Eighteenth Century Town Planning in France

In this century France took over the leadership from Italy in this field also. A number of schemes survive, still remarkably unspoilt and homogeneous. The most successful example is in the town centre at *Nancy*, which was mainly built in the years 1715–60. Boffrand had designed a royal palace when work was abandoned for political reasons. Later, in 1750, *Emmanuel Héré de Corny* carried out the grand scheme. He completed the palace (now the Palais Gouvernement) (**772**) and linked this by the tree-lined avenue, the *Place Carrière*, to the octagonal *Place Stanislas* (originally the Place Royale). A triumphal arch provides the entrance into the octagonal 'place' and on this side the buildings flanking it are only one storey high. At each lateral corner are beautiful sculptured fountains and iron gates (PLATES 80 and 81). The other three sides of the square are lined by taller buildings and opposite is the Hôtel de Ville. The whole scheme is in one style—rococo —one of the finest schemes of this type in Europe.

Others can still be seen in Lyons, Bordeaux, Rennes, Toulouse and Paris. The *Place Bellecour* (originally Louis le Grand) in Lyons was laid out by *Robert de Cotte* in 1713–38. It is an immense, tree-lined square which was unfortunately seriously damaged in the Revolution and was rebuilt in the early nineteenth century. The schemes in Rennes and Bordeaux are by the architect *Jacques-Jules Gabriel*, who was practising chiefly in the second half of the century by which time a reaction had set in from rococo and a return to a more severe and monumental classicism had become established. In Rennes, an extensive fire in 1720 made replanning necessary. Gabriel laid out the square round de Brosse's Palais de Justice and surrounded it with uniform classical buildings. Adjoining it, connected by an opening, he laid out another square containing the Hôtel de Ville and the theatre (1734–43).

Gabriel transformed the quayside area of the centre of *Bordeaux* in 1730–60 from a Medieval town to an eighteenth century classical one. This was his finest achievement, but the passage of years have not been kind to it. The *Place de la Bourse* (originally the Place Royale) is still there, with its fine buildings on an immense, shallow curve with a central fountain (**769**). Gabriel's nearby *Esplanade des Quinconces*, with its flanking Alleés (originally the Place de Bourgogne), still possesses its entrance triumphal arch, but it is a sad, neglected place today; the former glories have long since departed.

The *Place Capitole* in *Toulouse* is an impressive, homogeneous square with a 400 feet long town hall along one whole side. This was the work of a local architect *Guillaume Camnas* in 1750–3. It has an imposing, boldly articulated Ionic façade.

The eighteenth century building in the Place de la Concorde in Paris is the work of *Ange-Jacques Gabriel* (1698–1782) who was court architect to Louis XV from 1742 and made his

reputation in his designs for the *Petit Trianon* at *Versailles* (1762). Gabriel led the way in mid-century, together with architects like Jean Nicolas Servandoni (1695-1766) and Jacques Germain Soufflot (1714–80) away from rococo curves and to a return to symmetry, use of orders in a monumental manner and restraint in decoration. His Petit Trianon is a perfect, though small-scale example of this, while his *École Militaire* in the Champs de Mars in *Paris* (1751–68) is a larger, bolder one. These buildings have something in common with the contemporary English Palladians, but they are more vital, plastic and less stolidly monotonous.

It was decided in 1757 to develop a large square in *Paris* round the centrepiece of an equestrian statue of the King, to be called Place Louis XV (now *Place de la Concorde*). The square was to be laid out along the Seine with the Tuileries Gardens on its eastern side and the Champs Elysées on the west. The north/south axis would be formed by a new bridge on the south (not built till 1790, Pont de la Concorde) and a new road running northwards, the Rue Royale, which would terminate its vista with a church dedicated to S. Mary Magdalene (built in the early nineteenth century, the Madeleine). *Gabriel* built the two palaces in the square, flanking the southern end of the Rue Royale, 1761–70. They are twin palaces with Corinthian colonnades and pedimented end pavilions. The square itself was laid out to cover 810 by 565 square feet within the central space (though much larger to the building façades), and Louis XV's equestrian statue was placed in the centre. During the Revolution it was destroyed and the guillotine set up on the spot which today is marked by the obelisk.

Another fine work by Gabriel is the *Palace* at *Compiègne* which he rebuilt from the old château from 1751. This has similar qualities of monumentality and vitality to his Concorde palaces (**767**).

Eighteenth Century Churches

In France, as in England, this was not a great century for church building. The designs displayed the same tendencies as secular architecture; a return to symmetrical, monumental classicism. *Jean Servandoni* shows this quality in his façade for *S. Sulpice* in *Paris* (1733–45),

773 The Panthéon, Paris, J. G. Soufflot, 1757–90

while the *Madeleine Church* in *Besançon* (1766) is even more monumental. The outstanding church of the time is a pure example of neo-classicism: the *Panthéon* in *Paris*. It was begun in 1757, designed by *Jacques Germain Soufflot* and dedicated to the patron saint of Paris, S. Geneviève; the building became a Panthéon with the Revolution and great Frenchmen are buried here: Voltaire, Mirabeau, Rousseau, Victor Hugo and many more. It is a pure, cold, supremely classical building, based on its prototype and namesake in Rome but, being an eighteenth century structure, the dome is supported on a drum, which is carried on pendentives, in turn supported on the four crossing piers. The architect's idea was to provide a S. Peter's based on the Pantheon and to eclipse the other domes of Paris, notably that of Les Invalides. In fact,

Soufflot's dome is more like S. Paul's in London and, as a dome, much less fine than S. Peter's; it lacks the Baroque warmth of the original.

The exterior of the Panthéon is very plain. It is on Greek cross plan with four equal arms under a central dome. There is only one exterior feature, the great Corinthian portico. Apart from this, the one-storey exterior walls are plain, with only entablature and parapet.

The interior is in keeping, but a little less formal. There is still the same symmetry of an almost too perfect centrally planned church. All is light stone, apart from the wall paintings and sculptural groups. The wall paintings date from 1877 onwards. Some are very fine, particularly those by Puvis de Chavannes, representing the life of S. Geneviève. The Corinthian order is used throughout the building and a colonnade extends all round the church. Soufflot had intended columns to support the dome pendentives, but he died in 1780 before the church was finished and his successor, Rondelet, turned these into the present piers, making a more solid and serious centrepiece. The central drum with its rectangular windows creates a light interior. The cupola is coffered and the lantern painted as are also the pendentives. Over each arm of the church are coffered saucer domes (773).

England

Although English architects built in classical form during this whole period from 1625 onwards, it never became the style at which the English excelled as they had in Gothic. In the Middle Ages England created buildings which compete on equal terms with the work of any country in Europe, even France. Many fine classical buildings were produced also, especially in country houses and terrace architecture, but few examples compare to the Italian Baroque or the best of the French contribution. Apart from the work of certain outstanding, original architects such as Wren, Vanbrugh and Adam, English productions tended to be stolid, well designed and built but lacking in originality and vigour. S. Paul's Cathedral in London, the only great English classical church, cannot compare to the Medieval ones at Canterbury or York or Salisbury. It remains derivate and non-indigenous.

The English continued to create their best classical work in domestic architecture. In the years 1650–70 a more purely classical style of house was evolved from the Flemish-gabled brick buildings of the previous 30 years. This new type is often incorrectly termed a 'Wren-style house'; incorrectly because the style was developed before Wren was practising as an architect and because he designed little domestic work. The architects building this type of house, which was really a version of Dutch Palladian, were *John Webb* (1611–74), *Sir Roger Pratt* (1620–84) and *Hugh May* (1622–84). Pratt's finest house was *Coleshill*, Berkshire (1650–2), sadly destroyed by fire in 1952. It was a simple, symmetrical, rectangular block with no orders on the façade. Above the entablature was a hipped roof and tall chimney stacks. Hugh May's *Eltham Lodge, Kent* (1663–4) still exists. This is a brick and stone house with an Ionic giant order in the central portico. The house is strictly symmetrical and with a horizontal emphasis like Coleshill. Such designs were still Renaissance in character and Eltham Lodge closely resembles the Mauritshuis in the Hague (**691**).

Sir Christopher Wren (1632–1723)

To say that Wren was England's leading architect is an understatement. No other architect has ever held such a supreme position in England, while his reputation has remained uniformly high ever since his death. He was fortunate in that when he was beginning to practise great opportunities opened up before him, largely due to the Great Fire of London. He obtained commissions for civic and eccleciastical building as a result and he was early able to establish his reputation for original design. Other architects of genius such as Inigo Jones and Robert Adam had the ill-fortune to miss such opportunities.

Wren's work dominated the architecture in England of the second half of the seventeenth century. He was the vital force in all the important schemes, directing, influencing and controlling the design and execution of large projects such as the rebuilding of London after the fire of 1666 and the layouts at Hampton Court and Greenwich. His entry into the architectural profession was, by today's standards, unconventional. He was a brilliant young man, interested in many subjects but chiefly scientific matters. He was one of the founder members of the Royal Society and was described by John Evelyn, a fellow member, as 'that miracle of a youth'. Not till after he was 30 years old did he begin to practise architecture and, only a year or two later, was appointed principal architect to rebuild the City of London after its devastation. He designed a new layout on classical lines which was approved by King and Parliament, but foundered on the commercial city interests, which refused to yield up part of their rights for the general good of the city of London. Only an autocratic King or State like Louis XIV could have enforced acceptance of the scheme and, as a result, Londoners lost the chance of having riverside quays and walks by the Thames, as the Seine has, and broad boulevards with architectural vistas such as Paris achieved under Napoleon III. In the seventeenth century, London's city was re-created on the Medieval plan of narrow streets with tall, restricted, buildings. After two World Wars, the City's intransigence continues and we now have skyscraper blocks on the same ill-designed Medieval sites.

Despite the abandonment of his plan, Wren's part in the rebuilding was a large one. He was responsible for 53 churches and a new S. Paul's Cathedral. The *city churches* are, even in a career so full of great schemes and original architecture, an outstanding part of it. They show clearly his fertility of imagination and his ability to solve the most difficult problems of site, limitation of space and variation of style. None of the churches is quite like any other, although they are nearly all classical. Some have towers, some tall steeples and, one or two, cupolas. They are of stone and/or brick. Some are large and richly decorated, others are small and simple. The sites vary enormously and few are level or possess any parallel sides of equal length. The quality differs also; more money was available in some cases and Wren was more closely associated with the supervision of some than others. The most outstanding are *S. Bride*, Fleet Street (1680–1701), *S. Mary-le-Bow* (1671–80), *S. Stephen Walbrook* (1675–87), *S. Martin Ludgate* (1685–95), *S. Andrew-by-the-Wardrobe*, *S. Lawrence Jewry* (1670–86), *Christ Church*, Newgate Street (1704) and *S. Magnus the Martyr*, London Bridge (1670–1705). Most of these churches were damaged, some seriously, in the Second World War, but all are now fully restored.

Wren gathered a team of craftsmen to work for him in the churches and in other commissions. Some of the glass, carving, ironwork and painting is superb. *Grinling Gibbons* is the best known name among the carvers; he acquired a reputation for his naturalistic free-carved groups of flowers, birds and fruit. *Jean Tijou* was a French ornamental ironworker whose gates and grilles in the churches, S. Paul's and Hampton Court Palace are in the highest standard of craftsmanship (**780**). *Sir James Thornhill* carried out many of the great ceiling paintings as, for example, at Greenwich, Hampton Court Palace and in the dome of S. Paul's.

Wren made several designs for *S. Paul's Cathedral*, one of which, based on Greek cross plan, would have been much more original and impressive than the present building. It was rejected by the Church Commissioners (as Michelangelo's Greek cross plan for S. Peter's had been by the Pope, p. 316), because more space was desired and this would be provided by a Latin cross plan (**775**). The clergy in England also wanted a tall steeple. Wren compromised with a lofty, imposing dome and, by means of an inner brick cone to support the lantern and an inner shell to give a suitable shape to the interior cupola, solved the problems as other architects had done before him.

S. Paul's is one of a limited number of seventeenth century buildings in England to have Baroque characteristics. Wren often designed partly in Baroque manner; he had been most impressed on his only visit abroad by his study of Le Vau's Château de Vaux-le-Vicomte and the Institut de France in Paris (p. 382). The Baroque characteristics can be seen in the west front of S. Paul's, particularly in its western towers and in their juxtaposition with the dome. Due to the length of the church and the uphill slope of the ground from west to east, it is difficult to get a good view of the dome and towers from the west. Post-war building on Ludgate Hill has worsened this situation but this is more than compensated for in the fine view now available from the south-east; a view created by war-time bombing and fortunately preserved (**776**). S. Paul's is a straightforward example of a classical church built on Latin cross plan with dome and drum over the crossing. It is cool, clear, well-designed and built but lacking that spark, vitality

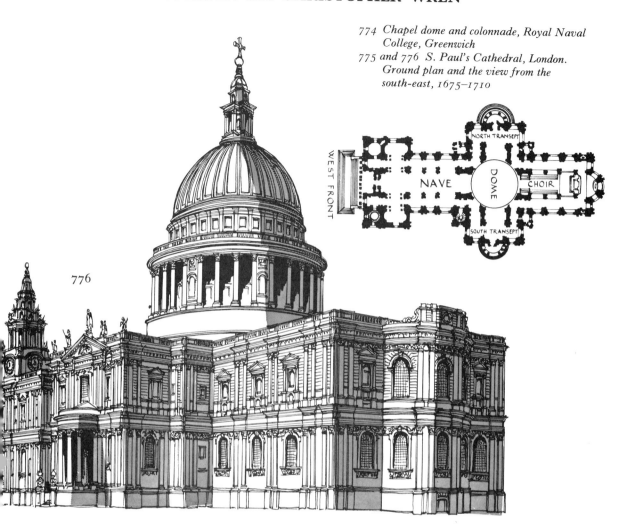

774 Chapel dome and colonnade, Royal Naval
College, Greenwich
775 and 776 S. Paul's Cathedral, London.
Ground plan and the view from the
south-east, 1675–1710

WEST FRONT

NORTH TRANSEPT

NAVE   DOME   CHOIR

SOUTH TRANSEPT

776

774

and warmth possessed by the great churches of the world in this style.

Much more of this quality is to be found in Wren's work at Hampton Court, Greenwich and the universities. *Hampton Court Palace* had been built in Tudor style for Henry VIII, but was in a neglected condition by the late seventeenth century. Wren was asked to enlarge the palace and he worked there from 1689–1701. He added new suites of fine rooms in buildings of brick and stone which, despite the very different styles, harmonise well with the Tudor brickwork. This is English classical domestic architecture at its best; a foreign style interpreted in indigenous materials by a great national architect, with no attempt to base the work on foreign models. Hampton Court Palace is unique; it could be seen in no other country but England.

The *Royal Hospital Greenwich* (now the Royal Naval College) was a larger project still. The Tudor Greenwich Palace was in decay. Inigo Jones' Queen's House remained and John Webb had begun a new palace but had only completed one block, the King Charles II building in 1669. The enterprise lapsed again. William and Mary decided to build here a naval counterpart to Chelsea Hospital (see Les Invalides, p. 382). Wren was put in charge of the project. He designed the whole scheme and carried out a fair part of it, though it was not finally completed till 1752. The layout is finest when viewed from the riverside as the visitor approaches the two main facing buildings with their colonnades and cupolas (which cover the hall and chapel respectively). At the end of the vista is Inigo Jones' Queen's House. The curving cupolas here contrast with the severe colonnades to illustrate Wren's version of Baroque (**774**).

Wren carried out a great deal of work at the two *universities*. At *Oxford* he designed the *Sheldonian Theatre* (1669) and, at *Cambridge*, *Pembroke College Chapel* (1663), *Emmanuel College* (1668) and, his best work here, the *library* at *Trinity College* (1676–84) (**783**).

Wren did not die until he was a very old man of 91, in 1723. Some years before this, styles in architecture had begun to change and new ideas were being put forward. The old master had lived too long. The work of the first quarter of the eighteenth century is more Baroque in general layout and massing of its architectural

forms than any seen in England before or since. Wren had used Baroque themes in the sense of 'movement', of curves, chiaroscuro and decoration. The architects of the early eighteenth century—*Vanbrugh, Hawksmoor, Archer*—were large-scale builders with a Baroque quality in their use of contrasting light and shade, mass against mass, though, in detail, the English version was unlike any other European Baroque; cube and rectangular blocks were more common than curves. Their contemporaries were divided, as have been their successors, in estimating their work. To study the creations of these architects is an experience which may excite and uplift or cause dismay and abhorrence; it cannot fail to make a strong impact.

Sir John Vanbrugh (1664–1726) had, like Archer and Hawksmoor, worked with Wren on a number of projects, at Greenwich, for example. When he designed his own great houses, he created grouped buildings of forceful, powerful masses, contrasting with one another, sometimes discordantly. This was quite different from his work under Wren. He was a master of handling masses of stone in a three-dimensional way, at creating exciting patterns in light and shade in settings of grandeur. His Flemish ancestry shows in his Baroque treatment of classical form, in the robustness of his porticoes, towers and wall articulation. His three famous houses are *Seaton Delaval* and *Castle Howard* in the north of England and *Blenheim Palace* near Oxford. All built in the early eighteenth century, they are large and imposing (**777**). Blenheim, for instance, has an entrance frontage of 856 feet, comprising an immense central block with portico and wings embracing a great court. These houses were the last of such gigantic residences, which became obsolete because of their size and cost.

Much of Archer's and Hawksmoor's work was ecclesiastical. *Thomas Archer's* (1668–1743) Baroque style was reminiscent of Wren's, as at the *Church of S. Paul, Deptford* (1730), but *S. John's Church, Westminster* (1721–8) was much weightier; this, his best and most typical work, was gutted during the war, but has been rebuilt. His *Birmingham Cathedral* (1709–25) is especially Baroque in its tower and lantern. *Nicholas Hawksmoor's* (1661–1736) designs, in church and university, were as controversial and forceful as Vanbrugh's. His best known churches are in the

777

778

779

780

7 *Entrance hall, Castle Howard, Yorkshire,*
  Vanbrugh, 1696–1712
8 *S. Mary-le-Strand, London, Gibbs, 1719*
9 *Ceiling, 20, Portman Square, London,*
  Adam, 1772–7
0 *Hampton Court Palace, iron screen, Jean*
  Tijou

781 Queen's College, Oxford, Hawksmoor, 1709–59
782 Camden Crescent, Bath, Jelly, 1788
783 Trinity College Library, Cambridge, Wren, 1676–84

781

782

783

East End of London and were damaged in the Second World War. *S. Mary Woolnoth* in the City survives to show his style clearly. He is also noted for his work at *All Souls' College, Oxford* (a Baroque Medievalism) and *Queen's College* nearby (**781**). Hawksmoor's architecture is highly original, especially his church steeples which are uncompromising and extremely bold.

Baroque architecture in England had been a foreign implant, duly anglicised. In the 1720s it died and was replaced by something much more English: *Palladianism*. The basis of this movement was also foreign—Andrea Palladio (p. 319) —but became, partly because it derived equally from the architecture of Inigo Jones (p. 334), particularly English. Palladian architecture in

784 *The hall, Houghton Hall, Norfolk, Colen Campbell, c. 1730*

784

England was the leading style from 1720–60; its chief patron, also an architect, was *Lord Burlington* and its leading architects *Colen Campbell* (d. 1729) and *William Kent* (1685–1748). The style developed into something neither Palladio nor Inigo Jones. It was more rigid and prescribed.

The outstanding contribution of the Palladian school was in country house building. The exterior of these houses was generally plain and monumental, almost severe. A porticoed central block would be connected to side pavilions by low galleries and colonnades. The whole scheme is fully symmetrical with careful attention to Roman classical proportion, orders and detail (as enunciated by Palladio). The houses appear to be four-square, solid and indisputably English. What makes them into masterpieces, on the exterior, is the siting and surroundings, for the parkland and gardens are in contrast and thus complementary to the architecture. The Palladian house was carefully set on rising ground, at the foot of a vista or by a stream or lake. The peculiarly English park was then laid out round it, with sweeping lawns, great spreading trees and natural landscape, decorated by classical temples and sculpture. Lancelot (Capability) Brown became famous as the chief exponent of this type of landscaping. He made lakes from streams and moved whole hillsides to where he needed them. This treatment is indigenous, very different from French or Italian gardens based on the geometrical formalities of Versailles. It was envied and copied later by other European nations, notably by Catherine the Great of Russia.

Typical of the large Palladian house are two examples in Norfolk: *Holkham Hall* designed by *William Kent* from 1734 and *Houghton Hall* by *Colen Campbell* (c. 1730) (**784**). The interiors are, in contrast to the plainness of the outside, masterpieces of Roman décor, or rather Roman orders and ornament adapted to the needs of English country house saloons, halls and dining rooms. The classical decoration is correct in proportion and handling; it is strong, three-dimensional and used in woodcarving as on doorcases and in stucco on ceilings and walls. There is nothing of the rococo delicacy in such interiors. Gilt and colours are used, though ceilings often have white grounds. Mahogany is employed for furniture and general woodwork and marble for chimney-pieces. At Holkham the hall and saloon are especially impressive. The Palladians also designed some houses more faithfully to Palladio's originals. Two examples are based on the Villa Capra (the Rotonda) near Vicenza (p. 321). Lord Burlington's *Chiswick House* is one of these; a symmetrical block surmounted by a central cupola.

James Gibbs (1682–1754) was an architect whose work is neither fully Baroque nor Palladian; it is individually 'Gibbs', but with an affinity to Wren. This shows especially in his church steeples, though his years working in Rome are also reflected in these buildings. Churches like *S. Mary-le-Strand* (**778**) (1714–17) and *S. Martin-in-the-Fields* (1722), both in London, are among his best work; they had a great influence on other architects, especially in the U.S.A. Gibbs carried out much university work; his *Senate House* and his *Fellows' Building* at *King's College*, both at *Cambridge*, are fine examples of his meticulous classical detail and sure instinct for taste and proportion.

The Classical Revival: 1760–1800

It was in these years that Greek classical architecture was discovered and studied. Travellers both professional architects and antiquarians as well as aristocratic young men on their 'Grand Tour', were setting out from all over Western Europe to see at first hand the masterpieces of the classical past. They now went further afield, not just to France and Italy as before but to Greece, Dalmatia, Egypt, Syria. Some returned travellers became ardent Greek enthusiasts, others retained a preference for Roman forms. In England, as in other countries, a 'battle of the styles' developed and some architects designed in only one or the other.

The two chief architects of these years were exactly contemporary, both Scottish, though in temperament and approach to architecture completely different from one another. *Sir William Chambers* (1723–96) was a close adherent to the Palladian tradition and designed most of his buildings in strictly Roman classical form. His work was of the highest standard, with fine proportion and an exacting excellence of detail and finish. He was the King's favourite architect and the Surveyor General, and thus in charge of all important building schemes. Among the public works of the time, Chambers was responsible for the new *Somerset House*, built on the site of the old palace. It was a difficult commission, being an unusual site: 800 feet on the river façade and only 135 feet on the north front in the Strand. There was then no embankment and the river elevation would be lapped by water, so Chambers built a masonry platform above tide level to support warehouses and offices and fronted it by a rusticated masonry arcade pierced by arches. The façade was divided into three blocks, with a central archway and two side watergates, so that the tide was controlled by the waters' entry into these archways. Contemporary drawings show that the building must have then been much more impressive as much of the height is now lost by the construction of the modern roadway and embankment. This is still one of London's finest waterfront monuments, of Portland stone, built and finished in Roman classical design.

In contrast to Chambers the Roman traditionalist, *Robert Adam* (1728–92) was an innovator, a seeker after new ideas and designs. In the years 1760–90, he carried out a vast quantity of work mostly in domestic architecture and drew his inspiration from a wide variety of sources. Like Wren in his city church design, no two houses by Adam are alike. He drew from sources such as Roman Imperial palaces or baths, Greek temples of Athens or Asia Minor, villas from Herculaneum. Also like Wren, he used such sources and then stamped his own personal interpretation upon them. Unlike the Palladians, he followed no rigid rule system. He abhorred such practice,

785 The dining room, Syon House, Middlesex, Adam, 1761–70

785

considering it limiting to an artist's creative ability. He adapted the older classical forms and interpreted them, so that the result was always clearly and recognisably Adam but also, despite his amendments, had more of the spirit of the original than Palladian architecture ever approached of Palladio.

Some of Adam's finest houses show these qualities clearly. *Syon House*, near London (from 1762) and *Kedleston Hall*, Derbyshire (1758–68) illustrate his palatial Roman style. There is rich colour, fine coloured and white marbles, gilt decoration with stucco, and layouts influenced by the great Roman halls and baths. At Syon these can be seen in the Hall, the ante-room (PLATE 83) and the dining room (**785**), while at Kedleston the hall and saloon are monumental master-pieces. At *Osterley*, Middlesex and the library at *Kenwood* the decoration is more delicate with the motifs nearer Greek origins: slenderer columns and pilasters and ceilings in pastel shades and white with arabesques in stucco. In the 1770s Adam's decorative work became very low relief and finespun, almost filigree, a tendency of which his ceiling in the music room in the *Portman Square* house in London is a classic example (**779**).

Like Wren, Adam had some fine craftsmen working for him, including the painters *Angelica Kauffmann* and her husband *Antonio Zucchi*, the stuccoist *Joseph Rose* and the sculptor and carver *Joseph Wilton*. The ceiling paintings, stucco work, metalwork, carving and furniture in the Adam houses are, in many cases, works of art in their own right. Adam was a perfectionist; he demanded and obtained high standards.

Terrace Architecture

As in France and Italy, a number of planning schemes were initiated, especially in the eighteenth century. Since the days of Inigo Jones London had been laid out in squares, but the buildings differed from one another. From the eighteenth century, terraces, crescents and whole squares were designed as an architectural unit, with façades alike or in keeping with their neighbours. The earliest developments were in *Bath* where *John Wood*, and his son of the same name, built first *Queen Square* (1728–35), then the *Circus* (1754)—a complete circle of 33

identical houses with superimposed orders over three storeys—and, most impressive of all, the *Royal Crescent* (1765–75). This is an immense curving terrace of 30 houses separated by a giant Ionic order of 114 columns. It is built on a hillside overlooking the city. Other schemes were begun in *Bristol, Cheltenham* and *Brighton* (**782**).

One of the most magnificent and enterprising town planning schemes was the *Adelphi* fronting the river Thames in *London*, near Westminster. This was the work of *Robert Adam* and his brothers, and consisted of a row of houses in the form of Roman Imperial palace architecture high on a terrace platform above the river; the land had previously been a muddy backwater. Almost the whole scheme was demolished unnecessarily in 1937. Adam also designed two city squares in the last years of his life. He did not live to see them built, and both have been altered though some complete elevations remain largely as he designed them: *Fitzroy Square, London* (east and south side) and *Charlotte Square, Edinburgh* (north side).

The eighteenth century in England was a time of high architectural standards in building design and detail. Of the many good architects who created fine buildings in different versions of classicism, as well as a touch of sham Gothic or Indian or Chinese, were *Thomas Leverton, Henry Holland, George Dance II, Sir Robert Taylor* and *James Wyatt*.

The Iberian Peninsula: Spain

The Renaissance came late to Spain and lasted well into the seventeenth century. Most of the architecture between 1670 and 1780 is Baroque, then in the second half of the eighteenth century came some more formal neo-classicism. Spanish Baroque reflects, like Spanish Gothic, the mixed heritage of the peninsula. There are strong influences from Italian Baroque, more limited ones from France, and still the fundamental underlying Moorish and Mujédar art forms which appear in the new designs as much as they had in the Medieval. The warm-blooded vitality, the lack of control and restraint, the plastic approach which had been seen in late Gothic and Renaissance plateresque architecture found most complete expression in the Baroque style. It was made to measure for Spanish exuberance and

786

788

787

789

790

786 *Plaza Mayor, Salamanca. (Town Hall centre), Alberto de Churriguera, 1729–40*
787 *and* 788 *Details of the Palace of the Marqués de Dos Aguas, Valencia, 1740–4*
789 *Façade, the Cartuja Church at Jerez de la Frontera, 1667*
790 *Façade, the University, Valladolid. Begun 1715, Diego and Narciso Tomé*

fanaticism, spilling out in the Counter Reformation. Not all Spanish Baroque architecture is uncontrolled and frenzied; this type of work is often called Churrigueresque. Some Baroque work, especially in the seventeenth century and the later eighteenth is much more restrained and formal. In general, though, Spanish Baroque is original, emotional and free. It does not resemble French, English or German Baroque at all. It is fiercely individual and Latin.

In the second half of the seventeenth century the Spanish love of decoration began to assert itself in reaction from Herrera's plain Renaissance architecture and found expression in early Baroque experiments. Much of Spain at this time was economically unsettled and poorly developed, the east and north-east regions flourishing most because of close trade links with the Neapolitan kingdom in Italy. In this region is the *Church* of *S. Catalina* in *Valencia* with its hexagonal tower (1688–1705) and the *Cathedral* of *La Seo* in *Zaragoza*. This is a Medieval church, its interior mainly reconstructed in the sixteenth century in late Gothic and early Renaissance style, but the façade is Baroque with a tower of 1682–90 designed by the Italian *Giovanni Battista Contini*.

In the south the façade of *Granada Cathedral* was designed by *Alonso Cano* (1601–67) and built after his death. This is a massive west front, Baroque in its heaviness but without orders and with little decoration. The most beautiful example of Spanish early Baroque workmanship can be seen in the façade added to the Medieval *Church* of the *Carthusian Monastery* (Cartuja) at *Jerez de la Frontera* (**789**). Dating from 1667, by an unknown architect, the façade combines a classic Baroque structure on Italian lines with southern Spanish decorative forms.

The Eighteenth Century

The term *Churrigueresque* is taken from the family of four brothers and three sons of de Churriguera who worked largely in Castile in the late seventeenth and early eighteenth century. *José de Churriguera* (1650–1725), head of the family, was chiefly a carver who specialised in designing the ornate, complex retablos essential to all Spanish churches. He worked chiefly in Salamanca, as did several members of the family

(all carvers and architects), transforming college churches and the New Cathedral with Baroque decoration inside and outside the building. There is irony in the fact that José's name became a synonym for all that is most extravagant in Spanish Baroque, for his own work, and that of several of his relatives, was restrained, even Herreran on occasions.

Alberto de Churriguera (1676–1750), a younger brother and the most talented member of the family, laid out the *Plaza Mayor* at *Salamanca* (**786**) with Andres García de Quiñones. This is a magnificent town planning scheme, a courtyard layout and, like that at Madrid (**730**) was closed to traffic by the four continuous sides of houses and arcades. Unlike Madrid, it is no longer traffic-free. Alberto also completed the façade of *Valladolid Cathedral* (1729) by adding the upper storey to the central portal. This is restrained, in keeping with yet a foil to Herrera's façade (p. 358), having plain pilasters and a pediment and side scrolls.

The Churrigueresque style, which was developed chiefly by other architects, is seen primarily in portal and frontispiece design on building exterior or retablo within. It is characterised by barley sugar columns, broken and arched pediments and entablatures, pilasters with more than one capital and a quantity of ornament in the form of flowers, medallions, figures, fruit and drapery.

Working in central Spain were two of the chief exponents of the style: *Pedro de Ribera* (Rivera) (c. 1683–1742) and Narciso Tomé. De Ribera was the principal architect to Madrid, where most of his work was done, though, unfortunately, not a great deal has survived unaltered. Among his churches still exist *Nuestra Señora de Montserrat* (1720) and *S. José*. The façade of the former is impressive, built in brick with stone facings. There is a Baroque tower and steeple. Inside, the church is not finished and is fairly plain. His centrepiece to the *Hospicio San Fernando* (1722–9) is typical Churrigueresque. Built in three diminishing stages, it is a riot of exuberant decoration, ebbing and flowing, yet controlled (PLATE 85). His *Toledo Bridge* (1723–4) is monumental; it has a richly sculptured shrine on each side of the centre arch.

Narciso Tomé worked under José de Churriguera at Salamanca, then carried out the decoration of the *University façade* at *Valladolid* with

Plate 82
Carved wood altar
rail detail. Church of
S. Michael, Louvain,
Belgium, 1650–6
Plate 83
Wall panel, ante
room, Syon House,
England, from 1762,
Robert Adam.
Stuccowork Joseph
Rose

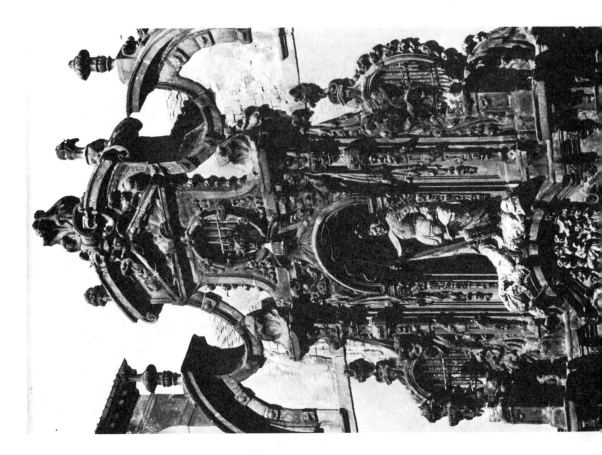

Plate 84
Gable detail, Palacio Mateus, Vila Real, Portugal. Early
18th century
Plate 85
Doorway detail, Hospicio de San Fernando, Madrid,
Spain. 1722, Pedro de Ribera

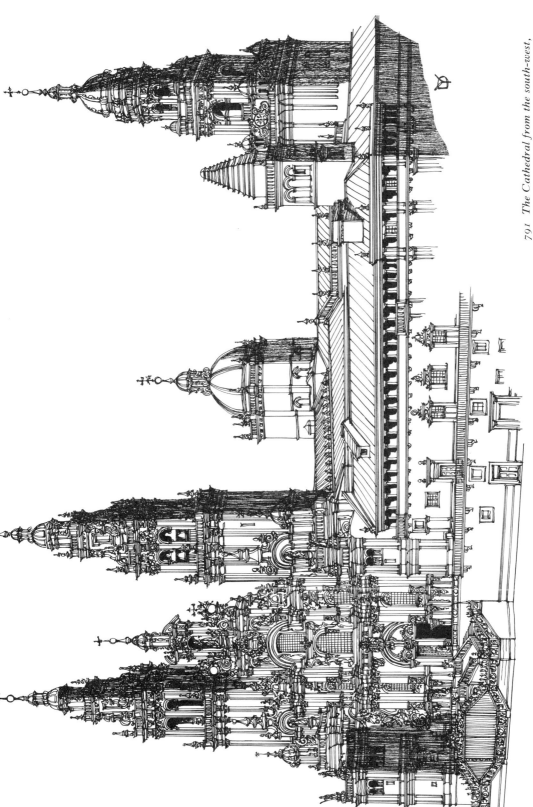

791 *The Cathedral from the south-west, Santiago de Compostela, Spain. Baroque towers and façade, Fernando Casas y Nuova, 1738–49*

BAROQUE CATHEDRALS IN SPAIN

792 *Façade, Valencia Cathedral, Rudolf and Vergara,
    1703*
793 *Façade, Murcia Cathedral, Jaimé Bort y Meliá,
    1740–54*
794 *El Pilar, Zaragoza (viewed from the river bridge t*
    the north-east). From 1677, Francisco de Herrera
    from 1750, Ventura Rodriguez

his brother Diego (**790**). This has a tall frontispiece decorated like a retablo. In 1721 Narciso Tomé was made the principal architect to *Toledo Cathedral* where he created the most fantastic monument to Churrigueresque art, the *Transparente*, behind the high altar (1732). This is a masterpiece of sculpture and painting, the two blending together as a carefully contrived theatrical creation. Tomé produced his special lighting effects by cutting a circular hole in one bay of the Gothic quadripartite vault in the eastern ambulatory, raising the ceiling height to permit a large plain glass window through which the easterly sun shines. The window opening is then framed with Baroque sculpture and the whole area blends in paint and stucco. As the light shines through, the whole sculptural tableau of the Transparente opposite comes to life; the brilliant sun on the upper part of cherubims, a lesser light on the Last Supper below, then it gradually diminishes as the eye descends past the golden rays radiating from the centre among the angels to the Virgin and Child at the bottom of the group. In a westerly light the whole tableau becomes dead and flat.

Contemporary with the Churrigueresque school in Castile was the Seville school led by the Figueroa family and, in the Granada area, the richly ornamental work of Hurtado Izquierdo. *Leonardo de Figueroa* (c. 1650-1730) worked in *Seville* with his two sons and nephew. They created a number of Baroque churches, very typical of the region and displaying the traditional Mujédar qualities of decoration. The area is stoneless, so brick was widely used, faced with brilliantly coloured ceramic tiling, especially on towers and cupolas. The *Church of S. Pablo* is like this, a Mujédar building rebuilt by Figueroa. The *Church of S. Luis* is more traditionally Italian Baroque, with its Greek cross plan and deep entrance narthex, but it has the Spanish Baroque decorative features of barley sugar columns, broken entablatures and rich decoration, as well as a brightly coloured tiled façade. Figueroa also built the *Seminary of S. Telmo* here which has an impressive frontispiece.

Francisco Hurtado Izquierdo (1669-1725) was the leading architect in the Granada area. Here, the strongest influence, even in the eighteenth century, was still Moorish. In the *Cartuja* at *Granada*, Izquierdo designed a *sacristy* (1713) based on the sumptuous richness of the Alhambra interiors, using the Arabic motifs and creating a masterpiece of flowing, vibrant richness in his all-over decoration. The walls are gleaming white marble, broken frequently with fantastically decorated pilasters and entablature. The ceiling is also riotously decorated and has a painted oval dome over the altar as well as painted pendentives. The materials used for ornamentation are all colourful and glowing: marbles, tortoiseshell, ivory, mother-of-pearl. It is extravagant, restless, beautiful and supreme Churrigueresque.

Izquierdo also designed the *Transparente* for the Monastery Church of *El Paular* (near Madrid) in 1718. This is in the tiny Capilla de Tabernáculo behind the high altar retablo screen. It is Baroque run riot and of much coarser, poorer workmanship than the sacristy at Granada. However, it was built by Izquierdo's pupils and it is at the moment in poor condition.

There is a considerable quantity of Baroque work in the *cathedrals* of Spain especially those in the south and primarily in façades added to Medieval or Renaissance buildings. The most impressive large-scale example, the *Cathedral of Santiago de Compostela* in north-west Spain, is also the most successful blending of a Romanesque masterpiece with a Baroque one. The interior is still almost entirely Romanesque (**319**) as is the famous Portico de la Gloria. The cathedral has simply been clothed almost all over with a Baroque dress, rich and articulated; the combination of the two styles is outstanding. The façade, with its lofty, multi-stage frontispiece and flanking western towers was begun in 1738 by *Fernando Casas y Nuova* and it encloses the Portico de la Gloria, which is now a second entrance inside the Baroque one (**791**). Work had begun before this on the south transept and the north side was not completed till after 1770 and in more neo-classical form. The whole cathedral, exterior and interior, is built in the local grey granite, lichen-covered from the damp Atlantic atmosphere. This aids the harmonising of the two differing architectural styles, as does the unusual verticality of the Baroque façade.

Baroque fronts added to southern cathedrals include those at Jaén and Murcia. The *Jaén west front* is also of vertical design. Built 1667-88, it has twin western towers and a strongly articulated centrepiece. *Murcia Cathedral* façade was added 1740–54. This is much more Baroque and southern with a horizontal emphasis, a richly sculptured screen and central broad niche (**793**).

The façade of *Valencia Cathedral* was added in 1713 to front the Gothic building by *Conrad Rudolf*, the Austrian architect. The decoration here is Spanish but the architecture is much more in the style of Borromini. The design problem was difficult as the cathedral façade is squeezed in between the Miguelete tower and the chapter house. The façade had to be narrow and tall but the architect has created such a Baroque impression of movement with his undulating curved planes that it gives the feeling of being about to burst out of the restriction of the flanking buildings (**792**).

Cádiz is the only completely Baroque *Cathedral* in Spain. Built on the edge of the harbour which juts out into the south Atlantic, it was begun in 1722 but not completed till 1853. The architect was *Vincente Acero* who had earlier designed the façade at Guadix Cathedral. The cathedral at Cádiz is a remarkable structure, large, monumental and very Baroque, especially in the interior massing and blending of the curved planes. The Corinthian order is used with grouped columns and ornamented entablatures broken forward. An ambulatory extends all round the nave, transepts and choir, giving a wide façade, which is extended further by the towers flanking the aisles. There is a dome and drum over the crossing and the sanctuary has a rotunda and surrounding chapels.

Eighteenth Century Palaces

The handling of these buildings was, in general, more restrained than the churches. Partly this was due to foreign influence. The two royal palaces, in Madrid and La Granja, were designed by Italians and some of the interior decoration was also by foreign artists, Tiepolo, for example. In 1734 the old fortress type of *palace* in *Madrid* was destroyed by fire. The king commissioned *Filippo Juvara* (p. 376) to design a new one. Juvara's plan was for a large and complex structure, with several courts and long façades. By the time the king had accepted the plans, Juvara had died. The successor he had recommended was commissioned to build the palace.

This was *Giovanni Battista Sacchetti* from Turin who, on request, constructed a smaller palace but kept faithfully to Juvara's designs. The palace is still large. It is built round one great court (**795**) and has long façades reminiscent of Caserta. There is a horizontal emphasis in the balustrade, entablature and two storeys spanned by a giant order of Doric pilasters, interrupted by Ionic engaged columns on the main pavilions. The whole stands on a rusticated basement. There are several fine apartments inside the palace, especially the throne room with its Tiepolo ceiling representing the greatness of the Spanish monarchy, its gilt and red wall decoration and rococo furniture. There is also the interesting small porcelain room with its entire walls and ceiling covered in glazed ceramics in white and green with gilt decoration: *putti*, portraits, medallions. This rich ornamentation was made at the royal porcelain factory. The staircase is based on that at Caserta. The decorative scheme is on white marble and stucco with gilt and coloured marble enrichment; above is a painted ceiling. It is finely proportioned Baroque but less monumental than Caserta.

The mountain palace retreat of S. Ildefonso, called *La Granja*, was built 1721–3 to a traditional Spanish fortress design by *Teodore Ardemans*, of German origin. In 1735 the king decided to enlarge and rebuild parts of the palace and commissioned Juvara who, with Sacchetti, turned it into a Spanish Baroque version of Versailles. The garden front of the palace is essentially Italianate, all gleaming white and pale pink, with giant pilasters and Baroque sculptural decoration (**796**). The setting is magnificent, carefully chosen in a sheltered hollow high in the range of the Guadarrama mountains towards Segovia. The gardens are extensive, laid out by the Frenchman *Étienne Boutelon*, on classic Versailles pattern with geometrical design and avenues radiating from the palace in different directions, leading to cascades descending from the hills and sculptural groups and fountains at all vista points. Much of the sculpture is also French; the best is by *René Carlier* (PLATE 86). The garden front of the palace looks out on the most impressive vista, extending uphill via cascades, steps and fountains into the far distance.

The *Royal Palace* at *Aranjuez*, south of Madrid, is less impressive. Built by Herrera (p. 358), it

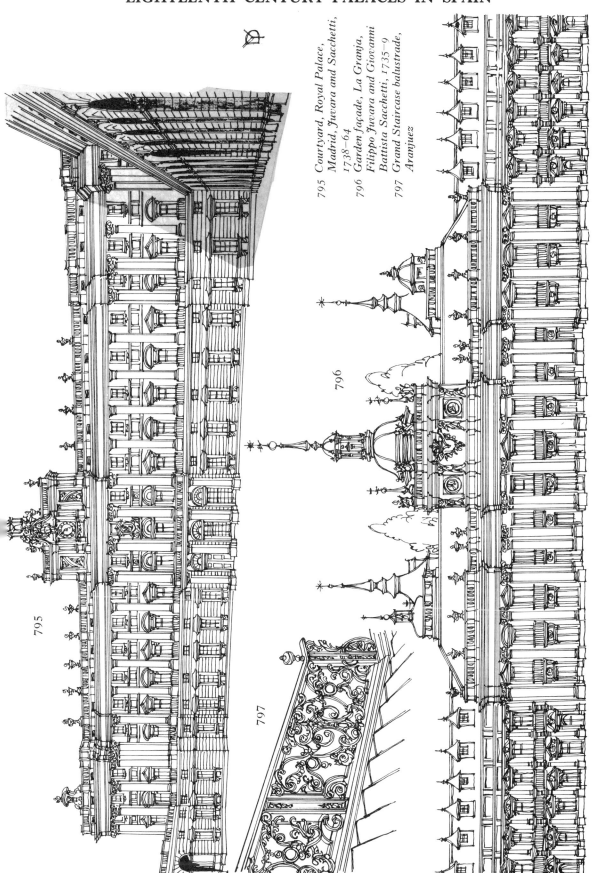

795 Courtyard, Royal Palace,
Madrid, Juvara and Sacchetti,
1738–64
796 Garden façade, La Granja,
Filippo Juvara and Giovanni
Battista Sacchetti, 1735–9
797 Grand Staircase balustrade,
Aranjuez

795

796

797

was enlarged and partly rebuilt in two periods in the eighteenth century: 1715–48 and in the 1770s. It now has a very large entrance court lined on three sides by classical ranges. Of the interior, the staircase is the finest part. The single central flight branches into two at the half-landing and these lead to the first floor. The steps are white marble and the balustrade decorative iron (797).

Among town palaces, the simple *Virreina Palace* in *Barcelona* (1722) was designed by *Manuel Arat*. The street façade is well pro-portioned and has ornament restricted to window frame cresting and balustrade vases. In complete contrast is the *Palace* of the *Marqués de Dos Aguas* in *Valencia*. This is a simple three-storey block building, but it is adorned in lively manner with rococo decoration round the windows and parapet. The painter *Hipólito Rovira y Brocandel* adorned the palace in 1740–4 with frescoes (which have now disappeared) over the walls and with the amazing entrance portal which was carved in white alabaster by *Ignacio Vergara*. This is carried out in a riotous use of rococo forms. The eye follows the nude figures on each side of the doorway, contorted and intertwined with pitchers, lions, palm trees and drapery up to the central figure of the Virgin and Child in a niche above, surrounded by further contortions and twirlings of figures, clouds, sun rays and plants (787 and 788).

Spanish Neo-classical Architecture

In the last decades of the eighteenth century there was a gradual abandonment of Baroque designs in favour of a return to a more severely pure classical structure with less decoration. One of the leaders of this movement was *Ventura Rodriguez* (1717–85). His earlier work, contributing with others on the Royal Palace in Madrid and in the design of his *Church of S. Marcos* in *Madrid* (1749–53) is partly Baroque. The church façade is severely plain, but has concavely curving side wings. Inside, it is Baroque. There is an oval dome over the crossing, painted and caissoned in panels, and an oval lantern above. The nave below is also oval and the church is aligned with the altar on the western side. It is a church closely dependent on Bernini's S. Andrea al Quirinale (p. 373).

The second *Cathedral of Zaragoza, Nuestra Señora del Pilar*, is an immense building. It was designed by Francisco de Herrera in 1677 and intended to be Baroque throughout. *Ventura Rodriguez* took over the work at the cathedral from 1753–66 and clothed the interior in more neo-classical form. It is dark inside as there are no windows in the aisle walls, only circular ones in the nave wall above the entablature which light the painted saucer domes but little else. There are also windows in the lantern of the dome over the crossing, but these too are few and small. The whole interior is treated with Corinthian piers and pilasters. The exterior is more satis-factory and is most impressive, especially when viewed from the bridge over the Ebro (794). There are four great corner towers with Baroque steeples and eight domes with lanterns. It is a Baroque design tempered with the neo-classical.

More purely and severely classical are the façades of Vich and Lugo Cathedrals. *José Morato* added a plain, neo-classical façade to *Vich Cathedral* in 1780–1803. This has only one decorative feature: the two-stage entrance portal. The Doric order is used throughout. The façade at *Lugo* was built 1769–84 by *Julian Sánchez Bort*. It is larger and less severe, with the Com-posite Order used across the main front. There is a central pediment and lofty towers which were completed in 1830.

Portugal

Portuguese architecture followed a similar pattern to Spanish in these years. There was not a great deal of building in the seventeenth century and most of that which survives dates from the later decades. At this time the Portuguese were experi-menting with the Baroque style which they developed fully by 1740. The buildings were simple in structure but, like the Spanish, richly decorated. The work is also free and exuberant but lighter and gayer than Spanish counterparts. The façade of *Alcobaça Abbey Church* dates from these years (797), as does the redecora-tion of the Gothic Church of *São Francisco* in *Oporto*. On the exterior a double-stage entrance portal has been added, with barley sugar columns, while the rather later interior is a riot of Baroque decoration—almost every inch is covered in gilded enrichment. The high altar is unbelievably

CLASSICAL CHURCHES IN PORTUGAL

798 *Basilica da Estrêla, Lisbon, designed Mateus Vincente, 1779–90*

799 *Alcobaça Abbey Church. Baroque façade, later seventeenth century*

800 *Carmelite Churches side by side in Oporto. (Left), Carmelite Church, 1619–28; (right) Terceiros do Carmo, 1756–68*

over-ornamented. Some of the village and small town churches are more successful, having an equally high level of decoration but used with greater restraint. Examples include the *Church of S. Vincente* at *Braga* (1691) and *S. Pedro* in *Amarante*. The triple-stage portal added to another Amarante church, *S. Gonçalo*, dates from this time also (**803**).

The twin *Carmelite churches* in *Oporto* (**800**) illustrate well the differences between the seventeenth and eighteenth century Portuguese work. The Baroque is fully advanced by the mid-eighteenth century with resultant richly ornamented exterior. The whole side of this church is covered in blue and white ceramic tiles. Such murals are seen all over Portugal especially in seventeenth and eighteenth century buildings. Another example is on the interior walls of the *Convent Church* of *Madre de Deus* in *Lisbon*. The décor of the interior of this church is by *João Frederico Ludovice* (1670–1752), a German architect (Johann Friedrich Ludwig) and illustrates the earlier Baroque style. This church dates from 1711 and is of high quality in workmanship and design. The ceiling is barrel vaulted and covered with painted panels in gilt frames. There is a triumphal arch approach to the high altar, very ornate in gilt decoration on white marble. Ludovice also decorated the *Chapel* of *S. John the Baptist* in the *Church* of *S. Roque* in *Lisbon* (1742–8). Much of the workmanship was done in Italy. The Corinthian Order is used and above is a central mosaic and caisson vault decorated with white marble *putti* and angels. The ornamentation of the small chapel is incredibly rich, all in precious materials: lapis lazuli, marbles, mosaic.

A genuine structural Baroque, as distinct from the decorative version which had been used in Portugal to date, was introduced by the Italian architect *Niccolò Nasoni* when he designed *Nossa Senhora de Assumpçao* (1732–50). This is an unusual building; it is situated on top of a hill near the centre of *Oporto*. Traffic now moves along a main road passing on either side of the church, which occupies almost an island site. The plan is long and narrow, with the tower (Torre dos Clérigos) at the far end and the oval nave at the other. The exterior (apart from the decorative tower) is simple. The entrance portico is more richly Baroque and the interior is en-

tirely oval, after Bernini. The church is entered through a vestibule which one approaches by climbing up further steps to the higher nave floor. The small choir leads off the oval nave and contains a heavily ornamented altar. The walls and vault are well-proportioned and controlled. There are Corinthian pilasters all round the walls and a panelled, oval dome above. There is no drum but oval windows in the lower cupola.

Two interesting later, fully Baroque churches, are those of *Nossa Senhora de la Encarnaçao* at *Milagres*, on a hill top six kilometres away above the town of *Leiria* and *Senhor dos Passos* in *Guimaraes*. The Milagres church has a wide, twin-towered façade with imposing curved gabled centrepiece. The façade is two-storeyed with Baroque windows above and simple arched openings below, providing a wide entrance gallery at the top of the approach steps. The Guimaraes church is quite different. It is tall and narrow with lofty steeples on either side of the convex front. It is approached by a monumental staircase. The churches are nearly contemporary, both having been completed in the 1790s.

Characteristic of Portugal are the *pilgrimage churches*. The famous examples at Lamego and Braga are dramatic. The theatrical quality of Baroque architecture is extended to landscaping. In each case the church is built on a hill top and is approached up the steep hillside by a terraced stone staircase, decorated all the way by finials and figure sculpture. The Pilgrimage Church of *Nossa Senhora dos Remédios*, designed by *Nasoni*, is the simpler of the two but is still a dramatic composition. Long flights of steps lead up from the town of Lamego by stages and platforms to the twin towered Baroque façade at the top. The upper part of the scheme is shown in Fig. **802**. Inside, the church is less impressive. In Baroque style, it is not large. It has a shallow curved ceiling decorated with rococo panels; the walls are articulated in the Composite Order with enriched entablatures. The altarpiece is gilded and ornate.

Bom Jésus do Monte is on a larger scale. The church has a magnificent situation on a hill top five kilometres away from the town of *Braga*. The hillside is wooded; the stone staircase ascends the escarpment through a gap in the trees. It is not as long a stairway as that at Lamego, but is more richly sculptured. The

BAROQUE IN PORTUGAL

801

802

803

801 *Palacio Mateus, Vila Real,*
1710–20
802 *Pilgrimage Church of Nossa*
Senhora dos Remédios, Lamego,
Nasoni, 1761
803 *Portal, Church of S. Gonçalo,*
Amarante

804 *Pilgrimage Church of Bom Jésus do Monte, near Braga, Portugal, Cruz Amarante, 1723*

804

Plate 86
Garden fountain.
Royal Palace of
La Granja, Spain,
1722–39

Plate 87
Gateway sculpture, Palace of Queluz, Portugal,
1758
Plate 88
Pilgrimage Church of Bom Jesus do Monte,
Braga, Portugal, begun 1723

Plate 89
Staircase Hall, Schloss Brühl, Germany. 1744–65, Neumann

church itself (**804**) has a more monumental façade and is a larger building. The best sculptured figures are on the terrace (PLATE 88). Inside, the church is plain and light, on tradiional Latin cruciform plan. The workmanship is somewhat provincial. As at Lamego, it is the dramatic exterior and setting which are remarkable.

Eighteenth Century Palaces

The two principal palaces of Portugal are at Mafra and Queluz. The *monastery—palace* at *Mafra* is an immense undertaking reminiscent, in its complexity and size, of the Escorial in Spain. *João Frederico Ludovice* had come to Lisbon from Rome in 1701. After designing the Madre de Deus convent church in Lisbon (p. 408), he was commissioned in 1711, by the king, to build the great convent-palace at Mafra. This is a mature Baroque structure, monumental and powerful; it dominates the vast square in front of the principal elevation, indeed, the whole town. The church façade is in the centre of this elevation (**805**), standing four-square with its Baroque twin towers, central pediment and crossing dome visible behind. The interior is brightly illuminated, well-proportioned Roman Baroque. It is entirely homogeneous, built in white and pinkish marble and with a patterned marble floor. The plan is Latin cruciform, with barrel vaulted arms and an apsidal east end. The Composite Order is used throughout the main church. The crossing dome is supported on pendentives. The drum is articulated with Corinthian columns and pilasters and the dome is coffered and painted.

Queluz is in complete contrast. This is the Portuguese La Granja, a summer palace for Lisbon, in gay insouciant pastel-coloured rococo. The palace itself is, however, no Versailles or La Granja. Designed by *Mateus Vincente de Oliviera*, it is smaller and less imposing. It has great charm and grace as well as an inconsequential, provincial air. Like La Granja, the garden façade, in particular, is white and pink in dainty rococo decorative form (**806**). The gardens are also French in design. They were laid out by the Frenchman *J. B. Robillion* in small-scale formal manner. There are fountains and lakes and some good, lead sculpture (PLATE 87).

A smaller, elegant, very Portuguese Baroque palace is that at *Vila Real*. The *Palacio Mateus* stands in attractive gardens fronted by a large lake. The façade has long, low wings and a central block which is approached by a small courtyard and a double entrance stairway (**801** and PLATE 84). The palace is, even more than Queluz, a little provincial, its sculptural decoration a little larger than life, but it possesses charm and compatibility.

The Germanic Influence in Central and Eastern Europe:
Germany

Baroque design was the paramount artistic expression over an extensive area of central and eastern Europe, but it did not fully develop under German architects till about 1700 and its use is predominant in the regions of Roman Catholic influence. The style transcended national frontiers so we find typical German Baroque workmanship in southern Europe, in Austria, in Switzerland, in Czechoslovakia, southern Poland and in Hungary. In the more northerly regions in Germany and Poland, the freer, rumbustious Baroque forms are more rarely to be found and, as in northern France, England or Holland, architecture is of a more severe, sparingly decorated, classical type.

The Baroque architecture which flourished with such vitality in Bavaria, for instance, carries the theme of pulsating life and movement further than either the Italian or Spanish versions had done. Italian Baroque, despite the undulations of alternately convex and concave curved planes, always gives precedence to the classical structure in orders, capitals, vaults, etc. The Spanish tends to obscure these by over-ornamentation and lack of coherence. The German achievement was to carry the Baroque principle of movement to the ultimate degree. Thus, though some churches are heavily ornamented, others are restrained in the use and area of decoration. It is not in the quantity of enrichment but in the flowing, undulating, always sinuously curving architectural forms that the summit of Baroque expression is obtained. Walls, vaults, capitals and piers, windows and doorways all contribute to this restless, surging movement and the delicate, pastel coloured, rococo ornament

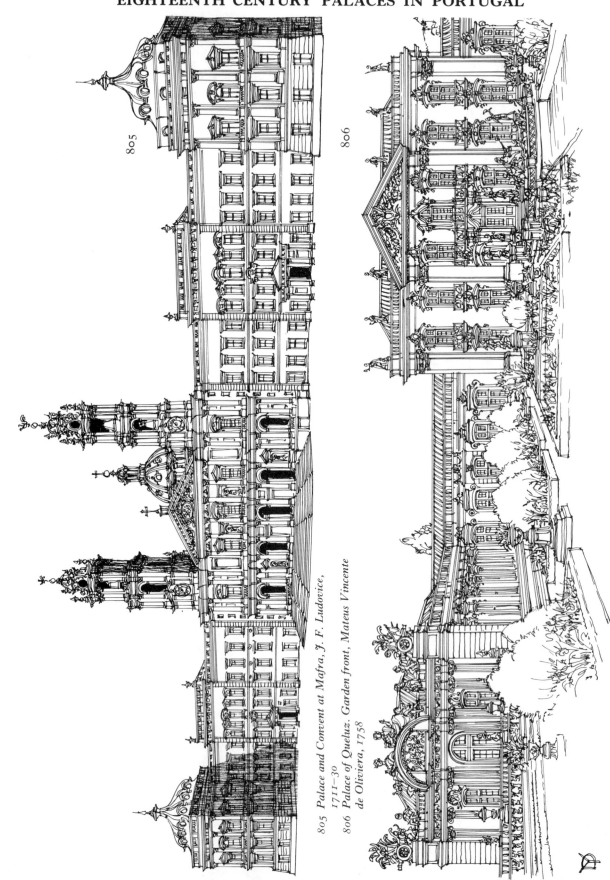

805 *Palace and Convent at Mafra, J. F. Ludovice,*
1711–30
806 *Palace of Queluz. Garden front, Mateus Vincente*
de Oliviera, 1758

completes the scheme. Church interiors illustrate the way in which craftsmanship in painting, sculpture and architecture, all of the highest quality, merge into one scheme of illusion and grandeur, so that it is often difficult to discern what is painted to represent three-dimensional form and what is three-dimensional reality. Motifs are taken from nature, from plant and animal life, but the treatment is not naturalistic. The leaf, tendril or stem is used as a design form. Though German rococo decoration is much more sensuous than the more delicate, subtle French prototype, both forms are sophisticated, not merely reproductions of nature's design.

In the seventeenth century building was either still Renaissance or Mannerist, like Holl's work in Augsburg (p. 340), or was carried out or influenced by Italian architects who designed in Roman Baroque. It was nearly 1700 by the time that German architects were ready to create their own Baroque buildings. *The Fountain Court* of the *Munich Residenz* is a good example of German work of the early seventeenth century. In simple classical style, it was laid out in 1612–18. The Thirty Years' War then followed (1618–48) and effectively frustrated building enterprises. In the second half of the century, under architects of Italian origin such as Barelli, Zuccali and Viscardi, construction of important buildings began again and, this time, in Italian Baroque form.

The *Cathedral* at *Passau* is a typical example. The interior was rebuilt from 1668 by *Carlo Lurago* (c. 1618–84). The basilican church has aisle chapels to the nave but none to the choir. The decorative scheme is all in white, with rich contrasting colour in the ceiling panels and pendentive spandrels. This is an early instance of the introduction of these transverse ceiling saucer domes which became such a feature of German Baroque churches in the eighteenth century. In Lurago's cathedral, the decoration is rich and Baroque; the quality of Carlone's stucco work is beautiful and both form and colour are expertly handled. But this is still Italian Baroque; the classical structure is paramount over the spatial movement.

Even more Roman Baroque is the *Theatinerkirche* in *Munich*, although it was not finally completed until the mid-eighteenth century (**810**). It was designed by *Agostino Barelli* on the lines of S. Andrea della Valle in Rome (**750**). It was built 1663–71 and decorated by *Enrico Zuccali* (1642–1724) from then until 1715. The interior is especially Italian Baroque; it is all white, with colour and gilt only in the altars. The church is correctly classical, on cruciform plan and with chapels in the thicknesses of the walls. A bold, enriched Composite Order is used. Above the entablature is a deep, sculptured frieze and windows. The barrel vaulted ceiling is sparingly decorated. The crossing dome stands on a sculptured drum, completing a finely proportioned, beautifully decorated interior.

Between about 1685 and 1710, *Enrico Zuccali* and *Giovanni Viscardi* (1647–1713) dominated the architecture of southern Germany. They designed in Italian Baroque style but gradually this became freer and less classical and thus more Bavarian. These two architects helped to set the pattern for the mature Austrian and Bavarian Baroque of Fischer von Erlach and Balthasar Neumann. From 1684, Zuccali enlarged and redecorated the *Palace of Schleissheim*, just north of Munich. Much of this has been rebuilt, but the three-storey central block (completed by Effner in 1726) with its giant Composite Order, remains. Inside is a magnificent staircase with centre flight which doubles back on each side. The stucco ornamentation here and in the saloon was carried out by *Joseph Zimmerman* from 1720. This rococo work is of very high quality. In 1702 Zuccali was commissioned to reconstruct the Medieval *Abbey Church* of *Ettal* near Oberammergau. This is essentially Roman Baroque in its pure classical lines and in its undulating façade (**811**). The dome and the interior décor are the work of *Joseph Schmuzer*, after 1745, but the treatment is similar throughout. The church has an oval nave covered by the immense dome; the chancel, leading off it, is a smaller oval.

Both Zuccali and Viscardi worked on the enlargement of *Schloss Nymphenburg* just outside Munich. Zuccali had designed the work and Viscardi was put in charge of carrying it out in 1702. He extended the façade by galleries and pavilions and began work on the saloon.

Southern Germany in the Early Eighteenth Century

While these Italian architects were developing

BAROQUE IN GERMANY

807 *Pilgrimage Church of
Steinhausen, Domenikus Zimmer-
mann, 1728–32*
808 *The Zwinger, Dresden, Daniel
Pöppelmann, 1711–20*
809 *Zwiefalten Abbey Church, J. M.
Fischer, 1740–65*
810 *The Theatinerkirche, Munich.
Begun Barelli and Zuccali 1663.
Completed Cuvilliés, 1767*

807

809

808

810

heir style of work, the Vorarlberg school of artists were also building and decorating, but n indigenous form. They worked mainly in families, of which the Thumb and Beer families built monastic churches in Germany as well as n Austria and Switzerland. The *Abbey Church* at *Kempten* is an early example. Designed by *Michael Beer* (*d.* 1666) and built 1652–60, it is large and monumental. It has a twin-towered, flat façade and a wide, low central dome. Inside, the four-bay nave has pilastered walls with flattened round arches between piers. There are chapels in the wall thickness. It is a simple, classical building, decorated sparingly. The *Abbey Church* of *Ober Marchtal*, on the Danube west of Ulm, followed. It was built 1686–1701 by *Michael Thumb* (*d.* 1690) and *Franz Beer* (1659–1726). The development into Baroque was here taken further, with the octagonal façade towers surmounted by cupolas and lanterns and, inside, the fine stucco decorated, panelled vault and carved pulpit.

The mature style of the Vorarlberg school can be seen in their masterpieces, the *Abbey Church* of *Weingarten*, begun 1715, and the *Abbey Church* at *Birnau* (1746–58). Many architects and artists worked at Weingarten. In connection with the architecture both *Franz Beer* and *Johann Jakob Herkommer* (1648–1717) had a share in the design and later Donato Frisoni and Joseph Schmuzer. It is an immense church, nearly 400 feet long, and rises above the town with an imposing façade of tall twin towers and, between, an undulating concavely and convexly curved front. It is built on a plinth and is articulated with the giant Corinthian Order. The inside is based, like many of the Vorarlberg type churches, on Il Gesù, but here the structure has developed further towards the later German Baroque pattern of free-standing piers. At Weingarten the piers project inwards from the wall, with their multi-pilasters and separate entablatures to support the barrel vault ribs of the nave. Galleries then connect the piers. The central vault is immensely wide, with arched ceilings—painted masterpieces by *Cosmas Damian Asam*. There are also painted saucer domes and a giant cupola and drum over the crossing.

The façade of the *Abbey Church* of *Birnau*, facing the shores of Lake Constance, is almost plain and only the tower displays Baroque

qualities. Thus far the church is typical Vorarlberg work and in contrast to the imposing façade of Weingarten. Inside is a different world. Here, the Vorarlberg masters created a mature Baroque on Bavarian pattern. The architect and mason in charge was *Peter Thumb* (1681–1766), son of Michael who had worked at Ober Marchtal. His interior at Birnau is a classic of its type. There is light and movement, spatial form in magnificently controlled curves. The broad flattened ceiling panels representing the Ascension are ideal for displaying the paintings of *Gottfried Götz* and the stucco framing, capitals and galleries of *Joseph Anton Feuchtmayer* are a wonderful foil. The interior is broad and open. There are no columns, aisles or screens to obscure the view. It is a fine vehicle for the high quality of craftsmanship with which it is decorated (PLATE 94).

Northern and Eastern Germany—Early Eighteenth Century

Two important centres in this area were *Berlin* and *Dresden*. Some outstanding artists were working in both cities; men who, like those of Renaissance Italy, often excelled in the handling of more than one medium. Andreas Schlüter in Berlin was sculptor and architect, as was also Marcus Dietze in Dresden. German architecture, and the world suffered a tragic loss in the almost total destruction of the eighteenth century work in both cities in the Second World War.

Little is known of the early life of *Andreas Schlüter*, who became one of Germany's greatest artists. It is thought that he was born about 1662 in Danzig (Gdansk). He came to *Berlin* from Warsaw in 1694 and quickly established a reputation. His most important architectural works were the *Arsenal* and the *Royal Palace*. The former, built 1695–1717, was damaged in the War, but is now restored. The Palace (1698–1707) was an even greater masterpiece. Designed in a bold, sculptural, Roman Baroque style, it was a fine design, superbly executed. It suffered only slight damage from bombing in 1945 but, in 1950, was razed to the ground by order of the Russians to create the Red Square (now called Marx Engels Platz) of East Berlin.

Schlüter's sculpture was equally of Roman Baroque quality. Again, little survives, but his magnificent equestrian statue of the Elector

BAROQUE CHURCHES IN GERMANY

811 Ettal Monastery. Designed by Enrico
    Zuccali; dome by Schmuzer, 1710-52
812 Aldersbach Abbey Church, Asam broth
    1718-29
813 Façade, Church of S. John Nepomuk,
    Munich, Asam brothers, 1733-46

EIGHTEENTH CENTURY PALACES IN GERMANY

814 *Schloss Charlottenburg, Berlin, von Knobelsdorff,*
   1740–6
815 *Palace of Sanssouci, Potsdam, von Knobelsdorff,*
   1741–7
816 *Schloss Solitude, Stuttgart, P.L.P. de la*
   Guêpière, 1763–7

814

815

816

Frederick Wilhelm I of Brandenburg was removed from its position near the Palace and now stands in the forecourt of Schloss Charlottenburg (**814**). Based on the Roman model of Marcus Aurelius in the Capitol in Rome, the statue is typical of Schlüter's vigorous, powerful style.

The chief work in *Dresden* was the rebuilding of the old part of the town after a serious fire in 1685. Disconcertingly called the Neustadt, it was laid out on classical pattern. Work began in the late seventeenth century under *Marcus Conrad Dietze* (d. 1704) and continued under *Daniel Pöppelmann* (1662-1736) and other architects until 1750, creating the Saxon Baroque style in buildings such as the Zwinger, the several palaces, the Frauenkirche and the Hofkirche. Almost all of this was lost in the Allied bombing raid in 1945, though some has now been rebuilt. Pöppelmann was the architect who set the pattern for Saxon Baroque. He took over the redevelopment of the Royal Palace in the Dresden Neustadt on Dietze's death in 1704. The *Zwinger** was the main part of this built. A court was constructed within the fortress walls of a Medieval bastion. The arcades and pavilions built by Pöppelmann were used as an orangery and accommodation for watching performances of festivals and tournaments which were held here. The famous wall pavilion (now reconstructed) from the Zwinger is shown in Fig. **808**. *Balthasar Permöser's* sculpture is an integral part of the design, acting as a foil to Pöppelmann's architecture. The building now houses a Dresden art collection.

In the north, the *Church of S. Michael* at *Hamburg* (now fully restored) is a good example of the tendency of this area towards Roman Baroque forms. It is a brick church, built 1751-61, by *Sonnini* and *Prey*, and has a lofty classical steeple. Inside, the décor of this oval planned building is in white and gold. The Composite Order, though in Baroque style, is dominant, the barrel vaults panelled and simple. In a monumental interior, the Baroque emphasis is displayed in the gallery curving sinuously round much of the church. At one end of the long dimension of the oval is the high altar, at the other the organ.

Central Germany — Eighteenth Century

The area around Bamberg, Nuremberg and

* *The word means a bailey or outer courtyard.*

Würzburg was a centre for outstanding Baroque art and architecture. The earlier work was created by the Dientzenhofer family and the later by Balthasar Neumann. There seemed to be as many members of the Dientzenhofer family working in the arts as there were de Churrigueras in Spain. In Germany three brothers were engaged in Baroque work: Georg, Leonhard and Johann. Another branch of the family created some outstanding buildings in Prague (p. 441). *Georg* designed the façade of *S. Martin's Church* in *Bamberg* (1681-91)—a monumental structure —and the *pilgrimage church* at *Waldsassen* (1685-9). *Leonhard* built the *Abbey of S. Michael* at *Bamberg* (1696-1702) and worked on the rebuilding of the *Schöntal Monastery* (1700-17). The most talented of the brothers was *Johann* (1663-1726). He rebuilt the *Cathedral* at *Fulda* (1704-12). This is very Roman, reminiscent of S. John in Lateran; it is an immense, monumental church with a twin towered façade and large dome over the crossing. His best works are the *Abbey Church* at *Banz* (1710-18), north of Bamberg and *Schloss Weissenstein* at *Pommersfelden* (1711-18). The church at Banz, which is situated on a hill near the edge of the River Main, has a bold German Baroque interior. A sensation of lively movement is produced by the ceiling of interlacing framed oval panels, causing constant conflict of curving planes. These vaults are all painted in symbolic manner with scenes from the New Testament. The architectural form of this church is broad and open, giving full rein to the decorative sculpture and painting; a mature example despite its early date.

In the *Schloss* at *Pommersfelden*, Dientzenhofer has created a monumental summer palace. On 'H' plan, it has boldly projecting wings and a plastic central portico with coupled Corinthian columns and pilasters and surmounted by a sculptured pediment. In front is an immense entrance court with, opposite to the façade, the curving sweep of the stable block. There are some fine interiors. Notable is the almost cube, three-storey, *staircase hall*. The first floor is articulated by coupled Corinthian columns while the second floor has caryatid figure supports. The beautiful coved ceiling is painted all over in allegorical manner, showing Apollo the sun god with the continents. The staircase ascends on both sides of the hall, its branches meeting at first floor level. Each newel is ornamented by vases and *putti* like Hildebrandt's Schloss Mirabell in Salzburg (**830**). Other notable interiors include the *Hall of Shells*, its whole surface covered with shells and stones and glinting touches of mica, and the *Festsaal*, the Marble Hall, which is a lofty imposing room.

Balthasar Neumann (1687–1753) was the leading genius of this period of German Baroque, taking an equivalent place to Fischer von Erlach in Austria. He was born in Eger in Hungary and was for many years an engineer in the Austrian Army. Like Sir Christopher Wren in England, his early training and thought were on scientific and engineering matters and, also like Wren, when he turned to architecture the aesthetic quality of his work was enhanced by his deep appreciation of things structural and scientific.

After some years in Paris and Vienna, he settled in *Würzburg* and here made his reputation in town planning in streets and houses, and also in the building of his chief work: the *Residenz*. His contribution covers several decades (in collaboration with von Hildebrandt) on buildings grouped round a *cour d'honneur* and a number of inner courtyards. Work was begun in 1719 and continued till his death in 1753. The elevations are all in Baroque style and the garden façades are particularly fine.

The Residenz had some magnificent interiors, but the disastrous air raid of 1945 caused great damage, especially to the Imperial apartments and the Hofkirche. Mercifully the great interiors of the staircase hall, the Kaisersaal and the Weisser Saal were more fortunate and today are once more in beautiful condition. These apartments are the result of the combined artistry of the architect, *Balthasar Neumann*, the stuccoist *Antonio Bossi* and the painter *Giovanni Battista Tiepolo* who came from Italy in 1750 to work for three years on these immense frescoes. The *staircase hall* is superb (**819**). The staircase ascends in a simple flight to the half landing, where it branches into two to climb to the galleried upper landing. The vaulted ceiling is immense, nearly 100 feet by 60 feet, and is unsupported. The architect Hildebrandt did not believe that it would survive, but not only did it pass the test of time but withstood the 1945 air raid also. Tiepolo here covered the vast surface with his allegorical painting of Apollo as patron of the arts, the personified seasons and the continents.

The *Kaisersaal*, on the first floor, is a large rectangular apartment with its corners cut off, the lower walls articulated by the Corinthian Order in column form with windows and doorways between; there are sculptured niches at each end. The coved ceiling, decorated by Bossi's stuccowork and Tiepolo's paintings, of which there is a central large oval panel with further paintings on the coved section, is pierced by oval windows. The *Weisser Saal*, next door, is, in contrast, all in white stucco and more Rococo than Baroque in treatment. The *Hofkirche*, the court chapel of the Residenz, was seriously damaged in the 1945 air raid but is now beautifully restored. It is a small but perfect interior, richly but not over-ostentatiously decorated and totally homogeneous. Designs for it were altered several times, but the present structure is predominantly Neumann's with decoration to Hildebrandt's design. The colours are strong and rich with an extensive use of gilt. The Composite Order is employed on the lower storey, mainly in column form, while above, in the gallery, is a rich profusion of gilded stucco and white sculpture with the painted cupola over all: a truly magnificent interior.

Apart from his extensive contribution at Würzburg, Neumann carried out a great deal of exceptional work in civic construction, palaces and churches. He collaborated with Hildebrandt at *Schloss Werneck* (1734–45) and at *Bruchsal* designed the wonderful staircase to the *palace* (1731–2), which was decorated by Feuchtmayer's rococo stuccowork. The palace itself is now largely restored, but the staircase was almost a total loss after war damage. *Schloss Werneck* is now in use as a hospital, though the park, on Capability Brown lines with a lake, is open to the public. The garden façade is fine, with a typical Neumann central curving mass, restrained yet powerful.

Schloss Brühl, in the Rhineland south of Cologne, was more fortunate. Neumann built the staircase here also (now fully restored), which is an impressive Baroque design in marble, wrought iron and stucco. The central flight is flanked by life-size sculptured figure groups; it culminates, at the half-landing, in a monumental centrepiece. The staircase then

PILGRIMAGE CHURCH OF VIERZEHNHEILIGEN, BEGUN 1743
BALTHASAR NEUMANN

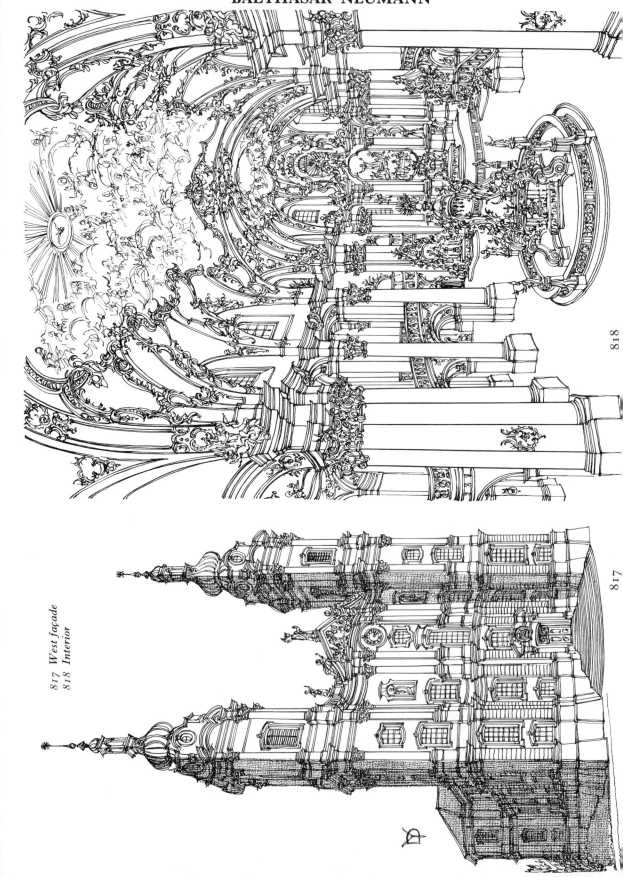

817 West façade
818 Interior

817

818

819 *The Staircase. Würzburg Residenz, 1734–53. Architect, Balthasar Neumann; painter, Giovanni Battista Tiepolo*

divides and doubles back to the galleried landing above, also in rich marble, ironwork and with beautiful sculptured figure-supports to the central, painted ceiling oval. The ceiling is illusory in that it is flat but appears, by its painted quality, to be concave (PLATE 89).

Neumann built several churches and chapels. His two supreme achievements are the pilgrimage church at Vierzehnheiligen and the abbey church at Neresheim; both of these are among the out-

standing examples of German Baroque. The *church* at *Vierzehnheiligen*, built 1743–72, faces Banz, which is on the other side of the river Main. It occupies a magnificent site on the crown of the hill. Its tall, striking exterior (**817**) has twin façade towers and a convexly and concavely curved centrepiece between. The church plan is basilican, on Latin cross, and has a drumless dome over the crossing. The interior is superb, a classic masterpiece of the best of German

Baroque workmanship in its architectural form, its stucco, iron and sculptured decoration. It is completely homogeneous, the ornament forming an integral part of the design and not, as in some examples, excessive (**818**). The scheme is in white, with the piers and columns painted to represent light coloured marble in mauve, cream and grey-green; bases and capitals are gilded. The ceiling is painted in curving panels which have scrolled, gilt borders. Colour is used sparingly throughout the church and to great effect. In form, the interior is in three ovals, the central nave being the largest oval. Curving galleries extend round the walls. It is very much a pilgrimage church, the magnificent 'fourteen saints altar' standing in the centre of the nave; this, the Mercy Altar (PLATE 90), was designed by *J. M. Küchel* and carried out, as was much of the stucco and sculpture in the church, by *J. M. Feuchtmayer* and *J. G. Übelherr*. All the craftsmanship is of superb quality (PLATE 93).

Neresheim Abbey Church is further south. It was one of the last works of the master, built 1747–92 and verges on the neo-classical. Nonetheless, the interior is still in the trend of spatial movement, based on ovals and curves, concave merging into convex. It is decorated in white except for the shallow saucer domes which cover all the open spaces and which are painted with Biblical scenes. A Composite Order is used throughout, with separate entablatures and the columns standing on plinths. There is an oval centre and semi-circular chancel as well as a corresponding semi-circle on the entrance side. The whole, as so often with Neumann's churches, is based on the oval structure, one curving form intersecting with another. This is a late Baroque version which displays the master's harmonious handling of these forms, acquired after a lifetime's experience.

Southern German High Baroque—Eighteenth Century

Several talented artists and architects were working here contemporaneously with Neumann. The most outstanding of these were the Asam brothers, the Zimmermann brothers and J. M. Fischer. Between them they built or rebuilt a number of abbey churches in the area of southern Germany, from lands just north of Lake Con-

stance in the west to just south of Regensburg in the east. Over the years 1715–60, under the guidance and skill of such artists, southern German Baroque reached the ultimate stage in its development. The exteriors of these churches were fairly simple, apart from the decorative steeples, concavely and convexly curving walls and ornamented portals. Inside, they were vehicles for rococo sculpture, stucco, paintings and carvings of the highest quality. The general architectural design was broad, superbly lit, designated by sweeping curves in vault and wall. No free-standing piers interrupted the view of the complex but unified composition. The enriched entablature and piers continued in the wall décor round the whole church, with designated space for the rich altars, culminating in the high altarpiece which swept up to the vault with its vibrant sculptural figures. The ceiling, designed in circular and oval patterns, was painted and stucco decorated all over. A magic world of perfection in human, animal and plant form is depicted in these gloriously alive, beautifully coloured and decorated interiors.

The *Asam brothers* were acknowledged masters at creating this supernatural world, *Cosmas Damian Asam* (1696–1739) was primarily a painter, his brother *Egid Quirin* (1697–1750) a sculptor and stuccoist, but both practised architecture. Sometimes they decorated churches for other architects as at *Osterhofen*, which was designed by *J. M. Fischer* 1726–40; on other occasions they carried out all functions themselves.

They worked at *Weltenburg* on the Danube near Regensburg from 1717, and at *Rohr* (PLATE 77) nearby (1717–25). They continued at *Aldersbach* from 1718 and created their most mature work, *S. John Nepomuk* in *Munich* (often called the Asamkirche) from 1733–46. The example illustrated in Fig. **812**, Aldersbach, is typical of all these in the harmony of the artistic parts: architecture, painting, sculpture. The architecture is basically simple; the stucco is rococo and decorated in white and pale, dull pinks with touches of gilt on the altars, which are very richly ornamented. The ceiling and altar panels (toned in the drawing) are all painted in full, rich colour, giving glowing life to the whole interior. Weltenburg and Aldersbach are the largest of these interiors, but the Asamkirche in Munich is the

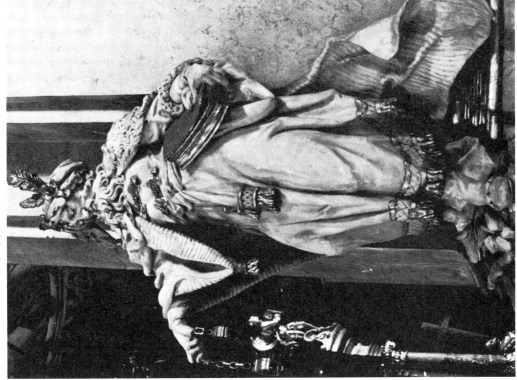

Germany. 1763, Küchel, Feuchtmayer and Übelherr

Plate 91

Church of S. Nicholas in the Lesser Town, Prague,
Czechoslovakia. 1703–53, C. and K. I. Dientzenhofer

Plate 92
Putti
Exterior entrance staircase, Church of S. George,
L'vov, U.S.S.R. 1738–58
Plate 93
Angel at the Francis altar. Church of
Vierzehnheiligen, Germany, 1763
Plate 94
Birnau Convent Church, Germany. 1746–50,

Feuchtmayer
Plate 95
Staircase. Schloss Mirabell, Salzburg, Austria.
1726, von Hildebrandt

most fantastic. It is a small church with a narrow façade decorated with Baroque sculpture (**813**). The interior is the essence of Baroque—all curves in planes and masses—there is no rigid classical grammar here. The church is divided into two tiers with galleries all round, curving alternately convex and concave. There are no aisles, no transepts, only one sumptuous room. The ceiling is painted in one large panel. The decoration is a riot of gilt and colour in barley sugar columns, sculpture and painted panels. The centrepiece over the altar is the *pièce de résistance*, as it is in all Asam churches. The sculptural figure group above floats away upwards without visible means of support. Their 'Ascension of the Virgin' at Rohr is the most incredible of these altarpieces. Here, the life-size figures below are struck in attitudes of astonishment and awe as the Virgin is borne aloft by angels. This central group seems to float ethereally despite the solidity of the sculptural material (PLATE 77).

Domenikus Zimmermann was chiefly a stonemason and his brother *Johann Baptist* a stuccoist and painter. Together, as with the Asam brothers, they decorated and also built a number of beautiful Baroque churches. The *pilgrimage church* of *Steinhausen* stands in open country north of Lake Constance (**807**). This is a simple but very Baroque church on both exterior and interior. It is oval in form with ten square piers supporting the oval dome, creating an ambulatory all round the church. The interior is decorated in white, pale pink and pale green with touches of gold. It is very light and restrained. The magnificent painted ceiling and altarpieces act as focal centres of colour.

Zimmermann's *Pilgrimage Church* of *Wies*, near Steingaden, south of Munich (1745–54) is very similar, but is larger and richer in decoration. There is the same oval nave but an added chancel. The exterior is very plain, in tremendous contrast to the interior.

Johann Michael Fischer (b. 1692) was one of the last of the great Baroque church builders of southern Germany. He designed the *Abbey Church* at *Osterhofen* (**422**), that at *Zwiefalten* 1740–65) (**809**) and that at *Rott-am-Inn* (1759–63): all are very fine Baroque churches, developed to the ultimate style of this type of decorative architecture. Fischer's masterpiece is the immense *Abbey Church* of *Ottobeuren* in Bavaria, north of Kempten. Begun in 1737, this is the largest in scale and most lavish of all the Baroque monasteries in this region. The church dominates the small town with its tall twin towers and convexly curving façade between. It is an imposing, cruciform church with shallow domes over all the bays and the crossing. The interior is extremely rich, all in white, blue-grey and gilt. This is more architectural and monumental than the Asam churches; there is something of Roman Baroque here, but the altar sculpture, saucer dome paintings and carved pulpits almost, though do not quite, dominate the architecture. It is a magnificent, coherent swan-song of Bavarian Baroque; a fine scheme of light and shade, white with colour, richness, but not cloying ornateness.

The Later Eighteenth Century

From 1740 onwards the influence of French rococo then, later, neo-classical forms began to supersede the German Baroque. A number of French architects were employed especially on royal and aristocratic palace structures. *François de Cuvilliés* (1695–1768) was court architect in Munich for many years where he worked in rococo style at the *Residenz* and the *Amalienburg* (PLATE 90) (Nymphenburg) in the 1730s and completed the *Theatinerkirche* (**810**). A beautiful example of his later work is in the *Residenz Theater*, which is in rococo style of 1751–3. The work of another Frenchman, *Pierre-Louis-Philippe de la Guêpière* can be seen at the country palace near Stuttgart, *Schloss Solitude* (**816**), a Baroque theme with central oval room but rococo in treatment.

In northern Germany, the greater part of the building work of the eighteenth century was destroyed by the bombing of the Second World War and, later, the advance of the Russian and Western armies. This applies especially to work in Berlin, Dresden, Leipzig, Kassel, Hamburg and Bremen. Only the buildings which survive in good or well-restored condition are discussed here.

The chief architect designing in rococo or neo-classical style in Prussia was not a Frenchman. He was *Georg Wenzeslaus von Knobelsdorff* (1699–1754), a Prussian aristocrat. He designed and carried out a number of town planning schemes and civic buildings for *Berlin*, especially in the area of the Unter den Linden (almost totally destroyed and now in East Berlin). His *Schloss Charlottenburg* in the western part of the city was damaged, but is now well restored (**814**). This is a large palace with extensive Versailles-type gardens. The equestrian statue of the Great Elector stands in front of the palace in the *Cour d'Honneur*.

Von Knobelsdorff then carried out extensive building at *Potsdam* in East Germany. He rebuilt the town palace (the *Stadtschloss*) in 1744 on monumental scale and an elegant palace nearby in rococo style, the smaller *Palace of Sanssouci*. The centre of the town of Potsdam was largely destroyed in the war and the Stadtschloss was a total loss. Sanssouci, fortunately, in its parkland, was untouched. The garden front (**815**) is approached up many flights of steps while the famous vines grow under glass on the terraces on either side. The palace façade is in white and yellow, with stone caryatid sculpture and detail. Inside, the finest rooms are the entrance hall, the music room and the oval saloon under the central cupola. The rooms are all in white with gold rococo decoration, and the Corinthian Order is used throughout.

Johann Boumann, a Dutchman, continued von Knobelsdorff's work in Potsdam. He built the *Old Town Hall* (1753), which was damaged but is now restored and used as a Museum of Culture, and in the park near Sanssouci, another large palace, the *Neues Palast* (1763–6). This also survives intact.

Along the Baltic coast of northern Germany, the old Hanseatic pattern of Medieval building with narrow house fronts and hall churches survived, though Baroque clothing encompassed the structures. Dutch architectural styles, especially from Amsterdam, were the prime influence here. Lübeck, Bremen and Hamburg had some fine examples of such work, but much of it was lost in the Second World War.

Switzerland

Medieval architecture lingered on in Switzerland, especially in ecclesiastical work. By the middle of the seventeenth century Jesuit influence began to be felt. The *Jesuit Church* at *Lucerne* (1666–73) is in restrained Baroque style (**822**). The interior

is a simple barrel-vaulted hall: no aisles, n crossing, dome or transepts. There are fou chapels along each side of the church. The whol interior is in white and gold with painted panel it is very light due to large windows in the vaul The *Jesuit Cathedral* at *Solothurn* has an im pressive Italianate Baroque exterior, raised on high podium with entrance steps (**821**). The ligh interior is well balanced and proportioned, simpl and not over-decorated. The choir and transept are apsidal-ended, with half domes over them There is a dome and drum over the crossing The influence here is partly Italian, partly th Vorarlberg school. It is also strongly influence by the type of cathedral as at Passau (**820**).

The Vorarlberg school of artists became para mount in the late seventeenth century. In fluenced by Bavarian Baroque, the families *Thumb, Beer* and *Moosbrugger* expanded thei influence and art. At the *Abbey Church* o *Disentis, Caspar Moosbrugger* produced a typicall Bavarian Baroque interior (**824**) in the grea monastery, finely sited lonely and high in th mountains at the head of the Lukmanier Pas which descends into Italy. At *Kreuzlingen* too a quite different area near Konstanz, the simpl exterior contains a rich Baroque interior (**825**).

The two outstanding eighteenth centur achievements were at *Einsiedeln* and *S. Galler* The *Benedictine Abbey* and Pilgrimage Church a *Einsiedeln* near Lake Zurich was rebuilt 1719–5 by *Caspar Moosbrugger*. The exterior is larg imposing but basically simple (**826**). Inside fantastic Baroque, comparable to Vierzehnheili gen in its quality of spacious architecture an decoration in white, mushroom, red, grey, gree and gilt. The domical vaults are magnificentl painted and these, with the rococo stucco wor are, characteristically, by the Asam brother who have given of their best in this superb Swis Baroque interior.

The *Abbey Church* of *S. Gallen*, only a fe miles away to the north-east, has a classi imposing Baroque exterior (**827**). This is a highl important work by the *Thumb* and *Beer* familie in the Vorarlberg tradition. The Abbey library a beautiful rococo room with painted ceiling an carved bookcases.

BAROQUE ARCHITECTURE IN SWITZERLAND

820   821

822   823

820 *Interior and* 821 *façade of
Solothurn Cathedral, Gaetono
Matteo Pisoni, 1762–73*

822 *Jesuit Church, Lucerne, Vogler,
1666–73*

823 *Eighteenth century houses,
Altstätten*

BAROQUE ABBEY CHURCHES IN SWITZERLAND

824 Disentis Abbey Church interior,
Moosbrugger, c. 1685
825 Chancel screen, Kreuzlingen
Convent Church
826 Convent Church at Einsiedeln,
Moosbrugger, 1719–50

825

824

826

the oval pattern followed; the *Church of the Servites* in *Vienna* (1651–77), for instance.

While the Austrian school of Baroque was slow to develop, the gap was filled by Italian influence. Most of the major buildings between 1640 and 1680 are by Italian architects. The most famous early church is the *Cathedral of Salzburg*, which was finally carried out to designs by *Santino Solari* and was consecrated in 1628. It is a cruciform cathedral on Latin cross plan, with apsidal ended transepts and choir and a dome upon an octagonal drum over the crossing. The façade is Roman Baroque with twin towers and superimposed orders in three stages. In front of the cathedral are the fine Baroque statues of S. Peter and S. Paul by *Mandl* (1697–8). Inside, the plan is much like Il Gesù in Rome, but the church is narrower and taller. It is a light interior, well designed and proportioned and very much on Roman Baroque lines.

The Carlone family carried out a number of

827 *Abbey Church at St. Gallen, Switzerland, Thumb and Beer, 1752–66*

827

Austria

As in Germany, the Thirty Years' War curtailed building activity till the second half of the seventeenth century. An indigenous Baroque slowly began to materialise in the Tyrol where the Gumpp family were court architects at Innsbruck. Several designs were based on centrally planned buildings and on the oval form (the Graz Mausoleum had been an early example of this). In 1647 *Christoph Gumpp* built the *Mariahilfkirche* in *Innsbruck*, which is a domed, circular structure with well-handled interior spatial forms. Other Baroque churches based on

projects; *Carlo Antonio Carlone* was the most talented. His work was fully Baroque, often Italianate, but the ornamentation had an Austrian flavour of richness and gaiety. Among his works are the *Abbey Church* of *S. Florian* (1686–1708), *Garsten Abbey Church* (**829**) (1677–85), the *Jesuit Church* of the *Nine Angelic Choirs* in *Vienna* (1662) and the *Esterházy Palace* at *Eisenstadt* on the Hungarian border (1663–72). The church interiors are especially Baroque, very richly decorated but always, in Italian manner, the classical architecture dominates the ornament, as at Passau Cathedral.

Johann Bernhard Fischer von Erlach (1656–1723)

Fischer von Erlach was the Bernini or Wren of Austria. Until he began to practise, Austrian Baroque was derived second-hand from foreign sources by largely foreign architects. He was born in Graz, the son of a sculptor. He left the town at the age of 22 and went to study for himself in Italy. He spent 12 years there, mainly in Rome and Naples. He returned to Austria and established himself in Vienna. Like Bernini and Borromini he had learned that full Baroque architecture is a successful merger between the three chief visual arts: architecture, sculpture, painting. Like his predecessors he established an architectural style which utilised all three as one unit, creating beauty and force in his handling of light and spatial effect. Like Neumann in Germany he carried the art of Baroque further than the Italians had done, producing powerful three-dimensional exteriors and interiors which were of exceptional dynamic beauty. He realised the exciting possibilities in the use of ceiling paintings in ovals and circles, framed by stucco sculpture which, in their curving planes, with the merging of the three arts, created a grand illusion of open sky effect.

Fischer von Erlach settled in Vienna by 1690, but carried out a great deal of work in *Salzburg* in this decade. His two famous *churches* here are the *Dreifaltigskeitskirche* (the Holy Trinity, 1694) and the *Kollegienkirche* for the Benedictine University (1696–1707). The exterior of the Dreifaltigskeitskirche is like that of S. Agnese in Piazza Navona in Rome (p. 375), with a large dome and drum flanked by two Baroque towers connected by a curving façade. This is a wider, lower front than the Roman example. The inside is more like Bernini's S. Andrea al Quirinale. A vestibule opens into a longitudinal oval church with recesses for altars in the centre and at the two sides. Corinthian pilasters continue round the walls and above is the drum and oval cupola with a painted ceiling.

The *Kollegienkirche* façade (east) is similar, but is taller and the central part is convex instead of concave. The site is more restricted so the building has to extend upwards not sideways. Inside, the cruciform church has no aisles or columns; tall Corinthian pilasters line the walls. The church is

barrel vaulted above the entablature. The altar is richly Baroque in its sculpture, culminating in billowing clouds.

Fischer von Erlach's church masterpiece is the *Karlskirche* in *Vienna* (**828**) (1716). Here he had the opportunity, on an open site, to put into practice his mature Baroque style. The church was dedicated to S. Charles Borromeo as a thank offering for deliverance from plague. The columns in front of the façade were designed by the architect with the minarets of eastern mosques in mind. They are based, decoratively, upon the Trajan Column in Rome and the spiral relief depict scenes from S. Charles' life. The exterior is fully Baroque in its curving façade, temple portico and vast drum and dome. Inside, the great oval space, articulated with Composite pilasters supporting an oval entablature, are surmounted by the drum and oval, painted dome with lantern above. The oval nave is recessed with three altars and one entrance; above this is the organ gallery. There is a great sense of dignity and harmony in the interior. The colouring is Roman, a little sombre, gilt and painted marbling with none of the light rococo treatment of Bavarian Baroque. This is Austrian Baroque monumentality.

Fischer von Erlach became the official architect to the Imperial Court at Vienna. His two chief works in this connection were the *Palace of Schönbrunn* and the *Hofburg*. He made impressive large-scale Baroque plans, but both structures were greatly altered from his original designs. At the *Palace of Schönbrunn* (the summer palace on the outskirts of the city) he was asked to modify his first great design on grounds of economy. In 1696 he made a second plan which was smaller and simpler. This was built, but was much altered by his son Josef Emmanuel and again in the eighteenth and nineteenth centuries. Schönbrunn is the Versailles of Austria, but the garden façade, as it stands today, is monotonous a long, flat elevation only slightly broken by the central block. The gardens are still fine and include raised terraces and fountains. The immense entrance *cour d'honneur* and front are much more characteristic of Fischer von Erlach's work.

The *Vienna Hofburg* (the royal palace) has been added to and altered many times between the building of the *Leopold Range* (1661–8) by

BAROQUE IN AUSTRIA

828 *Karlskirche, Vienna, Johann Fischer von Erlach, 1716*
829 *Pulpit, Garsten Abbey Church, Carlo Carlone, 1677–85*
830 *Schloss Mirabell, Salzburg. Staircase, Lucas von Hildebrandt, 1726*
831 *Façade, Mariakilfkircke, Graz, Josef Hueber, 1742–5*

IMPERIAL BUILDING IN VIENNA

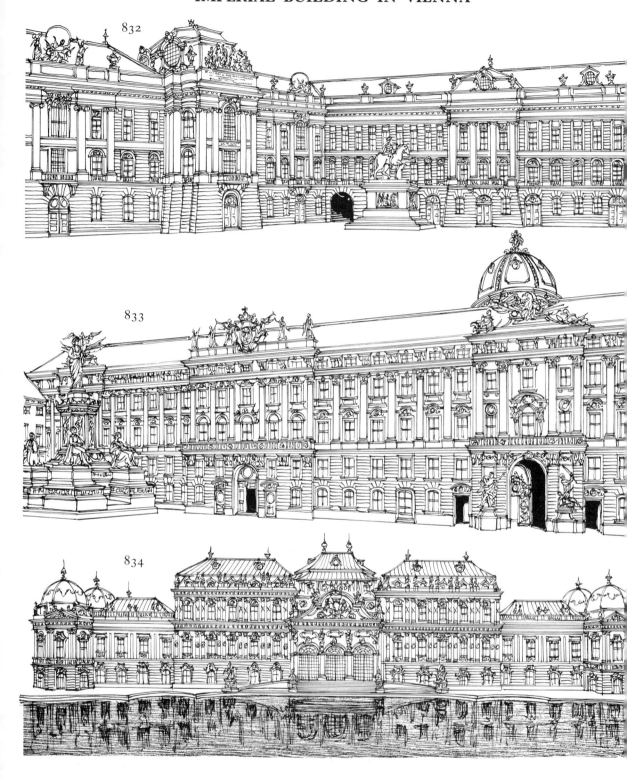

832 *National (formerly Imperial) Library, begun 1722, Johann Fischer von Erlach*
833 *Hofburg. Imperial Chancellery Wing, Josef Emmanuel Fischer von Erlach, 1729*
834 *Entrance front, Upper Belvedere of the Garden Palace of Prince Eugene, Lucas von Hildebrandt, 1721*

Philiberto Luchese and the later nineteenth century additions under the Emperor Franz Josef. The Leopold Range is simple, Renaissance to Mannerism, pleasant and dignified. Johann Fischer von Erlach designed far reaching plans for the Hofburg's extension, but he died before very much could be carried out. The *Imperial Library* (**832**) was begun in 1722 to his designs and, though largely built by his son Josef Emmanual, it is still the father's design. Here is shown his later phase of work, an abandoning of Baroque ground in favour of the rising tide of neo-classicism. It is still monumental but the projection of blocks and mouldings is less than before and decoration is restrained. The library was completed in 1735. The *Imperial Chancellery Wing* was entirely the work of *J. E. Fischer von Erlach*. Though it lacks the rich originality of his father's work, it is a competent, well-balanced design, with detail and decoration of high quality. It carries further the development towards neo-classicism (**833**).

After Fischer von Erlach came several outstanding Austrian architects. The most talented were *Johann Lucas von Hildebrandt* (1668–1745) and *Jacob Prandtauer* (1660–1726). Von Hildebrandt was born in Genoa and was half Italian. He studied in Rome for a number of years and his work always reflects this Italian background together with a preference for the light, French type of decorative design. He and Fischer von Erlach together embrace the whole spectrum of Austrian Baroque; one complements the other.

Von Hildebrandt began practice in *Vienna* in 1696. He designed the *Piaristenkirche* there (1698). This has a lofty, twin-towered Baroque façade with convexly curving two-stage frontispiece. The interior is much like his *S. Peter's Church* in the city (1702–33). There is the same central plan based on the oval motif, with painted saucer dome, without drum, overhead. Both interiors have beautifully handled spatial forms in curving planes.

Von Hildebrandt built and altered a number of *palaces*. The largest and most important of these commissions was the garden palace for *Prinz Eugen* in *Vienna*. There are two palaces here. The earlier one—the *Lower Belvedere*—was built at the foot of a slope in 1714–15. This is a modest, simple design. The Prince then commissioned a

more elaborate palace and von Hildebrandt built the *Upper Belvedere* on the crown of the slope, which is connected to the lower one by paths, steps, cascades and fountains. There is a considerable distance and difference in height of ground between the two structures. The Upper Belvedere is the magnificent palace; it is an elegant building with decorative pavilions and accomplished massing of the component parts of the elevation. On the entrance side of the Upper Belvedere is a large lake in which the palace is reflected (**834**).

Among von Hildebrandt's other palaces are the *Schwarzenberg Palace* (1697), near the Belvedere and now a hotel, and the *Daun-Kinsky Palace* (1713–16), also in Vienna. At *Salzburg*, he made a number of alterations and additions to the *Schloss Mirabell*, where his staircase is particularly successful (**830** and PLATE 95).

He carried out little ecclesiastical work, but one good example is his enlargement and remodelling at *Göttweig Abbey* (1719), which has, like a number of Austrian abbeys, a dramatic position high on a bluff above the river Danube, with a magnificent view of the plains below. The abbey buildings are set round an open court with the church as part of the group (**837**). The church interior is impressive; it is richly decorated with stucco ornamentation, ceiling paintings and painted marbling: a rich Baroque décor, part Austrian and part Italian; it bears little resemblance to the Bavarian Baroque of Ottobeuren or the Asamkirche. This is an ornate, late interpretation of Passau or S. Florian, with barrel vaulted ceiling.

Jacob Prandtauer came from the Tyrol. Like Fischer von Erlach, he was a sculptor and architect. Nearly all his work was in the great Austrian *abbeys*, generally enlarging or modernising existing structures. These are nearly all large-scale plans, of which the chief examples are at *Melk* and *S. Florian*.

He began work at *Melk* in 1702, extensively reconstructing the abbey from its Medieval origins. He separated the church from the surrounding conventual buildings so that its Baroque façade, with twin towers and central dome, serve as a landmark, perched on the escarpment at a bend of the river Danube (**835**). Melk and Göttweig share first place for dramatic siting along this river valley.

BAROQUE ABBEYS IN AUSTRIA

835 *Melk Benedictine Abbey, Jakob Prandtauer, 1702–36* 837 *Göttweig Abbey. Enlarged from 1719 by Lucas von*
836 *Zwettl Abbey Church, Matthias Steinl* *Hildebrandt*

At *S. Florian* he continued the work begun by Carlo Carlone (p. 427). Prandtauer's contribution is primarily the staircase block (1706–14) and the Marble Hall (1718–24). Both exteriors have Baroque pilastered fronts with rococo decoration. The monastery forms a large square court inside with the staircase block on the entrance façade and a fountain in front. The staircase is in two sets of flights, separating at the bottom and

838

838 University Church, Pest (Budapest), Hungary, Andreas Mayerhoffer, 1730–42

returning at the top. Square Doric pilasters are used and life-size sculptured figures are set in niches round the hall. The Marble Hall has a fine interior. Coupled Composite columns on plinths frame the windows along the two long sides; there is a coved, painted ceiling above.

A number of Baroque architects were working in Austria in the eighteenth century. *Joseph Munggenast* worked especially at Altenburg and Dürnstein; both are between Linz and Vienna. The *Abbey Church of Altenburg*'s interior is very Baroque, with an oval nave surrounded by Composite pilasters, the rectangular chancel barrel vaulted and entrance vestibule oval. There is a fine harmony of painting, stucco and carving. Over the nave oval is a beautiful painted cupola with small cupola and drum in the centre. The Library here is also remarkable. The room is large and rectangular, but it is covered by painted saucer domes and stucco decorated vaulting. Around the room is the Composite Order, its entablature returned over each column. It is a harmonious, colourful interior, the architecture by Munggenast and the decoration mainly by Sud-Tyrol artists.

Dürnstein Priory on the Danube was rebuilt 1716–33. Munggenast worked here, largely as a stonemason. Prandtauer also made designs and *Matthias Steinl* too contributed much to the architecture and sculpture. Steinl and Munggenast also worked at *Zwettl Abbey*. The church here has a tall Baroque façade decorated by sculptured figures, notably a group of S. Michael and the Devil (**836**). None of the original Romanesque interior remains; all is designed on Gothic hall church pattern, restored by Munggenast.

Buildings in Baroque style were being constructed or altered in a number of Austrian towns. In *Graz* there is *Joseph Hueber*'s *Mariahilfkirche* (**831**). In *Innsbruck* there are several and here the Gumpp family was active. A good example is *Georg Anton Gumpp*'s *Landhaus* (1725–8), which has a rich, dynamic façade. *S. Jakob's Church* (1717), by the Bavarian architect *Johann Jakob Herkommer* (p. 415), is dramatic and very much on the southern German pattern, as in its boldly concave, twin-towered façade. This is an unsophisticated version, but the interior is of high quality (**852**). The cruciform church is aisle-less, with apsidal terminations to the transepts, but the choir is square-ended on the interior. Three shallow domes cover the nave, while over the choir is a dome with lantern above and drum beneath. Herkommer had designed this beautiful church in 1712, but died soon after its commencement. The work was completed to the designs of the architect and the magnificent interior decoration is mainly by the *Asam brothers*, the beautifully painted ceilings by *Cosmas Damian* and the stucco work by *Egid Quirin* (p. 422).

The *Heblinghaus* nearby, a Gothic building, was redecorated in Rococo manner in 1775. It is a rich, plastic example (**849**).

Hungary

Because of the turmoil caused by war, and the Turkish occupation which continued till nearly the end of the seventeenth century, little classical architecture was produced in Hungary till the early eighteenth century. From this time reconstruction of the country began and some early classical buildings were produced in the capital. *Buda* was being extended and rebuilt when it suffered a serious fire in 1723. Few great buildings survived unharmed. One of these was the charming *town hall* (1692) with its corner oriel window and tiny lantern. The *Royal Palace* was built and extended by 1770, but, unfortunately little of it now survives. *Pest*, on the other side of the river Danube, was then expanded. The Roman Catholic Church was supporting an extensive programme of church building and a number of these structures were Baroque. The influence was Italian, for some time, under architects such as Martinelli, but soon the Austrian Baroque style percolated through. The *University Church* in *Pest* (1730–42) by the Austrian architect *Andreas Mayerhoffer* is the outstanding example of this type of work in Hungary. There is a fine Baroque exterior (**838**). The interior is simple architecturally, but it is richly decorated. The ceiling is painted all over, partly in panels and partly to represent architectural features in the vaulting. There is a triumphal arch entry to the chancel, which is apsidal ended. The church is rectangular, without aisles but with chapels in the nave walls. The pulpit and high altar are highly ornate but the standard of craftsmanship is high. Mayerhoffer also designed the *palace* at *Gödöllö* (1744–50) in rococo style.

Other good examples of Baroque churches can be seen in *Esztergom, Györ* and *Eger*. The *Jesuit Church* of *S. Ignatius* in *Esztergom* has a typical Baroque façade (**839**). Several Baroque buildings survive in Györ. The *Carmelite Church* (**840**) is a good example and there are a number of *houses* in Köztársaság Square. These, like those in *Eger* in Kossuth Lajos Street, are typical of Hungarian Baroque domestic architecture. They are unpretentious, low buildings with simple classical façades with or without orders. They have fine wrought-iron balconies and window grilles.

Eger, in the north-east part of the country, is still very much the unspoilt Baroque town created by *Jakob Fellner* and *Matthias Gerl*. Both architects adapted the Austrian pattern of Baroque to Hungarian needs and taste. Gerl's outstanding work here is the *Minorite Church* in the Market Square (now the Attila Jozsef College), which has a classic twin-towered façade and convexly curving front (**841**). Both Fellner and Gerl designed some of the houses just mentioned and Fellner was responsible for the *High School* (formerly the Ecclesiastical College) (**843**). He also designed the *episcopal palace* at *Veszprém* (**842**), which is an imposing building on top of the hill in the old town, next to the cathedral.

The best of the *palaces* remaining in Hungary is the large-scale layout at *Fertöd*, the *Eszterházy palace* (**844**). Fertöd is a small place between Sopron and Györ, till recent times called Esterháza. The palace was built by *Erhard Martinelli* from 1720 and was then extended by *Miklos Jacoby* (1762–6) and, again, later still. It has a magnificent horseshoe courtyard and entrance front, guarded by beautiful iron gates. In front of the central block is a double, curving staircase of stone and ironwork (**845**). The sweeping wings of the palace lead round to pavilions and then low stable blocks. The decoration of the façade is in low relief with simple decoration, mainly of rococo type. The palace contains 126 rooms, all rococo ornamented. It belonged to the Eszterházy family but is now an agricultural research centre, though open to visitors.

Yugoslavia and Rumania

The northern part of *Yugoslavia* remained under

BAROQUE CHURCHES IN HUNGARY

839 *Jesuit Church of S. Ignatius, Esztergom*
840 *Carmelite Church, Györ, 1725*
841 *Minorite Church (now the Attila Jószef College) Eger, Matthias Gerl, 1758–73*

BAROQUE IN HUNGARY

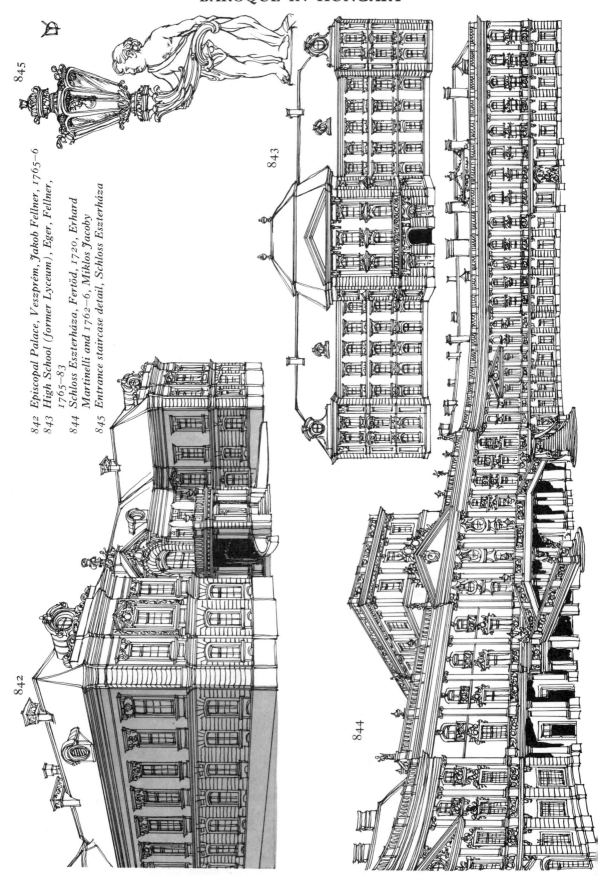

842 Episcopal Palace, Veszprém, Jakob Fellner, 1765–6
843 High School (former Lyceum), Eger, Fellner,
1765–83
844 Schloss Eszterháza, Fertöd, 1720, Erhard
Martinelli and 1762–6, Miklos Jacoby
845 Entrance staircase detail, Schloss Eszterháza

846

847

848

846 Church of S. Biagio (S. Blaise). Rebuilt 1706–15
847 The Cathedral, east façade, 1671–1713
848 The Jesuit Church, 1699–1725

Austro-Hungarian influence, the coastal region under Venetian. Inland and further south towards Greece the Turkish monopoly continued. The buildings illustrated on p. 437 of *Dubrovnik* from the seventeenth and eighteenth centuries show, therefore, the Italian style of building. All are ecclesiastical structures.

Rumania also has very few classical buildings dating from the seventeenth and eighteenth centuries. The majority of work is either Byzantine in approach or, as is shown in the Village Museum in Bucharest, of peasant, timber craftsmanship (p. 303). The *palace*, or villa, at *Mogosoaia* on the outskirts of Bucharest, is one classical structure from the eighteenth century. It is a modest, simple building, set in grounds laid out with a large lake.

Czechoslovakia

Baroque architecture was adopted enthusiastically in Czechoslovakia. It was influenced from several sources. The earlier work, in the seventeenth century, was primarily Italian: at one time at least 25 Italian architects were building palaces, churches and houses for the wealthy lay and ecclesiastical aristocracy. There was then a short period of limited French influence but, more strongly towards the later seventeenth and early eighteenth centuries, ideas came from Vienna and Bavaria, chiefly stemming from Fischer von Erlach, Hildebrandt and the Dientzenhofer family. There exists, therefore, a fine Baroque heritage in Czechoslovakia, in the remote country and mountain areas as well as in the towns, especially Prague.

The *Valdštějn Palace* had been begun in *Prague* in 1621 by *Andrea Spezza*. The loggia was in Renaissance style (p. 346) (**713**), but the façade and courtyard are boldly Baroque. Here was the beginning of the Italian influence, with the Czech characteristics only visible in smaller features such as the dormer windows. The courtyard is on the classic Roman Baroque pattern, with three orders superimposed, one above the other, articulating the three-storeyed ranges.

Italian Mannerism also came to Prague and was soon adapted to Czech design. It can be seen at the university, but more particularly in the extensive façade of the *Černin Palace* on castle hill (**856**). This was designed by *Francesco*

Caratti who created the façade, 465 feet long in 29 bays, its giant, three-quarter columns with their richly carved Mannerist capitals, standing on a rusticated base of diamond pattern. Inside he designed an immense saloon over two storeys high.

The Italian influence was strong in Baroque church design. A classic late example is the *Piarist Church of S. John* at *Kroměřiž* (**855**). On oval plan, it has a large oval dome, painted all over inside. There is no drum and circular windows pierce the lower part to provide adequate daylight. The oval nave has no aisles or transepts. There is a high altar at one long end of the oval and the entrance is opposite, at the other. The workmanship in marble, painting and gilded stucco is of a high standard and the concept is after Bernini at his most monumental.

Buildings in *Tábor* also show the Italian Baroque style, though on more provincial lines. The later seventeenth century *Convent Church* by *Antonio da Alfieri* is one example, while the *Convent Church* at *Klokoty*, outside the town on the opposite hillside, was built by architects of the school of *Giovanni Battista Santini*. The exterior is fine and occupies a magnificent site.

A French influence was provided by *Jean Baptiste Mathey*, who worked in *Prague* from 1675–94. His palaces are, in contrast to Caratti's Černin Palace, more subtle and less plastic, designed with low projection and pilasters rather than columns. He built some churches, such as the *Abbey Church* of S. *Josef* on the Malá Strana, which is on elliptical plan.

In the early eighteenth century *Johann Bernhard Fischer von Erlach* was working in *Prague*. He designed the *Clam-Gallas Palace*, which is typical of his work, bold and sculptural, especially in the famous doorways, the sculptured figures of which are by *Braun* (**854**).

The *Castle of Vranov* is romantically sited on a shelf of the steep mountainside above the gorge of the river Dyje (**850**). It was rebuilt in 1678–95 when the great oval saloon was designed by *Fischer von Erlach*. This is the chief room of the Baroque castle. The large oval cupola is painted all over, as is much of the wall area between the oval and rectangular windows, the coupled Corinthian pilasters and the sculptured niches. The sculpture is by the Viennese *Tobias Krackner* and the paintings by *Hans Michael Rotmayer*. It

BAROQUE IN AUSTRIA AND CZECHOSLOVAKIA

849 *Oriel Window, Heblinghaus, Innsbruck, 1775*
850 *Castle Vranov on the Dyje, Czechoslovakia. Rebuilt 1678–95. Oval Saloon, Fischer von Erlach*
851 *Church of S. Nicholas in the Old Town, Prague, K. I. Dientzenhofer, 1732–7*

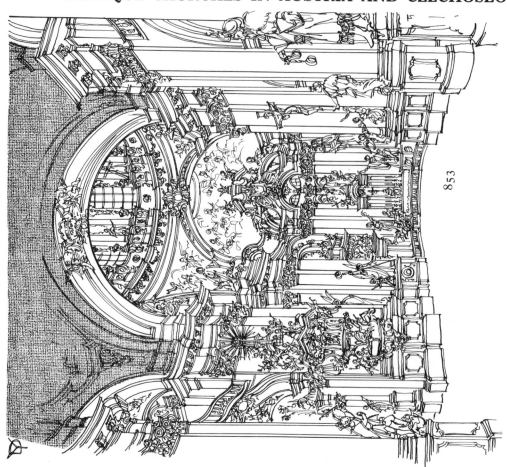

852 *Church of S. Jakob, Innsbruck, Austria. Begun 1717 to designs by Ĭ. Ĭ. Herkommer.*

853

852

is a fine saloon with good proportions, but the decorative work is not of the best Viennese standard. The Baroque Chapel of the Holy Trinity adjoins the saloon. Both it and the rest of the castle were completed by A. E. Martinelli between 1723 and 1732.

Hildebrandt also came from Vienna in the last years of the seventeenth century and worked on church design in Czechoslovakia. By the early years of the eighteenth century, the Austro-Bavarian influence on Czech Baroque architecture was asserting itself over the Italian. The change-over was completed with the establishment of some of the Dientzenhofers in Prague.

This remarkable Bavarian family were responsible for many fine Baroque buildings in Germany (p. 418). A branch of the family came to Prague in 1678 and set up practice there. The most outstanding of this generation of *Dientzenhofers* in Czechoslovakia was *Christoph* (1655–1722), who worked there most of his life. His best building is the *Church of S. Nicholas* in the Malá Strana at the foot of castle hill. This Jesuit church adjoining the monastery was begun in 1703. It is a very Baroque design, showing the influence of Guarini. The interior especially, with its curving balconies at gallery level and concave niches has a quality of perpetual movement, the walls undulating sinuously, articulated boldly in the Composite order. The large dome over the crossing is supported on a drum articulated with coupled Corinthian columns; between are windows and sculptured figures. The cupola interior is painted all over, as is also its lantern. The choir and transept apses are covered by semi-domes, while the nave is shallowly barrel vaulted and painted like Il Gesù in the Baroque movement manner. Though on Italian lines of structure and design, this is a Czech/Bavarian church in decoration and treatment. The pulpit and altars are typical, as are also the large figure statues ornamenting each pier (PLATE 91). The whole décor is in painted and gilded stucco, imitating white and coloured marble. It is rich but not over ornate: a superb, unified interior (**853**). The exterior is simpler, also Baroque with its undulating convex/concave façade and great dome and lantern but restrained in the ornamentation of its plastic monumentality. The Ionic order has a plain frieze, and decoration is confined to a few large sculptured figures and window tympana.

Christoph Dientzenhofer carried out a great deal of other work in Czechoslovakia, such as the monastic church at *Břevnov*. Other architects continued through the first 50 years of the eighteenth century designing in Baroque manner. The work of the Czech architect *Johann Santin-Aichel* is typical, as can be seen in such examples as his remodelling of the Cistercian *Abbey Church* at *Sedlec* and the Benedictine *Abbey Church* at *Kladruby*. The *Church of S. Saviour* in *Prague* and the remodelled interior of *S. Michael* at *Olomouc* are further instances of the wide spread of the Baroque style in Czechoslovakia.

The outstanding architect of this last phase of the Baroque in mid-century here was *Kilian Ignatius Dientzenhofer* (1690–1751), son of Christoph. He completed the Church of S. Nicholas in 1727, finishing the choir, dome and tower. He built many churches, using strongly Baroque, plastic forms and designing on octagonal, oval and circular ground plan. By mid-century, when the European tendency was towards classicism and away from Baroque, he still continued in his bold chiaroscuro designs. His churches in smaller towns and villages have mainly survived but, sadly, some of those in Prague are in poor condition. His Benedictine *Abbey Church of S. Nicholas* in the *Old Town* in Old Town Hall Square* has a fine monumental exterior (**851**), with a straight front but full of movement in its plasticity and ornament. Inside, the building is less successful. Kilian's Church of *S. John on the Rock*, in the city (begun 1730), has a fine position on the edge of a hillside. The building is in poor condition on the exterior and is ruined inside but, even in this state, the magnificence of the monumental design is clearly visible. A branching double staircase leads from the pavement steeply up to the façade doorways. The elevation itself is curved, articulated in massive Doric Order, with tall twin towers set inwards at an angle to the central portico.

Poland

Just as the Italian influence had brought the Renaissance architectural forms early to Poland, the same source was responsible for the introduction of Baroque architecture in the late sixteenth century. By this time Renaissance design had been assimilated and was in extensive use;

* *Not to be confused with his father's Church of S. Nicholas on the Malá Strana.*

BAROQUE ARCHITECTURE IN CZECHOSLOVAKIA

854

855

856

854 *Entrance doorway, Clam Gallas Palace, Prague,
J. B. Fischer von Erlach, begun 1707*
855 *Piarist Church of S. John, Kroměříž, 1737*
856 *Černin Palace, Prague, Francesco Caratti, 1669–92
(Now Ministry of Foreign Affairs)*

BAROQUE ARCHITECTURE IN POLAND

857

859

858

857 *Wilanow Palace, near Warsaw. Begun Agostino Locci after 1677; completed by Spazzio and Fontana 1725–33*
858 *Jesuit Church of S. S. Peter and Paul, Cracow, Giovanni Trevano, 1596–1619*
859 *High altar, Abbey Church of Trzebnica near Wroclaw, Gottleib Daene, 1780–5*

designers were ready for an early introduction of the new theme. The Roman Catholic Church brought about the creation of the first buildings, which were erected for the Jesuit and Cistercian Orders. The Jesuits had established themselves in *Cracow*, where at first they used the existing churches, then decided to build to their own designs, using their own architects of Italian origin. The *Church of SS. Peter and Paul* was one of the first of these and it is closely modelled on Il Gesù in Rome. The façade (**858**) is clearly based on Vignola's prototype, though his side scrolls are replaced by concave sweeps. The interior is Roman Baroque on the classic pattern. The Corinthian order, in coupled pilasters, is used all round the church as well as on the crossing piers. The dome stands on a drum and is capped by its lantern. Nave and transepts are barrel vaulted in monumental style and, in the apse, the conch is decorated all over with relief sculpture.

A later Jesuit example is the *Church of S. Matthew* (1689) at *Wroclaw*. Later called the University Church, it is constructed within the university group of buildings. The exterior is still in battered condition (after damage in the Second World War), but its classic façade remains, with Corinthian pilasters and concave sides to the upper gable. The interior is very fine and typical ornate Baroque of the late seventeenth century. The walls are articulated in the Composite order and there is a gallery round the sides of the church. Richly ornamented altars occupy each bay, while the monumental, Composite order high altar extends over the whole of the east end of the building. The barrel-vaulted ceilings are painted all over in one immense scheme. There is a quantity of good quality sculpture and gilded decoration. *Wroclaw University* is itself an outstanding Jesuit Baroque achievement. Begun in 1728, the river façade (**862**), designed by *Domenico Martinelli*, presents an elegant scheme, seen from the University Bridge over the Oder.

Elsewhere in Poland, Baroque church design developed in the seventeenth century on varied lines. Some examples had the southern German type of façade, with tall, twin towers and curving, undulating centrepieces. Others, especially the early buildings, still used Renaissance strapwork of Flemish type or Italian Renaissance orders.

In the later years of the seventeenth century,

Baroque church design illustrated the Polish love of rich ornamentation. The *Church of S. Anthony* at *Poznan* is an example. The façade is based on that of Il Gesù. The interior is aisled, an altar set at each Doric pier, and there are clerestory windows above. The barrel-vaulted ceiling is painted all over. An incredibly ornate, gilded high altar, with barley sugar columns, occupies the whole of the end wall of the church. The best example of these years is the *Church of S. Anne* in *Cracow*, built to the designs of the Dutch born *Tylman van Gameren* and supervised by *Francesco Solari*. Much of the sculpture on the façade and inside is by *Baldassare Fontana*. The façade is three-storeyed. Ionic pilasters are used on the ground level, concave scrolls set the sides of the storey above, while at the top is a plain gable. The exterior is monumental and on classic pattern, and its simplicity contrasts with the richly ornamented interior (**861**). This is on Roman Baroque lines with Composite pilasters (**861**) and aisles containing chapels. The barrel vaults are sculptured and painted. The cruciform church has similarities to S. Andrea della Valle in Rome (**750**), but the dome over the crossing is smaller and the standard of craftsmanship inferior to the Roman church.

Eighteenth century Baroque church design in Poland is generally on monumental lines and often large-scale and bold. In 1716, *Fischer von Erlach* introduced Viennese Baroque in his *Electoral Chapel* added to the east end of the *Cathedral of Wroclaw*. Designed in his classic style it has an oval dome, contrasting with the circular cupola of the Renaissance chapel next to it. In *L'vov*, now in the U.S.S.R., the *Dominican Church* is a bold design (**860**) on elliptical plan. This is surmounted by a large oval dome on its drum, both carried on eight piers. It is a mixture of styles, part Italian and part Bavarian; a fine, monumental, vigorous Baroque. On different lines is the Greek Catholic *Cathedral of S. George* in the same city (**863**). It has a fine position on the crest of a hill and is approached up a flight of steps with sculptured *putti* finials (PLATE 92). Also something of an architectural blend, it is a centrally planned church but cruciform. A tall, four-sided drum, capped by a low dome, rises over the crossing, while the four subsidiary domes are concealed by the attic mouldings. A magnificent Baroque façade, sur-

BAROQUE ARCHITECTURE IN POLAND

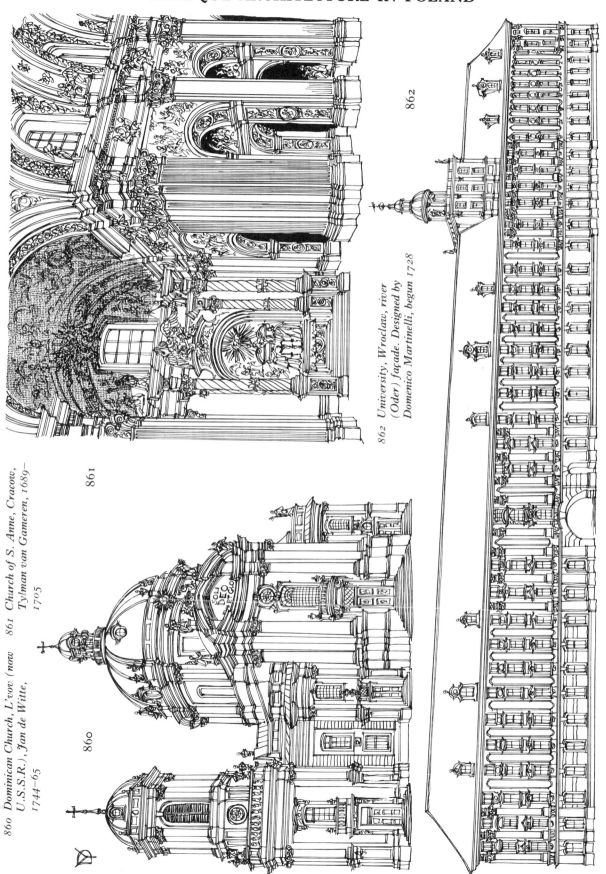

860 *Dominican Church, L'vov (now U.S.S.R.), Jan de Witte, 1744–65*

861 *Church of S. Anne, Cracow, Tylman van Gameren, 1689–1705*

862 *University, Wroclaw, river (Oder) façade. Designed by Domenico Martinelli, begun 1728*

863 *Cathedral of S. George, L'vov, U.S.S.R.,*
Bernardo Meretyn, 1738–58 (completed 1776)

863

mounted by a sculptured, equestrian group of S. George, fronts the building. It is an interesting blend of Italian and eastern European architectural traditions. A late example of a richly decorated Baroque interior is the *Abbey Church* at *Trzebnica* on the outskirts of Wroclaw. The building itself is all white inside and of monumental design, but the numerous altars, some of immense size and complexity, give an impression of gilded and sculptured richness to the whole interior (**859**).

A large proportion of the seventeenth and eighteenth century building of palaces and large houses has been lost in Poland due to the devastation of the Second World War. This is particularly so in Wroclaw and Warsaw. Typical was the *Krasinski Palace* in *Warsaw* (1676–97), built by *Tylman van Gameren*, with decoration by *Andreas Schlüter* (demolished 1944 but now rebuilt). In the later eighteenth century a number of rococo palaces were also built in Warsaw, but little survived the war.

The *Palace of Wilanow*, however, eight miles south of Warsaw, escaped severe damage. It was the royal palace of King John III Sobieski, who bought the village of Wilanow in 1677 and commissioned a country house near the capital. It began as a moderate sized house (its name derived from Villa Nova), designed by *Agostino Locci*, a Pole of Italian origin, and built 1677–96. The chief sculptor was *Andreas Schlüter* from Gdansk (p. 415), who carried out much of the rich, sculptural decoration and, possibly, influenced the architectural design. The building was enlarged between 1725 and 1733, by the Italian architects *Spazzio* and *Fontana*. Wings were extended and Baroque towers were added, while the entrance façade was considerably altered later in the century. The garden elevation (**857**), however, has retained much of its original appearance. The interior was seriously damaged in the War, but it has been largely restored and the palace is now part of the National Museum of Warsaw.

Northern Europe:
The U.S.S.R.

It is impossible to apply the same type of architectural labels and time scale to European Russia as to other countries of the Continent. Northern nations like Poland and even Sweden and Denmark had kept fairly strong links with western culture over the centuries, largely through the Roman Catholic and Protestant Churches; Russia remained aloof. The majority of outstanding buildings up till 1700 have, therefore, been discussed in Chapter 3 because, despite a sixteenth and seventeenth century date, they are of Russian Byzantine design. Some buildings, while reflecting the national style generally encouraged by the Tsars and Russian Church, began to include Medieval and Renaissance features, usually in fenestration and doorways. Those have been included in Chapters 5 and 6.

A number of interesting buildings, especially churches, have survived from the seventeenth century, still displaying this fundamentally Byzantine and national approach. The *Church of the Georgian Virgin* in *Moscow* (1634–54), for example, has much in common with the Putinki Church in the city (**246**). There is the same rich colouring and surface decoration, the rows of *kokoshniki* surmounted by grouped onion domes on tall drums. The windows and doorways show some classical influence, but the entrance porch is essentially Russian. The *Church of the Nativity* in *Gorky* (1699) is similar.

In the early seventeenth century the city of *Yaroslavl*, north of Moscow, became prosperous and a number of churches were built. Though plainer than the Moscow ones, they show the same construction and design as, for instance, the *Church of S. Elijah*. At *Rostov*, just south of Yaroslavl, the extensive Kremlin layout was built in the seventeenth century (p. 305 and Fig. **562**). This is a fortified monastic town with a great barbican Medieval type gatehouse, into which the church is incorporated; a not unusual procedure in Russia, which can be seen in the *Pechersk Monastery* at *Kiev* (**865** and **866**), though this is a more Baroque than Medieval example.

In the later seventeenth century the national Byzantine style was still in use, though classical features were now more obvious. The *Archangel*

Cathedral group at *Gorky* illustrates this tendency as does also the *Cathedral of the Assumption* (1693–9) in the *Riazan Kremlin* built by *Bukhvostov*. This Cathedral is still in the form of a tall block surmounted by grouped domes on tall drums, but the entrance doorway and window design combine classical detail with eastern cresting. The belfry of the Kremlin Cathedral group is purely classical as it was built later, in 1789–1840 (**869**).

The uniting of the Ukraine with Greater Russia in the late seventeenth century brought a timid westernisation of both clergy and culture. Baroque architectural ideas began to seep through from Austria, Hungary and Czechoslovakia. In *Moscow* this progress was slow and the Byzantine theme remained paramount for a long time, as is shown by the *Church of the Twelve Apostles* in the *Kremlin*. This has the five Russian domes on the cubical block structure like the early Kremlin cathedrals here (p. 124). The eighteenth century belfry in *Chernigov* in the Ukraine is much more classical, as is the Kiev example (**866**). There is one crowning dome, in both cases, but the columns and fenestration are entirely western.

Peter the Great: the Early Eighteenth Century

The eighteenth century in Russia saw a complete reversal of the earlier policies of the Tsars and the Church towards closing all frontiers against foreigners. As today in Intourist hotels, travellers from abroad had been kept separate from the native population by segregation in a different part of the city. Fear of infection from more liberal political and ecclesiastical views was then, as now, fundamental to Russian philosophy. The autocratic rule during the eighteenth century by three great Tsars (or Tsarisas), Peter, Elizabeth, Catherine, broken only by the short, unstable reigns of the ineffectual male line that descended from Peter, altered the whole picture. Russia became part of Europe again as she had been in the early days of Kiev's greatness.

Peter I returned to Russia after his first visit to western Europe in 1697. He planned to pursue vigorously a policy of trade and interchange of ideas and cultures with the west, which he saw as an advantage for Russia. He deemed it foolish for his country to be cut off from the development, social, political and artistic, which had been emerging in western Europe during the previous two centuries.

In architecture, his most important contribution was the foundation of *S. Petersburg* (now Leningrad). The site where this great city stands today was, in 1703 when Peter decided to build his capital there, as inhospitable and unpropitious as could be imagined. Situated at a latitude of 60°, the climate was bitterly cold in a long, dark winter, damp and misty in a short cold spring and autumn, and enjoying only a brief summer. The islands in the mouth of the River Neva, where S. Petersburg was founded, were of marshy ground; the water was shallow and unsuitable for large ships. The site was cut off from the rest of civilised Russia by extensive, dense forestation.

In spite of much criticism Peter carried on. He ordered works to begin on a fortress and sea-port based on the islands and necessary living structures were erected. He wanted a fireproof stone and brick city, but the area had only wood, so many of the early structures had to be in this material. He brought an enormous labour force from all over Russia, of whom thousands died from cold, hunger and exhaustion. He ordered a cessation of all building in stone and brick elsewhere in Russia in order to conserve sufficient supplies for his city. He ordered aristocratic, merchant and government official families to leave their homes and estates and come to live in the capital. Being an autocrat, with the power of the State behind him, and being Peter the Great, he succeeded. When he died in 1725, the foundation of a Baroque town was established. By the end of the century, S. Petersburg was one of the great classical cities of the world, a water city like Amsterdam or Stockholm though not, as is sometimes claimed, in the least like Venice.

All the great monarchs of the eighteenth century in Russia employed predominantly architects of foreign origin. This was because they were importing a foreign architectural style and needed to train their native artists in an unfamiliar manner. This influx from western Europe—chiefly Italy, France and Germany—not only of architects, but of their staffs of artisans in painting, sculpture, glazing, wood and stone carving, ironwork and stucco brought tremendous vitality to Russian art, but it also tended to curtail the national culture and crafts. These became unfashionable and many skills were lost, especially in timber and ceramic work.

Partly because much of the building was in wood and partly due to the shift from the original building on the islands in the Neva to the mainland, much of the architecture of the time of Peter the Great has been replaced or altered. But the planning of the city remains. This was carefully worked out from the beginning. The city centre was established on and near the waterline of the Neva, mainly on the north-facing bank. Here was a great central square with long, wide boulevards radiating southwards from it. The large islands opposite to the north bank continued to be used for important structures.

The first important architect whom Peter employed at S. Petersburg was *Domenico Tressini* (1670–1734) from Italian Switzerland. Tressini (in Russia: Andrei Petrovich Trezin) built the great *Peter and Paul Fortress* on the large island opposite to the Winter Palace. With foundations of earth and wood, on pentagonal plan, he used brick facings. Inside, in the great court, he built the *Cathedral of SS. Peter and Paul*; the burial church of the tsars. The present structure was restored in the later eighteenth century, to the original design, after earlier storm damage and neglect (**871**). From contemporary engravings it can be seen that it lacks some of the Baroque boldness due to its rebuilding in an age of neo-classicism.

Tressini carried out a great deal of other work —government buildings, hospitals, barracks, fortifications—but most of this has disappeared or been severely altered. He designed an ambitious plan for the Alexander Nevsky Monastery in 1715, for example but nothing of his work remains in the existing structure.

After Tressini came a stream of foreign architects of greater or lesser note. They include *Andreas Schlüter* from Berlin (p. 415), *Gottfried Schädel* and *Theodor Schwertfeger*. Much of their work has been lost or altered. A similar fate befell the contribution by the French architect *Jean Baptiste Alexandre Le Blond* (1679–1719). He was tempted to S. Petersburg in 1716 from Paris by an offer of a large salary but, like Schlüter, died after a few years. His chief work was Peter's great summer palace on the Gulf of Finland, nearly 25 kilometres west of S. Petersburg. This had been projected by Tressini 1711–14. It was begun according to Le Blond's designs in 1716, on restrained, French-classical pattern, with a two-storey central block with low,

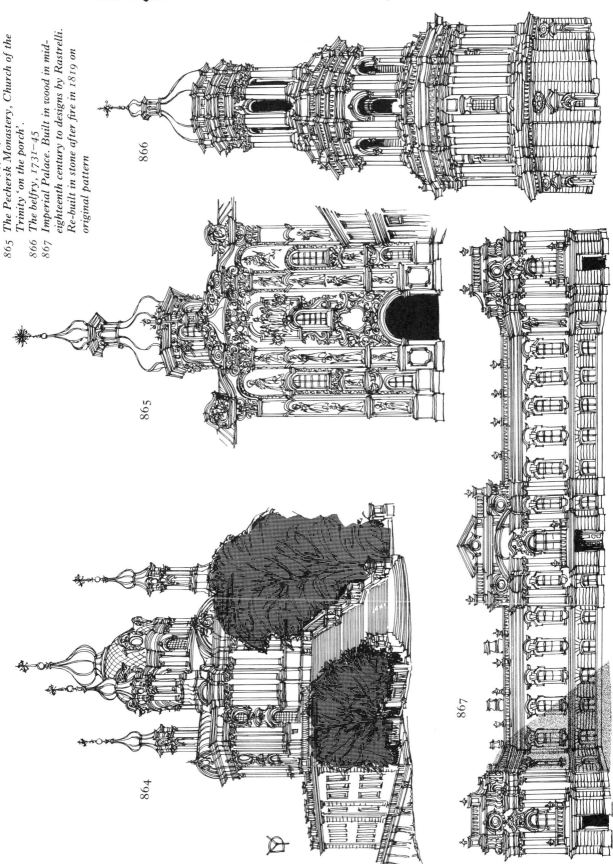

865 The Pechersk Monastery, Church of the
Trinity 'on the porch'.
866 The belfry, 1731–45
867 Imperial Palace. Built in wood in mid-
eighteenth century to designs by Rastrelli.
Re-built in stone after fire in 1819 on
original pattern

866

865

864

867

straight-wings terminating in pavilions. *Petrodvorets* (Peter's Palace), originally called by the German name of Peterhof, became the site for rebuilding and extension throughout the eighteenth and nineteenth centuries and a number of different palaces were built for the tsars and members of the aristocracy along this stretch of the Gulf of Finland (pp. 452, 455).

The Empress Elizabeth—Mid-Eighteenth Century

Elizabeth Petrovna (1709–1762) was Peter's younger daughter. In 1741 she succeeded in overthrowing the unsatisfactory government of the Regency and reigned for 20 years, displaying many of the characteristics of strength, wisdom and tact of her father. Architecturally, this period saw the establishment of Russian Baroque under the leadership of *Bartolommeo Francesco Rastrelli* (1700–71), who was born of an Italian family but who had come to Russia as a very young man with Le Blond. The son of a sculptor, Rastrelli soon showed his outstanding talent. He settled well in his adopted country as Bartholomei Bartholomeevich Rastrelli and was allowed to work and study for some years in Paris, Austria, Germany and Italy.

Rastrelli's opportunity came under Elizabeth. From 1741 to 1762 he designed all the important buildings in Russia, especially in S. Petersburg. His contribution was even more enduring than his own buildings, which in themselves established Russian Baroque architecture as of international standard. The younger school of Russian architects were trained in his ways and learnt their profession from him. A fully national school was established once more which kept pace with the stylistic changes in Europe but retained, like France, Germany or England, its national interpretation of them.

Rastrelli's buildings, churches and palaces, were always powerfully, three-dimensionally Baroque in form, with decoration which tended more to rococo as time passed. They were Russian in the greatness of their sheer size and in the use of colour on the exterior as well as inside. Some of his palaces have disappeared or have been much altered, but a great deal remains. The work in S. Petersburg was nearly all damaged in the Second World War, but much of it has been restored. It is doubtful that the modern standard

of craftsmanship in stucco decoration, painting and sculpture is anywhere near as good as it was on Rastrelli's original buildings, but the general impression is fine; it is only on closer inspection that the poverty of the finish and form becomes clearly apparent. Two particular examples of this decline are the Winter Palace and Petrodvorets.*

Of the many *palaces* which Rastrelli built for the aristocracy in *S. Petersburg* two examples especially survive: the *Vorontsov* (1743–5) and the *Stroganov* (1750–4). The latter (**872**) is typical of his work in its bold Baroque projection of the giant order together with rococo fenestration and ornament.

He built two imposing ecclesiastical schemes: the *Smolny Convent* in *S. Petersburg* and *S. Andrew's Church* in *Kiev*. The Smolny Convent is an immense layout with the great Cathedral of the Resurrection in the centre. This is a landmark over much of the city (**876**). The convent was started by Elizabeth for orphan girls. Rastrelli laid out conventual buildings on a Greek cross plan, with the cathedral in the centre. This, in particular, shows his restoration to Russia of its national Byzantine monastic church plan married to Baroque powerfulness and rococo decoration— a masterly combination. For colour and size its equal could be found in no other country in Europe. The interior was completed long after Rastrelli's death in cool, neo-classical form. It is now in poor condition and requires further restoration. The *Church of S. Andrew* in *Kiev* has a fine hill-top situation and is approached by long flights of steps. Once again Rastrelli's talent for combining a magnificent Baroque silhouette of a church on cruciform plan with the Russian traditional grouping and design of domes and tall drums is clearly shown (**864**).

Rastrelli's outstanding achievement is in his three great royal palaces for Elizabeth: the *Winter Palace* in *S. Petersburg*, *Petrodvorets* and *Tsarkoe Selo* on the Gulf of Finland. The Winter Palace along the edge of the south bank of the river Neva was the last and most successful of these (**874** and **875**). It has an immensely long façade to the river on the north side and to the vast palace square on the south, scene of the massacre of 1905. Rastrelli controls this length, retains the interest by his bold treatment while the white and green rococo gleams in the reflec-

* It is interesting to see in East Berlin that the rebuilding and restoration of old buildings in the devastated city, though slow in completion, are of a very high standard. The deficiency is obviously national not political. Examples here include the Royal Library, the Opera House and the Humboldt University.

LENINGRAD AND RIAZAN, U.S.S.R.

868 Palace of Peterhof (Petrodvorets) on the Gulf of Finland, about 15 miles west of Leningrad. Designed Le Blond 1716–17; remodelled by Rastrelli 1747–53. The drawing shows the palace as it is now, restored from war damaged condition, largely to the original design

869 Bell tower of the Cathedral of the Assumption, Riazan Kremlin, 1789–1840, completed Voronikhin

870 Bishop's Palace near the Cathedral, mainly seventeenth century

THE CHANGING FACE OF CLASSICISM: 1580–1800

871 Cathedral of S.S. Peter and Paul, Leningrad (in the Fortress on an island in the River Neva). Built 1714–25 by Domenico Tressini. Spire nearly 400 feet high. This drawing shows the cathedral as it is today. It is more severe and less Baroque than Tressini's work.

façade immensely, but retained its proportion b adding a new storey. Again, despite the fact tha it was not his new project, he infused a mor Baroque element into the French classical struc ture and decorated it with rococo fenestratior The extensive grounds were laid out in Frenc manner with *rond-points* and vistas, parterre terraces and fountains. These are of engineerin interest: the whole scheme is based on a gravit feed system of hydraulics as the great palace i on the brow of a hill and the central cascac descends directly to the sea (**868**). The palac was seriously damaged in the Second World Wa but is now fully restored on the exterior. It is a painted in yellow with white decorative feature The sculpture of the fountains and walks ha been replaced. These are copies, poor ones un fortunately, of the original subjects and group including the central Samson fountain. A numbe of classical buildings remain in the grounds, fc instance *Mon Plaisir* by *Le Blond* (c. 1717 where Peter lived while his palace was bein built, and Braunstein's Orangery of c. 1725. Mo Plaisir was later enlarged by Rastrelli an altered by Quarenghi.

The *Great Palace* of *Tsarkoe Selo* was built i the village of this name 32 kilometres from S Petersburg. The name means Tsar's (or Im perial) Village, taken from the original Finnis settlement there. It is now re-titled Pushkir Rastrelli also altered and enlarged this vas palace for Elizabeth. It had a frontage of nearl 1000 feet, rather monotonous on the mai elevation but carried out in Rastrelli's rococ style. Further alterations and additions wer made under Catherine, notably interiors b Charles Cameron. Tsarkoe Selo was almo totally destroyed in the war.

Empress Catherine II—the Late Eighteenth Century

Catherine the Great (1729–96), remarkable in heritor of the Romanov dynasty, was not Romanov or a Russian. She was born in Stetti (now Szczecin in Poland), a German princes called Sophia. The Empress Elizabeth approve of her and she married Peter in 1744, Elizabeth nephew and heir who became Peter III on he death. Within a few months of his accession h had shown himself unsuitable and incapabl

tions in the waters of the Neva. The Winter Palace has been altered and restored more than once, but Rastrelli's magnificent panache still shows through.

He began enlargement and reconstruction at Peter's *Petrodvorets* in 1747. Elizabeth wanted much more space and large reception rooms for her much greater court. Rastrelli lengthened the

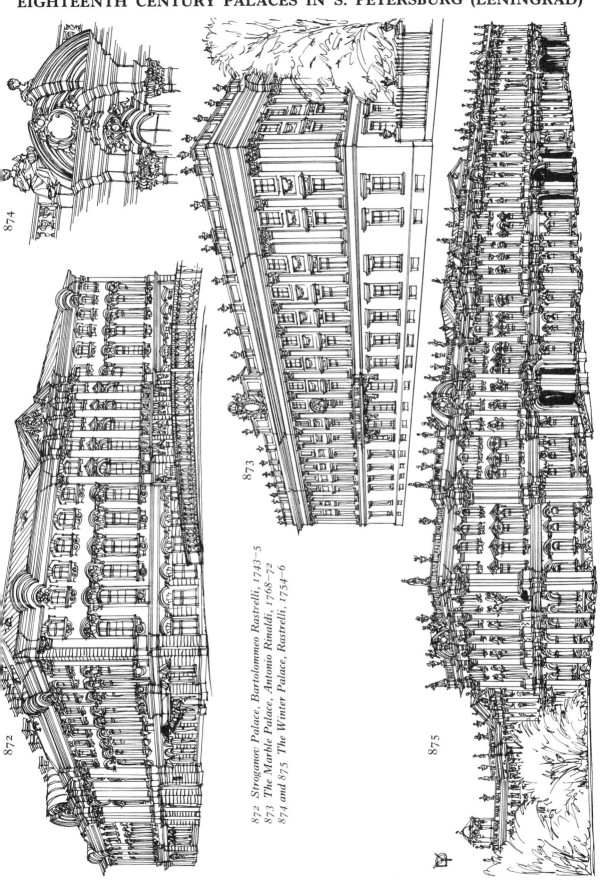

872 *Stroganov Palace, Bartolommeo Rastrelli, 1743–5*
873 *The Marble Palace, Antonio Rinaldi, 1768–72*
874 and 875 *The Winter Palace, Rastrelli, 1754–6*

874

873

872

875

876

876 *The Smolny Cathedral and Convent, Leningrad, Rastrelli, from 1748*

for the responsibilities of Tsar. Sophia, who had taken the name of Catherine on her acceptance into the Russian Orthodox Church in 1744, became Empress and ruled for 34 years. She identified herself completely with Russia and its people and became, more even than Elizabeth, natural successor to Peter the Great.

During her reign architecture and the other arts flourished and became completely professional, able to compete on level terms with western European countries. Catherine abandoned Baroque and rococo styles and embraced neo-classicism. This was the trend of the day in Europe as well as her own personal preference. Under her, different architects, foreign and Russian, evolved a pure Russian classical style.

Catherine employed a number of foreign architects, among them the Frenchman *Vallin de la Mothe*, the German *Velten* and the Italian *Rinaldi*. *Antonio Rinaldi* came to Russia from Rome in 1755. He built two large palaces, of which the *Marble Palace* in *S. Petersburg* survives (**873**). As can be seen, this is a much quieter elevation than Rastrelli's work, with only slight projections and a neo-classical emphasis on the horizontal members. It acquired its name from the red and grey materials with which it was faced. Rinaldi also began the great *Cathedral of S. Isaac*, an impressive design, but the building was not completed; it was finally erected by Montferrand 1817–57 (p. 502).

Of the Russian architects, *Vasili Ivanovich Bazhenov* (1739–99) built the *Arsenal* in *S. Petersburg* and a palace. In *Moscow* he was responsible for the *Pashkov Palace* which is built on an eminence near the centre of the city. It is now part of the Lenin Library (**879**). His *Church of All Mourners* is more classical and of later date (**880**).

In the last decades of the century *Ivan Yegorovich Starov* (1743–1808) built the impressive *Tauride Palace* and the new *Cathedral for the large Alexander Nevsky Monastery* in *S. Petersburg*. This, a monument of neo-classical design, was to replace the now decaying structure designed by Tressini.

Catherine then showed a preference for Western European architecture and employed *Charles Cameron* (c. 1740–1812), a Scot, to decorate a new series of private rooms for her at the *Palace* of *Tsarkoe Selo*. Cameron's style of work was after that of Robert Adam and he used this form of neo-classical décor in delicate stucco relief work, marble columns and wood panelling. Some of his interiors, like Adam's, were in Imperial Roman tradition and he employed beautiful materials such as marble veneers, agate, malachite and ceramics to produce a rich, glowing and colourful effect. Cameron was then employed as architect for the Grand Duke's *country house* at *Pavlovsk* (1781–96). Here again his interior work was highly successful, especially the two halls, one Greek, one Roman, which again show a marked affinity to Adam's Roman palace schemes. Cameron also laid out the park here on English (Capability Brown) lines. Catherine preferred such landscaping to the formal French (Versailles) pattern. Unfortunately much of Cameron's work here, as at Tsarkoe Selo, suffered greatly in the Second World War.

The best architect of this period was the Italian *Giacomo Quarenghi* (1744–1817), who worked in Russia from 1780 onwards. He designed the Palladian type structure, called the *English Palace*, at Petrodvorets in 1781–9, as well as a palace at Tsarkoe Selo. In *S. Petersburg*, he built the *Academy of Sciences* (1783–7) on Palladian pattern and, in 1782–5, the *Hermitage Theatre*. Quarenghi's work was on Italian lines but he followed different sources according to commission: Palladio, early Renaissance or Baroque. His buildings were monumental, well-proportioned and designed with taste and quality.

Scandinavia: Denmark

Scandinavia was still too cut off in the seventeenth century from the artistic centres of Baroque Europe to develop her individual approach to this form. On the northern fringe of Europe, Norway and Finland largely went their own way architecturally, using traditional materials and building styles. Sweden and Denmark initiated building programmes under royal patronage, trying to establish cities planned and decorated in contemporary manner, but Italy was too far away for the Baroque forms to percolate other than slowly and the northern cities had little to offer to attract Italian architects. In both countries the work in contemporary manner of the seventeenth and much of the eighteenth centuries was by foreign-born architects, chiefly French

EIGHTEENTH CENTURY CLASSICAL BUILDING IN MOSCOW

877

879

877 *Entrance porch and 878 Steeple of the Church of the Archangel Gabriel, I. P. Zarudny, 1705–7 (restored 1733–80)*

879 *Pashkov Palace (now part of th Lenin Library), V. I. Bazhenov 1784–6*

880 *Church of All Mourners, Bazhenov, 1790; rotunda rebuilt, 1828–33*

880

87

and Dutch. It was certainly the Dutch Palladian style which dominated the earlier classical work.

Typical of this style in seventeenth century Denmark is the *Charlottenburg Palace* in *Copenhagen*, built by the Dutchman *Evert Janssen* (**883**). Severe, symmetrical, restrained in brick, with sandstone reserved for decoration, this is characteristically Dutch Palladian.

A measure of how far the Danes were lagging behind in classical development is seen in the seventeenth century churches in *Copenhagen*. The interior of the *Trinislatis* (Trinity) *Church*, its white and light décor contrasting pleasingly with the dark, gaunt exterior, has classical, octagonal piers and Baroque furniture, but retains a Medieval style vault, despite the late date (**881**). The *Vor Frelser Kirke*, on the other hand, designed by *Lambert van Haven* in 1682, is fully classical. The brick exterior is essentially northern early Baroque with its tall western tower, rather than a dome, and its simple brick mouldings, doorway and fenestrations. (The strange spiral steeple is a later addition by de Thurah and based on Borromini's S. Ivo alla Sapienza in Rome). The interior, in vivid contrast, is sparkling, light and spacious. On Greek cross plan, this is spatial Baroque, northern in its plain, large, round-headed windows, simple Doric piers and broad curving vault, decorated only by restrained stucco work above each pier, but the altarpiece, with complete change of mood, creates a focus, after Bernini, its figure sculpture capturing the instant of movement, live and ardent. Quite different again is the richly carved organ loft at the other end of the church. This is in typical northern seventeenth century style, very fine, but more in the trend of Grinling Gibbons (**884**).

In the early eighteenth century, Frederik IV began a comprehensive building programme. He had been attracted on his travels in Italy to the larger villa type of design and commissioned two such buildings in Denmark. The *Palace of Frederiksberg* was begun in 1699 on the outskirts of Copenhagen (**886**). It was a long, simple block, on Roman pattern, in brick and painted stucco. A succession of architects worked on the palace during the eighteenth century, altering and enlarging so that the present building, now under military occupation, has lost some of its character and charm, particularly in the addition

of the extensive flanking wings. It is a pleasant building but provincial in appearance and standard.

Fredensborg, just south-west of Helsingör, was begun in 1719. Frederik this time commissioned a Palladian villa which was designed on symmetrical plan, with a domed, central hall. On either side of the main block, low wings extend round an octagonal courtyard. This building has also been added to and altered but retains its original design better than Frederiksberg. A pleasant structure, situated in a fine park, it is somewhat mediocre in design and finish. It is still used as a royal palace.

The finest eighteenth century building scheme in Denmark is the street layout in *Copenhagen* centred on *Amalienborg*, called Frederiksstaden (**885**). King Frederik V, on the throne from 1746–66, envisaged a distinguished residential area around Amaliegade and extending on either side from Bredgade to the harbour. The central open space, the Amalienborg Plads, or the Place Royale, was to be an octagon lined by palaces and divided by streets radiating from a central focal point. The scheme was begun in 1749 and the equestrian statue of Frederik, by the French sculptor J. F. Saly, was set in the centre of the piazza in 1768. The blocks around the octagon were designed to be of one scheme. Four of these are set on four of the sides and (later) Ionic colonnades connect the ranges. The scheme was conceived by Marcus Tuscher, but it was put into operation by the King's architect *Niels Eigtved*. He laid down the overall detailed plans for the buildings of the whole area round the Amalienborg as well as the design for the four palaces round the octagonal *place* which were to be occupied by noble families as town mansions. Now, all four are used as the royal town palace.

Facing the equestrian central statue on the chief axis intersection is Frederiksgade at the end of which *Frederik's Church* was to be built to terminate the vista. It was to be based upon Juvara's type of Baroque memorial church, a centrally planned building with a great dome surmounting the centre. Several designs were made, by Eigtved, by de Thurah and others, but that by the Frenchman *Nicolas Jardin* was finally accepted in 1756 and the church was begun. Building was much interrupted and delayed so that the church was not ultimately

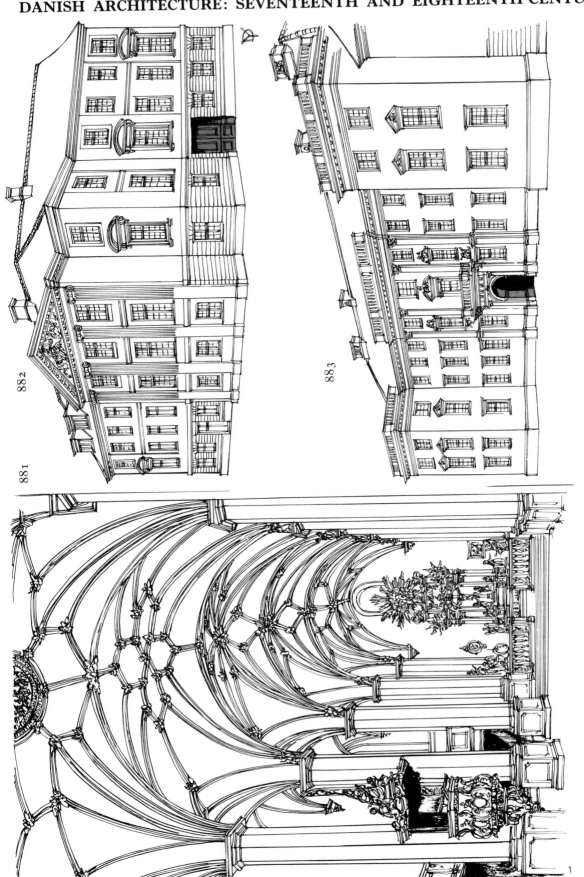

882

883

881

881 *Interior, Trinislatis Church, Copenhagen, 1637–56*

C. F. Harsdorff, 1770–80

884

884 Vor Frelser Kirke (Church of Our Saviour), Copenhagen, Lambert van Haven, 1682

completed until the nineteenth century (p. 505).

A number of country houses on simple, traditional classical pattern were built in the later eighteenth century. That at *Lerchenborg* (**887**) is typical. It is large, long and low, in whitewashed brick. It is unpretentious but well-proportioned and adapted to the flat, pastoral landscape in which it stands.

Town buildings in the later years of the eighteenth century were firstly rococo, of which there are one or two good examples in the Amalienborg area near Bredgade and, then, in line with the times, neo-classical. *C. F. Harsdorff* was an architect who often built in this latter style. His houses and apartments in Kongens Nytorv are one example (**882**), as is his Ionic connecting colonnades in the Amalienborg Plads (**885**).

Sweden

Seventeenth and eighteenth century architecture in Sweden was more distinguished than that in Denmark. Classical design was developed in the first half of the seventeenth century and consolidated in the second. This was largely due to the work of four architects, two families of father and son, of French origin. *Simon de la Vallée*, a Frenchman who had worked in Holland, spent the last five years of his life in Sweden. He died in 1642 but his work was admirably continued and improved by his son *Jean* (1620–96). *Nicodemus Tessin* (1615–81) was also of French origin but passed all his working life in Scandinavia. He became city architect for Stockholm and was the chief royal architect. His *son*, also *Nicodemus* (1654–1728), continued his father's work and inherited his positions. He was in effect Sweden's Christopher Wren. A fifth architect, who contributed considerably to later seventeenth century

PALACES AND HOUSES IN DENMARK: EIGHTEENTH CENTURY

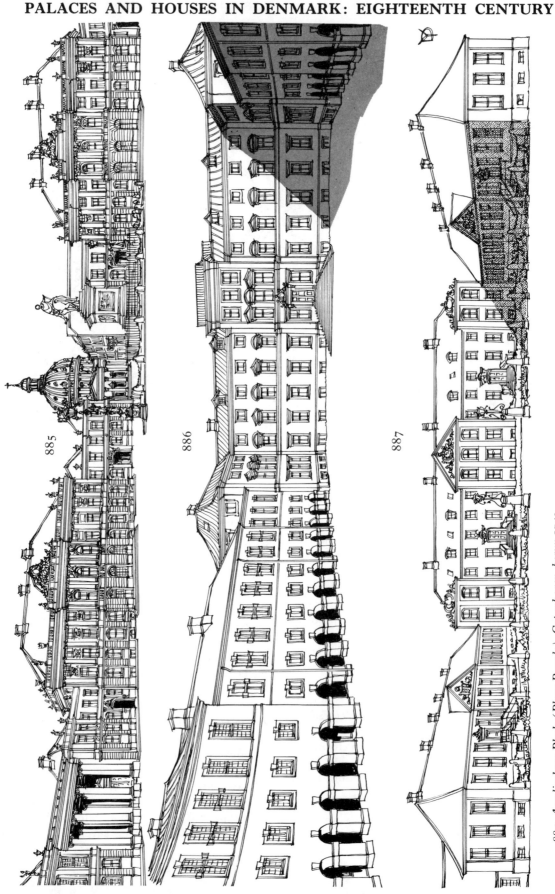

885

886

887

885 *Amalienborg Plads (Place Royale), Copenhagen, begun 1749*
886 *Frederiksberg Palace near Copenhagen. Italian style. 1699–1730*

work, was *Erik Dahlberg* (1625–1703), Swedish, nationalist and very much an individualist.

A good example of the earlier seventeenth century type of work is the severely plain brick building in *Göteborg* (Gothenburg) the *Kronhus* or Crown House. This has classical doorways and plain windows, but makes no concession to Renaissance decoration, let alone Baroque ornamentation.

The castle or palace at *Skokloster* (**888**), just south of Uppsala, is classical, but in the early Renaissance northern tradition of four-square severity with corner octagonal towers, reminiscent of Aschaffenburg in Germany (**699**).

In this period the Swedish nobility were becoming wealthier and began to build in a more contemporary manner: a Dutch Palladian style. *Joost Vingboons* came from Holland (p. 471) to work on some building projects, one of which was the Nobles' Assembly Hall or House of Lords, *Riddarhuset* in *Stockholm*. This is one of the most perfect Dutch Palladian buildings in Sweden. It was designed by *Simon de la Vallée* in 1641, Vingboons continued the work after the architect's death, but it was completed by Jean de la Vallée (**891**). The strongest influence here was probably Vingboons', as is shown in the simple pilastered front and central pediment though, inside, Jean de la Vallée's fine contribution is the double staircase.

Among the numbers of houses and palaces designed by *Nicodemus Tessin the Elder*, *Drottningholm Palace* is the most famous. Begun in 1662 as the summer royal palace (for which purpose it is still in use), the palace and gardens were laid out on the island of Lovö in Lake Mälaren about seven miles from Stockholm. The entrance front looks out on to the lake (**893**) while the garden façade (which is of very similar design) faces the park with its imposing terraces and parterres designed in the manner of Versailles. The house itself is very French and inside there is a beautiful hall, saloon and staircase. On Tessin's death in 1681, his son continued the work.

Nicodemus Tessin the Younger was a more cosmopolitan architect, accomplished and with an individualistic style. He had travelled widely in Europe and his best work is modelled on Roman Baroque, especially that in the style of Bernini. Tessin's chief work is the *Royal Palace* in *Stockholm*. This was a castle which the King decided to rebuild. Tessin reconstructed the north wing, but in 1691 a fire destroyed the castle leaving intact only part of the new wing. Tessin continued work, designing a new palace to incorporate the remains. The work proceeded during much of the eighteenth century long after the architect's death. Despite the mixture of styles in classical form resulting from the supervision of several architects, Tessin's Roman Baroque can be seen clearly overall. It is a large palace on Italian plan ranged round a great court. The south façade is vigorously Baroque with monumental Corinthian columned and sculptured centrepiece contrasting with the water elevation, which is severely classical. Equally, the courtyard is monumental and correctly classical while the *cour d'honneur* is boldly rusticated and articulated (**892**).

There is a markedly Baroque flavour about the best of both seventeenth and eighteenth century *churches* in Sweden. A pace-setter was the *Church of S. Katarina in Stockholm* by *Jean de la Vallée* (1656), a symmetrical, centrally planned building on Greek cross layout with dome over the crossing and four chapels at the corners each with a smaller cupola over it. Another centrally planned church in the city is that of *Hedvig Eleonora* (**889**), also by Jean de la Vallée. *Nicodemus Tessin the Elder* then designed the *Chapel of King Charles XII* (1671), a centrally planned, octagonal chapel added to the Riddarholm Church in Stockholm. (This was completed by Hårleman in 1743.) Also by Tessin is the imposing *Cathedral* at *Kalmar*. This is on oval, rather than circular plan. The east and west elevations are fronted by a façade, while on the north and south sides, which are shorter, there is an apse. The projected central dome was never built (**894**). The exterior is severe and monumental with good classical detail, while the interior is particularly fine eighteenth century Baroque. A rectangular hall, it has a simply barrel vaulted nave and choir with short barrel vaulted transepts midway. Coupled Ionic pilasters support a continuous entablature. At one end in the apse is the high altar, at the other, the organ. At the sides, in the transepts, seating galleries are carried on Composite columns. The decoration of the church is restrained but of high quality (**895**).

In much simpler vein, the centrally planned

SEVENTEENTH CENTURY ARCHITECTURE IN SWEDEN

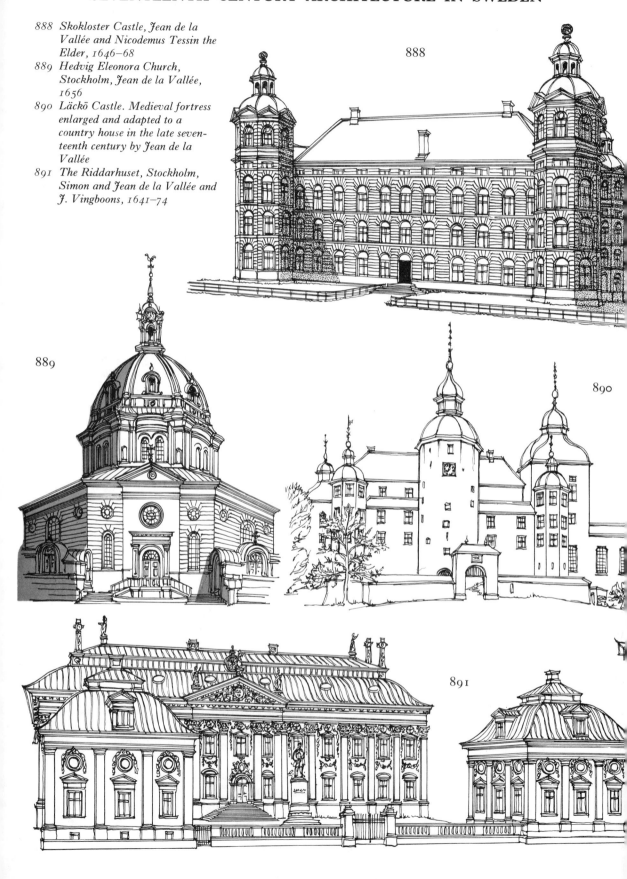

888 Skokloster Castle, Jean de la
Vallée and Nicodemus Tessin the
Elder, 1646–68
889 Hedvig Eleonora Church,
Stockholm, Jean de la Vallée,
1656
890 Läckö Castle. Medieval fortress
enlarged and adapted to a
country house in the late seventeenth century by Jean de la
Vallée
891 The Riddarhuset, Stockholm,
Simon and Jean de la Vallée and
J. Vingboons, 1641–74

888

889

890

891

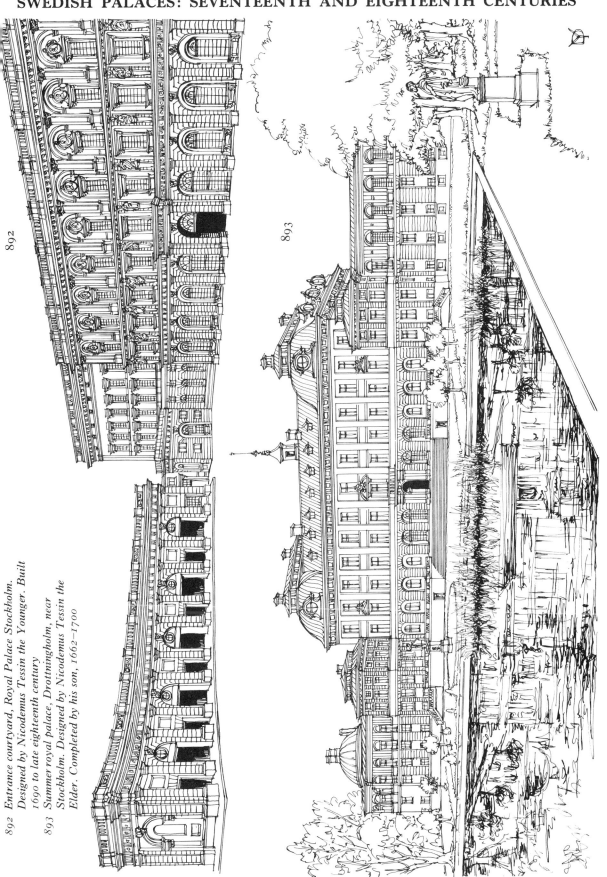

892 Entrance courtyard, Royal Palace Stockholm.
Designed by Nicodemus Tessin the Younger. Built
1690 to late eighteenth century

893 Summer royal palace, Drottningholm, near
Stockholm. Designed by Nicodemus Tessin the
Elder. Completed by his son, 1662–1700

894

895

894 Kalmar Cathedral, Sweden, Nicodemus Tessin the Elder, 1660–1703
895 Interior, Kalmar Cathedral, Sweden, Tessin, 1660–1703 (pews omitted)

church of S. Katarina was also used as a pattern for *Erik Dahlberg* in his late seventeenth century churches at *Karlshamn* and *Laxå*. The latter is entirely of wood, the walls and roofs being covered with shingles. It is octagonal, with four porches symmetrically placed.

Notable among the architects of the later eighteenth century were *Karl Adelcrantz* (1716–96) and *Erik Palmstedt* (1741–1803). Adelcrantz carried out much of the civic planning work, especially in *Stockholm*, where he implemented some of Tessin's original designs for the area round the royal palace. Tessin had planned the palace as a centrepiece for a large scheme. Adelcrantz initiated the *Gustav Adolf Torg* (Square) layout, designing the Opera House there (now demolished), while *Palmstedt* was responsible for the still existing palace which balanced it. The square is on the mainland and opposite to it to the southwards is the large island of Old Stockholm where the royal palace faces the mainland. Between the two is a small island, the Helgeandsholmen. A bridge connects this island northwards and southwards and is the *Norrbro* which was also begun at this time by Adelcrantz. Also in Stockholm, this architect was responsible for the *Adolf Frederik's Church* (1768–83), which is a traditional Baroque design with central dome and lantern. It has a well-proportioned exterior with good detail. Inside, like Il Gesù, it is on genuine Roman Baroque pattern, no aisles or piers and all four arms of the cross barrel vaulted. Typical of *Palmstedt*'s classical work is the *Exchange* in *Stockholm* (1767–76), built on Roman lines.

Norway

The pattern of development in Norway and Finland was different from that of Denmark and Sweden. The former countries were poorer, more remote from the art centres of Europe and in mountain and lakeland terrain which hindered communication and maintained isolation. Until after 1800, the great majority of building was in timber so that, even in the eighteenth century, when contemporary Baroque styles were percolating through, the derivation and adaptation of the time was governed by the medium and climatic conditions. Again, because nearly all structures were of wood, whole streets of build-ings, even towns, were periodically ravaged by fire, so that beautiful cities like Bergen, Trondheim and Oslo were constantly replacing their older buildings with new ones.

There is, in consequence, very little left in the towns dating from before 1700. Of eighteenth century work, the most interesting is in *Trondheim*, which was largely rebuilt after a severe fire in 1708. Norway was more prosperous in this century, and, though the new buildings were still of wood, the important ones were larger, more richly decorative and, within the possibilities of the medium, contemporary with design elsewhere. Typical of the best of these is the *Stiftsgården Palace* (**897**). This is the largest wooden building in Scandinavia. It is long, low and built in classical form round three sides of a court. Rather later, but also of wood and very typical, is the *Manor House* at *Lade*, on the outskirts of Trondheim (**898**). Several streets in the centre of Trondheim have a number of fine wooden houses (now sometimes adapted into shops) from the eighteenth and early nineteenth centuries. They are all low and have steeply pitched roofs to throw off the snow. Most of them have classical pedimented window frames and columned porticoes. The best examples are in *Kongens Gate, Munkegata* and *Olav Tryggvasons Gate*.

Other interesting wooden houses in classical style can be seen in *Bergen*, partly in the town and also nearby in Gamle Bergen, at Sandvik. Here, streets of old houses have been preserved as a museum. There are also many examples of domestic and agricultural architecture in wood construction, preserved in the Oslo Folk Museum from these years (p. 270). Particularly interesting structures come from Hallingdal and Heddal.

A few brick houses in *Oslo* date from the eighteenth century. These are more international in design, but are simple, restrained in decoration and with steeply pitched roofs. One such building is No. 2 Olsen's Gate (**896**).

Of especial interest from these two centuries in Norway are the *churches*. New churches built in the seventeenth century were designed for the Lutheran ritual. They were almost all of wood, on cruciform plan and with tall, slender spires. The stave method was abandoned in favour of logs or boarding. A typical and hardly altered example is *Kvikne Church*, standing on

NORWEGIAN DOMESTIC ARCHITECTURE

896 *Mr. Treschow's House. Fred Olsen's Gate, 2, Oslo, 1740*
897 *Stiftsgården, Palace façade, Trondheim, 1774–8*
898 *Garden front, Lade Manor House, near Trondheim 1811*

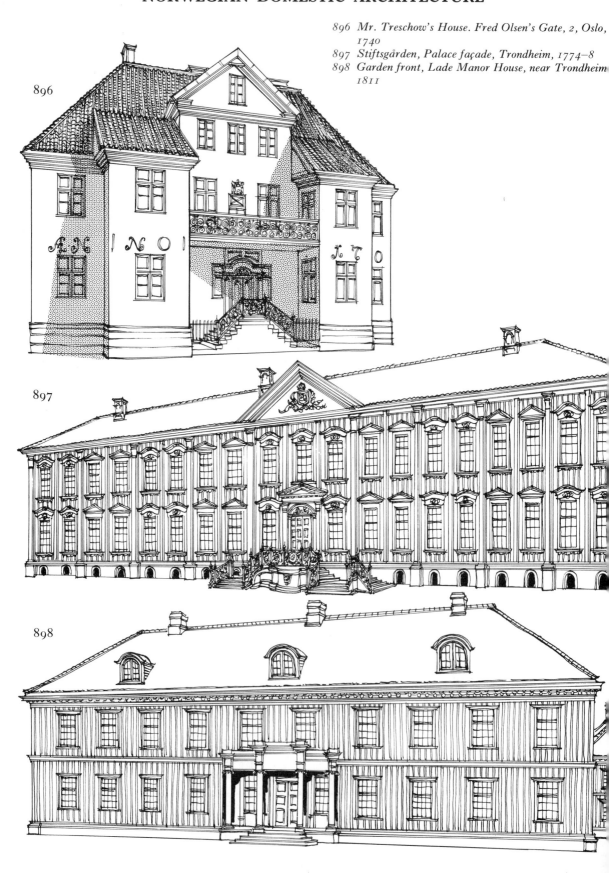

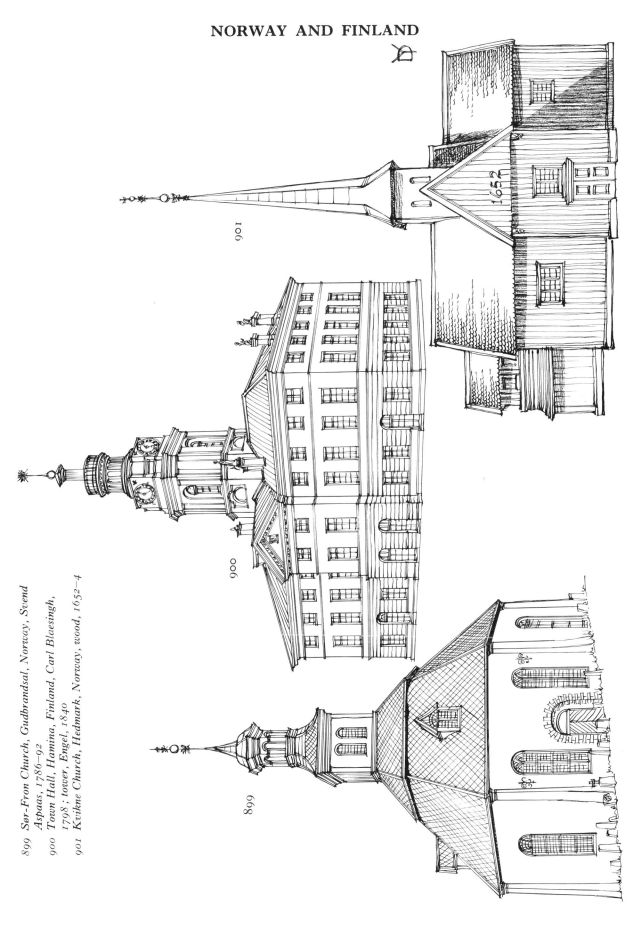

899 *Sør-Fron Church, Gudbrandsal, Norway, Svend Aspaas, 1786–92*

900 *Town Hall, Hamina, Finland, Carl Blaesingh, 1798 ; tower, Engel, 1840*

901 *Kvikne Church, Hedmark, Norway, wood, 1652–4*

902

902 Sør-Fron Church, Gudbrandsal, Norway, Svend Aspaas, 1786–92

the outskirts of a tiny village in a lonely valley in northern Hedmark (**901**). The exterior is of boarded wood. Inside, the church is painted all over the wood ceiling and walls in acanthus scrolled designs, incorporating panels depicting the Passion and the Life of the Apostles. Both these and the richly carved and painted pulpit are charmingly sophisticated and naïvely attractive—a remarkable testimony to mountain valley craftsmanship in this age. The work has much in common with the equally remote mountain churches of this date in Rumania and Bulgaria.

Though the majority of churches, even in the eighteenth century, were still of this type, after 1740 several examples were built which show a strong Baroque quality. This is clearly national in derivation, but an affinity with Baroque spatial and lighting effects, as well as an adherence to the octagonal, centrally planned form, is notable. Two outstanding octagonal churches are that at *Røros*, not far from Kvikne in northern Hedmark, and that at *Sør-Fron* in Gudbrandsal. Both were

designed by *Svend Aspaas* in the 1780s. Røros Church stands near the summit of a hill at the top of the small town's main street. It comprises an elongated octagon in plan with a square tower at the north-eastern side. It is a large church, painted white and with steeply pitched tiled roofs.

Sør-Fron Church, on the outskirts of a village much further south, is a simple octagon on the exterior, with no tower, only a central lantern (**899**). The interior is fully Baroque in its spatial handling and in altar and gallery detailing. The gallery, supported on columns, extends all round the church, its passage curtailed only by the high altar itself. The illustration in Fig. **902** shows the view from this level. This is a simple church, mainly in carved and painted wood; it is a Norwegian version of Borromini and, as such, charmingly successful.

The *Church* at *Kongsberg* dominates the town from the hillside above. The interior is very like that at Sør-Fron but on a more magnificent scale.

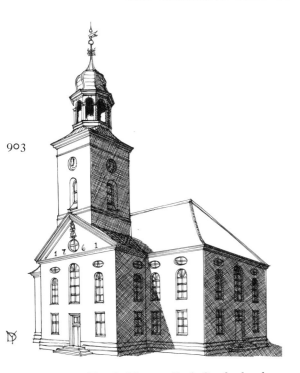

903

903 Kongsberg Church, Norway, J. A. Stuckenbrock, 1740–61

Here, though, the church is rectangular, with the high altar in the centre of the long side and opposite are enclosed boxes in the gallery for royal and important guests. It is a large church, with two galleries, one above the other, which can seat 3000 people. The decoration is all Baroque, in wood, carved, gilded and painted to imitate marble and other materials. The church exterior is of brick, large scale but simple in design (**903**).

Finland

Little notable Finnish architecture from these years exists. The great majority of building was in wood, which has perished or been altered during the country's political and military struggles with her larger neighbours. Impressive defence fortifications were built, of which *Sveaborg* was one of the largest. This is an island about three miles south-east of Helsinki. It was completely fortified all round, with strong walling, but the buildings are much altered now. A number of centralised, cruciform churches were built in the eighteenth century, but these were mainly of wood and have not survived well.

Very few civic structures on classical lines were built in towns until the extensive development of the early nineteenth century (pp. 508, 510). The old *town hall* in *Porvoo* dates from 1764, and is a simple, colour-washed building, now used as a museum. The finest example of such work is the *town hall* at *Hamina* (**900**). This little town, now on the Soviet border, was destroyed during the Russian occupation of 1713–21. After this date it was rebuilt by *Carl Blaesingh*, who laid out the new town on a classical, centralised pattern based on concentric octagons, after Scamozzi's sixteenth century prototype at Palmanova in northern Italy. In Hamina, the streets radiate outwards from the centre of the design where stands the town hall, which is a classical gem. It was built in 1798, but the tower was added later by Engel.

The Low Countries: Belgium

There is a marked difference in the classical architecture of this period in Belgium and Holland. The former, as a largely Catholic area, developed a Baroque style under the leadership of the Jesuits who built many churches. In Holland the trend was similar to that in England and northern Germany.

Seventeenth century work in *Belgium* is mainly ecclesiastical. The towns were prospering less than in the fifteenth and sixteenth centuries and little secular work of interest emerged. Even in the churches the late Gothic structural form was slow to die. Typical is the *Church of S. Michael* in *Louvain*, designed in 1650 by *Willem Hesius* (van Hees). The ground plan is Latin cruciform, transepts and choir are apsidal-ended, while the aisles are formed by free-standing Ionic and Composite columns, not classical piers (**905**). The decoration is Baroque and the columns support an entablature, but above is a Gothic-type ribbed vaulted ceiling. Barrel vaulting decorated with painted panels and stucco decoration is rare in Belgium. The quality of ornament in the interior, and on the exterior façade is good. There is some fine woodcarving and sculpture in the altar rail and confession boxes (PLATE 82).

The *eighteenth century*, on the other hand, is noted for the building of secular structures. The outstanding instance of this is the *Grande Place* in *Brussels*. The guild houses here (**908**)

BAROQUE ARCHITECTURE IN THE LOW COUNTRIES

904 *Nieuwe Kerk, The Hague, Van Bassen and Noorwits, 1665*
905 *Church of S. Michael, Louvain, Willem Hesius, 1650–6*
906 *Nos. 364–370, Herengracht, Amsterdam, Vingboons, 1662–5*
907 *S. Mary's Church, Leyden, A. van 's Gravensande, 1639–49*

908

908 Grande Place, Brussels, late seventeenth and early eighteenth centuries

were rebuilt on the narrow, Medieval sites which they had occupied before their destruction by bombardment in 1695. The treatment of the new buildings is entirely Baroque. Each house differs from its neighbour but they all form a homogeneous unit. The decoration is rich and varied, in gables, finials, columns and sculptured figures; it is a national form of Baroque, characteristic of the country.

After 1750 a more neo-classical style replaced the Baroque. A number of town-planning schemes were carried out in this medium. The most important of these was designed by a French architect, *Barré*. This was the *Place Royale* in *Brussels*, laid out on the site of the old palace. It has a fine position high up in the city, looking down upon the Mont des Arts with its terraced steps and, further away, the town hall and cathedral. *Gilles Barnabé Guimard*, also of French origin, carried out the work with façades round three sides of a square and the equestrian statue in the centre in front of the church portico (**910**).

Holland

The *seventeenth century*, in particular, was a period of building activity in Holland. There is little Baroque design and this is found chiefly in decoration. Classical architecture is mainly in brick, with correct use of pilasters and ornament. Stone is often used for orders, decoration and facings. Large parts of the centre of *Amsterdam* were built in the seventeenth century, especially in terraces of tall houses along canals like Herengracht, Keizersgracht, Prinsengracht. One of the chief architects was *Philip Vingboons* (1614–78) who built in the same basic style as had been used in the sixteenth century, but replaced the curved, stepped gables with simpler, pedimented ones with curving swags at the sides. Giant orders are used on a number of façades. Doorways are planned in pairs and the whole curved terrace is of one architectural composition. The examples shown in Fig. **906** of the Herengracht are typical. A fine palace at *29, Kloveniersburgwal* (1622) was designed by his brother, *Justus Vingboons*.

Vingboons was designing chiefly in the years 1640–60. In the later years of the century, *Daniel Marot* (1661–1751), a refugee Huguenot, brought a French flavour to Dutch architecture. His work is richer and more Baroque in decoration and structure. It can be seen at *The Hague*, where his *Royal Library* (**912**) and buildings in the *Korte Vijverberg* (such as No. 3), survive. No. 475 in the Herengracht in Amsterdam is also thought to be by him.

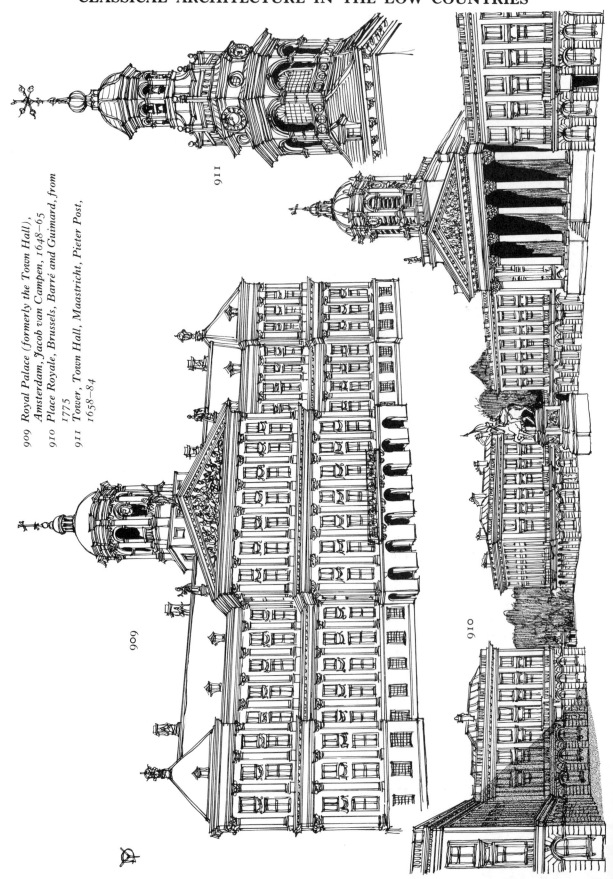

909 Royal Palace (formerly the Town Hall),
Amsterdam, Jacob van Campen, 1648–65

910 Place Royale, Brussels, Barré and Guimard, from
1775

911 Tower, Town Hall, Maastricht, Pieter Post,
1658–84

912 No. 34, Lange Vorhout (Royal Library), The Hague, Holland, Daniel Marot, 1734–8

Dutch Palladian architecture was still flourishing, particularly in mid-century. The prime example of this is the large *town hall* in the centre of *Amsterdam* by *Jacob van Campen* (**909**). This immense rectangular block contains two interior courts. A structure designed for prestige, it is one of the few Dutch buildings to be entirely of stone. Of similar style is the *town hall* at *Maastricht* (1658–84) by *Pieter Post* (**911**).

Apart from these specific examples there are many individual houses and, commonly, whole streets of seventeenth and eighteenth century Dutch houses surviving, little altered on the exterior. These are often in towns along the canals. Aside from those already mentioned in *Amsterdam*, there are some elegant, tall façades in the Leidsegracht and round the open Begijnhof, which is a quiet courtyard of unusual shape surrounded by seventeenth century houses. In *The Hague* is No. 74 Lange Vorhout (1760–4) by P. de Swart and in *Leyden* there are several streets, like the Rapenburg Quay and Papengracht, which have many distinguished houses.

The *churches* are also classical in vein though not very Baroque. Typical is the *New Church* at *The Hague* by *Pieter Noorvits* (**904**), which still has much in common with de Keyser's Amsterdam churches (p. 336). The *Marekerk* at *Leyden* is more Baroque in structure (**907**). It is centrally planned but is in plain brick with a minimum of decoration. It is octagonal and inside has a ring of eight columns supporting the central drum and dome and creating an ambulatory. The *Lutheran Church* in *Amsterdam* (1669–71) still presents a fine exterior and is a landmark in the centre of the city. Also of brick and centrally planned, it is circular with a giant order all round the exterior walls, the columns standing on a stone plinth. Above is an immense dome. Visitors attracted by optimistic descriptions of its classical interior in current books are surprised to find that it is now a sports store selling camping and boating equipment on three floors.

PART FOUR
THE MODERN WORLD

8

The Nineteenth Century: Eclecticism

Throughout Europe all architecture was based on what had gone before; the nineteenth century was exclusively an era of stylistic revivals. This is true to a certain extent of all buildings created since the fifteenth century, but the designers of the Renaissance, Baroque and Rococo eras, though inspired by earlier work, brought to their interpretation something new and personal; as can be seen in the variations on the classical theme produced by Brunelleschi, Bernini, Mansart and Wren. All these architects took their ideas from Ancient Rome, but their work included something new and different in its design and function.

It is only now that a balanced evaluation of nineteenth century architecture is being made. In the first half of the twentieth century historians and critics were too close to the previous age to assess its contribution fairly. Most condemned the work as derivative, mass-produced and in poor taste. A few, in contrast, praised fulsomely. It is undoubtedly true that the nineteenth century, all over Europe, perpetrated much ugly, tasteless building, permitted large, uncontrolled expansion of cities and created for posterity great areas of slums. Designers also experimented with mass production of building materials and decorative media, explored the possibilities of iron, glass, steel and prefabrication and, at the same time, produced a fair quantity of fine architecture, much of which, despite widespread demolition in cities and the holocaust of two world wars, survives today.

The Industrial Revolution, first in the eighteenth century and more fully in the nineteenth, was responsible for the movement of population from country to town. Improved standards of hygiene raised the total numbers of people to an undreamt of level. In all the industrialised regions of Europe, led by England and Germany and followed later by France, the Low Countries and the Austro-Hungarian Empire, a tremendous building drive got under way to provide factories, homes, schools and civic structures for the increase of population. Two major results of this—problems which still trouble us today—were the mass production development of the building industry and speculative expansion. In the early nineteenth century craftwork and hand made decoration, furniture, etc. were still common. By 1900, ceiling ornamentation and wainscot mouldings, fireplaces and decorative motifs of all types were mass produced and applied ready made to the inside and exterior of a building. A hardness of finish and a sameness of design invaded more and more the domain previously governed by aesthetic considerations; a process which has culminated in the module-based glass and concrete box architecture of our own day.

At the same time, speculative builders were profiting from the desperate need for housing. They bought land on the outskirts of industrial cities and built houses, packed close together in ugly rows, which lacked sanitation and all amenities. Life in these houses was miserable, standard of health and hygiene abysmally low. The countryside of Europe was slowly eaten into by areas of small ugly dwellings, factories, slag heaps and other debris from man's progress from an agricultural life to an industrial one.

But not all building of homes was like this. There were philanthropists, visionaries and architects of social purpose, ahead of their time and thought. In Germany there was Krupp at Essen; in England, Sir Titus Salt in Yorkshire and Lord Leverhulme at Port Sunlight. Such men built 'ideal townships' for their workers with housing, shops and amenities near to the factories. These were the pioneers of the 'new town' or 'garden city' concepts of the twentieth century.

In style, the architecture of the nineteenth century comprised a re-interpretation of all previous forms from Byzantine and Romanesque to eighteenth century Rococo; the architect tried them all. Romanesque, Byzantine and

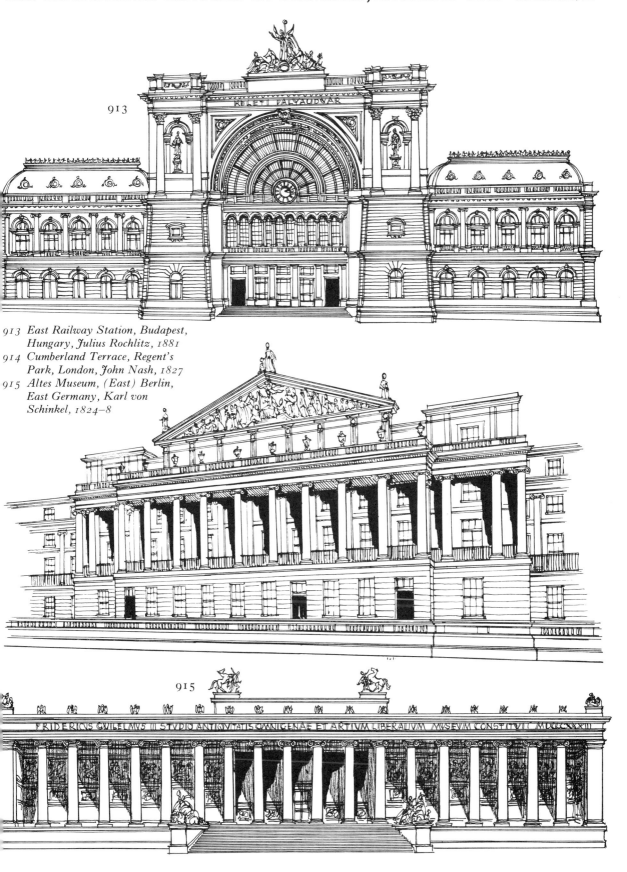

913 *East Railway Station, Budapest,*
Hungary, Julius Rochlitz, 1881
914 *Cumberland Terrace, Regent's*
Park, London, John Nash, 1827
915 *Altes Museum, (East) Berlin,*
East Germany, Karl von
Schinkel, 1824–8

Gothic styles were generally reserved for churches, schools, houses and universities and classical themes were applied to civic layouts and public building. Some countries, with a strong classical tradition, such as Italy, built primarily in this way. Others, with strong Medieval associations, such as England, favoured Gothic. The industrial nations developed structural design in iron and glass and some of the finest architecture of the nineteenth century stems from the engineering achievements of this age. England was the leader, followed closely by France, Italy and Germany.

In general, despite national and regional characteristics and development, certain trends were to be seen in most countries in specific decades. For instance, the early nineteenth century, up to about 1830, is marked by the prevalence of Romantic Classicism and also for neo-classical designs based upon Greek temple forms. These are simple, with clean, even severe lines. Germany was a leader in this field, followed by England, France and Denmark. In the 1840s and 1850s came the Romanesque and early Gothic designs leading to the High Gothic of the mid- and later century, especially in England. In the later decades of the century came a tremendous mixture of styles, architects trying all ideas and some reverting to a simpler, more stringent approach.

Strictly limited space has been given to this chapter in comparison with earlier ones because of the derivative nature of the work. The illustrations have been chosen from typical, good examples in their countries. There are, in most cases, one or two buildings in a country which are of exceptionally high standard, but they are rarely typical though they had a strong influence on other work. These have not usually been selected for illustration but are, of course, discussed in the text. The fact that most of the work of the century is derivative and often standardised does not mean that there is no fine architecture or buildings worth seeing. A great deal of this remains; a personal study of it is highly rewarding.

England

Among the countries and architects producing the best architecture of this century are England,

the Germanic countries and France. England was the natural leader for a large proportion of the century because its people were enjoying greater peace and economic stability than other European nations and because it was the leader, by several decades, in the development of the Industrial Revolution.

Like other countries, the architecture of the first 40 years of the century, late Georgian and Regency, is primarily romantic and neo-classical. The traditions of the 'golden age' of the later eighteenth century of Adam, Chambers, Leverton and Holland continued. *John Nash* (1752–1835) was a leading figure, known especially for his town planning in *London* of the *Regent's Park* and *Regent Street*. His terraces round the Regent's Park, though not as well built or finished as those by his eighteenth century predecessors, are fine town, terrace architecture and mainly survive today (**914**). While Nash was building in traditional classical style, *Sir John Soane* (1753–1837) was the last of the original architectural designers of Britain. His style is austere, astringent and often uncompromising. It does not appeal as readily to popular taste as do Nash's façades, but is more distinctive. Fine examples of his work still extant (and all in London) include the screen wall of the *Bank of England*, the *Dulwich Art Gallery and Mausoleum*, the *churches* of S. *John, Bethnal Green* and *Holy Trinity, Marylebone* as well as his *houses* in *Lincoln's Inn Fields* (now the Sir John Soane Museum) and *Pitzhanger Manor* at *Ealing* (now the public library).

Nash and Soane were building chiefly in the first and second decades of the century. Further classical work came from *William Wilkins* (1778–1839) and *Sir Robert Smirke* (1781–1867) in the period 1825–40. The former is especially known for the *National Gallery* in Trafalgar Square in *London* and his Gothic screen at *King's College, Cambridge*. Smirke's chief work is the *British Museum* in *London* with its severe, extended Ionic temple front (1825–47).

Several fine speculative estates were laid out in London and other cities in these years, mainly on classical lines. Typical is *George Basevi's Belgrave Square* and *South Kensington*, streets and layouts at *Bath, Cheltenham* and *Bristol*. The *Hove* and *Brighton* seafront terraces are particularly fine. Also of excellent standard are the estates laid out by the famous speculative builder *Thomas Cubitt* in Belgravia and Pimlico.

From 1840 English architecture turned towards Gothic design. The first great monument in this mode is the *Palace of Westminster*, rebuilt after the fire of 1834 by *Sir Charles Barry* (1795–1860), assisted in the decoration by *A. W. N. Pugin*. The Palace of Westminster, which includes the Houses of Commons and Lords, the Victoria Tower and the clock tower of Big Ben, has a magnificent riverside site. It is built in late Gothic style, panelled all over in stone and glass. It remains the greatest English neo-Gothic building, finely and dramatically designed and containing craftsmanship and ornament of the highest quality.

The question may be asked: 'What is the fundamental difference between architecture of the Gothic Revival period and that of the Middle Ages?' It is clear that there *are* differences, but these are not easy to define. This consideration is equally applicable to all countries in Europe which possess neo-Gothic and also neo-classical building. The chief difference is in the craftsmanship. Medieval and Renaissance work evolved over hundreds of years. A large body of craftsmen spent their lives carving, modelling, painting and working in plaster, glass, iron or wood. In the nineteenth century, after several hundred years of classical work there were no craftsmen in Gothic architecture. Barry and Pugin, in England, had to train a new school of craftsmen to build the Palace of Westminster. Their work was excellent, but after 1850 the pace of building accelerated and demands far exceeded supply in all forms of craftsmen. Thus means of mass production of decorative features had to be developed. This gives the hard, repetitious finish typical of a nineteenth century Gothic finial or capital. Medieval buildings took many years to erect: nineteenth century ones could be completed in months.

Another difference is in spirit. Medieval building arose from the religious feeling of its period. In the nineteenth century religious fervour was strong, but it was not the sole basis

916 Natural History Museum, London, Alfred Waterhouse, 1873–9

916

for life. Lord Clark* expresses this feeling vividly. 'Although the saints in a modern Catholic image shop are extremely virtuous, they are obviously the product of an utterly worldly civilisation, whereas the gargoyles of a Medieval cathedral, though monsters of vice, are alive with the spirit of a truly religious age.'

The Gothic Revival in England was at its height from 1855–85. This is the High Victorian Gothic period. Its chief architects were *George Edmund Street* (1824–81), known for the *Law Courts* in *London, Alfred Waterhouse* (1830–1905), the *Natural History Museum, London* (**916**) and *Manchester Town Hall, Sir George Gilbert Scott* (1811–78), the most prolific of all and famed for his controversial *Albert Memorial* and *S. Pancras Hotel*—both now coming back into fashion—and *William Butterfield* (1814–1900) of *Keble College, Oxford* and *All Saints' Church* of *London*'s West End. These architects and many others built in all styles of Gothic from Romanesque to Tudor, often in brick and generally with polychrome decorative features. The structures are sound, well designed and, with the patina of years, are acquiring respectability and appreciation.

In the last two decades of the century came a reaction among younger architects away from Victorian heaviness, over-decoration and spurious materials towards a simplicity and a return to undisguised stone, brick or wood. Leaders in this movement include *Philip Webb* (1831–1915), *Norman Shaw* (1831–1912), *C. F. A. Voysey* (1857–1941) and *Charles Rennie Mackintosh* (1869–1928). Shaw's work was exceptionally fine and varied. A number of his buildings survive: his houses and flats in London, country houses like *Bryanston*, Dorset and *Grim's Dyke*, Middlesex and, in the centre of London, *New Scotland Yard*† and the *Pall Mall Assurance offices*. Voysey and Mackintosh designed work which foreshadowed the modern approach of the twentieth century. *Mackintosh's Glasgow School of Art* verges towards Art Nouveau but in an uncompromising manner. *Voysey's houses* are simple, unpretentious and a return to the English country building style of the craftsman.

Iron had long been used as a building material, but it was only from the later eighteenth century that it was employed on a large scale. Developments in cast iron and steel followed and after 1850, glass and iron were used structually as well as decoratively. The *Crystal Palace* in *London* erected for the Great Exhibition of 1851 in Hyde Park, was the first prefabricated example on a large scale. Measuring 1851 feet by 450 feet it contained 900,000 square feet of glass and was supported on 3300 iron columns with 2224 girders. It was put up in five months and, in 1852, taken down and re-erected at Sydenham where it remained a London landmark until its destruction by fire in 1936.

The nineteenth century was the *railway age* in Britain. Many *stations* are fine architectural structures. Among these are *King's Cross* in *London* (1850–2) by *Lewis Cubitt, Paddington* in *London* by *Brunel* and *Wyatt* (1852–4) and the 1000 feet façade at *Chester* (1847–8) by *Thompson* and *Stephenson*. The great engineers of the first half of the century, *Rennie, Telford, Brunel* and *Stephenson*, led the way in structural design in iron with their railway, canal and bridge constructions. Much of their achievements survives as in *Brunel's Clifton Bridge*, high over the Avon Gorge at Bristol, and *Telford's* 1000 feet long *Pont-Cysylltau aqueduct* at *Llangollen* and his road bridges at *Conway* and the *Menai Straits* both in Wales. The structures of these engineers led the way to the structural use in architecture of iron and steel and glass as can be seen in Italy Belgium and France (pp. 491, 494, 496). Such structures constituted the original contribution to building of the nineteenth century, comparable in their way to the engineering achievements of Ancient Rome.

The Germanic Influence: Germany, Austria, Hungary, Switzerland, Czechoslovakia:
Germany

Germany, with England, produced the best work in the earlier decades of this century, when a number of architects specialised in neo-classical and Romantic Classical design. Centres of several major cities were rebuilt and laid out in extensive schemes, for example, Berlin, Munich and Karlsruhe. An early prototype of the severely Greek temple portico design is the *Brandenburg Gate*, built as an entrance to the city and the Unter den Linden in *Berlin* (1789–93) by *K. G. Langhans*.

* The Gothic Revival, *John Murray, 1962.*
† *The embankment building, not that in Broadway.*

A number of architects followed Langhans in this type of Grecian design. *David Gilly* (1748–1808) in *Berlin, Friedrich Weinbrenner* (1766–1826) in *Karlsruhe*. In *Munich* three outstanding architects re-designed the centre of the city: *Karl von Fischer* (1782–1820), *Leo von Klenze* (1784–1864) and *Friedrich von Gärtner* (1792–1847). Fischer laid out the *Karolinenplatz* in 1808 and designed the *National Theatre* in the *Max Josephsplatz*. *Von Klenze* rebuilt this to the original design after a fire in 1823. His chief work in the city was the laying out of the vast *Königsplatz*; an entirely Grecian scheme. He designed the *Glyptotek* on the left, a pedimented building with Corinthian portico and, incorporating *Ziebland's* similar *Picture Gallery* opposite, on the right, completed the scheme with his central *Propylaeon* (1846–63), derived from the Athens acropolis group. Differing from this severe Grecian work is von Klenze's façade for the *Königsbau* (1826–33, the royal palace) in Munich, fronting the Max Josephsplatz which, with its rusticated three storey, pilastered treatment, is like an early Renaissance Florentine palace.

Gärtner's chief contribution to Munich is the long, principal thoroughfare, the *Ludwigstrasse*, containing his elevations of the *University* (1834–40), the *Blindeninstitut* (1834–8), the *State Library* (1831–40) and dominated by the twin-towered *Ludwigskirche* (1829–40). The church is Italian Romanesque in style, but the other buildings are in the severe, round-arched manner of this period of Romantic Classicism (*Rundbogenstil*). The interior of the church is Byzantine in quality and atmosphere. The great barrel vaults and walls are painted all over in rich colours and gilt to represent mosaic, culminating in an immense painting on the entire east wall behind the altar. Even the capitals are in Byzantine basket form. It is an impressive interior. At each end of the long thoroughfare Gärtner has returned to Roman classicism with his triumphal arch at the top—the *Siegestor* (1843–50) and, at the city end, his replica of the Loggia dei Lanzi in Florence—the *Feldherrenhalle*.

The outstanding German architect of the first half of the nineteenth century was *Karl Friedrich von Schinkel* (1781–1841). He designed largely in neo-classical form and his masterpiece here is the *Altes Museum* in *Berlin* (**915**). This is now in East Berlin and its reconstruction after war damage is almost complete. Comparable in theme to Smirke's British Museum in London, the Berlin example is a finer building. It is beautifully proportioned and finished. Schinkel's *Neue Wache* in the Unter den Linden is nearby. This is in severe Greek-temple style reminiscent of von Klenze's Propylaeon in Munich. It too has been well restored.

Schinkel was also a great exponent of what Germany called the *Rundbogenstil*. The particularly German approach to Romantic Classicism was especially used in the period 1825–45. The elevations are commonly pierced by round arches and these features and other motifs are repeated regularly along the extensive façades. The design was also applied to other forms of eclecticism, including classical and Byzantine structures. It was a reaction from the more severe Greek type of neo-classicism and can be seen in, for example, the work of Gärtner in Munich and many others in cities like Stuttgart, Hanover and Darmstadt. A late example is the *Berlin Town Hall* (1859–70), in East Berlin, now restored in a too brilliant red brick.

Among other outstanding examples of Schinkel's work is the *Schauspielhaus* (theatre) in *Berlin* (1819–21) and many buildings at Potsdam. The Schauspielhaus (East Berlin) was seriously damaged in the war and reconstruction has not yet begun, but enough remains for this to be possible, and the work is being undertaken. His great *Nikolaikirche* in *Potsdam* (1830–50) was also damaged but is being restored. This is a centrally planned classical church based on the Pantheon in Rome. Above the great cube structure rises a drum and dome similar to Wren's S. Paul's in London.

A fair quantity of Gothic Revival building was carried out in the second half of the century, but most of it was in the form of restoration and completion of the Medieval heritage. *Cologne Cathedral* was the chief of these (1824–80), when the entire west front, with its tall twin steeples was added. New churches were generally weightier than English equivalents. The *Kaiser Wilhelm Gedächtniskirche* in *Berlin* was typical of these. The blackened shell was retained after the Second World War in memory of Berlin's experiences, and now a very modern church and bell-tower incongruously flank the ruins at the head of the Kurfürstendamm. Typical of the secular neo-Gothic style is the *Munich Town Hall* (**917**), an imposing structure. The view in the illustration is taken from the towers of the Frauenkirche nearby.

Late nineteenth century work in Germany was more often in monumental neo-Baroque form, with weighty, lavish ornamentation. An excellent example is the *Reichstag* in *Berlin* (1884–94). Designed by *Wallot*, it was set on fire in 1933 and is now cleaned and restored. At the other end of the Unter der Linden in East Berlin is the still unrestored new *Cathedral*. This is also a rich ornamental Baroque building, with imposing façades and a great central dome. The design, by *Raschdorf*, replaced Schinkel's Cathedral in 1894–1905.

Austria and Hungary

The most important nineteenth century building was in the replanning of the two capitals of the Austro-Hungarian Empire, Vienna and Budapest, under the aegis of Franz Josef. Since he did not accede until 1848, there are few examples of Romantic or neo-classicism. *Luigi Pichl's Diet of Lower Austria* at No. 13 Herrengasse in *Vienna*

917

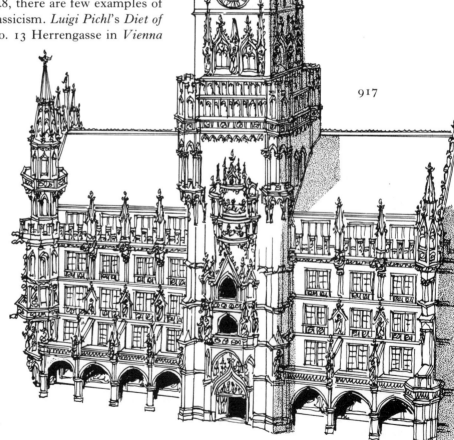

917 Neues Rathaus (town hall), Munich, G. J. von Hauberrisser, 1867–74

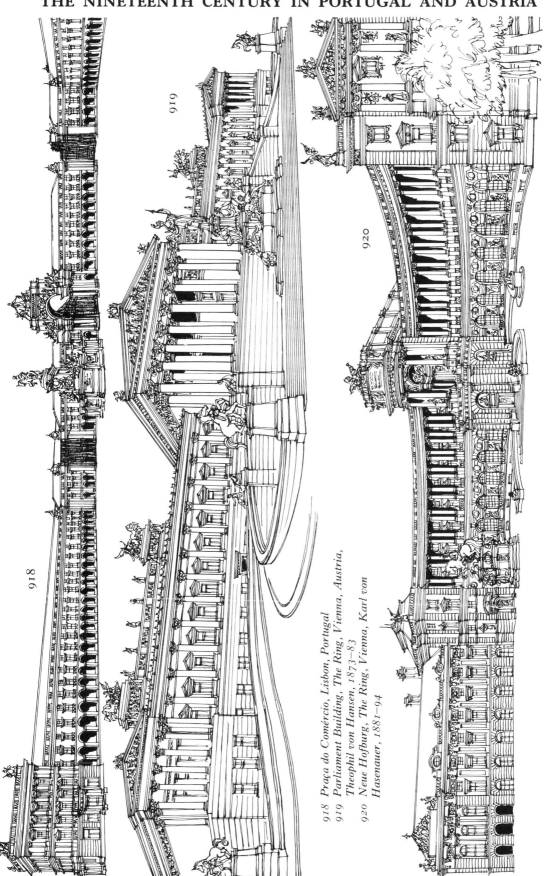

918 *Praça do Comércio, Lisbon, Portugal*
919 *Parliament Building, The Ring, Vienna, Austria,*
    Theophil von Hansen, 1873–83
920 *Neue Hofburg, The Ring, Vienna, Karl von*
    Hasenauer, 1881–94

(1837–44) is one such building. Other work of the time is in the German *Rundbogenstil* based on Renaissance forms, such as the neighbouring *Landeshauptmannshaft* at No. 11 Herrengasse (1846–8) by *Paul Sprenger*.

The Emperor Franz Josef made plans for his great reconstruction of Vienna in 1849. He intended to build a capital as fine as Napoleon's Second Empire Paris. Certainly Vienna is the only Western European capital to rival Paris in its thoroughgoing nineteenth century re-structuring which created broad boulevards, lined with harmonious buildings of good standard, obviously planned and executed under a régime powerful enough to overcome commercial and political opposition, thus attaining homogeneity. Neither the Prince Regent in London nor Kaiser Wilhelm I in Berlin were able to carry out so successfully their ambitious plans.

Vienna, on Franz Josef's accession, was still a fortified, largely Medieval city. Its fortifications were destroyed and the Emperor created his famous *Ringstrasse* which, with the Danube canal, completely encircles the Medieval city, containing S. Stephen's Cathedral, the old town hall and contemporary buildings. The 'Ring' took 30 years to build, from 1858–88. The structures around it are in keeping with one another, though not entirely uniform. Most of them are in High Renaissance style, a little heavy and with ground arcades and mansard roofs. Typical are the *Palais Epstein* (1870–3) by *Hansen*, the façades flanking the New Town Hall and the two great museums by *Semper* and *Hasenauer* on the Maria Theresienplatz, adjoining the Ring, the *Natural History Museum* and, opposite, the *Art Museum* (Kunsthistoriches) (1872–81). These have central domes rising above long ornate façades. A statue of the seated Empress provides a focal centre for the square.

These structures are typical but not of high quality. More interesting are those in and near the Ring which are based on a variety of styles. In neo-Gothic is the *Votivkirche* (1856–79) by *Ferstel*—a slenderer, smaller Cologne Cathedral, and the imposing *Neues Rathaus*, the new town hall (1872–83), by *von Schmidt*. Immediately opposite on the other side of the Ringstrasse is the attractive *Burgtheater*, a neo-Baroque building (1874–88) by *Semper*, reminiscent of the Paris Opera House. This, like the *Viennese Opera*

House (1861–9) by *Van der Null*, has been rebuilt since the War to the original pattern.

The examples illustrated show two of the most imposing structures on the Ring. One is the *Parliament House* (**919**) in Grecian style, which is a late instance of building in the Greek Revival manner. It is a pleasant structure on a fine site and with good detail and sculpture. Opposite, across the Ring and the gardens, is the new wing added by Franz Josef to the existing palace—the *Neue Hofburg* (**920**). By *Hasenauer*, this is eclectic but imposing with its panache of sweeping colonnades. Behind this range, on the opposite façade, the Michaeler elevation was completed in this century (1893) to the original designs of J. E. Fischer von Erlach (p. 428). The work is bold and Baroque, but nineteenth century in its hardness and heaviness.

The Hungarian capital of *Budapest* was also built up under Franz Josef in the second half of the nineteenth century. Unfortunately the city suffered greatly in the latter part of the Second World War when the German army defended it against the Russian advance. Further damage was done to buildings in the uprising of 1956 and the majority of structures are not yet in a good state of repair.

Mihály Pollack's *National Museum* is an example of the earlier work on Romantic Classical lines (1837–47). This has a central Corinthian pedimented portico above a rusticated base. There are flanking towers and side colonnaded wings. The building stands in a garden behind the immense *Parliament Building* on the riverside. This stems from the neo-Gothic movement, which reached Budapest late in the century. It is partly inspired by Barry's Palace of Westminster in London, but has a great central drum and dome, still in Gothic design. It is a strange but successful marriage of styles (1883–1902, *Steindl*).

In classical style and typical of the later years of the century are the *East Railway Station* façade (**913**) and the great *Heroes Square*. On the edge of the park to the north-east of the city, this is an immense layout, designed by *Schikedanz*, completing the vista at the end of the great Nepköztársasag Boulevard, flanked by imposing houses where most of the consulates are situated. In the centre of the open space is the *Milennium Monument* commemorating (in 1896) the thousandth anniversary of the occupation of the Danube

921 S. Stephen's Basilica, Budapest, Hungary. Begun 1851 ; dome rebuilt by Ybl ; interior completed twentieth century

basin by the Magyars. There is a central column surmounted by the archangel Gabriel and two flanking, curved colonnades, surmounted by horses and chariots and with statues of Hungarian Kings* below. At the foot of the column are groups of Magyar horsemen. These show great characteristic vitality (PLATE 99). Classical buildings flank either side of the monument. On the left is the Corinthian colonnaded *Fine Arts Museum* (1900–6) and on the right the *Exhibition Palace of the Fine Arts* (1894). This is in classical temple design with relief and mosaic decoration (*Schikedanz* and *Herzog*).

There are many nineteenth century churches in Hungary. Two of the large classical examples are *S. Stephen's Basilica* in *Budapest* and *Eszter-*

* In 1945 several reactionary kings, including Franz Josef, were removed and replaced by more suitable proletarian candidates.

gom Cathedral. S. Stephen's (**921**) is a traditional, well-proportioned Baroque design on the exterior, a massive, heavy building with temple front, flanking towers and central drum and dome. Inside it is at present rather dark as the drum windows are blocked up. It is built on Greek cross plan, the vast central dome supported on pendentives and immense piers. The Corinthian Order is used and the decoration is in marble, gilt, mosaic and painting. It is rich, heavy and ornate.

The *Cathedral* at *Esztergom* is very different. It is also immense, but has a wonderful site, high on a hill. Framed against the skyline, it rises directly above the Danube and dominates the town, instead of being sited in a busy city square full of parked lorries. The exterior is plain, almost totally undecorated. It has an immense Corinthian portico and Adam-type Composite columns surround the drum beneath the dome. The exterior, despite its siting, is a much less satisfactory design than S. Stephen's. It is ill-proportioned and too nakedly undecorated. The interior, in contrast, appears well handled. The dome, which is too small on the exterior, here seems effective, and both it and the drum and pendentives are decorated with paintings and mosaic. The interior is very light and in subtle colouring with a sparing use of gilt and blue and grey marbles. There are simple altar pictures based on Titian's work.

The French influence was strong in parts of *Switzerland* and French architects designed many buildings in the French-language-speaking towns like Neuchâtel, Geneva and Lausanne. The German *Rundbogenstil* was followed in many German-speaking areas. Little of the work is of outstanding interest and stylistically was often many years out of date. In Zürich *Winterthur Semper* designed several buildings, including the temple-porticoed *town hall* and the huge buildings of the *Polytechnic* begun in 1859 (**924**).

Work in *Czechoslovakia* was eclectic, but livelier and of more interesting design. In the later nineteenth century some imposing structures were evidence of the prosperity. This can be seen in *Prague*, for example, among other large cities. These are generally on neo-Renaissance or neo-Baroque lines, richly ornamented and of good quality workmanship. Typical are the immense *National Museum* (1885–90) by *Joseph Schulz*, standing on the crest of the hill at the top of Wenceslaus Square, which includes the Pantheon used for the lying-in-state of the city's great men, and the more elegant *National Theatre* (1881–3) by Joseph Zítek on the banks of the River Vltava (**922**). This is decorated by many artists of the period.

France

The French Revolution not only brought architectural construction to a halt but caused extensive damage to individual buildings, especially cathedrals and châteaux. Complete areas of centres of cities were also devastated in reprisal for royalist support; the Place Bellecour in

Lyons, for example, became a casualty. From 1806 Napoleon Bonaparte endeavoured to get a building programme re-started, partly because he aimed to leave some fine monuments in Paris and other cities as evidence of his reign and partly to ease the unemployment situation. He began many schemes, but most of these were completed after his death. His chief architects were *Charles Percier* (1764–1838) and *Pierre Fontaine* (1762–1853). Among their outstanding contribution to Paris in First Empire style, which was Romantic Classical, were the completion of the *Place de la Concorde* (p. 387), the nearby *Rue de Rivoli* (1802–55) and the extensions of the *Louvre* which included the elegant *Arc du Carrousel* set between the palace and the entrance to the Tuileries gardens. The arch, built 1806–8, is a marble version of that of Septimius Severus in the Rome Forum. It is delicately sculptured and well-proportioned. The original quadriga represented Napoleon and included the four Greek horses from S. Mark's Cathedral in Venice (p. 103). These were returned to their position there after Napoleon's fall, by the British. Percier and Fontaine also worked on the palaces of France at Compiègne, Fontainebleau and Versailles. Their work is of good standard, less finely detailed and designed than that of the eighteenth century but of higher quality than that of most of their contemporaries.

The best known monument of Napoleon's First Empire in Paris is the *Arc de Triomphe de l'Étoile*. Designed largely by *J. F. T. Chalgrin* (1739–1811), it is a vast arch, 162 feet in height, astylar and decorated with (on the left hand side facing the Champs Elysées) the famous sculptured group by *Rude* entitled 'Le Départ' (PLATE 96). The Place de L'Étoile* is a magnificent site; 12 great roads radiate from the central position held by the arch, which is on the highest point of this area. Under the arch is the eternal flame, marking the resting place of France's 'Unknown Soldier'.

Among notable examples of neo-classicism in Paris in the first 30 years of the century are the Exchange (1808–27), the Palais Bourbon (1807) and the Madeleine (1806–42). The *Exchange* (Bourse) is the Paris equivalent of Smirke's British Museum and Schinkel's Altes Museum. It is a large colonnaded structure in the Corinthian Order and was designed by *A. T. Brongniart*

* One French leader was replaced by another when it was renamed after General de Gaulle subsequent to his death in 1970.

THE NINETEENTH CENTURY IN CZECHOSLOVAKIA, POLAND AND SWITZERLAND

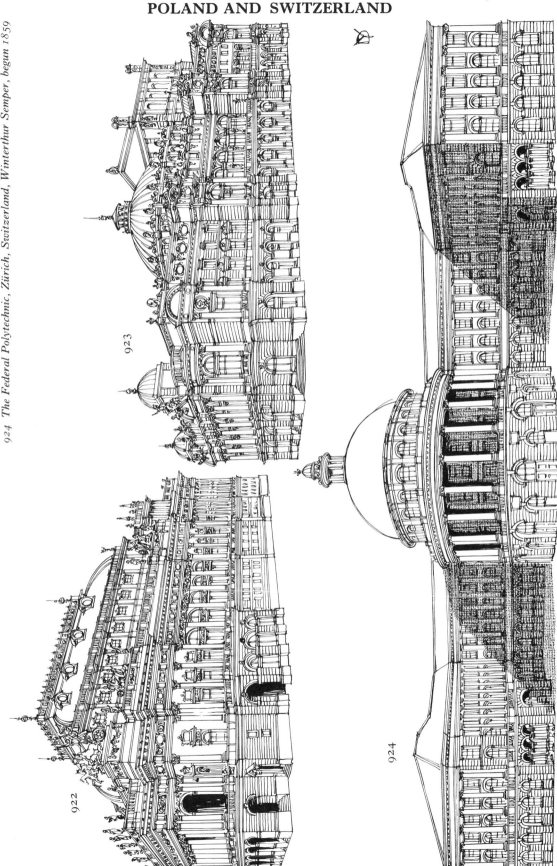

922 The National Theatre, Prague, Czechoslovakia, Joseph Zítek, 1881–3
923 The Municipal Theatre, Cracow, Poland, Zawiejski, 1893
924 The Federal Polytechnic, Zürich, Switzerland, Winterthur Semper, begun 1859

(1739–1813). The *Palais Bourbon* is now the Chamber of Deputies for France. Designed by *Poyet*, it is situated on the banks of the Seine; it has a large, Corinthian portico standing on a great flight of steps. It is surmounted by a sculptured pediment.

The site of a *church* to be dedicated to the *Magdalen* had been planned in the eighteenth century, when Gabriel designed the Place de la Concorde and the Rue Royale (p. 387). The church was to stand at the end of this vista. Napoleon decided early in the nineteenth century to build a temple of glory here on Roman Corinthian lines, standing upon a podium. It was designed on these lines in 1808 by *Pierre Vignon* (1762–1828) and is now a Paris landmark on this impressive site. The exterior is severe and saved only from being fully uncompromising by its fine proportions and pedimental sculpture. The interior (**927**), made into a church soon after its completion, is well designed and richly decorated, entirely classical and roofed by caissoned saucer domes and a barrel vaulted entrance vestibule. In notable contrast to the monumental exterior is this ornately gilded and painted interior.

An extensive influence on the architecture of the first half of the century was exerted by *Professor Durand*, professor of architecture at the École Polytechnique in Paris. His publications laid down guiding lines for eclectic design of the time and had an effect upon architects abroad as well as in France, especially Germany and Denmark

The quality of design and craftsmanship deteriorated in France, as elsewhere, after 1830–40. Among the better *churches* of the mid-century are the Parisian examples of *La Trinité* (1861–7), *S. Augustin* (1860–8) and, more severely classical, the church of *S. Vincent de Paul* (1824–44), designed by *Lepère* and *Hittorff*. This is a notable landmark, its great Ionic portico standing on a tall flight of steps with sculptured pediment above, and tall, square flanking towers.

The main layout of the centre of Paris (apart from the Medieval Île de la Cité and the Île S. Louis) is the product of the Second Empire. Napoleon III became Emperor in 1852 and for almost the next 20 years, under *Haussmann* and his colleagues, the Grandes Boulevards of Paris, with their *ronds-point* and flamboyant buildings set at significant places, were constructed. The

schemes were extensive, the quality of work high, the façades along the boulevards homogeneous and imposing. An urban masterpiece was created; the finest in Europe in this century Apart from one or two exceptions, the individual buildings are not outstanding. It is the town planning, the layout and the harmonious handling of the whole which is effective. The structures are mainly of stone or stucco, with shops on the ground floor, flats above, covered by mansard roofs. The roofline is even, the fenestration uniform. The whole is classical, often neo-Baroque. The *rond-point* of the Étoile, laid out by Haussmann, its buildings by Hittorff, is typical

One of the first large buildings to be constructed was the *New Louvre*, the extension to the existing palace. Started by *Visconti* in 1852, it was continued by *Lequel* (1810–80). The façades echo the design of the older work but are bolder and more plastic, especially in the sculpture and convex mansard roofs.

The most flamboyant and successful scheme of the period is the *Avenue* and *Place de l'Opéra* (**928**). The Place was laid out from 1858 onwards with buildings by *Rohault de Fleury* and *Henri Blondel*. The Opera House itself, designed by *Garnier* and built 1861–75, set the pattern for cities all over Europe. Strongly related to it is among others, the Burgtheater in Vienna (p. 484) the Rumanian Athenaeum in Bucharest (**925**) the Opera Houses of Odessa and L'vov (pp. 503, 500) and the Theatre in Cracow (**923**). The Paris Opera is sumptuous, imperial and very Baroque The exterior is three-dimensional and plastic more Italian than French. The sculpture on the façade by *Carpeaux* is noteworthy (PLATE 97) Inside, the foyer, grand staircase and auditorium are superbly luxurious in gilt with crimson velvet; the essence of the period in the wealthy countries of Western Europe.

Outside Paris a neo-Baroque layout of great magnificence is the *Palais Longchamps* at *Marseilles* (1862–9) by H. J. Espérandieu (1829–74). The monument constitutes an imposing entrance to the park, set into the hillside, with a central, sculptured cascade, flanked by a sweeping staircase and curving colonnades which lead, at each side, to square, classical blocks (PLATE 98)

France in the nineteenth century, like England thoroughly restored the monuments of her great Medieval heritage. The equivalent figure in

Plate 97
The Opera House, 1861–5. Sculpture by Carpeaux

Plate 96
Arc de Triomphe, 1806–35. Sculpture by Rude

Plate 98
Palais Longchamps,
Marseilles, France.
1862–9, Esperandieu
Plate 99
Detail. The Magyar
tribesmen. Milen-
nium Monument,
Budapest, Hungary,
1896

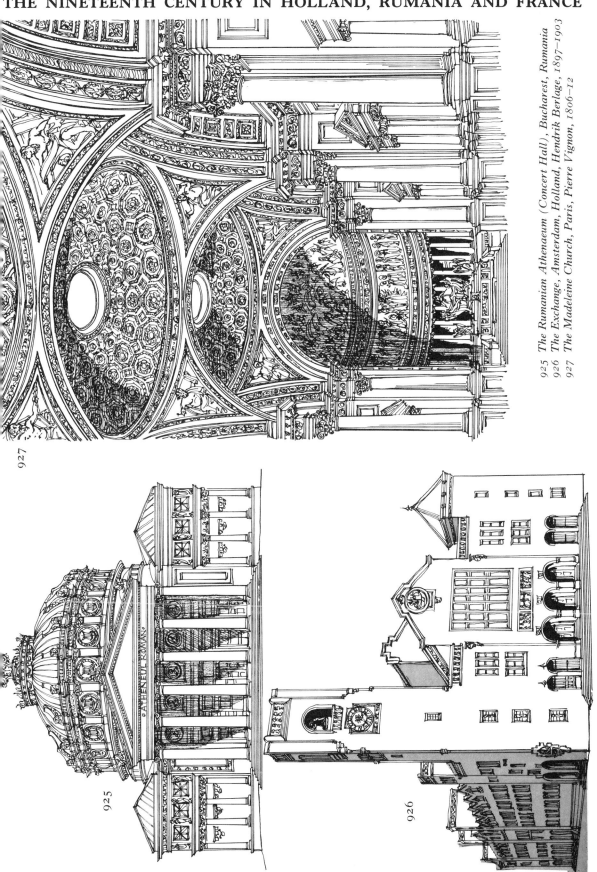

925 The Rumanian Athenaeum (Concert Hall), Bucharest, Rumania
926 The Exchange, Amsterdam, Holland, Hendrik Berlage, 1897–1903
927 The Madeleine Church, Paris, Pierre Vignon, 1806–12

928 Place de l'Opéra, Paris, de Fleury and Blondel, 1858–64. The Opera House (Académie Nationale de Musique), J. L. C. Garnier, 1861–74
929 Rila Monastery (75 miles south of Sofia), Bulgaria. Founded tenth century, rebuilt after fire of 1833

928

929

France to the English Sir George Gilbert Scott was *E. Viollet-le-Duc*, whose work was largely in the field of rebuilding and reconstructing Gothic masterpieces. Like Scott, he often·was over-enthusiastic and has accordingly been blamed by later generations. It is true nonetheless, that, but for the skilled work of such men in the nineteenth century, few of our own Medieval cathedrals would now be standing. Viollet-le-Duc's name is most closely associated in this respect with the Cathedral of Notre Dame, La Sainte Chapelle and the Abbey Church of S. Denis in Paris (p. 205), the Château of Pierrefonds and the walled town of Carcassonne (p. 212).

The *fin-de-siècle* brought a new wave of neo-Baroque buildings to Paris, when further grand-scale structures were built. Among these are the *Grand* and the *Petit Palais*. Completed at the same time, but quite different in style, was the great *Church of Sacré Cœur*, set on the hill of Montmartre, with its approach stairways and platforms. This church had been begun in 1874 by *Paul Abadie* (1812–84). It is in Romanesque/Byzantine style after the Church of S. Front at Périgueux (p. 107). A controversial building, but an arresting one.

It was in England that the possibilities of construction, as well as decoration, were studied and developed in the use of *iron, steel* and *glass* (p. 480). The first iron bridge in the world was built at Coalbrookdale in Shropshire, over the river Severn, as early as 1779. Further structures followed under the great engineers and in 1851 came the aptly-named Crystal Palace. The French were most interested in developing these techniques. They also, in the early nineteenth century, built iron bridges in Paris and elsewhere and went on, later in the century, to incorporate iron and glass into railway station construction, shopping galleries and even libraries. The most famous monument in iron in France is the Eiffel Tower in Paris, designed for the Paris Exhibition of 1889 by Gustave Eiffel (1832–1923). Eiffel was an engineer, but his researches and achievements, as with the English engineers, led later to the construction of metal structures clad in stone. The Eiffel Tower is 984 feet high.

Some of the Paris railway stations, like those in London, are architecturally fine. The *Gare de l'Est* (1847–52) by *Duquesney*, the *Gare du Nord* (1862–3) by *Hittorff* and the *Gare d'Orsay* (interior now disused) (1898–1900) by *Laloux* are three examples. Two famous libraries of Paris have interesting interior iron structures. The *Bibliothèque S. Geneviève* (next to the Panthéon) is a particularly elegant example. Built by *Henri Labrouste* (1845–50), it is especially original. In the *Bibliothèque Nationale* very slender iron columns with Corinthian capitals support the metal roof. This is divided into nine equal compartments, each with a saucer dome of glass and iron which illuminates the whole square room below. It is a functional and attractive interior.

Italy

By 1800, Italian dominance of the world of art and architecture had come to an end; there are no great names in nineteenth century Italian architecture. France was leading European design at the turn of the century and soon the impetus of new ideas and thought began to come from England and Germany. The Italians produced work quite comparable to other western nations and, indeed, created far fewer monstrosities to blight their cities than did other countries, but they had been pre-eminent for so long, their work had been so superb, that they themselves deprecated their nineteenth century efforts more than foreigners did. Italian architects felt the standards to be poor and thought little of having to follow on foreign lines.

Because of this deprecatory view, Italian nineteenth century work has been for long undervalued and it is only now being appreciated for its genuine worth. Designs were almost all classical. Italy's classical heritage was overwhelmingly strong; there was no Gothic Revival here. Among the works of the early part of the century, some interiors are particularly fine. At the *Royal Palace of Caserta*, some of the state rooms first built by Vanvitelli (p. 376) were redesigned. Of especial quality are the *Sala di Marte* and *Sala di Astra*, carried out by *Antonio di Simone* in 1807. This work is not just decorative but monumental in the serious, classical manner in the immense interiors, with coupled Ionic pilasters alternating with high relief sculptured panels extending from floor to entablature.

Deeply coved, sculptured ceilings echo the scheme above.

Also at Caserta, but later, comes the *Throne Room* designed in 1839–45 by *Gaetono Genovese* (1795–1860). This interior, rich and sumptuous, is craftsmanship of high quality, as is also the beautiful ornate interior of the famous Opera House of *La Scala* in *Milan*, decorated in 1830 by *Alessandro Sanquirico* (1774–1849). Both these interiors are in white and gold. Other theatres include the *San Carlo Opera House* in *Naples* (1810–12) by *Antonio Niccolini* and the Venetian Opera House, *La Fenice*, where the interior was redecorated in 1836 in neo-rococo style.

In one field of work the Italians excelled in the nineteenth century; that of *town planning* and civic schemes. In the first half of the century extensive layouts were completed in Turin, Trieste and Naples and, in the second half, in Rome. The work in *Turin* was the most far-reaching and, being of an early date, of the highest architectural standard and craftsmanship. The seventeenth and eighteenth century tradition of planning by streets and squares was continued (p. 376) and the city centre was expanded along lines already begun. Turin architecture had always had a French influence due to its nearness to the French border and its links with that country. The great schemes of the *Piazza Vittorio Veneto* and the Piazza Carlo Felice illustrate this. The former, designed by *Frizzi* and *Promis*, is an immense open space extending from the arcaded Via Po to the river, its vista being terminated by the *Church of Gran Madre di Dio*, built 1818–21 by *Fernando Bonsignore*, to commemorate the re-establishment of the Savoy monarchy to its capital at the end of the Napoleonic occupation. The church, based on the Rome Pantheon, is not outstanding, but the homogeneity of the piazza, in which it is included, is notable. On the other side of the city, the Via Roma divides into the two branches of the *Piazza Carlo Felice* and ends at the T-junction of the Corso Emmanuele II, its vista blocked by the fine glass and iron façade of the *Porta Nuova Railway Station* (1866–8, *Ceppi* and *Mazzuchetti*). The piazza is a scheme of the 1820s and

930 *Canale Grande layout with Church of S. Antonio di Padova at end of vista, Trieste, Italy, Peter von Nobile, 1826–49*

930

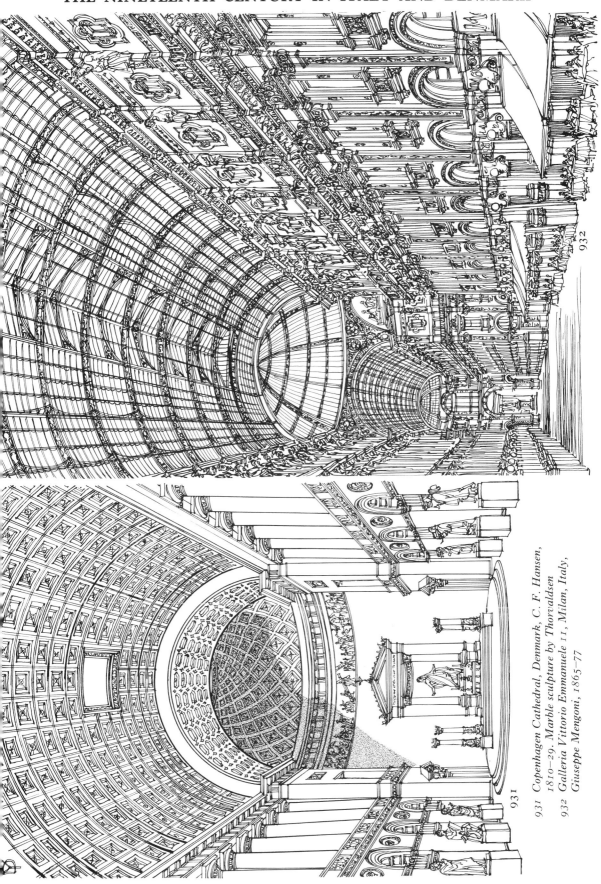

931 *Copenhagen Cathedral, Denmark, C. F. Hansen,*
1810–29. Marble sculpture by Thorvaldsen
932 *Galleria Vittorio Emmanuele II, Milan, Italy,*
Giuseppe Mengoni, 1865–77

1830s, also homogeneous and with decorative, elegant, well-proportioned façades.

In *Trieste* the waterfront area of the *Canale Grande* was laid out at much the same time. The *Church of S. Antonio di Padova* at the head of the waterway is another 'Pantheon' and has a fine situation (**930**). Along the waters' edge are excellently designed and finished palace façades.

In the great piazza near the harbour in *Naples* stands the *Church of S. Francesco dei Paolo* (1816–24 by *Pietro Bianchi*). An imposing church, it is doubly eclectic, the body being a Rome Pantheon and the curving side colonnades based on Bernini's S. Peter's. It is a successful, large-scale design.

After the unification of Italy, *Rome* became the capital and King Victor Emmanuel (like the Kaiser in Berlin) tried to give to his capital city suitably imposing architectural layouts. Berlin did not fully succeed and nor did Rome. The latter had, of course, been a great city in too many past ages—in Ancient Rome, in the Middle Ages, in the days of the Renaissance and Baroque. Victor Emmanuel in the nineteenth century could not hope to compete in any way with these; the days of great architecture were over. Of the civic schemes of the time, the *Piazza Esedra* is proably the most successful. Laid out in 1885 by *Gaetono Koch*, its façades sweep round in quarters of a circle at the head of the Via Nazionale, set off by the vigorous sculptured fountain in the centre.

The great *monument* to *Victor Emmanuel* in *Rome*, impossible to ignore, is that dazzlingly white marble edifice in the Piazza Venezia. This, like the Albert Memorial in London, is now accepted as an integral part of the city of Rome, scorned by the intelligentsia but a magnet for tourists of all nations, Italians included. It represents the epitome of the 1880s in all European nations. It is imperial, richly sculptured and decorated, dramatic and larger than life. Dedicated to King and country, it stands for sentiment and sacrifice, a true monument of its age (p. 480).

Italy, like other European nations, restored and completed her Medieval cathedrals in this century. The two chief examples were *Milan Cathedral*, where the façade was finally finished early in the century, and *Florence* where the façade was at last built in 1887 by *Emilio de*

Fabris. The latter achieves its object of carefully matching the Medieval marble veneers, colours and decoration, but it is still nineteenth century in feeling.

Italy made an important contribution to architectural design in iron and glass in its railway stations and galleries. The most famous of these is the *Galleria Vittorio Emmanuele II* in *Milan* (**932**), which extends from the Piazza del Duomo to the Piazza della Scala, an immense cruciform structure covered in glass panels in iron frames. It was built by an English firm, and with English professional advice, under the Italian architect Giuseppe Mengoni (1829–77). The decoration and sculpture is of the period, mostly in iron, painted and in good, if restored, condition. The arcade still fulfils its original function, as the meeting place where the people of Milan stroll, sit in the cafés and look in the shops. It is the Roman forum of its day, providing protection from rain and sun.

The Iberian Peninsula

Little of outstanding interest came from either *Portugal* or *Spain* in much of this century. Typical of the best work early in the century, is the *Praça do Comércio* district in *Lisbon* (**918**); this is the huge central square, open on one side to the estuary of the Tagus. The centre of the city was slowly rebuilt in squares and streets after the earthquake of 1755 and retains its late eighteenth century style.

In *Madrid* a number of classical buildings were erected during the century, such as the *Palace of the Congress* (1843–50) and the city gateway, the *Glorieta Puerta de Toledo* (1817). The immense *Cathedral, Nuestra Señora de la Almudena*, which was begun in 1880 by *Marquès Francisco de Cubas*, is still unfinished. The neo-classical exterior, next to the royal palace, has twin towers on the façade, joined by a two-storey colonnade, Ionic superimposed on Doric. Later building incorporated some Romanesque and Gothic work which blends satisfactorily with the whole. Typical of neo-Gothic design in *Spain* is the *Cathedral of San Sebastian*, begun in 1888. This has a German-type tall tower and perforated steeple of the Ulm or Freiburg type. It is a Latin cruciform church. Inside is a tall nave arcade with slender piers and early Gothic foliated capitals. Above is a blind triforium and clerestory windows. The choir is apsidal and contains some fine glass.

The outstanding figure of Spanish architecture in the nineteenth century and, indeed, the most original architect of the period in Europe, was *Antonio Gaudì y Cornet* (1852–1926). His name is generally coupled with the movement of Art Nouveau, but much of his work was carried out in the nineteenth century before the move-

ment commenced, and even his twentieth century work is so individual that it cannot be filed neatly under a general label. His career stems from the 1870s and he early turned away from neo-classicism, developing, for some years, a style on neo-Gothic lines. He was a Catalan and most of his contribution is to be found in and around *Barcelona*. He built palaces and houses and restored a number of Medieval monuments such as *Palma Cathedral* and the *Monastery of Montserrat*. In Medieval style, but essentially Gaudì, is his *Bishop's Palace* at *Astorga* (1887–93), adjoining the Medieval Cathedral. This has Gothic towers, battlements and fenestration, but the parabolic curve of the arches of the portal indicate the master's original touch. This feature can be found in much of his work.

The personal quality of Gaudì's building in this century can be seen clearly on the palace and park in Barcelona named after Don Eusebio Güell and the fantastic cathedral-temple of the Holy Family. The *Palacio Güell* (1885–9) is in the city in the street called Conde del Asalto just off the main Rambla Capuchino. It is a six-storeyed stone front, restrained and simple but unmistakably by Gaudì in its two entrances with characteristic, parabolic-arched doorways and decorative iron grilles. The *Parque Güell*, where Gaudì worked up to 1914, now the city's public

933

933 *Church of the Holy Family (Templo Expiatorio de la Sagrada Familia), Barcelona, Spain. Begun 1882. Antonio Gaudì y Cornet, 1884–1926*

park, is situated on a hill on the outskirts of the town. It contains a church, a house, arbours, sculpture and playgrounds. The motifs are chiefly natural ones; caves, rocks, plants, animals, but the architectural derivation is Gothic apart from the classical supports for the children's playground. These are Doric columns, but so vast that they resemble a cross between Paestum temples and the Nile palaces. The church, the grottoes and the garden layout are in coloured ceramic faced with inset stones. This is a fairy-tale garden with the marzipan and gingerbread house of Grimm's stories.

The temple dedicated to the Holy Family is still slowly and painfully being added to in the city of Barcelona. The *Templo Expiatorio de la Sagrada Familia* was designed by *Francisco del Villar* in neo-Gothic style and begun in 1882. In November 1883 the work was entrusted to his assistant *Gaudì*, who devoted himself to it during the rest of his life. By 1893 he had completed the crypt and the outer walls of the chevet, according to Villar's designs. This part can be seen in the right hand half of the drawing in Fig. **933**.

After this beginning Gaudì developed his own design, and the part built largely before 1914 is the façade to one of the transepts which includes the triple doorway and four towers shown on the left of the drawing. Here is the personal Gaudì, all curves and three-dimensional plasticity, but his treatment is quite different from that of any other architect. When he had been working at Montserrat, he was fascinated by the formation of the mountain peaks, rising vertically above the shelf on which the monastery stands, high above Barcelona. Anyone who has seen this mountain formation, resembling vertical, rounded pillars of solidified molten lava, will at once recognise the same molten stone effect in Gaudì's porticoes. Stalactitic deposits hang from each pointed arch; the sculpture has the same semi-liquid quality, each drip caught as in a snapshot, before it falls. There is the same instant quality of arrested movement that is seen in Bernini's work.

The Sagrada Familia was continued, after a break for the First World War, in 1919, but stopped at the architect's death in 1926. Since then the monument has remained for years a fragment (though an immense one). Work is now fully in progress again, but whether such a vast enterprise will ever attract sufficient funds to be completed must be in doubt. It is to be hoped that the Sagrada Familia will be finished. It is a unique, non-eclectic design, the greatest ecclesiastical structure since the eighteenth century. The building finished so far, though appearing large (the towers are 330 feet high), is still only a portion. It represents one transept façade and the outer choir chevet walling. Still remaining to be built are the nave and other transept, with similar towers, the choir *cimborio* and the great crossing group, the *cimborio* whose tower should rise to about 560 feet, higher than the tallest Medieval church in Europe: Ulm Minster, at 529 feet.

The Low Countries

Much of the *Belgian* civic work in this century is classical such as the *Théâtre de la Monnaie* in *Brussels* (1819). In the period 1860–90, boulevards and squares were laid out in the capital on the lines of the Parisian Second Empire. In general, though, the work is heavier and the detail coarser. Typical is the *Boulevard Anspach*, with its iron balconies and mansard roofs. This is now largely losing its character with alterations to individual premises.

The two chief examples of civic building in these years are the Exchange and the Palais de Justice. The *Exchange* (1868–73), by *L. P. Suys* (1823–87), stands in its own square half way along the Boulevard Anspach. It is in neo-Baroque style and has a heavy, ornate portico with approach steps and flanking lions. There is a wealth of sculpture typical of this date. The *Palace of Justice* (**936**) is also heavy, but is more original in conception. It was designed by *Joseph Poelaert* (1817–79) and built 1866–83. It has much of the feeling of Vanbrugh's work in its strong massing and three-dimensional weightiness. Standing on the highest point of this part of the city, it dominates the area as the blocks pile up to the tall dome. It is the most original building of its date in the country.

Belgium also produced some interesting structures in iron and glass. A surviving example in *Brussels*, is the *Galérie de la Reine* (formerly the Galérie S. Hubert), built in 1847 by *J. P. Cluysenaer*. This is an early city shopping gallery.

934 *Frederik's Kirke (the Marble Church), Copenhagen, Denmark. Designed by Jardin; begun 1749. Completed by Ferdinand Madahl, 1876–94*

935 *City Fish Hall, Göteborg (Gothenburg), Sweden, Gegerfelt, 1873–4*

936 *Palace of Justice, Brussels, Belgium, Joseph Poelaert, 1866–83*

and has delicate detail and good, subtle proportions. Doric pilasters line the walls of the
ground arcade. Above are two stages of classical
fenestration and the gallery is roofed in a semi-
circular vault of glass panels in iron frames. The
sculptural decoration is restrained and in a
classical Greek pattern.

There is little of note to record for the first
half of the century in *Holland*. Two exceptions
are the city gateway, the *Haarlemer Poort* (1840)
and the long façade of the *Palace of Justice*
(1846–52), both in *Amsterdam*.

By the 1860s, a number of architects were
creating prominent buildings of the neo-Gothic
or heavy, Second Empire Renaissance style.
Of the latter type of design is the work of *Cornelis
Outshoorn* (1810–75). A typical example is the
large *Amstel Hotel*, its four storeys and dormered,
mansard roofs lining the river bank in *Amsterdam*. Designing in equally heavy-handed manner,
but in neo-Gothic, is the Scott or Viollet-le-Duc
of Holland, *P. J. Cuijpers* (1827–1921). Two large
civic contributions of this architect are the
Rijksmuseum (1877–85) and the *Central Station*
(1881–9), both in *Amsterdam*. From the exterior,
these buildings are so similar that it is difficult to
know which is for trains and which for paintings.
Both are long, dark brick façades, with gables and
steep roofs broken by dormer windows. Each has
a centrepiece with flanking, gabled towers, a
central gable and main doorway and, at the ends
of the façades, terminal gabled pavilions. Only
the museum, however, on closer inspection, is
appropriately ornamented with panels of relief
sculpture and ceramic scenes.

Cuijpers, like his contemporaries in England
and France, also designed a number of *churches*
and these, too, bear great resemblance to one
another. The one illustrated, the *Vondelkerk* in
Amsterdam, like his *Maria Magdalenkerk* nearby
(1887), is very similar to numerous examples
produced in England at a similar date. The
Dutch examples are in brick, with striped or
polychrome decoration and the emphasis is on
height in sharp, hard turrets, spires and arches
(937).

At the very end of the century there was a
change of style. Brick remained (as it had been
since Hanseatic days in Holland) the usual
material, but a lead was taken (as in England,
p. 480) in simplifying the design and in creating a
more original line and detail. In *Amsterdam* the
Hotel Americain (1898–1900), by *Willem Krom-
hout* (1864–1940), is one example and this was
followed quickly by that excellent architect
Hendrik Berlage (1856–1934), who initiated a
specifically Dutch style. The *Amsterdam Exchange* is one instance of his work (926), as
another is his *Diamond Workers' Trade Union
Building* (1899–1900).

South-East Europe

Balkan countries had been restricted for centuries in developing their own architectural
expression by the overlordship of the Ottoman

937 *Vondelkerk, Amsterdam, Holland, P. J. Cuijpers,
1870*

Empire. In the nineteenth century, one by one these nations achieved their independence and began to build up their chief cities. From the late 1830s, civic building was re-started in *Athens*. The Hansen family, of Danish origin, who carried out so much neo-classical work in Europe, built here in this period. *Theophil von Hansen* (architect of the Parliament House in Vienna, Fig. **919**, p. 484), and his brother, created some fine buildings in the university area. They designed the *University* itself, a dramatic building in the Ionic Order (1837–42), and also the *Academy* and *National Library*.

The best building in Athens, dating from this time, is the royal palace, now used as the *Parliament House*, at the head of the main Syntagma Square. This is simple, with clean, classical lines and an elegant Greek Doric portico inspired, one would imagine, by the Parthenon at the other end of the road. This building, surprisingly enough, is by *Gärtner*, the architect of the Ludwigstrasse in Munich. It contrasts sharply with his Bavarian style.

In the rest of the century, streets in Athens became lined with typical classical façades of the day, as they did in the rest of Europe. In the years since 1950, however, due in part to the importance of the tourist trade, much of this building has disappeared and has been replaced by modern restaurants, shops and hotels. There is little of architectural note in modern Athens.

Even less building took place in the country now known as *Yugoslavia*. In the nineteenth century the northern part still belonged to the Austro-Hungarian Empire and so formed part of the building programme there, while the southern part of the nation, then Serbia, was under Turkish rule till after mid-century. Typical of the work at the end of the century is the *University of Belgrade*, which is a traditional Renaissance design of its period.

Bulgaria remained under Turkish domination till the later nineteenth century though the Church gained its freedom in 1870. Among the great *monasteries* of the country *Rila** (**929**) is one of the most famous. Set in a fine mountain landscape, it was founded in the tenth century, but the church was destroyed by fire in 1833. Later in the century it was rebuilt and the whole monastery restored and extended. The polysided courtyard is surrounded by arcaded galleries which contained cells. The galleries are painted in striped horizontal lines. After the fire a further storey was added and the new church was set in one corner of the courtyard. It is a five-domed basilica in Byzantine style, with an arcaded narthex on three sides, all covered by saucer domes. The interior is painted all over; it is in excellent condition and the standard of craftsmanship is high. Inside the church there are three large central domes on tall, fenestrated drums. It is a simple, three-aisled interior with marble columns but is painted on all surfaces, including the drums and cupolas of the domes. The chancel screen is a fantastic piece of decorative craftwork. The present church is much larger than the one it replaces. The exterior of the monastery is like a fortress with solid, very high walls rising out of a mountain stream. Tiny windows pierce this fastness.

Modern *Rumania* is a large country, but until the middle of the nineteenth century was composed of small provinces much of whose lands were controlled by the Austro-Hungarian Empire or by the Turks. Independence from the latter came in the 1870s. There are a number of classical buildings in *Bucharest*, dating from different periods in the nineteenth century. One of the best is the *Rumanian Athenaeum* (**925**) in the centre of the city, inspiration for which has clearly stemmed from Paris. Indeed the Rumanians call their capital the 'Paris of the Balkans'—an extravagant claim in spite of some fine boulevards. Among the more exceptional structures are the Palace of Justice, the Centre for Economic Development, the General Post Office and the Central Bank.

In towns such as *Sibiu* and *Cluj* there are also some good neo-classical buildings in the central streets, as well as some neo-Gothic ones. In *Sinaia*, the *Castle Peles*, the royal palace built in 1873, is a romantic turreted pile set in hilly parkland. It is reminiscent of romantic German or Swiss sixteenth century castles and, not surprisingly, the architect, *Wilhelm Doderer*, was *Viennese*.

In the nineteenth century church building was revived in Byzantine tradition, much as neo-Gothic was established in England. The *Greek Orthodox Cathedral* in *Constantza* (1884–95) is a large example as is also the *Domnita Balasa Church* in *Bucharest* (1881–5).

* *Rila Monastery is now a museum; no monks remain.*

Northern and Eastern Europe: Poland and the U.S.S.R.

Nineteenth century European architecture is predominantly found in the cities. In *Poland* a great proportion of this building was lost during the Second World War, as the major cities suffered more probably than in any other country. The war began by Hitler's invasion of Poland and the cities of *Wroclaw* and *Warsaw* were—amid an almost total state of destruction—among the last to find peace in 1945. The country was a buffer between the retreating Germany army and the advancing Soviet forces and only *Cracow* of the major cities survived fairly intact. It is, therefore, from a few surviving examples that nineteenth century Polish architecture can be judged.*

Designs in *Cracow* are strongly influenced by the Austro-Hungarian Empire directives and cities like *Gdansk* on the Baltic coast by Prussian ideas. The *Municipal Theatre* in *Cracow* (1891–3) by *Zawiejski* is another attractive variant on the Paris Opera House (**923**). There is also the elegant neo-rococo *Stadnicki Palace* in Grodzka Street, with its pleasant façade and doorway. The *Museum of Silesia* in *Wroclaw* is a large structure on typical late nineteenth century Renaissance lines. Standing on the river bank (River Oder) this vast block was damaged, but is now largely restored. It is of neo-Renaissance style, monumentally conceived and well executed.

The U.S.S.R.

The first half of the nineteenth century in Russia produced architecture of a design and quality which compares favourably with any in Western Europe. Much of this was created under Tsar Alexander I, who reigned from 1801–25 and was an enlightened patron of the arts, *au fait* with the modes of his day and a man of taste. In the first half of his reign he encouraged neo-classicism based on the Greek model, while later work, towards 1825, was more on the lines of Imperial Rome. Like all Russian architecture, the structures are large in scale, many part of extensive, civic schemes and set in immense squares and boulevards which offset the building size.

As under the patronage of Peter, Elizabeth and Catherine, foreign architects were still

employed, but Russian architects too were now making their full contribution to the beautifying of their cities and here *S. Petersburg* was, as ever, the prime recipient. Three architects contributed in the main in the years 1801–15: Voronikhin, de Thomon and Zakharov. *Andrei Nikiforovich Voronikhin* (1760–1814) was born a serf but, on showing promise as an artist, was sent to S. Petersburg Academy by his master to study, and later on the Grand Tour in Paris and Rome. He returned to S. Petersburg in 1790 and, after a few years began work on his large commission, the *Cathedral of the Virgin of Kazan* (**938**). This is an immense building, based on S. Peter's in Rome, with a domed church fronted by a great portico and with forward curving Corinthian colonnades on each side. Terminating these are *Orlovski*'s statues of *Barclay de Tolly* and *Marshal Kutuzov*. It is a finely proportioned, imposing cathedral, but monumentally cold, rather in the same manner as is the Paris Panthéon. The interior is richly ornate Baroque, with coffered barrel vaults supported by walls with Corinthian order entablatures. It is difficult to see below this level because of the exhibits; the building is laid out as a museum of the history of religion and atheism and it is now called the 'Temple of Atheism'. An instance of Voronikhin's severer Greek styles can be seen in his *Institute of Mines* in the city, which he built in 1803–7, based upon the Temple of Poseidon at Paestum. This has the characteristically sturdy Doric columns of the early Greek period and some fine sculptured groups.

Thomas de Thomon (1754–1813) was born in France but settled in Russia in 1790. His outstanding work in S. Petersburg is the *Exchange* (Birzha) (1810–16), which has a Doric portico, also closely deriving from the Paestum temples.

The buildings of *Adrian Dmitrievich Zakharov* (1761–1811) are much more Russian. He trained in S. Petersburg, then spent some years in Paris and Italy, but his style has all the breadth and hugeness, the ability to handle great masses and contrasts in chiaroscuro which characterises the best Russian architecture. This manner is not eclecticism but a national interpretation of the design of his day. His chief work in *S. Petersburg* is the *Admiralty* group of buildings, where he had to reconstruct older parts, retaining the landmark on the southern side of the river Neva,

* *Although a great proportion of the finer buildings have been or are being restored.*

THE NINETEENTH CENTURY IN THE U.S.S.R.

938 *Cathedral of the Virgin of Kazan, Leningrad, A. N. Voronikhin, 1801–11*
939 *General Staff Arches, Winter Palace Square, Leningrad, K. I. Rossi, 1819–29*
940 *State Department Store, GUM, Red Square, Moscow, A. N. Pomerantsev, 1889–93*

938

939

940

the tall steeple and certain features of the previous buildings, yet at the same time greatly extending the group. The façade facing the Neva has a Doric colonnade and square entrance pavilion blocks. On the southern elevation is the tall entrance tower, its square, Ionic colonnaded base and above the sculptured figures supporting the lofty steeple. Flanking the entrance below are the draped female figure groups (1812, *Shchedrin*) (PLATE 100).

A hiatus in building was caused by the Napoleonic invasion but, after the final retreat from Moscow, a new era of construction began under different architects: Stasov, Rossi and Montferrand. *Vasili Petrovich Stasov* (1769–1848) was a Russian architect who also studied and worked in Western Europe. He began his architectural career in Russia in 1808, working for the Tsar on the S. Petersburg palaces and at Tsarkoe Selo. He also designed a number of churches. His work was mainly on Greek lines such as the *Moscow Triumphal Arch* in S. Petersburg (1833–8).

Karl Ivanovich Rossi (1775–1849) had a different background. Of Italian descent, he was, however, Russian born. His contribution to *S. Petersburg* was in extensive civic schemes, based on Imperial Roman prototypes. He designed the beautifully delineated and finished *Alexandra* (now Pushkin) *Theatre* (1827–32) in Ostrovsky Square. Leading from the rear of the theatre, he laid out *Rossi Street* at the same period. This is a classical terrace reminiscent of Nash or Wood in England. A giant order of coupled Ionic columns extends the whole length of the long façade, broken only at the terminal pavilions. Below the order are simple arches containing windows, connected by rusticated walling.

A larger scheme was his *Senate and Synod* (1829–34), a long line of buildings near the Admiralty, adjacent to the Neva and looking out on to the equestrian statue by Falconet of Peter the Great, erected by Catherine. These buildings housed the supreme judiciary and ecclesiastical representatives. Rossi's design is in one long elevation comprising two identical façades joined by a central triumphal arch. The Corinthian Order in columns is used over the whole length of the elevation, above a rusticated lower storey. The proportions and handling are good and the interest is maintained along a very lengthy façade.

Rossi's most ambitious project, and his masterpiece, is his layout for the gigantic square opposite to the Winter Palace. This is a tremendously long façade of simple, unadorned fenestrated treatment, broken by an immense central, concavely curving sweep. In the centre of this area (which houses the buildings for the *General Staff*), is an equally large-scale triumphal arch, complete with surmounting chariot and six horses* (**939**). This great façade, monumentally and imperially handled, offsets admirably the fine Baroque of Rastrelli's Winter Palace opposite (**874**).

The achievement of *Ricard de Montferrand* (1786–1858), a French architect, was the building of *S. Isaac's Cathedral* in S. Petersburg (1817–57). He won the competition for this commission in 1817, but the cathedral was many years in the building, with consequent deterioration in craftsmanship and design during the period. Though French, Montferrand has produced a very Russian building, immensely large and monumental, in robust classical style. It is on Greek-cross plan, with a large central dome on Corinthian colonnaded drum and small cupolas set round it. The façades have weighty Corinthian porticoes, pedimented and sculptured. The exterior has been recently restored and cleaned and the gilt domes gleam in the pale northern sunshine. It is a solemn structure, lacking in warmth but gaining greatly from the richness of its materials, especially the granite columns with their gilt capitals and bases. There is also a quantity of sculpture typical of the mid-century date.

The best architecture of the period 1800–30 was certainly in S. Petersburg. But other cities were also being developed and laid out with civic schemes in neo-classical style. Interesting work of this type includes *Odessa* where, for example, buildings round the *Square of the Commune*, mainly by *Boffo* have elegant façades. Typical is the Archaeological Museum—now the Workers' Soviet—which has a well-proportioned Corinthian colonnaded front. Along the *Black Sea front* are terrace buildings which have much in common with contemporary work in Brighton and Hove in England. Numbers 7–8, for example (1827–8, designed by *Melnikov*), have plain, classically fenestrated façades broken by a curving crescent with Ionic pilastered front. The statue by *Martos* (1826) of Richelieu stands at the

* *Such classical groups, as the name quadriga indicates, had four horses. The vastness of the country encouraged Russian architects to design on larger scale than in Western Europe.*

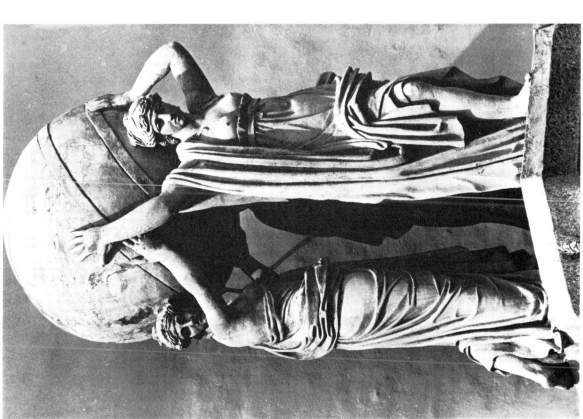

Plate 100
New Admiralty, Leningrad, U.S.S.R. 1812. Sculptor Shchedrin

Plate 101
The Opera House, Odessa, U.S.S.R., 1884–7

Plate 103
Detail sculpture, Alfonso XII Monument. Madrid, Spain, 1922

Plate 102
West doorway, Tampere Cathedral, Finland. 1902–7, Lars Sonck

central intersection of the curve.

The dominance of classicism in the official line in architecture continued unbroken in the period up to 1850. It is noted for the employment by the Tsar of German and Russo-German architects. The chief of these was *Konstantin Andreevich Ton* (1794–1881). He designed the *Grand Kremlin Palace* in *Moscow* (1838–49), a Russo-Renaissance building, classical in structure but with decorated windows and columns. It shows the common decline from early nineteenth century standards. The *Dutch Church* on the Nevski Prospekt in *S. Petersburg* (1837, by *Jacquot*) is more robustly and correctly classical. This is clearly modelled on the Mausoleum of Diocletian in the Palace at Split.

In the 1860s eclecticism came fully to Russia and, in addition to various classical themes, all the earlier styles were tried out too. These were not based on the Western European Medieval structures but on Russian ones. Next door to one another in the Red Square in *Moscow* are two typical examples, the Russian equivalents of work by Scott in England or Cuijpers in Holland: the *Lenin Museum* (originally the city hall) 1892, by *P. N. Chichagov* and the *History Museum* (1874–83) by the Anglo-Russian architect *V. O. Sherwood*. Both of these are very large, dark brick, overdecorated structures. They incorporate all the traditional Medieval and Byzantine Russian architectural motifs—tent roofs, *kokoshniki*, octagonal towers and pinnacles, ornate window surrounds and wall panelling—but this is all assembled together in a heavy, uninspired manner and with little comprehension of the Medieval type of massing and design.

On the other side of the Square* is the fantastic State Department Store, *GUM* (**940**), an immensely long façade opposite to the Kremlin walls and adjoining the Cathedral of S. Basil. The exterior has similar characteristics to the museums but is handled better and with more imagination. The interior is most interesting and a classic of its type in iron and glass, like the galleries of the period in Western Europe. GUM has three parallel, barrel vaulted galleries, each about 1000 feet in length, with balconies and walkways at different heights, all serving shops. There are then iron connecting walkways from one section to another. The interior is like the nave and aisles of a church, only the aisles are nearly as wide and as high as the nave. In the centre is a fountain and a very tall lamp, hanging from above, almost down to it. One can walk round the centrepiece at gallery passageway levels, covered by the iron and glass domed roof above. There are literally hundreds of shops and stalls in GUM, selling almost everything.

In ecclesiastical building the neo-Byzantine style of about the sixteenth century was prevalent in the 1880s. In *S. Petersburg, S. Saviour's Church in the Spilled Blood* was built 1883–1907 by *A. A. Parland* on the site of the assassination of the Tsar Alexander II. It is modelled on the Cathedral of S. Basil in Moscow, but its highly ornate façades and towers are overdone and the elegance and beautiful form of the prototype are missing. In *Kiev*, the *Cathedral of S. Vladimir* (1882) is a simpler example, taking its pattern from the Byzantine churches of the city. The interior is particularly fine, decorated on all surfaces with painted and marble veneer and paintings with gilt backgrounds in Byzantine style. The plan is cruciform, with barrel-vaulted arms, a tall drum and dome over the crossing and subsidiary smaller ones around. The piers are square and solid and there is a high gallery. With the wide narthex, the whole interior is very much in Russian and eastern Byzantine style rather than western.

Of the eclectic classical structures of the later years of the century, the *University* at *L'vov** (1880s) is a good example. The *Bolshoi Theatre* in *Moscow*, rebuilt 1886 by *Cavos*, and the *L'vov* and *Odessa Opera Houses* are in neo-Baroque style. The Odessa example is especially impressive; it is closely modelled on the Paris Opera. It was designed by *Felner* and *Gelmer* in 1884–6 (PLATE 101). It has a fine situation and, newly cleaned, sparkles in the sun. The interior, exceptional acoustically, is a rich and fine example of late nineteenth century décor. There are four rows of balconies, in gilt and cream, with red velvet seating and curtaining. The four-centred proscenium arch is ornamented in the spandrels by white sculptured figures. The magnificent ceiling has a circular centrepiece and is painted to depict scenes from Shakespeare's plays. A glass and gilt chandelier in the style of the English Regency hangs from the centre.

Originally Poland.

The Red Square in Moscow is an immensely wide street rather than a square. It was formerly called Market Square because of the stalls in and around it.

Scandinavia
Denmark

Of the four Scandinavian countries, the most notable large-scale development is in Helsinki in Finland, where it was initiated by the Russians and largely built by German designers. So far as indigenous architects were concerned, Denmark produced the best work, especially in Copenhagen. In the first half of the century many buildings were designed in Romantic Classical and neo-classical style by architects such as Hansen and Bindesbøll. Development was by streets and terraces, but the chief monuments are civic and ecclesiastical.

Christian Frederik Hansen (1756–1845) was the prime classical architect in the early years. His main contribution was in the *Cathedral* and the *Palace of Justice* in *Copenhagen*. The great fire in the city in 1795 caused extensive damage, as did also the English bombardment of 1807. Hansen rebuilt the *Cathedral, Vôr Frue Kirke*, 1811–29, using the old walls. The exterior is plain, with apsidal east end and a tall, square western tower rises above the Doric façade portico. The interior is most impressive (**931**). There is a caissoned, barrel-vaulted ceiling throughout and a plain screen in front of the organ (west end), with Doric colonnade above and simple arches below. This pattern of colonnaded gallery above an arched nave arcade leading to aisles is repeated all round the church, except at the east end where a great triumphal arch fronts the apse; this is decorated below the cornice with a frieze depicting Christ on the way to Golgotha. The altarpiece, set on a curving stylobate, contains, in a niche, *Bertel Thorvaldsen's* (1768–1844) figure of Christ. This and the other marble statues of the 12 Apostles standing round the church, as well as much of the remaining sculptural decoration are by this famous Danish sculptor. The work was done in Rome between 1820–40.

Hansen's work is based on Imperial Roman classicism. This influence can be seen clearly in his *Raad-og Domhus* (1803–15), which was built as a combined Town Hall and Court House. It now serves only as the Law Courts. It is a plain, monumental building with simple Ionic portico. Hansen also rebuilt the *Christiansborg Palace* in Copenhagen, again using the walls of the older structure. This was his most important commission but unfortunately it was, in its turn, burnt down in 1884 and the present immense structure, housing the Parliament, the Supreme Court and the Foreign Office, was built by Jørgensen in 1907–16.

After 1820 there was a reaction in Denmark against Roman classicism and a turning towards the purer Greek forms. Schinkel's work was a strong influence (the German architect, p. 481). *Gottlieb Bindesbøll* (1800–56), the most original Danish architect of the nineteenth century, was their leader. He built eclectically, in neo-Gothic, such as his *Church* at *Hobro* (1850), and in German *Rundbogenstil*, as in his *Agricultural School* (1856–8) in *Copenhagen*. His masterpiece, which is original not eclectic, is the *Thorvaldsen Museum* in *Copenhagen* (1839–48), which was built to house the collections and works of the sculptor, as well as to provide a suitable setting for his tomb. The tomb is set in a central court which, like the rest of the building, is severely simple, with something of Greek form but more of Egyptian. The astylar façade has Egyptian-styled doorway openings. Round the exterior are murals by Jørgen Sonne, depicting the story of the bringing of Thorvaldsen's sculpture from Rome to Copenhagen.

After this in Denmark eclecticism was prevalent for the rest of the century. Some of the work was strongly influenced by Germany, in *Rundbogenstil* and neo-Byzantine form. Other examples show the effect of Second Empire France. Many architects designed in more than one style, changing their approach according to commission. The *University of Copenhagen* (1835) is a typical work by *Peder Malling*. This is classical, but with a neo-Gothic flavour to the gables and dormers. It is in the same square as the cathedral and next door to it is Herholt's neo-Gothic *University Library* of 1856–61. This is in red brick and very typical of Danish neo-Gothic work. *J. D. Herholt* (1818–1902) was the most important architect in Denmark in the 1850–70 period. Much of his work was in the *Rundbogenstil* as, for example, his *Danish National Bank* in *Copenhagen* (1866–70). He also turned his hand to more traditional neo-Gothic, on Italian pattern, in his *Town Hall* at *Odense* (1880–3). This has a crenellated parapet after the Medieval type common in Ferrara and Verona and a frontispiece with clock above the doorway which is Florentine in origin.

A number of architects were designing in the heavy neo-Renaissance and Baroque work of the later years of the century. *Vilhelm Petersen* and *Ferdinand Jensen* used this style for the building of apartment blocks and offices such as *63–5 Bredgade* in Copenhagen (1886–7), while *Jens Vilhelm Dahlerup* built the *State Museum for the Fine Arts* (Glyptotek 1892–7) and the *Royal Theatre* (1872–4) in the city. These are both typical products of their age, heavy and unimaginative, but well constructed and large scale.

The leading architect of the period 1875–1900 in Denmark was *Ferdinand Medahl* (1827–1908). He was Professor at the Copenhagen Academy from 1864 and its Director for over 30 years. His work in the reconstruction of *Frederiksborg Castle* in 1861–75, after its severe damage by fire in 1859, is typical. It is competent and imposing but very heavy, hard and unimaginative. His most outstanding work was the Frederik's Kirke, or the *Marble Church*, in *Copenhagen* (**934**). This was finally built 1876–94, but it had been designed by Jardin and left as a fragment since the eighteenth century (p. 457). The exterior is very fine. The immense drum and dome, clearly modelled on S. Peter's in Rome, rather over-dominate the church; and this is more apparent in the interior, which is completely circular, with a circular ambulatory round the nave. The interior dome is flatter and painted in panels. It is in the inside of the church that the fact that the building was largely constructed in the later nineteenth century, instead of the mid-eighteenth, is so apparent; it lacks warmth, life and character.

As in some other European countries, the beginnings of a new national architectural style, reverting to simplicity and away from overt eclecticism, began to appear after 1890. Leader of this movement in Denmark was *Martin Nyrop* (1849–1923). His *Town Hall* in Copenhagen (1892–1905) is his chief work, which is in brick on similar lines to Berlage's style in Amsterdam (p. 498). In both cases the architects were reverting to the traditional building material used simply and clearly, without stucco covering or over-decoration, to reinstitute a national style.

Sweden

Architecture in the first half of the nineteenth century in Sweden was undistinguished. There were no outstanding architects designing in the field of neo- or romantic-classicism, as elsewhere, and financial means were not available to indulge large civic schemes or public buildings of note. Classical architecture was designed and built; it was adequate and competent, no more.

Typical were works like the *University Library at Uppsala* by *Karl F. Sundvall* (1754–1831) and the *Skeppsholm Church in Stockholm* (1824–42) by *Frederik Blom* (1781–1853). This is an octagonal building with shallow dome and lantern above; inside, the church is circular.

From the later 1840s a Gothic Revival was begun. The dull, derivative classical designs of the recent years were abandoned, especially in ecclesiastical work, castles and museums, in favour of Medieval inspiration. Sweden produced its own competent, energetic restorer and recreator of the Medieval heritage—*Helgo Zettervall* (1831–1907). Zettervall was as enthusiastic as Viollet-le-Duc in France or Sir George Gilbert Scott in England to restore the great cathedrals and churches of his native land to their former glories and, like his colleagues in these other countries, passionately believed that it was better to return the entire building to its original design and style rather than tolerate Renaissance, Baroque, or even late Gothic intrusions, however fine quality work they might be. Like his colleagues, his intentions were of the best, his work good, capable and correct; without his contribution, much of Sweden's Medieval heritage would by now have become lost. His hand was, however, a heavy one, especially on the fine cathedrals of Uppsala, Lund, Linköping and Skara.

Zettervall was versatile and his own contribution (apart from restoration work) varied from the neo-classic University House in Lund to the delicate, tall *Church of Oskar Frederik* in *Göteborg* (Gothenburg). This is an elegant but typical example of Gothic Revivalism of the 1870s, in deep red and black polychrome brickwork with green metal roofs and slender spires and gables. The interior is also lofty and slender (**941**) with delicate ribbed vaults over nave and aisles. Clustered, slim columns with small foli-

941

941 *Oskar Frederik's Church, Göteborg (Gothenburg), Sweden, Helgo Zettervall, 1870s*

ated capitals support the arches and vault springing. Like others of his age and belief, Zettervall had no objections to the spurious use of materials. Here, metal columns support the gallery and he often substituted cement for stone.

Quite different from Revivalist Gothic but finely designed and functional is the *Fish Hall* at *Göteborg* (**935**); a simple, northern interpretation of the style.

In the last 20 years of the century, in Sweden as elsewhere in Europe, eclecticism ran riot and all previous styles were re-introduced and experimented with. Typical of its period, and in classical vein is the *Central Railway Station* in *Stockholm* by *Edelsvärd*; a long, monumental façade with Ionic pilasters. In less sombre and richer style is *Anderberg*'s *Opera House* in Gustav Adolf's Square also in Stockholm (1898). An enthusiastic quality example is the Baroque *Church of Gustav Vasa* in the capital, designed by *Agi Lindegren* (1858–1927) at the end of the century. This is a large, opulent church on classic central Greek-cross plan, with tall drum encircled by coupled Doric columns and with dome and lantern above. Inside, the decoration

is of fine quality Baroque design with painted cupola and pendentives and stucco ornament between. Doric pilasters and piers are used throughout the church. The different standard of craftsmanship between this highly competent, late nineteenth century work and that which it imitates is seen clearly here when it is compared with the beautiful altar, made by Burchardt Precht in 1731 for Uppsala Cathedral, from where it was removed when Zettervall restored the cathedral to its Medieval origins. The eighteenth century altarpiece is magnificent, rich and ornate, with its Composite columns with gilt capitals and entablatures. Life-size figure sculpture is set in groups at the sides and above.

Also at the end of the century there emerged in Sweden, as in England and Denmark, a simpler, plainer type of architecture, still eclectic, but of astringent quality. The leading Swedish architect in this work was *Isak Gustav Clason* (1856–1930). One of his earlier works (1886) was the large block at No. 31 Strandvägen in Stockholm, at the edge of the harbour, called *Bünsow House*. It is dedicated to Frederik Bünsow, whose portrait plaque appears over the main doorway. Built in polychrome brick and stone, it is a well designed structure in early French Renaissance style. It is plain for its time, the ornament being restricted to the portals and gables. Another work by Clason is the *Nordiska* (northern) *Museum* in *Stockholm* (1890–1904). Based on the Danish palace design of Frederiksberg, this is a Dutch gabled building with central steeple and corner turrets. It also has much in common with English Jacobean work with its brick façades and stone facings. It is an elegant structure, a notable landmark across the waters of the lake.

Norway

Until the early nineteenth century, Danish influence on Norwegian architecture was extensive, due to the political union between the two countries. In 1814, this union was dissolved and the newly independent country of Norway began to establish an architectural tradition which was built up, in the early years, by architects from different lands: Germany, England, Holland as well as the other Scandinavian countries.

Oslo, till 1924 called Christiana, was small and lacking the large civic structures and street layout suitable for a capital city. Under King Karl Johan the years 1814–44 saw the establishment of such features. The Danish born architect *H. D. F. Linstow* was responsible for planning the

centre of the capital, with the royal palace at one end of the long boulevard, Karl Johansgate, and the university and parliament building further down. The *royal palace* is situated on an eminence in parkland at the top of the vista. Built 1835–48, it is a rectangular, classical building, with Ionic portico. It is simple, well-proportioned and finely sited. In front is the equestrian statue of the King.

Linstow's contribution was the street layout and the palace. *C. H. Grosch*, also born in Denmark, was responsible for the *University Buildings* (**945**), the Doric *Exchange* and the *Market Hall*. The first two of these are also classical buildings, a little heavier than the palace but of good quality, design and workmanship. The great German architect Schinkel (p. 481) advised on the designs for the University buildings, which are Grosch's best work here. They comprise three separate blocks, the central one having an imposing Ionic portico.

By the mid-century, Norwegian architecture had followed the general Western European pattern of eclecticism. Grosch designed the Market Hall, near the cathedral, in red brick in neo-Romanesque style, heavy in treatment and solemn in design. Also Romanesque, almost *Rundbogenstil*, is the *Parliament Building*, further down the Karl Johansgate. Designed by the Swedish architect *E. V. Langlet*, it was built in 1866 in yellow brick. It is a stolid building whose

942 Frognerseteren Restaurant, near Oslo, Norway, Holm Münthe, 1890

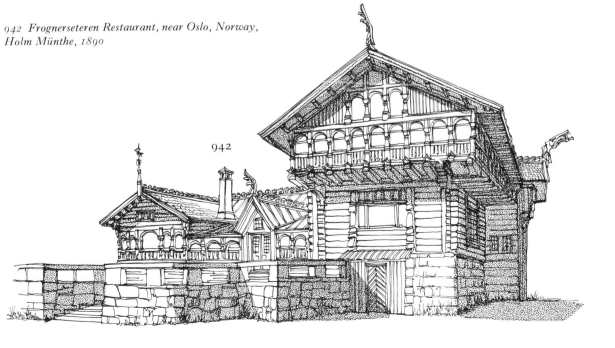

942

most interesting feature is the central, circular hall, flanked by projecting wings.

Apart from the capital, much of the building in Norway throughout the nineteenth century was still in the traditional building material of wood. This was especially so in the construction of houses and churches. Towards the end of the century the 'dragon style' was evolved, which was based on the Medieval stave church designs with their characteristic finials (p. 193). The style was popular as it was founded on a national type of structure, not a foreign import, like classical building. An interesting example of this work is the *Frognerseteren Restaurant* (942), built in 1890 by *Holm Munthe*. This has a magnificent site, 14 kilometres from Oslo. 1387 feet above the city and the fjord, it is reached by a mountain railway which, en route, passes by the Univeristy at Blindern. The restaurant is in good condition, though the building of a terrace and some additional structures have interfered with its with its original clean lines.

The *Kvikne Hotel* at *Balestrand*, far up the Sognfjord, is another typical Norwegian timber structure of the 1890s. This is not in 'dragon style', but is characteristic in its fretwork wooden gables and supporting posts and balconies. It is a large building, set at the water's edge and dwarfed only by the high mountains closing in behind.

Finland

The quality of classical architecture built here, in the first 40 years of the nineteenth century, is far finer than in any of the other Scandinavian lands and compares favourably with that in any European country at this time, even Schinkel's and von Klenze's Germany, Napoleon's Paris and Nash's London terraces. In 1809, Finland's centuries-old ties with Sweden were broken as the country became part of the Russian Empire. Until this time Turku (Abö) had been the capital.

In 1812, the Tsar, Alexander I decided to set up a new Finnish capital city at *Helsinki*; a site nearer to Russia and further from Swedish influence. At that time, Helsinki was a small fishing town of only 4000 inhabitants living in wooden buildings. Alexander decided on an imposing city, laid out on classical lines, with all the important civic structures to be designed specially in one, homogeneous layout. *Carl Ludwig Engel* (1778–1840), the German architect, fellow student with Schinkel, who had studied and worked in Italy, Berlin and S. Petersburg, was put in charge of the operation. He came to Finland, stayed there for a quarter of a century (the rest of his life) and carried out the Tsar's wishes. Helsinki was made into a fine capital city, magnificently laid out on monumental lines, with beautiful classical buildings, all in keeping with one another but varied and not monotonously similar. The city has been added to ever since but the original layouts are unaltered, well cared for and unforgettably impressive.

The chief of these, designed by Engel, is the great *Senate Square*, 560 feet by 330 feet, and near its centre the bronze monument to the Tsar Alexander II, erected 1894. The square is dominated by the vast *Lutheran Cathedral of S. Nicholas* (943). Built on a great podium, approached by an immense flight of steps and flanked at the corners by classical pavilions, it is a centrally designed church on Greek cross plan. Completely symmetrical, with a Corinthian portico on each of the four sides and with central drum and dome over the crossing, it is classical with Byzantine overtones. The interior is light, the whole in white and light stone colour. It is entirely classical. The immense, Corinthian crossing piers support the four semi-circular arches and pendentives with a shallow, plain interior dome without lantern. There are four apses, each with its Ionic colonnade, ambulatory behind and a hemispherical dome above. There is an elegant, simple pulpit with gilt classical decoration; the restrained altar is in keeping.

Engel designed classical buildings on other elevations of the square. The *Senate House* (now the Council of State Building) occupies the eastern side (944), the main *University Building* (1828–32) the western, with the domed *University Library* next to it, further north. The University Building is a simple, classical block, not dissimilar to the Senate House but with Ionic portico. The adjacent library has no portico, but Corinthian columns and pilasters across the front. Inside are three reading rooms; the central one is under the dome which is visible on the exterior. Though damaged in the Second World War, it is now restored, and is a fine interior. It is a rectangular room with a

THE NINETEENTH CENTURY IN FINLAND AND NORWAY

943 *Lutheran Cathedral of S. Nicholas, Senate Square,*
Helsinki, Finland, Carl Ludwig Engel, 1830–52
944 *Senate House, Senate Square, Helsinki,*
Engel, 1818–22
945 *University, Oslo, Norway, Christian Heinrich*
Grosch, begun 1840

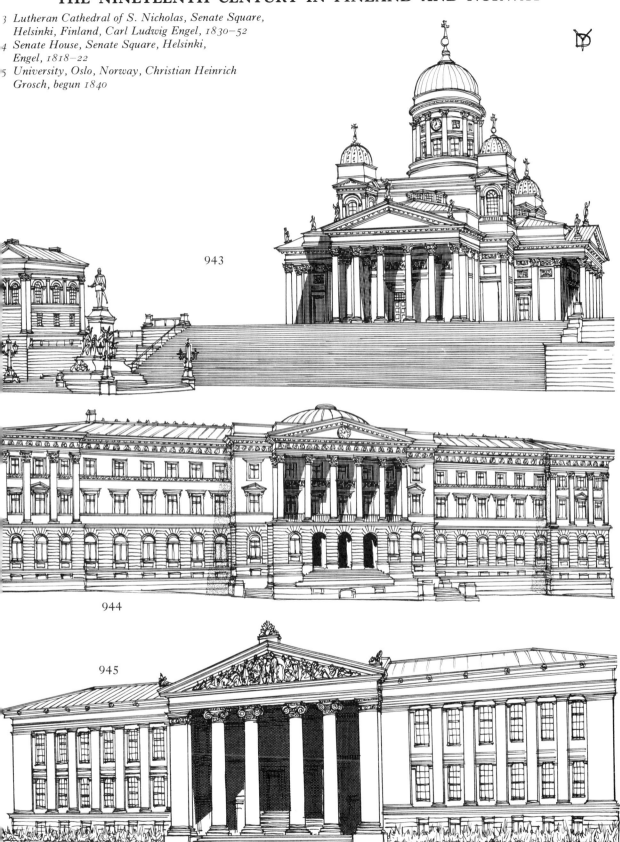

943

944

945

colonnade of 28 Corinthian columns supporting a gallery. The ceiling is domed with lunettes on the four sides. The decoration is all painted: caissons in the dome and figure compositions in the lunettes.

The Senate Square slopes gradually towards the Market Square and the *South Harbour*. Here, there is a long line of fine buildings fronting the harbour, mainly classical in design but dating from different decades in the nineteenth century. Facing the buildings, one's back to the harbour, from left to right they comprise the *City Hall*, 1833 by *Engel*, a large building with Corinthian pilasters in the central portico and end pavilions; a small classical building, 1815 by *Pehr Granstedt*; the *Swedish Embassy*, also classical though astylar, 1922 by *Torben Grut*; the *Supreme Court*, rusticated classical, 1883 by *E. A. Sjöström* and the *President's Palace*, 1813 by *Pehr Granstedt*. This was built as the Helsinki palace for the Tsar and has a central, Ionic portico. This homogeneous, curving elevation round the harbour's edge is of one theme, but has vitality and interest springing from its varied dates of construction. A taller structure, on higher ground beyond the palace, is in complete contrast. The classical buildings are white and pastel shades. This building, the *Orthodox Cathedral* is in deep red brick, Russian Byzantine in style, built in 1868 by *Gornostajeff*. The interior is surprisingly light considering the heavy Byzantine décor in gilt and colour.

Apart from the creation of the capital city, many other buildings were erected in Finland in these years, in classical style and of high quality in design and structure. In 1810, a national body for administering and constructing buildings was set up. Its first Controller of Public Works was the Italian architect *Carlo Francesco Bassi* (1772–1840). The few works by him which survive include the *Old Church* at *Tampere* (1824). Largely of wood, painted white, it is picturesquely sited, like so many of Finland's buildings, in a group of trees in the centre of the city. It has a separate bell tower and is a simple domed church with plain portico.

In *Turku*, the old capital, *Bassi* designed the *Abö Akademie* (the Swedish language University Building), which is near to the cathedral. It was built in 1832–3 and is a rectangular, classical block with a two storey Doric portico. *Carl Christoffer Gjörwell* designed the *Old University*

Building, not far away, in 1802–15, with Bassi's co-operation. Turku's classical heritage is less complete than Helsinki's due to the removal of its capital status, but *Engel*, who succeeded Bassi as Controller, laid out a new town here on the opposite side of the River Aura from the Medieval city centred on the cathedral. This was done after the fire of Turku in 1827. The centre is the large market square, the *Kauppatori*. On the north side is the low building of the *Orthodox Church*, with its immense dome and sturdy, Doric portico (1846) and on the west, the *Swedish Theatre* (1838), which has a façade ornamented by Corinthian pilasters.

In *Hamina*, since 1945 near the border with the Soviet Union, the small town centre possesses some beautiful classical buildings (p. 469). *Engel* built the circular, domed *Orthodox Church* (1837), though the separate campanile in mixed classical and Russian Byzantine style, was by *Visconti*. The *Medieval Church* nearby was restored by Engel in 1828 in simple classical manner. In *Hämeenlinna*, the classical church by *L. J. Desprez* (1798) still stands in the town centre. Surrounded by trees, it is in good condition, though the interior has been completely modernised. The Prefecture nearby is also a classical building, of 1833–6.

In the second half of the nineteenth century, Finland also turned to eclecticism, building in classical, Romanesque and neo-Gothic manner. Typical of the *fin de siècle* are *Gustav Nyström's* buildings in *Helsinki*; The *House of Estates* (1891) and the *State Archives Building* (1890). These are both of high quality classical architecture, well designed and proportioned with good detail and sculpture. In *Hamina*, the *Military Academy* (1898) is another excellent example, this time in the Doric Order.

Georg Theodor Chiewitz worked more in Medieval style. In *Loviisa*, his *Town Hall* is on simple, Romanesque lines (1856), reminiscent of Italian small town halls such as that of Montepulciano. His *church* nearby is in neo-Gothic vein (1865), in deep red brick. It is a large building of good quality, belonging to the same spirit as the Gothic Revival of England and Germany, on cruciform plan with a tall, eastern steeple. Chiewitz's best known work is the *House of Nobles* in *Helsinki*, near the Senate Square. Built 1861, this is red brick and stone in Gothic

Revival style. The exterior is solemn and pedestrian; the interior has an impressive stairway and assembly hall. Also in Helsinki, very typical of the period, is the heavily ornamented office building now used by the Forestry Board. Designed by *Carl Theodor Hoijer* in 1889, it is in neo-Renaissance style.

9
Twentieth Century Architecture

Modern architecture is a vast and complex subject. The function of this book is not to treat the subject in detail, but to complete the history of European architecture by tracing the steady evolution of style and structure up to the present day.

Although the architecture of the first 70 years of this century in the 23 countries of Europe is of complex variety, there is a pattern and a coherent development which has taken, indeed is still taking place. As in earlier ages, it is progressing at different speeds in various countries. The chief factors governing this pace of development in the twentieth century have been two-fold: the political system under which the country has been governed and the poverty or richness of its industrial development.

It is often said that there is no difference between the current architecture of any of the European nations, that the same glass, concrete and steel boxes, based on module construction, are erected everywhere. This is not quite true. Despite the international nature of present day building, and a prime characteristic of twentieth century architecture has been its internationality, national traditions still make themselves felt based, as they always have been, on climate, individual mode of living and economic necessity.

Modern architecture is the term universally applied to the building of the twentieth century which evolved in a number of countries after the First World War. No one has yet produced a better name to describe the type of structure and layout peculiar to this century. It owes nothing to the styles of the past. This does not mean that all, or even a majority of building since 1918 is modern architecture. In fact, until 1950, only a minority of work was in this form and the bulk of construction was in traditional, that is eclectic, manner. It is only the pioneers who created modern architecture before 1950 but, as has always been so, posterity tends to forget the majority of the work in favour of the new form

which, in its turn, becomes the accepted style. This it now is, all over Europe.

The development was inevitable, not just because architects wished to design in a new manner, but because of swiftly increasing European populations, the need to re-build quickly twice in the century, after two world wars, and the developments in materials and technology which made it possible to erect cheaply in mass production methods and prefabricated systems on a large scale. It is these factors, not primarily man's desire for change, which have brought about the transformation in the building scene and have killed for ever the building and architectural industry founded on craftmanship and an aesthetic basis. A number of outstanding men have tried in vain to turn the clock back. In England, William Morris was the first of these.

Until 1900, all architecture in Europe had been based on two great styles: classical and Gothic (or Medieval). The ancient classical civilisations of Greece and Rome had evolved the pattern; Byzantine and Romanesque took much from them, but also developed a Medieval style which developed into Gothic. The Renaissance re-discovered the classical world, the Baroque and rococo as well as the classic revival reinterpreted the theme until, finally, in the nineteenth century came eclecticism of all these forms, successively and in every possible reincarnation.

The strange, ephemeral movement of *Art Nouveau* brought a new form into existence. Manifesting itself in a number of countries from 1890, it burnt itself out by 1914. It was a decorative rather than architectural movement, though it showed itself in building, especially in the early years of the twentieth century. It was short-lived and, in later years, very much de-bunked but it is important historically in architecture as the first attempt to break away from eclecticism. It was not entirely successful in this but it was a deeply felt striving to do so.

Art Nouveau was known by different names in various countries; England and the U.S.A. termed it thus, Belgium the *coup de jouet*, Germany the *Jugendstil*, France the *style nouille* or style Guimard, Austria the *Sezessionstil*, Italy *lo stile Liberty* and Spain *Modernismo*. These names referred either to architects, journals or were descriptions.

The chief materials used in Art Nouveau were iron and glass, first employed ornamentally and later three-dimensionally. The characteristics were decorative, curved lines, floral and geometric. Further development included the use of faïence, stained glass, terracotta and veneers. In later, more architectonic examples, the whole façade became plastic and moulded as in Gaudì's twentieth century work.

Art Nouveau was in part an escape for architects who wished to break away from eclecticism but who also shied away from industrialisation and technology. They preferred the world of the individual, the craftsman, the cottage industry. It was an extension of the ideas of Morris and Ruskin. Based on a backward glancing, it could not last. The First World War created a power which finally broke down the illusions and post-1918 architects were either eclectics or modernists.

Modern architecture is quite different from Art Nouveau in principles and aims. A few architects were experimenting with new ideas before 1918 but, in general, it was an inter-war creation. These modern architects rejected ornament; in reaction to nineteenth century eclecticism they produced buildings that were stark, denuded of all softness and decoration. They were vitally concerned with function, the proper use of materials and architectural structure.

It is paradoxical that the countries where such men of original thought and courage to defy the tradition of the established architectural schools should mainly have been among those which, in the 1930s, submitted to totalitarian government, both communist and fascist. Totalitarianism made it impossible for such original artists to work, so that they emigrated, suffered in prisons and camps, died, or submitted to absolute power. These countries—Germany, Italy, the U.S.S.R.—produced much more than half of the original thinkers and designers of modern architecture. In all cases, the building in these lands in the 1930s became eclectic and sterile.

Many of the leaders of modern architecture were born in the period 1880–90. A large proportion of them lived to considerable or advanced age and, like Mies Van der Rohe, Gropius and Le Corbusier, worked till the end of their lives, creating original and interesting designs all over the world. Because so many of the most famous of them lived and worked on, this generation has become intermingled, in its creations, with the next, among which are also some outstanding contributors.

Until 1950, most European architecture continued to be traditional and eclectic. Much was pedestrian and will be ignored. It would be unjust and inaccurate, however, to label it all in this way. In Denmark, Sweden and in England as well as in France, strong reactionary elements combined with natural conservatism to keep out most of the modernists and give the commissions to the traditionalists. The work of some of these, such as Lutyens in England, is well designed, original within its terms of reference and of high quality.

There are many 'isms' to which modern architecture has been subject in its evolution since 1920. These are often incomprehensible to the layman, in themselves difficult to define and explain, and represent the stages through which many of the architects passed, often quickly and without regret. Like much twentieth century labelling, some of it is jargon and verbiage, and it is not important for the admirer of architecture to comprehend fully. For example, *'expressionism'* was current before and just after the First World War. Various influences are involved here; Art Nouveau, romantic nationalism, surrealism. Architectural examples are dramatic and powerful, like Fritz Höger's Chilehaus in Hamburg (1922), Gropius' theatre at Jena (1923) and Poelzig's rebuilding of the Grosses Schauspielhaus in Berlin (1919).

Constructivism originated in Moscow soon after the Revolution of 1917. It was essentially a sculptural movement, affecting architecture only marginally when it put the accent on the structure of a building, discarding ornament as trivia. Few constructivist buildings got off the drawing board, largely due to the troubled and economically difficult period in which they were evolved. Among the leaders were El Lissitsky and Leonidov.

These theories were allied to the most common

'ism' of the 1920s—*functionalism*. This, the need of a building to be designed suitably for its purpose, had always been a tenet of good architecture. The leaders of the modern school of the 1920s were impressed by the theme of structure, of making it visible and unashamed, not covered by a classical or other façade. They were intrigued by the new technology and engineering projects and the shapes evolved; spheres, cylinders, cones, cubes. They worked out the economics of building in these forms, endlessly repeated, to facilitate cheap production. Their careful, idealistic themes became lost and buried under the calculations of accountants, the mass of building required under municipal and parliamentary authorities and the amount of money available, so that everything became subject to the invincible theory that if a building was efficiently designed for its purpose then, willy-nilly, it must automatically be beautiful. Every country in Europe possesses thousands of examples to prove the fallacy of such a theory, which was never held by the originators anyway.

Since 1950 the pace of building has increased phenomenally; partly because of the need to replace war-destroyed structures and partly to house, educate and entertain growing populations with a rising standard of living. The style of architecture has become truly international. The housing estate with its terrace building or high-rise dwellings, the office skyscrapers, the low level schools; all are familiar in each of the European countries. The result presents a monotonous sight to the traveller, but architecture of an individual period has always had similarity. It is because the quantity of building today is so much greater that the monotony increases with it. That there are national differences will be shown in the discussion of the individual countries.

In the years just after the Second World War, glass curtain walling was *de rigueur*. It became the most ubiquitious façade treatment everywhere. In the later 1950s another 'ism' showed itself—*brutalism*. This is an architecture for architects, almost incomprehensibly ugly to the lay public. It represented a movement by younger architects in Britain in the later 1950s towards an honesty and visibility of structure—even plumbing—and materials. This was no new theme even then; its real origins are more clearly

the *béton brut* of Le Corbusier in his Unités and later work (p. 536). The chief material used is concrete, raw, exposed and left rough, though brick is included also in British examples. The cheaper the building, the easier it is to make it 'brutalist'. There are housing estates of it (Park Hill, Sheffield), new universities in number and even more numerous are the schools. The Germans and some other nations took it up in the 1960s, but created some vastly more original and interesting results with it, especially in church building. Their younger architects, coming in at a later stage, appear to have more to say in the field of design.

The most outstanding, original, attractive and functional modern architecture of the 1950s and 1960s is to be found firstly in Finland, then in Italy and latterly in Western Germany.

Western Europe:
Germany, Austria, Switzerland
Germany

The history of the twentieth century in Europe has been turbulent. This quality has been clearly reflected in its architecture, where fashion has fluctuated violently in 70 years from ornate eclecticism, through severe functionalism, to a dominance of civil engineering module construction. Nowhere in Europe is this more apparent than in Germany, which began the century a newly forged proud nation to suffer, after two world wars, once again a division of its peoples. Since 1945 this division has resulted in the architecture of the two Germanys taking a different path. The essential German characteristics of energy, industry, determination and a wealth of talent are, however, to be seen in both parts of the country. It was these qualities which made Germany into the leading nation in new architectural ideas for so great a part of the twentieth century.

It is not easy today for a student to follow the development of German architecture *in situ* because of the extreme devastation of so many German cities in the Second World War. Most of the damage was in the northern industrial areas and, naturally, it was in these cities, which were built up in the industrialisation programme of 1900–39, that the new architectural ideas were promulgated and came to fruition. The internationally famous buildings in Art Nouveau, Functionalist and Expressionist form, as well as those which stemmed from the Bauhaus ideas, have largely disappeared; only a few remain. The architects who experimented and built in these styles either emigrated in the early 1930s, or stayed at home to design in Fascist neo-classicism as directed, or remained commission-less.

Best known among the architects who embraced the Art Nouveau culture in Germany were *August Endell* (1871–1925) and *Alfred Messel* (1853–1909). The *Studio Elvira* in *Munich* was designed by Endell in 1897. Messel's chief contribution was the *Wertheim Department Store* in *Berlin* of 1896 (p. 516). He then went on to other forms of design.

Entirely new ideas in architecture were being experimented with by a number of designers in Germany even before 1914. The most famous name in this field is that of *Walter Gropius* (1883–1969), who began his architectural career in 1908, after training at the Technische Hochschule in Munich, then travelling in Europe for a year. One of his early works was the *Fagus Factory*, making shoe lasts, at *Alfeld-an-der-Leine* (**948**). Although today this building appears ordinary, in 1911 it was a revolutionary prototype, heralding the glass curtain walling systems so prevalent after 1950. It is one of the few of Gropius' buildings to have survived in Germany.

In 1919 Gropius was appointed at Weimar to head the Art College. Two institutions were amalgamated, the Grand Ducal School of Applied Arts and the Grand Ducal Academy of Arts. Under Gropius the new institution became the *Staatliches Bauhaus*. Here he was able to put into practice his strongly held ideas. He was so successful that this small college, which trained only a few hundred students in the limited years of its existence, became architecturally world famous, a Mecca which attracted the architects, artists and students from all over Europe who saw here something new which would free them from the straitjacket of designing in Medieval or classical idiom. This applied to all the visual arts. Artists of such stature as Paul Klee from Switzerland and Vassili Kandinsky from Russia were two who joined his orbit.

Gropius' idea was to set up an institution where students in all the arts and crafts could study and learn one from another. He abhorred the artificial barriers which existed between artists and craftsmen and between artists in different media; he believed that all artists should be craftsmen anyway. He saw them all as interdependent. He felt that the manual dexterity in the craft was as vital and necessary as the mental contribution of the designer. The phrase so often heard to denote lack of academic ability but compensating artistic dexterity, 'he is good with his hands', would have found no favour with Gropius. He knew only too well that the skill of the craftsman is as fundamentally directed by the brain as that of the original designer. So, every Bauhaus student, whatever his field of work or talent, took the same workshop training. He saw and studied what was necessary for the complete design. When qualified he was able to comprehend and oversee all the aesthetic and constructional processes needed in his field.

All this, of course, was nothing new. It had been practised by many, the architects of the Italian Renaissance and Baroque periods, for example, and by eighteenth century designers such as Robert Adam, who not only worked out every detail of a building but fully understood the arts and crafts, as well as the building science, which went into it. During the nineteenth century these down-to-earth ideals and practices had been somewhat lost. Gropius and his staff re-established them, aiming at collaborative design in a building. It is unfortunate that in their efforts to break the shackles which had tied architects for hundreds of years to the Medieval/classical design pattern, they went to extremes in reaction. Bauhaus building is today sometimes felt to be inhuman, mechanical. Its plainness is too obvious. It lacks warmth and colour. These qualities were far from the aims of the builders, but they were held in the grip of an intensity of desire to build something new, something functional, clean and stripped of tawdry decoration.

In the 1920s there were many different movements and all tended towards extremes. All were reactions from what had preceded them and from one another. The architectural styles of the period did not last long, but the effect of these movements was like a pebble dropped into a pool of water. The widening circles of ripples spread all over Europe and beyond and, after 1945, had a widespread and permanent effect. Architecture could never again be as it was before 1914. The tradition was finally broken. A measure of the influence engendered by the Bauhaus was clear in the intensity of reaction to it—for and against. Its opposers included architectural reactionaries in the 1920s, the Nazis in the 1930s, who described the work as art-Bolshevism, and the Russians, at the same time, who thought it bourgeois.

In 1925 Gropius was invited to leave Weimar to come to Dessau to re-establish the Bauhaus there in new premises. The buildings created for the Bauhaus themselves became prototypes for the new architecture, of which the glass-boxed studio block was the most famous. Gropius left the Bauhaus in 1928, after which it was transferred to Berlin, and continued his own work, which for some years had been largely in the field of low-cost housing estates for industrial workers. Much of this was in *Dessau* (now in East Germany) and also at *Karlsruhe*. His best known work in this field was in *Berlin* in *Siemens-stadt*, from 1929, an immense estate housing the workers from the Siemens Co. This was the prototype on which estates all over Europe were modelled. It is a mixed development of tall slab blocks interspersed with long lines of terrace building in three and four storeys. The estate survives and Gropius' work as well as that of his colleagues like Sharoun can be seen in streets like Goebelstrasse and Jungfernheidweg.

Gropius' views on architecture became so unpopular under Nazi rule that he left Germany in 1934 and settled in England (p. 532). Finding himself underemployed, he moved on to the U.S.A. in 1937, where he accepted the post of Professor of Architecture at Harvard University. There his influence was chiefly in the educational field. At the end of his life he returned to Europe to carry out a number of commissions, notably the *Bijenkorf Store* in *Rotterdam* (p. 530) and the *UNESCO Building* in *Paris* (p. 538).

Other original architects in Germany in the years 1910–30, included Behrens, van der Rohe and Mendelsohn. *Peter Behrens* (1868–1940), the eldest of the group, is best known for his industrial work in Germany. Before 1908 his designs were simple, clean-cut and interesting, but generally on the lines of romantic classicism. After his appointment as architect to AEG, he developed original schemes in the industrial field. His *Turbine Factory* in *Berlin* (1909), which still exists, was a breakthrough in design.

It is undecorated and built in concrete, steel and glass. Two more factories followed in Berlin in 1910, then in 1913 he built the large AEG plant at *Riga* in the U.S.S.R. He became in demand for industrial architectural work, completing an office building for the Mannesmann Steel Works in *Düsseldorf* (destroyed) and an extensive scheme for I. G. Farben at *Frankfurt*. Behrens was one of the founders of modern architecture in Europe and his pupils include the most famous of modern architects—Le Corbusier, Gropius and van der Rohe.

The third of this talented triumvirate, *Mies van der Rohe* (1888–1969), developed his full potential later in life, especially after he had left Germany. He was less influential than Gropius in the 1920s. His chief work at this time was the *Weissenhof housing estate* at *Stuttgart* (which still exists), where he was General Director from 1927. Other architects, like Behrens, also worked here, but van der Rohe's contribution is the most interesting and advanced.

In 1930 he became Director of the Bauhaus in Berlin. After the Bauhaus was closed in 1933, he was unemployed under a hostile government, so, like Gropius, he settled in the U.S.A. Here, he found immense opportunities to develop his architectural style, and his many and varied buildings had a great influence on architects both there and in Europe. His work is original, sometimes severe, always finely proportioned and elegant. Typical is his Seagram skyscraper on Park Avenue in New York (1956–8). Like Gropius, some of his last works were for Europe, notably the *New National Gallery* in *West Berlin* (1965–8) and his design for a Piazza Tower in the City of London near the Bank of England.

Erich Mendelsohn (1887–1953) quickly adapted himself to the possible uses of the new architectural materials of concrete, glass and steel. His earlier works are of the Expressionist style, like his *Einstein Tower* at *Potsdam* (1920–1), which is highly plastic. In the 1920s he worked more in steel and glass, to a rectangular pattern, in his designs for department stores and office blocks.* Unfortunately little remains of Mendelsohn's work in Germany. He emigrated to England in 1933 (p. 532), then left for Palestine in 1939, and finally for the U.S.A. in 1941.

The fame of these outstanding men tends to overshadow the work of other pre-war architects

* The largest and best known of these was the Columbus House *in the* Potsdamer Platz *in* Berlin *(1931). This, like the Art Nouveau* Wertheim Department Store

(page 515), has disappeared from the devastated, once famous square.

ARCHITECTURE IN GERMANY, 1900–1939

946 *Chilehaus, Hamburg, Fritz Höger, 1923*
947 *Stuttgart Railway Station, Paul Bonatz and F. E. Scholer, 1914–27*
948 *The Fagus Factory, Alfeld-an-der-Leine, Walter Gropius and Adolf Meyer, 1911–14*

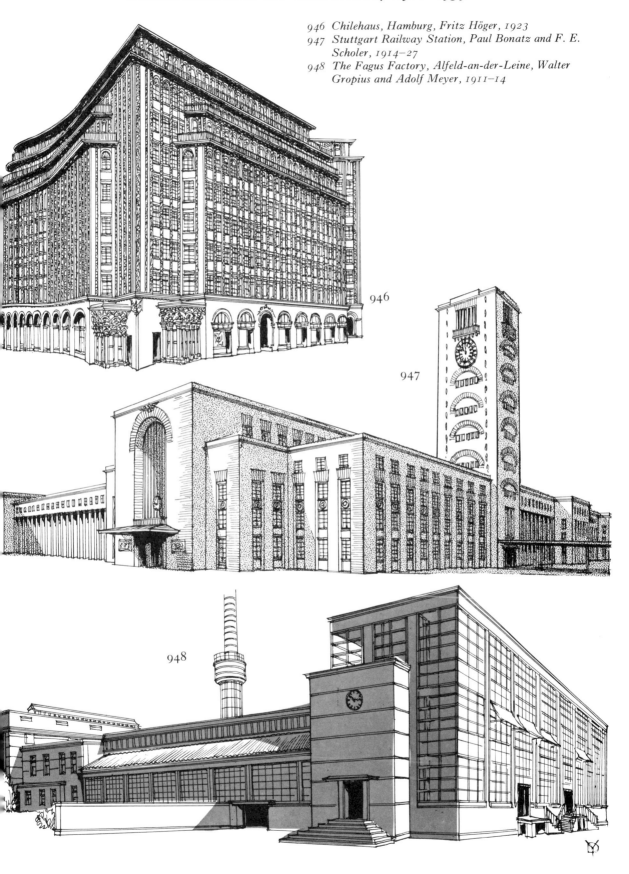

in Germany, several of whom produced talented and original work. As elsewhere, the years before 1914 saw the designing of eclectic buildings on romantic classical lines. The *Town Hall* at *Berlin-Charlottenburg* is a chunky example (1905, by *Reinhardt-Sessenguth*). There were also several instances of more forward-looking modern work, such as *Bonatz's* (1877–1951) *Stuttgart Railway Station* (**947**); a bold design in plain large ashlar blocks. Expressionism flourished in the 1920s. *Hans Poelzig* (1869–1936) was the chief architect in this field and his remodelling of the *Grosses Schauspielhaus* in *Berlin* (1919) was a dramatic example. The circular stage had a ceiling of Arabic influenced stalactite decoration. The building, in East Berlin, is still unrestored, but sufficient of it exists in a ruined condition to make the proposed re-building possible. Expressionist design was also incorporated into tall blocks. The *Chilehaus* in *Hamburg* (which still survives), is a striking example (**946**) by *Fritz Höger* (1877–1949). The influence of Sullivan's designs of the 1890s in the U.S.A. can be seen here, despite the Expressionist curves.

From about 1925–33, some building in the modern idiom, but of plain box-like type was erected in Germany. Better examples include the *town hall* at *Berlin-Schöneberg* (1930, the *Katreiner Hochhaus* nearby (1929–30), the *Hochhaus-am-Hansaring, Cologne* (1925), *Poelzig's Radio Building* in *Berlin* (1931), and *Fahrenkamp's Shellhaus* (1931) and curving office blocks in the *Fehrbelliner Platz* (1930), both in *Berlin*.

Some interesting churches were built, of which two Expressionist examples should be mentioned. One is the *Kreuzkirche* in *Berlin-Wilmersdorf*, built 1930 by *Paulus*. A brick church, it has an immense tower, like the fortified Romanesque churches of Germany, with a purple ceramic-faced, sculptured porch. The interior is on eight-sided oval plan with the parabolic arch dominating the constructional design. *Dominikus Böhm* (1880–1955) designed a number of Expressionist churches of which *S. Engelbert* at *Cologne-Riehl* (1931–3) is especially notable. It is on circular plan (with a separate tall bell tower). The exterior is of brick walls on the parabolic arched faces; each has a circular window set near the top of the arch. A later church is the more modern *Gustav Adolfkirche* in Berlin (1934) by *Bartning*. It has a vertical accent in angular stages and is built in brick and concrete

Until 1933 German architecture had been vigorously capable of expansion and development. The government of the Third Reich under Adolf Hitler ended this state of affairs. From then on until after 1945, modern architecture was not permitted; the official expression in architecture was neo-classicism of a heavy, monumental, uninspiring type.

After 1945 Germany was in a bad economic state and many of her cities lay in ruins. Until the early 1950s only essential structures were put up, in poor materials. With American aid the economy was started up again and a large building programme was initiated. Because of the urgent need for city buildings of all types, there was no time for the planning or reorganisation of towns. Buildings were erected on the old sites and traffic problems are now acute.[*]

Housing was given low priority and, when begun, the programme continued along pre-war lines. The *Hansaviertel* of *West Berlin* is an example. It has a fine site in the Tiergarten. Although, thanks to the prestige of the Interbau Exhibition scheme of 1957 which initiated it, it possesses some fine blocks of flats designed by internationally famous architects—Le Corbusier, Alvar Aalto, Walter Gropius, etc.—it is all haphazard, with no basic planning scheme. The most interesting church here caused some controversy when first built. It is the *Kaiser Friedrich Gedächtnis Kirche*, designed by *Ludwig Lemmer*. The grey exterior is drab and has weathered poorly, though the see-through bell-tower still has an ethereal quality viewed through the Tiergarten trees. The interior is pleasant, its walls of wood slats and attractively coloured in abstract paint and mosaic designs. One large wall is mainly of coloured glass in greys, greens and blues.

The best architecture in the 1950s was in government building, civic architecture and offices. The designs were severely rectangular in glass curtain wall or concrete blocks. Steel and module construction set this pattern, as in the U.S.A. and England. Typical of the better examples are the *Thyssenhaus Hochhaus* (1956–60) by *Hentrich* and *Petschnigg* and the *Mannesmann Hochhaus* (1956–8) by *Schneider-Esteban* both in *Düsseldorf*. There are a number of city centre schemes in the traditional pattern of the

---

[*] *This is not, of course, a peculiarly German problem. Italy, France and England suffer in a similar manner, though England has built some New Towns to siphon off population from big cities.*

MODERN ARCHITECTURE IN GERMANY

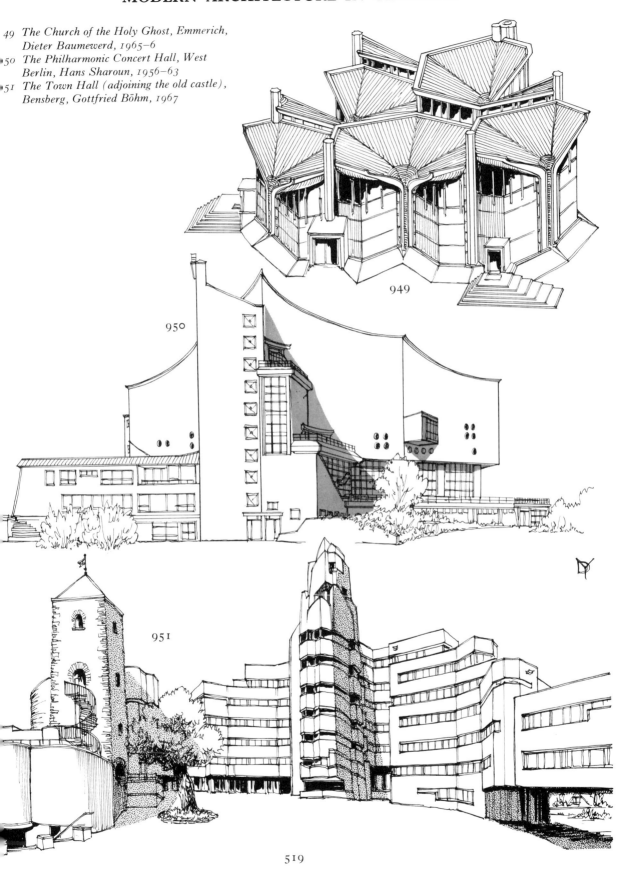

949

950

951

period, like the *Europa Platz* at the head of the Kurfürstendamm in *West Berlin* (1963–5) by Hentrich and Petschnigg and the more interesting *Ernst Reuter Platz* also in the city.

In the 1960s West German architecture has become more varied and of better quality in building. The tall glass box is still being constructed, but more architects are, where the opportunity permits, designing in more interesting and unusual styles. Some 'brutalist' buildings are being put up in great concrete cubes and masses, showing the same desire as in England for the 'honesty' of exposed concrete. West German architects have taken the theme further and produced some more original and exciting variants, using a greater selection of materials, surfacings and facings to provide contrast and interest. A good example is *Gottfried Böhm*'s *town hall* at *Bensberg* (**951**). Set on top of a hill above the town, the new building is amalgamated in one scheme with the old castle, blending admirably.

Architects were tending away from the rectangular box and hard right angles. This is particularly seen in the many theatres and concert halls built all over West Germany. Examples include the *Beethovenhalle* at *Bonn* (1959, *Wolske*) and the nearby town theatre, the *city theatre* at *Münster* by *Deilmann* and the *theatre* at *Düsseldorf*, 1967–9 by *Bernhard Pfau*. This last design takes further the breakaway from rectangular boxing, with its undulating curving façade.

Churches also provide a greater opportunity for variety in form and treatment. There are many interesting examples, but four, in particular, illustrate this. In *West Berlin*, the *Sühne Christi Church* in Siemensstadt has an original interior. Built 1962–4 by *Hansrudolf Plarre*, it is on octagonal plan and has brick walls inside, decorated by cavity brick facings. Above, the roof is of metal struts, criss-crossing one another with metal spheres at the intersections, in the manner of the structure of a crystal. Nearby is the *Church of Maria Regina Martyrum*, built 1961–3, by *Schädel* and *Ebert* in memory of Catholic Martyrs who died in the years 1933–45. It is a severe, concrete church with a separate bell tower and large, open atrium in front of the church, round which are some very modern sculptured 'Stations of the Cross' by *Hajek* and a

metal relief of Joseph, Mary and Christ on a donkey. Downstairs is the memorial chapel and, above, is the main church, severe and very plain. There are no windows; the light comes from the ceiling between the beams.

Helmut Striffler's *Church of the Atonement* at the site of the previous concentration camp at *Dachau* was built 1965–7. It is long and low, a finely shaped and proportioned 'brutalism'. In contrast is *Baumewerd's Church of the Holy Ghost* at *Emmerich*. Built in boarded concrete, the lighting and spatial forms are unusually designed, with changing planes and angles. The interior walls are faced with abstract patterned glass. The planed concrete pillars are capped in spreading lotus forms, opening up into the roof. This formation can be seen in a view of the exterior shown from above (**949**). The altar cross, in blood red metal, made from burnt and devastated war materials, is a symbolism of our age.

Germany lost all her great architects in the 1930s and the post-war period has not produced men of equivalent talent or stature. There are, however, some designers who, as young architects in 1933, stayed in their homeland and are now senior men in their profession. Of these, two in particular have established a link in architectural excellence from the pre-war days till now. One of these is *Hans Sharoun* (1893–1972) who studied and worked chiefly in Berlin as a young man. He contributed to the *Weissenhof Estate* in *Stuttgart* under Mies van der Rohe in the 1920s and extensively to *Siemensstadt* in *Berlin* in the 1930s. He was allowed little latitude under the Third Reich and designed few buildings. In 1945 he was appointed to lead the Department for Building and Reconstruction in *West Berlin*. Among his numerous contributions there since then are the *American Memorial Library* and the *Philharmonic Concert Hall*, built almost on the 'wall', near the Brandenburger Tor (**950**).

Another such architect is *Egon Eiermann* (b. 1904), among whose post-war contributions are a number of interesting churches. Germany lost so much of its earlier architectural heritage during the Second World War that there was the greater inducement to restore and adapt what remained. A common practice in ecclesiastical building has been to retain the surviving tower and add a new church to it. Some of these schemes are not successful marriages: for example, the Church of S. Rochus in Düsseldorf or the Christikirche in Bochum. The most dramatic of these conceptions is Eiermann's *Kaiser Wilhelm Gedächtnis Kirche* in the Europa Platz in *West Berlin*. The old church was a typical product of the later nineteenth century German Gothic Revival—large, ornate and not a work of beauty or elegance. It was decided after 1945 to retain the blackened and truncated tower as a war memorial for West Berlin. In 1955–63 Eiermann made the tower safe and weather-proof, restored its barrel vaulted interior mosaics and sculptured panels and added, on one side, an octagonal bell tower and, on the other, an octagonal church, both in plain, honeycombed concrete; a brutal and emotional change of style. The interior of the new church is most effective, the honeycomb pattern showing as myriads of tiny glass windows, in square panes, on all eight sides of the building, in rich colourings of which deep blue predominates. There is a simple altar table, above which is a modern metal sculptured, crucified Christ; it is very large and has no cross. Opposite the altar, above the entrance door, is a fine organ and a platform gallery, suspended over the doorway, to accomodate a whole orchestra and choir.

The development of *East Germany* since 1945, under the aegis of Moscow, has been different, but the energy, talent and capacity for thorough workmanship is equally apparent here as in the western half of the country. In East Germany, work was held back till after 1960 and little building was done, apart from one or two show schemes like *Stalinallee* (now Karl Marx Allee) in *East Berlin*. These were in the official Soviet style as seen in Kiev and Moscow (p. 553); a sterile, provincial version of modern classicism.

In the 1960s the rebuilding of cities was begun, notably East Berlin, Leipzig, Dresden, Frankfurt-an-der-Oder and Karl Marx Stadt (Chemnitz before 1945). Here, the buildings are dull, in rectangular blocks, unenterprisingly designed round large squares or wide boulevards, which are left open for mass parades. The *Unter den Linden* and *Alexander Platz* in *East Berlin* are typical. Here, as in Leipzig and Dresden, the restoration of the great buildings of the past is being carried out to a characteristically German

high standard, but work is slow compared to western achievements. Also, in Berlin especially, the whole of the original centre of the city, containing therefore all the fine buildings, is now East Berlin. It was devastated, with a consequent need for wholesale restoration and rebuilding.

Since the late 1960s more modern designs are appearing, and also more enterprising ideas. The heavy hand of the planners is less apparent. Hotels in western style are being built to attract the tourist from Western Europe, the *Hotel Berolina* in *Berlin* for example. Even so, standardisation is still much stronger than in the West, resulting in much greater urban monotony.

Austria

Before 1914 Austria, with its empire extending over much of central and eastern Europe, was an important power and many fine buildings were erected, especially in Vienna. Since the Treaty of Versailles, Austria has been a small, not rich country and her architectural influence has been correspondingly less than that of Germany.

One or two architects used Art Nouveau decoration at the end of the nineteenth century. The chief of these was *Otto Wagner* (1841–1918), who introduced the ornamental style into the ironwork of his Vienna Stadtbahn stations, rather like Guimard in Paris (p. 534). That at the *Karlplatz* is one example, but it is now in a ruinous condition. His block of flats in the city, usually called the *Majolika Haus*, was decorated across the façade in floral designs, as was the ironwork of the balconies and grilles.

The use of Art Nouveau in Austria was, nevertheless, only decorative and ephemeral. After 1900 Wagner, like his colleagues, turned to different designs. His best work is probably the *Postal Savings Bank* in *Vienna* (1904–6), which has restrained decoration and a more modern treatment. His *workers' flats* in the city at No. 40 Neustiftgasse and No. 4 Doblergasse (1910–11) were plainer, simple facades.

Much of Wagner's work was in and around Vienna and has suffered consequent destruction and damage from the Second World War. This also applies to the contribution by *Adolf Loos* (1870–1933), the other well-known Austrian architect of this time. Loos was born in Brno, then studied in Germany and worked in the

U.S.A. He returned to Europe and lived in Vienna from 1896. His work was plain and severe. He abhorred ornament, particularly Art Nouveau. He developed his style in using reinforced concrete, and most of his commissions were for houses, where he often employed this medium. He built houses in Vienna, Paris, Montreux, Brno and Plzen, many of which have been lost. Typical examples included the *Gustav Scheu House* in *Vienna-Hietzing* (1912), the *Rufer House* in *Vienna* (1922) and No. 14 Av. Junod, *Paris* (1926). Some of his houses show a strong influence from Voysey in England and Frank Lloyd Wright from the U.S.A.

Architecture in Austria since 1945 has not produced outstanding originality or quality, and has generally followed the pattern of other smaller countries. Typical of the better work is the *Church of the Holy Blood* at *Salzburg-Parsch*, by *Holzbauer*. The exterior is uninteresting. The more successful interior is divided into two parts; one is large and light with a gable roof, part wood and part glass, and a simple altar under this. The other section is much lower, supported on ribbed columns under a groined roof, like the ancient crypt design of the early Romanesque period. A stained glass window on either side of this area gives a lower light, in rich hues, in contrast to the brightness of the main part of the church.

Switzerland

After lagging behind in the field of architectural design in the nineteenth century, Swiss architects began to take advantage of modern architectural thought in the early 1920s. The work of Le Corbusier, himself a Swiss, and that of the Bauhaus impressed younger Swiss architects

952 Church of S. Anthony, Basle, Switzerland, Karl Moser, 1926–31

THE TWENTIETH CENTURY IN HOLLAND AND SWITZERLAND

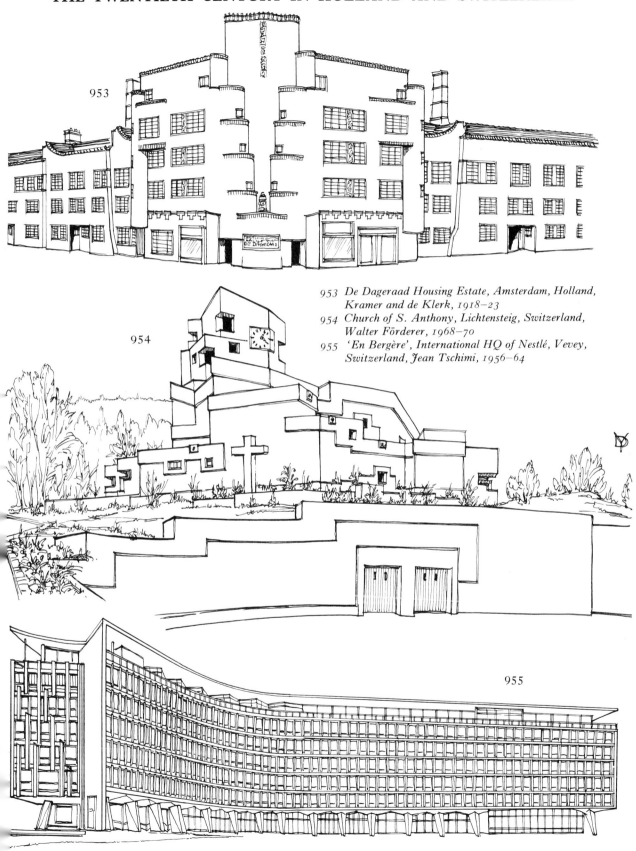

953 *De Dageraad Housing Estate, Amsterdam, Holland, Kramer and de Klerk, 1918–23*

954 *Church of S. Anthony, Lichtensteig, Switzerland, Walter Förderer, 1968–70*

955 *'En Bergère', International HQ of Nestlé, Vevey, Switzerland, Jean Tschimi, 1956–64*

greatly and several of them began to develop original themes in the new materials of concrete, glass and steel. *Robert Maillart* (1872–1940) was chiefly noted for his structural approach in the civil engineering problems of using concrete and metal for bridges and blocks of buildings. *Hannes Meyer* (1889–1954), Director of the Bauhaus for a time, produced some early examples of functional design. Many architects developed advanced methods of town planning and layout of housing estates. The *Zürich* scheme of *Neubühl* (1930–2) is one of these, where the architects *Paul Artaria* and *Hans Schmidt* introduced standardisation of units and carefully sited the buildings to create open space between.

The new style was brought to the design of churches and in this field *Karl Moser* (1860–1936) was the leader. He was the Swiss equivalent of Auguste Perret in France and his *Church of S. Anthony* in *Basle* (1926–31) has much in common with Perret's example at Le Raincy (**967**). The Basle church is also in concrete, with large areas of glass panelling and it has a tall tower, more original than Perret's and one which was widely emulated in both Switzerland and Germany. Inside it is less glowingly lit and is heavier in treatment, but the reticulated, parabolic vaulted ceiling, supported on the uncompromisingly square-sectioned reinforced concrete pillars, is monumentally impressive (**952**). The windows are in rectangular panels of coloured glass with figure groups depicted in them. There is a simple, bronze pulpit covered by a plain, flat canopy; the side panels are sculptured in low relief.

There are two examples of this type of church in *Lucerne*, by pupils of Moser: *S. Charles* by *Fritz Metzger* and *S. Joseph* by *Otto Dreyer*. The Church of S. Charles stands on the edge of the River Reuss, not far from its exit from Lake Lucerne. The exterior is in concrete, severe, with a two-storeyed, columned porch fronting the river bank. At the side is the familiar lofty, square-sectioned tower and, at the rear, the church ends in an apsidal curve, the plain concrete broken only by the window which extends all round the upper part of the building. The interior is unusual and spacious. It comprises one vast open space with flat concrete ceiling supported by concrete columns faced with strips of dark, polished marble; gaps are left between these strips effectively representing classical fluting. There are no capitals, bases or entases, however. The columns extend all round the church, giving aisles and ambulatory. Above, in the walls, is the long, continuous band of window panes in coloured glass of abstract designs, creating a rich glow to the interior when the sun is shining. The pulpit is of wood with metal, sculptured panels.

The *Church of S. Joseph* has a separate campanile, Italian style, and this (like the similar church at Altstetten on the outskirts of Zürich, 1938–41), has a perforated design all over it and a clock and belfry in the top part. The interior is very simple. There is an almost flat ceiling and plain walls with simple, stocky columns. The stark altar table has a draped baldacchino over it and the wall behind is draped also. The colouring is all in grey curtaining, black, unpolished stone and light wood. It is an effective interior but more neutral and less dramatic than the other examples.

In the immediate post-war years, Switzerland constructed far fewer buildings than other countries, since her cities had not been devastated in the war. By the early 1960s Swiss architects began again to show initiative in modern building and designs for churches, apartments and office blocks, illustrating interest and originality.* There are many unusual church schemes; two of the more outstanding are the Catholic churches at Buchs and at Lichtensteig. The *Buchs Church* (*Brütsch*, 1966–8), has a plain exterior with tall tower: a more up-to-date version of Moser. The interior is, on the other hand, spatially, finely handled. The church is entered near the bell tower, via a sloping passage, along which are set stone and bronze sculptural 'Stations of the Cross', and this connects to the church, in a separate building. The interior is in boarded concrete and wood, plain, but outstanding in the carefully angled planes and the handling of both natural and artificial lighting, indirect and reminding the observer of Le Corbusier's convent at Eveux-sur-l'Arbresle (p. 537). There is some modern sculpture of unusual design and high quality in the interior, placed carefully as part of the architecture and not merely as decoration.

The *Church of S. Gallus* (**954**) at *Lichtensteig*, built 1968–70 by *Walter Förderer*, is sited on a hill at the edge of the small town, pleasantly landscaped behind, with gardens and a cemetery.

* *It is notable that French Switzerland (birth-place of Le Corbusier) and, even more, Italian Switzerland, have fallen behind in this respect.*

The building is constructed in stepped blocks in concrete, a design imaginatively handled as these masses approach the original form of the tower. The interior is all of straight lines in light coloured wood. Under the tower is a traditional form of wood structure, its beams radiating from a wheel set asymmetrically; artificial lighting is incorporated in the beams. The altar stands beneath, plain and in traditional materials.

Förderer has designed a number of schemes in Switzerland, developing his ideas on group purpose building of church combined with discussion rooms (like the scheme at Sussex University Meeting House, by Spence, p. 534), also with theatre, concert hall and lecture theatre, providing a multi-purpose structure where people can exchange ideas and experience. His ecclesiastical community scheme at Hérémence, near Sion, is of this type. He is also noted for his *Swiss Graduate School of Economics* and *Administration* at *S. Gallen* (1960–3).

In other fields of work, the terraced flats at *Zug*, set in to the steep hillside, are an interesting development, built 1957–60 by *Stucky* and *Meuli*. The tower block scheme in *Zürich (Zur Palme)* by *Haefeli, Moser* and *Steiger*, 1960s, containing offices and shops round a piazza, is typical of the better designs of this type. It is of boarded concrete on the lower part and of steel and glass above. The *Nestlé's International HQ* building is attractively situated, fronted by lawns spreading down to the shores of Lake Geneva at *Vevey* (**955**). It is on similar plan to the Y-shaped UNESCO Building in Paris.

Despite the large number of hotels which Switzerland already possesses, the demands of the vital tourist trade have caused the building of new ones. At *Interlaken*, for instance, the *Hotel Bernerhof* is a pleasant example, combining in its design and treatment the traditional Swiss intimate, mountain hotel style with modern materials. It is on a suitable scale in dark red brown and white rubble finish, sympathetic in feeling to this town. This is in contrast to the nearby '*Hochhaus*' in concrete, the new Hotel Metropole, which intrudes upon this attractive setting.

Italy

Art Nouveau (*lo stile* Liberty, named after the Regent Street Store which was displaying patterned fabrics of this type) was introduced into architecture here in the early years of the twentieth century. *Basile, d'Aronco, Cattaneo* and *Sommaruga* were architects who built in this mode. Giuseppe Sommaruga's (1867–1917) apartment block in the *Corso Venezia* in *Milan* still exists (1903). It is typical of the extrovert Italian approach to Art Nouveau. The doorway and lower windows appear to be hewn from the living rock, the decorative window panels swirl and curve and the second floor *putti* in pairs cling precariously to their window frames.

If Italy was not one of the major exponents of Art Nouveau, she did produce some of the earliest and most talented protagonists in *modern architecture*. Even before the First World War, *Antonio Sant'Elia* (1880–1916) was creating his designs for cities years ahead of his time. He was a visionary of future architecture, fascinated by the romantic aspects of technology, especially in the U.S.A., and planned cities for Italy. His *Città Nuova*, projected in 1914 was exhibited in Milan. It envisaged skyscrapers, pedestrian precincts and traffic moving on overhead roadways at two or three different levels. He was a socialist and developed these schemes as part of his suggestions for an ideal society. Tragically, his talents were cut short in 1916 when he was killed in action. His drawings and designs survive and have strongly influenced later work.

In the early 1920s it was *Giuseppe Terragni* (1904–43) who led Italy's modern school of thought. His life too was abbreviated, this time by the Second World War, and his working years were few between his graduation from Milan Polytechnic in 1926 till his call-up in 1939. This was long enough for him to produce a number of original buildings which brought him international acclaim and became prototypes in Europe. In 1926 he helped to found the '*gruppo sette*', seven architects who joined the '*Movimento Italiano per l'Architettura Razionale*'. They enunciated a new architectural theme, searching for clarity, order, honesty in use of materials and an end to eclecticism. They were all young and were inspired by the Bauhaus project in Germany (p. 515) and the work of Frank Lloyd Wright in America.

Terragni's chief buildings include the *Casa del Fascio* (1932–6) and his *apartment house* (**958**), both in *Como* and the *Casa Rustici*, another block of flats in the Corso Sempione in *Milan* (1934–5). These are all simple, unornamented structures.

Other Italian architects who designed in modern style in the period 1919–36 include Pagano, Michelucci, Ridolfi, Montuori, Ponti, Figini and Pollini. Some of the work of *Giuseppe Pagano* (1896–1945) and *Mario Ridolfo* can still be seen in the *Città Universitaria* in *Rome*. In particular, there is Pagano's *Istituto Fisico* (1930–5) (the Department of Physics Building) and Ridolfo's *Library* (*c.* 1935). *Giovanni Michelucci* (*b.* 1891) is best known for his *S. Maria Novella Railway Station* in *Florence* (1933–6); a simple, well-proportioned structure in advance of its time.

Some architects tried, not very successfully to pursue modern design under fascism, others, like *Ponti*, endeavoured to follow a middle line, which enabled them to survive professionally to build in modern style after 1945 (**957**), but many adopted the government's policy and patronage. Totalitarian governments rarely advocate new designs or change in the arts. Mussolini was no exception. He saw himself as the head of a new Italian state which would revive the glories of the Roman Empire. The only suitable architectural expression for such a power was, of course, Roman classicism, albeit in simplified, modern dress. His enforcement of his desires was much less stringent than Hitler's, or structures like Michelucci's railway station would not have been built, but architects seeking and accepting government patronage were expected to produce works fundamentally classical. Much of this was not only eclectic but profoundly dull. Among the best, well-proportioned, and lively are *Eugenio Montuori's* (*b.* 1907) fantastic *Railway Station* in *Milan* (begun 1931) and *Marcello Piacentini's* (*b.* 1881) extensive layouts such as the *Città Bassa* of *Bergamo* (1922–4) and the completion of *Turin's Via Roma* (1938).

In 1945 the need for reconstruction was urgent in a country whose cities had been so badly damaged. A quantity of buildings was put up, of poor quality, in dull, block design, as fast as they could be completed. This was necessary but, in the 1950s, it was realised that future slums were being created. The pace of building slowed and much better standards of design and structure were encouraged and enforced.

From the late 1950s the Italian contribution to original and interesting modern architecture has been considerable. Traditional Italian craftmanship has been modified to unit and mass-production methods, using coloured marbles, granite and mosaic partly for decoration and facing. There is more variety in colour and shape than in the modern work of most European countries. A greater use of curves, both linear and three-dimensional, is usual and the brilliant colours traditional to Italy's building over the centuries, so aptly complementary to the sunshine, are still to be seen.

Italy has also been a leading nation in developing the most ubiquitous of modern materials, available to all countries whatever their natural resources—reinforced concrete. Partly for economic reasons, this has been preferred to steel and the results have shown a greater variety of design. Over emphasis on steel leads to rectangular tower blocks as in the U.S.A., England and Germany. Italian derivations from concrete have produced an infinite range of self-supporting roofs, vaults and shell coverings to all types of buildings.

The most important figure in the development of reinforced concrete is the engineer *Pier Luigi Nervi* (*b.* 1891). He early established a reputation for this work in 1930 in his *stadium* at *Florence* and his later *hangars* at *Orvieto* and *Orbetello*. He has continued till the present day, creating original, beautiful concrete structures of infinite variety of which the *Palazzetto dello Sport* (**956**) is typical. Among his other structures are the *hall* at the *Lido di Roma, Ostia*, the *terme* at *Chianciano*, the other Olympic constructions in Rome—the *Palazzo dello Sport* and the *Stadium*—and the *Exhibition Hall* in *Turin*. In 1960 Nervi returned to Turin to build his imaginative *Palace of Labour* for the centenary celebrations. This vast hall, like the English Crystal Palace of a century earlier (p. 480), had to be built quickly and to be suitable for later adaptation. It was, therefore, constructed partly in steel. The metal columns have palm leaf capitals reminiscent of ancient Nile palaces.

Nervi's aim has been to create functional buildings which, at the same time, act by their aesthetic qualities as an effective educational influence. Functionalism, for Nervi, has never become 'brutalism'. In consequence, his work is admired by the lay public as well as by the

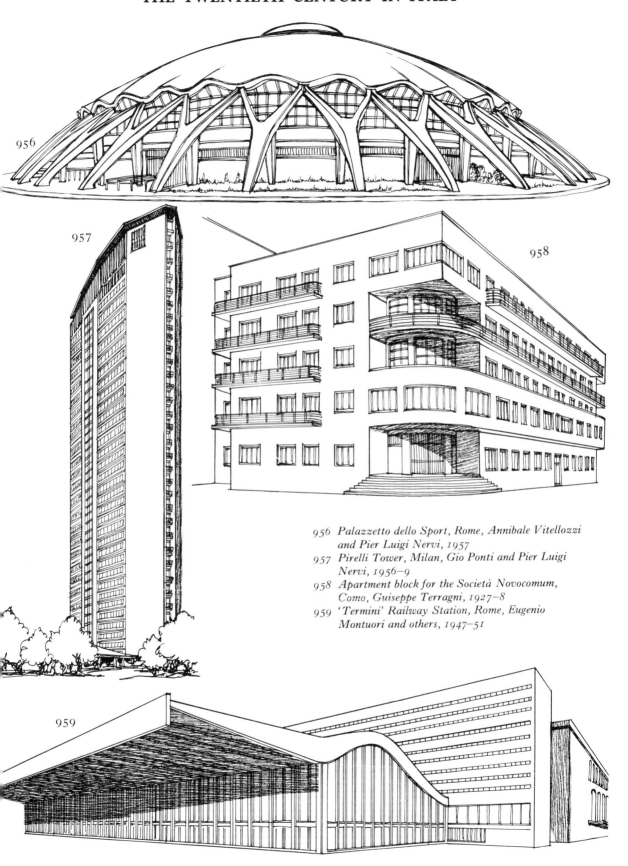

956 *Palazzetto dello Sport, Rome, Annibale Vitellozzi and Pier Luigi Nervi, 1957*

957 *Pirelli Tower, Milan, Gio Ponti and Pier Luigi Nervi, 1956–9*

958 *Apartment block for the Società Novocomum, Como, Guiseppe Terragni, 1927–8*

959 *'Termini' Railway Station, Rome, Eugenio Montuori and others, 1947–51*

architects.

Of the outstanding work of the 1950s in Italy, which have influenced other work internationally, is the *Pirelli Tower* in *Milan* (**957**), architect *Gio Ponti* (*b.* 1891), engineer *Nervi;* the *Termini Railway Station* in *Rome*, finally completed in 1951 by *Eugenio Montuori* and others (**959**); the *Olivetti Building* in *Milan* (1954, *Bernasconi and Partners*) and the *Faculty of Architecture Buildings* at the *Milan Polytechnic (Morasutti and Mangiarotti)*.

Interesting work of the 1960s includes the curving concrete façades of the *Technical College* at *Busto Arsizio* (1963–4) by *Castiglione* and *Fontana* and the many interesting and original churches, especially the *Church of S. Giovanni* on the *Autostrada del Sole* at *Florence*. This was built in 1962 by *Giovanni Michelucci* and dedicated to the memory of those who lost their lives in the construction of this famous autostrada through the mountains. Built with coarse rubble block walls and copper roofing, it is an unusual design, plastic, honest and basic in its tent-like form.

The Low Countries:
Holland

From the beginning of the century there developed a national modern architecture in Holland which, if not as original as that of men like Gropius, Mies Van der Rohe or Le Corbusier, was unusual, completely non-eclectic and ingenious in its adaptation of the traditional Dutch building material of brick to the modern idiom.

The leader of this national school of the late nineteenth century was *Hendrik Berlage* (p. 498, Chapter 8). After his outstanding civic structures of the *fin de siècle*, he launched, in the early twentieth century, into laying out housing estates of the low-cost type as well as city planning. He was followed by the architect *J. M. Van der Meij* (*b.* 1868), whose work was national and as near to Art Nouveau as was ever approached in Holland. A typical example of his contribution at this time is the *Scheepvaarthuis*, the Dock Offices or Terminal, on the Prins Hendrik quay in *Amsterdam* (1913). This is a most unusual building, angular, powerful, dramatic and intimately personal. It is built of dark brick with decoration in iron scrolls and twirls. The roof is covered by lighter coloured ceramic tiling.

From just before the First World War till about 1925, the leading architects were *Michael de Klerk* (1884–1923) and his colleague *P. L. Kramer* (*b.* 1881). Their work was of the expressionist school like that of their contemporary German counterparts. They laid out a number of large housing estates, especially in *Amsterdam* as in, for example, the *Eigen Haard Estate* from 1913. The buildings are all in brick with unusual, simple, three and four storey façades employing the material skilfully in curves and rounded corners. The work is national, romantic and, even now, does not appear old-fashioned. Certainly, such buildings, low-cost as they were, have stood up to the extensive wear and tear which they received much better than their post-war equivalents—a tribute to the building standards of the time. A little later, in 1918–23, came the *De Dageraard Estate* in Amsterdam, of similar treatment (**953**).

In more modern and somewhat functionalist vein came the work of Oud and Dudok. *Jacobus J.P. Oud* (1890–1963) worked on a number of housing estates, chiefly in *Rotterdam*, where he became city architect in 1918. He also designed a fine estate at the *Hook of Holland* in 1926–7, very simple and advanced for its period. In later years, his work mellowed, became less functionalistic and more ornamental. Typical of this design is his *Shell Building* in *The Hague*, begun 1938.

Willem Dudok (*b.* 1884) was an architect with a modern but personal, particularly Dutch style. He was city architect at *Hilversum* for a number of years and his *town hall* here (**961**), one of his best works, was much imitated all over Holland. The building, in brick, is plain, almost stark, but beautifully proportioned and designed. His other contributions to the city include the *Bavinck School* and the *public baths*.

In the post-war period, architecture began to get under way again after 1950. The first major task which the Dutch had to face was the rebuilding of the devastated city of *Rotterdam*, where so much fine architecture by men such as Oud and Dudok had perished. In the centre of the city it was a case of starting from scratch. Unfortunately, as in the case of Germany and Italy, the need was so great that architectural and planning opportunities were missed in an endeavour to house the population and build

THE TWENTIETH CENTURY IN GREECE AND HOLLAND

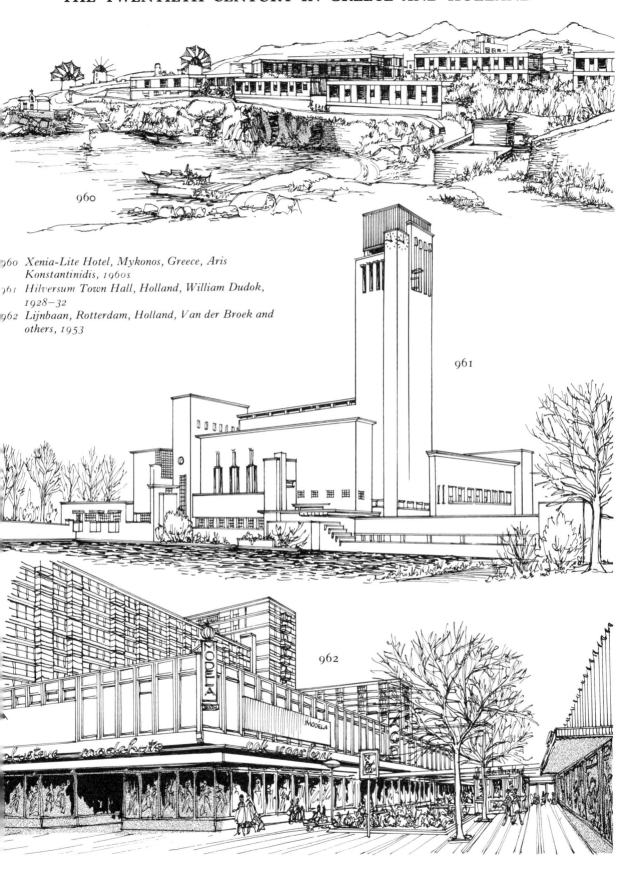

960 Xenia-Lite Hotel, Mykonos, Greece, Aris
Konstantinidis, 1960s
961 Hilversum Town Hall, Holland, William Dudok,
1928–32
962 Lijnbaan, Rotterdam, Holland, Van der Broek and
others, 1953

offices and civic structures quickly. This work, and that of later decades, is not of the original character that had been shown in the inter-war years in Holland. It is reasonably good but not outstanding.

One new factor was developed here in the early 1950s, the *pedestrian precinct*, of which the *Lijnbaan* is the prototype (**962**). Such precincts have now become commonplace in the cities of Western Europe, but in 1953 this was an unusual and progressive development. Much of the work of reconstruction here was under the leadership of *J. H. Van der Broek* and *J. B. Bakema*. Also of interest, in the centre of Rotterdam, is *S. Paul's Church,* the *Central Station*, the *Exchange* and the new *Bijenkorf Store*, which was one of the later works of *Walter Gropius* in 1955–7. It is very plain on the exterior except for a metal, sculptured decoration in contemporary style on the Coolsingel façade. This contains motifs appropriate to Rotterdam such as fisherman's netting, anchors and lines of rigging, all in iron and copper. Inside, all the floors are the same as one another, with wood framed ceilings containing light panels. Columns support this ceiling and the walls are plain. The restaurant, on the top floor, is simple and attractively coloured and decorated.

Belgium

The most important exponent of Art Nouveau in the field of architecture was *Victor Horta* (1861–1947) of Belgium. From 1892 he developed this theme, especially in *Brussels*. His first building was the *Tassel House* (1893) and he continued with the *Hôtel Solvay* (1895). His chief contribution was in the *Maison du Peuple* in the city (1896–9). This building occupies an unusually

formed site within an irregularly-shaped open square. The façades are curved and generally concave. Art Nouveau is used here both architecturally and in the decorative handling of the work in metal, stone and brick. Horta's most famous building was the *Innovation Department Store* (1901), destroyed only a few years ago by fire. The front was entirely of glass and iron, set in a granite frame.

Following the Art Nouveau theme, came the introduction of modern architecture, wherein an early exponent was *Henry van der Velde* (1863–1957), who was born in Antwerp. He was especially interested in Functionalism and the development of a pure form in architecture. He had spent many years studying in the field of painting as well as industrial design before returning to architecture about 1895. He spent much of his working lifetime in Germany helping in the foundation and development of the Weimar School of Applied Arts from 1906, a school which Gropius finally took over to create the Bauhaus. Van der Velde went to Switzerland in 1917 and returned to Belgium in 1925. His influence after this was chiefly in the academic field.

963 Église des Pères du S. Sacrament, Sleihage, Belgium

963

Post-war architecture in Belgium is not noteworthy. Among the more interesting examples is the *Church* of the *Pères du S. Sacrament* at *Sleihage*, built in the early 1960s. It is a 12-sided church and has triangular windows all round. The ceiling is entirely in dull black and the rest of the church interior is in black marble, stainless steel and glasswork. There is no colour. The exterior has steel roofing and a flèche (**963**).

England

Like Holland, England showed little inclination to dabble with *Art Nouveau* in architecture, though in interior decoration, fabric design, stained glass, painting and craftwork it was a temporary phase. The nearest approach to Art Nouveau in architecture was the work of such architects as *C. Harrison Townsend* as in his *Whitechapel Art Gallery* (1900) and *Bishopsgate Institute* (1893–4), both in London and that of *C. R. Mackintosh* (1869–1928), the Scottish architect, whose outstanding contribution was the *Glasgow School of Art* (1898–1907). This type of work, though only on the fringe of Art Nouveau, was an attempt to refute eclecticism.

Most architecture in England until after the Second World War was eclectic. Some fine traditional buildings, erected in brick and stone, and predominantly in a simplified form of classicism, were however created. Up till 1914 the best work was in neo-Baroque style, similar to the Paris Grand and Petit Palais. The extensive layout of the *Cardiff City Centre*, the *Central Hall, Westminster* and the *Town Hall* at *Deptford* are all by the firm of *Lanchester, Stewart and Richards*. They are good designs, with excellent detail and the city centre in Cardiff, in particular, has stood the test of time well.

In the years 1918–39, within the eclectic framework, fine buildings were produced by architects like *Sir Reginald Blomfield, Sir Ernest Newton* and *Sir Guy Dawber*.

The outstanding figure of the time was *Sir Edwin Lutyens* (1869–1944). His work was traditional, generally on a classical basis, streamlined and simplified and, as with the work of all great architects, definably personal. He worked in all fields: civic, housing, ecclesiastical. Like Sir Christopher Wren, he adapted the simplified classicism of his day to essentially English patterns. He showed this at first entirely in house building. These were the last of the great country houses, following on the tradition of Norman Shaw and C. F. A. Voysey. His best houses, mostly built before 1914, were *Heathcote, Ilkley*, 1906, of local stone, the *Deanery, Sonning*, 1899–1901, of brick, and *Tigbourne Court*, Hambledon, *Surrey*, 1899, also in brick. He built few town houses but, of contrasting styles in his housing estates, were the traditional brickwork of *Hampstead Garden Suburb*, begun 1908, and his low-cost council scheme in *Page Street, Westminster*, begun 1928. The Hampstead work was the central area of the suburb, comprising the two churches and the Institute Buildings. It is well designed and attractively blended into the surroundings. The Page Street scheme, on the other hand, is much more original. Lutyens used light grey bricks, Portland stone and white cement to produce a chequer board pattern in successive rectangular blocks on courtyard layout. The effect is austere, modern, entirely non-eclectic, apart from its white, painted sash windows. It is one of his most original works.

In the early 1920s Lutyens turned to large civic schemes and developed his classical theme. One of his best works is *Britannic House* in Finsbury Circus, London (1920–6). Typical of his simpler, more streamlined approach, in the next decade, is the *Reuter Building* in Fleet Street (**966**). He built a number of these large, plain, yet elegant classical structures, particularly as architect to the Midland Bank.

Outstanding examples of Lutyens' industry vary from the extensive scheme at *New Delhi* in *India* to the *Cenotaph* in *Whitehall*. One of his last works was the *Metropolitan Cathedral of Christ the King* in *Liverpool*; an immense classical/Byzantine structure of which only the crypt was built and survives under the modern cathedral podium (p. 532).

Another traditionalist was *Sir Giles Gilbert Scott* (1880–1960), grandson of the nineteenth century Sir George. In a large number of churches, work on abbey, cathedral and university chapel restoration and rebuilding, Scott evolved a simplified Gothic style rather as Lutyens had done in classical form.

His outstanding contributions were in widely different fields: the *Anglican Cathedral of Liver-*

pool and in *power station* design. Scott won the competition for Liverpool Cathedral in 1901 at the age of 21. It is a fine design, Gothic in modern dress, but much more alive and rich than the emasculated version at Guildford Cathedral. It is a red sandstone building with a high vault and impressive tower. The high cost and difficulty of finding sufficient funds and the skilled labour has delayed its completion; now the nave is the only major part unfinished. It is undoubtedly the last of the great cathedrals in Gothic style and, though perhaps an anachronism, is a worthy swan song.

In 1929, Scott set the pattern for *power station* design in Britain with his brick building at *Battersea*, fronting the river Thames in London. He continued with this type of work till late in life; at the age of 79 he was consulting architect for the nuclear power station at *Berkeley*. In 1937–42 he built the new *Waterloo Bridge* in London and was later consultant for the *Forth road bridge* near Edinburgh.

The work of *Sir John Burnet* was more modern. *Adelaide House* at London Bridge (1924) and the *Kodak Building* in Kingsway (1911) are early examples of steel framing with the structure visible in the façade design. In the period 1920–39 came the plain block architecture evidenced by *Senate House, London University* (1933–7). The best example of this type is the *Headquarters* of *Transport Executive* (**965**).

Genuine modern architecture was unusual in England before 1945. The few examples built were chiefly by foreigners who were political refugees and came to seek asylum in Britain. Although they would have liked to stay in the country, they mainly emigrated further, mostly to the U.S.A., because the architectural opportunities for modern architecture in England were so limited. They included *Walter Gropius* who came in 1934, designed buildings at *Impington Village College*, Cambridgeshire with *Maxwell Fry* and departed for the U.S.A. in 1937. *Erich Mendelsohn* came in 1933, built the *De la Warr Pavilion Bexhill-on-Sea* in 1936 with *Serge Chermayeff* (from the Caucasus), then departed for Palestine and later to the U.S.A. Others included *Peter Behrens* and *Berthold Lubetkin*. Lubetkin, also from the Caucasus, founded the firm of *Tecton* which built the well-known *Highpoint Flats* at *Highgate* in North London (1938). Other flats of a modern type include the *Isokon*

Flats at *Hampstead* (1933–4) by *Wells Coates* and *Kensal House* (1936) in *Ladbroke Grove*; a low-cost scheme by *Maxwell Fry* (b. 1899). Also ahead of its time in England was the *Peter Jones' Department Store* in London (1936–9) by *William Crabtree*. This is an early example of glass curtain walling reminiscent of Mendelsohn's earlier work in Germany (p. 516).

Modern architecture in the post-war years in England compares favourably with that of other countries in quality of building, planning and layout—general housing schemes, civic structures and schools, and especially in the New Towns. These are, in general, better built and more imaginatively planned and designed than the Swedish prototypes, for instance (p. 544). There is, however, a general monotony in the great quantity of building and an over emphasis on the rectangular block, due to the dependence on the steel construction method. As in Germany, most of the outstanding examples have come in the later years, since 1960.

Among the skyscraper blocks, the *Millbank Tower* on the Thames Embankment in *London* (1963), *Ronald Ward and Partners* and *Centrepoint*, also in London, at *S. Giles' Circus* (1962–6), *R. Seifert and Partners* are the most unusual and interesting. The Millbank Tower is of steel and glass, Centrepoint of reinforced concrete. This honeycomb patterned, 370-feet tower is a London landmark. The same architects have designed a lower, but not dissimilar structure for Grand Metropolitan Hotels in Knightsbridge.

The most original building in Britain is the new *Roman Catholic Cathedral* of *Liverpool*, built 1962–7 by *Sir Frederik Gibberd* (b. 1908) to replace Lutyens' abandoned design. It is constructed on circular plan—the centrally planned church of Renaissance ideals—but this is no eclectic building. It is like an immense marquee, with a glass lantern and metal crown above (**964**). The cathedral is built on the podium of the intended classical cathedral and has an outside sacrament chapel and altar where open air services can be held on the great podium space in front. Inside, the cathedral emanates, by the handling of its spatial features and both natural and artificial lighting, the spiritual quality to be felt in the great Medieval cathedrals. There is no white light. The natural lighting comes entirely from the lantern, whose glass ranges through all

THE TWENTIETH CENTURY IN ENGLAND

964 *The Metropolitan Cathedral of Christ the King, Liverpool, Sir Frederick Gibberd, 1962–7*
965 *Broadway House, London, Adams, Holden and Pearson, 1929*
966 *HQ. of the Press Association and Reuter Building, London, Sir Edwin Lutyens, 1935*

the spectrum colours, and the narrow strips of coloured glass in the nave walls. Chapels are inserted into these walls all round, squeezed in between the great sloping buttresses which offset the thrust of the 2000-ton lantern. This lighting is rich and glowing, even on a dull, wet Liverpool day. In sunshine, it becomes magical. The altar is set in the centre of the circular, grey patterned floor. Round it are concentric rings of pews and, above, is suspended the delicate metal baldacchino.

From the mass of dull building created to house the new universities, extensions and technical colleges of Britain, more interesting well-designed examples include the *Arts Faculty Buildings* in Sidgwick Avenue, *Cambridge* (1961), by *Sir Hugh Casson* (b. 1910) and *Neville Conder* and the new *University of York* by *Robert Matthew* (b. 1907). This lay-out was well planned and landscaped on a new site and has some pleasant, attractive buildings. More original is the work at *Durham University* where some of the new buildings front the A1 trunk road. These façades have been kept blind to cut out noise and dirt, and advantage is taken of the natural lighting on the opposite elevation.

The most publicised of the *new Universities*, that of *Sussex*, is built on a fine site of rolling country between the Downs and the sea, at Falmer, near Brighton. The chief architect, *Sir Basil Spence* (b. 1907), has used a brick and concrete format, combining the two media skilfully in an arcaded style. This can be seen in the first building here, *Falmer House* (1962–3), which has a central court on traditional English University pattern. The flattish arches are repeated, though the balance and proportions differ, on each of the three floors. The architect's *Meeting House* is also interesting, especially inside. There are two floors, the lower one for relaxation and reading and the upper is a circular chapel, illuminated through the coloured glass extending round the walls. As at Liverpool Cathedral, the colours run through the whole spectrum gamut. There is an oculus above in the sloping ceiling.

Sir Basil Spence has repeated his brick and concrete arched theme in the newly completed *Household Cavalry Regiment Buildings* in *Knightsbridge* in London. This façade is successful: a sophisticated improvement on the buildings at Sussex University, though the controversial tower is more mundane.

The Durham University buildings and these two Spence examples are sometimes designated as 'brutalist', but none of them obtrudes offensively and they possess a refinement which seems to be absent in more classic 'brutalist' buildings such as the *Park Hill Development, Sheffield* (1961), the *Tricorn Centre* at *Portsmouth* 1967 (*Owen Luder*) and the *Queen Elizabeth concert hall* on London's riverside. All of these are of raw, unrelieved concrete in massive thrusting blocks.

France

French architects did not take *Art Nouveau* seriously. Some of them experimented with ornamental ironwork and used the motifs for carving and interior decoration. *Hector Guimard* (1867–1942) was the most enthusiastic and his Métro entrances in Paris, designed at the turn of the century, are typical. Little remains of French work in the Art Nouveau style, only remnants and restorations, in some of the Paris restaurants, to give atmosphere. The Vagenende Restaurant in the Boulevard S. Germain in the Latin Quarter is one of the most successful of these.

Two of the earliest exponents of *modern architecture* were practising in France: *Auguste Perret* (1874–1954) and *Tony Garnier* (1867–1948). Perret's was the greater contribution in actual building and he is especially noted for his development of the technique of building in reinforced concrete. His early work was in Art Nouveau style as in, for example, his tall apartment block in *Paris, 119, Avenue Wagram*, built in 1902. He soon turned his attention to concrete and produced a much more original design in another block of flats in the city, *25 bis, Rue Franklin*. It is from this building that his reputation began to be established for original contribution to architectural construction.

While iron and steel were the chief structural developments of the nineteenth century, reinforced concrete belongs to the twentieth. This is concrete strengthened by the insertion of metal rods. The technique had first been tried in the mid-nineteenth century but was not developed until the *fin de siècle*. It was Perret who established the viability of the material for structural design. His first concrete apartment block was faced with faïence mosaic and the structure hidden. He then went on to the modern concept of

THE TWENTIETH CENTURY IN FRANCE

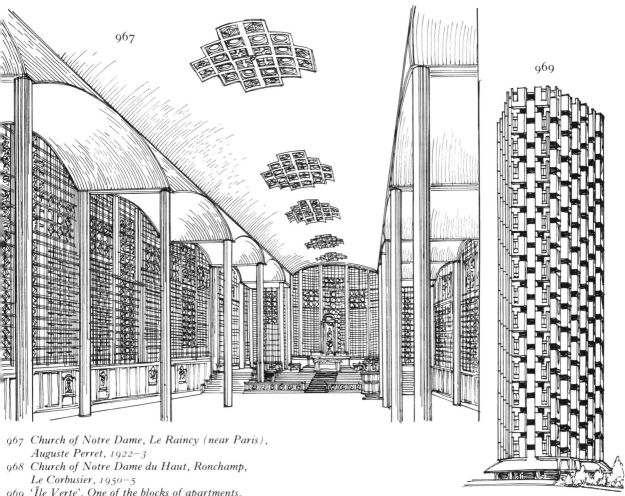

967

969

967 *Church of Notre Dame, Le Raincy (near Paris),*
Auguste Perret, 1922–3
968 *Church of Notre Dame du Haut, Ronchamp,*
Le Corbusier, 1950–5
969 *'Île Verte'. One of the blocks of apartments,*
Grenoble, Anger and Puccinelli, completed 1969

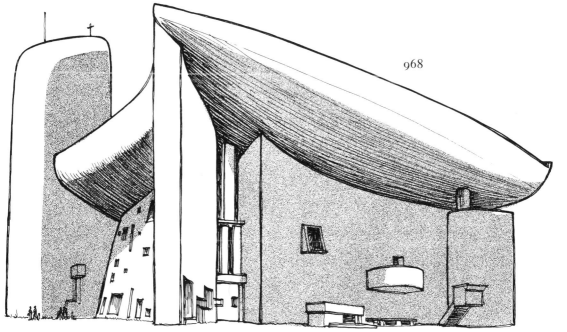

968

'honest structure' in further blocks of flats and other buildings.

Perret's most original concrete structure is the *Church of Notre Dame* at *Le Raincy* on the outskirts of Paris (**967**). The exterior is well designed, with a tall tower of diminishing stages, but it is the interior which is magnificent. It is a wide, light church, the shallow vaulted roof supported on slender columns. The whole structure is in concrete apart from the glass window panels which extend the full height of the walls all round the church. They provide a symphony of colour, culminating in deep blue behind the altar. Because of the slenderness of the columns and the richness of the glass, this church possesses a spiritual atmosphere and unimpeded sight and sound of and from the altar for everyone. It became the prototype for churches all over Europe for decades, from Moser in pre-war Switzerland to Spence's post-war Coventry Cathedral and recent churches in France such as the Church of S. Rémy at Baccarat.

Tony Garnier is known chiefly for his project for an industrial town designed in the early years of the century. He called it the *Cité Industrielle* and it represented his ideas for an ideal city in the age of technology. It was, like Sant' Elia's *Città Nuova*, years ahead of its time. Garnier illustrates glass curtain walling, building on *pilotis* and with flat roofs. The shapes are simple blocks and the material chiefly concrete. Garnier envisages pedestrian precincts, community centres, and schools. Traffic and industry are separated from leisure and living areas. He was city architect in Lyons for many years and tried to use some of his themes during his working life in practical structures. He was full of new ideas and had a fertile imagination.

Since 1920 French architecture has been dominated by the world famous Swiss architect Charles Edouard Jeanneret (1888–1965), usually known as *Le Corbusier*. He was one of the four great world leaders in modern architecture in the first half of the twentieth century. The others were the American Frank Lloyd Wright and the Germans Walter Gropius and Mies Van der Rohe.

Le Corbusier became established as an architect with advanced, original ideas immediately after the First World War. He specialised in house design and in low-cost housing and planning on flats and estates. He envisaged the housing unit as a 'machine for living in'. Extraneous and unnecessary features were stripped off, leaving a very simple structure with flat roofs and plain walls. He evolved the *piloti* system. These, at first, were free-standing, concrete columns upon which the house or apartment-block stood. This box-like building on stilts theme has been with us ever since. He was absorbed in the social problems of housing people in cities and developed his ideas in his book *'Urbanisme'*, published in 1925.

In the 1930s the economic depression hit France badly and building was severely curtailed. In these years Le Corbusier worked out many projects but most of his actual building was outside France. He worked in South America, North Africa, India on such designs as the Ministry of Education Building in Rio de Janeiro (1936–45) and the Centrosoyus in Moscow (1930, p. 552).

Immediately after the Second World War Le Corbusier won even greater international fame for the development of his *Unité d'Habitation* theme. The first of these was built in the Boulevard Michelet on the outskirts of *Marseilles* in 1947–52 (**970**). It was his answer to the problem of successfully accommodating large numbers of people in a small space at a low cost. The scheme comprises one immense rectangular block, carried on a double row of massive, central supports rather than slender *pilotis*. It contains 350 flats in eight double storeys, with a storey for shops half way up and communal facilities on the roof. This is certainly a 'machine for living in'. Claimed as an architectural masterpiece, it nevertheless strikes a chill to the heart to imagine living in such a 'machine'. Whether the building is aesthetically satisfactory is very much a matter for personal taste. Though posterity will no doubt accord both to Le Corbusier and the *Unité* an important place in the history of modern architecture, it may well re-write the excessive eulogies with which the first *Unité* was greeted by the architectural world. A second was built in Nantes 1952–7, a third in West Berlin (1957) and the fourth at Briey-la-Forêt (1960).

In 1950 Le Corbusier turned to ecclesiastical architecture. First he built his world famous, highly personal and original *pilgrimage Church of Notre Dame du Haut* at *Ronchamp* (**968**).

Finding much more universal favour than the *Unités*, the church is massive, rough-cast, essentially plastic. An interesting silhouette is seen from all angles and each form and mass is balanced exactly to give a satisfying design. The interior is also unusual. The surfaces are all of rough-cast concrete. The lighting is carefully arranged to shine through the tiny windows set in the thick walling. These are of irregular shapes and sizes and are filled with coloured glass. The whole interior is curved or sloped at differently designed angles, all dominated by the massiveness of the curved, tent-like roof. The studied sophistication of the work soon becomes apparent after the first fleeting impression of rural simplicity.

Le Corbusier's second ecclesiastical commission is quite different and has more in common with the stark, raw concrete of his *Unités*. This is the *Dominican Convent* of *La Tourette* at *Eveux-sur-l'Arbresle*, near Lyons, begun 1956. The entire layout of conventual buildings and church are of plain concrete inside and out. The exterior is particularly 'brutalist'; stark and uncompromising. The interior of the church is a large rectangle, tall and rather narrow, the choir at a higher level than the nave. The crypt is painted in rich, strong colours and is lit by oculi in the ceiling. The colours from this chamber, which can be seen from the plain grey main church, contrast vividly with it. The whole church has atmosphere, much of which is due to the carefully planned indirect natural lighting. The artificial lighting is equally necessary and carefully thought out. Much of it comes from the floor, angled in many directions to illuminate varied vistas and planes. Nearly all the surfaces

of walls, window openings and floor are subtly sloped, the angles being meticulously worked out to give the optimum visual effect.

The work of men like Perret and Le Corbusier was, however, untypical of architecture in France until after 1950. The resistance mounted by the establishment in architecture was formidable. Led by academic centres such as the École des Beaux Arts in Paris, the commissions were successfully kept out of the hands of younger architects trying to establish modern architecture. Building in France in the first half of the twentieth century was more traditional than anywhere except England and the quality of this traditional work was inferior, especially compared to work by such architects as Lutyens. Typical of the 1930s is the vapid emptiness of such structures as the *Palais de Chaillot* and the *Museum of Modern Art*, both built in 1937 in *Paris*.

After the Second World War the State provided financial support for housing schemes and modern architecture became the accepted style. Little advantage was gained from this. A number of planned estates were built on the periphery of cities and a few new centres established. Architecturally the designs are often original and interesting, but the quality of workmanship, building and landscaping and the shoddiness of the materials employed is poorer in France than

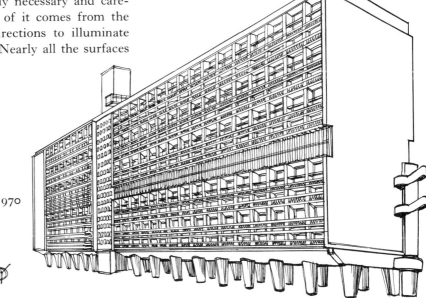

970

970 L'Unité d'Habitation, Marseilles, Le Corbusier, 1946–52

in any country in Europe, including some like Greece, Yugoslavia and Rumania, which are genuinely poor countries.

Typical of these housing estates is the *Cité des Courtillières* at *Pantin*, a suburb of *Paris*. Built not many years ago, it is fast becoming a slum. The design is ingenious and unusual, with six storey long blocks winding sinuously around the site, interspersed with traditional tall blocks. The appallingly low standard of workmanship and materials more than cancels out, from the point of view of living conditions, any architectural merit which the scheme may have had. Carefully taken photographs, with calculated lighting effects, of the models and the buildings when brand new give a false impression of the arid reality.

Another such instance is the new town of *Marly-le-Roi*, just west of Paris. It is small with an unimaginitive centre, monotonously laid out with low-level, poorly constructed shops round an apology for a piece of sculpture. As a new design for living, it compares unfavourably with most European examples, especially such English ones as Crawley or Stevenage New Towns. Also the subject of praise from architectural critics, but a no less unimpressive new town is that at *Bagnols-sur-Cèze*, twinned with the pleasant old Provençal small town. A privileged layout, built for the workers from Marcoule nuclear power station and awarded the 1960 *Prix d'Urbanisme*, the story is one of similar mediocrity and lack of quality. The best new housing development in France seen by the author is the new town built to house the workers from the site of the natural gas discovery at *Lacq* in the *Pyrenees*. This is a much better scheme, using high quality materials and workmanship, especially in the church, the town hall and individual houses on the upper slopes.

Apart from Le Corbusier's work and the layout by the aged *Auguste Perret* in the rebuilding of *Le Havre* (the Place de l'Hôtel de Ville and S. Joseph's Church), the most interesting examples of modern architecture in France are in some new churches and the UNESCO building in Paris. Interesting new churches include that of S. *Agnes* in *Fontaine-les-Grès* by *Michel Marot*, the *Church* of *Sacré Coeur* at *Audincourt* by *Maurice Novarina* and, by far the most interesting, the *Church of Notre Dame en son Immaculée*

Conception at *Royan*. Designed by *Guillaume Gillet*, built in 1954–9 entirely in reinforced concrete, this is the modern successor to Perret's work at Le Raincy and has much in common with the present-day Finnish churches, like that at Tampere (p. 550). It is a dramatic successful design outside and in the interior. It is large and on oval plan. It possesses two features from Medieval, southern French/Spanish origins; on the exterior the base splays outwards like the castle at Coca in Spain and, inside, the two levels of galleries are set into the thickness of the piers and buttresses like the chapels in Albi Cathedral in southern France (p. 208). The interior décor is most effective. All is in grey concrete except for the focal point of rich light shining through the coloured glass behind the altar.

The *UNESCO Headquarters Building* in *Paris* (1953–8) is notable. Designed and built by an international group of architects, *Marcel Breuer*, born in Hungary but a citizen of the U.S.A., *Bernard Zehrfuss* a Frenchman and *Pier Luigi Nervi*, Italian, it is a Y-shaped building, eight storeys high. It is an interesting conception, containing some fine halls and rooms, finely built and finished with quality materials.

The Iberian Peninsula
Spain

Art Nouveau in Spain is embodied in the work of *Antonio Gaudí*, but in a manner which is personal to the architect and which went much further towards individual and original design than the Art Nouveau movement ever achieved. Gaudí's work of the late nineteenth century, including his masterpiece, the Sagrada Familia, has been described in Chapter 8 (p. 496). In the twentieth century his style developed, becoming more plastic and flowing, as is evidenced in his later portal on the Sagrada Familia (**933**) His two chief buildings showing these characteristics are the apartment blocks in *Barcelona*, the *Casa Battló*, at 43 Paseo de Gracia, and the *Casa Milá* at number 92 (**972**). Both were built 1905–7. The former is a tall and narrow block of six storeys; the latter much larger. It occupies a corner site and contains two courts. The façades are undulating like waves. There are no horizontal or vertical lines or planes; all is movement. The chief motif is the sea, not only in waves but

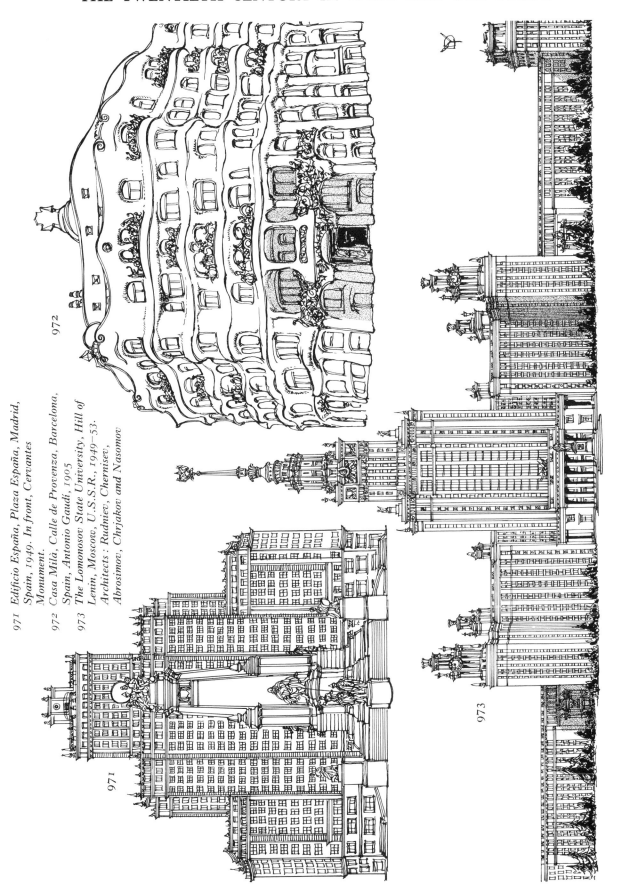

971 Edificio España, Plaza España, Madrid,
    Spain, 1949. In front, Cervantes
    Monument.
972 Casa Milà, Calle de Provenza, Barcelona,
    Spain, Antonio Gaudí, 1905
973 The Lomonosov State University, Hill of
    Lenin, Moscow, U.S.S.R., 1949–53.
    Architects: Rudniev, Chernisev,
    Abrosimov, Chrjakov and Nasomov

971

972

973

in fronds of plant life, seaweed and rocks. This maritime element is seen mainly in the iron balconies on each floor. The building is not to everyone's taste but it is one of the few genuinely original and different works of the time and completely non-eclectic.

Although Gaudì was famed and respected in his own time, he had no real followers. His was an individual contribution, not the basis of a large movement, as was, for example, the Bauhaus. Most of the other architectural work in Spain before the Second World War was traditional. Typical is the vast Baroque pile of the *General Post Office* in *Madrid* (1913, *Palacios*), the classical monument to *King Alfonso* in the *Retiro Park* in the city (1922) (PLATE 103) and the neo-Gothic *Cathedral* at *Vitoria*, begun 1906 and continued after a long period of inactivity, after 1946. This is a large cathedral, well-designed and built on traditional cruciform lines with apsidal choir ending. It is, despite the high quality workmanship, an unenterprising, uninteresting building.

Since 1950 most of Spanish architecture has been in the modern idiom, though the totalitarian régime controlling the country has still shown a tendency towards traditional building. One example of this is the *National Monument* of *Santa Cruz* of the *Valley of the Fallen*, built near the Escorial in the Guadarrama Mountains. Initiated by General Franco, it was consecrated in 1960. Covering three and a third acres and situated at nearly 6000 feet above sea level, the monument comprises a great sculptured cross above a curving, arcaded entrance which leads into a basilica hewn out of the mountain side. The whole scheme is on the gigantic scale and in the simplified classical style, both so beloved of dictators, whether fascist or communist. The interior of the basilica is a rectangular chamber, barrel vaulted and with an immense cupola at the far end, decorated all over by mosaic pictures in the Byzantine tradition of style and subject. The work is treated in a fairly modern manner, but is based entirely on traditional precepts. The quality of the materials is good and the craftsmanship technically adequate.

In the genuinely modern style Spanish work is of fair quality only, and there are few outstanding examples. Typical are the tall blocks in the *Plaza España* in *Madrid* (**971**), modern hotels such as the *Grand Hotel Zurbaran* in *Badajoz*, banks such as the *Banca Catalana* (1965–8) in *Barcelona*, blocks of flats like that in the *Calle Muntaner* in *Barcelona* (1965–7) and new university building such as that at *San Sebastian*, begun 1964 by *Miguel de Oriol*. Prolific development schemes abound along the miles of coastline of the Mediterranean from Barcelona in the north-east to Cádiz in the south-west. *Gandía*, near Valencia, and *Benidorm*, nearer Alicante, are typical. These architectural mushroom growths are appearing all round the warm sandy beaches of Europe, especially those undeveloped before 1945. Such work is monotonously similar from Spain to Bulgaria.

Modern buildings in Spain which have received some particular architectural acclaim include the apartment blocks called the *Torres Blancas* on the Avenida de América at the entrance to *Madrid*, built 1965–8 by *Saénz-Oiza*, and one or two churches. The Torres Blancas have balconies made in flat, cylindrical shapes which, when piled one above the other, give a superficial resemblance to the famous Chicago cylindrical towers. The Spanish examples are, unfortunately, much more impressive on the photographic page than in reality, as they are poorly proportioned, dull and dark.

There are two churches of some interest in *Vitoria*. The finer of these is the *Church of the Coronation of Our Lady* by *Miguel Fisac*. The interior is very plain, of natural wood and stone. The surfaces are curved in Baroque fashion to give movement, but the effect is different due to the excessive simplicity of the décor. The lighting from the slit windows on one side is effective. The *Church of Our Lady of the Angels* by *Ferrer* and others has an unusual form. The exterior is a pyramid covered with blue-grey tiling with a separate, concrete campanile which is an integral part of the neighbouring apartment block. One wonders how the occupants of the latter appreciate the ringing of the bells. The interior of the church is vast and barn-like; it is much less interesting.

Portugal

As in Spain, the totalitarian régime shows its preference and power in such buildings as the immense, austere *Pantheon* in *Lisbon*, inaugurated by Dr. Salazar as a temple to honour great Portuguese citizens for example, Vasco da Gama. This is a perfect, centrally planned church on classical principles with drum and dome rising on pendentives supported on Composite Order piers. It is correct but cold and uninspired. In post-war modern architecture are examples such as can be seen in any city of Europe, for example, the housing development on the *Avenida Infante Santo* in *Lisbon* by *Pessoa*. More original and of general interest is the *Discovery Monument* at *Belém*, overlooking the Tagus, on the fringe of the city of Lisbon. Completed in 1960, it commemorates the great Portuguese explorers of the fifteenth and sixteenth centuries. The architect was *Cottinelli Telmo* and the sculptor, *Leopoldo de Almeida* (PLATE 105).

Northern Europe: Scandinavia
Denmark

The development of the Danish and Swedish architectural styles in the twentieth century proceeded on similar lines in both countries. Before the First World War, Danish architects tended to turn away from eclecticism towards Nyrop's (Chapter 8, p. 505) style of romantic nationalism, or to a mixture of this and Art Nouveau. One of *Nyrop*'s later works is his chunky, personal version of Romanesque decorated with Art Nouveau, the *Elijah Church* in *Copenhagen* (1906–8). Another architect whose work is individually personal and national is *P. V. Jensen Klint* (1853–1930). Sometimes he benefited from Gothic inspiration, sometimes Art Nouveau. His style is plastic and monumental. His best known work is the *Grundtvig Church* in *Copenhagen*, built as a memorial to N. F. S. Grundtvig, the hymn writer, educationalist and priest. The church is entirely of brick (between five and six million of them), including the altar, pulpits and decoration. The tall façade (**976**) is unusual in design, but the rest of the exterior and the interior are in a beautiful, unadorned version of Gothic. The interior, in particular, has a magnificent simplicity in its tall piers rising in unbroken line to the lofty vault. It is a moving interior of great dramatic intensity; one of the last monuments to the Gothic style comparable, though in different mood, to Scott's Liverpool Cathedral (p. 531).

From about 1915–6 the Danes, like the other Scandinavian countries, returned to *neo-classicism*. Leading architects in the years up to 1930 included *Carl Petersen* (1874–1923) and *Hack Kampmann* (1856–1920). Petersen designed the *Faaborg Museum* in simple classical style. Kampmann is best known for his *Police Headquarters Building* in *Copenhagen* (1918–24). A stark, grey structure on the exterior, built on a triangular site, it contains two beautiful courts, especially the circular one. This is handled in a plain but correct classicism, with coupled Doric columns on the ground arcade and plain classical windows on two storeys above. It is reminiscent of the courtyard of Charles V's Renaissance palace at the Alhambra (**732**).

In the 1930s Denmark, like Sweden, turned towards Bauhaus designs and *functionalism*. Architects explored the possibilities of reinforced concrete and adapted their national material—brick—to similar designs. Typical examples built in this decade were *Broadcasting House* in *Copenhagen* (1937–45, by *Vilhelm Lauritzen*), the *Copenhagen Stadium* (1934, by *Hansen* and *Jørgensen*) and housing estates and blocks of flats like those on *Tuborvej*, a suburb of Copenhagen (1940–2, by *Baumann* and *Hansen*).

A good quality example of brickwork in this plain style is *Aarhus University*. A competition was held for this in 1931 and *Kay Fisker, C. F. Møller* and *Poul Stegmann* were appointed to design a number of buildings. The university, which is still being added to, is pleasantly situated on a rolling site about two kilometres from the centre of the city and is laid out with a lake, trees and flowers. Although building has continued intermittently between 1932 and 1958, designs are remarkably homogeneous. Only the very latest buildings are noticeably different; the remainder are all in yellow brick, very plain block designs with tiled roofs and rectangular simple fenestration. Much of the original work of the 1930s has had to be rebuilt. The R.A.F. bombed the buildings because they were occupied by the Gestapo.

The best known Danish architect of the period 1935–1970 is *Arne Jacobsen* (1902–71). He was strongly influenced by the work of Le Corbusier and Mies Van der Rohe. He early adopted functionalism and produced a series of buildings during these years. His designs became even

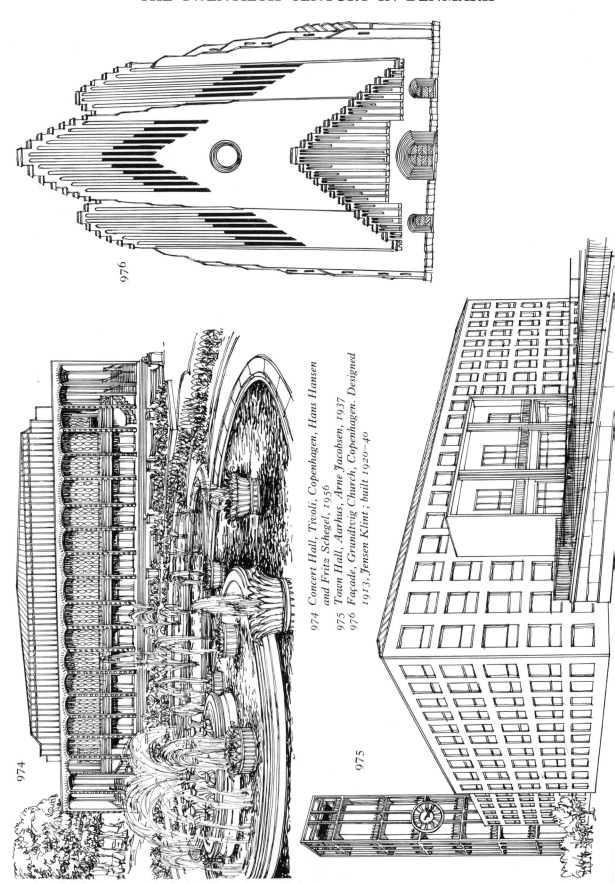

974 Concert Hall, Tivoli, Copenhagen, Hans Hansen
and Fritz Schegel, 1956
975 Town Hall, Aarhus, Arne Jacobsen, 1937
976 Façade, Grundtvig Church, Copenhagen. Designed
1913, Jensen Klint; built 1920-40

plainer as time passed, as is evidenced by the starkly plain, repeated glass walling of the façade of his *Rødovre* (new suburb of Copenhagen) *Town Hall*, built in 1956. Jacobsen's work, like that of all Danish architects of quality, was very national. Within the confines of plain, modern architecture, his buildings are notable for their excellence of materials, of finish and superb quality of proportion. He worked in concrete— plain or marble faced—brick and glass and steel curtain walling. His designs are recognisable for their individuality, their sparing use of decoration and careful calculation of scale. His best known pre-war building is *Aarhus Town Hall* (**975**). It is interesting to compare this with the one at *Søllerød* (1942) and the final example at *Rødovre*. He also designed the 21-storey steel and glass skyscraper in *Copenhagen* for *Scandinavian airlines*, combining their needs with the *Royal Hotel* (1960), as well as an even plainer glass office block in *Nyropsgade* (1955).

Other modern work of interest, all in or near *Copenhagen*, is the *Restaurant* and *Club Pavilion* along the waters' edge at *Langelinie* (1958, *Eva* and *Nils Koppel*), the *concert hall* in the *Tivoli*, a replacement for one lost during the war (**974**), the interior of the *Church* of *S. Knud Lavard* in the suburb of *Lyngby* (1956–7, by *Carl Frederiksen*) and the *town centre* of the new scheme at *Rødovre*, which has a particularly attractive under-cover shopping precinct laid out with cafés round fountains, trees and seats (PLATE 106).

Sweden

The early years of the twentieth century were a time of romantic nationalism here, as in Finland. Sweden became known for her simple, brick, clean-lined structures, built mainly between 1910 and 1930. At the same time, in the first decade of the century, Swedish architects were still building (like their colleagues elsewhere in Europe) in styles more closely derived from the past. *Ferdinand Boberg* (1860–1946) evolved a Swedish form of·Art Nouveau, an example of which can be seen in his *General Post Office* in *Stockholm* (1903). Its newly cleaned pale pink façade gleams in the evening sunshine, clearly delineating the Art Nouveau decoration on the principal entrance and the wall panelled ornament. The *Royal Dramatic Theatre* in *Stockholm*

(1907) by *Frederik Lilleqvist* (1863–1932) is a rich, ornate example of a simplified classicism. In its articulation and column supports the exterior shows the influence of Wagner's work in Vienna (p. 521).

In the years 1910–30 Swedish architects tried to break away from eclecticism into a more modern approach. They developed a romantic nationalist style which, while still eclectic, was couched in such simple, elegant terms that it was not so obviously derivative. As in Denmark and Finland, there was an emphasis on a return to national materials, clearly displayed. In Sweden, this was generally brick, designed on clean lines with carefully rationed use of ornament. In the 1930s and 1940s such architecture was classified as modern. It is now seen to be fully traditional and has much in common with the works of traditional architects in other countries, Sir Edwin Lutyens in England, for instance. In both cases, the designs are essentially national.

The best known work in this style is the *Stockholm City Hall*, begun in 1911 and opened in 1923 (**979**). It was built to the designs of *Ragnar Östberg* (1866–1945) and is a brick structure with a tall, elegant tower. The buildings are grouped round two courtyards. The interiors are interesting, especially the Golden Hall, 144 feet long and decorated with mosaic. The City Hall is Stockholm's most famous landmark. It has a magnificent setting; the waters of Lake Mälaren enclose it on two sides. Less imaginative and elegant but similarly in simplified eclectic vein is the work of *Carl Westmann* (1866– 1936), which can be seen in his *Law Courts* in *Stockholm* (1912–5). This also shows Medieval origins; its interiors are vaulted and darkly mysterious.

In the 1920s a number of architects returned to neo-classicism in a modern simplified form. *Ivar Tengbom* (*b.* 1878) was a leader in this respect[*] and his *Concert Hall* in *Stockholm* (1926) is a prototype. This has a lofty, simple portico of Corinthian columns which have multi-sided shafts. In front is the Orpheus Fountain by Carl Milles (1936) (PLATE 107).

Two ecclesiastical buildings which belong to the period of romantic nationalism but which, though partly eclectic, are essentially original works are the *Engelbrekt Church* in *Stockholm* and the *Masthugg Church* in *Göteborg*. Both have

[*] *Tengbom earlier had designed in romantic nationalist mood as in his brick Högalid Church in Stockholm; a landmark with its tall Baroque towers.*

some affinity with the Grundtvig Church in Copenhagen (p. 541) (**976**). The Engelbrekt Church (**978**) is very tall and powerful. In its setting on the top of a rocky hill, it reminds one of Lars Sonck's Finnish churches (p. 549), though the exterior is less plastic. The Stockholm church by *Lars Israel Wahlman* (1870–1952) is of brick. Built in 1910–4, it has one tall, simple tower. The interior is reminiscent of Sonck, with the great parabolic arches spanning each arm of the cross. The decoration is restrained, chunky and imaginative. The altar wall is painted and gilded, the originally designed wooden pulpit set in stone. Granite is used for the arches and pillars, wood for the barrel vaulting. There is considerable contrast between the massive, arched interior and the soigné verticality of the outside.

The *Masthugg Church* in *Göteborg* (Gothenburg) (**980**) was designed by *Sigfrid Eriksson* (*b.* 1874) and built in 1914. It is unusual, massive and severe, its monumental tower rising on the skyline of the hills bordering the river. The exterior is of red brick on a base of granite blocks on an L-shaped plan. Inside, the brick is whitewashed. Piers support semi-circular, plain arches and the roof is of open timber construction in whole logs, not rafters. It is an interesting church, original and monumentally simple.

From 1930 onwards some Swedish architects were beginning to design in functionalist style, to try out such newer materials as glass and concrete, and to model their works on those of Le Corbusier and Gropius. A leading architect of the period 1920–40 was *Erik Gunnar Asplund* (1885–1940). He had studied extensively in Italy and Greece and his earlier work was a severe interpretation of neo-classicism. His best known design in this form is the *Stockholm City Library* (1924–8) (**977**). The lending library in the rotunda has a fine interior. He then advanced to glass and steel construction and developed a modern style. His extension to the Göteborg Town Hall dates from 1937.

Also in Göteborg (Gothenburg) is the civic layout in the *Götaplatsen* where architectural development over the years 1923–36 can be seen in one scheme. A number of architects were employed here where, in the centre, is the *Art Museum* (1923), flanked by the neo-classical *City Theatre* (east), built by *Carl Bergsten* in 1934

and (west), the *City Concert Hall* (1935–6) by *Einar Eriksson*. The sculpture of the central fountain and the theatre caryatids is typical of the date.

Osvald Almqvist (1884–1950) was one of Sweden's early functionalist architects, as was also *Sven Markelius* (*b.* 1889), whose best known work is the *Concert Hall* at *Hälsingborg* (1932).

Post-war architecture in Sweden received considerable acclaim in the 1960s. Swedish architects were praised for their high standards in building, planning and research, their use of prefabricated unit construction and, especially, for their new towns such as those on the periphery of Stockholm at Vällingby and Farsta. But, as with the romantic nationalism of the 1920s, it was realised later that this work was less originally planned and conceived than had been thought. It appeared so outstanding because Sweden, a neutral country in the 1939–45 war, had been able to develop her building of this type much earlier than the countries which had suffered the devastation of their cities.

In fact, Swedish post-war architecture has produced some remarkably banal results from such high powered planning and automation. The advanced methods of construction seem to have created only dull, circumscribed buildings, markedly so in contrast to the lively, original and beautifully finished work of the Finns. *Vällingby New Town*, for instance, today gives an impression of a small, unnotable town centre, with functional and well-constructed buildings, but drab in both style and hue. The whole town displays a marked lack of imagination, in appearance and in design. Everything is in grey and dun. Concrete and dull brown brick prevail. The churches are as un-ecclesiastical as garages and as unwelcoming. They look as though they were produced as cheaply and quickly as possible. *Farsta New Town* is similar but poorer, both architecturally and in quality of building and workmanship. Though later, already it is shabbier than Vällingby. In both towns the main housing near the centre is in stark, high-rise concrete blocks built, like so many others in different countries, before the planners of Europe 'discovered' that most people prefer, and need, to live in low rise blocks, or even small houses.

TWENTIETH CENTURY ARCHITECTURE IN SWEDEN

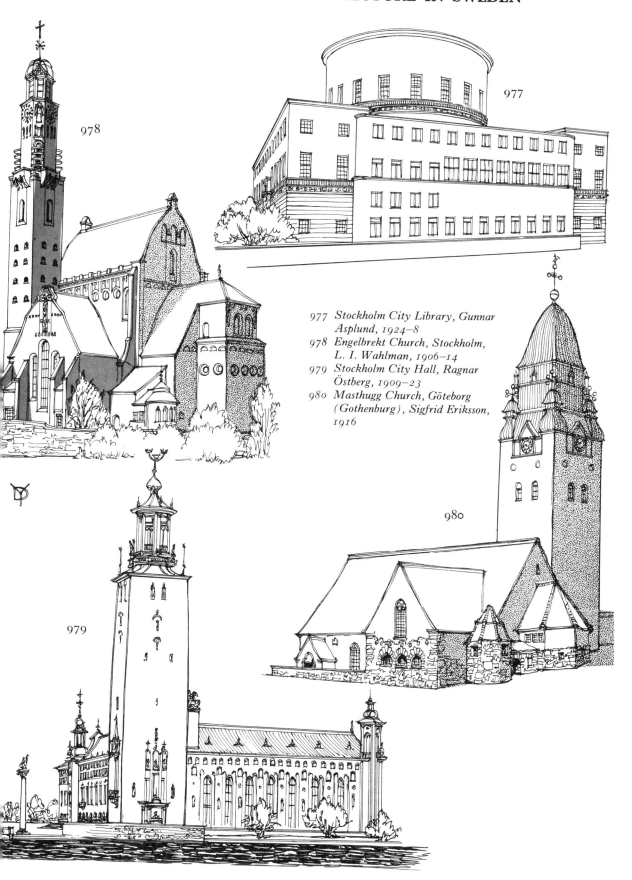

977 *Stockholm City Library, Gunnar Asplund, 1924–8*
978 *Engelbrekt Church, Stockholm, L. I. Wahlman, 1906–14*
979 *Stockholm City Hall, Ragnar Östberg, 1909–23*
980 *Masthugg Church, Göteborg (Gothenburg), Sigfrid Eriksson, 1916*

THE TWENTIETH CENTURY IN NORWAY AND THE U.S.S.R.

981 *Rjukan Power Station, Norway, Olaf Nordhagen,*
    c. 1920
982 *Eystein Church, Norway, c. 1970*
983 *Kazan Railway Station, Moscow, U.S.S.R., A. V.*
    Shchoussev, 1914–40

982

981

КАЗАНСКИ ВОКЗА

983

Norway

During the first 30 years of the twentieth century traditional forms of architecture held the field. There were two bases: first, the tradition, mainly on wood, of Norwegian building through the centuries; second, that based on an international revival of Gothic or classical form. In the first of these, the *'dragon style'* continued from the *fin de siècle* movement (Chapter 8, p. 508) (**945**). Private houses, large and small, were built in this manner, especially in the mountains.

In an international traditional manner *Bredo Greve* designed the *Technical University* at *Trondheim* in 1910. A Gothic Revival building, this is very northern European in its dour, monumental façade, solidly built in rough-hewn granite blocks. Chief architect of this school of work was *Olaf Nordhagen* who carried out the extensive restoration and reconstruction work necessary at this time on *Trondheim Cathedral*, the great Gothic monument of Norway (p. 267). Nordhagen built the *Library* at *Bergen*, which is also of rough-hewn blocks, in a simplified Romanesque style. His most interesting achievement is in the immense hydro-electric *power station* at *Rjukan*, deep in the mountains of central/southern Norway. This is in a modern Baroque, a monumental design in large stone blocks, set into the hillside (**981**). It has columns with modern capitals and sparing classical decoration. The village *church* of 1914–5, is in similar vein of Norwegian style blending suitably into the wild landscape.

A simplified form of classicism, akin to the contemporary English kind, was used for public buildings. *Haugesund Town Hall* (1931, *Munthe-Kaas*) is one example, *Magnus Poulsson's Shipping Offices* in the railway station square in *Oslo* (1917) is another.

In the late 1920s and early 1930s the ideas of the Bauhaus and functionalism percolated through to the north. An early skyscraper building of this

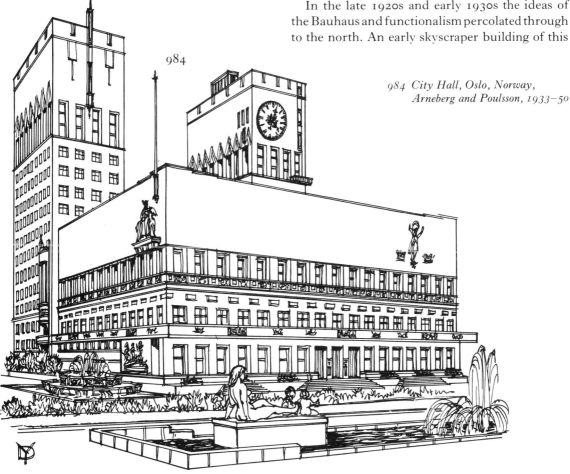

984

984 City Hall, Oslo, Norway, Arneberg and Poulsson, 1933–50

type in *Oslo* is the *Horn Building* in Egertorvet (1929). Other structures weré built by *Lars Backer, Gudolf Blackstad* and *Munthe-Kaas*. The outstanding example, which illustrates the Norwegian national approach, is the famous *City Hall* of Oslo (**984**). This immense building in red brick stands near the waterfront, where the whole area is laid out with lower buildings, fountains and gardens (PLATE 104). It was begun in 1933, but the interior was not completed till 1950. The walls of the large hall and galleries are covered with paintings and tapestries. These depict Norwegian life and art. They are of varying standard, some naïve and garish, others most successful. The latter are refreshingly charming and show nothing of the decadence to be seen in more recent mural work in the civic buildings of capitals further south, for example the UNESCO Building in Paris.

Post-war Norwegian architecture is entirely modern, and takes several of the accepted forms. A good and well-designed example of the very simple approach is the large government building complex in *Oslo* in Henrik Ibsen's Gate, by *Erling Viksjø*, from 1958. There is a tall 14-storey block, with decoration incised on the plain end wall, adjoining low curved blocks which include the new post office. The treatment is of good quality, light-coloured pebble rough concrete. The first new buildings for the *University of Oslo*, at *Blindern* outside the city had been built in the late 1930s, in red brick, by *Bryn* and *Ellefsen*. These are in plain, functionalist style. The whole complex has been greatly enlarged since the war in the usual pattern of tall and low rectangular blocks in glass, steel and brick. The layout is successful, the quality of building good: very similar to new universities in other northern countries.

In more nationally traditional style is a late work by *Magnus Poulsson*; the modern *church* at *Gravberget*, in the woods near the Swedish border (1955). Here is Norwegian church-building in timber at its best, using traditional methods but on modern lines. Another, more recent, church is the one at *Eystein* on the E.6 Arctic Highway near Hjerkinn. This is of white rubble covered concrete with purplish grey roofing and a wooden sculptured figure under the rose window (**982**). It is a charming, well-built church, entirely suited to its lonely sur-roundings on the high mountain plateau.

Norway has built several satellite towns since the war; *Lambertseter* near Oslo, for example, and new towns to replace those destroyed by the Germans in the invasion of 1940 at places like *Kristiansund* and *Molde* in the lonely island area west of Trondheim. While the designs are good, but not outstanding, the workmanship, quality of materials and landscaping is excellent.

Finland

Russia finally conquered Finland and removed the country from the sphere of Swedish influence in 1809, at the same time granting autonomy to the Finns. In architecture a renascent nationalism was reflected in a return to building in local materials and traditional structural methods. Three architects, in particular, showed great talent and originality in this work: *Sonck, Saarinen* and *Lindgren*. Their buildings are strongly plastic, with dramatic massing. The material, whether stone or timber, is ruggedly handled and left in great blocks or beams. There are picturesque towers and roofs based on Finnish Medieval churches and castles. *Lars Sonck* (1870–1956) is the most personal of the group. His buildings are always clearly stamped with his characteristic style and handling. His *Cathedral* at *Tampere* is his best work, built 1902–7 in rough hewn granite blocks. It is a large building, finely built and proportioned, sited on a hill. The grey of the granite contrasts pleasingly with the red tiled roofs and spires (**985** and PLATE 102). The interior is quite different. It is a Gothic structure, but decorated in a mixture of Byzantine and Art Nouveau motifs. The quality of workmanship, the lighting, colour and spatial handling, are magnificent.

Sonck's other great church is the *Kallio Church* in *Helsinki* (1909–12). It also is very large, crowning a steep hill, and it has an immensely tall central tower and eastern apse which dominate the Helsinki skyline. This church too is built of rugged, grey blocks. The exterior is dramatic and sombre; the interior, in contrast, is wide and brightly lit. Its interior is plainer than that of Tampere Cathedral, but it has a characteristic gallery and capitals. It shows Sonck moving away from national romanticism towards a more modern approach. Highly personalised is his

Plate 104 Detail, Discovery Monument, Belém, Portugal, 1960. Sculptor De Almeida

Plate 105 Detail, Oslo City Hall, Norway. 1933–50. Arneberg and Poulsson

Plate 106
Detail of fountain in shopping precinct, Rødovre, near Copenhagen, Denmark. Post 1956

Plate 107

Telephone Exchange in *Helsinki* (1905), a building constructed of vast, rugged granite blocks and with his individual style of decoration in window shafts, especially in the oriel window in the tower.

Eliel Saarinen (1873–1950) joined Lindgren in partnership. Until his emigration to the U.S.A. in the early 1920s, Saarinen was the most outstanding architect in Finland in this period of fine building. His most famous structure is the *Railway Station* at *Helsinki* (**986**), for which he gained an international reputation. This too is in granite blocks, rugged, dramatic and stark. Inside, the decoration is somewhat Art Nouveau, superimposed on great Romanesque arcuated construction. Saarinen's *National Museum* in *Helsinki* (1905) is typical of the Finnish national style of the time, but his *Town Hall* at *Lahti* (1912) shows his progression towards the internationality of modern architecture.

In the 1920s, as in the other Scandinavian countries, neo-classicism returned to Finland, this time in a plainer version comparable to Lutyens in England and the earlier work of Asplund in Sweden. *Kallió's Municipal Theatre* in *Tampere* (1912) is a traditional example, but *J. S. Sirén's Parliament Building* in *Helsinki* (1927–31) is typical of the formal, simplified classicism. The monumental block is approached by an immense flight of steps on which is an impressive, lofty colonnade.

Finland had gained independence in 1917. The urge of her artists to express their national

985 *Tampere Cathedral, Finland, from the south-west. Granite blocks. Lars Sonck, 1902–7*

985

feelings in their several media evaporated. By 1930, the neo-classical phase was passing and Finland adopted modern architecture. In the years before the War, the country was beginning to establish its position as a leading nation in this field; after 1945 its European pre-eminence was confirmed.

Finland's greatest modern architect, *Alvar Aalto* (b. 1898) studied at the Helsinki Polytechnic and graduated in 1921. After a few early designs in simple classical form, he soon moved towards functionalism, setting aside all purely decorative features and concentrating on fundamental structure. Two of his works of the inter-war years became classics in modern architecture and made him internationally famous. Highly original was his *City Library* at *Viipuri* (1927–35), where he first used his acoustic system of insulating wood strips in ceiling design. Viipuri was Finland's second city, but was lost to the country when it was ceded to the Soviet Union in the Second World War. The library was seriously damaged but has now been rebuilt. Aalto's other outstanding building of the time is the *Tuberculosis Sanatorium* at *Paimio* (1929–33); a most original, plastic design.

Another important contributor to Finland's modern building before 1939 was *Erik Bryggman* (1891–1955). He graduated from the Helsinki Polytechnic in 1916 and spent much of his working life in *Turku*. In the years 1930–40 he designed his best works, which include the *Library* for the *Abô Akademie* in 1935–6 and

986 Railway Station, Helsinki, Finland, Eliel Saarinen, 1904–14

many houses. His most original and successful work is the *Cemetery Resurrection Chapel* at Turku (1939). Built in the cemetery on the outskirts of the city, it is a simple, white, rectangular structure with a colonnade and tower. The interior is most effective. Covered by a flattish barrel vaulted ceiling, there is a colonnade and windows along one whole side, while beside the altar at the far end is a tall, large, plain window which not only floods the whole interior with light but makes one feel as though the pine woods outside are really part of the interior. This ability to blend and affiliate architecture with natural surroundings is an especial and beautiful quality of Finnish architecture and one not confined to modern work alone.

A number of other architects were designing good quality modern structures in the 1930s. *Pauli Blomstedt* (1900–35) was responsible for the *Finnish Savings Bank* in *Helsinki* and the pleasant, distinguished, luxury hotel at *Hämeenlinna*, the *Aulanko Hotel*, which is built beside the lake in most beautiful surroundings. This, like most of Finland's buildings of the period, is plain, white and well-proportioned. A good example of the years just before the war is the

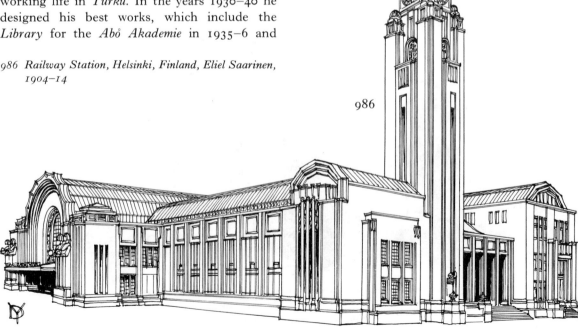

986

Stadium at *Helsinki*, built for the Olympic Games of 1940 (though the games had to be cancelled). This and the Olympic Village were the most modern structures of their kind at this time.

After 1945 Finnish architecture began to realise the promise of originality which had shown itself in the 1930s. The modern style has continued a steady progress since. Led by Alvar Aalto, supported by his talented colleagues, a Finnish school of architecture has evolved. It is characteristic and national, expressing in what to the Finns is the most important of the arts, a contemporary fulfilment of both functional and aesthetic perfection. In Finland, as in other countries, there is a quantity of average, typical modern architecture in simple but monotonous block formation, but the proportion of interesting, vital ideas, schemes and projects is greater than elsewhere. The Finns have adapted their modern architecture to suit their difficult climate and not to obtrude on their landscape. The architecture is, as it should be in any age, an integral part of the environment, providing what is needed for the comfort, inspiration and efficiency of mankind, but never offending or causing distress to the beholder and user. Finnish modern architecture, apart from its fine designs, interesting form and detail has an unusually high standard of quality in building and finish. It maintains a uniform standard not reached by any other European country. That this is possible in a country most of which is in extreme cold and darkness for much of the year, where the population is less than five million and not wealthy, should shame those richer lands of the west whose performance has been markedly so much lower.

After a war in which Finland lost a large section of her territory to the Soviet Union, the country faced the problem of housing and employing, within its reduced borders, over 400,000 people who had been displaced by the Russians. This represented, at that time, one eighth of the population. In addition, Finland, like other countries participating in the war, had lost many buildings and had several years of leeway in building to make up. The task of so much building by so small a nation was formidable and work of the 1950s is accordingly noted more for quantity than quality, though the

standards here never fell as low as in a number of similarly placed European countries at this time. The work of the 1960s, now that the urgency is abating, has shown much more originality and enterprise. Finnish architects are skilled in the handling of wood—their national material—and also brick and reinforced concrete. Shortage of steel means a greater use of these materials and less rectangular block skyscraper building.

Of the new towns and housing centres, *Tapiola* is justly famous. About eight kilometres from Helsinki, it covers a large area of land and is spread out to make attractive use of existing trees and the countryside. The houses and other buildings are sited naturally and pleasantly, not laid out in formal rectangles. The satellite town was begun in 1952, its chief architect *Aarne Ervi* (*b.* 1910), who designed the central area. The lay-out comprises a large lake with swimming pools and fountains and behind it a pedestrian precinct shopping area and a 13-storey tower block, which has a restaurant and terrace on the top floor. The housing is of mixed development, pleasingly planned and built. The only poor building is the church, its exterior mercifully hidden by trees. The interior is a bright cube, devoid of any atmosphere, in grey breeze blocks and boarded concrete.

Among the many other fine new town centres and housing developments are the *Central Square* at *Vaasa* (1963) by *Viljo Revell* (1910–64), the island site at *Säynätsalo* (1950–2) by *Alvar Aalto*, the development at *Kotka* and nearby *Sunila* and the *town centre* at *Seinäjoki*. This is an extensive complex, begun in 1951 and still continuing. A number of buildings of the civic centre are by *Aalto*, of which the *Church* and the *Theatre* have been built. There are also two libraries and halls. The church is of brick, painted white and has a tall, slender, separate campanile. The theatre is faced with purple ceramic tiling. It is an unusual shape and a most effective design supported on its simple colonnade.

Alvar Aalto has contributed extensively to the high quality of the architecture of post-war Finland. Among his other works are the *Church* at *Vuoksenniska*, near Imatra (1959), the *Enso-Gutzeit* office block at *Helsinki* (1962) and his *House of Culture* there (1958). At the end of the war, he was responsible for planning the new town development at *Rovaniemi*, the capital of

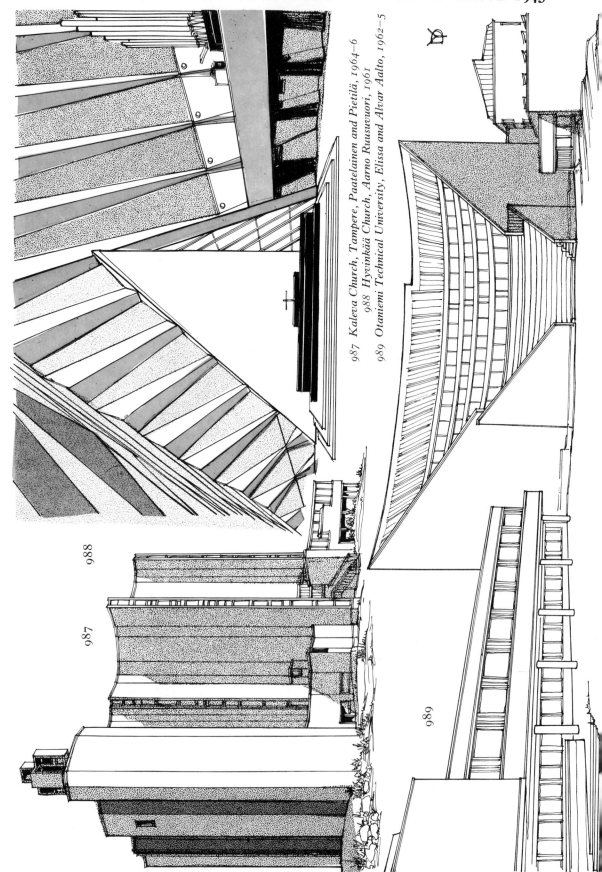

987 *Kaleva Church, Tampere, Paatelainen and Pietilä, 1964–6*
988 *Hyvinkää Church, Aarno Ruusuvuori, 1961*
989 *Otaniemi Technical University, Elissa and Alvar Aalto, 1962–5*

Finnish Lapland. Just within the Arctic Circle, this remarkable town is now a developing industrial area. All the skills and knowledge of the technological age have gone to make living and working in the buildings of the new development comfortable and pleasing during the long winter ice and darkness. Aalto's versatility and national qualities are shown particularly at the new *Technical University* at *Otaniemi*, between Helsinki and Tapiola. There are many buildings of red brick and grey granite laid out on a large, rolling and wooded site. There are close affinities here with Sussex University in England. Quite different, however, are Aalto's university centre and auditorium group which dominate the scene (**989**).

Of the many great post-war Finnish architects must be mentioned *Aarne Ervi, Aarno Ruusuvuori, Reima Pietilä* and *Raili Paatelainen*. Ervi's work at Tapiola has been referred to. He was also responsible for some new *University* buildings at *Turku* where he built the *Library* in 1954. Among other works, the other architects have been responsible for designing two of the most original and satisfactory churches in modern materials and idiom erected anywhere in post-war Europe. Acoustically, liturgically and aesthetically they are exciting and functional. The *Church* at *Hyvinkää* (just north of Helsinki) is an unusual triangular tent-like form, in white, shining concrete and glass, set in the woodlands on the edge of the town. The interior is striking (**988**), with its windows, galleries and roofing echoing endlessly, but not repetitively, the triangular motif. In sunlight especially, the interior lighting effects are dramatic, through the beautiful glass panels.

The *Kaleva Church* at *Tampere* (built on a grassy mound in the suburb of that name), stands on a triangular site in a new housing estate. The walls of multi-planes and curves are of uniform height and are faced with cream coloured, composition tiling, which gives a glowing, oatmeal consistency all over and delineates clearly the undulating character of the exterior (**987**). The interior is rather like the church at Royan in France (p. 538), but here there is no gallery. The immense height lends an overwhelming impression of light and space. This is Baroque architecture in a modern idiom. The simple materials of concrete and pale

coloured, plain wood are handled imaginatively and in a fine tradition of craftsmanship. The undulating ceiling is in a darkish concrete and ribbed. The walls are white and plain concrete, the window glass is plain. The pews, choir stalls, organ casing and altar sculpture are of beautifully finished wood.

The U.S.S.R.

Before the First World War Russian architecture was still based on the classical tradition, generally in a heavy, over-ornamented Baroque style which was tinged with oriental and Byzantine forms. Typical is the *Kiev Opera House* of 1901 by *Shretera*. It is set in a square laid out with four-storey apartment blocks in the same decorative style. *Art Nouveau* was seen chiefly in paintings, interior decoration and, above all, choreography. In architecture, its effect was limited, its chief exponent Schekhtel. The finest structure of the period is the *Kazan Railway Station* in *Moscow* by *A. V. Shchoussev* (**983**). It is derivative, but its origins are manifold, eastern and western, ancient and Medieval. It is a richly decorated, colourful and successful design.

The Revolution of 1917 caused a total upheaval in the arts as well as in the rest of life in Russia. The old traditions and links with the west were swept away. After the chaos of the first few years, it was realised that not only would society need to be reformed but that this was a tremendous opportunity, artistically, to break with eclecticism. The younger architects, in particular, saw this as a great chance to create an art form in building worthy of the ideas of a Workers' State. From 1920 it became clear to all such architects that modern architecture was the building style for socialism. The State now took responsibility and handled the financial support for all building: civic, town planning, industrial, technical, housing and education.

There was, for some years, more discussion than action. Partly this was due to administrative disorganisation and Russia's economic position after the war and the Revolution. Money was not available in sufficient quantity. 'Constructivism' was one of the themes of the new architecture, led by such men as Eliezer M. (*El*) *Lissitzsky* (1890–1941), who had studied at Darmstadt before the war. The theory was that this new architectural form would express the collective aims and desires of the masses in art and building. Materials must be produced by Soviet industry. New materials—glass, steel, concrete—were correct and nothing must be on or in a building not strictly functional or useful. The exponents of this theme were convinced that such buildings would have beauty and satisfaction which would inspire and educate all the people. The structures would be a blend of the greatest achievements of man in science, technology and art. Unfortunately not a great deal was ever built and experience showed, as decades passed, that 'the masses' resolutely preferred their buildings in familiar traditional style, of traditional materials not glass and concrete and with plenty of decoration on them: a revelation manifested to well-intentioned modern architects not only in Russia.

The years 1925–32 were a time of trial and experiment in modern architecture in the U.S.S.R. There was not a great deal of contact with the west and therefore little to guide architects in these new theories. Of the older men, established in their profession before 1917, some began to adapt themselves to the new régime and continued to build in a semi-traditional vein. These included *Shchoussev, Shchouko* and *Zholtovsky*. Many others emigrated to the west.

Of the younger men who established themselves and designed in modern manner were the *Vesnin brothers* (Alexander, Leonid and Victor), who evolved a number of projects of which little was actually built. The most successful of these younger men was *Konstantin Melnikov*. With the radical changes in social structure and methods of government, the types of buildings erected had changed too. Private houses, churches, cathedrals were now no longer needed. Instead were built palaces for the Soviets (probably the nearest equivalent to town hall and council offices), communal housing and, a specifically communist type of building, the *workers' club*. This was the class of building for which Melnikov became well-known; he built seven between 1925 and 1929, of which several survive, including the *Club Rusakov* in *Moscow* (**990**), 1925–6. A workers' club was a multi-purpose building. It included theatre, cinema, library, facilities for study, reading, discussion and light entertainment. Melnikov's designs for these and

other structures were, since he and his colleagues had so little contact with the west, surprisingly similar to the functionalist ideas of the Bauhaus. The Moscow club is very plain, angular and of modern materials.

Later modern architects in Russia had some western examples to study, as, for example, the *Centrosoyus*, now the Ministry of Light Industries, built in *Moscow* 1928–36 by *Le Corbusier*. This large building of glass and steel curtain-walled façades and terminal blocks of concrete on *pilotis* still survives. It is now a familiar design, but was a prototype in 1928.

Several new projects were designed in the 1920s by younger architects, but by the early 1930s support for modern architecture began to weaken. The Soviet Union lost its first idealistic fervour for communist principles and became a dictatorship. As in the parallel contemporary régimes in Germany and Italy, attenuated classical architecture became the accepted style. To the frustration of the modern architects, the 'masses' much preferred this. In the nineteenth century classicism had been the prerogative of the privileged classes. Now, in simplified form, it was available, with thanks, for all. Chief examples in the 1930s were the *Moskva Hotel* (1936, *Shchoussev*), the *Supreme Soviet of the Ukraine* at *Kiev* (1938, *Fomin*), the extensive layout of shops and apartments in *Gorki Street*, the main street of *Moscow* (1938, *Mordinov*) and the *Lenin Library* in *Moscow* (1938, *Shchouko* and *Helfreich*). These are all well-designed and -built classical structures comparable with western examples of the time.

The most impressive construction in this style was to be the *Palace of the Soviets* in *Moscow*. A competition was held; 200 architects entered, many from western Europe; famous international names included Gropius, Mendelsohn, Le Corbusier. The Soviet hierarchy decided on a traditional building and appointed *B. Iofan, V. Shchouko* and colleagues to carry out their Russian design. This was in 1934. The model showed a fantastic, vast-scale, classical structure in diminishing stages, overlooking the Kremlin and dwarfing it. The total height of the building was to be 1365 feet, the tallest in the world. This included a totally out-of-scale, immense statue of Lenin, 325 feet in height. The Palace was to contain museums, an amphitheatre, halls, an

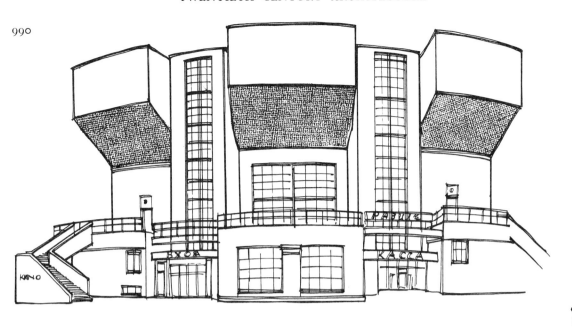

990 Workers' Club, 'Club Rusakov', Moscow, U.S.S.R., K. Melnikov, 1925–6

auditorium, library and government rooms. The work had not progressed far when Hitler's armies invaded the Soviet Union. After 1945 the climate of opinion had changed, the building was never erected and Moscow gained a large open air swimming pool on the site.

However, the Stalinist form of classical architecture, a mixture of Baroque, nineteenth century heavy grandeur and the inevitable large-scale approach traditional to the Russians continued to develop after 1945 and lasted until the early 1960s. Typical are the immense skyscrapers, owing something to the early twentieth century American pattern, which were erected as universities, government offices and hotels, not only in the Soviet Union but in all the eastern European satellites as well. In *Moscow* is the greatest of them all, the *Lomonosov State University*, built on the Lenin Hills on the fringe of the city (**973**). There is also the very similar *Hotel Ukraina* in *Moscow*, the apartment block in *Vassaniya Square* and the *Traffic Ministry* at the Red Gate, all of the 1950s. In *Kiev*, the main street, the *Kreshchatik*, was rebuilt in this style in the 1950s, after almost total destruction during the War, with many civic buildings, as was also *Stalinallee* in *East Berlin*. This was the first main street to be rebuilt after the War; it is now Karl Marx Allee. All this work is classical in basis, especially in

fenestration and decoration, but there is an oriental and Byzantine quality also, blended with the American skyscraper central tower and steeple designs of the period just before the First World War in New York. The Woolworth Building (1913) is of this type.

An admirable achievement in the U.S.S.R. has been the building of the *Moscow Underground Railway* system or Metro. It was begun before the war and has been continued since. Apart from being technically and administratively an efficient system (a rarity in the Soviet Union), it is aesthetically the most original in the world. Each station is different in design and décor. The most interesting pre-war station is *Dynamo*, built 1938 by *Tschetschulin*, which has a fine sculptured exterior building on classical pattern. Of the post-war stations, Komsomol and Botanic Garden are among the best. *Komsomol* was built 1952 by *Shchoussev* and *Warwarin*. It is of fine quality in materials and craftsmanship, but more Edwardian than of 1952 vintage. The ceilings are of rococo and Baroque decorated plaster; the semi-apsidal entrance for the trains is ornamented by ceramic tile murals representing Soviet work and achievement on one side and, on the other, the story of the building of the Metro showing both men and women labouring at laying track. The *Botanic Gardens Station* (1952, *Helfreich* and

THE TWENTIETH CENTURY IN EASTERN EUROPE

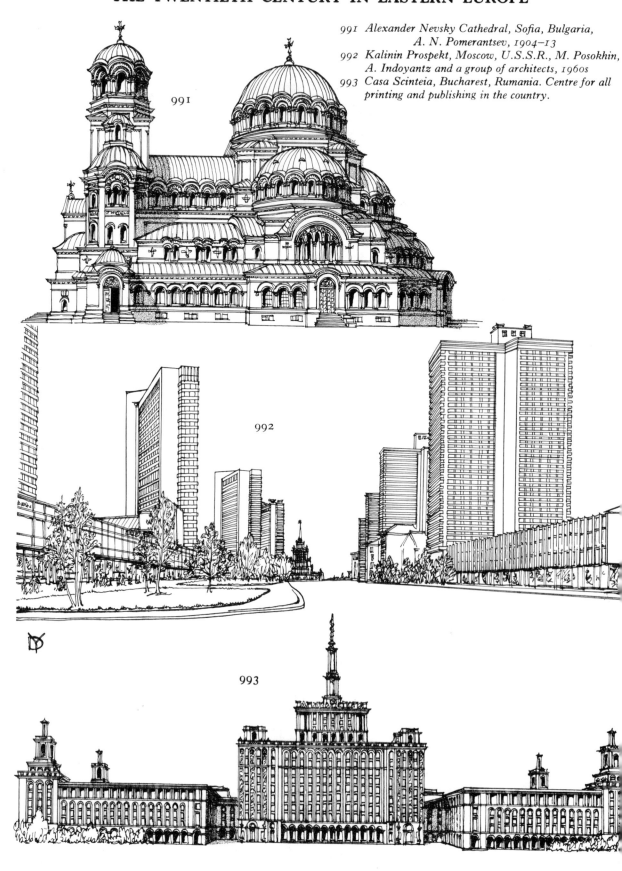

991 *Alexander Nevsky Cathedral, Sofia, Bulgaria,*
A. N. Pomerantsev, 1904–13

992 *Kalinin Prospekt, Moscow, U.S.S.R., M. Posokhin,*
A. Indoyantz and a group of architects, 1960s

993 *Casa Scinteia, Bucharest, Rumania. Centre for all*
printing and publishing in the country.

991

992

993

Minkus), now re-named Prospekt Mira, is in Baroque/Byzantine classical form, with a lattice patterned barrel vaulted ceiling in stucco supported on immense, squat columns with vast Corinthian type, figured capitals. The scheme is in white marble and glazed white ceramic tiling with gilt decoration. The upstairs booking hall is like an ornate, Edwardian version of a Nile temple with Egyptian lotus columns and capitals. All the stations are derivative but the variety, quality and robust vitality compel admiration.

Since 1960 the Russians have turned to the international mode of modern architecture. They have taken to glass, steel and concrete boxes which differ little from those elsewhere in Europe except that what is now being built in Moscow is similar to what was erected in Western Europe a decade or so ago. The *Kalinin Prospekt* in *Moscow* (**992**) is the show boulevard of shops, offices and apartments. It looks much like a street in any capital of Western Europe, but the road is far wider and longer and the individual flats are much smaller and less well equipped, especially with bathrooms, heating, hot water systems and kitchens. But they represent progress to Soviet citizens. There is also, in the centre of the city, a *'cluster block'* type of building. Erected 1968–9 by *Posokhin, Indoyantz* and others, it contains offices, a conference hall and hotel. It is an elegant, well-designed structure of glass and steel. A link between these latest achievements and the Stalinist building era is provided by the *Palace of Congresses* in the *Kremlin*, built 1960–1 by *M. V. Posokhin*. This is of the plain, functionalist type of modern building, with much in common with Arne Jacobsen's town halls. It is a beautifully finished structure in fine materials.

Eastern Europe:
Rumania and Bulgaria

The development of architecture during the twentieth century in both these countries shows the strength of influence from Russia and from the west. In Rumania, the stronger influence has probably been from the west, in Bulgaria, from the east. Classical-style architecture from the inter-war years still survives in *Bucharest*. This is of the same type of plain classicism, stripped of decoration and using only the orders and fenestration, that was usual in the U.S.S.R. in the 1930s.

In post-war years *Rumania* took up modern architecture earlier than the U.S.S.R. Certainly Stalinist skyscrapers were built under Soviet influence; the immense *Casa Scinteia* in *Bucharest* (**993**) is the chief example. This occupies a fine site but the proportions are less satisfactory than the Moscow examples; it is too stumpy and squat. Apart from these buildings, which are not numerous, much of Rumanian modern architecture is of good quality. In *Bucharest* there is a simple, elegant *Exhibition Pavilion* at the entrance to the Village Museum. The *State Circus* has a waved concrete roof after the style of Nervi in Rome (**956**). In the centre of the city, in the *Piata Palatulei* (Palace Square), is an entirely modern layout comprising a domed *Congress Hall* and apartment blocks of different proportions and sizes. The ensemble is an attractive one with plenty of space and excellent landscaping of trees, lawns and flowers. This is in marked contrast to French equivalents (p. 537–8). The Congress Hall is faced with cream coloured stone set in stainless steel framing. Below the shallow dome are blue-grey mosaic panels.

There are many new *hotels* in the country built to attract the fast-growing tourist trade. The *Carpaţi* in *Braşov* is a good example. On the beaches round the Black Sea coast entire new resorts have been created on mere sand spits. The building of the large hotels and blocks of flats, together with the landscaping and successful growing of trees and flowers, especially roses, has been a remarkable technical and scientific feat. Like the Israelis, the Rumanians have made the sand to blossom. *Mamaia* is the best known of these resorts, five miles north of Constanţa. Its sea front extends over a great distance along the sand spit, while the great lake of Siutghiol lies inland behind. In building more than 30 hotels here, as well as apartments, the Rumanians had to begin from nothing and provide drinking water, electricity and drainage. The sea front is laid out in gardens and with shops, post office, hairdressing salons, supermarkets; only cafés and restaurants are rare. The quality of building is good, if a little monotonous.

Bulgaria, a nearer neighbour, has for centuries been more strongly influenced by Russian art and architecture. The great *Cathedral of Sofia, Alexander Nevsky* (**991**), was built by a Russian architect in honour of the Russian liberators of the day. It is a large, flamboyant, impressive cathedral, its newly gilded domes gleaming in the sunshine. The exterior is well-proportioned and architecturally simple in structure, though richly decorated in Byzantine tradition. The interior is even more Byzantine. Ionic marble columns divide the narthex from the five-aisled nave with its vast square piers. The windows are small but numerous. The entire interior is painted with scenes from the Bible; the style of these paintings varies from Byzantine formality to modern realism. From the interior of the great crossing cupola the bearded Pantocrator gazes down sternly like a Russian Tsar admonishing his people. The marble archbishop's throne has an impressive canopy over it, supported on columns with Byzantine drilled hole capitals (p. 89) which, in turn, stand upon the backs of lions.

In *Sofia* also is the *Russian Church* of *S. Nikolai* (1913, by the Russian architect *Preobrajensky*). Much smaller than the cathedral, this is an interesting architectural pile, tall, dramatic and very Byzantine. With its small gilded onion domes surrounding the tall steeple topped by another such cupola, it is reminiscent of the cathedrals in the Moscow Kremlin (p. 122). There is a fine tall entrance porch decorated with paintings and mosaic.

As in the U.S.S.R., classical architecture in different guises has been built for much of the twentieth century. The style before the First World War was, as in Russia, heavily ornamented Baroque, for example the *National Theatre* of *Sofia* of 1907. An inter-war example is the *University*, built in 1931 by the French architect *Breançon* on Petit Palais lines. The building has much more the appearance of belonging to the 1900–10 era in Paris than 1931. After 1945, the massive skyscraper classicism of Stalinism came to Sofia in the buildings in *Lenin Square*, while the *Stadium* shows the very plain version of the Palace of Congresses type in Moscow.

Since 1955–60 modern architecture has been built in quantity in Bulgaria and, in particular, along the Black Sea coast in resorts like *Varna*, which are much like their Rumanian equivalents.

Greece and Yugoslavia

Greek architecture has developed along western lines. A poor country, the quantity of building was not extensive until after 1945 when the tourist trade began to increase quickly. A number of the better-known examples of modern architecture in Greece, especially in *Athens* are by foreign architects; the *U.S.A. Embassy*, for example, by *Walter Gropius* and his Collaborative, and also the *Hilton Hotel*. Many of the numerous *hotels* built all over the country are well designed, comfortable and fine. They are by Greek architects, who have created varied designs on original lines and all carefully suited to their location. The interior décor is particularly attractive and unusual. The *Xenia* chain of hotels is a good example as at, for instance, the *Island of Mykonos* (**960**) and at *Nauplia* in the Peloponnese. A hotel on more 'brutalist' lines in its exterior structure and appearance is the *Amalia Hotel* at *Delphi*, built 1966 by *Valsamakis*. This is particularly well designed for its magnificent site and for the interior, which is ideally suited to the climate.

Yugoslavia has followed a similar pattern. Again, the poverty of the country has been restrictive and, poised politically between east and west, the western influence has been slower to develop than in Greece. Modern architecture of the 1950s in Yugoslavia was drab and dull, lacking good materials and original ideas. The work of the 1960s is much better, though the quality of finish and plumbing is still not always good. There has been much new building along the resorts of the whole *Adriatic Coast*, with problems of terrain even more difficult than those of the Rumanians at Mamaia. Here the mountains make communications, transport and siting a problem, but the Yugoslavs are overcoming the difficulties and making some fine resorts.

Hungary, Czechoslovakia and Poland

Hungarian architecture before the First World War was still strongly influenced by Austria. There was some sign of Art Nouveau and still much eclecticism. A typical building surviving in the war-damaged city of *Budapest* is that now occupied as headquarters by *Ibusz*, the State Tourist Organisation, built in 1909.

In the years since 1945 Hungary has, like the

other countries of the communist bloc, been influenced by the U.S.S.R. A severe, but late use of classicism is the *Railway Station* façade at *Györ* (1959), which has completely plain columns like Piacentini's Via Roma in Turin of 1938. Above the columns is a sculptured panel notable for its Soviet influence. The *National Theatre* in *Budapest* is a structure of the 1960s. This indicates the now completely modern approach with its semi-abstract, all-over decoration to the rectangular block façade.

Czechoslovakia

The pattern of architectural design followed here had much in common with that in Austria. The *Art Nouveau* manner, in vogue at the turn of the century, was led by *Jan Kotěra*, a pupil of Wagner (p.521). He and his colleagues designed a number of houses and stores.

Soon after the First World War, the ideas of *modern architecture* percolated to Czechoslovakia and, from 1921 onwards, a number of 'functionalist' architects were practising. These included *Josef Fuchs, Jaromír Krejcar* and *F. M. Černy*. The Prague Sample Fairs Palace, built 1924–8 by Tyl and Fuchs, was an early example of glass curtain-walling.

By 1925–7 modern architecture was establishing itself in Czechoslovakia and designs were in advance of most countries of Western Europe with the exception of Germany, Switzerland and Italy. Buildings such as department stores, hotels, churches and civic structures were being erected under such architects as *Polaček, Gočár*, and *Bohuslav Fuchs*, whose Avion Hotel at Brno (1927) was typical.

In the 1930s, as in many Western European countries, large *housing estates* were planned and built. A modern example of the time was the 'Baba' residential district of Prague, laid out 1928–32 by *Pavel Janák*. This still exists, though it appears old-fashioned today in its severe 'functionalist' blocks, almost totally devoid of decorative or architectural relief. A new town was planned at Zlín—now *Gottwaldov*—where both industrial development and appropriate housing with educational and shopping needs were provided. It was designed by *František Gahura** and *Vladimir Karfík* and largely built 1928–39; an innovation at this time.

* *Gahura was also responsible for the glass and steel department store* Centrum *in Brno, built in 1946–52.*

The Second World War did not cause great devastation to most Czech towns and cities and, as architects had not been forced to emigrate for political reasons to the same extent as in Germany, the modern architectural tradition survived in Czechoslovakia. In 1945, however, the power of the new régime from the east established the usual stranglehold on artistic endeavour and enterprise. A period of architectural stagnation followed from which there was only just emerging a new energy and initiative when the Russian occupation of the country in 1968 put an end to hopes of its success.

In the 1960s a new generation of younger architects were beginning to design in the current modern mode. Before this the Stalinist Moscow style of skyscraper blocks had been *de rigueur* for large commissions in Czechoslovakia as elsewhere in Eastern Europe (**973** and **993**). The International Hotel in Prague is a typical example, being a facsimile, on smaller scale (as befits a satellite country) of the Hotel Ukraina in Moscow. Among the talented new group of architects was *Karel Prager*, who designed the glass curtain-walled *Institute of Macromolecular Chemistry* of the Czechoslovak Academy of Sciences in the Petřiny district of *Prague* in 1964. This is an area of the city which has been developed as a new dormitory suburb since 1955. Another building, this time of low-level design, planned in a curving elevation, is the *Soviet Chamber of Commerce* in *Prague*, designed in 1964 by *Holuša, Kulišták* and *Leniček*.

The most interesting of Prager's designs is the new *Parliament House* in *Prague*, next to the National Museum at the head of Wenceslaus Square. The new building is an interesting one, square in form and carried out in glass, metal and stone. Tragically, the architect, still in his thirties, has been deprived of his commission and disbarred from his profession because of his sympathetic support for the previous, Dubcek, régime.

Poland

Because of the extensive devastation of nearly all Polish cities in the Second World War, it is difficult to find good examples of twentieth century architecture. Naturally, the Poles, when rebuilding their cities, have attempted to restore and re-create the great periods of their architectural heritage—the Middle Ages, Renaissance and Baroque eras—and twentieth century work has been replaced by contemporary building.

Modern architecture did not develop early in Poland and most of the buildings in the modern style erected in the inter-war years were by foreigners. These included *Hans Poelzig*'s water tower in *Poznan*, 1910, *Hans Sharoun*'s hostel at *Wroclaw* (1929) and *Erich Mendelsohn*'s store in the same city. The last of these, built by Mendelsohn as the *Petersdorff Store* in 1927 (p. 516), miraculously survives and illustrates how far ahead of its time this design was, with its glass, metal and concrete construction, horizontal emphasis and curving corner turning.

Little new building of note appeared in the years after 1945; too great an effort was needed to provide shelter and work for the homeless population. This was especially true of the capital, Warsaw, 80 per cent of whose buildings were destroyed or gutted. In the late 1950s and early 1960s Polish architecture, as elsewhere in Eastern Europe, was dominated by Moscow. The *Palace of Culture* in Warsaw, designed 1952–6 by *Rudniev*, one of the architects of the Lomonosov State University in Moscow (**973**) shows the usual approach of this type of building. In the later 1960s, modern building, also very much on Soviet pattern, has been erected. Workers' flats in housing estates are, like those in Leningrad and Moscow, dull and blockish, while the boulevards of Warsaw, like Marszalkowska, show offices, flats and cinemas, etc., laid out just like Moscow's Kalinin Prospekt (**992**) and East Berlin's Karl Marx Allee.

There are now signs that more interesting architecture is being designed and studied. The interior of the main hall at *Warsaw airport*, for example, shows a livelier approach, as do also one or two of the new churches. In certain cities the slowly developing tourist trade with the west is encouraging more interesting designs in hotels on western pattern. The *Cracovia Hotel* in *Cracow* is one example; the *Orbis-Monopol* Hotel in *Wroclaw* another.

Glossary

The bold reference figures in brackets refer to line drawings.

Abacus The top member of a capital, usually a square or curved-sided slab of stone or marble (**47**).

Abutment Solid masonry acting as support against the thrust or lateral pressure of an arch (**610**).

Acanthus A leaf form used in classical ornament (**94**).

Acropolis A city on a hill. A Greek term usually implying also some fortification (**29**).

Acroteria Blocks resting on the vertex and lower extremities of a pediment to carry carved ornament (**34**).

Agora A Greek term for an open air place of assembly, generally the market place.

Alcázar A Spanish word for a castle or fortress.

Ambulatory A passage or aisle giving access between the choir, with high altar, and the apse of a church (**544**).

Antefixae Carved blocks set at regular intervals along the lower edge of a roof in classical architecture.

Anthemion A type of classical ornament based on the honeysuckle flower (**62**).

Apse Semi-circular or polygonal termination to a church most commonly to be found on the eastern or transeptal elevations (**321**).

Arabesque Classical ornament in delicate flowing forms, terminating in scrolls and decorated with flowers and leaves (**105**).

Arcade A series of arches open, or closed with masonry, supported on columns or piers (**287**).

Architrave The lowest member of the entablature (**23**).

Arcuated construction Wherein the structure is supported on arches (**121**).

Arris The vertical sharp edges between the flutes on a column (**23**).

Articulation The designing, defining and dividing up of a façade into vertical and horizontal architectural members.

Ashlar Hewn and squared stones prepared for building.

Astragal A moulding at the top of the column and below the capital.

Astylar A classical façade without columns or pilasters (**651**).

Atrium An entrance court in Roman houses but, in Early Christian and Byzantine church architecture, an open square or courtyard in front of the entrance (**145**).

Attic A term applied in Renaissance and later classical architecture to the upper storey of a structure above the cornice.

Baldacchino A canopy supported on pillars set over an altar or throne.

Barbican Outer defence to a city or castle. Generally a double tower over a gate or bridge (**546**).

Barrel vault A continuous vault in semi-circular section, like a tunnel (**319**).

Basilica In Roman architecture a hall of justice and centre for commercial exchange. This type of structure was adapted by the early Christians for their church design. It was a rectangular building generally with an apse at one end. It was divided internally into nave and aisles by columns, not piers, and these supported a timber roof. There were no transepts. The basilican plan continued in use, with modifications, especially in Italy and France, for several centuries (**173**).

Bema In Ancient Athens a raised platform in a place of public assembly. Adapted later into Early Christian church design as a raised stage, generally at the apsidal end, of a basilica for use of the clergy.

Caisson see coffer.

Caldarium A hot room in a Roman Baths.

Cantilever A specially shaped beam or other member (e.g. staircase tread) supported securely at one end and carrying a load at the other free end or with the load distributed uniformly along the beam. A cantilever bracket is used to support a cornice or balcony, etc., of considerable projection. The cantilever principle is frequently adopted in designs of large bridges, e.g. the Forth Railway Bridge, near Edinburgh.

Capital The crowning feature of a column or pilaster (**27**).

Cartouche Ornament in the form of elaborate scrolled forms round shields, tablets or coats of arms.

Caryatid Sculptured female figure in the form of support or column (PLATE 6).

Ceiling cove Curved part of ceiling where it joins the wall.

Cella The enclosed, central part of a Roman temple (**112**).

Centering A structure, usually made of timber, set up to support a dome, vault or ceiling until construction is complete.

Chevet Term given to circular or polygonal apse when surrounded by an ambulatory from which radiate chapels (**428**).

Chevron ornament Romanesque decoration in zig-zag form (**395**).

Cimborio Spanish term for lantern or fenestrated cupola (**472**).

Clerestory The upper storey in a church generally pierced by a row of windows (**532, 544**).

Coffer Panel or caisson sunk into a ceiling, dome or vault—often ornamented (**108**).

Conch The domed ceiling of a semi-circular apse (PLATE 22).

Corbel table A projecting section of wall supported on corbels (carved blocks of stone or wood) and generally forming a parapet.

Cornice The crowning member of the classical entablature (**23**).

Coupled columns In classical architecture where the wall articulation is designed with the columns in pairs (**763**).

Crocket A projecting block of stone carved in Gothic foliage on the inclined sides of pinnacles and canopies.

Crossing The central area in a cruciform church where the transepts cross the nave and choir arm. Above this lofty space is generally set a tower (with or without spire) or a cupola (**494**).

Cruciform A plan based on the form of a cross (**422**).

Curtain wall In modern architecture this English term is in universal use and commonly describes an external, non-loadbearing wall composed of repeated modular elements generally of glass in metal framing. These are pre-fabricated and erected on the site.

Cusp Point forming the foliations in Gothic tracery (**457**).

Cyclopean masonry Walling composed of immense blocks of stone as seen in building at Tyrins or Mycenae. Named after the Cyclops (**9**).

Cyma A moulding in a section of two contrasting curves—either cyma recta or cyma reversa—used in classical architecture especially (**26**).

Dentil Classical form of ornament (**26**).

Domical vault A vault covering a square or polygonal compartment and shaped like a dome.

Domus Roman private house.

Dosseret A deep block often placed above the Byzantine capital to support the wide voussoirs of the arch above (PLATE 21).

Drum The circular or poly-sided vertical walling supporting a dome (**181**).

Echinus A curved, moulded member supporting the abacus of the Doric Order. The term is derived from the Greek *echinos* meaning sea urchin. The curve resembles the shell of the sea urchin (**23**).

Engaged column A column (in classical architecture) which is attached to the wall so that only a half to three-quarters of its circumference stands visible.

Entasis Taken from the Greek word for distension, is an outward curving along the outline of a column shaft. It is designed to counteract the optical illusion which gives to a shaft bounded by straight lines the appearance of being curved inwards, i.e. concave.

Fillet A narrow, flat band which divides mouldings from one another; also separates column flutes.

Finial Ornament finishing off the apex of a roof, gable, pediment, pinnacle, newel, canopy, etc (**610**).

Flèche French term for a slender spire commonly found over the crossing on a Gothic church (**427**).

Flute Vertical channelling in the shaft of a column (**24**).

Forum The Roman place of assembly for markets, courts of justice and business (**85**).

Fret ornament Classical decoration.

Frieze The central member of the classical entablature (**23**).

Frigidarium The cold water swimming bath in a Roman Baths.

Frontispiece The two- or three-stage entrance feature applied to the principal façade of a court or building (**676**).

Giant order Used in Mannerist and Baroque architecture wherein the order spans two storeys of the façade (**657**).

Greek cross plan A cruciform plan where the four arms of the cross are of equal length (**209**).

Guilloche Classical ornament in the form of an intertwined plait.

Guttae Small cones under the mutules and triglyphs of the Doric entablature (**23**).

Hall church A rectangular church, generally of Gothic design, where the vaulting height of the entire building is the same. Such a church has, therefore, neither triforium nor clerestory. Most commonly found in Germany and Scandinavia (**522, 538**).

Hypocaust A hollow space under the floor in which heat from the furnace was accumulated for warming rooms and hot water system. Used in Ancient Rome.

Insula A Roman multi-storeyed tenement block (**151**).

Intercolumniation The space between columns. (**34**).

Intersecting vault Where two vaults, either of semi-circular section or of pointed form, meet and intersect one another at right angles. Most usual instance is in the crossing of a church where the transepts cross nave and choir.

Kokoshniki Term used in Russia for the series of arches set in rows generally in Byzantine construction. Derived from kokoshnik, the name for a traditional headdress for Russian women which the arch is thought to resemble (**246**).

Lantern Structure for ventilation and light. Often surmounting a dome or tower (**660**).

Latin cross plan A cruciform plan where the nave is longer than the other three arms (**423**).

Lierne From the French *lier* = to tie. A short, intermediate rib in Gothic vaulting which is not a ridge rib nor rises from the impost.

Lintel The horizontal stone slab or timber beam spanning an opening and supported on columns or walls (**10**).

Loggia Open sided gallery or arcade (**662**).

Machicolation A parapet in Medieval fortified buildings with openings between supporting corbels for dropping missiles upon the enemy (**482**).

Manoeline Portuguese decorative architectural style of the early sixteenth century, named after Dom Manoel I (**1495–1521**) (PLATE 53).

Metope The space between the triglyphs of a Doric frieze. Often decorated with sculptured groups or carved ornament (**23**).

Module A unit of measurement based on proportion by which the parts of a classical order are regulated. Generally taken from the half-diameter of the column at its junction with the base. In modern architecture, a standard unit adopted for the convenience of mass production.

Monolithic column One whose shaft is of one piece of stone or marble in contrast to one made up in hollow drums.

Mozarabic A style of architecture in medieval Spain named after the Mozarabs, who were Christians owning allegiance to a Moorish King but allowed to practice Christianity.

Mutule Blocks attached under Doric cornices from which the guttae depend (**23**).

Naos Chamber in a Greek temple containing the cult statue (**48**).

Narthex The western portico or ante-nave in Early Christian and Byzantine churches railed off for women and penitents (**209, 242**).

Necking The space between the astragal of a column shaft and the actual capital (**608**).

Orchestra Space where the chorus danced and sang in a Greek theatre (**55**).

Pediment The triangular feature in classical architecture which resembles the Gothic gable. Supported on the entablature over porticoes, windows and doors (**34**).

Pendentive Spherical triangles formed by the intersecting of the dome by two pairs of opposite arches, themselves carried on four piers or columns (**175, 190**).

Peristyle A row of columns surrounding a temple, court or cloister, also the space so enclosed (**34, 144**).

Piano nobile An Italian Renaissance term, meaning literally the 'noble floor'. In classical building it is the first and principal floor of a house.

Pilaster A column of rectangular section often engaged in the wall (**734**).

Pilaster strip Low relief vertical strips with the appearance of pilasters but with only decorative not constructional purpose (**251**).

Pilotis A term in modern architecture taken from the French word for pile or stake. Introduced by Le Corbusier in his designs of flats and houses supported on columns or piles (**970**).

Plateresque A form of rich, surface ornament in Spanish architecture used in both Gothic and Renaissance buildings. The term is derived from platería = silverwork (**625**).

Podium A continuous projecting base or pedestal (**657**).

Pozzolana A substance used in Roman building. A volcanic ash found near Naples and named after a nearby village. Mixed with lime from the local stone it formed a very hard concrete used in construction of vaults.

Propylaeum An important entrance gateway in Greek architecture as, for example, the entrance to the acropolis at Athens (**29**).

Putto A term used to describe the cherubs and babies

sculptured in Baroque architecture. From the Italian word meaning child (PLATES 92–5).

Retablo An altarpiece or framing enclosing painted panels above an altar. A Spanish word used especially when referring to Spanish architecture.

Relieving arch A relieving or discharging arch or slab is constructed to prevent the weight of masonry above it from crushing the lintel stone below (**5, 10**).

Rotunda Building of circular ground plan often surmounted by a dome; a circular hall or room (**171**).

Rustication A treatment of masonry with sunk joints and roughened surfaces. Used in classical architecture (**651**).

Set-off Sloping or horizontal member connecting the lower and thicker part of a wall with the receding upper part (**478**).

Shaft The column of an order, between the capital and base (**14, 15**).

Spandrel Triangular space formed between an arch and the rectangle of outer mouldings as in a doorway. Generally decorated by carving or mosaic (**388**).

Solar Medieval term for an upper room, usually the private sitting room of the owner of the house.

Squinch Arches placed diagonally across the internal angles of a tower or base of drum to convert the square form into an octagonal base to support an octagonal spire or circular drum (**175**).

Stave church Medieval, wooden stave or mast churches of Scandinavia constructed in self-contained units. The walls, the stave screens, rest upon the timber sleepers below, but do not take weight or thrust. This is taken upon the skeleton framework of poles, or masts, which are set into the timber ground sills then attached to the staves (**365, 371**).

Stilted arch An arch having its springing line higher than the level of the impost mouldings. It is then connected to these mouldings by vertical sections of walling or stilts (**300**).

Strapwork A form of ornament using straps or lines of decoration intertwined and forming panels. The straps are flat with raised fillet edges. Used on ceiling or wall decoration, especially in early Mannerist type Renaissance work in Flanders, Poland or England (PLATE 70).

String course A moulding or projecting course set horizontally along the elevation of a building.

Stucco A plaster used for coating wall surfaces or moulding into architectural decoration or sculpture.

Stylobate A basement, generally of three steps, supporting a row of columns in Greek temple design (**34**).

Tepidarium Room of moderate heat in a Roman Baths.

Tholos A circular, classical temple (**53**).

Tierceron A third rib in Gothic vaulting.

Trabeated construction A structure composed of horizontal lintels and vertical posts as in Greek architecture (**34**).

Tracery The ornamental stonework in the head of a Gothic window (**456**).

Transept The arms of a cruciform church set at right angles to the nave and choir. Transepts are generally aligned north and south (**339**).

Travertine An Italian building stone of a porous yellowish type.

Triforium The central, or first floor stage, of a Medieval church between the nave arcade and the clerestory. The triforium is usually arcaded and may have a passage behind at first floor level extending continuously round the church (**293**).

Triglyph The blocks, cut with vertical channels, which are set at regular intervals in the frieze of the Doric Order (**23**).

Trumeau A French term which is used to refer to the pier between two openings or, more commonly in Gothic architecture, the pier dividing a large portal in two parts (PLATES 40, 45).

Tympanum The triangular space between the sloping and horizontal cornices of a classical pediment (**34**).

Undercroft The chamber partly or wholly below ground, generally in a Medieval building. In a church this would be a crypt, in a house or castle it would be used for storage.

Vault Arched covering in stone, brick or wood.

Vaulting bay The rectangular or square area bounded by columns or piers and covered by a ribbed or groined vault.

Vaulting boss A carved, decorative feature set at intervals in a ribbed vault to hide the junctions between one rib and another (**453**).

Vault springing The point at which the vault ribs spring upwards from the capital, corbel or arch impost (**550**).

Volute A spiral or scroll to be seen in Ionic, Corinthian and Composite capitals (**25**).

Voussoir The wedge-shaped stones which compose an arch (**71**).

Bibliography

A select list of books, classified by style and country, recommended for further reading.

GENERAL

ALLSOPP, B., *A History of Classical Architecture,* Sir Isaac Pitman and Sons Ltd., 1965

ALLSOPP, B., BOOTON, H. W. and CLARK, U., *The Great Tradition of Western Architecture,* A. and C. Black, 1966

BLUM, A. S., *A Short History of Art,* B. T. Batsford Ltd., 1926

CAMESASCA, E., *History of the House,* Collins, 1971

CICHY, B., *Architektur und Baustile,* E. E. Thoma, Munich, 1959

COPPLESTONE, T. (Ed.), *World Architecture,* Paul Hamlyn, 1963

DYNES, W., *Palaces of Europe,* Paul Hamlyn, 1968

FLETCHER, BANISTER, *A History of Architecture on the Comparative Method,* The Athlone Press, 1961

GLAZIER, R., *A Manual of Historic Ornament,* B. T. Batsford Ltd., 1926

GLOAG, J., *Guide to Western Architecture,* George Allen and Unwin Ltd., 1958

GLOAG, J., and BRIDGWATER, D., *A History of Cast Iron in Architecture,* George Allen and Unwin Ltd., 1948

HARRIS, J. and LEVER, J., *Illustrated Glossary of Architecture 850–1830,* Faber and Faber, 1964

HINDLEY, G., *Castles of Europe,* Paul Hamlyn, 1968

HOAR, F., *European Architecture,* Evans Bros. Ltd., 1967

JORDAN, R. FURNEAUX, *A Concise History of Western Architecture,* Thames and Hudson, 1969

MAGUIRE, R. and MURRAY, K., *Modern Churches of the World,* Studio Vista Ltd., 1965

MANSBRIDGE, J., *Graphic History of Architecture,* B. T. Batsford Ltd., 1967

MEYER, F. S., *A Handbook of Ornament,* B. T. Batsford Ltd., 1896.

MUSCHENHEIM, W., *Elements of the Art of Architecture,* Thames and Hudson, 1965

PEVSNER, N., *An Outline of European Architecture,* Penguin Books, Jubilee Ed., 1961

POTHORN, H., *Styles of Architecture,* B. T. Batsford Ltd., 1971

RICHARDS, I., *Abbeys of Europe,* Paul Hamlyn, 1968

ROSENAU, H., *Social Purpose in Architecture,* Studio Vista Ltd., 1970

At all the major monuments and sites in Europe, excellent guide books are available. These are too numerous to list here.

SIMPSON, F. M., *A History of Architectural Development,* Longmans, Green and Co., 1909. (See under separate sections for modern revised version.)

SITWELL, S., *Great Houses of Europe,* Weidenfeld and Nicholson, 1961; *Great Palaces,* Weidenfeld and Nicholson, 1964

STATHAM, H. H., *A History of Architecture,* B. T. Batsford Ltd., 1950

STRZYGOWSKI, J., *Early Church Art in Northern Europe,* B. T. Batsford Ltd., 1928

Belgium and Holland

SITWELL, S., *The Netherlands,* B. T. Batsford Ltd.

Britain

BATSFORD, H. and FRY, C., *The Cathedrals of England,* B. T. Batsford Ltd., 1960

BRAUN, H., *English Abbeys,* Faber and Faber Ltd., 1971

CLIFTON-TAYLOR, A., *The Pattern of English Building,* Faber and Faber Ltd., 1972; *The Cathedrals of England,* Thames and Hudson, 1967

COOK, G. H., *The English Cathedral,* Phoenix House Ltd., 1957; *English Monasteries in the Middle Ages,* Phoenix House Ltd., 1961

COOK, O. and SMITH, E., *English Abbeys and Priories,* Thames and Hudson, 1960

CRUDEN, S., *Scottish Abbeys,* H. M. Stationery Office, 1960

DUNBAR, J. G., *The Historic Architecture of Scotland,* B. T. Batsford Ltd., 1966

GODFREY, W. H., *A History of Architecture in and around London,* Phoenix House Ltd., 1962

HARVEY, J., *The English Cathedrals,* B. T. Batsford Ltd., 1956

HUTTON, G., and SMITH, E., *English Parish Churches,* Thames and Hudson, 1957

LINNELL, C. L. S. and KERSTING, A. F., *English Cathedrals in Colour,* B. T. Batsford Ltd., 1960

LITTLE, B., *English Historic Architecture,* B. T. Batsford Ltd., 1964

O'NEIL, B. H. ST. J., *Castles,* H. M. Stationery Office, 1954

PETZCH, H., *Architecture in Scotland,* Longman Group Ltd., 1971

PEVSNER, N., *London* (Buildings of England Series), Penguin Books, 1962

SIMPSON, W. D., *Castles in England and Wales*, B. T. Batsford Ltd., 1969

VALE, E. and KERSTING, A. F., *A Portrait of English Churches*, B. T. Batsford Ltd., 1956

WEBB, M., *Architecture in Britain Today*, Country Life Books, 1969

YARWOOD, D., *The Architecture of England*, B. T. Batsford Ltd., 1967; *The English Home*, B. T. Batsford Ltd., 1964; *English Houses*, B. T. Batsford Ltd., 1966

Czechoslovakia

HEJNA, A. and KLEIBL, A., *Tábor*, Státi Nakladatelstiví Krásné Literatury a Umění, Praha, 1964

KNOX, B., *Bohemia and Moravia*, Faber and Faber Ltd., 1962

KOZÁK, B. and KOŽÍK, F., *Poklady Prăzské Architektury*, Orbis, Praha, 1965

KÝHOS, K., and NOHA, J., *Praha*, Sportovní a Turistické Nakladatelstiví, Praha, 1964

France

BIÉ, M., *Les Châteaux de la Loire*, Editions Sun, Paris, 1961

BLOMFIELD, R., *A History of French Architecture*, G. Bell and Sons, 1911

BONY, J. and HÜRLIMANN, M., *French Cathedrals*, Thames and Hudson, 1954

DUTTON, R., *The Châteaux of France*, B. T. Batsford Ltd., 1957

HOWGRAVE-GRAHAM, R. P., *The Cathedrals of France*, B. T. Batsford Ltd., 1959

RODIN, A., *The Cathedrals of France*, Hamlyn Publishing Group, 1965

WEST, T. W., *A History of Architecture in France*, University of London Press Ltd., 1969

Germany

BAUM, J. and SCHMIDT-GLASSNER, H., *German Cathedrals*, Thames and Hudson, 1956

Greece

TSIMBOUKI, P., *Rhodes*, Leonti Bros, Piraeus, 1960

Italy

BERGÈRE, T. and R., *The Story of St. Peter's*, Dodd, Mead and Co., New York, 1966

BRIGGS, M. S., *Architecture in Italy*, J. M. Dent and Sons Ltd.

COARELLI, F. and SANTUCCI, U., *Arte nel Mezzogiorno*, Editalia, Roma, 1966

FRANKLIN, J. W., *The Cathedrals of Italy*, B. T. Batsford Ltd., 1958

GODFREY, F. M., *Italian Architecture up to 1750*, Alec Tiranti, 1971

GUNTON, L., *Rome's Historic Churches*, George Allen and Unwin, 1969

LEES-MILNE, J., *Saint Peter's*, Hamish Hamilton, 1967

MÂLE, E., *The Early Churches of Rome*, Ernest Benn Ltd., 1960

WEST, T. W., *A History of Architecture in Italy*, University of London Press Ltd., 1968

WILLEMSEN, C. A. and ODENTHAL, D., *Apulia*, Thames and Hudson, 1959

YARWOOD, D., *The Architecture of Italy*, Chatto and Windus Ltd., 1970

Poland

DMOCHOWSKI, Z., *The Architecture of Poland*, The Polish Research Centre, 1956

DOBRZYCKI, J., *Cracow*, Dom Stowa Polskiego, Warsaw, 1967

GALL, E., *Danzig und das Land an der Weichsel*, Deutscher Kunstverlag, München, 1953

KNOX, B., *The Architecture of Poland*, Barrie and Jenkins, 1971

Rumania

CIOCULESCU, S. and others, *Romania*, Meridiane Publishing House, Bucharest, 1967

GUSTI, G., *Arhitectura în România*, Editura Meridiane, Bucureşti, 1965

Monuments of Religious Art in Rumania, Carpati, Bucharest

Russia (U.S.S.R.)

HAMILTON, G. H., *The Art and Architecture of Russia*, Pelican History of Art Series, Penguin Books, 1954

Kiev, Publishing House for Political Literature of the Ukraine, 1966

MICHAILOW, B. P., *Architektur der Völker der Sowjetunion*, Henschelverlag Berlin, 1953

VOYCE, A., *Russian Architecture*, Philosophical Library, New York, 1948

Scandinavia

FABER, T., *A History of Danish Architecture*, Det Danske Selskab, 1964

GIEDION, S., *Architecture in Finland*, R.I.B.A., 1957

HAHR, A., *Architecture in Sweden*, Alb. Bonniers Boktryckerie, Stockholm

KAVLI, G., *Norwegian Architecture*, B. T. Batsford Ltd., 1958

MARÉ, E. de *Scandinavia*, B. T. Batsford Ltd., 1952

PAULSSON, T., *Scandinavian Architecture*, Leonard Hill Ltd., 1958

RICHARDS, J. M., *A Guide to Finnish Architecture*, Hugh Evelyn, 1966

SITWELL, S., *Denmark*, B. T. Batsford Ltd., 1956

Spain and Portugal

BEVAN, B., *History of Spanish Architecture*, B. T. Batsford Ltd., 1939

DIETERICH, A., and BOGER, B., *Portrait of Spain*, Oliver and Boyd, 1958

HARVEY, J., *The Cathedrals of Spain*, B. T. Batsford Ltd., 1957

SERNA, G., Gómez de la, *Toledo*, Noguer, Barcelona, Madrid, 1967

WEISSMÜLLER, A. A., *Castles from the Heart of Spain*, Barrie and Rockliff, 1967

Ancient Greece

AYRTON, E., *The Doric Temple*, Thames and Hudson, 1961

BOSSERT, H. T. and ZSCHIETZSCHMANN, W., *Hellas and Rome*, Zwemmer, 1936

DINSMOOR, W. B., *The Architecture of Ancient Greece*, B. T. Batsford Ltd., 1950

GROMORT, G., *L'Architecture en Grèce et à Rome*, Vincent, Fréal et Cie, Paris, 1947

HOEGLER, R., *La Grèce Éternelle*, Europa Verlag A. G., Zürich, 1956

LAWRENCE, A. W., *Greek Architecture*, Pelican History of Art Series, Penguin Books, 1957

MARTIENSSEN, R. D., *The Idea of Space in Greek Architecture*, Witwatersrand University Press, Johannesburg, 1964

MARTIN, R., *Manuel d'Architecture Grecque*, A. and J. Picard et Cie, Paris, 1965

PLOMMER, H., *Ancient and Classical Architecture* (Simpson's History of Architectural Development), Longmans, Green and Co. Ltd.

RICHTER, G. M. A., *Greek Art*, Phaidon Press, 1959

ROBERTSON, D. S., *Greek and Roman Architecture*, Cambridge University Press, 1969

SCRANTON, R. L., *Greek Architecture*, Prentice-Hall International

TAYLOR, W., *Greek Architecture*, Arthur Barker Ltd., 1971

Etruscan and Roman

ANDERSON, W. J. and SPIERS, R. P., *The Architecture of Ancient Rome*, B. T. Batsford Ltd., 1927

BOËTHIUS, A. and WARD PERKINS, J. B., *Etruscan and Roman Architecture*, Pelican History of Art Series, Penguin Books, 1970

BOSSERT, H. T. and ZSCHIETZSCHMANN, W., *Hellas and Rome*, Zwemmer, 1936

BRION, M. and SMITH, E., *Pompeii and Herculaneum*, Elek Books Ltd., 1960

BROWN, F. E., *Roman Architecture*, Prentice-Hall International

CALZA, G. and BECATTI, G., *Ostia*, Istituto Poligrafico dello Stato, Roma, 1958

CALZA, R. and NASH, E., *Ostia*, Sansoni, Firenze

GRIMAL, P., *Rome of the Caesars*, Phaidon Press

GROMORT, G., *L'Architecture en Grèce et à Rome*, Vincent, Fréal et Cie, Paris, 1947

KÄHLER, H., *Rome and Her Empire*, Methuen, 1963

MACDONALD, W. L., *The Architecture of the Roman Empire*, Yale University Press, New Haven and London, 1965

MAIURI, A., *Pompeii*, Istituto Geografico de Agostini, Novara, 1960

PICARD, G., *Roman Architecture*, Oldbourne, 1965

PLOMMER, H., *Ancient and Classical Architecture* (Simpson's History of Architectural Development), Longmans, Green and Co. Ltd.

ROBERTSON, D. S., *Greek and Roman Architecture*, Cambridge University Press, 1969

VIGHI, R., *Villa Hadriana*, Nardini, Roma

WHEELER, M., *Roman Art and Architecture*, Thames and Hudson, 1964

Early Christian and Byzantine

BOVINI, G., *Ravenna; its Monuments and Works of Art*, Fratelli Lega, Faenza

HAMILTON, J. A., *Byzantine Architecture and Decoration*, B. T. Batsford Ltd., 1933

HODDINOTT, R. F., *Early Byzantine Churches in Macedonia and Southern Serbia*, Macmillan and Co. Ltd., 1963

KÄHLER, H. and MANGO, C., *Hagia Sophia*, A. Zwemmer Ltd., 1967

KRAUTHEIMER, R., *Early Christian and Byzantine Architecture*, Pelican History of Art Series, Penguin Books, 1965

MACDONALD, W. L., *Early Christian and Byzantine Architecture*, Prentice-Hall International, 1962

MICHELIS, P. A., *Byzantine Art*, B. T. Batsford Ltd., 1955

STEWART, C., *Byzantine Legacy*, George Allen and Unwin Ltd., 1959; *Early Christian, Byzantine and Romanesque Architecture* (Simpson's History of Architectural Development), Longmans, Green and Co. Ltd.; *Serbian Legacy*, George Allen and Unwin Ltd., 1959

TALBOT RICE, D., *Constantinople*, Elek Books Ltd., 1965; *Art of the Byzantine Era*, Thames and Hudson, 1963

Pre-Romanesque and Romanesque

ALLSOPP, B., *Romanesque Architecture*, Arthur Barker Ltd., 1971

BUSCH, H. and LOHSE, B., *Romanesque Europe*, B. T. Batsford Ltd., 1960

CONANT, K. J., *Carolingian and Romanesque Architecture*, Pelican History of Art Series, Penguin Books, 1966

DECKER, H., *Romanesque Art in Italy*, Thames and Hudson, 1958

FISHER, E. A., *The Greater Anglo-Saxon Churches*, Faber and Faber Ltd., 1962

GANTNER, J. and POBÉ, M., *Romanesque Art in France*, Thames and Hudson, 1956

KÜNSTLER, G., *Romanesque Art in Europe*, Thames and Hudson, 1969

NEBOLSINE, G., *Journey into Romanesque*, Weidenfeld and Nicolson, 1969

STEWART, C., *Early Christian, Byzantine and Romanesque Architecture* (Simpson's History of Architectural Development), Longmans, Green and Co. Ltd.

STOLL, R., *Architecture and Sculpture in Early Britain*, Thames and Hudson, 1967

VERZONE, P., *From Theodoric to Charlemagne. A History of the Dark Ages in the West*, Methuen, 1967

Medieval and Gothic

BRANNER, R., *Gothic Architecture*, Prentice-Hall International, 1961; *Burgundian Gothic Architecture*, A. Zwemmer Ltd., 1960; *St. Louis and the Court Style in Gothic Architecture*, A. Zwemmer Ltd., 1965

BRAUN, H., *An Introduction to English Mediaeval Architecture*, Faber and Faber Ltd., 1951

BUSCH, H. and LOHSE, B., *Gothic Europe*, B. T. Batsford Ltd., 1959

COOK, G. H., *English Monasteries in the Middle Ages*, Phoenix House Ltd., 1961

FRANKL, P., *Gothic Architecture*, Pelican History of Art Series, Penguin Books, 1962

HARVEY, J., *The Gothic World*, B. T. Batsford Ltd., 1950; *The Master Builders*, Thames and Hudson, 1971; *Henry Yevele*, B. T. Batsford Ltd., 1944; *Gothic England*, B. T. Batsford Ltd., 1948

HOFSTÄTTER, H., *Gothic Architecture*, Macdonald, 1970

HUBERT, G., *L'Architecture Française du XIIᵉ au XVIIIᵉ Siècle*, La Bibliothèque des Arts, Paris, 1968

LINCOLN, E. F., *The Medieval Legacy*, MacGibbon and Kee, 1961

SAALMAN, H., *Medieval Architecture*, Prentice-Hall International

SITWELL, S., *Gothic Europe*, Weidenfeld and Nicolson, 1969

STEWART, C., *Gothic Architecture* (Simpson's History of Architectural Development), Longmans, Green and Co. Ltd.

VOYCE, A., *The Art and Architecture of Mediaeval Russia*, University of Oklahoma Press, Norman, 1967

WEBB, G., *Architecture in Britain, the Middle Ages*, Pelican History of Art Series, Penguin Books, 1956

WEST, G. H., *Gothic Architecture in England and France*, George Bell and Sons Ltd., 1927

Renaissance and Mannerism

General

ALLSOPP, B., *A History of Renaissance Architecture*, Sir Isaac Pitman and Sons Ltd., 1959

BUSCH, H. and LOHSE, B., *Renaissance Europe*, B. T. Batsford Ltd., 1961

HUGHES, J. Q. and LYNTON, N., *Renaissance Architecture* (Simpson's History of Architectural Development), Longmans, Green and Co. Ltd., 1965

LOWRY, B., *Renaissance Architecture*, Prentice-Hall International

England

DOWNES, K., *Christopher Wren*, Allen Lane, the Penguin Press, 1971

DUTTON, R., *The Age of Wren*, B. T. Batsford Ltd., 1951

GIROUARD, M., *Robert Smythson and the Architecture of the Elizabethan Era*. Country Life Ltd., 1966

HIND, A. M., *Wenceslaus Hollar and his Views of London and Windsor in the Seventeenth Century*, The Bodley Head Press Ltd., 1922

LEES-MILNE, J., *The Age of Inigo Jones*, B. T. Batsford Ltd., 1953; *Tudor Renaissance*, B. T. Batsford Ltd., 1951

SEKLER, E., *Wren and his Place in European Architecture*, Faber and Faber Ltd., 1956

WHINNEY, M., *Wren*, Thames and Hudson, 1971

France

BLUNT, A., *Philibert de l'Orme*, A. Zwemmer Ltd., 1958

WARD, W. H., *The Architecture of the Renaissance in France 1495–1830* (2 Vols.), B. T. Batsford Ltd., 1926

Italy

ACKERMAN, J. S., *The Architecture of Michelangelo,* A. Zwemmer Ltd., 1961

ARGAN, G. C., and other authors, *Michelangiolo Architetto,* Giulio Einaudi, 1964

BALZARETTI, L., *Ville Venete*, Tamburini, Milano, 1965

BONELLI, R., *Da Bramante a Michelangelo*, Neri Pozza, Venezia, 1960

BRUSCHI, A., *Bramante Architetto*, Laterza, Bari, 1969

DECKER, H., *The Renaissance in Italy*, Thames and Hudson, 1969

FÖRSTER, O. H., *Bramante*, Anton Schroll and Co., Wien and München, 1956

GADOL, J., *Leon Battista Alberti*, The University of Chicago Press, Chicago and London, 1969

GAZZOLA, P., *Michele Sanmichele*, Neri Pozza, Venezia, 1960

GOLDSCHEIDER, L., *Michelangelo*, The Phaidon Press, 1953

LUPORINI, E., *Brunelleschi*, Edizione di Comunità, Milano, 1964

MONETTI, A., *The Life of Brunelleschi*, Pennsylvania State University Press, University Park and London, 1970

MURRAY, P. J., *The Architecture of the Italian Renaissance*, B. T. Batsford Ltd., 1963

TAFURI, M., *Jacopo Sansovino*, Marsilio, 1970

Spain

PRENTICE, A. N., *Renaissance Architecture and Ornament in Spain 1500–1560*, Alec Tiranti, 1970

SERRANO, M. L., *El Escorial*, Patrimonio Nacional, 1969

Baroque, Rococo and other Seventeenth and Eighteenth Century Classical Work

General

BAZIN, G., *The Baroque*, Thames and Hudson, 1968

BUSCH, H. and LOHSE, B., *Baroque Europe*, B. T. Batsford Ltd., 1962

HUGHES, J. Q. and LYNTON, N., *Renaissance Architecture*, (Simpson's History of Architectural Development), Longmans, Green and Co. Ltd., 1965

MILLON, H. A., *Baroque and Rococo Architecture*, Prentice-Hall International

Central Europe

BOURKE, J., *Baroque Churches of Central Europe*, Faber and Faber, 1958

HEMPEL, E., *Baroque Art and Architecture in Central Europe*, Pelican History of Art Series, Penguin Books, 1965

Belgium and Holland

GERSON, H. and TER KUILE, E. H., *Art and Architecture in Belgium 1600–1800*, Pelican History of Art Series, Penguin Books, 1960

ROSENBERG, J., SLIVE, S. and TER KUILE, E. H., *Dutch Art and Architecture 1600–1800*, Pelican History of Art Series, Penguin Books, 1966

England

ADAM, R. and J., *The Works in Architecture of Robert and James Adam*, Alec Tiranti Ltd., 1959

DOWNES, K., *Hawksmoor*, Thames and Hudson, 1969

FLEMING, J., *Robert Adam and His Circle*, John Murray Ltd., 1962

HARRIS, J., *Sir William Chambers*, A. Zwemmer Ltd., 1970

ISON, W., *The Georgian Buildings of Bristol*, Faber and Faber Ltd., 1952; *The Georgian Buildings of Bath*, Faber and Faber Ltd., 1948

JOURDAIN, M., *The Work of William Kent*, Country Life Ltd., 1948

LEES-MILNE, J., *The Age of Adam*, B. T. Batsford Ltd., 1947

SITWELL, S., *British Architects and Craftsmen 1600–1830*, B. T Batsford Ltd., 1948

STROUD, D., *George Dance Architect 1741–1825*, Faber and Faber Ltd., 1971; *Henry Holland*, Country Life Ltd., 1966

SUMMERSON, J., *Architecture in Britain 1530–1830*, Pelican History of Art Series, Penguin Books, 1953; *Georgian London*, Pleiades Books, 1945

WHIFFEN, M., *Stuart and Georgian Churches 1603–1837*, B. T. Batsford Ltd., 1948

YARWOOD, D., *Robert Adam*, J. M. Dent and Sons Ltd., 1970

France

BLUNT, A., *Art and Architecture in France 1500–1700*, Pelican History of Art Series, Penguin Books, 1957; *François Mansart*, The Warburg Institute, 1941

BOURGET, P., *Jules Hardouin Mansart*, Vincent, Fréal et Cie, Paris, 1956

JOSEPHSON, R., *L'Architecte de Charles XII, Nicodème Tessin*, G. Van Oest, Paris et Bruxelles, 1930

Italy and the South

BLUNT, A., *Sicilian Baroque*, Weidenfeld and Nicolson, 1968

COUDENHOVE-ERTHAL, E., *Carlo Fontana*, Anton Schroll and Co., Wien, 1930

FAGIOLO DELL' ARCO, M. M., *Bernini*, Mario Bulzoni, Roma, 1967

GANGI, G., *Il Barocco nella Sicilia Occidentale*, De Luca, Roma, 1968

HIBBARD, H., *Bernini*, Penguin Books, 1965

LABO, M., *Guarino Guarini*, Astra Arengarium, 1956

LEES-MILNE, J., *Baroque in Italy*, B. T. Batsford Ltd., 1959

SITWELL, S., *Southern Baroque Re-visited*, Weidenfeld and Nicolson, 1969

WITTKOWER, R., *Art and Architecture in Italy 1600–1750*, Pelican History of Art Series, Penguin Books, 1965

Spain and Portugal

CORREA, A. B., *La Arquitectura en Galicia durante el siglo XVII*, Instituto Padre Sarmiento, Madrid, 1966

KUBLER, G. and SORIA, M., *Art and Architecture in Spain and Portugal 1500–1800*, Pelican History of Art Series, Penguin Books, 1959

LEES-MILNE, J., *Baroque in Spain and Portugal*, B. T. Batsford Ltd., 1960

The Nineteenth Century

General

HITCHCOCK, H. RUSSELL, *Architecture, Nineteenth and Twentieth Centuries*, Pelican History of Art Series, Penguin Books, 1958

HOWARTH, T., *Nineteenth and Twentieth Century Architecture*, Longmans, Green and Co. Ltd., 1959

England

CLARK, K., *The Gothic Revival*, John Murray Ltd., 1962

COOK, J., MORDAUNT, *Victorian Architecture*, Johnson Reprint Co. Ltd., 1971

FERRIDAY, P., *Victorian Architecture*, Jonathan Cape, 1963

GOODHART-RENDEL, H. S., *English Architecture Since the Regency*, Constable and Co., 1953

HITCHCOCK, H. RUSSELL, *Early Victorian Architecture in Britain* (2 vols.), Architectural Press Ltd., 1954

HOBHOUSE, H., *Thomas Cubitt the Master Builder*, Macmillan, 1971

MARGETSON, S., *Regency London*, Cassell, 1971

PILCHER, D., *The Regency Style*, B. T. Batsford Ltd., 1948

POPE-HENNESSY, J. and WILD, H., *The Houses of Parliament*, B. T. Batsford Ltd., 1945

PUGIN, A. W. N., *Contrasts* (Repub.), Leicester University Press, 1969; *Specimens of Gothic Architecture* (2 vols.), M. A. Nattali (original edn. J. Taylor, 1821), 1825

RICHARDS, J. M. and MARÉ, E. de, *The Functional Tradition in Early Industrial Buildings*, Architectural Press Ltd., 1958

STANTON, P., *Pugin*, Thames and Hudson, 1971

STROUD, D., *The Architecture of Sir John Soane*, Studio, 1961

Greece

Neo-Classical Architecture in Greece, The Commercial Bank of Greece, Athens, 1967

Italy

PORTOGHESI, P., *L'eclettismo a Roma 1870–1922*, De Luca, Roma

Twentieth Century and Modern

General

BANHAM, R., *The New Brutalism*, The Architectural Press, 1966; *Guide to Modern Architecture*, The Architectural Press, 1962

HITCHCOCK, H. RUSSELL, *Architecture, Nineteenth and Twentieth Centuries*, Pelican History of Art Series, Penguin Books, 1958

HOWARTH, T., *Nineteenth and Twentieth Century Architecture*, Longmans, Green and Co. Ltd., 1959

KIDDERSMITH, G. E., *The New Architecture of Europe*, Penguin Books, 1962

KULTERMANN, U., *New Architecture of the World*, Thames and Hudson, 1966

PEHNT, W., *Encyclopaedia of Modern Architecture*, Thames and Hudson, 1963

PEVSNER, N., *The Sources of Modern Architecture and Design*, Thames and Hudson, 1968

RICHARDS, J. M., *An Introduction to Modern Architecture*, Penguin Books, 1956

SCULLY, V., *Modern Architecture*, Prentice-Hall International

WHITTICK, A., *European Architecture in the Twentieth Century*, Crosby, Lockwood and Son Ltd., 1950

WINTER, J., *Modern Buildings*, Paul Hamlyn, 1969

Austria

ACHLEITNER, F. and others, *Neue Architektur in Österreich 1945–1970*, R. Bohmann, Vienna, 1969

BACULO, A. G., *Otto Wagner*, Edizione Scientifiche Italiane, Napoli, 1971

MÜNZ, L. and KÜNSTER, G., *Der Architekt Adolf Loos*, Anton Schroll, Wien und München, 1964

Czechoslovakia

DOSTAL, O., PECHAK, J. and PROCHAZKA, V., *Modern Architecture in Czechoslovakia*, Nakladatelstiví Československých Výtvarných Umělců, Prague, 1967

HLADKY, M. and others, *Slovak Building Development in Socialist Czechoslovakia*, Czech Union of Architects, 1963

JENŠTERLE, J., *Recent Architecture in Slovenia*, Moderna Galerija Ljubljana, 1968

England

BOOTH, P. and TAYLOR, N., *Cambridge New Architecture*, Leonard Hill, 1970

HUSSEY, C., *The Life of Sir Edwin Lutyens*, Country Life Ltd., 1950

LAMBERT, S., *New Architecture of London*, The Architectural Association, 1963

LUTYENS, K., *Sir Edwin Lutyens*, Country Life Ltd., 1942

WEBB, M., *Architecture in Britain Today*, Country Life Books, 1969

France

BESSET, M., *New French Architecture*, The Architectural Press, 1967; *Who was Le Corbusier?*, Albert Skira, Geneva, 1968

BLAKE, P., *Marcel Breuer*, Longmans, Green and Co. Ltd., 1956

BOESIGER, W., *Le Corbusier* (8 vols.), Thames and Hudson, 1970

CHAMPIGNEULLE, B., *Perret*, Arts et Métiers Graphiques, Paris, 1959

CHOAY, F., *Le Corbusier*, Mayflower, 1960

JONES, C., *Marcel Breuer*, Thames and Hudson, 1962

LE CORBUSIER, *Towards a New Architecture*, The Architectural Press, 1970; *The City of Tomorrow*, The Architectural Press, 1971

PAWLOWSKI, C., *Tony Garnier*, Centre de Recherche d'Urbanisme, Paris, 1967

Germany

BURCHARD, J., *Post-War Architecture in Germany*, Massachusetts Institute of Technology Press, Cambridge, U.S.A., 1966

CONRADS, U., *Modern Architecture in Germany*, The Architectural Press, 1962

DREXLER, A., *Ludwig Mies Van der Rohe*, Mayflower

ECKARDT, W. VON, *Erich Mendelsohn*, Mayflower, 1960

FEUERSTEIN, G., *New Directions in German Architecture*, Studio Vista, 1968

FITCH, J. M., *Walter Gropius*, Mayflower, 1960

GROPIUS, W., *Scope of Total Architecture*, George Allen and Unwin Ltd., 1956

HEUSS, T., *Hans Poelzig*, Ernst Wasmuth, Tübingen, 1948

KASPAR, K., *New German Architecture*, The Architectural Press, also Gerd Hatje, Stuttgart, 1956

PEHNT, W., *German Architecture*, The Architectural Press, 1970

PETER, H., *Modernes Deutschland*, Mosaik Verlag, Hamburg, 1968

TEUT, A., *Architektur im Dritten Reich 1933–45*, Ullstein, Berlin, Frankfurt/m, Wien, 1967

WHITTICK, A., *Eric Mendelsohn*, Leonard Hill, 1964

Holland

BLIJSTRA, R., *Dutch Architecture after 1900*, P. N. van Campen and Zoon, Amsterdam, 1966

FANELLI, G., *Architettura Moderna in Olanda 1900–1940*, Marchi e Bertolli, 1968

William M. Dudok, G. Van Saane, Amsterdam, 1955

Italy

GALARDI, A., *New Italian Architecture*, The Architectural Press, 1967

GREGOTTI, V., *New Directions in Italian Architecture*, Studio Vista, 1968

HUXTABLE, A. L., *Pier Luigi Nervi*, Mayflower

JOEDICKE, J., *Pier Luigi Nervi*, Edizione di Comunità, Milano, 1957

LABÒ, M., *Giuseppe Terragni*, Il Balcone, Milan

MELOGRANI, C., *Giuseppe Pagano*, Il Balcone, Milan

Milano Oggi, Milano Moderna, Milan, 1958

Minoletti, Milano Moderna, Milan, 1959

NERVI, P. L., *New Structures*, The Architectural Press Ltd., 1963

PAGANI, C., *Archittetura Italiana Oggi*, Ulrico Hoepli, Milan, 1955

PICA, A., *Recent Italian Architecture*, Edizioni del Milione, Milan, 1959

Poland

DWORAKOWSKI, Z., *Warsawa*, Arkady, 1960

Rumania

CAFFÉ, M. and SEBESTYÉN, G., *Development of Constructions in Rumania*, Meridiane Publishing House, Bucharest, 1964

Scandinavia

FABER, T., *New Danish Architecture*, The Architectural Press, 1968

FLEIG, K., *Alvar Aalto*, Les Editions d'Architecture, Artemis, Zürich, 1970

GUTHEIM, F., *Alvar Aalto*, Mayflower

HOLMDAHL, G. and others, *Gunnar Asplund Architect 1885–1945*, Svenska Arkitekters Riksförbund, Stockholm, 1950

PEDERSEN, J., *Architekten Arne Jacobsen*, Architekens Vorlag, Copenhagen, 1957

RAY, S., *Il Contributo Svedese all'Architettura Contemporanea e l'Opere di Sven Markelius*, Oficina Edizioni, Roma, 1969

SALOKORPI, A., *Modern Architecture in Finland*, Weidenfeld and Nicolson, 1970

THELAUS, E., *New Architecture in Sweden*, Svenska Arkitekters Riksförbund, Stockholm, 1961

Spain

COLLINS, G. K. *Antonio Gaudì*, Mayflower

GIRBAU, L. D., *Arquitectura Española Contemporanea*, Editorial Blume, Madrid, 1968

Switzerland

ALTHERR, A., *New Swiss Architecture*, Gerd Hatje, Stuttgart, 1965

BACHMANN, J. and MOOS, S. VON, *New Directions in Swiss Architecture*, Studio Vista, 1969

U.S.S.R.

FEO, V. da, *U.R.S.S. Architettura 1917–1936*, Riuniti, 1963

KOPE, A., *Town and Revolution. Soviet Architecture and City Planning 1917–35*, Thames and Hudson, 1970

LISSITZKY, EL, *Russia: An Architecture for World Revolution*, Lund Humphries, 1970

QUILICI, V., *Architettura Sovietica Contemporanea*, Cappelli

Index

Buildings are listed under the names of towns or villages. Persons are generally listed under the surname or second name. Line illustration references are printed in bold type; plate references in italic.